I0236021

HIDDEN ATROCITIES

A Nancy Bernkopf Tucker and Warren I. Cohen Book on American-East Asian Relations

Edited by

Thomas J. Christensen

Mark Philip Bradley

Rosemary Foot

Michael J. Green, *By More Than Providence: Grand Strategy and American Power in the Asia Pacific Since 1783*

Nancy Bernkopf Tucker was a historian of American diplomacy whose work focused on American–East Asian relations. She published seven books, including the prize-winning *Uncertain Friendships: Taiwan, Hong Kong, and the United States, 1945–1992*. Her articles and essays appeared in countless journals and anthologies, including the *American Historical Review*, *Diplomatic History*, *Foreign Affairs*, and the *Journal of American History*. In addition to teaching at Colgate and Georgetown (where she was the first woman to be awarded tenure in the School of Foreign Service), she served on the China desk of the Department of State and in the American embassy in Beijing. When the Office of the Director of National Intelligence was created, she was chosen to serve as the first Assistant Deputy Director of National Intelligence for Analytic Integrity and Standards and Ombudsman, and she was awarded the National Intelligence Medal of Achievement in 2007. To honor her, in 2012 the Woodrow Wilson International Center for Scholars established an annual Nancy Bernkopf Tucker Memorial Lecture on U.S.–East Asian Relations.

Warren I. Cohen is University Distinguished Professor Emeritus at Michigan State University and the University of Maryland, Baltimore County, and a senior scholar in the Asia Program of the Woodrow Wilson Center. He has written thirteen books and edited seven others. He served as a line officer in the U.S. Pacific Fleet, editor of *Diplomatic History*, president of the Society for Historians of American Foreign Relations, and chairman of the Department of State Advisory Committee on Historical Diplomatic Documentation. In addition to scholarly publications, he has written for the *Atlantic*, the *Baltimore Sun*, the *Christian Science Monitor*, *Dissent*, *Foreign Affairs*, the *International Herald Tribune*, the *Los Angeles Times*, *The Nation*, the *New York Times*, the *Times Literary Supplement*, and the *Washington Post*. He has also been a consultant on Chinese affairs to various government organizations.

JEANNE GUILLEMIN

HIDDEN ATROCITIES

Japanese Germ Warfare and American Obstruction of Justice at the Tokyo Trial

COLUMBIA UNIVERSITY PRESS *New York*

COLUMBIA UNIVERSITY PRESS

PUBLISHERS SINCE 1893

NEW YORK CHICHESTER, WEST SUSSEX

cup.columbia.edu

Library of Congress Cataloging-in-Publication Data

Names: Guillemin, Jeanne, 1943- author.

Title: Hidden atrocities : Japanese germ warfare and American obstruction of justice at the Tokyo Trial / Jeanne Guillemin.

Description: New York : Columbia University Press, 2017. | Series: The Nancy Bernkopf Tucker and Warren I. Cohen books on American-East Asian relations | Includes bibliographical references and index.

Identifiers: LCCN 2016057961 (print) | LCCN 2016059683 (ebook) | ISBN 9780231183529 (cloth : alk. paper) | ISBN 9780231544986 (electronic)

Subjects: LCSH: Tokyo Trial, Tokyo, Japan, 1946-1948 | War crime trials—Japan. | Biological weapons—Japan—History.

Classification: LCC KZ1181 .G85 2017 (print) | LCC KZ1181 (ebook) | DDC 341.6/90268—dc23

LC record available at https://lccn.loc.gov/2016057961

Columbia University Press books are printed on permanent and durable acid-free paper.

Printed in the United States of America

Cover image: Xinhua News Agency © GettyImages

The history of the world is the judgment of the world.

—Friedrich Schiller

CONTENTS

PROLOGUE

GENERAL ISHII AND GERM WARFARE

IN THE AUTUMN OF 1940, THREE YEARS INTO ITS WAR WITH CHINA, Japan reached a stalemate. In 1937 the Japanese military had begun a drive south from northeastern China, where it ruled the puppet government of Manchukuo (the "state of Manchuria"). Its forces had occupied Beijing, Tianjin, Shanghai, and the Chinese capital, Nanjing, and gained control of key southern ports. Yet resistance in central China was blocking a total conquest and thwarting the vision of Japanese leaders for a "New Order in East Asia" that would extend to Indochina, Burma, the Pacific, and beyond.[1] The war had thrown Japan's economy, newly under the threat of American oil and steel embargos, into a crisis.[2]

To break the impasse, the Japanese high command accepted an innovative proposal from the Kwantung Army in Manchukuo, then led by General Umezu Yoshijiro. The army, created in 1918 to guard Japan's interests in Manchuria, grew to rule the area like a fiefdom and, in addition to other exploits, oversaw a covert biological warfare research center at Pingfan, just outside the city of Harbin.[3] Dr. Ishii Shiro, its founder and director, had developed a technique for infecting enemy populations with bubonic plague: planes flying at low altitude could spray millions of plague-infected Oriental rat fleas (*Xenopsylla cheopsis*) on city targets.[4] The fleas would be released with bundles of grain; the rats attracted to the grain would be bitten by the fleas, sicken, and die; then, as in a natural outbreak, the fleas would find human hosts. Or the biting fleas would directly infect the targeted humans, a method of transmission tested with success on captive Chinese and Manchu "guinea pigs" at Pingfan.

Ishii, a major general in the medical corps, had long relied on powerful supporters like General Umezu to promote his secret program.[5] One of his early mentors was Dr. Koizumi Chikahiko, a strong advocate for chemical weapons who became minister of health and welfare.[6] Another was General Araki Sadao, a former minister of war and in 1940 the minister of education. At the highest level was General Tojo Hideki, the new minister of war. Tojo had spent three years in Manchukuo under General Umezu, first as head of the Secret Police and then as the Kwantung Army chief of staff, and was familiar with Ishii's secret research and mission.

To the Japanese public and to many in the military and government, General Ishii was known only as the head of Pingfan's Anti-epidemic Water Purification Bureau (Boeki Kyusuibu), a beneficent supplier of clean water and vaccines for troops in battle. A filtration device Ishii had invented could turn urine into potable water, an invention he liked to claim he had demonstrated to Emperor Hirohito himself.[7] From its beginning in 1932, Ishii's Manchukuo enterprise, an offshoot of the Army Epidemic Prevention Research Laboratory in Tokyo, intended to exploit the region's subjugated peoples to explore human reactions to wartime hazards for troops, such as freezing temperatures, shrapnel wounds, cholera, and syphilis. "Comfort women" coerced to serve the sexual needs of Japanese soldiers were infected, along with other women and men, with venereal diseases; in a special project in remote Qiqihar, Ishii subjected Chinese captives to blistering chemical agents.[8] His foremost objective, though, was to conduct experiments with infectious diseases that had potential as germ weapons, like plague, anthrax, cholera, typhus, and glanders.

In 1936 Ishii's venture was reorganized as the Epidemic Prevention Department of the Kwantung Army, with an animal disease branch (under the army's Unit 100) just outside Changchun, the capital of Manchukuo. Ishii moved his research group from its original site at Beiyinhe, 100 kilometers southeast of Harbin, to a new center 30 kilometers outside the city, the complex called Pingfan, where a dozen contiguous villages, including the one called Pingfan, were razed to make room for it. The modern, gated enclave, designated a closed military zone in 1938, covered more than a thousand acres, with 150 buildings, its own airfield, a railway line to Harbin, and a testing ground for model bombs. Pingfan was sustained by medical researchers recruited largely from the Kyoto Imperial Medical School and the Tokyo Army Hospital. Hundreds of soldiers guarded the center and hundreds of Chinese slave workers kept it in working order. The Kempeitai, the local military police, kept General Ishii supplied with captives from jails, Chinese insurgents who had been captured, and unlucky individuals, including Russians, abducted off the street in Harbin into black vans or herded into trains as cargoes of *marutas* (logs) to the fictional lumber mill behind Pingfan's barbed wire.

Ishii's Water Purification Bureau earned him notable government awards.[9] It was commended for its clean water and vaccine assistance in the 1939 Nomonhan conflict between Japan and the Soviet Union at the contested Mongolian border marked by the Khalkin-gol River. During the fighting, which lasted five months, Ishii dispatched a "suicide squad" of twenty-two men to contaminate the river, a source of water for the enemy, with cholera, typhus, and paratyphus. Although the sabotage results were inconclusive and the Soviet Army won the battle, Ishii's detachment received a special army service citation, and in Tokyo he was decorated with the Third Order of the Golden Kite and the Middle Cord of the Rising Sun. In 1940 Ishii oversaw not only Pingfan, designated as the center for Kwantung Army Unit 731, but its branches in Beijing, Shanghai, and Nanjing that employed nearly five thousand officers and rank-and-file soldiers.[10] A facility in Nanjing, run by the army's Unit 1644 (also called the Tama Detachment), and an outpost in Shanghai positioned him for attacks in central China.

By July 1940 Ishii's plague plans were approved. General Umezu ordered 5 kilograms of infected fleas in metal canisters to be shipped from Pingfan to Unit 1644, along with 70 kilograms of cultures of typhoid pathogens (*Salmonella typhi*) and 50 of cholera (*Vibrio cholerae*) for possible backup.[11] Ishii had ready a team of vaccinated experts to handle the infected fleas and a small plane fitted with a crude spray device that could unload the insects and grain.

Ishii's first aerial attack was on October 4 and the target was Quzhou, a commercial hub in southeastern Zhejiang Province. After two weeks passed with no reports of a plague outbreak there, Ishii went forward with a plague attack on the port of Ningbo, an ancient trade center dating back two thousand years and in 1940 an important conduit for shipments of Chinese arms to the interior. Despite repeated aerial bombings, it had resisted Japanese conquest.

Since the mid-nineteenth century, Ningbo had been a center for the American Presbyterian mission and its medical outreach. On the afternoon of October 27, 1940, Archie Crouch, a young minister from Ohio, watched a small Japanese aircraft approach the city. In his diary he described what happened next: "As this lone plane circled slowly over the heart of the city a plume of what appeared to be dense smoke billowed out behind the fuselage. I thought it must be on fire, but the cloud dispersed downward quickly, like rain from a thunderhead on a summer day, and the plane flew away."[12]

The "thunderhead," deposited as mounds of wheat with some scraps of cloth (the fleas had dispersed), mystified the city's residents. Then, on October 29, local health officials diagnosed the first cases of plague. According to Crouch's diary, ten people died of the disease on November 1 and sixteen more the next day.[13] While hospital staff identified and treated more cases, public health teams imposed quarantines, disinfected homes, burned bedding and clothes, evacuated the worst-afflicted neighborhood, and posted newspaper alerts to the distressed public; a small payment was offered for each rat turned in, alive or dead. Officials mobilized vaccinations throughout the city, including for Crouch, his wife, and their two young children, one a newborn girl. In early December, as a final precaution, health officials burned down the evacuated section of the city, an area of just over an acre, where most of the mysterious wheat had fallen. The epidemic persisted for thirty-four days and killed at least a hundred people, not counting victims who may have fled to the countryside.

Traveling across war-torn China from Chongqing, plague experts from the National Health Administration took weeks to reach Ningbo. Once there, they were unable to find laboratory proof of any link between the fallen grain and the plague bacilli or to find any infected fleas. Despite suspicions that the Japanese airplane had caused the epidemic, the Chinese press drew no firm conclusions. Then, on November 8, plague finally broke out in Quzhou, Ishii's first target, replicating the Ningbo epidemic and validating Ishii's germ warfare tactic.

Having avoided detection, General Ishii proceeded with more attacks. On November 26 he launched a plague attack on Kinhwa (Jinhua), also in Zhejiang Province, but the mixture of fleas and grain dropped there somehow failed to cause an outbreak.

In April 1941 Ningbo finally fell to the Japanese. The Crouch family followed the many Westerners and Chinese who fled the port city by boat; as a precaution against the spread of plague, the gangplanks were soaked with disinfectant. People also fled Quzhou and Jinhua as they became part of the battle zone contested by the Chinese Kuomintang (KMT) government troops and Japanese forces.

Waiting until November 4, 1941, General Ishii mounted a carefully prepared fourth aerial plague attack. The target was Changteh (Changde), an important railway center to the west, in Hunan Province, which was being bombed daily by the Japanese. Ishii assigned Colonel Ota Kiyoshi, from Nanjing's Unit 1644, to organize the details. Again, a single, low-flying airplane sprayed the city center with plague-infected fleas mixed with wheat and rice. Within a week a virulent epidemic began; only a rapid public health response kept the deaths to fewer than a hundred. The already besieged city was thrown into a panic, again with no proof that the Japanese were the perpetrators.

To make its case against Japan, China's National Health Administration compiled the records on the bizarre attacks into a report it circulated among the Allied embassies in Chongqing.[14] This first instance of germ warfare in modern history, the Chinese insisted, was in violation of international rules of war. The report was forwarded to the US and British experts who were secretly developing biological weapons to use against Nazi Germany. They reacted with skepticism. Theodor Rosebury, a leading scientist in the American program, questioned why laboratory tests had failed to reveal the plague bacilli in the grain and on cloth materials dropped by the Japanese planes. The lack of data, he thought, left the Chinese allegations "incompletely proved" by medical science.[15]

The Chinese government then staged a press conference in Chongqing to publicize its plague attack charges against Japan, but to no avail. Going a step further, China's ambassador in London, Dr. Wellington Koo, brought the plague charges and, with them, accusations of Japanese chemical warfare to the newly formed Pacific War Council; his goal was to inspire action by the US-UK Combined Chiefs of Staff. Again the effort failed. Just a few months before, Pearl Harbor had been attacked, and the United States, embroiled in the war against Nazi Germany in Europe and against Imperial Japan in the Pacific, had little attention to spare for China.[16] The Japanese, their goals of regional domination nearly achieved, were a formidable foe: "At the peak of its expansion in early 1942, Japan bestrode Asia like a colossus, one foot planted in the mid-Pacific, the other deep in the interior of China, its ambitious grasp reaching north to the Aleutian Islands and south to the Western colonial enclaves of Southeast Asia."[17]

To concentrate its forces on fighting the United States, Japan sought more than ever to terminate hostilities in China.[18] At this point, General Ishii stood ready to offer the Imperial Army an upgraded germ weapons capability, augmented by a wide array of pathogens, improved production, and trained teams of scientists, pilots, and saboteurs.

In the spring of 1942, Ishii's ambitions for a major military role seemed about to be fulfilled. The Japanese Army was planning a campaign to engage KMT forces in Zhejiang and the adjacent Jiangxi Province. In part, the campaign involved a retort to US forces that had reacted to Japan's attack on Pearl Harbor in December 1941.[19] In April 1942, in a symbolic retaliation, twenty-five B-29 bombers, launched from US aircraft carriers in the Pacific, reached Japan's Home Islands and bombed Tokyo, Yokohama, and other major centers. In the United States the raid boosted national morale, and the mission's leader, Lieutenant Colonel Jimmy Doolittle, and his men became instant heroes. After the attack, the fuel in their aircraft spent, the Doolittle pilots headed west and most ditched their planes in China's mountainous southeastern provinces. Doolittle and his crew bailed out near Quzhou, where, like many other fliers, they were protected by local townspeople and led west by guerillas to safety. For the Japanese government, this US aerial invasion was a warning of what might happen if more powerful US bombers (with four engines instead of two) were ever based in China. The counterstrategy was to destroy all Chinese airfields and railways and lay waste to the entire area to prevent any future buildup.

General Ishii's germ weapons would add a secret weapon to the Zhejiang-Jiangxi campaign, one guaranteed to increase civilian terror and death, at relatively little expense or diversion of military resources. It was important that the true source of the epidemics be disguised, as with the plague attacks, to avoid international criticism of Japan or the provocation of massive American retaliation with chemical weapons, a feared possibility. With bombs, sprays, and sabotage, Ishii's teams of experts were to spread disease over thousands of miles, following the railway line that linked Shangrao in Jiangxi Province eastward to Quzhou and Jinhua in Zhejiang Province, and north to the provincial capital Hangzhou, the port city near Shanghai.

In organizing his team, Ishii drew on his most loyal and tested staff. He put Dr. Karasawa Tomio, a young microbiologist from Unit 731, in charge of logistics. Karasawa had learned from the earlier plague attacks how to coordinate biological warfare with the army's field command. In command of Unit 1644, Dr. Masuda Tomosada, Ishii's close friend and protégé, stood ready with large-scale stocks of pathogens, specially outfitted planes, and crews and pilots trained in germ attack methods. At Pingfan, Dr. Kawashima Kioshi, Ishii's senior scientist in charge of mass production, could ship more pathogens as they were needed.

Starting in May 1942, Japan's Expeditionary Army of 175,000 men, led by Field Marshal Hata Shunroku, quickly overwhelmed the 260,000 poorly equipped Chinese troops and forced their retreat, while bombarding the air bases and railways in the provinces. Unable to hold its ground, the Japanese army then embarked on a "scorched earth" campaign to leave General Chiang Kai-shek little to reclaim. Along with sacking and burning towns, the Japanese searched out and executed any Chinese suspected of helping the Doolittle airmen.

The Zhejiang-Jiangxi campaign lasted from May through August. Ishii's germ bomb raids and low-altitude spraying were coordinated with the conventional bombings and the troop rampages through towns and villages. His saboteurs infected wells with cholera and distributed poisoned food and drink among targeted civilians.

From Japan's perspective, the campaign was a success. An estimated 250,000 Chinese civilians died, in addition to the 30,000 Chinese soldiers killed.[20] Among these fatalities, in poorly documented numbers, were the victims of Ishii's disease attacks. Sprays of anthrax and glanders along roadways killed many farmers as well as livestock. Continuing epidemics of plague and cholera later added to the total of people who suffered and died. As the campaign ended, the Japanese military in Shanghai put on trial eight captured Doolittle fliers and executed three of them for attacking civilian targets.

One part of General Ishii's attack plan, though, was not a success. After inadvertently entering hazardous infected zones, around ten thousand Japanese soldiers came down with cholera and nearly two thousand died. Ishii was reposted to an army hospital at Beijing and Dr. Kitano Masaji, his rival at Unit 100, became commander at Unit 731 for the next two and a half years, after which Ishii returned. In the most intense years of the war, research and production under Unit 731 continued to grow, and its branch initiatives multiplied along the Manchurian border with Soviet Siberia. Officers at the General Staff in Tokyo proved amenable to germ warfare plans for the Pacific, in the Philippines and beyond.[21] Still in the army's good graces, in 1943 Ishii was given another award for his water purification and vaccination work, which, the public was told, had been extended to Burma and Singapore, in fact the sites of new biological weapons centers. In Singapore, a large secret facility, masked as a vaccine research facility, was replicating Pingfan experiments with humans and mass pathogen production. Dr. Naito Ryoichi from the Tokyo Army Hospital was put in charge of it.

In 1944 General Umezu left for Tokyo to become army chief of staff. By then the war had turned against the Japanese. Weakened by conflict in China and by the US offensive in the Pacific, in the spring of 1945 Japan was being devastated by repeated US bombings of its cities; in desperation, its leaders turned to kamikaze suicide air attacks and a last-ditch mobilization of civilians to take up arms and fight to the death. After the United States dropped atomic bombs on Hiroshima and Nagasaki in August 1945, Japan's defeat was inevitable, and with it a Soviet invasion from Siberia into Manchukuo. Before Soviet troops could reach Harbin, General Ishii ordered that explosives be used to destroy Unit 731's offices, barracks, mess halls, laboratories, prison, crematorium, gas chamber, warehouses, and other buildings. In the process, its records and medical samples, proof of its criminal activities, went up in smoke. To prevent the survival of any victims of its medical experimentation, the several hundred captives still alive at Pingfan were forced to choose between suicide by hanging or by taking cyanide.[22] Laboratories and records were similarly destroyed at the Unit 100 site at Changchun. The Unit 1644 facility in Nanjing was emptied of incriminating files and equipment, as were the other centers in China and in Burma and Singapore, and any surviving captives were killed. Ishii fled to Japan, where he went into hiding. Most of his top scientists, like his protégé Masuda, also escaped to Japan, as did Dr. Kitano and Dr. Naito. Less lucky, Dr. Kawashima, head of Unit 731 production, and Dr. Karasawa, former organizer of the 1942 germ attacks on China, were captured by the advancing Soviet troops.

In September 1945, as Ishii arrived back in Japan, the victorious Allies started arresting high-level Japanese officials for war crimes prosecution. Among them were Japan's former premier Tojo, highest on the list, former minister of health Koizumi, and former war minister Araki, with General Umezu likely to be apprehended. Although Ishii remained in hiding and was presumed dead, he had done a great deal to protect himself from criminal charges should he be discovered. The clandestine nature of his germ attacks had left the enemy without proof; all his captive victims had been murdered, and the documentation of his program of inhumane medical experiments and mass germ attacks had been destroyed. In Japan Ishii and the hundreds complicit in his projects relied on mutual silence to protect themselves from public exposure, scandal, or prison. If the silence could be maintained, without disturbance by the Occupation, he and his cohort could put the past behind and resume normal lives in their homeland.

HIDDEN ATROCITIES

INTRODUCTION

LASTING PEACE AND THE PROTECTION OF CIVILIANS

WITH THE WAR OVER IN 1945, CHINA HAD EVERY INTENTION OF prosecuting Japan for the plague attacks dismissed by the Allies in 1942. Yet any jurist would have to search history for relevant criminal law applicable to weapons that had never before been employed in industrial-age warfare. The inquiry would have to begin with defining the hostile use of "poison," with its connotations of surreptitious harm to the body, and how treaty makers in the nineteenth century, alerted to the use of chemical poisons as weapons, anticipated biological weapons.

In May 1899 delegates from more than three dozen nations met in the Netherlands at The Hague to confront the new epoch of wars without boundaries, wars in which technology was fast outstripping morality and law. The rise of state armies in the previous half century had relied on the technological advance of weapons; machine guns, mobile heavy artillery, and better-designed rifles had replaced Napoleonic guns and cannons. From the Crimean War of 1853–1856 to the American Civil War in the 1860s to the Franco-Prussian War of 1870–1871, large competing armies were increasing battlefield carnage, destroying environments and economies, and seriously harming civilians. Defying this trend, the delegates aimed to reinforce the idea that the "right of belligerents to adopt means of injuring the enemy is not unlimited."[1] The words were lifted nearly verbatim from article 12 of the Brussels Declaration of 1874 on the laws of war. This accord had echoed the rallying cry of the 1868 Declaration of St. Petersburg that the sole legitimate end for states at war is to disable the greatest number of the enemy's forces, not to "uselessly aggravate the sufferings of disabled men, or render their death inevitable." Wars would continue, but civilized nations had the duty to alleviate their "calamities."

For a legal model, the delegates in The Hague turned to the Lieber Code, adopted by President Abraham Lincoln during the American Civil War to instruct the Union Army in rules of land warfare.[2] The code required the humane treatment of prisoners of war, the battlefield injured, and defenseless civilians, and it stipulated that violators would be subject to trial and punishment, including the death penalty. The resulting Hague Convention of 1899 supported the same humanitarian rules in war. Going further, it promoted peace by banning military aggression against undefended nations and created an international court of arbitration to settle disputes. The idealistic expectation was that, given the wreckage war was causing, sovereign states would subject themselves to self-evident laws of humanity and public conscience that united them as "a family of nations."[3]

The framers of the Hague Convention also tentatively attempted to pass moral judgment on warfare technology, introducing the option for states to reject unethical innovations that deprived the enemy of any means of defense and made war an unfair contest lacking in honor. A prime example was the use of armed balloons to attack civilian populations, which was prohibited by convention 4 (1).

Although yet to be developed, poison gas weapons fell into this onerous category. As early as the 1860s, ideas were circulating to exploit the science of chemistry to turn chloroform, hydrochloric acid, hydrogen cyanide, arsenic, and nausea-causing smoke into battlefield weapons.[4] Other toxic substances poised for military use were chlorine, cyanogen chloride, phosgene, and mustard agent, all discovered or synthesized in the late eighteenth and early nineteenth centuries. Advocates for poison gas weapons, among them a few scientists, claimed that such toxic clouds could revolutionize land warfare. The treaty makers at The Hague wanted to prevent a futuristic, science-driven arsenal that could cause needless suffering among defenseless troops and might randomly harm civilians. Thus convention 4 (2) stated, "The Contracting Powers agree to abstain from the use of projectiles the sole object of which is the diffusion of asphyxiating or deleterious gases."[5] With the exception of the United States, the major Western nations along with China and Japan signed the agreement.

The Hague Convention of 1907 extended the 1899 provisions beyond their original five-year limit and refined certain restrictions; for example, in convention 4 it became "forbidden to employ poison or poison weapons," not just projectiles for diffusion. In addition, convention 3 of 1907 banned "the crime of surprise attack," that is, one state's unprovoked armed assault on another, and presented a model for a clear, five-point declaration of war.[6] This time, the United States, along with the other major Western powers and, again, China and Japan, committed themselves to the accord.

In 1914 World War I began and, without regard for treaties, a new phase in international conflict and the unrestrained development of weapons technology started. This time, long-range mortars, tanks, submarines with torpedoes, and fighter aircraft expanded the dimensions of warfare by blurring the distinction between the front lines and civilian targets behind the lines.

Despite the bans on poison weapons, World War I saw widespread employment of chemical weapons, invented to overcome the impasse of trench warfare.[7] On April 22, 1915, at the Second Battle of Ypres in Belgium, the German military released 167 tons of chlorine gas from a lineup of 5,700 pressure cylinders. Carried by the wind, the toxic emission passed in minutes to French colonial troops, causing asphyxiation and blindness as the terrified soldiers either held their positions in the trenches or attempted to run for safety. This stunning attack and another one two days later marked the start of a vigorous, unprecedented arms race.[8] Laboratories in all the belligerent nations—Germany, Britain, Italy, Russia, Austro-Hungary, and later the United States—competed for increasingly potent chemicals, with tens of thousands of candidate agents analyzed for their potential as poisons.[9] So-called harassing agents—tear gas (lachrymators) and agents that caused sneezing (sternutators)—were added to the arsenals. Phosgene, a lung irritant like chlorine but six times more toxic, was the Allies' preferred agent, while the Germans relied on the less volatile diphosgene. By far the most important chemical agent was mustard gas, a blistering agent (vesicant) that could penetrate cloth and linger in the environment and was introduced and produced in mass quantities by the Germans after Ypres. The Allies quickly built their own mustard gas factories, with dangerous consequences for workers who were accidentally exposed.[10] Despite the development of gas masks and protective clothing for combatants (and cavalry horses), chemicals and their "killing clouds" became a symbol of the war's worst terror.[11]

The cost of World War I in human lives, environmental destruction, and political and economic upheaval outstripped all previous conflicts. Entire regions of Europe and many areas of the world dominated by Western powers felt the impact.[12] With such a scale of devastation and suffering, it was questionable how social order could be restored, the terrible damages to victims recompensed, or retribution for war crimes justly exacted.

The 1919 Treaty of Versailles between the Allies and Germany ended the war, but nearly all the signatories walked away dissatisfied.[13] The treaty formally arraigned the defeated German emperor, Wilhelm of Hohenzollern, but he escaped charges of unprovoked war (in violation of the Hague Convention 3) by fleeing to neutral Holland. Instead of Allied military tribunals, German court trials imposed light penalties on only a handful of errant soldiers.[14] Unique among the participants, the Japanese, who had joined the Allies against Germany, requested that a clause assuring racial equality be inserted in the treaty, a petition denied by the Western powers. Japan, though, was rewarded by being allowed to retain its control of Germany's island holdings in the northern Pacific—the Marianas, the Carolines, the Marshall Islands, and Palau.[15] In addition, Japan was awarded the German concession on the Chinese peninsula of Shandong overlooking the Korean Peninsula, which it already occupied. This arrangement appeared to so anger China that its delegate refused to sign the treaty.[16]

Germany's use of chemical weapons, identified with its aggression in war, became a focal point during the peace negotiations. The Treaty of Versailles revived the language of the Hague Conventions against the use of poison gas and, in article 171, banned Germany from producing or importing toxic agents. A further amendment gave the Allies the right to monitor German chemical plants, forcing transparency on its advanced industries in the name of international security.[17]

In the midst of global uncertainty, the creation of the League of Nations in 1920 by the signers of the Treaty of Versailles heralded a new, institutional approach to peace, centered on the political resolution of state conflicts.[18] The sense of an existential crisis, coupled with agreement on fundamental principles of justice, created a historic "constitutional moment" for progressive action.[19] US president Woodrow Wilson, supported by other visionaries, led the initiative to unite "the family of civilized nations" to oppose the barbarities of war. Rather than resort to warfare, sovereign states would submit their conflicts to arbitration; in addition, they promised to act in one another's defense in the event of unprovoked aggression. In 1922 the establishment of the Permanent Court of International Justice at The Hague allowed member nations to settle their disputes through legal procedures, which they did for the next decade, at the rate of five cases per year.[20] In 1924 the league directed its Commission of Experts for the Progressive Codification of International Law to explore the role of a criminal court, so no future kaiser, after violating peace accords, could escape justice.[21]

The league also promised a new, optimistic era of disarmament. Article 8 of its covenant affirmed that "the maintenance of peace requires the reduction of national armaments to the lowest point consistent with national safety and the enforcement by common action of international obligations."[22] Member states agreed to "full and frank information as to the scale of their armaments, their military, naval and air programs and the condition of such of their industries as are adaptable to warlike purposes."

Although the United States refused to join the league, US representatives maintained an active presence in its meetings and selectively supported international agreements that protected American interests. One of those interests was controlling Japan, the rising force in Asia and the Pacific.

Japan had come late as a force in Asian colonization, with its growing economy and population pushing it toward greater expansion. It had taken over Korea in 1910 and, keeping it under military rule, significantly built up its industry while suppressing any independence movements.[23] Japan's trade presence in northeastern China, in the area it and other foreign nations called Manchuria, was well established. Within the restrictions of the League of Nations mandate, Japan had effectively colonized the former German islands in the Pacific. Japan's naval power, with an advanced fleet that had improved on British engineering, also threatened Western investors and China's future autonomy.[24]

In 1921 the United States took the lead in organizing a series of League of Nations conferences to promote peace and disarmament and, as part of the Western agenda, to keep the status quo in Asia. In addition to other important attempts to restrict dissension, in 1922 three key treaties resulted. The Four-Power Treaty signed by the United States, France, the United Kingdom, and Japan clarified their mutual alliance, confirming that in any conflict Japan would stand by the Allied nations. The Nine-Power Treaty (which added China, Italy, Belgium, the Netherlands, and Portugal as signatories) was another restraint on Japan. It supported an "Open Door" policy that guaranteed Chinese autonomy in negotiating trade and other international relations, which meant that Japan had to temper its involvement in Manchurian and Chinese trade. After years of delay, Japan and China signed the Shandong Treaty, whereby China resumed control of the province and its railway system, a change that Japan only reluctantly accepted yet one that still allowed it economic dominance in the area.[25]

With a focus on disarmament, the Five-Power Treaty (the Four Powers plus Italy) entailed an agreement to restrict ship and submarine construction and, in its article 5, to prohibit the use in war of "noxious gases," as stipulated in the Hague Conventions and the Treaty of Versailles.[26] In an unexpected way, American influence guaranteed that the ban on chemical weapons would be internationally supported.

Immediately following World War I, the US War Department was set to demobilize the Chemical Warfare Service (CWS) by transferring its research and development to the Army Corps of Engineers. The wartime founder of the service, General Amos A. Fries, launched a campaign to reverse that decision. A dedicated advocate, Fries in 1918 saw the potential for strategic US gas bombing of Germany, an escalation to civilian targeting rejected by his superiors.[27] Reaching outside the military, he convinced two key members of Congress to delay the dissolution of the service until he could garner political support. Fries then persuaded the US chemical industry that it shared the CWS mission: the strong defense of America through technical preparedness.[28] A US chemical industry technically superior to that of Germany (the perceived threat) would, Fries argued, be the backbone for a weapons-ready CWS. Convinced, executives from Dow Chemical and DuPont went on speaking tours and, with Fries, inundated the press with scaremongering articles and books about surprise gas attacks from a superior enemy that only the chemical industry could counter. The propaganda backfired. As one historian put it: "By 1921, [gas] had become the bête noire of World War I, a symbol of the inhumanity of modern war."[29] In 1922 pressure from the public made US delegates promote a complete ban on chemical weapons, the last outcome Fries wanted.

The French failed to ratify the Five-Power Treaty, and it never came into force. Even so, like the Hague Conventions, the treaty's ban on chemical weapons paved the way for the Geneva Protocol of 1925, the international prohibition of the use of chemical weapons in war. The protocol repeated the 1922 Washington text nearly verbatim, forbidding "asphyxiating, poisonous or other gases, and of all analogous liquids, materials or devices" already "justly condemned by the general opinion of the civilized world" and "universally accepted as part of International Law, binding alike the conscience and the practice of nations."[30]

The authors of the protocol included a parallel restraint on bacteriological warfare, then an imagined threat. Over the previous three decades, the revolutionary new science of microbiology, based on the work of pioneers such as France's Louis Pasteur and Germany's Robert Koch, had improved the means to prevent if not cure smallpox, anthrax, malaria, typhoid, tuberculosis, and other infectious diseases that for centuries had ravaged the world. A special League of Nations Committee on Chemical Warfare, meeting in Paris in July 1924 to estimate "the probable effects of chemical discoveries in future wars," extended its discussion to possible bacteriological warfare.[31] While the committee members believed that public health measures, such as vaccinations, quarantines, and sanitation, would limit any attempted intentional spread of disease, they also admitted that progress in medical science, as in chemistry, might be used by states for hostile purposes. As an example, during the early years of World War I, German Army saboteurs had infected Allied pack animals with anthrax, and curious evidence had emerged of other plots, including German plans to infect Romanian cavalry horses with glanders (caused by the bacterium *Burkholderia mallei*).[32] The committee cautioned that bacteriological weapons "would reach civilian populations, would cross frontiers, and might reappear or continue even after the cessation of hostilities."

In 1922, two years before this discussion, France's military had begun testing germ aerosols using sturdy anthrax spores, to respond in kind to possible German germ attacks on their shared border.[33] The Soviet Union was on the same track, exploring the offensive and defensive aspects of microbiology—a disconcerting fact that influenced delegates to the Geneva Protocol deliberations to recommend a ban on bacteriological warfare.[34] On the agreement that the future might hold new risks, the prohibition was extended to "the use of bacteriological methods of warfare."

The Geneva Protocol was widely embraced: forty-three nations became parties, with the British Empire, France, Italy, Germany, and the Soviet Union leading the way.[35] It could not, though, provide a complete guarantee against proliferation. The option was given state parties to develop and produce chemical and germ weapons if they believed (as did the French) that they were under enemy threat and needed to reserve the right to retaliate in kind to a first attack by an enemy power.

As exceptions to the international consensus, the United States and Japan signed but did not ratify the protocol. In the 1920s an isolationist US Senate voted against joining the League of Nations, and Congress similarly moved toward policies that favored General Fries and the Chemical Warfare Service and were supported by industry and a few congressional leaders.[36] Despite nearly unanimous opposition within the military, the CWS was established by the National Defense Act of 1920, which specified that its chief should have the rank of brigadier general, and that there should be ninety officers in grades colonel to second lieutenant plus fifteen hundred enlisted men. Its duties comprised all aspects of "the investigation, development, manufacture or procurement and supply to the Army of all smoke and incendiary materials, all toxic gases, and all gas-defense appliances."[37] Munition plants and proving grounds and the training of troops in offensive and defensive chemical warfare were under its jurisdiction, as were the organization, equipment, training, and operation of special gas troops.

At the same time, US government policy favored the Geneva Protocol prohibitions, with allowance for preparation for the use of chemical weapons in reprisal—in contrast to the European Powers, which generally urged a prohibition that disallowed preparedness.[38] General Fries, who saw the protocol as a threat to the survival of CWS, campaigned within the army against its ratification, arguing that such a treaty undermined US military strength. That argument so convinced the majority in the Senate that the issue was not even put to a vote.

Japan refused to become a party to the Geneva Protocol for different reasons. As its political ambitions grew, so did its interest in modern, science-based weapons.[39] During World War I the Japanese military was more intrigued than repulsed by European chemical warfare. Rather than be bound by the Geneva Protocol, it moved ahead to research and develop chemical weapons with knowledge acquired after the war on investigative trips to Germany and the United States.[40] In 1928 Japan built a major production facility at Okunoshima, near Hiroshima, mainly for mustard and tear gas production. By then, its Army Institute of Scientific Research included forty chemical weapons laboratories, twenty affiliated workshops, and an annex staffed with hundreds of scientists and technicians.[41]

For decades Japan had developed its medical sciences, based largely on Germany's advances, and was poised to develop biological weapons. To enhance the education of its military physicians, the Japanese Army customarily sent its best military physicians on tours of the world's major research centers, especially Berlin, Paris, London, Geneva, and New York. During his tour, Major Ishii Shiro (his rank in 1930) became convinced of the possibilities of germ warfare. When he was afterward appointed to the Tokyo Army Medical School, Ishii found a patron in Dr. Koizumi Chikahiko, the school's dean and Japan's future minister of health and welfare. Koizumi, a major proponent of Japan's chemical weapons program, helped fund Ishii's vision for an entirely new category of weapons—infectious airborne bacteria—and helped him gain an entrepreneurial foothold in the Kwantung Army after Japan established Manchukuo.[42]

Ishii's germ warfare vision, at first limited to sabotage, was enlarged by the development of airplanes and bombs for strategic attacks. In the early interwar years, the potential of air power was driving the modern concept of total war, that is, a state's fight to full victory by annihilating the enemy's industrial base—its factories, rail and shipping lines, and labor force.[43] All that was needed was the development of heavier, long-range aircraft. In 1921 the Italian general Giulio Douhet, a pioneer of strategic bombing, imagined the unrestricted future of war: "Air power makes it possible not only to make high explosive bombing raids over any sector of the enemy's territory, but also to ravage his whole country by chemical and bacteriological warfare."[44] On the alert, representatives at the League of Nations composed a draft treaty to restrict air warfare—the Hague Rules of Aerial

Warfare (1923)—but the convention lacked international backing and remained in draft form.

In 1928, in a grand gesture toward peace, sixty-three nations, including Japan and the Soviet Union, signed the Kellogg-Briand Pact. Also called the Treaty of Paris, the pact condemned the use of war for the resolution of international conflicts and pledged instead the recourse to "pacific means."[45] The US Senate voted to approve the pact but not with high hopes that it would prevent war.[46]

At this juncture in international affairs, the protection of prisoners of war was also reinforced. Based on a draft by the International Committee of the Red Cross, the Geneva Convention of 1929, improving on earlier treaties, clarified the standards for the humane treatment of captives, including women, who were owed adequate food, shelter, clothing, sanitary conditions, and compensation for their labor.[47] Along with the other major powers, Germany, although intent on rearmament, became a party to this treaty, but Japan, increasingly militarized and antagonistic to the West, failed to do so.

At the 1932 World Disarmament Conference in Geneva, sponsored by the League of Nations, the United States delegation declared itself for "the total abolition of lethal gases and bacteriological warfare." But in Washington, General Douglas MacArthur, then the army chief of staff, and Secretary of State Henry Stimson agreed that the delegation had to stop short of a ban on peacetime preparations, which would have shut down the CWS.[48] The final conference resolution was more restrictive than the United States wanted, in that it extended the ban to nonlethal agents such as tear gas, and it also prohibited the manufacture, trade, and possession of the "appliances or substances exclusively suited to chemical or incendiary warfare."[49] The US Chemical Warfare Service survived but in a political atmosphere full of ambivalence about its future and whether chemicals could be competitive with conventional explosives.

The Path to World War II

In the early 1930s the legal means to lasting peace created after World War I was losing ground to ultranationalism and the rise of fascism. The impetus for the league's codification of international criminal laws disappeared.

Germany quit the World Disarmament Conference. Before Japan reneged on the Washington Treaty, it took a radical turn against other peace accords. In September 1931, claiming that Chinese troops had attacked the Japanese Kwantung Army, the Japanese military aggressively reacted to what they called the "Mukden Incident" and began its conquest of Manchuria.[50] The emperor and his cabinet advisors approved the move; as much as they feared jeopardizing trade relations with the West, they feared a military coup more.[51] Japan's moderates and militarists were struggling over how to achieve supreme power in East Asia, while the World Depression, which had halved Japan's trade, continued to erode its economy.[52] Manchuria offered Japan the opportunity to experiment with a new and profitable vision of state-controlled corporate industry, with inspiration from German and Italian fascism, as well as the Soviet five-year plans and US New Deal projects.[53] The availability of Chinese "coolies" and slave labor, an efficient railway system, and ample minerals and coal added to the incentives to invade and conquer.[54]

China immediately protested Japan's aggression to the Council of the League of Nations. Its most influential members, particularly Great Britain, had important commercial interests in both countries but, unfortunately for China, not much stake in Manchuria. From the beginning, the council hesitated to become involved as long as China proper—south of the Great Wall and Beijing—was not violated.[55] Japan's explanation for its aggression, communicated via diplomatic channels, was that its troops had acted in self-defense against chronic violent attacks and that, given the disorder inherent in Chinese society, Japan's expanded presence would help Manchuria become a successful independent nation. With Japan's consent, five months after the Mukden Incident the league appointed the Lytton Commission to investigate the conflict on site.[56] Although he initially encouraged a diplomatic settlement, Secretary Stimson soon switched his sympathies to China.[57] Incensed at Japan's violation of both the Open Door agreement and the Kellogg-Briand Pact, he tried to mobilize international support on the corrective basis of the "Stimson doctrine," but with no success.[58] Even the Soviet Union, which felt threatened by a Japanese presence on its Siberian border, was unwilling to provoke Japan.[59]

Ignoring all treaty obligations, the Japanese military extended its conquest of Manchuria and even dared to briefly engage China near the Great

Wall. Suddenly, in January 1932, in retribution for a Chinese trade embargo, the Japanese military provoked an armed conflict in Shanghai's Chapei district. Its aerial bombing raids, the first total war attack of the epoch, killed thousands of Chinese civilians living there and sent over 250,000 others rushing for safety to the city's International Settlement.[60] Faced with international outrage, the Japanese pulled back, but Japan's capacity and will for armed aggression beyond its borders were clear. On March 1 of that same year, having installed the Kwantung Army as its ruling force, Japan declared the creation of the independent state of Manchukuo and made Henry Pu Yi, the twelfth and last Qing dynasty emperor, its puppet "chief executive." In September the Japanese officially recognized Manchukuo as a new nation and later designated Pu Yi as its "emperor."

Soon after, on October 1, the Lytton Commission released its report condemning Manchukuo as an illegitimate puppet state and advising a multilateral conference to demilitarize it.[61] Nothing was done until, at a February 1933 meeting in Geneva, the other league members unanimously voted for Japan's withdrawal from Manchuria. Japan's delegate to the league was the diplomat Matsuoka Yosuke. Matsuoka, raised in the United States, was fluent in English and had a law degree from the University of Oregon. In a planned riposte, he argued that this new acquisition was vital to Japan's existence and resigned from the league on Japan's behalf. Before its delegation exited, Matsuoka's parting thrust was that the United States would be just as unwilling to give up control of the Panama Canal or the British to relinquish Egypt.[62] Japan then abrogated its naval pacts with the West and began a major buildup of its naval forces and its army. It also tightened colonial control of Korea and Taiwan and amplified its repressive rule at home—a centralization of authority resembling European fascism.[63]

In 1933 Nazi-controlled Germany also quit the league, claiming that the World Disarmament Conference had acted with prejudice by denying Germany arms parity with France.[64]

Fascist Italy was the next to turn against the international community. In 1934, under Prime Minister Benito Mussolini, Italy attacked Ethiopia with the intention of increasing its colonial holdings in Africa. Since Italy had not ratified the Third Hague Convention, no criminal charge of a "surprise attack" could be made. The league attempted reconciliation between the two nations but to no avail. Starting in December 1935, Italy aggressed again, in a new way. In violation of the 1925 Geneva Protocol, which Italy had ratified in 1928, it began using asphyxiating and mustard gases on unprotected Ethiopian troops and civilians.[65] The response of league members was to vote for economic sanctions, which had no impact. Despite personal protests from Ethiopia's emperor Haile Selassie, whose country had belatedly joined the league, and documented proof of gas casualties from Red Cross physicians, the league failed to move to deter further gas attacks, making the Geneva Protocol a "dead letter," a treaty in effect but ignored. The war ended in May 1936 with Ethiopia's defeat and its incorporation into Italian East Africa, after which Italy decided to exit the league. The lesson, not lost on Japan, was that the international community would tolerate the use of chemical weapons by major states on lesser, undefended countries for expansionist ends. In November Germany and Japan signed the Anti-Comintern Pact to solidify their alliance against international communism and the Soviet Union.

World conflict was escalating in ways the League of Nations was unable to arbitrate. In July 1937 the Japanese initiated war against China. It started with a clash between Japanese army units and Chinese garrison forces, in what became known as the Marco Polo Bridge or Liutiaogou Incident. Although the conflict was initially settled by an armistice, Kwantung Army forces were brought from Korea and three divisions transported from the homeland to fortify the Japanese presence. The emperor and cabinet approved, after the military decisions were made.[66] In effect, the Second Sino-Japanese War had begun, much longer and more brutal than the one in 1894–1895. The Japanese, fearful of jeopardizing trade agreements with the West, particularly the United States, insisted on downplaying it as the "China Incident" or the "holy war" (*seisen*).

Quickly gaining control of Beijing, the Japanese battled for three months against entrenched Kuomintang government forces before capturing Shanghai. Then, moving inland, on December 13 their troops took over Nanjing, China's capital, from retreating KMT troops. Their conquest of the city set loose a seven-week rampage of mass executions, brutal assaults, and burning and looting, which became infamous in the West as the "Rape of Nanking." League members protested, but none rushed to openly confront belligerent Japan in China's defense.

In October 1937 China's delegates to the league formally protested Japan's use of chemical weapons (identified as mustard gas) on unprotected Chinese troops on the route from Shanghai to Nanjing and presented evidence of the attacks.[67] The weakened league could only express sympathy and remind its members that "the civilized world" had rejected chemical warfare. In 1938 the Chinese returned with additional charges: the Japanese had expanded their chemical attacks to northern Jiangxi Province, injuring and killing undefended KMT troops under siege. Demanding accountability, they identified General Hata Shunroku, commander of Japan's forces in China, as the "defendant" responsible for the crime.[68] China's delegate offered an impassioned warning:

> Peace is indivisible. Aggression in one region, however remote, if not effectively checked by collective action, encourages similar aggression in other parts of the world. Has 1931 in Asia no direct relation to 1938 in Europe? . . . He who imagines that a flood of aggression and deluge of unreason could be held in water-tight compartments lives in a fool's paradise.[69]

As in the case of Italy's earlier attacks on Ethiopia, league members failed to rise to the mutual defense they had idealistically pledged, with the British delegate especially skeptical of the Chinese accusations. "All elements of cooperation which are necessary," the league resolution noted, "are not yet assured."[70] Treaties had been violated—the Nine-Power Treaty of 1922 and the Treaty of Paris were cited—and individual states were encouraged to give China support, but no collective action was forthcoming.

On September 1, 1939, Germany invaded Poland and the catastrophic war that would quickly surpass World War I began. Germany, Italy, and Japan, intent on armed expansion, found common ground as the Axis powers, their alliance sealed by the Tripartite Pact of 1940. Matsuoka, who had become Japan's foreign minister, vigorously helped broker the agreement.

Writing in early 1941, American sociologist Robert Park looked back on the changes since World War I:

> Since that time warfare, with the rapid advance in the technology of war, has assumed ever vaster proportions and achieved an ever more terrible efficiency. International politics, meantime, has become more realistic

> and more cynical. Total warfare, so called, is limited neither to the heavens above nor to the waters under the earth, and with the advent of the new "strategy of treachery and terror," war has invaded the realm of the spirit—the last stronghold of free souls.[71]

The December 1941 Japanese attack on Pearl Harbor and the US entry into the war began an even more intense phase of destruction, proving ultimately that, armed with advanced weapons, warring industrial nations could in a few years wreck the globe. From 1939 to 1945 some sixty million people were killed, once-thriving cities and natural environments were laid waste, major states went bankrupt or nearly so, masses of people were forced to migrate and died of epidemics, exposure, or starvation, and political upheaval and oppression became a norm.[72] In Germany, Poland, and the Soviet Union, entire populations were murdered in Nazi concentration camps and in mass executions in cities and towns. Allied troops died by the hundreds of thousands on the western front, German and Soviet soldiers by the millions in the East. In the Pacific and in Asia, the estimated body counts, although difficult to reckon in disadvantaged, war-torn countries, were on the scale of those in the European Theater. A difference, though, was race: the victims in the east were nearly all Asian, mostly colonized populations, with proportionately few among them Europeans.[73] Between eight and ten million were killed in China and millions more died in the Philippines, Indochina (struck by famine late in the war), the Dutch East Indies, Malaysia, and the Pacific Islands.

As the war intensified, civilians took the brunt of aerial attacks made more lethal by advanced technology. German V-2 rockets used against the British in 1944 were part of the dangerous drive toward strategic weapons. That same year the United States and Great Britain began relying on heavy bombers and improved incendiary munitions to target Germany's major cities and manufacturing centers. This "carpet bombing" killed hundreds of thousands of civilians and reduced many urban terrains to rubble. With Germany near defeat, the same Allied strategy was directed at Japan, where, in a matter of months, some sixty cities were set aflame and much of Tokyo and the surrounding area, raided twice, was reduced to ashes.[74] The death tolls from the raids reached the hundreds of thousands, with millions made homeless.

The war's culminating air strike was the US atomic bombing of Hiroshima on August 6, 1945, followed three days later by the atomic bombing of Nagasaki. The two unprecedented blasts leveled the landscape, killing over 200,000 Japanese and burning and sickening thousands more. Even before the Axis powers surrendered, the urgent question became whether the world could survive any more ultranationalism and unrestrained violence. Would there be a role for international legal institutions to preserve peace when it came—and do better than the idealistic solutions devised after World War I?

Firing Squads or War Crimes Tribunals?

In November 1943 at the Teheran Conference of the Big Three, UK prime minister Winston Churchill, US president Franklin Roosevelt, and Joseph Stalin, head of the Soviet Union (with the title "Party general secretary"), debated how, once they had achieved victory, they might punish the Axis leaders.[75] One proposal was to capture Hitler and his cronies and execute them by firing squad, an expedient solution favored by Churchill and others within the British government and by some US government leaders.[76]

The alternative to summary execution was an international tribunal. The precedent for this legal solution was not encouraging. In 1919, after the First World War, Allied attempts to prosecute Kaiser Wilhelm II and other Germans for war crimes had ended in a fiasco, leaving the German public angry and humiliated, their own attempts at trials a shambles, and the kaiser living in comfortable exile in Holland.[77] Nonetheless, a USSR representative had proposed an international tribunal to the other Allies in 1942, in line with Soviet development of concepts of international crimes against peace.[78]

In addition, a Soviet law to prosecute Nazi war criminals—the Moscow Declaration of October 30, 1943—had just reaffirmed an earlier fiat.[79] As Stalin well knew, public trials could serve political ends: the Soviet "show trials" of 1936–1938, which purged thousands of dissidents on the basis of false evidence, had demonstrated the state's punitive power. The prosecution of Nazi leaders, whose crimes needed no fabrication, could have a profound socializing impact on the defeated German people, introducing them to a new political framework.

In July 1943 the Soviet Union had tested its tribunal proposition in the liberated city of Krasnodar, where its jurists charged eleven collaborators with being instruments of the German government in the murders of seven thousand Soviet citizens. Eight of the eleven defendants were convicted and publicly hanged in the city square before a crowd of thirty thousand.[80] Newsreels of the trial and the hangings were distributed in local cinemas to bolster support for the war against Germany. As Stalin conferred with Roosevelt and Churchill at Teheran, Soviet officials were preparing a grander version of the Krasnodor trial in Kharkov (Kharkiv) in the Ukraine.[81] The Soviet Union also anticipated cooperating with Poland on war crimes investigations, to prepare for future war crimes trials.[82]

President Roosevelt preferred a judicial solution in the form of the major international war crimes tribunal as proposed by his secretary of war, Henry Stimson, who had been secretary of state under President Herbert Hoover.[83] After Roosevelt died, on April 12, 1945, the US decision about retribution was left to his successor, former vice president Harry S. Truman, who favored a major international trial. The timing for international criminal tribunals was right. Dreadful accounts were emerging about the Nazi mass murders of Jews, Roma, Poles, Ukrainians, and Russians, demanding the addition of the word genocide to the modern lexicon.[84]

Revolted by the war's atrocities and with victory in sight, the Allies strengthened their commitment to a future of global peace and justice. At Teheran, Roosevelt, Churchill, and Stalin had supported the creation of a United Nations organization, a more robust version of the League of Nations. After Roosevelt's death, President Truman followed through on this resolve, which culminated in the San Francisco Conference of June 1945, attended by 850 delegates. The debates about how to structure the organization were often contentious. To promote stability a Security Council was created, made up of the United States, Great Britain, the Soviet Union, France, and China. Another decision was to have member states pledge armed support for the council's initiative on behalf of undefended nations. Still another was to create an International Court of Justice in The Hague to replace the league's Permanent Court of International Justice, which had been terminated with the 1940 Nazi occupation of the Netherlands. In a reaffirmation of the league's peace-making ambitions, the goal of establishing "a system for the regulation of armaments" was given a mandate in article 26.[85]

On June 25 the final draft of the UN charter was unanimously approved. Gathered at the San Francisco Opera House, each delegate stood to indicate assent, and "so too did everyone present, the staff, the press, and some visitors, and the hall resounded to a mighty ovation." The next day the charter was signed by the members of the Security Council and forty-five other nations, all of them resolving to protect succeeding generations from "the scourge of war." In his address at the final meeting of the conference, President Truman told the over six thousand assembled, "Between the victory in Europe and the final victory [over Japan], in the most destructive of all wars, you have won a victory against war itself."[86]

The Allies agreed that the leaders of the defeated Axis powers should be tried in military tribunals. The call had been sounded in 1941 in London, when eleven nations in exile, along with the United Kingdom, formed the Inter-Allied Commission on the Punishment of War Crimes and issued the Declaration of St. James Palace, which urged the prosecution of those responsible for war crimes "through the channel of organized justice" and established the United Nations War Crimes Commission (UNWCC) to facilitate the process.[87]

Near the war's end, Secretary Stimson persisted with a plan for an Allied tribunal, an experiment in justice to be conducted when the Third Reich was defeated.[88] An international military tribunal, it was soon agreed, was the right venue to judge violations of the laws and customs of war.[89] The initiative was carried forward by a small working group of jurists, notable among them Jewish-Polish immigrant Hersch Lauterpacht from Cambridge University. Together they formulated the London Charter, which mapped the goals and structure of an International Military Tribunal (IMT) to prosecute individual major Nazi war criminals; the venue would be Nuremberg, a symbolic gesture against the Nazi's anti-Semitic Nuremberg Laws.[90]

The extravagant scope of World War II—truly "the most destructive of all wars"—was a challenge to the Allied legal experts crafting the final version of the London Charter, the basis for the Nuremberg tribunal and, later, for the International Military Tribunal for the Far East (IMTFE) in Tokyo. In defining war crimes, they decided to hold Axis leaders responsible as individuals for war crimes and focused on three general issues.

First was the unprovoked military aggression on other nations, the crime against peace. They drew on the precedent of the Kellogg-Briand Pact (1928) and other prewar treaties, notably the Third Hague Convention, which banned the "surprise" initiation of war. Added to this concept was a related and ultimately controversial war crime: conspiracy in the planning, propaganda, and staging of political coups that presaged the decisions to wage aggressive war.[91]

Second, the London Charter allowed the prosecution of conventional war crimes, based on precedents established by treaties and laws and therefore less vulnerable to legal debate. For example, the Allies were entitled to prosecute defendants for Axis abuses of prisoners of war expressly banned in the treaty of 1929 and earlier accords. Established rules of war also forbade economic exploitation, the unwarranted destruction of infrastructure and the environment, and failure to control the criminal conduct of troops in land, air, and naval forces.[92]

As a third war crime category, the authors of the London Charter addressed the Nazi systematic killing of civilians by introducing the new concept of "crimes against humanity." Specifically, these were "murder, extermination, enslavement, deportation and other inhumane acts committed against any civilian population."[93]

Little in the charter deliberations supported the legal regulation of armaments, which had preoccupied the framers of the Hague Conventions and internationalists after World War I. The emphasis in 1945 was on the intent and actions of the Axis leaders in waging aggressive war, not the accelerating technological means of warfare. Had ethical judgments of weapons been raised, for example, about the targeting of defenseless civilians in war, the Allies, especially the Americans, would have had more to answer for than their defeated enemies. Even before the atomic bombing of Hiroshima, the US incendiary bombings of European and Japanese cities, justified as retaliation for Axis aggression, made it nearly imperative to shape legal arguments with defensive watchfulness. In Berlin to prepare the indictments for Nuremberg, British lawyers rejected as "inappropriate" any charges against Germany for the use of V1 and V2 rockets on England and the civilian deaths they caused. The defense argument, they believed, would veer awkwardly "outside the range of the trial." As US prosecutor Telford Taylor commented, "It was only necessary to look out the windows at bomb-ravaged Berlin to divine what the 'argument' would have been."[94] The Nuremberg Charter was signed just after Hiroshima, which had less import for the Nazi trials than it would for the Tokyo trial, where the defense counsel would intermittently lash out at the United States for the bombings of Hiroshima and Nagasaki.

The architects of the London Charter were the inheritors of a progressive humanism that had its roots in the previous centuries of European thought, following the liberal ideals of the Enlightenment and natural law.[95] Law rooted in human reason and based on universal moral principles has long driven movements for supranational jurisdiction to balance the scales of justice.[96] The ancient roots for this faith in rationality go back to the golden age of Greece, to the *Oresteia* of the playwright Aeschylus. In that great drama, the rational court of Athena is chosen over the vengeful Furies to judge the crime of matricide committed by the hero Orestes. Through the deliberations of this ideal court, generations of violent conflict are ended and social order is restored.[97] In the great disorder that followed World War II, it seemed that international criminal law offered a necessary, restorative solution. In his opening statement at Nuremberg, Robert Jackson, US chief prosecutor, articulated Allied trust in the rule of law: "That four great nations, flush with victory and stung with injury stay the hand of vengeance and voluntarily submit their captive enemies to the judgment of law is one of the most significant tributes that Power ever has paid to reason."[98] Yet, as Jackson warned, the victors' prosecution, once etched in juridical history, was itself liable to future criticism if its standards slipped: "We must never forget that the record on which we judge these defendants is the record on which history will judge us tomorrow, to pass a poisoned chalice is to put it to our lips as well." But could such a standard be met?[99]

The International Military Tribunal for the Far East

As after World War I the United States emerged with the strongest claim to wealth and world hegemony; by extrapolation, it had the power to determine how the war crimes tribunals would be carried out.[100] The preservation of "civilization" and a world united as a "society of nations" were the ideas of social order that dominated in 1945. The notion that the victorious Allies had liberated the German people from fascism for a higher democratic future carried weight at the Nuremberg IMT. The trial finished within less than a year, with the prosecution aided by the "Teutonic penchant for meticulous record keeping."[101] New technology, such as the IBM machinery that allowed simultaneous translation, helped accelerate the proceedings.[102] The judges from the Four Powers (the United States, United Kingdom, the Soviet Union, and France) agreed on their verdicts before what Winston Churchill called the "Iron Curtain" had fully divided Western Europe and the Eastern Bloc.[103]

The Tokyo trial began six months after Nuremberg, in May 1946, in a radically different geopolitical context, one where the United States ruled securely as the Occupation power and relations between European and Asian nations were in flux. Nine Allied signatories to the Japanese surrender agreement were entitled to participate at the IMTFE: the Four Powers plus China, Australia, Canada, New Zealand, and the Netherlands. Having fought alongside the Allies, India and the Philippines were each subsequently allowed a judge and chief prosecutor.

Each representative nation had a different historic and wartime relationship to Imperial Japan and a different role in the region. The Americans had been stung by Pearl Harbor and were headed toward taking a dominant position in Asia, to fill the vacuum left by the European end of empire. Australia and New Zealand looked to the Americans as a substitute for British protection. Canada, fatigued by service on two fronts of the war, had a lesser stake in the region. Like Great Britain, the French and Dutch had de facto lost their colonial holdings but would still fight to retain them. The Soviet Union had maintained a wartime neutrality pact with Japan until August 1945, when it invaded Manchuria. Stalin awaited the outcome of the civil war in China, to see if Mao Zedong's Chinese Communist Party (CCP) would expand on its northern base or if Generalissimo Chiang Kai-shek, whose Russian-speaking son had consulted with Stalin in Moscow, would triumph despite poor decisions and corruption. The Philippines, about to achieve independence, would remain a dependent of the United States. India was still struggling for its freedom. Twenty thousand of its soldiers, taken as Japanese POWs, had fought the Allies as the Indian National Army; after the war those veterans were alternately tried as war criminals and celebrated as heroes of the independence movement. In sum, the "peace" that Imperial Japan was accused of violating had been that of an Asian Pacific region dominated by Western interests.[104] The old European empires in East Asia and the Pacific, disintegrating into civil wars and ethnic violence, were destabilizing the region.[105] The atomic age had begun, even though information about Hiroshima and Nagasaki was being withheld from the Japanese people.[106] As a result, the IMTFE struggled—as did the IMT in other ways—with the impossibility of using criminal law to restore a prewar political order that no longer existed.[107]

The principles guiding the Tokyo trial were as straightforward as East Asia politics were complex. The Japanese Instrument of Surrender, signed on September 2, repeated the Allied call for criminal prosecution made in the Potsdam Declaration of July 26, 1945. Signed by the United States, Britain, and China, this declaration was communicated to Japan as part of the terms of unconditional surrender. "We do not intend," it stated, "that the Japanese shall be enslaved as a race or destroyed as a nation, but stern justice shall be meted out to all war criminals, including those who have visited cruelties upon our prisoners." Legal retribution would be complemented by a political transition to democracy. "The Japanese Government," the agreement stipulated, "shall remove all obstacles to the revival and strengthening of democratic tendencies among the Japanese people. Freedom of speech, of religion, and of thought, as respect for the fundamental human rights shall be established." Unconditional surrender meant that the emperor and the Japanese government had to submit entirely to the victors' authority, although that authority was meant to liberate them.

The implementation of the Potsdam Declaration, including the organization of the Tokyo trial, was assigned by the Allies to General of the Army Douglas MacArthur, Supreme Commander for the Allied Powers (SCAP) and in charge of the Occupation of Japan. For many Americans, MacArthur was a revered war hero, one with a flair for the dramatic.[108] After a bitter defeat at Corregidor in 1942, in early 1945 he liberated the Philippines from Japan and fulfilled the promise of "I shall return" he had made to the seventy-five thousand abandoned American and Filipino troops. At age 65, he had behind him a career in which he had succeeded best with a minimum of supervision. As SCAP he was given the chance to govern Japan with considerable autonomy, within Washington guidelines, but under no one's thumb. As one diplomat put it, the government authorities in the West, preoccupied with postwar Europe, were "very remote" from the politics of postwar Tokyo.[109]

The China Brief

Of all the nations represented at the IMTFE, China had the most extensive case against Imperial Japan. Its history of conflicts with its more prosperous, aggressive neighbor went back at least to 1928, with the Japanese assassination of an important Manchu warlord, and lasted until September 1945. Although the United States often appeared as China's champion, its well-intended declarations, like the Open Door policy and the Stimson Doctrine, were more about words than actions. Immediately after Pearl Harbor, Generalissimo Chiang had declared war on the Axis Powers and President Roosevelt welcomed China as one of the "Four Policemen" united against Japan in alliance with the United States, Britain, and the Soviet Union.[110] Funding and resources for Chiang's Kuomintang government army increased, but the Americans and British kept firmly to a policy of "Germany First."[111]

Struggling since the 1920s to become a modern, unified nation, China was still affected by decades of being divided by foreign concessions, legal arrangements whereby Great Britain, Japan, Russia, Germany, France, and the United States controlled its major ports, rivers, and trade centers.[112] For some, China remained a semicolony, even though, in January 1943, the Americans and the British each officially agreed to end the old colonial system of extraterritorial interference. After the 1943 Cairo Conference, where Chiang met with Churchill and Roosevelt to discuss the postwar return of Manchuria and Taiwan to the Republic of China (ROC), the British and American press mocked the idea of China as a world power.[113] Less than respectful, the Soviet Union barred Chinese diplomats from meetings about the future of coveted Manchurian seaports and otherwise complained about their participation at conferences. When China sought assistance for early war crimes trials from the UN Commission for the Investigation of War Crimes, the British chairman, suspicious of the Chinese allegations, turned it down, with the support of the Free French, Belgian, and Dutch delegations.[114]

With Japan's defeat, the United States hoped "that China could emerge from the chaos of war as a strong, unified, democratic nation and take the place of Japan as a powerful stabilizing force in the Far East."[115] The hopes for this stable sovereignty were not bright. In addition to the civil war, in areas formerly occupied by the Japanese, leftover puppet militias were fighting both the nationalists and the communists.[116] Postwar inflation and unemployment were rampant and food was scarce; epidemics of cholera and plague were pervasive.

Against that background, the IMTFE held out the promise of a forum in which the Chinese would find respect and vindication. Its belief in legal redress was firm. As early as January 1942 China had signed the "Declaration by United Nations," affirming with the United States, the United Kingdom, the Soviet Union, and twenty-two other nations a common resolve to fight against the Axis powers for freedom, human rights, and justice.[117] Before that, China had committed itself to the idea that the same principles for punishing the Nazis should apply to Japanese war criminals.[118]

Eager to participate in Tokyo, China's designated prosecutor, Hsiang Che-chun (Xiang Zhejun), arrived in early February. Like other well-educated but inexperienced lawyers later sent by the KMT to assist him, he underestimated the burden of proof the prosecutors had to bear.[119] As feared by the British, China was ill-prepared to present credible evidence. Official records from the wartime capital of Chongqing were still being shipped by barge back to Nanjing, the newly reclaimed capital. As an assist, the United Nations War Crimes Commission, prompted by US delegate Herbert C. Pell, Jr., was working with local Chinese courts to organize their data into a national profile.[120]

The burden fell on China to present war crimes that were already solidly documented and organized for prosecution in a Western criminal court. Japan's 1931 and 1937 military incursions, reported to the League of Nations, were obvious choices for its "aggressive war" charges. Its strongest "crimes against humanity" charge was for the Japanese "Rape of Nanking" that started in late 1937. A half-dozen well-educated Americans, most of them missionaries, had been eyewitnesses to the atrocities, and their vivid accounts of the massacres, rapes, and lootings had been reported in the West since 1938.[121]

In addition, the Chinese intended to prosecute Imperial Japan's widespread promotion of opium sales in occupied China, which had enslaved urban populations and caused many deaths solely to fill the imperial war chest. The subject was sensitive, given the long history of the British opium trade and the two colonial-era Opium Wars fought to keep the lucrative supply flowing—a history that still rankled Generalissimo Chiang.[122] For more than a hundred years, opium had helped define China as "the sick man of Asia."[123] The Chinese believed that Japan's continued exploitation constituted a crime against humanity, systematically widespread and devastating.

China also planned to resurrect two grievances left over from the war years. One was the charge of Japanese chemical warfare first made to the League of Nations in 1937 and repeated in 1938. The league statement in 1938 had defined the attacks as "illicit." China had also had support from President Franklin Roosevelt. In a June 1942 press conference, he had referred to "authoritative reports" of Japan's use of "poisonous or noxious agents" on China and warned that if this "inhumane form of warfare" continued, the United States would retaliate in kind "to enforce full retribution." In fact, the US Army had verified Japanese chemical attacks on the city of Ichang (Yichang) in October 1941 that killed six hundred defenseless Chinese troops.[124] For China, the Tokyo court offered a historic opportunity to show that that the Geneva Protocol of 1925 was not a "dead letter" but a living instrument for peace respected by "the civilized world."

China's other grievance concerned the Japanese plague attacks, the accusation broadcast by its public health officials in 1942 and quickly dismissed by its allies. For the Chinese, the unusual attacks fit the category "crimes against humanity," on a par with Nazi atrocities in that they showed Japan's repeated murders of defenseless civilians.

For the Chinese, the strength of their overall case against Japan gave them hope that the IMTFE, representing the world community, would finally give China its full measure of justice.

1

MacARTHUR IN JAPAN

"PUNISH THE WAR CRIMINALS"

In a national broadcast on the evening of August 14, 1945, President Truman announced that the emperor of Japan had accepted the "unconditional surrender" demanded in the Potsdam Declaration. With the atomic bombings of Hiroshima on August 6 and Nagasaki on August 9 behind him, Truman spoke with the authority of the world's only nuclear power. The official "V-J" day, Truman cautioned, would have to wait until the surrender document was officially signed. He was putting General of the Army Douglas MacArthur in charge of the event and designating him the Supreme Commander for the Allied Powers (SCAP)—a decision cleared beforehand with the British, Chinese, and Soviets. During the prior week, Truman's chief of staff, George C. Marshall, another five-star general of the army, had kept up a steady flow of "eyes only" communications to MacArthur, dictating the terms of Japanese surrender and details about his command.[1] The situation in the Pacific was far from stable. After Nagasaki, 150 US B-29 bombers had staged massive bombing raids on the Japanese Home Islands, dropping 700 one-ton bombs on Osaka, the densely populated port, and five other cities.[2] Fears persisted that Japanese soldiers and civilians were mobilized to fight to the death.

Five days after Truman's announcement, sixteen representatives of the Imperial Army and Navy arrived at MacArthur's headquarters in Manila. MacArthur made it a point not to meet the delegates.[3] Instead he let his chief of staff, Lieutenant Richard K. Sutherland, and his head of combat intelligence, General Charles A. Willoughby, and a team of translators communicate the Washington directives. The directives emphasized the liberation of prisoners of war and the cooperation of civilian and military officials, who should remain in their positions until notified of their dismissal by MacArthur, to whom the emperor and the Japanese government were subject.[4]

On August 20, after a day and night of meetings, the Japanese contingent left Manila and returned to the emperor with the translated text of the Instrument of Surrender, to which Hirohito agreed. General MacArthur decided to position himself as soon as possible in Japan as the supreme commander, to show he was in charge of the Occupation. Although he first planned for a surrender ceremony on August 30, a typhoon delayed his trip for two days and the ceremony was rescheduled for September 2. A steady stream of policy directives from the State-War-Navy Coordinating Committee (SWNCC) in Washington instructed him how to proceed in bringing Allied forces in the Pacific to assemble in Tokyo. Created in 1944, this interagency body deliberated decisions on top national security issues, including Axis war crimes prosecutions, and had a special subcommittee on Far East affairs.

The authority behind SWNCC was the Joint Chiefs of Staff (JCS), the presidential advisory group organized at Marshall's suggestion in February 1942. Led by Admiral William Leahy, the JCS members were the senior officers of the army, navy, and army air force. Its wartime purpose was to defeat the Nazis by working jointly with the United Kingdom and its service heads as the Combined Chiefs of Staff.[5] President Roosevelt grew to rely greatly on the Joint Chiefs, and especially Admiral Leahy, for advice about US grand strategy.[6] President Truman after him did the same, and, when the war ended, he kept Leahy, promoted to fleet admiral in 1944, as head of the JCS and a close advisor. Also on the JCS was Army Chief of Staff Dwight D. Eisenhower, who in the 1930s had spent seven years assisting MacArthur in the Philippines; like MacArthur and Marshall, Eisenhower had been made a five-star general of the army late in the war.[7]

Just before General MacArthur left Manila for the Atsugi Air Base in Yokohama, he received more SWNCC orders regarding postsurrender policy for Japan. On route in his new C-54 transport plane *Bataan II,* he summarized the agenda to an aide:

> First, destroy the military power. Punish war criminals. Build the structure of representative government. Modernize the constitution. Hold free elections. Enfranchise the women. Release the political prisoners. Liberate the farmers. Encourage a free economy. Abolish police oppression. Develop a free and responsible press. Liberalize education. Decentralize political power. Separate the church from the state.[8]

The first item, "destroy the military power," involved gaining control over Japan's seven million armed imperial troops scattered over an enormous area. Nor did all the imperial commanders agree with the surrender terms. On August 11 a group of army field officers in Tokyo were caught in a plot to kidnap the emperor and assassinate the delegates who had negotiated for peace. Between August 15 and August 29 a spasm of more failed coups, arrests, suicides, and protests rocked Tokyo. In the aftermath, the government's army minister and a rear admiral committed suicide.

Through the emperor's intervention, the chaos ended in time for MacArthur's arrival.[9] As had been typical of him throughout the war, the general always wanted to be first on shore, no matter what the danger.[10] On this day a contingent of photographers he brought with him captured the historic image of the supreme commander in his trademark sunglasses, a corncob pipe clenched between his teeth, wearing a khaki uniform and gold-braid cap.

Allied security in and around Tokyo was necessarily high. The Eighth Army had secured Atsugi Air Base with 7,500 US troops; the US Third Fleet, under Fleet Admiral Chester W. Nimitz, and the British Far East Fleet had converged at ports near Tokyo Bay. US Marines joined two parachute regiments to control the docks of Yokohama and nearby Yokosuka. A small contingent from the Royal Australian Navy took over three fortresses at the entrance to Tokyo Bay, where they hoisted a Union Jack. The battleship *Missouri* was moored in the bay. In deference to Admiral Nimitz and his essential contribution to Japan's defeat, President Truman had given firm orders that the surrender ceremony would take place on its deck and outlined the details of the ceremony.[11]

Without incident, MacArthur went from Atsugi to his temporary headquarters in Yokohama, where he was put up at the New Grand Hotel and established an advanced base at the Customs Building. Then and on his later entrance into Tokyo, his cavalcade passed quiet crowds of destitute civilians and a flattened landscape of ashes and the ruins of factories.

On September 2, on the deck of the *Missouri*, MacArthur officiated at the historic signing of the Instrument of Surrender. With over two hundred Allied vessels anchored nearby, four destroyers were kept busy shuttling guests to the ceremony. Dozens of reporters were positioned on scaffolding alongside the veranda deck (which the crew called "the surrender deck"). Only one Japanese photographer was allowed, kept under armed guard lest he have suicidal kamikaze impulses.[12] On the deck, a large table with two chairs had been set up; on the table were the documents to be signed (one copy for the Japanese, one for the Allies).

At 9:00 a.m., General MacArthur and representatives from the nine Allied nations (Australia, Britain, Canada, France, the Netherlands, New Zealand, the Republic of China, the Soviet Union, and the United States) assembled, along with their staffs and guards. Thanks to MacArthur, Australian, Canadian, and New Zealand officials were allowed to sign individually rather than cede their authority to the British.

In time to meet the Allied representatives, an eleven-person Japanese retinue had been ferried from the mainland and carefully escorted up to the deck. Leading them was Foreign Minister Shigemitsu Mamoru, dressed in a top hat, white gloves, a morning coat, and striped trousers. Shigemitsu, who had lost a leg in a Korean terrorist attack in 1932, leaned awkwardly on a cane. At his side, in full dress uniform, peaked cap, and riding boots, was General Umezu Yoshijiro, known to his troops as the "Ivory Mask" for his implacable demeanor.[13] In 1944 Umezu had risen from commander of the Kwantung Army in Manchuria (where he oversaw Unit 731) to chief of the Imperial Army General Staff.

Standing at a microphone, General MacArthur, his hands shaking slightly, began the ceremony by reading his speech. Its conclusion resounded with postwar idealism: "It is my earnest hope and indeed the hope of all mankind, that from this solemn occasion a better world shall emerge out of the blood and carnage of the past—a world dedicated to the dignity of man and the fulfillment of his most cherished wish—for freedom, tolerance and justice."[14]

Foreign Minister Shigemitsu signed Japan's surrender on behalf of the imperial government and was followed by General Umezu, who signed for the Imperial General Headquarters. General MacArthur signed next as the supreme commander. After MacArthur, Fleet Admiral Nimitz, the commander of the Pacific navy, signed for the United States. General Xu Yongchang, the Chinese chief of general staff, was first among the Allies to sign after Nimitz. The representatives of the United Kingdom, the Soviet Union, and the other parties followed in order.[15]

As the ceremony ended, nearly two thousand B-29 bombers and navy fighters flew in formation over the harbor, a symbol of the victors' military might. Nonetheless, a Japanese diplomat who witnessed the proceedings credited MacArthur with creating "an altar of peace" on the *Missouri*'s narrow quarter deck.[16]

Soon after the surrender ceremony, MacArthur was taken on a tour of the Tokyo Bay area, which had been leveled by US bombing raids. His immediate conclusion was that the war had brought Japan near to economic and industrial collapse, making it unable to wage war. Assured by General Umezu that Japan's 2.25 million soldiers in the Home Islands would be demobilized by October 10, MacArthur halved the estimated number of regular army troops needed for the Occupation, from 400,000 to 200,000. He felt, and correctly so, that the Eighth Army, set to add between 100,000 and 130,000 in the next several weeks, would suffice.[17] That he announced this decision to the press before consulting Washington raised hackles at the White House, where President Truman and his military advisors were already worried over the postwar drop in soldier recruitment.[18] Even more troublesome was the thought that MacArthur's temperamental resistance to Washington, a problem during his wartime command, would undermine US goals for the Occupation.

On September 8 MacArthur moved to the refurbished US embassy in Tokyo, with his wife, Jean, and young son, Arthur. At a private ceremony with an honor guard, the same American flag that had flown over the White House when Pearl Harbor was attacked was raised over the compound.[19] MacArthur's temporary headquarters remained a large, barracks-like room in the Customs Building in Yokohama. There, on September 12, he announced to an assembly of army and navy officers and a team from the War Crimes Office in Washington that he envisioned prosecution of Japanese war criminals in both the major tribunal and minor trials: "The Trials must be conducted in the full light of publicity. They must be fair and free from vengeance or politics. They must be examples to the world of law and justice. We shall be criticized but we shall strive for the verdict of history."[20]

Looking for Biological Weapons

Lieutenant Colonel Murray Sanders, a specialist in bacteriology from the US Army's Chemical Warfare Service, was in the third jeep behind MacArthur in the army cavalcade that brought the SCAP contingent to Tokyo.[21] Age 35, he was head of an infectious disease research division at Camp Detrick in Frederick, Maryland, the center of the secret US biological warfare program, and he was well known to military intelligence in Washington.[22]

Months before, General MacArthur with Lieutenant Sutherland had laid the groundwork for incorporating US scientists like Sanders into the final push for victory over Japan.[23] They began with the creation of the Pacific Branch of the Office of Scientific Research and Development (PBOSRD), an offshoot of the Washington OSRD, which oversaw both the Manhattan Project and the US biological warfare program. Physicist Karl T. Compton, president of MIT and also the head of OSRD field operations in Washington, was appointed its leader. At first the idea was to mobilize scientific assistance for the final assault on Japan, with the recruitment of several hundred engineers and 300 tons of special laboratory equipment to be sent to Manila, where PBSORD would provide "an advanced echelon of scientific support."

With the dropping of the atomic bombs and Japan's surrender, the goal of the Pacific Branch became investigative, in line with the larger Alsos Mission, created by US intelligence in partnership with leaders of the Manhattan Project.[24] The Alsos Mission's original goal was to secure Germany's uranium stores and capture its atomic physicists before the Soviets, who were advancing from the east, could apprehend them. In

1944, as Nazi troops retreated, the Americans, with British assistance, expanded the search to rocketry and chemical and biological weapons, looking for laboratories, production plants, munitions, instructional records, and German scientific experts.

At times previous Allied intelligence about German weapons was proved wrong by the Alsos results. Owing to technical mistakes and underfunding, Nazi physicists had failed in their atomic bomb plans; compared to the US program, it was, as the mission's leader Samuel Goudsmit put it, "small-time stuff."[25] The real prize was German rocket science, the expertise behind the Nazis' armed V-2 rockets. A second surprise was that Germany had virtually no biological weapons, despite years of Western intelligence reports to the contrary. Perhaps because of his germophobia, Hitler had banned his military from pursuing biological warfare capability; only a few small experimental efforts had been made, without the führer's knowledge.[26]

Still another surprise for Allied investigators in Europe was the extent to which the Nazis had developed chemical weapons. In addition to manufacturing huge quantities of mustard, phosgene, and other chemical weapons, the Germans had invented three organophosporous-based nerve agents—tabun, sarin, and soman—and started the mass production of suitable munitions.[27] The extraordinary lethal impact of the invisible, odorless gases—sudden convulsions followed by paralysis and death—impressed the Allies, who, east and west, rushed to round up scientific and industrial experts and any abandoned technical equipment.

As early as May 28, 1945, Undersecretary of War Robert Patterson contacted Admiral Leahy at the JCS to ask how the United States could secure the expert knowledge of Nazi weapons scientists without incurring the "strong resentment of the American public."[28] Patterson's idea was to have the SWNCC take charge and put selected scientists in protective military custody, just on a short-term basis, to find out what they knew. By July the Military Intelligence Division of the War Department oversaw the "exploiting" of German specialists in science and technology, hundreds of whom, including 115 rocket scientists, were slated for military hiring. The goal was to select "chosen, rare minds whose continuing intellectual productivity we wish to use."[29] Motivated by fears of Soviet competition, on September 3, 1945, President Truman authorized contracts for as long as five years for expert German scientists. In line with this policy, JCS directive 1067, which ordered US authorities to arrest Nazi war criminals, left an immunity loophole for individuals who might be "useful for intelligence or other military reasons."[30]

Expectations of what Japan could yield in terms of advanced weapons were much lower than for Germany, which for a century had led the world in science and technology. Japanese scientists were known to be capable of preliminary atomic bomb research and of producing standard chemical weapons like mustard and phosgene.[31] Little was known about their potential biological weapons, until, in 1944, breakthroughs in decoding and decrypting of Japanese communications opened new windows on Japan's germ warfare ambitions.[32]

As commander-in-chief of the Pacific (CINCPAC), General MacArthur relied on two intelligence officers to make sense of this new information. Closest to him was Brigadier General Willoughby, who directed US Army intelligence (G-2) in the Pacific and was in charge of combat intelligence.[33] Born in Germany in 1892, Willoughby immigrated as a teenager to America, joined the army, and served in World War I. Afterward, deciding to become a career officer, he earned a degree from the US Army War College, became a lieutenant colonel, and wrote books on military history.[34] In the mid-1930s MacArthur met Willoughby, then teaching at Fort Leavenworth, Kansas, in the US Army Command and General Staff School. Six foot two and weighing over two hundred pounds, Willoughby impressed his fellow officers with his erudition, his authoritarian "Prussian" demeanor, his monocle, and his custom-tailored uniforms. Even though he was a supporter of Spain's fascist dictator Francisco Franco, he made a good impression on MacArthur.[35]

In 1940 MacArthur, then field marshal of the Philippine Commonwealth, responded to Willoughby's many letters of petition by appointing him his G-4 (logistics) assistant chief of staff. In mid-1941, when MacArthur took charge of the Far Eastern Command, he made Willoughby his assistant chief of staff for intelligence. In 1942 Willoughby was one of the few who accompanied MacArthur on the escape from Corregidor to Australia. Although at crucial times Willoughby erred in his estimates of Japanese forces, MacArthur could count on his unwavering loyalty, just as Willoughby counted on his.[36]

Five years younger than Willoughby and a more congenial personality, Colonel Elliott Thorpe commanded MacArthur's Counter-Intelligence Corps (CIC), a Far Eastern branch of the European operation initially based in Australia. Thorpe's CIC responsibilities ranged widely, from monitoring troop mail and guarding Allied officers in transit to running a spy network that included New Guinea tribesmen and Mormon missionaries. As the Japanese retreated from the Pacific islands, CIC secured thousands of Japanese documents and its officers interrogated hundreds of collaborators and Japanese prisoners of war. For help with translation and interrogation, Thorpe relied on Willoughby, who at G-2 had created the Allied Translation and Interpreters Service (ATIS), which employed several hundred second-generation Japanese Americans (Nisei), many from Hawaii and California, to work as translators and compile intelligence data.[37] They were sent into the field with combat forces and accompanied troops in all initial landing operations—sometimes paying with their lives. In addition, ATIS conducted its own interviews with Japanese prisoners.[38]

As Allied forces advanced westward toward Japan, both these intelligence units received increasing reports about secret biological weapons and began consulting with the Chemical Warfare Service and its intelligence officers. Memos from the Pacific Theater about Japanese germ weapons were soon circulating at the War Department—passing from its Intelligence Division to the Joint Biological Weapons Subcommittee, the Joint New Weapons Committee, and the Joint Intelligence Committee, a top secret entity that reported to the JCS.[39] CIC informants spoke early of a Japanese germ weapons facility identified with the Kwantung Army's Unit 731 in Manchukuo, outside the city of Harbin, and run by a military physician, General Ishii Shiro.

In May 1944 a captured document revealed an unsuspected Japanese potential: a diagram of a Japanese Mark 7 experimental bacillus bomb, likely for anthrax and similar to munitions being developed by the United States and Britain in their biological warfare (BW) programs.[40] The information, from the notebook of an "enlisted Japanese trainee," also described twelve other bomb types for conventional explosives and incendiaries. Highlighting the discovery to MacArthur, Willoughby characterized the diagram as the "first factual evidence that Japan actually has a munition for BW." A drawing of the bomb with a green tip and a purple and gray body was circulated to all Allied commanding officers in the Pacific, to aid with identification in case the Japanese had left a cache behind with its other discarded weapons. G-2, CIC, and the CWS staff in the Pacific also increased surveillance for any suspicious bombs and unusual disease outbreaks. The Mark 7 finding, corroborated by another captured document, was discussed with George Merck, the civilian leader of the US War Research Service, which oversaw the US Army's biological weapons program, and with CWS intelligence officers. Willoughby's ATIS warned General MacArthur about the enemy's germ weapons threat. "The JAPANESE," it stated, "would use this type of warfare as a surprise weapon without the slightest hesitation."[41]

A December 15, 1944, summary report from CWS intelligence included a detailed map of an affiliate of Unit 731 located in Nanjing, called the Tama Unit. The source was an x-ray specialist in the Japanese military who was considered "very intelligent and sincere."[42]

Six months later, in June 1945, General Willoughby gave General MacArthur the ATIS summary statement on *Japanese Violations of the Laws of War,* compiled to assist the Australians in their efforts to prosecute war criminals.[43] Citing units and divisions and the names of commanding officers, ATIS was able to supply ample information on cannibalism—the Japanese military rules forbade starving troops from eating their own war dead but not from eating the flesh of captives—and on the torture and killing of Allied prisoners in the Philippines, New Guinea, and Burma. About "bacterial warfare," however, the US report offered only a fragment: a Japanese prisoner of war, a bacteriologist who had worked in Canton in 1941, had heard of a Major General Ishii Shiro who was conducting bacillus bomb tests at a branch of the Army Medical College in Harbin.[44]

As the defeat of Japan grew imminent, all ATIS data and more from other sources were compiled in a July 26 report by the War Department's Military Intelligence Division in Washington. It noted that the Japanese had used plague in at least one instance, on the Chinese city of Changde, although a lack of epidemiological data and reliable samples of BW agents weakened the case made by China's public health officials.[45] The Japanese, it was thought, would be most likely to use cholera, dysentery, typhoid, anthrax, plague, or glanders in small-scale attacks where there would be "little or no possibility of its detection." Buried in the report, along with suggestions that rats and fleas with plague might be dropped in containers and that dogs with rabies might be parachuted down on enemy targets, was a POW account of bacteria disseminated by airplanes sent from the Nanjing Water Supply and Prevention Headquarters, described as a front for an army biological warfare facility. If desperate, the War Department's report concluded, the Japanese might attack with a combination of chemical and germ weapons.

In an article retrieved from defeated Germany, a Japanese officer downplayed the restraints of the Geneva Protocol: "In the case of a victorious enemy such a moral agreement might possibly be only a dead letter." "Bacterial warfare," another discovered document asserted, "is a new form of scientific combat in modern war, in which the most advanced discoveries of modern scientific research are put to practical use for attack and defense, and therefore methods of attack and defense depend on scientific progress."[46]

Advised of this intelligence, in early August 1945 Colonel Sanders arrived in Manila with the other Pacific Branch investigators. There he met MIT's Karl Compton, the project leader, and General Willoughby. On August 14, with the confirmation of the Japanese surrender, the night sky of Manila was filled with skyrockets, colored flares, and searchlights that played on the clouds as whistles blew. After Manila's all-night celebration, Compton, with MacArthur's approval, wired Washington to cancel all further preparations for the Pacific Branch. Instead, he was asked to help organize a Scientific Intelligence Mission staffed by scientists who, like Sanders, were already in the Pacific Theater.[47]

Although not the new mission's designated leader, Compton posed the essential question: "What technical ideas or developments of the Japanese could we advantageously incorporate in our own future national security program?"[48] To miss no opportunity, the Scientific Intelligence Mission team accompanied MacArthur as he proceeded to Japan.[49]

To establish his base in Tokyo, MacArthur chose the large, modern, undamaged Dai-Ichi Mutual Life Insurance Building in central Tokyo. From his sixth-floor office, which overlooked the Imperial Palace moat and gardens and had views of Mount Fuji, he created and ruled the new, complex organization of the Occupation. SCAP became an institution, the embodiment of McArthur's Supreme Command, and General Headquarters (GHQ) the large bureaucracy that housed its civil and military divisions.[50]

Focused on intelligence and national security, MacArthur put General Willoughby in charge of G-2 in Tokyo and appointed Elliott Thorpe, who had been promoted to brigadier general, to run a revised and expanded CIC, both under SCAP auspices. Murray Sanders was also given an office at the Dai-Ichi Building, near G-2 and its technical intelligence staff. Several times in the coming weeks, he and Willoughby visited MacArthur in his sixth-floor inner sanctum to update him on the investigation into Japanese germ weapons. At times Karl Compton joined them.

To start his inquiry, Sanders was guided by Dr. Naito Ryoichi, represented to him as a surgeon with a private practice in the suburbs of Osaka who was fluent in English and had been affiliated with the Tokyo Army Hospital. Unknown to Sanders, Naito, with the rank of lieutenant colonel in the medical corps, had directed the Singapore extension of General Ishii's germ weapons program. His name had also appeared in US prewar intelligence records. In 1939 he had embarked on a failed effort to obtain samples of the yellow fever virus from a laboratory at the Rockefeller Institute in New York City, a venture that became the subject of an FBI report passed to army intelligence and the Office of the Surgeon General in Washington.[51] Later in 1939 Dr. Miyagawa Yonetsugi, an internationally famous bacteriologist with ties to members of the Imperial Cabinet and also involved in Ishii's program, contacted Rockefeller with the same request, which was again refused.[52]

After the war Naito maintained his network of BW scientists. The first contact he brought Sanders to interrogate was his esteemed colleague, Dr. Miyagawa. Miyagawa repeated what Naito had already claimed: that Unit 731, headed by General Ishii (now reported deceased), had been a purely defensive venture to protect troops against infectious diseases and unsanitary conditions in foreign climes. Naito then introduced Sanders to another half-dozen scientists who repeated this description, even as several described biological bomb prototypes developed, they said, as purely defensive measures.[53]

With help from SCAP, Naito arranged for Sanders to interview General Umezu, still in uniform, at least for another month, as he assisted the Occupation with Japan's demobilization. Like the others interviewed, Umezu assured Sanders that Unit 731 activities were solely for troop protection against epidemics and distanced himself from any implication that the unit might have conducted germ weapons research. "From the beginning to the end of the war," he said, "I entertained no thought of using it offensively." He also reminded Sanders that, for humane reasons, "The use of bacterial agents is forbidden by international law."[54]

SCAP and the Major War Criminals

While Sanders was conducting interviews, General MacArthur was under pressure from the Joint Chiefs to organize the prosecution of major Japanese war criminals, commensurate with the Nuremberg International Military Tribunal, scheduled to begin that fall. A September 4 radiogram from Washington had ordered the supreme commander to arrest and detain a broad range of suspects: top army and navy leaders, all commissioned officers of the military police (Kempeitai), key ultranationalists, and those high government officials who had played an active role in aggression.[55] MacArthur, though, was ambivalent about staging a major trial.[56]

The understanding at SCAP was that the major Japanese war crime had been the strike on Pearl Harbor, which had left almost 2,500 dead and destroyed or damaged eighteen US ships and three hundred aircraft. For Americans, December 7, 1941, was truly "a date that would live in infamy," as President Roosevelt had told the nation in his radio address the next day. MacArthur's staff came up with a list of ten foremost members of Japan's cabinet in 1941, which was then enlarged to thirty-eight officials. On September 10 SCAP ordered Thorpe at CIC to begin a blitz campaign to arrest them all. At the top of the list was former prime minister Tojo Hideki. As Tojo was about to be arrested at his home, he attempted suicide by shooting himself in the chest.[57] With press reporters on hand to staunch the blood flow (and to photograph him) and emergency American medical intervention, Tojo survived and, after his recovery, was incarcerated at Sugamo Prison in Tokyo. Two of his cabinet members committed hara-kiri before they could be apprehended. One was Koizumi, the former minister of health and welfare who had befriended General Ishii, Dr. Miyagawa, and others associated with Unit 731 germ weapons.[58] Other suicides followed, leading the Soviet journal *New Times* to criticize the clumsy American tactics that were permitting Japanese war criminals to escape justice.[59]

More suspects were added to the list and, with the assistance of Japan's police, more arrests were quickly made.

While Sugamo Prison was filling up, the SWNCC wanted MacArthur to move toward a major tribunal. On September 22 he received a radiogram from the committee that spelled out the "Identification, apprehension and trial of persons suspected of War Crimes." Among other details, it offered three categories from article 6 of the Nuremberg Charter, denoting them as (A) Crimes Against Peace, (B) War Crimes, and (C) Crimes Against Humanity:

A. Planning, preparation, initiation or waging of a war of aggression or a war in violation of International treaties, agreements or assurances, or participation by a common plan or conspiracy for the accomplishment of any of the foregoing.
B. Violations of the laws or customs of war. Such violations shall include but not be limited to murder, ill treatment or deportation to slave labor or for any other purpose of civilian population of, or in, occupied territory, murder or ill treatment of prisoners of war or internees or persons on the seas or elsewhere, improper treatment of hostages, plunder of public or private property, wanton destruction of cities, towns or villages or devastation not justified by military necessity.[60]
C. Murder, extermination, enslavement, deportation and other inhumane acts committed against any civilian population, before or during the war or persecutions on political, racial or religious grounds in execution of or in connection with any crime defined herein whether or not in violation of the domestic law of the country where perpetrated.

These categories presented the basis for formulating a Tokyo Charter following the lines laid out by the London Charter for Nuremberg. The emphasis was on the "Class A" crimes against peace, for which top individual leaders would be prosecuted, with the B and C crimes as added possibilities that might or not be included in the charges against a specific defendant.

Well before the Tokyo Charter was written, British and Commonwealth nations were prosecuting the Japanese military for the mistreatment of

POWs.[61] In 1944 soldiers returning from Asia and the Pacific to Great Britain, Australia, New Zealand, and Canada brought home firsthand accounts of Japanese abuses—of brutal beatings, torture, starvation, forced marches, and murders that violated the international rules of war, particularly the Geneva Convention of 1929 for the protection of prisoners of war. In June 1944 the Australians established a War Crimes Commission in Canberra and appointed Sir William Webb, chief justice of the Supreme Court of Queensland, to lead an investigation of these firsthand accounts of Japanese war crimes. A partial release of the results, which confirmed the gruesome POW stories, caused an uproar. Japan was vilified as Australia's "number one enemy" and Emperor Hirohito as its "number one war criminal."[62] Subscribing, though, to the principle of justice over revenge, the Australians embarked on a long series of military tribunals—over six hundred in the next five years. However uneven in practice, their procedures followed the general standards for military tribunals and allowed counsel for the defense and appeals.

In the fall of 1944, having regained Singapore from the Japanese, who had captured it in 1942, the British set up a War Crimes Branch there and, relying on domestic criminal law, traced suspects, gathered evidence, conducted victim interviews, gathered photographs, and created fingerprint files to help identify the potential criminals. The project was hindered by the postwar repatriation of Allied troops, which put potential witnesses at a great distance, and the enormous scale of Japan's wartime empire. The British eventually created seventeen military courts, from Singapore to Rangoon, Hong Kong, Malaya, and British North Borneo; and they cooperated with the Americans, Dutch, and French on their separate war crimes cases.[63]

For MacArthur, the Japanese military's abuse of POWs was the most "heinous" of war crimes.[64] His first SCAP directive was the freeing of Allied prisoners of war, in dire need of food and medical care, from the over fifty camps in Japan. While under pressure to organize the IMTFE, he moved to prosecute two assaults on Americans that had wounded their national pride. The first was the October 10, 1942, Japanese execution of three downed US airmen who had been part of the famous Doolittle Raid conducted earlier that year.[65] On August 13, 1942, in a post facto legal response to the raid, the Japanese passed the Enemy Airmen's Act, requiring the death sentence for enemy fliers who bombed civilian and nonmilitary targets, which the Doolittle Raiders had done. (As Doolittle's copilot later recalled, "Since we had a load of incendiaries, our target was the populated areas of the west and northwest parts of Tokyo."[66])

Although all fifteen Doolittle planes were afterward abandoned or destroyed in crash landings in occupied China (or, with one exception, in the Soviet Union), nearly all the airmen made it to safety. Eight crew members, though, were captured by the Japanese, flown to Japan for nearly two months of solitary confinement and torture, and then brought to Shanghai for a quick sham trial in late August 1942.[67] Five of the eight Americans were sentenced to prison. The other three were executed by a firing squad and buried in a nearby cemetery. The news of their fate was unknown in the West until April 23, 1943, when the White House released the details. Not surprisingly, "the response the story provoked in the United States was comparable to the rage that greeted the news of Pearl Harbor."[68]

A second source of outrage for MacArthur personally and for many Americans was the fate of US soldiers in the Bataan Death March. The brutal 60-mile trek involved 76,000 prisoners (12,000 Americans and 64,000 Filipinos) left behind after the April 1942 surrender of Corregidor. Those captives who lagged or resisted were shot; nearly half the prisoners did not survive; the rest were sent by "hell ships" to forced labor camps in Japan and Manchuria, with many dying en route.[69] MacArthur, the Pacific commander forced to flee and leave his troops behind, felt a special anguish. In January 1944 the official report on the march went public with details of the torture and killing of the American and Filipino captives that matched similar accounts of forced labor on the Burma-Siam "railway of death" and the mistreatment and deaths of other POWs transported on "hell ships" to Japanese camps. A few months before the war's end, anti-Japanese feeling among the Allies had risen to such a pitch that "the true goal of the war seemed to be the enemy's extermination."[70]

As SCAP MacArthur had the authority to seek quick retribution in both cases. To begin, he turned to the Allied Legal Section (LS) under his jurisdiction at General Headquarters (GHQ). Legal Section had five divisions: Administrative, Law, Legislation and Justice, and a division each to handle communication with the Philippines and Australia. Throughout the Occupation, LS, especially its Legislation and Justice Division, became "SCAP's primary watchdog for civil rights."[71] The role of Legal Section in assisting war crimes prosecution was more vulnerable to bias and ultimately secretive.

As his LS chief of section, MacArthur chose the 43-year-old Colonel Alva C. Carpenter, a lawyer educated at Northwestern University and described in the press as heroically "tall" and "square-jawed."[72] Like Willoughby, he was one of MacArthur's trusted "Bataan Gang" officers. Following MacArthur's instructions, Carpenter quickly authorized the trial of General Homma Masaharu, who had been in command in the Philippines at the time of the Bataan Death March. In cooperation with the Republic of China, another tribunal was arranged to take place in Shanghai, to prosecute the Japanese military who had captured the Doolittle pilots and executed three of them in August 1942.

MacArthur, whose ties to the Philippines went back to his first visit as a lieutenant in 1903, wanted another score settled. In the 1945 battle to regain Manila, some 30,000 trapped Japanese marines and sailors had slaughtered an estimated 100,000 or more civilians in Manila seeking refuge in churches, schools, and their homes. Reports of atrocities in the final days were shocking: "Hospitals were set afire after their patients had been strapped to their beds. The corpses of males were mutilated, females of all ages were raped before they were slain, and babies' eyeballs were gorged out and smeared on the wall like jelly."[73]

MacArthur blamed the Japanese general Yamashita Tomoyaki, leader of the Japanese forces in the final year of the Pacific war, for what became known as "the Rape of Manila." Yamashita had ordered his troops to retreat from Manila, but, with a breakdown in communication, he lost control to an admiral who decided to defend the city to the death. Nonetheless, MacArthur had Carpenter arrange Yamashita's prosecution for war crimes, charging him with a failure of "command responsibility," an important distinction regarding a dereliction of duty rather than giving a direct order or permission for criminal acts in war. Like Homma, Yamashita was found guilty and executed.[74] Ignoring the international controversy about officer liability that ensued, MacArthur lauded the decision with a bombastic speech about "due justice."[75]

Solving the Problem of the Emperor

In these early months of the Occupation, trust in MacArthur ran high. As Assistant Secretary of State John J. McCloy wrote him, "You have a job at the windy corner of our policy and I do not know of anyone as well qualified to take us around it."[76] On December 26, 1945, at the Moscow Conference, the major Allied leaders (the United States, United Kingdom, and Soviet Union) also gave MacArthur their vote of confidence as "the Supreme Commander who is the sole executive authority for the Allied Powers in Japan."[77] MacArthur was also given "full responsibility for the administration of Korea south of 38 degrees latitude." The Soviet Union, an occupying force since the previous summer, maintained jurisdiction above that line. By agreement, the two nations would confer on the administration of the two zones, although nothing would prevent the inevitable ideological split.[78]

In theory, it was possible that the Allies' new Far Eastern Commission (FEC), based in Washington, could contest SCAP's decisions. The Moscow Conference made sure that the FEC would be represented in Tokyo by the Allied Council for Japan (ACJ), composed of the supreme commander as the US delegate and chairman, one representative each from the Soviet Union and China, and a fourth member representing the UK, Australia, New Zealand, and India. MacArthur appointed George Atcheson, Jr., his chief policy advisor from the State Department, as his deputy to the ACJ. He then gave the council delegates a two-hour speech outlining his goals for the Occupation, while declaring himself equally loyal to each of the Allied powers and open to their assistance. The British delegate, although he found MacArthur's style "somewhat florid," judged the performance "most impressive and statesman-like."[79] After that, MacArthur generally ignored the council's opinions.

The September 1945 order from Washington had urged MacArthur to hold the highest Japanese leaders accountable for war crimes. But MacArthur delayed in switching his focus from field commanders in the Philippines to the power structure of Imperial Japan. The main issue was whether Emperor Hirohito should be indicted. Australia, China, France, and the Soviet Union, along with members of the US Congress and many Americans, were in favor of Hirohito's prosecution as a war criminal. Two Axis leaders had already escaped Allied justice. The previous April, Hitler had committed suicide in Berlin and, in the same week, fascist Italy's deposed leader Benito Mussolini was captured and shot by partisans in northern Italy. The punishment of the third Axis leader seemed essential.

In opposition, the British were wary of toppling any monarch, and, like American officials, including MacArthur, they had academic advisors arguing against robbing the defeated nation of a stabilizing icon.[80] Early in the Occupation MacArthur's psychological warfare staff, along with Foreign Minister Shigemitsu, convinced him that preserving the emperor's position was essential to his mission.[81] So far, the Japanese reaction to defeat in the Home Islands had been placid, thanks to respect for the emperor's authority. By October 15, in accordance with the schedule laid down by SCAP, all tactical Japanese Army groups had been dissolved and some seven million Japanese soldiers had reportedly laid down their arms. Japanese public opinion also supported MacArthur's protection of the emperor.[82] In a closed meeting, MacArthur told representatives of the FEC that Hirohito had been nothing more than a ventriloquist's dummy for fanatical militarists.[83]

Yet in late November the Joint Chiefs of Staff position, communicated to MacArthur by the SWNCC, was that, while the institution of the emperor could be preserved, Hirohito as a person was not "immune from arrest, trial, and punishment as a War Criminal."[84] Further, "any decision not to try him should be made in light of all available facts." Barely acknowledging MacArthur's authority, the message said that he should gather criminal evidence against the emperor with strict security and transmit it to the Joint Chiefs for submission to the SWNCC. "In due course," the cable ended, "you will be asked to recommend as to conditions which may warrant or permit proceedings against Hirohito as a War Criminal."

The cable foresaw that a move to indict the emperor might come from one or more of the Allies. The next month, in fact, Alan Mansfield (later the lead Australian prosecutor at the Tokyo trial) presented a report to the United Nations War Crimes Commission in London that put Hirohito at the top of a list of sixty-one major Japanese war criminals. Washington and MacArthur would prove slow to react.

The International Prosecution Section and the Counsel in Chief

In Tokyo, MacArthur moved forward with plans for organizing the IMTFE, which was threatened by the same problems with coordinating the Allied cases that at first troubled Nuremberg. The Four Powers' three different legal traditions—Anglo-American, Continental European, and Soviet—were early on recognized as obstacles to cooperation. The American and British jurists, sharing roots in English common law, presumed the IMT would use an adversarial system, in which the trial judge knew only the charges and let opposing prosecution and defense lawyers act to present evidence and examine and cross-examine witnesses. The French espoused the "inquisitorial system" of Continental law, in which an examining magistrate is given all criminal evidence in a dossier and decides whether an indictment is warranted. If so, the evidence would be given to the defendant and the court and the trial would proceed with all concerned parties informed of the facts. The Soviets saw law more as the servant of state order and ideology.[85]

With China and the Netherlands added to the mix, plus input from Burma and Portugal, friction in Tokyo could be worse than at Nuremberg, where the four judges negotiated their differences.[86] MacArthur decided that the IMTFE would need a chief of counsel to prevent a judicial Tower of Babel, and that he should be an American. Truman agreed and to fill the role selected Joseph B. Keenan, a New Deal democrat with a Harvard Law School degree (Class of 1913) who had served in the army in World War I.[87]

From 1933 to 1939 Keenan had worked at the Department of Justice, reaching the level of assistant attorney general in charge of the Criminal Division; his immediate superior had been Tom Clark, now Truman's attorney general and trusted advisor. Keenan's antiracketeering cases against figures like "Machine Gun" Kelly had put him on the front pages, and he had authored the Lindbergh antikidnapping law and guided it through Congress.[88] President Roosevelt had chosen him as a liaison to Capitol Hill and nicknamed him "Joe the Key" for his insider connections. At one time in line to run for senator from Ohio (when he lived and had a law practice in Cleveland), Keenan was ambitious to be Tokyo's answer to Supreme Court Justice Robert Jackson, the chief prosecutor at Nuremberg whose eloquent opening speech had just made world news. He knew Jackson on a first-name basis from his work at the Justice Department and did not hesitate to ask his advice about his new role in Tokyo. Yet Keenan, with his red face, polka-dot bow ties, and stories about gangsters like John Dillinger, Baby Face Nelson, and Bonny and Clyde, had little of Jackson's stature and gravitas.

In preparation for Keenan's arrival in Tokyo, on November 29 MacArthur instructed Alva Carpenter at Legal Section to create a new subdivision, the International Prosecution Section (IPS), to organize interrogations and search for war crimes evidence. This new entity would concentrate on Class A war criminals, the top leaders, leaving Legal Section to pursue lesser suspects. Legal Section at that time was also home to an Investigation Division, created solely to identify and gather evidence on Japanese leaders responsible for Pearl Harbor. Moved to IPS, that division's mission expanded to major war crimes suspects in general.[89]

Joseph Keenan left Washington for Tokyo on December 2, just as his appointment at IPS was announced to the press. Accompanying him on the secretary of state's aircraft *The Statesman* were fifteen lawyers whose recruitment, known as Project K, had been kept secret. For the news photographers invited to the send-off, Keenan, short and burly, stood on the first step of the gangway to look as tall as or taller than his team members gathered with him. One of them, a rangy older man in a trench coat, was Colonel Thomas Morrow. Morrow, a highly-decorated veteran of World War I, had rejoined the army after Pearl Harbor, leaving behind a judgeship in Ohio. Another lawyer of the same generation, Carlisle Higgins from North Carolina, was on board the flight; he would serve as Keenan's deputy chief of counsel at IPS.[90] Captain Luke Lea, Jr., the son of a former democratic senator from Tennessee, would serve as Keenan's military aide.

The Project K recruits were men of mixed backgrounds and ages but qualified by education or experience or both. Solis Horwitz, a Harvard-trained lawyer, had served during the war as a Japanese language specialist with US Army Intelligence; one of the brainiest of the project recruits, he would be appointed a deputy prosecutor. Other recruits were Henry Hauxhurst, an experienced corporate lawyer from Ohio; Colonel Gilbert Woolworth, who had come out of retirement from the Army's Judge Advocate General's Department; and John Fihelly, from the Justice Department, who was widely considered the best trial lawyer in the United

States.[91] Also on Keenan's team was Navy Captain James J. Robinson, another Harvard-educated lawyer and advisor on criminal law to the US Supreme Court. Robinson had recently headed the Investigation Division at Legal Services and had been at Yokohama on September 12 when General MacArthur proclaimed that the tribunals would be "fair and free from vengeance or politics."[92]

Once in Tokyo, Keenan found the neophyte IPS organization waiting for him. To it, he added his team, after its members had been settled in quarters at the Hattori House estate and in offices at the elegant Meiji Building, close to MacArthur's Dai-Ichi Building headquarters. The IPS would house the Allied prosecution teams from all participating nations, in addition to offices for the Chief of Counsel, Administration, Investigation Division, and Documents Division.

Once in Tokyo, Chief of Counsel Keenan was responsible for orchestrating the entire prosecution, supervising everything from translating and evaluating evidence to selecting defendants and integrating the different national cases against the accused into a single indictment. Keenan himself seemed not to know who all the defendants might be or how the indictment might be phrased. The twenty-three IPS lawyers (fifteen civilians and eight US military personnel) were also novices. As Solis Horwitz later recalled, "Rarely has any group of men undertaking a project of similar size and scope been less prepared for their task than were the original twenty-odd members of the legal staff of the prosecution when they began their labors on 8 December 1945."[93]

Keenan divided the assignments for his IPS lawyers into thirteen categories, with each individually or with a partner expected to concentrate on a different time period and subject area.[94] Colonel Morrow was put in charge of investigating conflicts in China from late 1936 onward and identifying the members of the five Japanese cabinets from 1934 to 1939. Fihelly and Higgins were to analyze treaties involving the Axis powers and relations with the Allies, plus the five cabinets that ruled from 1939 through October 1941, when Tojo came to power. The remaining groups concentrated on suspects in influential "cliques." Hauxhurst and Horwitz concentrated on the corporate industries (*zaibatsu*), while two military officers, Colonel Woolworth and Captain Robinson, focused on army cliques (*gumbatsu*). To Robinson would go the plum assignment of arguing the criminality of Japan's attack on Pearl Harbor.[95] Another officer, Colonel Douglas L. Waldorf, was assigned to combing the central Counter-Intelligence Corps files.

The net for criminal suspects was cast wide. Legal Section helped with suggestions, as did SCAP's Counter-Intelligence Section under General Thorpe. SCAP's Office of the Political Advisor (POLAD) compiled a list of one hundred suspects from a copy of *Who's Who in Japan* and other sources.[96] Ministries in Australia and China and various Allied agencies also made suggestions. Some Nazi German files from Nuremberg were added to the data on Axis ties. From Washington, the State-War-Navy Coordinating Committee sent its recommendations, based mostly on lists of past cabinet members.[97]

Finding official Japanese documents for evidence to prosecute suspects emerged as the first and worst of IPS's problems.[98] Just as Keenan and his team arrived in Tokyo, SCAP was informed that, on August 14, with the news of the surrender agreement, the Japanese government had ordered the destruction of all potentially damning files—those related to foreign affairs, counter-intelligence, thought, peace preservation or materials by which national power might be estimated and those relating to "secret history."[99] First the cabinet, then the Ministry of Foreign Affairs, and finally the military branches destroyed so many files that the clouds of smoke from incinerations reportedly "darkened the skies."[100] More documents were burned in the early days of the Occupation, before its counterintelligence agencies were in place.[101] The persistent refusal of Japanese officials to give IPS access to their remaining documents made its work even harder. Finally, a direct request by MacArthur to the emperor allowed IPS staff to pick out what it needed, but it took a month after Keenan's arrival to receive the many requested documents. The destruction of files necessarily shifted IPS to witness interrogation, a labor-intensive way of gaining information, which required translators who were in short supply and already needed to process documents.[102]

In December 1945, after the earlier arrests of Tojo and most of his cabinet, SCAP approved the same dragnet approach to arrest the members of the two cabinets that had preceded Tojo's. This sweep of suspects brought the possible timeline for prosecution back to 1937 and the start of the Second Sino-Japanese War. On December 16 Prince Konoe, who had led both these cabinets, killed himself with potassium cyanide.[103] Imprisoned in this second set of arrests was Marquis Kido Koichi, former Lord Keeper of the Privy Seal and so close to the emperor that he was perceived as a kind of surrogate for Hirohito. Kido handed over his diary, 5,920 entries dating from 1930 to the war's end, a record that gave the prosecution a playbook for understanding political events and identifying suspects.[104] But the final list of defendants remained undetermined.

Australia's earlier demand to the UN War Crimes Commission that the emperor be prosecuted was still at issue. It circulated from the commission to the Allied Council in Japan, to the Far Eastern Council in Washington, and was even passed to the IPS. MacArthur's firm intent, though, was to convert Hirohito from a deity to his subjects to a beneficent secular monarch. Thus on January 1, 1946, at MacArthur's request, Hirohito issued what became known as the "Humanity Declaration." The relationship between the emperor and the polity, he declared, rested on mutual trust and affection, not on "the false conception that the Emperor is divine, and that the Japanese people are superior to other races and fated to rule the world."[105] His emphasis on pre-existing Meiji values of citizen participation allowed him to support the goals of the liberal, democratic constitution that SCAP was formulating for Japan. The emperor was already appearing at public events in Western garb to convince his awed constituents that he was an ordinary citizen of the new Japan.

Gathering evidence to indict Hirohito was of no interest to MacArthur, nor was listening to Allied critics. Instead, in a blasting cable to General Eisenhower at the JCS, he argued that to indict the emperor would cause "a tremendous convulsion among the Japanese people, the repercussions of which cannot be overestimated. He is a symbol which unites all Japanese. Destroy him and the nation will disintegrate."[106] MacArthur also raised the risk of a future communist Japan. Communist activists, released from Japanese jails, were gaining popular support; by Occupation rules, their freedom of speech was guaranteed as long as they did not criticize the Occupation or the Allies, but they might pose a threat. "Should the emperor be indicted," MacArthur wrote, "I believe all hope of introducing modern democratic methods would disappear and than [*sic*] when military control finally ceased some form of intense regimentation probably along communistic lines would arise from the mutilated masses."

Faced with a politically sensitive decision, SWNCC members passed the issue to their network of consultants throughout the War Department and at the Department of State. Months of inconclusive deliberations followed, slowed by high-level reluctance to cause controversy, either by prosecuting the emperor or by exonerating him.[107] Bureaucratic inertia gave MacArthur what he wanted: the time, without headlines, to make Hirohito into a figurehead for the new, democratic, pacifist Japan.

The Tokyo Charter

That first winter in Tokyo, in consultation with Keenan and the SCAP legal staff—and avoiding input from other Allied nations—MacArthur edited the Nuremberg Charter to the purposes of the IMTFE.[108] In the new version, the Tokyo Charter, he respected the Nuremberg war crimes definitions, with some minor changes. For example, to Class A war crimes, he added a phrase that targeted the "leaders, organizers, instigators and accomplices" who had conspired in the Axis criminal plans. This addition underscored the understanding that during the war the Japanese public, increasingly isolated from the outside world, had been manipulated by government propaganda and Thought Police. To crimes against humanity, he added imprisonment, torture, and rape—three categories already associated with the excesses of Japanese warfare. He also kept throughout the emphasis on "murder," so that top Japanese leaders would be held responsible for the intentional, premeditated killings authorized by their government and be identified as common criminals not above domestic law.

With the authority granted him by the Allies, MacArthur inserted provisions into the Tokyo Charter that directly or indirectly enhanced his control. For example, he reserved for himself the right to approve the judges nominated by each of the participating nations and to appoint the president of the tribunal; Washington had stipulated that the number of court judges could be nine or as many as eleven, depending on which Allied nations decided to participate and whether India and the Philippines would be allowed judges, which was not yet decided. MacArthur set the quorum for the court at six judges, with no alternates allowed.[109] Decisions about the convictions of individual defendants would be made by majority vote (in Nuremberg, three out of four votes were decisive), and he gave the president of the tribunal the power to break any ties.

MacArthur would have the ultimate say over the sentencing of defendants, who, as in Nuremberg, had no right of appeal. In Nuremberg, sentencing authority had been accorded to the Control Council of Germany, the political entity created by the four occupying powers to oversee denazification and which also authorized the IMT in Nuremberg. Setting himself up for possible criticism, MacArthur took this prerogative for himself; although he could not impose greater penalties than the court decided, he could lessen a penalty, by changing a death sentence to life imprisonment or decreasing the term of a sentence. In a small but important revision to the charter, MacArthur deleted the reference to "heads of state" as criminals, which would include the emperor, and substituted the phrase "high officials."

MacArthur also created a General Secretariat for the IMTFE, to assume overall managerial responsibility, for example, for the employment of court clerks and court reporters, travel and housing, document reproduction, and the translation of court documents and records. Japanese and English were designated the tribunal's two official languages, putting the Soviet Union and France at a disadvantage not found at Nuremberg, and leaving China and the Netherlands to adapt as they could.

On January 19, 1946, MacArthur declared the creation of the IMTFE:

> I, Douglas MacArthur, as Supreme Commander for the Allied Powers, by virtue of the authority so conferred on me, in order to implement the Terms of Surrender which requires the meting out of stern justice to war criminals, do order . . . there shall be established an International Military Tribunal for the Far East (IMTFE) for the trial of those persons charged individually, or as members of organizations, or in both capacities, with offenses which include crimes against peace.[110]

The tribunal's legitimacy would be determined by its independence from SCAP, a concept on which its judges agreed. Initially, MacArthur envisioned giving the court's opening address and continuing to give direct advice to the court. President Webb and the other judges refused both suggestions.[111] Backing off, MacArthur reassured them that he would in no way trouble the legitimacy of the court, a promise he did not keep.

2

SPOILS OF WAR

SECRET JAPANESE BIOLOGICAL SCIENCE

According to US postwar defense policy, the acquisition of an innovative weapon could override moral or legal judgments. In 1944 and 1945 the US military shipped a hundred German V-2 rockets to America and appropriated tons of technical documents. With the recruitment of Wernher von Braun, Arthur Rudolph, and other Nazi rocket scientists, a bright future for American missile development was assured.[1] Finding new lives in America, these scientists were left unaccountable for the consequences of rocket attacks—the killings of defenseless British civilians, the destruction of cities, and the exploitation of slave laborers, including the thirty thousand captives who died in the years of building the German rockets in cave factories at Nordhausen.[2]

Rocket science was just one example. Although the Germans did not use battlefield chemical weapons in World War II, by the spring of 1942 they were mass producing the nerve agent tabun, exploiting slave and forced laborers, subjecting them to illness or death from accidental exposure. The US and British joint search for expert German chemists continued, despite the report that one IG Farben executive had admitted to tabun and sarin testing on concentration camp inmates at the IG Elberfeld factory to determine lethal dosages.[3] Other reports surfaced of fatal human experiments with phosgene, mustard gas, and another potent World War I vesicant, lewisite, at the Natzweiler and Neuengamme concentration camps, to test antidotes.[4] The resemblance of these experiments to other Nazi atrocities cast doubt on whether any scientific researchers involved should be given immunity. After the war, when this inhumane research was uncovered by military intelligence, Allied researchers who reviewed the data responded with technocratic comments that, in their lack of humanity, echoed Nazi norms.[5] They disparaged the Nazis' "poor methodology" and "surprising lack of originality" and wondered why more tests had not been conducted using mechanically sprayed poisons.[6]

Providing explicit legal protection, the loophole in the JCS directive 1067 allowed Germans who possessed "information of value" to be exempted from war crimes prosecution by the United States, a significant guarantee for individual candidates seeking immunity. Some fifteen hundred German scientists were given new biographies (attached to their real files) in an Office of Strategic Services cover-up called Project Paperclip.[7] The national security value of scientific knowledge, especially when viewed in competition with the Soviet Union, gave the victors the right to invent justifications for technology transfer that sidestepped questions of ethics.[8] At the worst, scientists with records linked to atrocities posed the threat of embarrassing publicity in the midst of the major and minor war crimes trials, but the risks were taken anyway.[9]

Arriving in Japan with MacArthur, the US Scientific Intelligence team was mainly made up of physicists, including Karl Compton, a small battery of chemists, and Colonel Murray Sanders as the lone biologist. The physicists started their inquiry at Japan's Institute of Physical and Chemical Research, which had overseen wartime atomic research in laboratories throughout the country. They interviewed around three hundred of their Japanese counterparts and made inspection visits to a sample of institute laboratories, finding that many of them had been damaged during the war.[10] The team's conclusion was that Japan had little in the way of nuclear science that rivaled US expertise; their physicists were capable, but, lacking resources, including uranium, they had decided in 1943 that they could not develop a fission bomb during the war. Instead, they had been exploring the use of nuclear energy to replace coal, a venture that ended when the main laboratory in Tokyo was destroyed by bombing.

With assistance from the US Navy Technical Mission to Japan, the Chemical Warfare Service, and General Charles Willoughby's G-2 in Tokyo, the survey team reviewed Japanese chemical weapons production and defenses.[11] Together they assessed Japanese types of chemical agents and their formulas, production techniques and facilities, stockpile and dump sites, munitions (including tear gas grenades), decontamination methods, and gas masks. They also sent samples of agents like lewisite and mustard gas to the United States for analysis. The US investigators discovered that the island of Okunoshima, near Hiroshima, had been Japan's secret center for the mass production of chemical weapons. Arrangements were made to have the factory destroyed and its stockpiles dumped into the sea; its grim history of accidents and injuries to workers was kept secret for decades. More stockpiles of mustard, tear gas, and other agents were uncovered on Shikoku Island, at a station midway between Hiroshima and Nagasaki. The team's conclusion was that Japanese chemical weapons were technologically less advanced than those of Nazi Germany, whose scientists had not shared their nerve gas formulas with Japan.

In his solitary inquiry into Japanese germ weapons, Murray Sanders, working from his office at the Dai-Ichi Building, continued to rely on Dr. Naito Ryoichi and his network. Before the war Sanders had taught at Columbia University's College of Physicians and Surgeons, and he was due to return there soon. Within weeks after Pearl Harbor, two other Columbia faculty, Theodor Rosebury and Elvin Kabat, along with a medical student, had written an important prospectus for a US biological weapons program.[12] They advised that microbes and toxins should be studied based on their availability and the enemy's likely vaccine or antisera defenses. Anthrax and botulinum toxin were first on the list—they were lethal and hardy pathogens (anthrax spores had been tested successfully as bomb fill), and no enemy was likely to be invulnerable to them. Biological warfare, as they saw it, suited total war strategy: "the disorganization of industrial areas behind the lines or of army centers and camps; for use as part of a 'scorched earth' policy, and against valuable animals, food plants, and industrial crops."[13]

In the spirit of patriotism, Sanders, like Rosebury and Kabat and many others, volunteered to work for the highly secret US biological weapons initiative. By early 1945, when intelligence showed there was no German BW threat, nearly all the senior scientists expected to resume their academic careers. Rosebury was eager to publish what he had learned about airborne diseases, Kabat to continue his research on immunology, and Sanders to explore the curative potential of snake venom, the direction his wartime lab work had taken him. In the interim, in Tokyo Sanders was as comfortable as any army officer could be, with a room at the Frank Lloyd Wright–designed Imperial Hotel (in the part not demolished in the bombings), where MIT president Karl Compton and many US generals and Allied officials were staying. Coupled with his access to General Willoughby and, through him, General MacArthur, Sanders was enjoying a stay in Tokyo that contrasted sharply with life at Camp Detrick, the center of the US BW program located in Frederick, Maryland. At the war's end, with hundreds of its employees returning to civilian life, morale at the base had plummeted. The program's staff reduction occurred in the overall context of postwar attrition, during which troop numbers fell to half their wartime peak and the War Department had difficulty recruiting replacements. No sooner had victory been claimed than Congress began issuing harsh criticisms of the conduct of the war. The Senate Special Committee to Investigate the National Defense Program, started by Truman when he was a senator, lashed out against graft, corruption, and excessive expenditures in the military.[14] Wartime military promotions were especially criticized as a drain on the military budget.

At the Chemical Warfare Service, the question became whether Camp Detrick's biological warfare program, which it oversaw, had any future at all; in three years of wide-ranging research and at a cost of $4 million, it had failed to meet its promise of producing a viable strategic weapon. Much hope had been invested in the anthrax pathogen *Bacillus anthracis*. Historically, the bacterium had caused ancient plagues in livestock that spread to humans through animal contact and the consumption of infected meat. As late as the mid-nineteenth century epizootics in Europe had devastated herds, ruined meat and tanning industries, and made textile workers handling wool vulnerable to inhaling the deadly spores. Louis Pasteur's discovery of effective vaccines for livestock in 1881 finally protected workers from skin infections and meat-eating consumers from intestinal outbreaks. Even so, it was understood that a vaccine for humans was dangerous and that the inhalation of anthrax spores remained exceptionally lethal, which assured its value as a weapon.

In the early 1940s British tests on Gruinard Island in Scotland demonstrated that those same spores dispersed by exploding bombs caused death to sheep, usually in a few days. By 1945 the US program had built a factory in Vigo, Indiana, intended to produce large volumes of anthrax spores to pack into British-designed munitions. In March 1944, intrigued by this new weapon, Prime Minister Winston Churchill approved an order of 500,000 anthrax bombs, which was beyond the factory's capacity to fulfill before the war's end.[15]

A fundamental problem at Detrick was ignorance about the human response to specific doses—about how many anthrax spores, for example, it took to kill a single individual or, from that data point, how to predictably gauge the devastation of a large urban population. The obvious missing element was research on human beings; since no cure could be offered, infecting test subjects via anthrax aerosols was tantamount to a death sentence.

On August 11, while Sanders was in Manila, the commanding general of the Army Services Forces ordered the BW program's complete termination, which meant laying off around a thousand workers. All industry contracts and research and development at Camp Detrick and most of the bomb testing at Dugway Proving Ground, Utah, were to be canceled.[16] The army's larger plan was to incorporate the Chemical Warfare Service into Army Ordnance, as a supplier of munitions like incendiary bombs but without control over their tactical employment by field forces.

The 1945 move to downgrade CWS was a reprise of the War Department's post–World War I effort to relegate chemical weapons to the Army Corps of Engineers. This time, no General Fries had to campaign among industrial leaders to save the service. Instead, it found an advocate in the new secretary of war, Robert P. Patterson (who in September had replaced Henry Stimson); Patterson wanted to maintain postwar capability during this "difficult period of readjustment," so that America would be prepared with advanced weapons for the next global war.[17] He was impressed by a letter from the head of CWS, Major General William N. Porter, in defense of its research innovations and the postwar combat-readiness training that the service offered.[18] As undersecretary of war in 1940–1945, Patterson had mobilized US industry for the war effort, and he appreciated how successfully Porter and the CWS staff had worked then with large corporations and managed the production of incendiary munitions essential to US war plans.

Through Patterson's influence, an independent CWS survived, but it was much reduced, and the US BW program continued to be cut back. The insect research site at Horn Island, Mississippi, the Vigo, Indiana, anthrax bomb factory, and the Granite Peak testing site were shut down and the industry contracts supporting them terminated. The CWS would center most of its biological weapons research and development, once spread over dozens of universities, industries, and government facilities, at Camp Detrick. This program shrinkage came with a 40 percent reduction in the FY1946 budget for biological weapons.[19]

Brigadier General Alden Waitt, then the CWS executive director, was assigned the promotion of Detrick's postwar mission.[20] Waitt had earned his undergraduate and master's degrees in chemistry from MIT for research on methane. He joined the army in 1917 and served as a gas warfare officer during World I in France, the scene of many horrific chemical battles. After that war, when public antipathy for chemical weapons ran high, Waitt joined the campaign of General Fries to sustain the CWS. Eventually he became a US Army instructor at the Air Force Tactical School at Maxwell Field, Alabama, where Curtis LeMay learned about the incendiary weapons that, as a general in the Pacific, he would use to devastate Japan.[21]

In 1934, as fears of German rearmament grew, the Joint Board of the War and Navy Departments authorized the first use of chemical weapons by the United States, its option since it had not ratified the Geneva Protocol.[22] Still, President Roosevelt's revulsion for chemical weapons worked as a restraint. Resonating to antipathy toward chemical weapons among rank-and-file officers, Roosevelt influenced a decrease in the CWS budget, kept the service from becoming an upgraded Army Chemical Corps, and forced a retreat from the first-use provision. "It has been and is the policy of this Government," Roosevelt declared in 1937, "to do everything in its power to outlaw the use of chemicals in warfare. Such use is inhuman and contrary to what modern civilization should stand for." To the dismay of CWS, he went further: "I hope the time will come when the Chemical Warfare Service can be entirely abolished."[23]

In 1939 Waitt met Lieutenant Chiang Wego (General Chiang Kai-shek's son), then in military training in United States. From him Waitt learned in detail how in 1937 the Japanese had used mustard gas on Chinese troops at Shanghai and that they still continued with chemical attacks. Never doubting Chiang's account, Waitt afterward argued that Japan's CW aggression meant that the United States must be prepared to use its own chemicals with a force that would "overshadow that of any possible opponent."[24] Not surprisingly, he remained a consistent, vocal critic of the Geneva Protocol. "All good people who still believe in international honor and good faith," he wrote in 1942, "should understand that the United States has refused to tie its own hands with an anti-gas treaty."[25]

In 1944, as the assistant chief of CWS for field operations, Waitt traveled with Allied troops as they advanced across Germany and unexpectedly discovered stockpiles of the Nazi nerve gas tabun buried in concrete bunkers.[26] The first American reaction was surprise. During the war its scientists had tried without success to develop organophosphates as chemical weapon agents but decided instead to concentrate on mustard gas testing and production.[27]

Earlier, in December 1943, CWS began considering how its existing chemical stockpile could be used in all-out gas attacks on the Axis powers, an idea that General Waitt floated to his Canadian colleagues in Ottawa.[28] In July 1944 Prime Minister Churchill ordered the British Chiefs of Staff to make a "cold-blooded calculation" as to how poison gas could reinforce the recent Normandy invasion.[29] The estimate came back that a combination of mustard and phosgene bombs would kill most of the 1.5 million people in Hamburg and also the three million in central Berlin. Professing to be wary of German retaliation, the Chiefs of Staff balked at the plan, to Churchill's chagrin.

In March 1945 the CWS staff proposed a similar mass chemical weapons attack on the Japanese.[30] It was known that Japanese civilians (like Germans) generally lacked gas masks and other protections, and that the Imperial Air Force was too weak for any significant counterattacks on Allied troops. Since the Japanese had used chemical weapons against China, the US attacks could be considered retaliatory, within its policy boundaries.

The resulting CWS proposal for "Operation Olympic" (part of the overall US final strategy "Operation Downfall") was called "Operation Sphinx."[31] It targeted the key Japanese cities and estimated the civilian deaths from repeated chemical attacks (mostly with mustard gas) at five to eight million with perhaps equal numbers in injuries. The Joint Chiefs were amenable and had public support. After the February–March 1945 battle for Iwo Jima, where US troops suffered twenty-six thousand casualties, with nearly six thousand killed, almost half the Americans polled favored gas warfare against Japan.[32] But the plan was ultimately judged unfeasible, given the lack of troop training and the predictable resistance of the armed forces to replacing conventional bombs with chemical ones. The US Allies—China, the United Kingdom, and the Soviet Union—would all have had to agree, and the US Navy remained opposed to strategic chemical attacks.[33] Top Department of War analysts, privy to classified information about the atomic bomb, dismissed the CWS plan.

As part of his postwar vision for Camp Detrick, Waitt invited the army and navy to develop projects in microbiology that would utilize its scientists, laboratories, and buildings. Since progress had been made at Detrick in understanding plant and animal diseases, Waitt invited the Department of Agriculture to join as a federal partner. Further, his plan made a bid to demonstrate transparency, as a way of recruiting a new generation of scientists. He proclaimed that more than two hundred technical articles by the program's staff, based mostly on wartime research, were ready for publication. His plan reached out to the National Academy of Sciences and the National Institutes of Health to support quality research.

This promotion of openness was mainly for public consumption. Waitt's true agenda was laid out in a November 4, 1946, top secret report called "Appreciation of Biological Warfare," which advocated total war attacks on civilians.[34] Its main assertion was that the Soviet Union might have "significant quantities of biological agents" as well as ambitions to turn germ warfare from a secondary to a primary means of waging war, with results as "disastrous" for the United States as any atomic bomb. Taking a page from General Fries, Waitt argued that the only hope was US preparedness. "Our superiority in long-range air craft and possession of advanced bases," the report stated, "will give us an advantage enabling us to strike our enemy's populated areas." The War Department was urged to develop training doctrine, new disease and toxin agents, techniques, and weapons for the waging of offensive and defensive warfare. In its recommendations, the report was emphatically against adherence to the Geneva Protocol and urged that the US limitation (still in force) to retaliatory attacks on enemies be omitted in favor of a first-use option.

Just a year before, the United Nations Atomic Energy Commission had declared the goal "to make specific proposals for the elimination from national armaments of atomic weapons and of all other weapons adaptable to mass destruction." The phrase "all other weapons" had been added with particular reference to biological weapons.[35] Seeing the commission as a threat to his service's BW mission, Waitt urged that "no action be initiated by the War Department to seek an international system of control of Biological Warfare" and that "any War Department publicity on this subject which might result in public pressure for the establishment of an international system of control of Biological Warfare be given careful consideration before being released." His rationale was simple: "It must be assumed that another war will become a completely total war. There will be no restrictions on weapons, tactics or strategy used by the enemy and hence by ourselves. Biological Warfare must play an important part in such a war."[36]

In that spirit, BW program officials from the United States, Britain, and Canada agreed to sign a tripartite agreement to continue their wartime cooperation on germ weapons. The concern to restrain the massive harm that might be done to civilians was counterbalanced by incentives to possess the most destructive strategic weapons, which now, in theory, included biologicals.[37] Behind the scenes, advocates made moral arguments in favor of germ weapons over conventional explosives—for example, a BW victim might have a "fighting chance" of recovering from an infection, and some good antidotes might result from defensive research.[38]

Deceiving Colonel Sanders

Simultaneous with Sanders's investigation in Tokyo, the Alsos Mission in Germany reported its findings on Nazi efforts to achieve germ weapons capability, attempts that were thwarted by Hitler's ban on testing and the failure to develop coordination between medical scientists and the military.[39] Plans, though, had included research on "humans for experimental purposes," with an offer from Heinrich Himmler to use concentration camp inmates to study the offensive use of plague.[40] In addition, unknown to the führer, Hermann Göring had approved the construction of a BW research facility near Poznan, which advancing Soviet troops had discovered. The four authors of the Alsos report, which was 133 pages long, benefited from ample documentation and long discussions with key scientists.[41]

On his own in Japan, Murray Sanders was disappointed by the lack of progress in his inquiry—his sources offered little information on their microbiology research and kept repeating that their program had only defended the health of Japan's troops. After consulting with Willoughby and MacArthur, Sanders decided to call Naito's bluff by saying that the lack of wholehearted cooperation was causing him to "lose face" with his superiors. Sanders also spun a story about possibly having to involve the Soviets, whose brutality to captives the Japanese expected and feared. Some of these Unit 731 scientists had just missed being among the many thousands of Japanese apprehended by Soviet forces in Manchuria.

Apparently the ploy worked. The next day Naito gave Sanders twelve handwritten pages describing Unit 731 in its entirety.[42] At the top of the organizational chart he put the emperor; beneath him were the various war departments and the Army Medical College; near the bottom was Lieutenant General Ishii Shiro as the founding director of the Harbin research and production center (under Unit 731), with his subalterns below him. In a written statement to Sanders, Naito declared that his reasons for coming forward were altruistic. He sought no "recompense" for the information he was offering; rather, he feared that the secrecy about Japan's BW program would lead to later revelations damaging to his "poor nation." He said he had shared his concern with the chief of Japan's Bureau of Medicine, who was unfortunately reluctant to make any disclosures. According to Naito, "the higher officers of Japanese Head Quarter" had recently debated whether to reveal the existence of the biological weapons program and decided against it, "out of concern for Emperor Hirohito's reputation." It was not that the emperor knew about the program, they insisted, only that its existence might be negatively interpreted. Among those who joined the debate, Naito said, was General Umezu. Sanders's other informants had told him that General Ishii had answered directly to General Umezu and then, in 1944, to his successor, Major General Yamada Otozo, missing in Manchuria.

Naito begged Sanders to keep his outline secret and not ascribe it to him or to any of the higher officials he had mentioned. "I shall be killed," he pleaded, "if anyone knows what I have done with this information. My only hope is to rescue this poor, defeated nation." Sanders asked Naito if "human guinea pigs" had been used in Japanese BW experiments. Naito vowed "this has not been the case."

Sanders took the organizational outline, his best yield to date, to a meeting with General MacArthur, General Willoughby, and Karl Compton in the supreme commander's office in the Dai-Ichi building. He recommended to them that, to get the maximum information, Naito should be assured that none of the BW scientists would be prosecuted for war crimes. In 1944 the SWNCC had ruled that if a German could offer "information of value" to the US government, then immunity from prosecution was guaranteed, and for hundreds of Nazi scientists it had been.[43] In October 1945 no such SWNCC provision existed to protect Japanese weapons scientists, whose contribution lacked luster—until their secret biological weapons research began to look promising. According to Sanders, MacArthur encouraged him to make a verbal promise, saying, "Well, you're the man in charge of the scientific aspects of this. If you feel you cannot get all the information, we're not given to torture, so offer him that promise as coming from General MacArthur—and get the data."[44]

Whatever Sanders said to Naito, the doctor became more forthcoming about Unit 731's technical achievements. For example, he told Sanders that the most successful offensive research of Japan's BW program involved plague. One breakthrough was the discovery of how to easily infect the *Xenopsylla cheopsis* flea with bubonic plague. Rather than making the connection to the plague attacks on China, Sanders let the statement pass.

Naito also described the mass production of pathogens for plague, cholera, dysentery, salmonella, and anthrax, which he characterized as a "challenge." The organisms the Japanese considered prime BW candidates were plague, anthrax, and glanders. Of these, glanders was the most unusual. Caused by *Burkholderia mallei,* it was a bacterial disease affecting horses and mules that, from an American perspective, had limited utility. A sophisticated enemy that relied on trucks, trains, and planes for transport, rather than pack animals, would hardly feel the impact, although it could decimate livestock in farms and villages. Like anthrax, glanders could be contracted through skin abrasions and could kill human targets by an overwhelming general infection. Or, unlike anthrax, the disease could become chronic, leaving victims with painful abscesses.

Seeking more substantive revelations, Sanders next interviewed Colonel Masuda Tomosada (Ishii's protégé), who identified himself as a Unit 731 administrator, and Major Kaneko Junichi, described as a bomb expert. Together they impressed on Sanders the large investment the Japanese military had made in Pingfan, the center outside Harbin. Separately they sketched maps of Pingfan as it had been in 1939–1940, when it was a garrison for three thousand residents, mostly soldiers, they said, and included houses, laboratories, pathogen production facilities, a vaccine factory, clinics, a large testing area, and its own rail line to Harbin. The maps, which Sanders afterward had copied, showed an enclave that looked more developed than Camp Detrick, which had built quickly during the war on an unused national guard air field. Pingfan's industrial capacity stood out. As Sanders wrote: "Perhaps no better indication of the magnitude of the Pingfan project can be gained than consideration of the fact that in addition to various offensive activities, the vaccine production of the plant was of the order of twenty million doses annually."[45]

Sanders then pursued the subject of Japanese BW bombs and whether they had been extensively tested. When Sanders asked his informants about the Mark VII bomb (whose diagram had alarmed Willoughby in 1944), they denied it had ever been manufactured. This was odd, since US Navy investigators had just found a document describing the testing of the Mark VII in Tokyo Bay in 1943.[46] That issue aside, the Japanese scientists were almost enthusiastic in telling Sanders about other munitions and their development and field tests in Manchuria. In all, approximately four thousand bombs were dropped from planes on the large test area at Pingfan. At least eight types of bombs were produced and tested there, one of them an innovative "mother-and-daughter" radio cluster bomb. More than two thousand of another bomb, the *Uji* type 50, which had a payload of 10–100 liters, were tested in field trials. A third bomb, called *Ha,* was invented to spread lethal anthrax spores. As Sanders's informants explained, it was tested on many animals, which Sanders took as a sign that the program had been exceptionally well funded.

> The immediate effect was gained by shrapnel bursts with secondary consideration given to ground contamination. The statement has been made that a scratch wound from a single piece of shrapnel was sufficient to produce illness and death in 50–90% of the horses, and in 90–100% of sheep exposed in experiments. More than 500 sheep were used in such field trials and estimates of horses similarly expended vary from 100 to 200.[47]

Despite Naito's vow that no human guinea pigs had been used, Sanders had a strange experience that suggested otherwise. One night, a man dressed in a beret, sweatshirt, and trousers knocked at the window of his hotel room. The interloper had shimmied down the drainpipe to the window ledge. On guard, Sanders reached for his revolver before he let him in. Then he listened as the intruder described the design and production of the *Uji* bacteriological bomb. The man told Sanders that, to test the bomb, "they had staked out prisoners at varying distances from the bomb when it had exploded, to see the impact on them. Some of the prisoners had died."[48]

Sanders told MacArthur and Willoughby about his visitor, to ask if the deal with Naito was off. After hearing the story, MacArthur reportedly raised his eyebrows, lit his pipe, and commented, "We need more evidence. We can't simply act on that. Keep going. Ask more questions. And keep quiet about it."[49]

Although Sanders pressed his informants for data about human experiments, he made no progress and centered his evaluation on Japanese technical information and its limits. As he wrote in his report, "Japanese offensive BW was characterized by a curious mixture of foresight, energy, ingenuity, and at the same time, lack of imagination with surprisingly amateurish approaches to some aspects of the work."[50] The Japanese scientists had failed, for instance, to develop (as the British and Americans had) sophisticated cloud chamber experiments to calculate dose response in test animals. From Sanders's perspective, the Japanese could have researched a greater variety of bacteria and toxins—especially since they said they had propagated a great number of mice, rats, marmots, rabbits, and goats for their experiments.

In their interviews, Masuda and Kaneko insisted that they had worked primarily to defend soldiers at war by providing improved water purification and better vaccines and antisera. They claimed that they began this work because they believed the Soviets and the Chinese had used germ weapons in sabotage. Sanders's informants agreed that General Ishii Shiro was the driving force of the entire enterprise, within Japan and outside the homeland, and "was able to carry on in an unhampered fashion so long as he satisfied the commanding general of the Kwantung Army."[51]

Much had been hidden from Sanders. Focused on Pingfan, he had been diverted from the scale of the program beyond Harbin and the real wartime roles of Masuda and Naito. In 1939 Masuda was chosen to head the Ei 1644 Tama Division based in Nanjing. Inside its gates, scientists produced a range of pathogens, cultivated plague-infected fleas, and conducted experiments on Chinese captives. After the Zhejiang-Jiangxi campaign in 1942, Masuda moved to a facility in Burma, around the same time that Naito ran the Singapore enterprise. Their interviews with Sanders over, Naito and Masuda collaborated on strategies to encourage all former BW scientists tell US investigators what they wanted to know but reveal nothing about their human experiments, germ warfare preparations, or any plans to attack the United States with disease agents.

The Sanders Report, about sixty pages long, was forwarded to the British Inter-service Sub-committee on Biological Warfare, which added it to other material in its file on Japan's bacteriological weapons. The skeptical British reaction was that a "more detailed interrogation" might get better technical details and, more seriously, that the "report throws little light on the policy of the Japanese Supreme Command." Their intelligence officials believed that the Kwantung Army, in the 1930s the rogue extremists of Japan's military, had "done many things independently of the Tokyo authorities" and might provide "useful scapegoats" for other official bodies.[52]

SCAP's Intelligence Operations

In September 1945 MacArthur had placed Willoughby and Thorpe and their separate AFPAC intelligence operations within the complex organization of General Headquarters, with offices on the second floor of the Dai-Ichi Building. Willoughby had been promoted to major general, superior to Thorpe's rank of brigadier general, but his authority was limited. At GHQ he oversaw ATIS and its continued translation services, a small

War Department team tasked with evaluating operational, civil, and theater intelligence, and was tracking the Scientific Intelligence Survey teams.[53] Using the limited authority he had, General Willoughby had been resourceful. At the presurrender meeting held in Manila on August 19–20, 1945, he had met Japan's Army Military Intelligence chief, Lieutenant General Arisue Seizo, and afterward hired him to create a secret spy network to report on communist agents in Japan, Korea, and Manchuria. In early September he put Arisue and other former Japanese military on salary at G-2 in Tokyo in an operation masked as historical research.[54] But these were all minor responsibilities.

In contrast, Thorpe was head of intelligence at the Counter-Intelligence Corps and at SCAP's Civil Intelligence Section (CIS). This dual role gave him broad authority in affecting the Occupation, with influence over press and media censorship, intellectual trends, preparation for purges of former regime activists, the freeing of political prisoners, the monitoring of public safety, police behavior and prison reform, and the arrest of war crimes suspects, plus the key civil reforms that SCAP intended to introduce quickly.[55]

Contrary to MacArthur's democratic reforms, Willoughby believed that the Japanese imperial government and the rule of the emperor should be preserved and that secret policing and restraints on free speech were necessary for social order. SCAP's civilian staff sometimes mocked his stiff Prussian mannerisms and his claim to German aristocracy; behind his back, they called him "Sir Charles" and "Baron von Willoughby" and even "Little Hitler." MacArthur himself jokingly referred to him as "my lovable fascist."[56]

As part of the Military Section, Willoughby occasionally obstructed the aims of SCAP's powerful Government Section (GS) as it implemented civil reforms. GS had privileged offices on the sixth floor of the Dai-Ichi Building, next to MacArthur's. The head of GS, Major General Courtney Whitney, trained as a lawyer, had been with MacArthur in the Pacific, in charge of civil affairs in the Philippines. Although an ultraconservative, he was as committed as MacArthur to liberal Occupation goals, and they spent two or more hours a day conferring—which did not please Willoughby.[57]

In September 1945 Willoughby refused to give clearance to the text of the Civil Liberties Declaration, "The Removal of Restrictions on Political,

Civil and Religious Liberties." The declaration was the centerpiece of MacArthur's reforms, a "Magna Carta" for Japan, as he called it. Willoughby's objection was that removing civil restrictions would allow the suppressed Japanese Communist Party to reorganize as a legitimate political force, just as new rules permitted the release of hundreds of communists from prison. He foresaw the rise of a Soviet-backed ideology in Japan that could spell the failure of the Occupation. General Thorpe and Lieutenant Colonel Charles K. Kades, Whitney's deputy chief of the Government Section, finally persuaded him to approve the declaration.

The Civil Liberties Declaration (also known as Japan's Bill of Rights) was announced on October 4, two days after GHQ was inaugurated, and it had profound consequences. All laws were abolished that "restricted freedom of thought, religion, assembly or speech" or that worked "unequally in favor of or against any person by reason of race, nationality, creed or political opinion." The Japanese secret police forces were abolished, and as a result nearly five thousand officials in the Home Ministry and law-enforcement agencies were dismissed. The Japanese were permitted to have free and critical discussions of the emperor and imperial institutions, including the government. In reaction, the existing Japanese cabinet, dedicated to protecting the emperor, resigned and was replaced by those willing to support a new order; among the new members were government ministers who had been in prison or under house arrest for opposing the war.[58]

Willoughby never changed his mind about the threat of communism, although, at this point in his career, he had little power to influence decision-making processes at GHQ. Nor did he change his mind about Courtney Whitney, who, along with Kades, went on to help revise the imperial Japanese constitution.[59] That revolutionary document not only mandated democratic representation but introduced article 9, the no-war clause that resurrected the altruism of Kellogg-Briand Pact of 1928, while allaying the fears of those nations that had suffered from Imperial Japan's aggression:

> Aspiring sincerely to an international peace based on justice and order, the Japanese people forever renounce war as a sovereign right of the nation and the threat or use of force as a means of settling disputes with other nations.

> For the above purpose, land, sea, and air forces, as well as other war potential, will never be maintained. The right of belligerency of the state will not be recognized.[60]

Although neither Willoughby nor Thorpe had been in favor of the IMTFE, their intelligence operations assisted the tribunal as needed. ATIS staff employees, many of them Japanese American, were reassigned as interpreters and translators and, at times, as investigators and language officers, while ATIS became the repository for G-2 documents. Thorpe's CIC contributed to the initial arrests of Class A suspects (which later were handled by the Japanese government), and if IPS had an inquiry about a missing witness or suspect, CIC would usually make the necessary inquiries.

The head of Legal Section, Alva Carpenter, was responsible for assessing criminal suspects, which involved his staff in poring over the many hundreds of letters that Japanese citizens, feeling empowered by the Occupation, wrote to General MacArthur about a wide variety of subjects that personally concerned them. After they were translated for SCAP, the letters would be reviewed and sent to LS if they seemed to offer leads to war criminals. If an investigation led to evidence that appeared credible and seemed to merit prosecution, Carpenter would assign a case number and prepare for a minor tribunal within SCAP's jurisdiction, as he had done with the General Yamashita and other cases.

Beginning with the Occupation, a series of letters from Japanese individuals (most of them anonymous) made specific accusations about the Imperial Army's germ weapons—about Pingfan, about another center for Unit 100 in Manchukuo, and about the torture of prisoners in medical experiments.[61] The names of General Ishii and other scientists were cited, and in a few instances the writers confessed their own guilt, usually in vague terms. Carpenter filed these letters but held off assigning a case number.

A Marginalized CWS

His research done, Colonel Murray Sanders returned to Camp Detrick, where, mostly relegated to defensive research, its scientists were concentrating on vaccines and antibiotics. But Detrick was lagging behind the competition. As funding increased for the new National Institutes of Health, most of it went to universities and medical centers, which were entering a new era of government-supported research expansion. With its reduced budget and loss of civilian scientists, Detrick was hobbled by poor recruitment. To help, the National Research Council of the National Academy of Sciences sponsored science fellowships for the program. Some of the program's wartime research was published in open, peer-reviewed journals, as General Waitt had promised, but the bright new generation of biologists still did not apply.

On the chemical science side, the CWS wartime legacy was lackluster. The Office of Scientific Research and Development had promoted the Manhattan Project and the US biological weapons program as twin projects in advanced weapons innovations. But Vannevar Bush, the MIT-trained engineer and businessman who headed OSRD, saw little potential in chemical weapons.

Although scientifically marginalized, CWS chemists and engineers made significant technical improvements that fit the war's strategic aims. The CWS staff, for example, contributed to the invention of the firebomb, a combination of incendiary and flame thrower. At first it was just an extra gasoline tank that a plane could drop on a target, but CWS technicians adapted a small white phosphorus grenade to fit inside the tank and ignite its contents when it hit the ground. As General Waitt later enthusiastically described: "When the tank was filled with thickened gasoline and dropped at low altitudes, it produced a nerve-shattering sheet of flame 90 or 100 yards long and some 25 or 30 yards wide that started large fires and instantly killed those it touched."[62]

Another CWS invention was a bomb with a steel shell containing a mixture of powdered aluminum and iron oxide known as thermite; this was the bomb used in the Doolittle Raid on Tokyo in 1942. Another assist to the army air force from CWS was the building of model enemy housing—authentic stone houses for Germany and wooden houses for Japan—to develop incendiary bombs best suited to their respective targets. An "iron nose" was put on the magnesium bomb for Germany, while the bombs for Japan were kept light. Once just crude rag-and-gasoline concoctions, improved incendiaries became the war's major destroyers of human habitat, and, technically not categorized as chemical weapons, they could be and were used for first strikes.

Devising a lighter incendiary bomb appropriate for Japan was made easier by Harvard University scientists who in 1942 invented napalm, a metallic soap to thicken gasoline. CWS followed through by developing the 6-pound M-69 bomblet and the heavier 100-pound M-47. These two innovations exponentially increased the efficiency of incendiaries and made them the choice of "carpet bombers" in the European and Pacific theaters. As the war continued, over 60 percent of the bomb loads dropped on enemy targets were incendiaries of one kind or another.

In Japan, the US use of incendiaries represented a radical shift from precision to strategic bombing on a scale never before known.[63] The March 10, 1945, dawn incendiary raid on Tokyo ("Operation Meetinghouse"), ordered by Major General Curtis E. LeMay, was the turning point. Three hundred B-29 superfortress bombers dropped six thousand incendiary bombs, mostly M-69s, on Tokyo; the ensuing firestorms, intensified by brisk winds, killed more than 100,000 people and injured perhaps as many more, leaving over a million homeless. The bombing destroyed 15 square miles of city's core, starting with the port area; surveillance photographs taken afterward revealed 44 square miles of smoking gray ashes.[64] The attack proved more destructive than any in the European Theater and was accomplished relatively quickly and with only minor losses to the bombers. His success celebrated in newsreels and newspaper photographs, LeMay went on to lay waste sixty more Japanese cities.[65] The ultimate goal of LeMay's superior, General Henry "Hap" Arnold, commander of the US Army Air Forces, was to give the air force autonomy from the army and navy, a goal LeMay helped achieve.

Before the decision was made to drop the atomic bomb on Hiroshima, General MacArthur argued that US ground forces could take Japan's four Home Islands and win the war. The head of the Joint Chiefs of Staff, Admiral William Leahy, fearing the precedent that the use of the atomic bomb would create, sided with him. With the support of General Arnold, General LeMay believed that incendiary bombs were the better, proven alternative.[66]

President Truman was persuaded otherwise. His decision to use the atom bomb, in addition to its immediate consequences, profoundly influenced the trajectory of state weapons development. Physics, "the queen of sciences," became forever linked to instantaneous mass murder and catastrophic environmental destruction, and to competition for international and regional power. In comparison, biology and chemistry and their usefulness in weapons development were eclipsed.

On August 6, the day of the bombing of Hiroshima, when Secretary of War Stimson addressed the American public about the event, he heaped accolades on the scientists of the Manhattan Project, who most people assumed were physicists:

> No praise is too great for the unstinting efforts, brilliant achievements, and complete devotion to national interest of the scientists of this country. Nowhere else in the world has science performed so successfully in time of war. All the men of science who have cooperated effectively with industry and the military authorities in bringing the project to fruition merit the very highest expression of gratitude from the people of the nation.[67]

That same day, in an extraordinary gesture of openness, Secretary Stimson released a long statement to the press describing the enormity of the atomic bomb project: its $2 billion budget; its centers at Hanford, Washington, Oak Ridge, Tennessee, and Los Alamos, New Mexico, among others; its links to elite universities and major corporations; and its tens of thousands of employees. On August 11, after the August 9 bombing of Nagasaki, the War Department allowed the publication of the Smyth Report, which described the Manhattan Project in more detail and became a best seller.[68] This transparency "appalled the British, enlightened the Soviets on which approaches to isotope preparation not to pursue and . . . defined what might be public and what secret about the atomic bomb program, thereby forestalling information leaks."[69]

There were no accolades for CWS's invention of the M-47 and M-69 bombs, except from a few advocates on Capitol Hill. The service had no significant capability, even with a buildup in chemical stockpiles toward the war's end.[70] And a scandal loomed about kickbacks from wartime government contractors.[71]

Nor could CWS take credit for the biological weapons program, under its aegis since 1944. Even though in 1944 a scaremongering book purporting to reveal both the US and Japanese programs achieved some notoriety, the secrecy surrounding the US BW program was as intense as for the Manhattan Project and persisted after the war.[72] Few outside a small circle in government knew that an anthrax bomb might be mass produced or that the United States possessed the means to destroy an enemy state's livestock or crops. Behind the scenes, advocates for the program argued that the time given to develop germ weapons (less than three years) had been too short for significant results and that the unexplored strategic capability of biological weapons—the intentional spread of disease among enemy masses—still held promise. British promoters, too, believed that biological weapons could match the impact of nuclear ones, given more time and funding.[73]

During an early October 1945 visit to President Truman, Karl Compton briefed him on the Scientific Intelligence Survey, nearly completed, with its follow-up investigations assigned to Willoughby at G-2 in Tokyo. With the president's encouragement, Compton wrote a follow-up letter about his trip, a summary he shared with General MacArthur.[74] His overview started by describing the impact of US bombings of Tokyo: half of Tokyo was "a level ash heap." Compton then went on to dismiss the importance of Imperial Japan's nuclear and chemical weapons and to describe its radar capability as three years behind that of the United States.

Yet Compton saw potential in Japanese germ weapons: "In only one field, bacteriology, had our mission uncovered any Japanese scientific work which added anything to our own state of knowledge or art. . . . Thus far they have denied any intention of inaugurating or preparing for offensive bacteriological warfare, but we doubt this denial and are pursing the subject further."[75]

Compton's caution about offensive germ weapons likely resonated with Truman. Just two weeks before, presidential advisor Clark Clifford, in submitting his estimate of the Soviet threat, urged that the United States should prepare for nuclear and biological warfare with its former ally.[76]

On November 1, 1945, as part of the larger *Scientific Intelligence Survey in Japan* report, Sanders's observations were circulated to a short list of government officials and science advisors. General Willoughby at G-2 and his Scientific and Advisory Section, now responsible for coordination of the exploitation of Japan's weapons information, were on that list. Like

Compton, Willoughby saw the potential offensive value of Japanese germ weapons as a national security issue.

G-2 and Chemical and Biological Warfare

In late 1945 news of Imperial Japan's germ weapons began to show up in the press. The first story, in the Japanese communist newspaper *Red Flag*, described how, in anticipation of the Soviet invasion of Manchuria, Japanese planes had bombed the secret biological weapons enclave outside Harbin from which attacks on China had been launched. The Japanese communist network also became the source for a January 5, 1946, *New York Times* article that ran under the headline "Bubonic Tests on Americans and Chinese Charged to Japanese." The article reported that members of the Japanese medical corps had inoculated American and Chinese prisoners with bubonic plague in experiments in Harbin and Mukden. It named Dr. Ishii Shiro, a lieutenant general in the Japanese surgeon corps and former head of the Ishii Institute in Harbin, as the director of the tests. The Sanders report, rather than the last inquiry on Pingfan, would be just the first, preliminary one.

The US wartime program, although kept strictly secret, was also about to make the news. In classified briefings within the government, George Merck had summarized its offensive achievements—the mass production of pathogens, the testing of pathogenic aerosol sprays, and the pilot production of anthrax bombs. Months before, Merck had warned President Truman about possible global proliferation of germ weapons and the need for international cooperation to prevent it. Vannevar Bush and the nation's top science advisor, James Conant, president of Harvard University, had joined Merck in this plea, which merged into the arms-control mandate of the UN Atomic Energy Commission.[77] Yet US policy was, in fact, to increase its production of nuclear weapons. Its postwar policy for biological weapons, still ambiguous, was at a crucial juncture.

Then, in early January 1946, the veil of secrecy around the wartime BW program was partially lifted. Aiming to gain public support for Camp Detrick's defensive research, Merck released a sanitized overview of its wartime achievements.[78] The January 6, 1946, *Washington Post* covered the press conference announcing Merck's report. After noting the US invention of vaccines against rinderpest and chicken cholera, the *Post* article turned alarmist. Quoting Merck, it reported that "the development of agents for biological weapons is possible in many countries, large and small, without vast expenditures of money or the construction of huge production facilities."[79] This effort could be conducted "perhaps under the guise of legitimate medical or bacteriologic research." The *Post*'s attention-grabbing headline read "Germ Warfare Called Worse than Atomic." Writing for *Life Magazine*, journalist Gerard Piel reported on Detrick and its wartime research sites in Mississippi, Indiana, and Utah.[80] Piel, who had interviewed Waitt for background, infuriated the general by describing the program's past offensive research and the poor chances of ever controlling the international spread of such weapons.[81] Scenarios of Soviet germ attacks on America filled the press.[82] Little of substance, though, was revealed to the public.[83] There was no Smyth Report for US biological weapons, which, even without being used to fight the Axis powers, managed to frighten the public.

In an addendum to his report, which was also released to the press, Merck observed that he had just received military intelligence about Japan. "Intensive efforts," he wrote," were expanded by Japanese military towards forging biological agents into practical weapons of offensive warfare." He noted, "These efforts were pursued with energy and ingenuity."[84] Just as emphatically, he added, "There is no evidence that the enemy ever resorted to this means of warfare." So far this was true, but General Willoughby at G-2 in Tokyo was intent on discovering more, with CWS cooperation.

In late 1945 General Waitt, chief chemical officer at CWS, had already chosen Lieutenant Colonel Arvo Thompson of the Veterinary Corps to conduct a follow-up to the Sanders BW interviews. One of seven children of Finnish immigrants, Thompson had grown up in the Midwest and during the Depression found his calling in the army, as a veterinarian at CWS. After Pearl Harbor, when the United States was preparing to start its secret germ weapons program, Thompson was made an assistant to George Merck, then director of the War Research Service, the organization under the Federal Security Agency that initiated the germ warfare program.

In December 1942 Ira Baldwin, head of bacteriology at the University of Wisconsin, accepted the job of laboratory director for the project, which as yet had no laboratories or even a physical plant. With Thompson's help, Baldwin searched outside Washington for an isolated site and found what he liked in the old national guard airfield in Frederick, Maryland. Years before it had been named Detrick, in honor of the guard's retired surgeon. Having selected the site, Baldwin directed the development of Camp Detrick as a center for pilot-plant production and basic research. Thompson, who became his assistant, moved with his wife to Frederick and participated in Detrick's rapid growth—the new laboratories, production facilities, testing areas, animal breeding buildings, and expanded barracks, and the opening of extensions in Utah and Mississippi and accelerated cooperation on open-air testing with Canada. Then, in the spring of 1945, the boom was over and Baldwin went back to Wisconsin, while Thompson, now answerable to General Waitt, remained at Detrick.

In 1946 Thompson was given from January 11 to March 11 to complete his interrogations in Tokyo. Before he left, he visited Sanders, who was ill with tuberculosis, and discussed the Japanese model bombs and possible human experimentation.[85]

On December 3, 1945, General Thorpe's Counter-Intelligence Corps reported that one of its informants believed Ishii's death was a hoax and that he was hiding on the coast, at Kanazawa University, in the home of a former employee, a Professor Ishikawa. On January 17, 1946, CIC discovered that General Ishii was living at his country home in Kamo, 300 kilometers from Tokyo, with his wife and daughter.[86] His death certificate and the enshrinement of his ashes and bones had been faked. CIC ordered Ishii to return to his Tokyo address and, since Thompson had arrived, to make himself available for interrogation. When G-2 summoned Ishii to its Central Liaison Office, he claimed he was unable to come because he was a patient in the First National Hospital of Tokyo, suffering from a gallbladder inflammation and dysentery. He was shortly released, though, and Thompson, assisted by G-2 translators, was allowed to interview him but only at his Tokyo home.[87]

The initial meeting did not go well. General Ishii insisted on being addressed as "General" and, openly disdainful of Thompson's rank, questioned why the army hadn't sent a more senior officer. He took over his first interrogation by bragging about his invention of a portable decontamination device which he said could turn urine into potable water. "It was to help the Japanese Imperial Army do battle in other countries," he explained, "especially unhygienic ones." Eventually Ishii began drawing different types of bomb prototypes developed by his unit, although, he insisted, only for reasons of defense against the Soviets and Chinese.

Thompson then persuaded Ishii to sketch a map of Pingfan, which matched the map drawn for Colonel Sanders by Dr. Masuda and the bomb expert Kaneko. With pride Ishii pointed out the location of his office in the main building. Then he identified the other buildings: the housing reserved for himself, his officers, and visiting scientists; the research buildings where experiments were conducted; the small Buddhist temple where they worshipped; and the brothel, with Korean and Chinese women provided by the Kwantung Army. To the unsuspecting Thompson, he said nothing of the prison for the victims of medical experimentation or the crematorium where their bodies were disposed.

Feeling emboldened, Thompson asked the general if he would contact any of his former scientists who might be interested in answering purely technical questions. Ishii willingly recruited about a dozen, all loyal to him, and Thompson spent the next month interrogating them. When he started his project, the general opinion in Allied military intelligence was that the Japanese had investigated germ weapons but not used them. In his inquiry, Thompson might revise that estimate—or be convinced by Ishii that Unit 731 had never crossed that line.

3

INTERNATIONAL PROSECUTION SECTION

TOWARD THE "SWIFT AND SIMPLE TRIAL"

ON JANUARY 28, 1946, DAVID NELSON SUTTON, A CORPORATE LAWYER with a private practice in coastal West Point, Virginia, received his travel orders from the Department of War to serve in the International Prosecution Section of the IMTFE as an assistant prosecutor for the chief of counsel.[1] Fit and energetic, the 54-year-old Sutton packed two suitcases (weight limit total 65 pounds) with custom-made suits and shirts from his tailor in Richmond. Then he took a train to Washington, where, at the Overseas Branch Office at the Pentagon, he completed the necessary paperwork. On February 2, courtesy of the army, he flew to Hamilton Field in California and from there to Tokyo.

Sutton's loyal participation in the Virginia Democratic Party had given him the right contacts for the appointment. Principal among them was Senator Harry F. Byrd, Sr., who kept a tight rein on "the Organization," as the Virginia party machine was known; another was a state Supreme Court judge. For what he thought would be a four-month adventure, he left behind his wife and two children (his son studying at the University of Richmond, his daughter in high school); a gracious house called "The Outlook" on the banks of the Pamunkey River; his law firm, in the capable hands of Louise

Medlin, his secretary, and a colleague, Paul Causey; and his Disciples of Christ congregation in West Point, where he taught Sunday school and which had a mission in Tokyo.

By February 8 Sutton was settled in his office at the Meiji Building, a steel-reinforced architectural gem completed in 1934, near the main Tokyo Station, not far from the Imperial Grounds and in sight of the Dai-Ichi Building, where General MacArthur reigned. Chief of Counsel Joseph Keenan and his core group of International Prosecution Section attorneys occupied the seventh floor of the Meiji Building. The other Allied divisions, including the Chinese, were housed on the sixth floor, where Sutton, a newcomer, was assigned an office. More offices for IPS staff were being constructed on the third floor of the former Japanese War Ministry building, in Tokyo's Ichigaya District, where the trial would take place.

To Sutton's delight, a fellow Virginian, Frank Stacy Tavenner, was due to arrive soon at IPS. Tavenner was well known in the state's Democratic Party. In 1939 Senator Byrd had nominated him for a federal judgeship, a bid that failed. A "pay as you go" fiscal conservative, Byrd had been at odds with President Roosevelt over New Deal programs; not surprisingly, Roosevelt bypassed Tavenner for another candidate.[2] Still, with Byrd's influence, Tavenner became the US district attorney for western Virginia; after the war he was assigned to the National War Crimes Office, created by Secretary Stimson to organize evidence against the Axis leaders, until his appointment as an IPS assistant prosecutor.

While waiting for Tavenner to arrive, Sutton met another southerner, Roy Morgan, a native of Greensboro, North Carolina. Like Tavenner and Sutton, Morgan was a University of Virginia Law School graduate. He came to the IPS from the FBI, which he joined in 1932 right after law school, when he was 26. Most of his career at the bureau was spent tracking communist activities in the United States; after Pearl Harbor, he monitored German, Italian, and Japanese diplomats temporarily interned at the luxurious Greenbrier Hotel resort in White Sulphur Springs, West Virginia, and made friends with a few of them. Keenan had just appointed Morgan head of the new Investigation Division (ID) at IPS, the office that served as a center for all the prosecution's case information.

Since the list of defendants was still open for additions, Morgan was authorizing new interrogations of suspects. The number of those indicted might be as many as fifty, compared to the twenty-two in the dock at Nuremberg. Without much supervision, IPS lawyers continued seeking information on potential suspects from Tojo Hideki's cabinet and the previous ones, under Prince Konoe Fumimaro, prime minister from 1938 to 1941.[3] Over a thousand Japanese were in Sugamo Prison (constructed by the Japanese for sixty inmates). Around eighty of them were designated suspects of "high interest."

Morgan's search for suspects relied on tips from Legal Section and certain confidential sources he had within the imperial family.[4] A disappointment for him was a lack of qualified lawyers on his staff. GHQ, for example, had sent him two US Army lieutenants who had not completed law school and another who was a former state trooper with no legal training. He immediately suggested, when he met Sutton, that he might interrogate two former Japanese government ministers who were under suspicion for Class B war crimes, specifically for "plunder of public or private property."

Morgan's offhand proposal to Sutton reflected the improvisational ethos that dominated at IPS. Keenan left his team of attorneys to do what they deemed best, without clear objectives or firm deadlines. Although UK representatives had yet to arrive in Tokyo, British officials were already anxious about how the Americans at IPS were progressing, especially with the selection of trial defendants. As one UK Foreign Office official put it, the list of those indicted should "be as short as possible because the shorter the list the shorter the trial." An official from its Far Eastern Department echoed the sentiment: "All that is really wanted to satisfy the public is the trial of the few real major criminals which is conducted in such a way that the public can follow the proceedings and does not take so long so that the public completely loses interest."[5]

For the British government, rapid, decisive tribunals were a way to reassert its lost colonial authority and revive prestige for its empire, especially in China.[6] In 1946, under the jurisdiction of the Allied Land Forces Southeast Asia (ALFSEA), the coordinating legal office in Singapore, the British began holding trials in Hong Kong, twenty-three of them in total, to prosecute 123 Japanese (the majority of them military officers or members of the Kempeitai) for war crimes committed in Hong Kong, Shanghai, and Formosa (Taiwan) and on the high seas. A major though unstated goal was to convince their remnant colonial populations that Britain, now a victor, could protect their security, even if its empire had been shattered by the war.[7]

Confident, if not arrogant, about their upcoming participation in the Tokyo trial, the British assumed that China was "likely to be pliant" and "hoped that the Chinese, Dutch, French and Russians will send men who will use English!"[8] The Chinese prosecutor, Hsiang Che-chun, was already in Tokyo, maintaining the presence of a polite observer, but the other nations had been slow to respond. In the weeks after the creation of the International Military Tribunal for the Far East, the Soviet Union was initially silent and then on February 7 communicated through diplomatic channels that it had felt shut out of discussions about the charter and the organization of the IMTFE.[9] Confirmation of Soviet participation became so delayed that Keenan speculated how to proceed without them.[10]

The laissez-faire atmosphere at IPS began to change in February when the British, Australian, and New Zealand prosecutors established their presence, more than a month before the jurists from France, the Netherlands, and the Soviet Union arrived. The Australians and New Zealanders, motivated by regional interests, were enthusiastic for the Tokyo trial to commence. During the war both had felt gratitude for American defense and yet also resentment for being excluded as second-class allies from military and diplomatic decisions.[11] Arriving in Tokyo on February 5, their representatives were immediately hosted at a luncheon given by General and Mrs. MacArthur at the American Embassy, with Joseph Keenan also invited. The guests included Sir William Webb, the judge from Australia, and Australia's prosecutor Alan Mansfield, who had recently promoted the indictment of Hirohito in Geneva, which Webb also supported. With them were New Zealand's Judge Erima Harvey Northcroft, Brigadier Ronald Quilliam, the New Zealand prosecutor, and Arthur Comyns Carr, the British prosecutor.

Although the Anglo arrivals received "the utmost kindness and assistance" from the Americans, they were dismayed by how little had been accomplished. As Judge Northcroft reported to his foreign office:

> I understand material for the prosecutors has not yet been collected with any completeness. Indictments are now being drafted, but here again there is difficulty, as it has not yet been decided who in fact are to be

> arraigned. Naturally, of course, defense counsel have not been appointed, as criminals to be tried have not yet been determined upon. The court building itself is only now being planned.[12]

While describing "excellent personal relations" with IPS staff, the UK liaison to the Foreign Office agreed that "it cannot be said that the Americans had really got to grips with their task before our arrival."[13]

In creating the Tokyo Charter, MacArthur had left the door open to procedural improvisations and innovation—just as at Nuremberg, whose charter contained no detailed prescriptions for organization or defendant selection or indictment. Judges were expected to follow the lead of the court president, his name not yet announced, and the prosecutors to follow Keenan's. With few organizational directives, the Tokyo trial risked becoming a continual contest for decision-making powers.[14]

Yet as allies of the victorious Americans, the British, Australian, and New Zealand prosecutors had no hesitancy in taking charge. They immediately began gathering evidence on Japanese abuses of their POWs and internees and other treaty violations to which they resonated and pressed for a rapid start of the trial in advance of the date of April 15, which Keenan was then proposing. They became concerned that, compared to Nuremberg, Tokyo offered much less documentary evidence, which might lead to difficulties with pinning "definite responsibility on the accused."[15] It was also obvious that the court's General Secretariat was straining to assemble support staff and arrange for housing in the few parts of Tokyo not destroyed by bombs. The large new courtroom for the tribunal, modeled after Nuremberg's, was under construction (not just planned as Northcroft believed) in the Tokyo headquarters of the former Imperial Ministry of Defense, a symbolic choice by SCAP.

On February 15, when General MacArthur announced the final list of judges for the trial, several Anglo appointees stood out.[16] The British delegate Lord Patrick was a judge at Scotland's College of Justice, its highest court, and a king's counsel. New Zealand's Justice Northcroft was a member of its Supreme Court.[17] Among the judges, Sir William Webb was the most experienced in Japanese war crimes adjudication, having been president of the Australian War Crimes Commission in 1944–1945, and he and MacArthur were well acquainted. On February 20 MacArthur appointed

Webb president of the IMTFE, the figure of highest authority on the bench. Sir William initially felt "his position might be prejudiced by the fact of his authorship of the report on Japanese atrocities which bears his name."[18] Yet MacArthur kept to his decision. In accepting the role of IMTFE president, Webb was obliged to keep his personal opinion about Hirohito's guilt private until the court proceedings ended; the same, of course, held true for the other judges and IPS staff like Alan Mansfield.

Voicing no disagreement, MacArthur also approved the other judicial nominations. The Soviet judge, Major General I. M. Zarayanov, was a member of the Military Collegium of the Supreme Court and had served as head of the Red Army Military Academy of Law—which was about all that the other Allies knew about him. (As later revealed, he had participated in the Stalinist "purge" trials of 1936–1938.) Since Zarayanov knew neither English nor Japanese, the court's two official languages, his candidacy was something of an affront to the court. The Netherlands offered Bernard V. A. Röling, a professor of law at Utrecht who, like China's Judge Mei Ju-ao (Mei Ru-Ao), was just 40 years old, more than a decade younger than most others on the bench and lacking in trial experience. Also lacking courtroom experience, Judge Mei had other assets; he had been a Phi Beta Kappa undergraduate at Stanford University and had a law degree from the University of Chicago. Fluent in English, he made the representation of China at the IMTFE his primary goal. The first French judge appointed, Henri Reimburger, former legal counsel to the Ministry of Foreign Affairs, stepped aside for personal reasons; with minimal disruption, MacArthur approved his replacement, Henri Bernard, a judge who had participated in Nazi war crimes prosecutions in the French colonies in Africa. Bernard's spoken English, unfortunately, was less than fluent. A political appointee, Canada's Edward Stuart McDougall lacked a distinguished record as a jurist, having served only a few years on the Court of King's Bench of Quebec, but he had a distinguished military record from both World Wars and MacArthur approved him.[19]

One judicial appointment provoked bitter complaint from Chief of Counsel Keenan, although from few others. This was President Truman's selection of John P. Higgins, a chief justice of the Massachusetts State Superior Court, as the United States judge. The progressive Higgins, a former member of the US House of Representatives, had strong backing from Speaker of the House John McCormack, another Boston Irish Democrat.[20] Keenan saw the Higgins appointment as an insult to the status of the IMTFE; at Nuremberg, Attorney General Francis Biddle had been Truman's choice for the US judge.

Prior to Higgins's appointment, Keenan had lobbied Attorney General Tom C. Clark, his former boss at the Justice Department's Criminal Division, to urge the nomination of prestigious candidates, among them Willis Smith, president of the American Bar Association (who declined), and Keenan's former professor, Roscoe Pound, dean of Harvard Law School. After Truman's selection of Higgins became known, Keenan complained to MacArthur that the US appointment to the court bench should be at least a federal judge or a military officer with the rank of major general. Despite Keenan's criticisms, MacArthur still backed Truman's selection. Keenan remained irked and did not hesitate to complain to Tom Clark and his other contacts in Washington.[21]

Following common law, outside the courtroom the IMTFE judges were expected to avoid the IPS and its prosecutors. In line with that assumption, the judges were housed separately at Tokyo's Imperial Hotel. Yet the divide between judges and prosecutors and their staffs proved something of an artifice. Most judges knew their associate prosecutors personally. The Soviet judge Zarayanov was close to the associate prosecutor S. A. Golunsky, a minister in the Foreign Service. President Webb had served on the same court in Australia as Alan Mansfield, and the two had worked together on a war crimes commission in the Pacific. Prosecutor Hsiang and Judge Mei were well acquainted. For these jurists and others, little that their country's prosecutors would present in court would be new, and the charges introduced by other nations were at least generally familiar. The exception was China, whose long war with Japan had not been fully chronicled or appreciated in the West.

The expatriate world of Occupied Japan often blurred the lines between IMTFE divisions and between the court and General Headquarters.[22] The more gregarious judges and attorneys (prosecution and defense) met at private parties and receptions or at the round of cultural events sponsored by the Allied embassies and the Japanese government. Military officers from GHQ intermingled with IMTFE judges and staff. President Webb's preferred mealtime companions were US Army officers (not his fellow judges);

he and Judge Higgins, devout Catholics, attended mass together at the Jesuit Sophia University in Tokyo. Jurists and generals played golf at resorts once frequented by Hirohito and the royal family and now run by the US Army. Judge Röling, especially athletic, went horseback riding with defense staff, and he and G-2's General Charles Willoughby became tennis partners.[23] The housing shortage in Tokyo made it difficult for most spouses to accompany IMTFE employees. Even President Webb, who suffered from neck and shoulder ailments, was refused permission to bring his wife, despite a personal appeal to MacArthur. Many American women signed on to serve in the Occupation as secretaries, stenographers, and translators; whether in military uniform or as civilians, they proved a mainstay of the Occupation organization and often a force for the liberalization of women's rights in Japan, this in a context of Japanese and Occupation support of brothels for Allied troops.[24] In addition, a handful of American women lawyers were attracted to the trial and defied the conservative expectations of their colleagues and the Japanese.[25] Sponsored by the Occupation, films and live musicals played regularly at the Ernie Pyle Theater, the former women's drama school named for the Pulitzer Prize–winning journalist killed by a sniper on Okinawa. Although meant primarily for US troops, the theater events attracted wider audiences, at times even members of the imperial family.

Order by Committee

Chief of Counsel Keenan's role model was the Supreme Court Justice Robert Jackson, the lead US prosecutor at Nuremberg, who was known as a "solo performer rather than a conductor."[26] Keenan's reputation was that, more than overseeing his office, he enjoyed embassy receptions and cultural events—like Japanese theater—and playing golf at hotel resorts. When possible, he engaged in conversation with MacArthur or sought the company of the top brass, among them Major General Robert Eichelberger, commander of the Eighth Army and second in command to SCAP, who also golfed. As Keenan wrote a friend who worked in a Senate office, "We have splendid living quarters, good offices, good food and fine transportation services. As this is a combination that I have not experienced at home during the war years, I deeply appreciate them."[27] Until the Anglo contingent arrived, no one contested his authority or demanded that he become a "conductor."

In the first IPS draft of the indictment, shared with the British on February 8, Keenan proposed a new idea: that Japan would be represented at the IMTFE by a judge, sitting alongside the Allied jurists.[28] Japanese government officials had apparently impressed on SCAP their willingness to join in the prosecution of those leaders they felt had misled them; their participation would demonstrate that the IMTFE was more than "retribution by the victors against the vanquished."

Opposition from the UK attorney general and Foreign Office was quick and vigorous. They saw no reason to give the impression that Japan was "in fact [a] wronged party": "As soon as the trials are over we should be faced with the argument that the guilty have been punished, that Japan has been purged of all sin, and that what remains is a population of seventy-five million entirely innocent people whom it would be our duty to help in every possible way."[29]

Why, the British asked, raise the question of why a similar step had not been taken at Nuremberg, and why the hostile reaction of the many whose relatives had suffered at Japanese hands should be provoked. "If the Japanese judicial system," one official commented, "enjoyed a prestige similar to our own (which unfortunately it does not) there might be something in the idea. In actual circumstances . . . the disadvantages outweigh the advantages."[30] And, as a final objection, it was doubted how one could justify adding a Japanese judge while denying one for India. With the weight of these complaints, Keenan's innovative suggestion (certainly approved by SCAP) was scrapped, and attention shifted to including judges at the court from India and the Philippines, which were already allowed prosecutors.

By mid-February, with the French, Dutch, and Soviet prosecutors still absent, the British and Commonwealth prosecutors in Tokyo saw no reason to wait before making important moves to speed the trial. IPS decision making was supposed to be collaborative, but relative state power made a difference, plus the credibility of the charges to be brought against Japan also counted. The most deference was granted those whose troops had battled for years against the Japanese—the Chinese, the Americans, and the British and Commonwealth nations, the least to those at the sidelines of conflict.

The French war crimes charges, for example, would predictably stem from its role as a defeated colonial power in Indochina. Yet the Nazi occupation of France from June 1940 to the spring of 1944 and its rule by the Vichy government had made for a complicity between France and Japan in Asia. The extension of the Vichy government in Indochina had allowed tens of thousands of Japanese soldiers to occupy the country's eastern frontier until March 1945, when, following the liberation of France, the Japanese military took control. Several months of intense Japanese-French fighting and the Japanese capture and abuse of soldiers and civilians would certainly figure in France's IMTFE case, but these charges would pale in comparison to the Bataan Death March, the punitive transport of Allied POWs on "hell ships," and the hundreds of thousands of civilians slaughtered in China and the Philippines. In 1942 the Netherlands, under Nazi occupation from May 1940 until it was liberated in May 1945, staged a brief and failed defense of its East Indies. Its prosecutors would have plenty of civilian deaths and prison camp and forced labor abuses to present, but the Dutch had not lost many thousands of soldiers in the war.

Although a major world power, the Soviet Union had little to charge Japan in the way of aggressive war crimes, except for two border conflicts. The first was in the summer of 1938 at Lake Khasan, a brief "brush-fire war" over the boundaries of Manchuria, Japanese-held Korea, and Soviet Siberia that ended in Japanese defeat.[31] The second, the Battle of Nomonhan at the Khalkin-gol River in 1939, was a longer, more serious conflict over a contested Mongolian border; the Japanese were routed and turned their expansionist goals southward.[32] On April 13, 1941, the Soviet Union and Japan signed a five-year neutrality pact. In the agreement, each side "undertook to maintain peaceful and friendly relations between them and mutually respect the territorial integrity and inviolability of the other contracting party."[33] The pact held until the Soviet "lightning" invasion of Manchuria on August 9, 1945, and the Soviets new expanded presence in northeastern China.

Without the missing jurists from France, the Netherlands, and the Soviet Union, the Anglo contingent moved forward with its criticism of the American method for choosing defendants. Under Keenan, the IPS staff had concentrated on the interrogation of likely suspects to explore individual criminal records. The British and Commonwealth prosecutors preferred the

Nuremberg approach, which had been to pick a few individuals whose actions were representative of the most egregious instances of war crimes—whether conspiracies to wage aggressive war, aggressive warfare itself, the abuses of prisoners of war, or the murders of civilians. The Americans had enlarged the defendant list by pinning criminal responsibility on four or five or more suspects rather than just one or two iconic ones. The previous December the UK Foreign Office had sent the US State Department its recommended list of eleven major Japanese war criminals.[34] Such a minimum list, the British argued, would avoid the burden of lengthy or multiple major tribunals.

The Anglo criticisms also extended to the finer details of prosecutorial work. For example, the British criticized the IPS lack of explicit standards for interrogation that could be applied across national legal traditions. Suppose Americans asked questions one way, the British and Australians another, and the French and Dutch and Soviets relied on other approaches to inquiry?

Another criticism was the lack of a working definition of trial-worthy evidence. In the Nuremberg Charter, the criteria for evidence was intentionally left vague and unconstrained by "technical rules." Instead, it was written that "[the tribunal] shall adopt and apply to the greatest possible extent expeditious and nontechnical procedure, and shall admit any evidences which it deems to be of probative value." Probative value meant that whatever was presented should contribute as proof to the case argument—as the four judges agreed. This general phrasing acknowledged the difficulties of acquiring evidence after the chaos of war and from culturally and linguistically different sources. In Tokyo, at least nine judges would be weighing the evidence, which was in much shorter supply and possibly more troubled by the differences between Japanese and Western society.

Presuming that their shared legal tradition would dominate at the IMTFE, the British and Commonwealth prosecutors and their American counterparts at IPS assumed that the "best evidence" criteria recognized in common law should pertain at the IMTFE. The criteria traditionally had three aspects: the source of information had to be officially verified; it was best if it was firsthand and not hearsay; and it should be directly relevant to the charges at hand. Keenan had done nothing on an organizational level to implement these or any general standards, leaving evidence from throughout the vast Asia-Pacific region mixed with rumor, lies, disinformation, and ambiguous facts about the guilt of individual defendants.

A great amount of work certainly needed to be done at IPS. To start, the processing of documents at IPS—their evaluation, certification, translation, duplication, distribution, and centralization—lacked oversight.

Accurate, efficient translation was essential not only to document processing but to witness testimony and other court proceedings. Due to what were described as "inherent difficulties in the Japanese language, which speaks in an opposite way from the English," it was decided that the IBM technology for simultaneous translation that was working at Nuremberg could not be fully adapted for Tokyo. Instead, the court would have to rely on consecutive translation, a laborious, phrase-by-phrase process of relaying spoken communication, including statements by attorneys, witness testimony, cross-examination, arguments, and comments from the bench. Document translation was faster but still labor-intensive; a single page might take hours to translate from Japanese to English and still have debatable meaning.[35] For weeks, the General Secretariat had been recruiting translators of mixed Japanese and American or Japanese British parentage to keep up with the boxes of requested government documents now crowding offices at IPS.[36]

Keenan's response to the Anglo complaints was to delegate responsibility to committees and put his critics in charge. The most important of these was the Executive Committee for general oversight, to which Keenan appointed the British prosecutor Arthur Comyns Carr as chairman. Comyns Carr, a trial lawyer, seemed a model of discretion, with a near horror of the press, a counterbalance to Keenan's enjoyment of the news spotlight. Keenan then authorized an Evidence and Defendants Committee to review methods of obtaining and verifying trial evidence for charges against the accused; a general agreement was reached that no more than twenty defendants should be indicted. He appointed the Australian prosecutor Alan Mansfield its chair.

As a further measure, Keenan created a Drafting Committee to concentrate on the final list of defendants; the indictment text would specify by number the charges against each of them, with number 1 referring to the category "war of aggression." Unfortunately for the prosecutors, the timeline for Japan's war crimes was set back to 1928, the year of the

Kellogg-Briand international peace agreement and the alleged first signs of Japanese military aggression in northeastern China. The lead prosecutors had to familiarize themselves with a long history of changes in Japan's government—coups, assassinations, resignations, and many cabinet turnovers, with a large, circulating cast of political actors. The one stable figure in this seventeen-year timeline was Emperor Hirohito, whose possible indictment, under discussion in Washington at the State-War-Navy Coordinating Committee, was beyond IPS authority.

The Executive Committee created a special Sub-Committee on Documents to address the disorganized state of translation and duplication. Keenan then authorized an Interrogation Committee (made up of three attorneys, two Americans and one British) to implement relevant decisions reached by the Executive Committee.

The Executive Committee's first concern was achieving consensus on the standards for conducting and reporting interrogations and deciding how information from them would be used in the upcoming trial. The first question was how prosecutors would select passages from interviews that would be most effective in court. There were other questions, too, concerning how much prosecutors would be allowed to rely on affidavits as a substitute for actual witness testimony, what amount of documentary evidence judges would allow to be read into the record, and the best way to ensure that the necessary translations of documents would be ready in time.

Sutton Passes the Test

That February David Nelson Sutton, or Nelson, as he was called, acclimated himself to Tokyo. His room at the Hotel Koronada was spare but comfortable. Every day he read from his Bible and did his morning calisthenics. In this and other American billets, the Japanese staff, nearly all women, took care of laundry, pressing, and shoe shining. As Roy Morgan, who shared the same accommodations, wrote a friend: "At my residence we have possibly twenty-five to thirty servants, all of them are far superior to our negroes. . . . They wait on you hand and foot and never a complaint. They are very gentle and the type of servant that would make a housewife very happy. It appears that the Japanese have trained their women very well."[37]

Sutton's modest $90 per week compensation proved adequate. With Morgan and other Americans, he ate US Army meals next door at Hattori House on the gated Seiko company estate—scrambled eggs, toast and coffee for breakfast, hamburgers on buns for lunch, and noodle casseroles for dinner; Japanese restaurants were off limits, as were Japanese hotels. A car pool service ferried him back and forth to the Meiji Building. After his first shock at Tokyo's ashen landscape where people lived in makeshift hovels, he learned to ignore the devastation and grew used to the street crowds of Japanese, so recently the hated enemy and now destitute, with the gangs of orphaned children and the heavily made-up prostitutes in full view. Soon after Sutton arrived, a black-market gang had a shootout near the Tokyo Station, and, shortly after, thousands of Japanese amassed in front of the Imperial Palace to protest food shortages until police broke up the crowd.

Still, order prevailed, thanks in part to the visible Occupation presence and Allied troops patrolling the city. During the war many Americans were star struck by General MacArthur, which was the intent of much of the wartime propaganda coming from the Joint Chiefs and the White House.[38] In Tokyo, MacArthur effectively promoted his leadership image by sequestering himself in his office and limiting interaction with the public—he was august and remote, like a second emperor. Each morning just before ten o'clock, the traffic lights between the Dai-Ichi and the American embassy were turned green to allow his black Cadillac to speed past the crowds of Japanese bowing in deference at the curbside. At the building's front steps, crowds of Japanese and of Allied soldiers waited to glimpse him as he arrived. Even on Sundays, the general came to his office, went home for a two-hour lunch at the embassy, and then returned to work.

Sutton had the same work ethic, yet in his first days at IPS, he had little to do until Roy Morgan followed through with the proposal that he should interrogate the two businessmen (one in Sugamo Prison and the other under surveillance) suspected of wartime "plunder." The notion of pursuing leaders of industry could be controversial; unless they had sponsored forced labor or become high-level officials promoting war, they might be indistinguishable from American industrialists who had contributed to the war effort. On the other hand, the Soviet press was already fuming that the IMTFE was a capitalist sham in league with Japanese leaders of industry, "the giant monopoly octopuses."[39]

Morgan had already sent two experienced American lawyers to interrogate Hoshino Naoki, a former secretary to the Tojo Cabinet and a likely defendant; by his own admission, Hoshino had assisted in the drafting of the 1941 Declaration of War signed by the emperor.[40] The two businessmen he wanted Sutton to interview were not at Hoshino's level of notoriety. Nonetheless, Morgan wanted complete files on them, on the chance that they might implicate others.

On February 26 at 9:00 a.m., with permission from SCAP, Sutton arrived at Sugamo Prison to interrogate Murata Shozu—as if there were nothing unusual in having a small-town American lawyer interrogate a criminal suspect who, six months earlier, had been Japan's minister of transportation. Directed to the room set aside for the interrogation, Sutton found an elderly looking man in drab prison garb. Murata, age 68, had spent several years in the United States before World War I and spoke passable English and so, without a translator or stenographer, Sutton took his own notes on the interview.

Sutton learned that Murata had risen in the ranks from clerk to president at the Osaka Mercantile Steamship Company, which he described as the second largest steamship company in Japan. His explanation of Japan's wars was that his country had been unable to support its expanding population, which reached seventy million in the late 1930s. Sharp limits on immigration imposed by Australia, the United States, and other countries, compounded by tariff restrictions, thwarted Japan's efforts to industrialize. At no time, Murata said, had he favored the use of armed force to resolve the problem. As Sutton noted: "Representing big business interests, he is opposed to the interference of government in the conduct of business."[41] On the darker side, Murata had served as ambassador to the Japanese puppet government in the Philippines and as consultant to the Japanese Fourteenth Area Army there, before becoming minister of transportation in early 1945. Captured soon after the war ended, he had been transported to Tokyo from Yokohama with General Homma, who was on his way to Manila to be tried for the Bataan Death March.

After conferring with Morgan, Sutton summarized his interrogation of Murata in a brief memo to Keenan that ended with this evaluation: "I find nothing from the examination of this man or from my study and investigation of his activities, which leads me to the conclusion that he should be included as a war criminal and I respectfully recommend that he not be included in the list and that he be released from confinement."[42]

Sutton's first direct communication with the Chief of Counsel was rewarding in that Murata was eliminated as a possible Class A defendant, although he remained at Sugamo, along with hundreds of other suspects, for nearly two more years.

Starting on February 27 Sutton used his office at room 619 in the Meiji Building for a series of interviews of Hatta Yoshiaki, a high-level railroad executive and business developer in Manchukuo and the minister of transportation and communication in the Tojo Cabinet. SCAP had already purged him from public office. Since Hatta, age 64, spoke little English, Sutton was helped by an interpreter and a stenographer. His questions were short and simple, and Hatta replied with equal brevity. The interrogations, five in all, were slowed by translation, so that on average six hours of questioning yielded less than twenty pages of double-spaced typed transcript. The interviews were Sutton's first lesson in how translation slowed interrogation and in the value of English-speaking witnesses.

Although Sutton judged Hatta "a top flight business man," he was wary of his beliefs regarding Pearl Harbor and war with the United States. "His speedy replies to questions along this line and complete denial of any information or knowledge of war, leads me to the conclusion that his statements on these matters are not true." Sutton recommended that Tojo and others should be interrogated about Hatta's 1941 involvement in cabinet decisions. His bottom-line message to Keenan was: "In my opinion, he bears responsibility for the successive, aggressive wars undertaken by Japan but does not have that degree of responsibility which would include him within a list of the Japanese war criminals restricted to not more than 20 persons."[43] Again, Keenan listened and Hatta, too, was stricken from the list of possible defendants.

During this time, Keenan officially assigned Sutton to work for Roy Morgan at the Investigation Division to conduct more interrogations of suspects. From there, Sutton's position was quickly upgraded: he was assigned to assist the Chinese Division at IPS in organizing its Class C crimes against humanity charges against Japan.

On March 2 Frank Tavenner finally arrived at IPS. As reported in the *Washington Post*, his voyage was an adventure. He had flown to Tokyo as the only passenger on a US cargo plane carrying smallpox vaccine for American troops headed to Korea, where an epidemic had erupted.[44]

Both loyal Virginia Democrats, Tavenner and Sutton were from different backgrounds and had not met before. Like Senator Harry Byrd, Tavenner could trace his ancestors back to settlers in the 1660s and to owners of slave plantations whose descendants after the Civil War made their livings from apple orchards and newspaper chains and ran the political empires of white gentlemen. Tavenner's father had been a state senator; his seat had passed to Byrd early in Byrd's career, before he became a US senator. Sutton's father had been a grocer in Tidewater Virginia, his mother one of two teachers in the little schoolhouse where Nelson learned his ABCs. A self-made man, Sutton had worked his way through high school, college, and law school.

Although both men were born in 1892, Sutton was class of 1920 at the University of Virginia law school, while Tavenner, who took time for graduate study at Princeton and to work in his family's newspaper business, was class of 1927. In World War I Sutton stayed stateside as a riding instructor in the US Cavalry, while Tavenner went as army staff to England and France.

Above Tavenner in the IPS hierarchy was Keenan's deputy counsel Carlisle Higgins, another World War I veteran, although he had spent most of his service ill with Spanish influenza. In 1934 Higgins (no relation to the court's US judge) had been appointed by Roosevelt as US district attorney to the Middle District of North Carolina, and he stayed in that position until he left with Keenan for Tokyo in December 1945. Tavenner and Higgins became fast friends, dining together and even getting their haircuts at the same Japanese shop. When Higgins became bogged down in administrative duties, Tavenner acted as his emissary at staff and committee meetings.

The China Brief

Just after Tavenner's arrival, Nelson Sutton met with the Chinese prosecutor Hsiang Che-chun to review the China case. On January 11, before the IMTFE was formally announced, China notified SCAP that Hsiang was its first choice for judge. He had earned an undergraduate degree in American and English literature at Yale and a law degree from George Washington University. Chief prosecutor at the Shanghai High Court in 1945, he had held high positions in China's Ministries of Justice and Foreign Affairs. Rather than be China's judge, Hsiang preferred the role of prosecutor, which he felt gave him greater responsibility.[45] In his place, he suggested substituting the younger, also American-educated Mei Ju-ao, a member of China's Legislative Yuan. MacArthur approved Mei as China's judge and Hsiang became its associate prosecutor and thus head of the Chinese Division. When he met Sutton, Hsiang had been in Tokyo for several weeks, accompanied by his secretary Henry Chiu, a lawyer and businessman from Shanghai who was fluent in English.

Keenan, influenced by Roosevelt's high regard for China, had decided that Japan's invasion of Manchuria in 1931 would be "the opening salvo" for the prosecution's aggressive war charges, even before Pearl Harbor. And he wanted Hsiang to be the first associate prosecutor to argue his nation's charges to the court. Postwar China was struggling to develop a coherent national judicial system; its history of foreign legations, prolonged war, and Japanese occupation had left it legally unprepared for the tribunal.[46] Missing documents were another problem. Before losing Nanjing in 1937, the KMT transferred its files to Hankow (Hankou), on the Yangtze River near Wuhan. When Wuhan and Hankou were besieged (they fell in bloody battles in 1938), the files were shipped west to Chongqing. In March 1946 crates of documents from Chongqing were still being shipped on barges to Nanjing. In addition to searching those files, the Nanjing procurator's office was interviewing captive Japanese soldiers, but a good number of defeated troops had escaped, going renegade or joining the forces of the Chinese Communist Party. Far from having trial-ready information, the Chinese were in the process of organizing an immense volume of scattered data, some of it in boxes in the Chinese Division office. Despite the war's disruptions, China had begun trying to organize its own tribunals, one to prosecute for the Nanjing Massacre of 1937–1938, but its efforts lagged behind the IMTFE's, and it had yet to pass national war crimes legislation.[47]

Despite these obstacles, by using a typology of thirty-two war crimes developed during the Paris Peace Conference at Versailles in 1919, China's Ministry of Judicial Administration had composed a chart showing the occurrence of these crimes in twenty provinces and three cities.[48] The figures were based on 678 cases confirmed by the Far-Eastern and Pacific Sub-Commission of the United Nations War Crimes Commission. Among the designated crimes were murder, torture, rape, forced labor, pillage, wanton destruction of property, and abuse of prisoners of war. Created soon after the widespread use of chemical warfare in World War I, the list also included the "use of deleterious and asphyxiating gases." The United Nations counted eleven wartime incidents in this category, two in Zhejiang Province and nine in Hunan.

A second chart given to Sutton showed the numbers and distribution of Japanese war crimes based on data from China's own government institutions, using 620 of their confirmed cases. The distribution generally matched the UN chart; murder, rape, and pillage in war zones topped the list, while fourteen incidents of the use of poison gas, dispersed over seven battle zones, were recorded. Another chart in the same report gave the number of government institutions in major cities and regions where, from August 1945 to March 1946, Japanese war crimes had been investigated. For Zhejiang, the scene of Japan's 1942 "scorched earth" campaign, sixty-three investigating committees had been organized and 35,365 case incidents recorded. Kwantung (Guangdong) Province was next, with thirty-six committees and 14,081 cases. Shanghai followed, with one investigating committee and 13,186 cases. The total number of Chinese committees was 405, with 95,791 cases reported and more under investigation. "Judicial institutions," the report stated, "on account of [China's] recent resumption of administration in liberated areas, are still continuing investigation of war crimes cases." As with many wartime atrocities, the numbers were only estimates, not confirmed tallies. The report cautioned: "Each case, referred to in this chart, includes crimes committed against one person, or a whole family, or a whole village. Hence no total number of victims should be inferred from the number of cases herein."

The Japanese "Rape of Nanking," seven weeks of killing and looting that started in December 1937, would be the centerpiece for the Chinese Class C criminal charges; trial-worthy evidence for the atrocities was most needed. Like many Americans, Sutton was familiar with the 1938 press stories and the best-selling book about the onslaught, *What War Means,* by the journalist H. T. Timperley. For many outside China, the active role of American missionaries in communicating the victims' suffering and deaths had been inspiring. But popular writing and inspiration were not evidence. To assist, the UN War Crimes Commission had sent Hsiang some relevant material on civilian deaths, which awaited translation into English. Imprisoned at Sugamo, General Matsui, the Japanese commander who had entered the defeated city in triumph, would be held responsible for the Nanjing Massacre, as it was also called. The Nanjing prosecutor had sought to extradite him for its own tribunal, but had to settle for lower-level Japanese military when the Occupation's Legal Section refused.[49]

Hsiang brought Sutton up to date on China's two other Class C charges. The first was the Japanese commercial promotion of opium among the Chinese, a system that enslaved entire populations in occupied cities, while the profits from it supported the Kwantung Army and the Japanese war effort and personally enriched top leaders, such as Tojo, who were sure to be indicted.

The other charge concerned Japanese airplane attacks that had caused unusual plague outbreaks in three Chinese cities; the events had been written up in a medical journal in 1942.[50] Sutton knew nothing of the attacks and little about plague. During his youth, epidemics of malaria and yellow fever had swept through the South, and, like many veterans of World War I, he had witnessed the ravages of the 1918 Spanish flu epidemic. In his lifetime, though, plague had become a rarity in the United States, nearly eliminated by shipping and port sanitation regulations.[51]

To assist Sutton, Keenan appointed Colonel Thomas Morrow from the original Project K IPS team. A World War I war hero, Morrow was 55 at the time of attack on Pearl Harbor and a new district court judge in Hamilton, Ohio. He immediately rejoined the Army and was posted to Washington and then North Africa. When he was in full military dress, his chest was blanketed with medals: a Silver Star, a Legion of Merit, a Bronze Star, the French Croix de Guerre, and ten battle ribbons. Morrow had already without success tried to locate the mysterious Dr. Ishii whose name kept surfacing in reports and even the press. For personal reasons, he was also interested in Japan's chemical warfare in China, publicized in the West in the late 1930s and in 1941, at the time of verified mustard and lewisite attacks on Ichang. His Silver Star was for heroism in the Meuse-Argonne offensive at the end of World War I. That horrific September–November battle started with German use of heavy smoke screens, followed by repeated attacks with phosgene (the poison that killed more soldiers in the war than any other), highly persistent, blistering mustard gas, and two types of tear gas (chloropicrin and bromoacetone). The Americans troops, untrained in chemical defenses, had struggled with masks that fogged their vision and often discarded them; over 19,000 soldiers were gassed, which contributed to the 117,000 overall casualties.[52]

Rather than chemical or biological weapons, Chief of Counsel Keenan was focused on the Rape of Nanking, which he intended to showcase as the premier example of a Japanese Class C war crime. Aware that the Chinese Division badly needed help, Keenan proposed sending Sutton and Morrow on a fact-finding mission to China, under the direction of prosecutor Hsiang, with Henry Chiu as guide and translator. MacArthur agreed to the plan. The team could go to Nanjing to retrieve official documents and interview potential witnesses and, if necessary, stop off in other cities, Beijing and Chongqing, for example, for more general information on Japanese military aggression.

The Committees Take Action

On March 5 at 4:30 p.m., a special IPS Executive Committee meeting was held at the Meiji Building to announce new rules on interrogation and evidence.[53] There Sutton and Tavenner were joined by Colonel Morrow and Henry Hauxhurst, the corporate lawyer from Cincinnati who had come to Tokyo with Keenan and would travel to China to gather evidence on economic exploitation. Although usually only associate prosecutors were invited, Sutton, Morrow, and Hauxhurst were allowed because of the assistance they were directed to provide Prosecutor Hsiang, who was unable to attend.

Chairman Alfred Comyns Carr, precise and soft-spoken, started the meeting with a discussion of the IPS "chicken-and-egg" dilemma. Until the selection of defendants was complete, the indictment could not be finished; yet, following the Nuremberg model that made each of the accused a representative of major criminal offenses, the selection of defendants was waiting on the formulation of the indictment. By necessity, a March 15 deadline for its full text was moved to March 20. The Anglo-dominated Evidence and Drafting Committees were still fixed on a low number, from fifteen to twenty defendants. Still, many files had to be reviewed and final decisions made. Some nations, it was noted, "might not see their choices honored."

Comyns Carr read out seven "decisions on interrogation" that the committee had reached. The decisions, some of them merely exhortations, urged the prosecutors to do everything they could to make the trial "manageable." They were told to focus on case essentials, minimize details, and think of ways to shorten witness testimony, for example, by having key defendants double as witnesses.[54]

The committee gave the prosecutors only another ten days to conclude all major interrogations. To meet this goal, they would have to narrow the scope of their inquiries and concentrate on suspects who were in power just before Pearl Harbor and the start of the war in the Pacific. For efficiency's sake, IPS prosecutors had to begin submitting reports to the committee that assessed the likely court performance of every prospective defendant—for example, how they might perform under pressure, given advanced age or illness or mental condition. In addition, their reports should stipulate whether each chosen witness possessed "proper information" and was "fairly reliable" and would hold up under cross examination—or find another who could.

Prosecutors had to keep these summary reports up to date, either daily or every other day, and complete them by the ten-day time limit. Four copies of each report were to be submitted to the committee's secretary, who would see that all committee members received their copies.

The Executive Committee also introduced the issue of Japanese abuses of prisoners of war, a war crime its members agreed played "more than a nominal part" in the overall criminal charges. Although Japan had signed but not ratified the 1929 Geneva Convention for the protection of POWS, the charge would appear in the indictment as a violation of customary law to vindicate captured Allied soldiers who had been abused and killed, even though many minor trials in the Pacific had or were in the process of trying Japanese military for these crimes.

A point of general agreement was that charges of Class A "crimes against peace" would be entered by every nation represented at the IMTFE in their indictment of top government officials. The final number of counts in the indictment would depend on the detail given in the charges against each defendant.

As a follow-up, the next day Alan Mansfield, the committee chair, convened the first meeting of the Evidence and Defendants Committee.[55] Except for Prosecutor Hsiang from the Chinese Division, all thirteen IPS lawyers in attendance were American or from the British and Commonwealth divisions. Mansfield's primary concern was that ground rules be laid out before the projected onrush of more IPS lawyers and staff in the weeks before the trial began.

At first the committee became bogged down in details: how many document copies should be printed in English and in Japanese (two hundred and seventy-five, respectively, it was agreed), the proper way to certify Japanese government documents, and how to organize photostating and mimeographing. Out of frustration, Mansfield made a quick decision to create a new Subcommittee on Documents to handle these practicalities. Reacting quickly, after the meeting, Keenan created the position of documents officer at IPS and circulated a memo to the staff that each division should quickly submit to the Evidence Committee a list of documents that it would introduce as part of the overall case. The committee would review the list and then give it to the new documents officer (Captain Lindsay Williamson), whose duty was to assure proper authentication, by certificate if possible or by oral evidence.[56] Keenan then created another new post, that of translation and duplication officer, to work with the Documents Subcommittee to speed this process.

Shortly after, at the Evidence Committee's second meeting, Mansfield focused the discussion on document evaluation and selection. One problem was how to organize and mine the Japanese documents that had been on the increase since January, when government officials, under pressure from MacArthur and Emperor Hirohito, began responding to IPS requests. Translations of official Japanese documents had to be authenticated to ready them for submission at the trial; a certificate, it was decided, needed to be attached to each. The committee resolved to compose guidelines for how IMTFE defense attorneys would obtain documents and agreed that they would need document translations as well.

Still unclear were IPS guidelines for gleaning best evidence from interrogations so that it could be coordinated into the overall case argument. The committee turned to Roy Morgan and asked him to write a memo about his methods, learned at the FBI and the Department of Justice. A roundabout system for evidence evaluation then emerged. Morgan's advisory memo would be distributed to all prosecutors and to the new documents officer, Captain Williamson, with whom Morgan would coordinate his work on centralizing the IPS evidence files. Meanwhile, Solis Horwitz, deputy assistant to Keenan, would select the data on defendants and incidents that should be included. Captain Williamson and Horwitz together would review that information and send it to Morgan. Morgan would then extract the passages that he judged most relevant as evidence, whether against the person interrogated or other defendants. All this information would then flow to Horwitz. In addition to copies of Morgan's relevant case files, Horwitz would in due course receive copies of all documents of evidentiary value, a summary of IPS interrogations, and Morgan's extracts of key points. From this information, Horwitz would coordinate and refine the prosecution's case—or at least try to organize its many facets.[57]

Alan Mansfield, though, had one main resolve: to finalize a short list of defendants, to him the most crucial of the IPS collective decisions. On March 8, after reviewing the top suspects selected by the Americans, he gave Keenan a list of eighteen defendants.[58] Promotion of "aggressive war" by each of the accused was foremost in this judgment. General Tojo, the wartime premier who also controlled the Ministries of Foreign Affairs, Home Affairs, and Education, was an obvious choice. Still under interrogation at Sugamo, he was, unlike others, taking responsibility for the war. One of his right-hand men, General Muto Akira, had troops under his command at Nanjing in 1937 and had served under General Yamashita during the Rape of Manila. General Araki Sadao, one-time minister of war and an important advisor to Tojo, was another principal suspect, followed by others with similar histories. Admiral Nagano Osami was blamed for Pearl Harbor and the simultaneous surprise attacks on Hong Kong and Manila. Former foreign minister Matsuoka Yosuke, who had led the Japanese exit from the League of Nations in 1933, was listed for his role in creating the Axis alliance; General Oshima Hiroshi and diplomat Shiratori Toshio were also listed for their closeness to Nazi leaders and for support of Japan's military expansion.

Three other diplomats made the list. Togo Shiganori had briefly been ambassador to Germany, but his perceived crime was that, involved in peace negotiations with the United States in 1941, he had failed to warn the Americans in time about the surprise attack on Pearl Harbor. Baron Hirota Koki, foreign minister during the Nanking Massacre, was also implicated in cabinet warfare plans. The third diplomat was former foreign minister Shigemitsu. A belated peace advocate and already designated as a witness for the prosecution, he had been purged from government soon after he signed the Instrument of Surrender in September 1945.

In the selection, deference was paid to China's history. Colonel Hashimoto Kingoro was linked to planning the aggression at Mukden in 1931. General Matsui Iwane was held responsible as field commander during the Nanjing Massacre. Just as the city fell, Matsui, sick with malaria, had temporarily ceded his command to Prince Asaka, a member of the imperial family, but Matsui remained in the city for weeks afterward and, in any case, made no attempt to blame Asaka, whose relationship to the emperor protected him from prosecution.[59]

Violations of customary rules of war were also acknowledged. Regarding the treatment of prisoners of war, General Doihara Kenji was cited for running brutal POW camps in Malaya, Sumatra, Java, and Borneo, as well as for drug trafficking in China. Admiral Shimada Shigetaro was known for massacres of surviving crews of Allied warships and for the "hell ships." Criminal economic exploitation was represented by Hoshino Naoki, the chief cabinet secretary in 1941–1944, whose interrogation Morgan had recently arranged. In addition to promoting war against the Allies, Hoshino had directed opium trafficking to finance the Kwantung Army. General Suzuki Teiichi, an important government advisor, had mobilized the Japanese wartime economy and was known to have promoted the lucrative opium trade in China.

Two other selections were patently representational. Marquis Kido Koichi, Lord Keeper of the Privy Seal and the emperor's close advisor during the war years, appeared to be the obvious stand-in for Hirohito; as a member of the imperial family he had wielded high-level influence—and he was Chief of Counsel Keenan's pick as well. Okawa Shumei, a well-known propagandist who had never held government office, fit the description of an "instigator" who had conspired with Axis powers to wage aggressive war.

In his cover letter to Keenan, Mansfield urged him to submit the "Suggested List of Defendants" to the Executive Committee "at the earliest possible moment." He succinctly summarized the stringent Anglo strategy:

> As there are many reasons in favor of a swift and simple trial of few representative men, it is asked that the attached list be regarded as about the maximum number. The question for consideration, therefore, is not what names might be added, but rather what names, if any should be substituted for those in the List, so that a list of fifteen to twenty names may cover as fairly as possible the directive forces which posterity will hold responsible for the acts committed by Japan.[60]

The Executive Committee accepted the suggested list and allowed for some revision, for example, the elimination of former foreign minister Shigemitsu's name.

Following the solving of this basic problem of defendant selection, case preparation was next on the IPS agenda. The greatest pressure was on the Chinese Division, due to figure prominently in the opening of the prosecution's arguments and yet still needing to organize a coherent case based on trial-worthy evidence.

4

THE INVESTIGATION FOR EVIDENCE IN CHINA

THE TRIP TO CHINA BY DAVID NELSON SUTTON AND THOMAS MORROW was the most ambitious fact-finding expedition to be made on behalf of any IPS Division.[1] It was also, as Chief Prosecutor Joseph Keenan and General MacArthur agreed, highly necessary: China's case, central to the prosecution, lacked trial-worthy evidence, coherently and persuasively organized. Without it, no war crime could be fixed in history; with it, the world would remember the judgment of law. The two investigators would concentrate on the Class C crimes against humanity, with license to acquire pertinent information about the Class A war of aggression crimes and the Class B violations of treaties and laws of war. The two investigators were given a month, from March 12 to April 12, to complete this mission.

As details for the Sutton-Morrow trip were being finalized, Lieutenant Colonel Arvo Thompson of the Chemical Warfare Service was still in Tokyo finishing his interviews with General Ishii and his Unit 731 cohort. All went well for Thompson's project until a leak to United Press journalist Peter Kalischer blew his cover. In the February 27 issue of *Pacific Stars and Stripes,* Kalischer reported that US military intelligence had located General Ishii, sought on suspicion of having conducted experiments on

American and Chinese POWs in Manchuria, and that, over the course of seven weeks, Thompson had interviewed the general and twenty-five of his scientists.[2] According to Kalischer, Ishii denied "conducting experiments on prisoners of war or planning any large-scale attempts to develop offensive biological warfare" and that no more than a small fraction of the six million yen his institute received each year had gone to bacterial field tests. The article described Ishii as "a determined, almost ruthless individual" who since 1936 had been conducting experiments in bacteriology with the Japanese Army. The liberties taken by *Stars and Stripes* occasionally rankled MacArthur, but this article went further than most in its threat to G-2's investigation of a top secret issue.

Surprised by the news, on March 2 Morrow wrote a memo to Keenan, reminding him that months before he had tried to locate Ishii—and here the general was, practically on the IPS doorstep.[3] Morrow also reminded Keenan that chemical and biological weapons were both "prohibited methods of warfare." Japan's use of poison and bacteriological weapons, he pointed out, "assumes importance because of the obvious impossibility of developing such methods of warfare on the field of battle or through the resources of an army general in the field, and indicates that such methods of warfare were carried on by the Tokyo Government and not the field commanders." The leaders of the Imperial Army at the cabinet level, he reasoned, must have approved the military doctrine that allowed the manufacture of munitions, the training of soldiers, and the outfitting of planes—even if on a small scale.

Morrow called attention to page 679 of the *China Handbook 1937–1943*, in which a Dr. P. Z. King had written that "rice, wheat, and fleas were scattered over certain towns and Bubonic Plague appeared soon after, causing a number of deaths."[4] Morrow recommended that "if alive, Dr. King be procured for interrogation; also that the other experts who worked with him be located with a view to presenting all those persons as witnesses at the trial."[5]

Morrow was unclear whether Japan was party to the 1925 Geneva Protocol, which legally made a difference. The Japanese had agreed to The Hague Conventions of 1899 and 1907 that condemned the use of poisons in war, which gave the prosecution an edge. A ban against attacking with plague might apply—or the Chinese might be correct in arguing it was a crime against humanity.

After talking to Roy Morgan at the IPS Investigation Division, who seemed to know everyone, Morrow arranged to meet with Arvo Thompson at the G-2 office. There they were joined by an officer from General Charles Willoughby's Technical Intelligence staff, whose follow-up to the 1945 science survey was focused on chemical and biological weapons. The upshot was that, as an IPS prosecutor, Morrow was denied access to Ishii and the other Unit 731 scientists being interrogated. In a March 8 memo to Keenan, Morrow described his meeting with Thompson as "negative in its results." He had been told to follow up with the head of the CWS office in Tokyo, a meeting he decided to put off as he concentrated on preparing his trip to China.[6]

Nelson Sutton was working overtime on his trip plans, with notes and memos piling up on his desk. On an oversized National Geographic map of China, he marked in pencil the four cities he wanted to visit: Shanghai, Beijing, Chongqing, and Nanjing, scene of the 1937–1938 massacre. Prosecutor Hsiang had already gone ahead to Shanghai, where he lived, to lay the groundwork for the investigation.

As March 12 approached, Sutton's list of people to interview on the expedition grew to include Chinese generals, British policemen, a former Japanese drug dealer, Japanese Foreign Ministry personnel (in China to negotiate the repatriation of Japanese POWs), American Embassy personnel, and officials at the United Nations Relief and Rehabilitation Administration (UNRRA), which, in carrying out its humanitarian aid agreement with China, had accumulated war crimes evidence.[7] In his file, Sutton had an affidavit from UNRRA about three schoolgirls who were taken prisoner by Japanese gendarmes during the massacre in Nanjing and for two months had been "tortured, insulted and repeatedly raped."[8] As a result, two had died. As for investigating the plague attacks, Dr. Peter Z. King (Jin Baoshan), author of the 1942 report, turned out to be the current director-general of China's National Health Administration in Chongqing, where Sutton would interview him.

Through Prosecutor Hsiang, the War Crimes Commission in Nanjing was arranging for Sutton and Morrow to interview as many as fifty survivors of the massacre as potential witnesses. An IPS colleague gave Sutton the names of a dozen more sources to seek out and cheerfully signed his memo, "Good hunting!"[9] Henry Hauxhurst, the corporate lawyer from Cincinnati, would travel with them to China to find Class B economic exploitation evidence, which could include the highly profitable Japanese opium trade. Prior to World War II, the Japanese had agreed to a series of international accords restricting the manufacture and distribution of narcotic drugs, at junctures when the protection of China became an international goal. The Treaty of Versailles incorporated the prewar International Opium Convention, which was reinforced in 1925 when the League of Nations created a Permanent Central Board for the Suppression of the Use of Opium and Other Drugs. But the persistence of the drug trade in China made a mockery of the board. Japan signed the Convention for Limiting the Manufacture and Regulating the Distribution of Narcotic Drugs in 1931 and ratified it in 1935.[10] In 1938, though, Japan officially quit its already nominal place on the league's board. It then created an Asia Development Board (Koa-in) and began a highly organized system of opium and heroin distribution and profiteering that benefited a cartel of eight cabinet shareholders.[11] The Chinese Division was intent on including this chapter of Sino-Japanese relations in its case.

On March 6 Chief of Counsel Keenan directed Sutton to go to China to "procure and have properly authenticated pertinent documents and records" concerning Japan's aggressive warfare and atrocities committed by Japanese troops in China. The understanding was that Prosecutor Hsiang would be directing his secretary, Henry Chiu, and Nelson Sutton in the investigations, with Colonel Morrow assisting. An official order from SCAP quickly followed. By command of General MacArthur, Sutton was to travel "to Shanghai, Nanking, and such other places in the China Theater as may be necessary on temporary duty not to exceed thirty (30) days for purpose of interrogating witnesses, screening and analyzing documents and obtaining evidence about war crimes. Upon completion of this temporary duty he will return to his proper station."[12]

On March 9 Sutton went to SCAP's General Dispensary to obtain the bill of health needed for travel to China. He had remained healthy since arriving in Tokyo, avoiding the colds and food poisoning that troubled some of his IPS colleagues.[13] His immunizations as required by the War Department were in order. In addition, he was certified free from vermin and from the "quarantineable diseases" of cholera, plague, smallpox, yellow fever, epidemic (louse-borne) typhus, anthrax, psittacosis, and leprosy, and from other diseases "which might seriously prejudice the health of contacts en route."[14]

That travel in China might pose a health hazard to Sutton was apparent from the Tokyo English-language newspapers whose headlines were featuring the recent outbreaks of cholera in the Yangtze River Delta, coincident with the repatriation of Japanese soldiers. The press also brought news of other suffering and disruptions: droughts had destroyed crops, the Yellow River had flooded its banks in the North, 450 million Chinese were starving and 50 million displaced. The war had wrecked China's roads, bridges, and railways. In addition to wartime battle damage, Chiang Kai-shek's KMT troops had sought to contain Japanese troops by destroying highways and rail lines and creating floods. Random armed conflict persisted in China, especially in the North between KMT and Chinese Communist Party (CCP) troops.

Throughout his trip, Sutton was promised protection and privileges by the Department of War, as he was in Tokyo. He would be transported by US Army aircraft, billeted with army officers, and chauffeured by army drivers or, at times, by KMT officers. Translators and stenographers would assist him and the Chinese Division team. In each city he and Colonel Morrow would be invited to official receptions and dinners that could open doors for them.

Chief of Counsel Keenan decided to take a trip to China on his own, a two-week jaunt separate from Sutton and Morrow's. His agenda was to meet with General George C. Marshall, then in Beijing attempting to broker peace between the KMT and the CCP. Keenan also planned a private conference with Generalissimo Chiang Kai-shek in Chongqing and a visit to Shanghai, where Japanese soldiers were on trial for executing the three captive Doolittle pilots.

Off to China

On the afternoon of March 12, the Chinese Division team flew from Tokyo over the East China Sea to Shanghai. As the plane approached Kiangwan Airport, Sutton had his first view of the city, located at the mouth of the Yangtze River, with the Huangpu River adding to its waterfront. An exceptionally rainy winter had flooded the marsh to the city's west, making

Map 1 Japan, China, and neighboring countries, 1945–1946

The former Japanese colony Manchukuo, "the state of Manchuria" (known in China as the Three Eastern Provinces), is highlighted and the postwar division of Korea indicated.

Shanghai look like a small island surrounded by muddy water. In the harbor, a US battleship was anchored, with small fishing boats and junks bobbing nearby.

US Army drivers met Sutton, Morrow, and Hauxhurst at the airport and brought them through the city to their hotel. Large puddles in the street indicated drainage problems, and the smell of open sewers permeated the air. In contrast to Tokyo, most of Shanghai's buildings—the apartment houses, legations, offices, pagodas, and large department stores—were intact. Downtown was a noisy mix of Chinese crowds and street vendors, rickshaws and bicycles, and American soldiers in jeeps. General Albert C. Wedemeyer, commander of the China Theater since 1944, made his headquarters in Shanghai. Critical of US support of negotiations with the CCP, he was about to quit his post for an assignment in Washington.[15]

Sutton, Morrow, and Hauxhurst were billeted at the Cathay House, a fourteen-story hotel in the run-down French sector. The sector had a history relevant to the Nanjing Massacre. When Shanghai was under attack by the Japanese in 1932 and then again in 1937, the Jesuit priest Jaquinot de Besange created a safe zone in the French sector for Chinese civilians.[16] The plan became a model for the Nanjing Safety Zone created in 1937 by the German businessman John Rabe, American missionaries, and other foreigners.

Along with his large map of China, Sutton brought a supply of pencils and the small brown notebooks he used to record his observations.[17] The morning after the division team's arrival in Shanghai, Sutton and Morrow started the day early with an interview of a 47-year-old survivor of the Nanjing Massacre, a man named Wang Yien Sze.[18] Through a translator, Wang described how in the winter of 1937 Japanese soldiers had invaded one of the city's refugee camps where he and his brother were members of a local volunteer corps organized to prevent looting. Mistaking his brother for a Chinese soldier, the Japanese killed him by bayonetting him three times in the head and several times in the spine. Sutton made a note to consider Wang as a witness. After his testimony was typed from handwritten notes and read back to him for verification, Wang signed it with his fingerprint, and Morrow also signed. This authentication process—the interview, transcription, translation, and witnessed signature—would be repeated many times in the coming month, for survivors who had escaped anonymity.

This day and the rest of the week in Shanghai were given over to a hectic combination of planned and spontaneous efforts to make contacts and find evidence. While Morrow went off to question military sources, Sutton had lunch with S. Francis Liu, former chief justice of the Shanghai Supreme Court. Henry Chiu from the IPS China Division was at the lunch, but his translation skills were not needed. Like the IMTFE's Judge Mei and Associate Prosecutor Hsiang, Judge Liu was another Western-educated Chinese jurist; he had been an undergraduate at Oberlin College and then earned his law degree at Yale. Following that, he studied philosophy at the University of Berlin to better understand the differing East-West concepts of justice.[19] While Sutton took notes, Liu told him about the "Rape of Nanking." He spoke of girls stripped naked and bound with ropes being put on display to laughing Japanese soldiers—the photographs became Japanese military souvenirs. Liu also spoke of the humiliation of Chinese men in Nanjing. For example, those who failed to salute passing Japanese military had to kneel for twelve to thirty hours to pay for this disrespect. Finally, he described the mass slaughter of men suspected of being part of Chiang's army. "It was terrible," he told Sutton.

After lunch, Sutton met with Morrow and the two conferred briefly with Captain George Plotkin, director of the army's Criminal Investigation Division. The meeting, a detour from their Class C crimes investigation, had to do with Frank Tavenner's special interest in count 5 in the current indictment, "Japan's conspiracy with Nazi Germany for world domination." The previous week, Plotkin had received a letter from Captain Frank Farrell, a marine from the War Department's Strategic Services Unit in the China Theater, who urgently wanted to meet with Chief of Counsel Keenan. Farrell believed that Nazi corporations had conspired with the Japanese to exploit China's resources and that these same German business moguls were running a postwar network of spies. On the chance that this information might incriminate former prime minister Togo or other defendants, Sutton and Morrow agreed to meet with Farrell the following evening.

The next day, March 14, the two prosecutors went from one US Army and consular office to another explaining their mission. They also fit in a visit to the office of the International Christian Convention, long a sponsor of anti-opium campaigns in China and able to offer two volumes of files on the Nanjing Massacre and the similar attack on Hankow (Hankou) in 1938. Charles L. Boynton, its director, told them that Professor Miner Searle Bates, an American witness to the atrocities, had returned to Nanjing after three years in hiding with other university faculty and students. "Dr. Bates," Boynton advised, "will perhaps be the best witness."

Sutton and Morrow then located the Australian journalist H. J. Timperley, author of the book *What War Means* about the Rape of Nanjing and now employed by UNRRA.[20] Since he himself had not witnessed the massacre, Timperley offered little as a witness. Another strike against him was that he had written propaganda for Generalissimo Chiang during the war, a bias to which any reputable defense counsel would object. Timperley's book, though, was a valuable composite of the diaries and letters written by safety zone eyewitnesses who might offer powerful testimony.

The already-mentioned Dr. Bates, a member of the Nanjing International Red Cross Committee, had been Timperley's main source of information. Timperley added the name of John Magee, an Episcopal minister who had taken some 500 feet of films of the massacre. Selections from the films, widely circulated in the United States, had documented horrific carnage and the looting and physical destruction of the city. Other names stood out: the YMCA's George Fitch, the surgeon Robert Wilson, sociologist Lewis Smythe, and James McCallum, pastor at the South Gate Church in Nanjing—all of them Americans and, to Sutton's mind, good witness prospects.

According to US Army officers Sutton spoke to later that day, John Rabe should have been on his Nanjing witness list.[21] In addition to his courageous leadership of the Safety Zone Committee, Rabe had sent daily reports protesting the massacre to Japanese, American, British, and German Embassy officials. Then, in February 1938, he was recalled to Germany by Siemens, his employer. After the war, because he had been a member of the Nazi Party, he was subject to the Occupation purge and was now unable to travel and bear witness in Tokyo.

That night, as planned, Sutton and Morrow met with Captain Farrell, who gave them a long exposition on a supposed German spy ring involving Walther Stennes, a former Nazi captain, General Chiang's close advisor, and once head of Hitler's Storm Troopers.[22] As Farrell recounted, Stennes was still conniving in every way to disseminate anti-American propaganda and might be plotting a German government-in-exile in China. Captain Farrell was also trying to make a case against Heinrich Stahmer, one-time economic advisor to Japan and, in 1943–1945, ambassador to Tokyo, for his role in exploiting China's resources, for example, with the unregulated export of tungsten.[23] Sutton and Morrow promised to make IPS aware of Farrell's investigation, but they doubted that Farrell had any evidence that would implicate former prime minister Togo. A benefit of this diversion was that they had made a good connection with Captain Plotkin, who promised to be in touch about other leads.

In a lengthy meeting the next day, a group of US Army officers spoke passionately to Sutton about the importance of POW war crimes, and not just the murder of the Doolittle pilots. They talked about Bataan, the Philippines, Formosa, and Korea, and especially the prisoners at Mukden in Manchuria, where over a thousand had died from beatings, disease, and starvation. At SCAP's Legal Section, Alva Carpenter had already received twenty to thirty Mukden POW affidavits. At still another meeting that day in Shanghai, an American lawyer gave Sutton a more general insight, telling him that what China needed was technical help "as never before." Sutton earnestly took notes. "[China] has the brains," the lawyer told him, "Her resources are her people. Small industries should be developed."

That same day, Sutton met with Colonel David Barrett, a near celebrity in American military circles. A short, heavy-set man a few years older than Sutton, he was already listed as a key witness for the Chinese Class A aggressive war charges. In 1937, with General Joseph Stilwell, then the US military attaché in Beijing, he had witnessed firsthand the Marco Polo Bridge "incident" of June 7, which he described to Sutton as "a cooked-up job" by the Japanese to invade China. Barrett, fluent in Mandarin and a variety of Chinese dialects, was afterward stationed as a military attaché to the US Embassy in Chongqing, the Chinese government's provisional capital after the fall of Nanjing. In 1943 he was tapped to lead a special mission that placed him for nearly a year at Mao Zedong's headquarters in the remote Northwest.[24] His objective was to encourage Mao to forge a coalition with General Chiang. Caught in a conflict between the coalition plans of his army superior and those of a US ambassador, Barrett missed being promoted to brigadier general. After the war, General George Marshall, who had been Barrett's commanding officer in 1927 at Tientsin (Tianjin), his first posting in China, recruited him as an aide, his present position.

Barrett advised Sutton that if he really wanted to know about "the Japs in Shanghai," he should find John B. Powell, the American editor of the *China Weekly Review*, who would make a good witness for the prosecution.[25] Held captive for nearly a year at Shanghai's Bridge House Jail, Powell lost half his body weight and contracted gangrene that led to the amputation of both his feet. His son, John W. Powell, had taken over editing the review after his father returned to America. Sutton jotted the recommendation in his little brown notebook. While recognizing the importance of Barrett's 1937 experience, Sutton described him with lawyerly ambivalence: "A fair witness but inclined to argue."

It was late afternoon, but the day was not over. Sutton had arranged to meet Colonel Morrow at the British consulate in the Bund, where Shanghai's legations and large corporate offices were concentrated. There they would interview the former head of the Narcotics Division of the Shanghai Municipal Police, Harold Frank Gill, about the opium trade under Japanese governance. Gill, who was a British subject, ran the Narcotics Division from the end of 1939 until his internment in February 1943. With him was his Chinese assistant, Su Yeh Yueh, who had run the division's detective force.

Gill took the lead in describing the worsening situation after the defeated Chinese government forces withdrew. In 1938, once the Japanese controlled Shanghai, itinerant Korean vendors appeared, well supplied with the drug, which was exclusively for the Chinese; it was illegal to sell it to any Japanese or Europeans. Certain Japanese, notorious for running the opium business, could not be questioned or charged without the cooperation of the Japanese police, cooperation that was promised but never given. The opium sales continued with disastrous results. Since addicts would rather have opium than eat, they died by the dozens every day of starvation and their corpses piled up in alleyways. To buy opium or heroin, they stole money or sold themselves into prostitution, and they often ended in jail. Detective Su corroborated Gill's version of events. Impressed, Sutton arranged for both men's statements to be typed and witnessed as affidavits by the consular staff.[26]

After this, Sutton and Morrow left for still another interview, bringing Henry Chiu as their translator. A young Mr. Hsu, a textile merchant captured by the Japanese on the far southwest Burma-Yunnan (Kunming) Road, described the slaughter of hundreds of Chinese men like himself; he had narrowly missed being machine-gunned by falling to the ground just seconds before the bullets hit his group. Sutton thought him credible, although he spoke only halting English, and put him on his witness list.

That weekend, Judge Mei of the IMTFE arrived in Shanghai and checked into the Hotel Metropole, the elegant 1930s high-rise near the Bund. He invited the Chinese Division team to meet there on Sunday, in a conference room he had reserved. For the American trial lawyers, such an invitation from a sitting judge was unusual, but they followed the lead of Prosecutor Hsiang (or Judge Hsiang, as he was known). At the conference room, the dapper Judge Mei, with a trimmed moustache and wearing round spectacles and a well-tailored Western suit, greeted the team courteously and gave out his embossed visiting card, printed in English on one side, Chinese on the other. He invited Sutton to sit next to him at the table. Joining them were Prosecutor Hsiang, Colonel Morrow, Henry Hauxhurst, Henry Chiu, and two more additions, Jack Crowley, a staffer from IPS, and Captain Luke Lea, Chief of Counsel Keenan's military aide.[27]

Younger and more outspoken than Hsiang, Judge Mei believed that China had a strong tradition of natural moral codes (*li*) and of every individual's equality before the law (*fa*).[28] The Chinese penal code, he explained, was equitable, and therefore even Emperor Hirohito should be indicted, an opinion about which he was publicly silent.

At Mei's request, Sutton and Morrow reviewed the expedition's efforts so far and its plans going forward. They had made some progress in identifying prospective witnesses. In three days they would depart for Beijing, where they expected to discover more witnesses and information on Japanese opium trafficking and chemical warfare. Depending on what leads they found, they would spend a week or ten days there. On his own, Sutton would go to Chongqing for another week, after which he would meet Colonel Morrow and Henry Chiu in Nanjing. There, the last six days of their trip would be devoted to securing sworn testimony from a sample of Nanjing Massacre survivors and to selecting some to give testimony at the tribunal. On April 10 Sutton and Morrow would return to

Shanghai to pick up any loose threads, and they would be back in Tokyo by April 12. Not much time was left. The IMTFE was scheduled to open with the reading of the indictment in a few weeks, followed by the overall presentation of the prosecution's case, in which Chinese charges would figure strongly; barring delays, the trial would open in early May and the argument for the Chinese case might begin in June.

Sutton and Morrow spent most of the next day attending the high-profile trial of Japanese soldiers for the execution of the three downed Doolittle pilots.[29] The choice of venue, the Ward Row Jail, was intentional; the jail, built before the war by the British, had been used by the Japanese to incarcerate POWs. Inside, an improvised courtroom had been set up, with simple chairs and tables. The proceeding offered a glimpse of the tense atmosphere that might pervade the Tokyo trial. While hefty US military guards loomed over the diminutive Japanese defendants, a Doolittle flier from the original eight captured in China railed against the long months of torture, starvation, and solitary confinement they endured at the hands of the Japanese.

Most at issue was whether the principal defendant, Lieutenant General Sawada Shigeru, former commander of the Thirteenth Army in China, and his three subordinates had been acting on their own authority or had been obeying orders from above. The defense presented a statement from the imprisoned former premier Tojo (a friend of Sawada's), affirming that he took responsibility for the trial of the pilots. It had been, he argued, in conformity with the Japanese law enacted August 13, 1942, after the Doolittle raid, to criminalize foreign air attacks on "ordinary people" and the destruction of nonmilitary property in Japan and its territories in violation of international law.[30] Another affidavit, from Field Marshal Hata Shunroku, one-time head of the expeditionary force in China and also minister of war, affirmed that Sawada had had "no choice."[31] That the ultimate responsibility lay with two designated IMTFE defendants was all the IPS attorneys, who would introduce the Doolittle case at the IMTFE, needed to know.

That evening Judge Mei and Prosecutor Hsiang hosted the IPS attorneys at the lively Cum Luck Restaurant on Bubbling Well Road, the city's main artery, in the International Settlement, where the specialty was Cantonese dishes. (Sutton slipped a paper napkin into his pocket as a souvenir.) The next night Shanghai's mayor, Chien Ta-Chun, hosted Mei and the Chinese Division team at a cocktail reception at his official residence.

Early the next morning, Sutton and Morrow flew to Beijing, leaving Judge Hsiang behind. They were welcomed with a banquet at the mayor's residence attended by an eclectic crowd of Asians and Westerners. There Sutton ran into Walter Robertson, a banker from Richmond who was in line to become the assistant secretary of state for Far Eastern affairs.[32] Elated to find another Virginian, that night Sutton telegraphed the news to his wife Frances back in Virginia and signed it, "love, Nelson."

For his trip to Beijing, Sutton had packed a thirty-page guide to the city, with an introduction by Chiang Kai-shek that bid visitors to enjoy its wonders: the Forbidden City, the Sky Gods Temple, the ancient cedar trees, a trip to the Great Wall, and a renowned collection of insects at the zoo. Beijing had a dozen theaters—the operas were much recommended—and five movie houses, along with many Chinese and foreign restaurants.

Aside from a visit to a jewelry store at the Hotel de Peking to buy presents, though, Sutton took little time for touring. Not only was his investigative schedule busy but the current atmosphere in Beijing was tense. General Marshall's cease-fire negotiations had faltered and, without meeting Chief of Counsel Keenan, he had just flown to Washington to confer with President Truman. US Marines, who had accepted the Japanese surrender of the city in 1945, were still repatriating an estimated 300,000 Japanese soldiers and civilians. Marines were also guarding nearby railroad lines and ammunition stockpiles that Communist Party militia were persistently sabotaging. In addition, the US Army was committed to transporting tens of thousands of KMT soldiers north to Manchuria as a stabilizing force. Just days before the Chinese Division team arrived, Soviet forces had finally ended their six-month occupation of Manchuria, leaving a void that either side in the civil war might fill.

Sutton and Morrow's first interview in Beijing was with Peter J. Lawless, a British citizen who from mid-1938 to December 1941 had been the chief of police in the city's Legation Quarter. Prior to that, he had been inspector of police with the British Municipal Council in Tianjin. Lawless recounted how, as early as 1930, the Japanese had organized the opium trade in China. In 1937 a great influx of Japanese and Koreans arrived to promote contraband opium transport from Mongolia and its sale in occupied cities. "The death rate amongst these addicts," he added, "was very heavy, caused by drug poison or starvation. The addict would sooner die by an injection than [buy] food."[33] Lawless had no doubt that the Japanese Embassy staff knew of the magnitude of the narcotics trade and were complicit with people in the "ring." Sutton put Lawless down as a good potential witness, a solid police officer who, like Gill, could meet the best evidence criteria: official, firsthand, and relevant to the crime.

The rest of the week Sutton was chauffeured around the city to various military offices, while Morrow searched for evidence about Japanese chemical warfare. Then, on Saturday, the two of them spent three hours interrogating a former Japanese lieutenant general who in 1940–1941 had been president of the North China Liaison Office of Koa-in, Japan's Asia Affairs Board, and had few qualms about documenting the system while pointing an accusatory finger at others. Interviews with Chinese witnesses followed; a judge from the Beijing military court, an army colonel, and two men who had run opium dens each confirmed all previous accounts of the trade.

Through medical contacts, Sutton and Morrow found a European witness to the opium disaster, Dr. Leo Kandel, a dental surgeon. A Jew, Kandel had fled from Austria to Beijing in March 1939. Although he corroborated other testimony, he lacked the right credentials, and Sutton left him off the potential witness list. There was good news, though. As promised, the municipal government of Beijing had ready its summary report on opium, dated March 1946, which connected Japanese transgressions in China to the Koa-in.[34]

In Beijing Sutton reconnected with Colonel David Barrett, Marshall's aide and an invaluable firsthand witness to the Mukden incident, even if he did tend to argue. Barrett's recollection of the Japanese opium trade corroborated the other accounts. The Nationalists in the 1920s had virtually eliminated opium use; anyone caught trafficking could be beheaded. After 1931, he recalled, any city the Japanese occupied became littered with the bodies of dead addicts.

Interested in the plague charges against Japan, Barrett strongly suggested that Sutton locate Dr. Robert Lim (Lin Keshang), the Chinese Army's surgeon general, in Shanghai. According to Barrett, Lim was "one of the biggest men in China." During the war, he had brilliantly organized the Chinese Red Cross to provide emergency aid teams and transportation on battle fronts while promoting improved sanitation and vaccinations for civilians.[35] Near the war's end, Lim was brought to Burma by General Stilwell to help the Allied troops. As Barrett assured Sutton, "He knows all about the plague attacks. He's skeptical that the West will ever believe they happened."

Barrett's parting words to Sutton were meant to be helpful. "Never say 'Chinamen,'" he told him, "always say 'Chinese.'" Sutton wrote the advice down in his notebook.

King's Account

Since the plague attacks had been categorized by the Chinese as crimes against humanity, it fell to Sutton to investigate them, rather than to Morrow, who was more focused on Japanese military aggression and treaty violations. On March 27 Sutton left Beijing by plane for Chongqing, 1,300 miles inland, at the juncture of the Jialing and Yangtze Rivers. Set amid mountains and gorges, Chongqing was called "the City of Fog" and it was rainy and chilly when Sutton's plane arrived. The years of intense Japanese aerial bombardment had turned entire quarters of the city to rubble.

Sutton's first objective was to interview Dr. Peter King, the lead author on the plague attacks report. On March 28 he met King at his office in the government building that housed the National Health Administration. Trained as a physiologist in England, King had spent thirty years promoting public health in China and was known as a tireless administrator.[36] At the time of Sutton's visit, a fact-finding commission from the Rockefeller Foundation was on site reviewing China's health status. King had only grim statistics to offer on pervasive malnutrition, the extreme shortage of physicians and nurses, and epidemics of typhoid fever, dysentery, and malaria. Cholera was spreading from the central area north; an outbreak had just been reported in a town near Chongqing. Plague had erupted in northeastern China, south in Fujian, and on the Burma border.

As King saw it, his official Health Administration report in 1942 on the plague attacks was proof enough of Japan's complicity. It recorded that, on October 27, 1940, a low-flying Japanese airplane had attacked the city of Ningbo, dropping a "considerable quantity of wheat grains over the port city." On October 29 the first case of plague was clinically diagnosed. For centuries, the disease had been identified by its symptoms: painful swellings in the groin (called buboes), skin lesions, and intense fever and vomiting. At Ningbo, all laboratory tests confirmed that the plague bacterium, then called *Pasteurella pestis*, had caused the disease.

Then, on November 12, bubonic plague erupted in the western part of the city of Chu-hsiang (Quzhou) in Zhejiang Province, southwest of Shanghai, the result of an October 4 attack with wheat and rice grains on exactly that area.[37] The epidemic lasted twenty-four days and caused twenty-one deaths; a later reckoning by public health officials found that, by the next year, 184 more people had died of plague in the city, and the spread of the disease to two local villages (noted as I-wu and Tungyang) caused 218 more deaths. Owing to wartime conditions, laboratory tests were delayed, perhaps past the point when *Pasteurella pestis* could survive, and none of it was found in fleas or grain. Like Ningbo, Quzhou had been plague-free before the outbreak; hence the Japanese were assumed to be the cause—despite the lack of clear evidence.

For Sutton, the next attack scenario was even more perplexing. On November 26, 1940, while plague epidemics were terrifying Ningbo and Quzhou, three Japanese planes flew over Kinhwa (Jinhua), an important commercial center between those two cities. According to residents, the planes dropped a large quantity of small granules, about the size of shrimp eggs. Examined in the local health laboratory, the strange material yielded gram-negative bacilli that resembled *Pasteurella pestis* under the microscope, but the laboratory was ill-equipped to verify this suspicion. More than a month later, in January 1941, a team of scientists from the Ministry of Health arrived at Kinhwa to test the microbes on rodents. No infection resulted, nor did anyone there seem to come down with plague. Perhaps this Japanese "experiment" failed to preserve the virulence of the bacteria.

The final alleged attack was at Changteh (Changde) in Hunan Province. At about 5 a.m. on November 4, 1941, an airplane flew low over the city through the morning mist and scattered wheat and rice grains, pieces of paper, cotton wadding, and some unidentified particles. Some city residents brought samples of the dropped material to the local Presbyterian Hospital, where tests revealed microorganisms that looked like *Pasteurella pestis*.

Seven days later, on November 11, the first plague victim was diagnosed, followed by five more the same month. There were two more cases in December and a final one on January 13, 1942. As in the other cities, the public health system was mobilized: rats were hunted and killed, victims' homes were disinfected, and the population was vaccinated. Without these interventions, King believed, the impact would have been much worse. His worry then, as now, was that China lacked the rat poisons, disinfectants, and vaccines to stave off more plague epidemics.

On December 29, 1941, King's report on the attacks was delivered to Ambassador Clarence E. Gauss, stationed in Chongqing, but the State Department and Washington made no public comment, nor did the other Allies whose embassies were given the information. Chinese officials then staged a press conference, at which a military spokesman described the germ attacks as "the first use of bacteria as a weapon in the Japanese-Chinese war." The story, carried by Associated Press, competed with news that hundreds of unprotected Chinese soldiers, many barefoot or in sandals, had been killed in October by bombs of mustard and lewisite while defending the city of Ichang in Hubei, east of the capital. On March 2, 1942, a short article appeared in the *New York Times* with the headline "Chungking Fears Attack with Gas; Airplanes Said to Spread Plague."

On March 31 China's Foreign Ministry took a sterner note and officially notified all Allied embassies and legations that Japan's germ attacks were "ruthlessly in violation of the principles of international law and the principles of humanity." The final version of the King report was distributed. In its first paragraph, King asserted that "in the last two years sufficient circumstantial evidence has been gathered to show that the Japanese have tried to use our people as guinea pigs for experimentation on the practicality [of] bacterial warfare. They have tried to produce epidemics of plague in the Free China by scattering plague-infected materials with aeroplances."[38]

The *New York Times* carried the story of the plague attacks and cited a quote from the Foreign Ministry statement: "Such atrocities and barbarisms can terminate only though the ultimate defeat of the Japanese militarists by combined efforts on the part of the United Nations." In May 1942 the gist of the King report was published in English in the *Chinese Medical Journal*, with simultaneous reporting in the *China Press*.[39] By then, the plague had re-erupted in Quzhou, killing 147 of the 157 people infected. Changde also suffered a reoccurrence, with sixteen fatalities among one hundred people infected.

Distracted by other wartime crises, the international community responded tepidly to the appeals, with King's allusion to human guinea pigs largely ignored. China's efforts to publicize the plague attacks were doubted in Washington and London as desperate propaganda to win more Allied support for Generalissimo Chiang. When the King report circulated to Camp Detrick in Maryland and its companion UK program at Porton Down, its findings were dismissed.[40] As Dr. Paul Fildes, head of the UK biological weapons program, concluded, "There is no proved, or reasonably suspected, connection between the aircraft and the cases of plague, nor is the evidence convincing that the district was normally free from plague."[41]

Sutton, eager for sound facts, was having the same reaction. Dr. King, who had not participated in any of the field responses, urged him to speak with two physicians who had been on site at Changde. One was Robert Pollitzer, an Austrian physician considered China's foremost authority on plague. At the moment he was traveling extensively, putting down a new plague outbreak on the border between Jiangxi and Hunan Provinces, in a coal-producing area, and another one south, in Fujian's agricultural region. King offered to locate him on Sutton's behalf and help arrange a meeting. The other physician was W. I. Chen, medical director of the Methodist Union Hospital in Chongqing, who at that moment was awaiting Sutton at his office.

At the time of the attacks, Dr. Chen, a pathologist, had been head of the Department of Laboratory Medicine at the Chinese Ministry of War's Emergency Medical Service Training School in Guiyang, south of Chongqing, and a consultant for the Red Cross Medical Relief Corps. He traveled to Changde after the epidemic started and there autopsied the body of a 28-year-old man named Kung Tsao-shang, who had died November 24 after a short, severe episode of high fever and enlarged inguinal lymph nodes at the top of his right thigh. Kung worked in a village outside the city but had returned the previous week to visit his mother who was dying of a chronic illness. Along with several pages of autopsy and test data, Chen's results were presented in the public health report as "The Proven Case of Bubonic Plague in Changteh." Chen told Sutton that Dr. Robert Lim had ordered the Changde field response—the same Bobby Lim praised by Colonel Barrett—and endorsed the report. On the lookout for witnesses with credentials, Sutton wrote Lim's name in his notebook and underlined it twice.

Before leaving, Sutton obtained a typed affidavit from Chen to verify that his material in the King report was exactly as he had submitted it to the health authorities in 1941.[42] Chen would be a good witness, but any decent defense lawyer would seize on the gaps in his account. He had not witnessed the plane flying over on November 4, and his autopsy did not connect the young man's death to any grains the plane had dropped.

Later that day, Dr. King sent Sutton a note telling him that Dr. Pollitzer was in Nanjing for a conference and could meet at his office there. "He has been notified that you wish very much to see him," King wrote. "I have asked him to place at your disposal all the available material he has concerning our case against the Japanese in connection with bacteriological warfare in China."[43] Pollitzer was scheduled to leave April 4 for Manchuria, to help combat the plague outbreak there. King, reluctant to have Sutton delay his best plague expert, politely expressed his concern: "I shall be much obliged if you would try and stop at Nanjing on your way to Shanghai. This would allow him more time with you without changing his plans."

To make sure he met with Pollitzer, Sutton arranged to fly to Nanjing earlier than planned, on April 2. This cut short his stay in Chongqing, but he still fit in time to track other leads. In November 1944 the United Nations War Crimes Commission had set up an office in Chongqing, and it had been receiving evidence on alleged Japanese war crimes from the Chinese National Office.[44] China's International Department of the Ministry of Information was another possible source of information, and personnel still remained at the US wartime embassy. None of these sources met expectations. Still, on his last night, full of energy, Sutton attended an official city dinner.

About Dr. Pollitzer

Dr. Robert Pollitzer's address was the National Health Administration complex, in the center of Nanjing, which included the Central Hospital. The city had been off-limits to him since 1937 and his new office, located at the rear of the hospital, was still full of unpacked files and books. His modest job title, senior technical expert, belied the twenty-five years he had devoted to fighting plague, cholera, and other epidemics in his adopted country.

In 1918, from an educated Jewish family and with a new University of Vienna medical degree, Pollitzer was drafted into the Austrian Army as a medical reserve officer; soon after, he was captured by the Russians and sent to Siberia to treat wounded Russian soldiers and any locals who needed care. At the war's end he helped repatriate fellow Austrians, but, young and adventuresome, he preferred to explore North China. In 1921, while he was in Northeast China, a major plague epidemic broke out and he volunteered his services—and found his life's calling.

The disease was ancient, but laboratory knowledge of it was rudimentary and still evolving. Its modern history started in 1894, during an outbreak in Hong Kong, when the Swiss scientist Alphonse Yersin identified plague's bacterium (then called *Bacterium pestis*) by examining the germs from the swollen buboes of dead patients under a microscope.[45] With that, the microbial cause of the disease became known and the medical quest for vaccines and antisera began.

Other scientists soon showed that fleas are the common carriers of plague, especially one species called *Xenopsylla cheopsis*, later traced to the Black Death.[46] Unaffected by the disease, the fleas inject the bacilli they have in their stomachs into their hosts, often rats. When the rats die, the fleas leave the rats' nests for human bedding and, by biting humans, infect them. Other kinds of fleas and other kinds of rodents or mammal hosts can be involved in the transmission of plague. The inhalation of airborne bacilli could also cause the particularly virulent form called pneumonic plague.

In 1921, with the plague epidemic raging in Harbin, Dr. Wu Lien-teh, head of the city's Plague Prevention Service Laboratory, hired Pollitzer. Born in Malaya, Wu had studied medicine in England at Cambridge University, then in France and Germany, and also in the United States, where he spent a fellowship year at Johns Hopkins University. He was sent to Harbin in the winter of 1910 to combat a plague outbreak that was raging throughout China's northeastern provinces, from the northwestern border with Siberia to Beijing.[47] In four months Wu ended the epidemic by mobilizing the right public health responses—quarantines, disinfection stations, the monitoring of railways and ports, and public education. Although the outbreak caused at least sixty thousand deaths, Wu was hailed as a hero who had prevented an even worse catastrophe among the millions at risk. He then created the Manchurian Plague Prevention Service, the model for China's modern public health system. For the 1921 outbreak, having learned from his 1910 experience, Wu mounted an aggressive campaign that combined the mobilization of local public health teams with laboratory science and hospital care, a strategy that limited the number of deaths to around eight thousand and helped prevent the disease from spreading or recurring among the twenty-two million people in the region.

After 1921 Pollitzer stayed in Wu's laboratory, conducting research on the transmission and containment of the disease. He discovered, for example, that plague bacillus was unstable outside its host and could be killed by exposure to sunlight and by competing microbes.[48] In 1928 China's new Nationalist government under Chiang Kai-shek created the Ministry of Health, which established strong connections to the Rockefeller Foundation and the League of Nations Health Organization. Both supported Dr. Wu in building modern hospitals in Beijing and in Nanjing, as well as the northeastern provinces. The city's old plague lab in Harbin was upgraded to the Plague Prevention Laboratory of the League of Nations, and Wu put Pollitzer in charge of it. It was a productive period in a beautiful city founded on international commerce—Harbin was known as the "Paris of the North." Pollitzer and his colleagues published a comprehensive history of plague reservoirs throughout China.[49] Wu, who believed that China was on the brink of a golden age of medicine, coauthored a major work on how Western science and traditional Chinese medicine could be combined.[50]

In 1932 the idyll ended. As the Kwantung Army took control of Manchuria, Wu and Pollitzer fled to Shanghai, abandoning the Harbin public health offices, its new hospital, and the plague laboratory to a regime that would secretly support General Ishii Shiro's germ weapons program. They no sooner reached Shanghai than the Japanese bombed the Chinese sector and destroyed its public health offices there. Dr. Wu kept up his efforts to promote modern health standards, but as China succumbed to Japanese aggression, he retreated to a small town in Malaya where he remained until the end of the war, even throughout the Japanese occupation that began in 1942. Pollitzer stayed in China to work for its National Quarantine Service. In an honorary capacity, he also served under the Shanghai Municipal Council as a medical officer assisting the Chinese displaced by the 1932 bombing. After the Marco Polo Bridge incident in 1937, he worked for two years for the League of Nations before becoming a full-time employee of the Chinese Health Service. Then, in 1941, Dr. Lim sent him to Changde to investigate the plague outbreak.

Sutton Meets Dr. Pollitzer

On the morning of April 2, 1946, Sutton flew from Chongqing to Nanjing and was met by a US Army car and driver.

In 1937 millions of Americans in local movie theaters saw shocking newsreels of the fall of Nanjing. The two American camera operators, Norman Alley and Eric Mayell, who took the historic footage, chronicled the city's bombed buildings and women weeping over dead bodies in the rubble; then they found themselves in peril.[51] On December 12, as the city was about to fall, the USS *Panay*, a gunboat, rescued them and a dozen American diplomats and journalists and sailed up the Yangtze River to what should have been safety. Suddenly Japanese planes attacked the *Panay* and forced the stunned crew and passengers to scramble into life boats. The cameramen kept filming, recording the sinking of a Standard Oil tanker in billows of black smoke and their own desperate flight on land. The USS *Oahu*, with help from HMS *Ladybird* (also attacked but still afloat), ultimately transported the *Panay* victims to Shanghai. The Japanese, claiming the *Panay* sinking was an accident, insisted that they were not at war with the United States. On January 8 American diplomats were allowed to return to the Nanjing embassy, in the midst of the massacres and lootings. The *Panay*'s sinking, again a controversy, would be part of the US case against Japan.[52] The State Department's George Atcheson, Jr., MacArthur's deputy and chair of the Allied Council of Japan, had been onboard the *Panay* and might testify.

Nine years later, liberated Nanjing was a busy river-front city patrolled by KMT and American soldiers. Sutton was billeted at the Number 7 Hostel, War Area Service Corps, once the Metropolitan Hotel. By two o'clock Sutton was at the Central Hospital, his brown notebook and pencil in hand, meeting with Pollitzer. About Sutton's age, Pollitzer, dressed in a rumpled uniform, spoke English with an Austrian accent, like Dr. Kandel, the dental surgeon in Beijing. When he began talking about his career, Sutton realized that, although he might be China's foremost expert on plague, he had lived the life of a wanderer and ended in rather bleak circumstances in a war-damaged hospital amid unpacked boxes.

Sutton turned the conversation to the plague attack on Changde. In response, the doctor showed him a hand-drawn map of the city, which was walled like Nanjing but much smaller. An arrow drawn in red pencil indicated the direction of the Japanese plane on November 4, 1941, as it flew from the northeast, parallel with the Yuan River, and passed over the city. Two red circles indicated where most of the infective material had been dropped, near two city gates. Pollitzer pointed out that all the Changde cases were from those specific areas. Then he indicated a small red circle within one of the larger ones, at the western end of the city, where Kung Tsao-shang, the young worker autopsied by Dr. Chen, had visited his mother's house.

Having researched and written extensively on the subject, Pollitzer was sure that Changde and the central part of China where it was located had never suffered plague outbreaks, which were usually confined to southern port cities and areas or to Manchuria and Inner Mongolia. In 1941 he had considered whether plague could have spread from a neighboring region, but at the time the nearest epidemic was taking place at Quzhou, about 2,000 kilometers away. Changde was situated on a river system entirely different from those in the East, with no direct traffic by boat that could have led to the transport of infected rats and fleas. Since the Changde region was an exporter not an importer of rice and cotton, those vectors would not have reached the city in cargo. In any case, infected rats had not helped spread the disease; the two hundred caught and examined in November and December 1941 showed no signs of plague. Only months later did Pollitzer return and find infected rats. The best argument against any spread of plague from outside, he believed, was that all those stricken were local inhabitants, not travelers.

Pollitzer's theory about the Japanese attack method was that it began with plague-infected fleas, specifically the *Xenopsylla cheopsis* type prevalent in China and Manchuria, which the Japanese had occupied. The infected fleas were likely protected by cloth or paper and dropped along with the grain, which was to attract rats, a common rodent. In the Changde attack and at Ningbo, the fleas seemed to have found their human hosts first, before any rats, and nested first in closets, bedding, and blankets. Some people perhaps were bitten when, out of curiosity, they inspected the fallen grain or when they helped sweep up the grain from the streets and rooftops.

Pollitzer had answers for the proof missing from the King report for why sometimes no fleas were noticed (they had hopped away) or why dead fleas found with grain tested negative for plague (wartime laboratories lacked adequate technology). It was unfortunate that no infected "material" had been preserved, but the disruptions of war had made this impossible. Pollitzer emphasized the facts he felt were important, notably the occurrence of new cases in sequence after the aerial attack on Changde—with the first case presenting eight days later and the others following soon after. The pattern was nearly the same at Ningbo. The long delay of the epidemic in Quzhou was explicable if the infected fleas had found rat hosts before infecting humans, probably originally intended by the Japanese. As for the Kinhwa failure, given the innovative nature of the Japanese attacks, three out of four "successes" was a military achievement—and a war crime.

Despite these explanations, Sutton was concerned about the lack of eyewitnesses for the attacks and the absence of victim testimony. Pollitzer believed that there had been such witnesses in all the targeted cities. In Changde, for example, its inhabitants had agreed "unanimously" that the Japanese plane and its scattering of grain had caused the plague epidemic.[53] But those testimonies had not been recorded and could not be now, given the wartime dispersal of populations from the affected cities and the short period of time Sutton had for his inquiry. Pollitzer, though, pointed out that the King report included an eyewitness statement by E. J. Bannan, identified as a 60-year-old American nurse supervisor at Changde's Presbyterian Hospital. Bannan had stated

> that unhulled grain and wheat found on the streets and roofs of houses in the city of Changteh following the visit of an enemy plane on the morning of November 4th were dropped from that plane. I might say in this connection that I watched the flight of the plane closely that morning. In appearance it was somewhat like an hydroplane and flew low over the city—lower than any plane has yet flown in the more than 20 bombings I have witnessed here.[54]

Bannan had followed the ensuing cases (the first an 11-year-old girl) and corroborated the death by plague of the young villager, Kung Tsao-shang, autopsied by Chen. After thirty years of living in the city, Bannan had never known there to be a plague outbreak. "If the facts be true," went the nurse's closing observation, "as I believe they are, there can be only one conclusion drawn and that is—that the enemy is now carrying on a ruthless and inhuman warfare against combatants and non-combatants alike. This is truly a new way of spreading Japanese 'culture.'"

Although the credibility of an American medical missionary could help the Chinese charges, Pollitzer had never met Bannan. Sutton knew that the Presbyterian Church had maintained a strong presence in China; perhaps it had records of Bannan's whereabouts. He made a note to inquire.

Meanwhile, Pollitzer offered Sutton a report by his colleague, Dr. Winston Yung, about the first three plague targets—Ningbo, Quzhou, and Kinhwa (Jinhua)—where Yung had been part of the national public health response. His report might prove helpful. In it he wrote that "reliable witnesses" in Ningbo attested that on October 27, 1940, a Japanese plane had mysteriously scattered wheat "in a well circumscribed area in the heart of the city."[55]

Sutton's time was short, and Pollitzer was leaving soon for the far Northeast (Manchuria), where plague had broken out. Since Dr. Yung would be going with him, Pollitzer suggested that if they passed through Shanghai, they could meet with Sutton there and discuss the problem of evidence. Meanwhile, Sutton asked Pollitzer to have Yung sign and date a copy of his three-city report, with Pollitzer as a witness, and then send the document to him in Shanghai, care of the US Theater Judge Advocate's office. Sutton also asked Pollitzer to provide a written summary of his professional experience and qualifications. Pollitzer agreed and said he would drop it off the next day at the hostel. Before they parted, he gave Sutton a copy of the Changde map with its two red circles.[56]

The next day, Pollitzer left a two-page summary of his career for Sutton at the hostel.[57] With it, he included a letter from the undersecretary of the League of Nations at the time, Thanassis Aghnides, who confirmed his service. Dated June 7, 1941, in Geneva, the secretary's letter ended with praise: "During the whole period of the above-mentioned activities [1939–1941], Dr. Pollitzer has proved himself to be a very capable and extremely reliable expert, to whose excellent technical work, often performed in very strenuous circumstances, a warm tribute should be paid."[58]

So far, Sutton had learned two things since arriving in China. One was that the opium enslavement charges implicating defendants on the IPS list (cabinet cartel members like Tojo, Doihara, Hoshino, and Suzuki) could be backed by credible witnesses. The other was that the plague allegations lacked fundamental proof of cause and effect. Were the epidemics just instances of China's chronic public health and sanitation problems made worse by the war? Or had the Japanese used germ weapons, as Colonel Morrow suspected? So as not to disappoint his Chinese colleagues, he resolved to find Nurse Bannan, who had apparently left Changde after the 1941 epidemic.

In March 1946, while Nelson Sutton was conducting his investigation, Reverend Archie Crouch, witness to the plague attack in Ningbo in 1941, arrived in Seattle on the US troop ship *Marine Adder* after serving two years in China.[59] Like many Presbyterian missionaries, he was dedicated to the Chinese, but after the fall of Ningbo, his church refused him permission to stay. In 1944 he volunteered as a conscientious objector to help Allied pilots in remote western China, under the command of General Joseph Stilwell. He knew nothing of the Chinese Division charges and would not for nearly fifty years.

5

THE BEST WITNESSES

WITH ONLY EIGHT DAYS LEFT IN NANJING, DAVID NELSON SUTTON turned his attention from the ambiguities of the plague attacks to finding evidence for the 1937–1938 massacre in that city. To start, he went to the city's district court, where he was expected at the Procurator's Office. The Kuomintang government was mobilizing its own war crimes tribunals in its newly reclaimed capital. The trial of Lieutenant General Sakai Takashi, a field commander in China from 1939 to 1945, was due to start in late May.[1] The second major Chinese tribunal would concentrate on the Nanjing Massacre, and its preparations were an advantage for the IPS.

The Procurator's Office had prepared for Sutton a comprehensive folder of documents on the massacre's death statistics. It included photographs of twenty-one burial sites (described, for example, as "the hill behind the Ko Ling Temple," "under the Pagoda Bridge," and "outside the Chung Hua Gate next to the Kwangchow Public Cemetery at Mo Tso Lake"). A note was made that the Japanese had destroyed many other grave sites. Also verified by the procurator was a nine-page list of burial figures, including a list from the Red Swastika organization.[2] The total number of individuals buried by the Teung shan-tang (Chong Shan Tang) burial society was recorded as 112,266; the Red Swastika, 43,071; the Shia Kwan District, 26,100. The number of burials stated by Mr. Lu Su was 57,400; by Messrs. Jui, Chang, and Young, 7,000 or more; as stated by a Mr. Wu, 2,000; and, according to the epitaph on the Tomb of the Unknown Victims, the bodies of 3,000 or more who had died were buried there. The procurator's estimate was that, over the course of six or seven weeks, 47,000 victims had been buried inside the city and 78,000 outside its gates. Refugees fleeing the Japanese to Nanjing had also been killed; some thousands of nameless victims had been killed in the suburbs or by the river. The overall total of the dead (taking in all sources) was estimated at approximately 260,000.

Two *Reader's Digest* articles in 1938 about the Rape of Nanking had already broadcast these overwhelming figures.[3] The first article, full of death counts, was criticized by some readers as trumped-up Chinese propaganda. The second article, which featured the letters and diaries of the anonymous American eyewitnesses, did better at convincing the public. Having consulted with the journalist H. J. Timperley, Sutton knew the names of those Americans and saw the importance of having them cast off their anonymity at the IMTFE—if he could find them. Sutton's first contact in Nanjing was Miner Searle Bates, professor of history at the University of Nanjing, who had been the main source for Timperley's book.

Meeting Dr. Bates

On the evening of April 3, Sutton met with Bates at his home near the university, in the city's Gulou (Bell Tower) District. The university faculty and students had been in exile in the South but had now returned. Despite the disruption, and to Sutton's relief, Bates had preserved many of his papers and records.

Over tea, Bates explained that the Safety Zone Committee had been at first truly international, with a Danish chairman and British, German, Soviet, and American members, but at the time of the Japanese invasion only Germans and Americans still remained in the city. John Rabe, the German manager for Siemens, became the new chairman and Lewis Smythe, an American professor of sociology at the university, the secretary. The American, British, and German Embassies helped inform the Japanese and Chinese armies that a circumscribed area within Nanjing would be created to help civilians avoid the dangers of fighting and the imminent attack. The goal of the safety zone was to provide housing and if necessary food while the city was under siege. Its committee helped create the International Red Cross Committee, of which Bates had been a member. After Rabe was recalled to Germany in February 1938, the Safety Zone Committee's vice chair, Wilson Plumer Mills, became chair.

In addition to Rabe, another missing figure in this story was Wilhelmina (Minnie) Vautrin, chair of the emergency committee in charge of the Ginling College campus, which she turned into a shelter for women. With a master's degree from Teachers College, Columbia University, Vautrin hadn't the heart to flee when she saw the refugees pouring in from the east. The Nanjing atrocities deeply troubled her and, soon after returning to the United States in 1940, she committed suicide.

Bates was willing to testify that he had witnessed a series of unprovoked shootings of civilians, including within the safety zone where he lived. Japanese soldiers, after raping the wives of two of his Chinese neighbors, shot their husbands and threw the bodies into the pond at the edge of his property. He had seen other bodies piled on nearby streets. Bates believed that as many as thirty thousand soldiers who had laid down their arms, instead of being taken as POWs, were slaughtered in the first seventy-two hours after the Japanese conquest. The Safety Zone Committee hired laborers to bury them. More bodies were dumped in the river and carried away by the current or buried by others. Still convinced that Chinese soldiers were hiding in the city, the Japanese spent three weeks rounding up suspects from the safety zone and refugee camps, where most of the city's population was seeking shelter; they apprehended and shot large groups of able-bodied men who had callouses on their hands, presumably from using rifles. Bates admitted that a few Chinese combatants had thrown away their uniforms and dressed as civilians, but the great majority of those executed, he believed, were simple laborers.

About the fate of the Chinese women, Bates spoke of hundreds of rapes by gangs of soldiers, usually fifteen or twenty in each, who invaded the grounds of the university and Ginling College and even forced their way into private homes. In two instances, Bates himself intervened to stop the rapes of two women at his university by Japanese officers. From Minnie Vautrin at the college and from others, Bates heard dreadful stories of girls being taken captive and raped continually for days. He had seen photos of Chinese women stripped naked and humiliated by the insertion of sticks into their vaginas. He could attest with certainty that, at his university, Japanese soldiers had raped a girl of 9 and a grandmother of 76.

Bates could also describe the Japanese looting and pillaging of the city. As chairman of the university's Emergency Committee, he had drawn up a chart summarizing the costs of the plundering and destruction to buildings, which he reckoned at over $30,000.[4] The Nanjing Theological Seminary was similarly looted, with food, clothes, and furniture taken away. The American Church Mission, whose parish house had been damaged by shelling before December 12, was looted and burned. Various American businesses—a lumber company, a theater, and a trade transport warehouse—were robbed of equipment, trucks, and gasoline. Homes left to Chinese caretakers when their owners fled were routinely looted and then set afire. American flags, no matter where they were flying, were ripped down.

In most instances, gangs of soldiers randomly stole what they wished. In other instance, the theft was well organized, as when, backed by fleets of army trucks, officers emptied bank vaults and pillaged factories, shops, and homes. Anything moveable was fair game. After a few months, several foreign residents with influence were given the opportunity to retrieve their pianos and found them in a warehouse among more than two hundred others that had been stolen.

Sutton had a crucial question: how far up the chain of command had the complaints of the Safety Zone Committee gone? Bates was clear that he and others had personally informed the Japanese Embassy in Nanjing; he himself wrote letters that he copied for US Embassy diplomats. But he had no proof that the US State Department had used the information in their communications with Tokyo.

Bates and the Opium Charges

In addition to all Bates knew about the Nanjing Massacre, he had also made a study of the Japanese opium and narcotics trade and how it had devastated Shanghai, Nanjing, and other cities.[5] Bates took the initiative to survey officials of the Shanghai government (both Chinese and Japanese) and went so far as to approach inspectors and dealers within the Japanese organization that controlled distribution. On November 22, 1938, Bates sent the US Embassy a message about the new appearance of the opium trade (worth $2 million in Chinese dollars) and the heroin trade (worth $3 million), with 50,000 addicts of both sexes in a population of 400,000. (Sutton would later learn that Bates was characterized by the embassy staff as "an experienced investigator and a man of unquestioned integrity."[6]) The professor didn't claim his research was exhaustive or without flaws, but he had tried to be careful with his generalizations and write with scientific disinterest, although that was difficult.

He found that the main supply of opium came from Manchukuo, a secondary supply came from Iran and was brokered by the Japanese, and small amounts were brought in from a few points along the northern Chinese border. Transportation was inexpensive, except along certain exposed trade routes where the Japanese had to provide soldiers or hire mercenaries to protect their investment. The revenue was around three million per year in Chinese dollars, this before inflation set in, and it was the main support of the Japanese Reformed Government in China, the occupiers.

The drug commerce relied on a large, profitable system, with opium selling wholesale for $300 per pound, with substantial markups by vendors. In the spring of 1938, one of the most lucrative Japanese businesses in Nanjing was the exclusive sale of opium to the Chinese. Estimates were that a quarter to a third of Chinese adults, many of them young people, were addicted. They would bully or steal to find money for their habit. They would die of starvation rather than miss their drug.

Heroin from the North, which could sell for $300 an ounce, ended up competing with opium. Lower grades, priced for as little as $130 an ounce, were adulterated with caffeine or with chemicals and sold in tiny packets for as low as 20 or 30 cents. Nearly a dollar a day was required to provide satisfaction, but addicts considered the results superior to the same amount of opium, even though the chemical additives could be toxic or even fatal. The chief merchants in Nanjing were notorious; four of them were known as the "great kings of heroin." Their selling organization included some 2,400 vendors, and the number of heroin addicts reached well into the tens of thousands.

The Chinese were supposed to buy their opium legally, at the public stores, but Korean street vendors sold heroin more cheaply on the black market. The spread of addiction became a catastrophe for the police and the criminal courts, with a sharp increase in addicts and in related cases of theft and assault. One police officer told Bates that his department averaged thirty heroin-related arrests per day. Since the jails were crowded and practically without food, most of the accused were released within five days. As with opium, using the drug became more important than eating. Another police officer told Bates that twenty to thirty bodies of starved heroin addicts were reported daily for burial.

Fortunately, Bates had included all this information in reports and articles. He agreed that he would bring them to the US Embassy, which had just been reopened, where copies would be made, signed, and authenticated for submission as court evidence.

Sutton was optimistic that Bates would indeed be his "best witness." The professor's credentials were exemplary. After undergraduate study at Hiram College (where his father was president), he became a Rhodes Scholar and earned a bachelor's degree from Oxford University. In 1920, at age 23, he was commissioned by the United Christian Missionary Society to teach history at the University of Nanking, where he met his future wife, a teacher at Ginling College. From then on, the city and the university remained at the center of his life. Later he was the recipient of a Rockefeller Foundation Fellowship at Harvard University and, in 1935, earned a Ph.D. degree in Chinese history from Yale.[7] In January 1938, to help him negotiate with the Japanese, he was made vice president of Nanking University. Another plus was that he might save the court time by giving testimony about both the massacre and the opium enslavement.

Occupied Nanjing

Sutton and Bates talked about Bates's experience with the journalist Timperley. In January 1938 Timperley, then the *Manchester Guardian*'s correspondent in Shanghai, tried twice to telegraph a story on the massacre to his newspaper and was twice censored by the Japanese. The rebuffs fueled his determination to do a book presenting eyewitness accounts of the atrocities. To that end, he wrote Bates, whom he already knew, pitching the project. He promised to select material carefully, from the standpoint of "authenticity and fairness." His intention was to provoke a reaction. "To my mind," he told Bates, "it is not sufficient that our Government officials should be informed of the facts. If the moral indignation of the man in the street is to be properly aroused he must be given a chance to know the facts too."[8]

Bates and his colleagues Lewis Smythe and the Reverend Mills felt that the anonymity of the individuals who offered their personal accounts had to be preserved. If not, the Japanese could punish or deport any they felt had defamed them, which would undermine the Christian missions in all occupied areas and their mission to help Nanjing survivors find food, clothing, and shelter. Timperley could not promise perfect anonymity. All he could offer was a careful editing of material to minimize any definite identification.[9] Bates and the others decided to take the risk. Timperley's book was an instant success and roused international anger against the Japanese conquerors and sympathy for the victimized Chinese.

The outside world's moral indignation came too late to have much impact in Nanjing. In the aftermath of the invasion, the Japanese installed a puppet government of Chinese officials and at its head put Wang Jingwei, once heir apparent to Sun Yat-sen, the founding father of the Republic of China, and a bitter rival of Chiang Kai-shek. By the end of spring 1938 the city was calm, and by September its population, which had been 276,745 in June, stabilized at about 350,000.[10] The Japanese were part of this population. Around eight hundred Japanese entrepreneurs came to Nanjing to replace British commerce on the Yangtze—and to profit from the drug trade.

As a base for military operations in the region, the Japanese troop presence became permanent and Nanjing became a closed city, whose residents needed a special pass to travel outside its boundaries. Those who stayed behind, like Bates and Smythe, were under tight regulation. The Japanese soldiers and the city police continued the practice of randomly stopping Westerners to check their papers. The Japanese were openly hostile to them and to the members of the Safety Zone and Red Cross Committees. The few foreigners allowed to visit (most of them affiliated with the American, British, and French Foreign Ministries) were closely watched, and their visits were kept short. That September one visitor described Nanjing as "a dead city compared to its more flourishing days of the not so distant past" when the British dominated trade and Chinese shops filled the downtown area.[11] Instead, the Japanese exerted military control over the center of Nanjing and Chinese vendors were found only in "the most squalid and out of the way streets, where Japanese soldiers are not likely to be encountered."

At this same time, in the center city near the river, the Japanese built a small replica of Unit 731, with laboratory and production buildings, barracks, a prison, a hospital, a crematorium, and an airfield. The sign in front of it identified it as the Central China Anti-Epidemic Water Supply Unit. In reality it was the base for Unit Ei 1644, also called the Tama Unit.[12] For three years Dr. Masuda, the protégé of General Ishii, who was interviewed by Colonel Murray Sanders in September 1945, was its director and oversaw research on deadly pathogens (including anthrax, cholera, glanders, and snake poison) that were tested on Chinese captives. The Unit 731 techniques for infecting fleas with plague (by having them feed on sick rats) and reproducing them in volume were imported to Ei 1644.

Unit Ei 1644 was mobilized intermittently, first for the plague attacks of 1940–1941 and then for participation in the Zhejiang-Jiangxi campaign of 1942. Yet its activities remained a mystery to the city's inhabitants. The Chinese puppet government officials looked the other way or, drugged on opium, knew nothing. By 1942 all the Americans had decamped and the university went into exile. Later, in 1945, as Japan's defeat loomed, the military at Ei 1644 trashed the equipment and buildings and fled. If there were captives still held there, they did not survive.

Class B War Crimes and Smythe's Report

At 8 a.m. the day after their first meeting, Bates and Sutton met again, this time to talk about Lewis Smythe, another university professor, who was an eyewitness to the Rape of Nanking but unfortunately out of the city for another month. Smythe had also documented the widespread physical destruction and economic harm caused during the Japanese conquest of Nanjing. Although it was more Henry Hauxhurst's area than his own, Sutton saw how this information, separated from the crimes against humanity, could add more Class B charges to the China brief.

Smythe's wife had been born in Nanjing, and in 1928, when the Christian Missionary Society of Indianapolis, Indiana, offered to send him to teach at the university there, he agreed. He had just earned his doctorate at the University of Chicago, where the founders of American urban sociology—Louis Wirth, Robert Park, Robert Redfield, and others—had been his teachers. Smythe hardly anticipated that less than a decade later he would witness and then document the most unusual destruction of a city in war, one that took place *after* military surrender.[13]

For Sutton, Smythe's input would be an ideal source of evidence for Class B or C war crimes. As secretary of the Safety Zone Committee, he and John Rabe, the chair, took turns filing twice-daily itemizations of the injuries being inflicted on the Chinese. They did this for six weeks after the Japanese troops entered the city on December 13, 1937. Smythe was meticulous in numbering and cross-checking the accounts of atrocities as they began to pour in, and he submitted only those cases that he believed had been accurately reported. Like other members of the committee, he wrote letters to his wife, who had left the city before the invasion, which he kept to give her later when they could be reunited. To her he described how, for the first three days of the invasion, he and Rabe struggled in vain to keep the Japanese from the wholesale killing of men they suspected of being Chinese soldiers, on the basis of callouses on their hands from holding rifles or short hair or simply because they appeared able-bodied.

He described the Japanese sexual assaults on Chinese women as horrific. On December 21 he wrote his wife: "At the peak of the disorder Saturday and Sunday we estimated there must have been over 1000 women raped every night and on those two days, probably as many by day, in the Safety Zone! Any young women and a few old women were susceptible if caught."[14]

In the spring of 1938, with the city calm, Smythe began an ambitious survey project in the Chicago School style. As reported to the US Embassy, the survey was carried out under the auspices of the Nanjing government, but the city's Chinese and Japanese officials did not know that Smythe, with help from Bates, was directing it.[15] The major categories reported on ranged from those typical of urban sociology, such as population, employment, and earnings, to those relevant to warfare, such as deaths and injuries due to hostilities, lost family, and lost homes and farms.

Through his assistants, Smythe recruited 13,530 "applicant families" in the city proper and in the suburbs. The family investigation part of the inquiry lasted from March 9 to April 2. In a separate inquiry, Smythe organized the inspection of the damage done to buildings and farms. In the city sample, investigators were assigned a city area and filled out a questionnaire for every family in every fiftieth inhabited home, whether an apartment or a house. For damage estimates, the building investigators were sent out in pairs, with one a construction contractor. They were instructed to make an estimate of loss on every tenth building and to indicate whether it had been done by military operations (e.g., bombs or shells) or by looting or fires (a common practice among Japanese soldiers was to loot a shop or home and then set it on fire). The estimates of loss of contents in the uninhabited buildings were reckoned by the nature of the edifice (whether a home, a factory, a store, or a service center) and by asking neighbors. A control map was used to check if certain areas had been overlooked and needed further investigation.

According to Smythe's survey, 24 percent of the city's buildings were destroyed by fires set by soldiers. As for looting within the city, some 73 percent of buildings were affected, with rates of 85–96 percent for downtown commercial areas, where many Chinese shops had been located. In contrast, only 9 percent of the buildings in the safety zone were destroyed.

To conduct the agricultural part of the survey, investigators working for Smythe obtained passes to go outside the city and off the main roads. They sampled every third village on their routes and one of every ten farms. In every market town, they filled out a price schedule.

Smythe's final report included thirty-two tables of survey results and two maps. Yet accurately reckoning the death statistics proved a problem. Smythe drew a distinction between those killed "in military operations," that is, by shells, bombs, or bullets fired in battle, and those "killed by military action," that is, by Japanese soldiers after the city's surrender.[16] The postconflict deaths appeared sharply weighted toward men; the disproportion of Chinese males killed was what Smythe called "terrific." Men under 45 years of age accounted for 84 percent of deaths. For women, 83 percent of the deaths occurred among those over 45. Older women, his report noted, stood guard at home, not expecting to be killed, while young women were hidden or migrated to safety. The suburbs outside the city walls were especially affected. The normal death rate for China was usually 27 per 1,000 per year. In the suburbs of Nanjing, Smythe estimated that it in 1938 it was 106 per 1,000.

Although Smythe was systematic in his approach, the Chinese people interviewed, intimidated by Japanese rule, hesitated to answer questions about injuries and deaths. Families and especially male relatives proved reluctant to talk about cases of rape or the deaths of children, crimes openly reported by inhabitants during the massacre. As a result, Smythe's research presented lower figures for civilian deaths than the statistics from burial societies and other sources given to Sutton—on the order of tens of thousands rather than the two or three hundred thousand reckoned by the Procurator's Office. Nor could he calculate who had died in homes wrecked or burned to cinders.

Bates told Sutton that he had confidence in the Nanking burial society records, for two reasons. First, the Chinese traditionally honor their dead; the civilians in the city would necessarily want that tradition respected. Second, despite the tumult at that time, the city's burial societies had been relatively efficient. Underestimating the number of civilians killed would be more likely, in that displaced refugee families had likely buried their dead without burial society assistance or any records at all. In the march west from Shanghai, many villages and towns were burned down and their residents killed before they could escape. That much Sutton had heard. From US intelligence, Alva Carpenter at Legal Section had received the diary of a Japanese medical officer describing how, on November 29, 1937, on the march toward Nanjing, eighty residents of a small town were lined up and machine gunned, on army orders.[17] In Nanjing the men whose bodies had been dumped in the river and swept away could not be counted, nor could the Chinese soldiers whose bodies had been abandoned. In her diary for April 2, 1938, Minnie Vautrin had written, "Dr. Rosen [from the German Embassy] reports that there are still many unburied bodies of Chinese soldiers out in the National Park."[18]

Sutton put aside the calculation of death statistics—slaughter on a large scale had definitely occurred, no matter what the numbers. He wanted Smythe's report authenticated and sent to him in Tokyo. Since Smythe would not return to Nanjing for some weeks, Bates volunteered to pass on Sutton's instructions.

In addition, Sutton wanted Bates to help him reach as many of Timperley's sources as possible. The first name on Sutton's list was John Magee. Magee was an Episcopalian minister with degrees from Yale and the Episcopal Theological School in Cambridge, Massachusetts (affiliated with Harvard University), and he had been a principal organizer of the safety zone. After initiating the creation of the International Red Cross Committee of Nanjing, he used his role as chair to set up the Red Cross Hospital, which protected injured Chinese soldiers from being murdered, and he proved tireless in keeping watch over all the city's hospitals and refugee centers. In his diary and in letters to his wife, he described the horrific events of those seven weeks, especially the hospital treatment of hundreds of women who had been raped. Without being spotted by Japanese authorities, Magee had used his 16-millimeter camera to record the consequences of the atrocities. Later in 1938, on a furlough from his ministry, he smuggled out reels of his films and showed them while traveling in the United States, lecturing on the Nanjing Massacre. From Bates, Sutton learned that Magee, who left China that same year, had become a chaplain at Yale University.

Also on Sutton's list was James H. McCallum, another missionary, who had a bachelor's degree from Yale Divinity School and a master's from the Chicago Divinity School. In 1931 he began serving at the South Gate Church in Nanjing. In November 1937, after a majority of the University Hospital staff had been evacuated, McCallum agreed to take over the hospital's emergency management, although it meant he could not join his wife and children who had escaped to Shanghai. In working at the hospital and as an ambulance driver, he witnessed the impact of the mass atrocities and wrote about them in diary letters that, like those of George Fitch, were smuggled anonymously to the West. McCallum's whereabouts were unknown.

Fitch was another important potential witness. Secretary of the Young Men's Christian Association (YMCA) in Nanjing, he had coined the term "Rape of Nanking" in a letter on January 6, 1938, and later used it in speaking tours in the United States.[19] He was born in China to missionary parents and, after graduating from Wooster College in Ohio, attended the Union Theological Seminary in New York. After that, he dedicated his life to missionary work in China. In February 1938 his diary of the violence in Nanjing, dating from December 10, 1937, to January 11, 1938, was smuggled to the West and circulated widely as an anonymous account. It was read at the Department of State and at the British Foreign Ministry and cited in US intelligence reports. According to Bates, George Fitch had returned to China and was at present working for UNRRA on famine relief in Henan Province, west of Nanjing.

Sutton also wanted to find Dr. Robert O. Wilson, who had been a surgeon at the University of Nanjing Hospital and a member of the Red Cross Committee. The son of Methodist ministers, Wilson was born and brought up in Nanjing. He received his bachelor's degree from Princeton University and in 1933, when he was 27, earned his M.D. degree from Harvard Medical School. During the massacre he was the only surgeon available to civilian victims. His eyewitness experiences were preserved in his diary and in letters to his wife. Wilson, it turned out, had gone to live in Arcadia, California.

The former chair of the Safety Zone Committee, Reverend Wilson Plumer Mills, had returned to Nanjing, and Bates promised to introduce Sutton to him. With still much to discuss, Bates and Sutton decided to meet again early the next morning. Before Sutton left, Bates invited him to the Sunday morning service at the university chapel, organized each week by the students. Sutton accepted gratefully.

Meanwhile, at the hostel, two new messages were waiting. From Beijing, Colonel Morrow wired that he had, from the point of view of chemical weapons evidence, struck gold. He had found a former Japanese soldier willing to talk about attacks he had witnessed, and he had met a Chinese general who had created a museum of Japanese chemical munitions retrieved from battlefields. It was hard not to be impressed by Morrow, whose experience at the Meuse-Argonne offensive in 1918 helped explain why he chose to pursue chemical weapons evidence when he could be living comfortably as a district judge in Ohio.

From Tokyo, Frank Tavenner had sent a telegram giving Sutton a new assignment. In addition to his summary of Class C crimes, Sutton would draft the "economic aggression" part of the China brief, in consultation with Henry Hauxhurst. With the team's information on opium trafficking and the wanton pillaging and looting in Nanjing, Sutton saw how the pieces would fit together.

The Eyewitnesses to Atrocities

The night of April 4 Colonel Morrow, Henry Chiu, and an assistant from IPS, Jack Crowley, arrived in Nanjing and checked into the Metropolitan. At 10 p.m. Sutton met with them to review the week's plan.

Starting the next day, Friday, April 5, through the following Wednesday, a series of several dozen Chinese survivors would come to the hostel, to room 312, which was set up with chairs, tables, and typewriters. Henry Chiu would be the lead translator; the Nanjing procurator was offering a bilingual KMT officer to assist; and, with prodding from the IPS, the US Army would provide a typist and stenographer. Each interview should be a page or so long, enough to gauge the potential value of the testimony while allowing as many victims as possible to tell their stories. Each statement would be typed in English, with a carbon duplicate. Chiu would read it back to the witness, who would correct any mistakes and then sign, with Chiu, Morrow, Crowley, or Sutton also signing as witnesses. For those who were illiterate, an inkpad had been provided to make a thumbprint.

In addition to clear written statements that could be submitted to the court as affidavits, the team would search for witnesses convincing enough to testify at the IMTFE. The importance and complexity of the China brief, Sutton believed, demanded a full roster, dozens perhaps. He knew already that he wanted Professor Bates, the Shanghai and Beijing policemen, and the textile merchant Hsu, who had narrowly escaped being machine-gunned but hesitated about adding the plague experts.

The next morning at 8:00, the first group of Chinese survivors arrived in the Metropolitan lobby and were shepherded by Henry Chiu to room 312. Many had come with family members and were dressed against the chill in padded jackets and pants. They could have been any people in the crowds on the Nanjing streets. Their testimony, though, was the stuff of nightmares.

To begin, two Chinese men described how in December 1937 they were living in a house on the outskirts of the city. There were two families, fourteen people altogether. On the first day the Japanese troops came into the city (which would have been December 13), around eighty soldiers came to the house and ordered the families to line up outside. After accusing the three adult men in the household of being Chinese soldiers, they shot one, bayoneted the two others, and then kicked to death the first man's pregnant wife.[20]

Next, a young man of 27 testified that the Japanese examined the right hand of a man who was a cook and, finding it had callouses, shot him, claiming that he must have acquired them as a soldier handling a rifle. The young man, having no callouses, was let go. He also saw two Japanese soldiers dragging a struggling, weeping Chinese woman into a house, presumably to rape her. About two weeks later he saw soldiers dragging a girl about 13 years old into another house. He was told later she was raped there.[21]

Another witness, Shang Teh Yi, gave striking testimony of narrowly avoiding a Japanese machine gun massacre by falling down just before the shots were fired and five hours later climbing out of the pile of corpses.[22]

That night Bates brought the Reverend Mills to meet Sutton. A craggy South Carolinian with deep-set eyes, Mills had been a Rhodes Scholar like Bates and ended up following in the footsteps of his father, a Presbyterian minister. The journey took from 1921, when he earned his master's in theology from the University of South Carolina, to his ordination in 1932, after he had earned another master's from New York's Union Theological School. The years in between Mills and his wife spent in China, where he worked for the YMCA. In 1932 he was sent to the Northern Presbyterian Mission in Nanjing, where he served on the Presbyterian Foreign Mission Board. As vice chair and then chair of the Safety Zone Committee, he had worked to protect the Chinese and protest the atrocities to the Japanese Foreign Ministry. Mills stayed in Nanjing until September 1942, after which he was interned by the Japanese at the infamous Pudong prison camp in Shanghai, across the Huangpu River from the Bund.[23] By a diplomatic agreement, he was repatriated to the United States in December 1943. China, though, was his passion, and he returned in 1944 to work in Chongqing and then moved in 1945 to the liberated Nanjing.

Both Mills and Bates had harsh words for General Matsui, the Japanese field commander, who on December 17, 1937, had paraded into the vanquished city on a chestnut horse and, according to the missionaries, waited five weeks before even attempting to restore order. By then thousands had been murdered, the population terrorized, and many Chinese homes, shops, and businesses looted and burned. The two men insisted that the Japanese authorities knew all about the atrocities, for they themselves had personally protested to them from the very start.

On December 16, 1937, for example, Bates had written to Japanese Embassy officials: "I beg leave to approach you informally about problems of order and general welfare upon the property of the University next to your Embassy building." He then enumerated looting and rapes from the day before—in the Library Building where fifteen hundred Chinese were being sheltered, four women were raped, three were carried off, raped, and released, and three were carried off and not returned. He concluded by asking for empathy, urging, "for the reputation of the Japanese Army and the Japanese Empire, for the sake of good relations between Japanese authorities and the common people of China, for your own thought of your wives, sisters, and daughters, that the families of Nanking receive protection from the violence of soldiers."[24]

The Safety Zone Committee had systematically updated even more detailed reports to Japanese Embassy officials and sent protests to the Shanghai consulate. It was not until late January 1938, after the State Department released a dispatch from John Moore Allison (then third secretary at the American Embassy in Nanjing), that Japan reacted. Two weeks later General Matsui finally "told his soldiers to behave themselves."[25] Not long after, he was required to hand over his command to General Hata and retired from the military. Although not a top leader, he was being held in Sugamo Prison, certain to be a defendant at the IMTFE for his notoriety alone—to the frustration of Nanjing officials who wanted field commanders like him for their own trials.[26]

The Interviews Continue

On Saturday, April 6, the interviews in room 312 at the hostel resumed. Some individuals had the kind of credentials that interested Sutton. For example, Sutton was able to interview Hsu Chuan-Ying, age 62, vice chair of the Nanking branch of the Red Swastika Society, the Chinese philanthropic organization that took charge of many burials after the massacre. The interview was in English; in 1917 Hsu had earned a Ph.D. degree from the University of Illinois, but his English was rusty. He affirmed what Sutton already felt: that the Nanjing mass killings were part of "a pattern of warfare" typical of the Japanese military in other locales, like his home province, Anhui, to the west, and Jiangxi to the south. Hsu gave Sutton a signed description of the massacre, a solid basis for testimony in court.[27]

Other, more personal testimony followed. A Mrs. Chang described how, when the Japanese entered Nanjing, they burned her family's home, and worse. As the family fled, they were met by twelve Japanese soldiers. It was in broad daylight, around ten in the morning. As she recounted:

> One of the soldiers wearing a sword, whom I thought was an officer, grabbed my sister-in-law, and raped and then killed her in the presence of her husband and children, who were killed at the same time. The husband was killed for trying to defend his wife and the two children were killed because they wept when their mother was being raped. The five year old girl was suffocated by having her clothing stuffed into her mouth, and the boy was bayoneted. The father and mother were both bayoneted and thereby killed. My mother-in-law was bayoneted and died twelve days later. I fell to the ground, and escaped later with my two children.

"I went to the refugee camp," she continued, "and on the way saw many corpses of women and civilian men. The women had their apparel pulled up and looked like they had been raped. I saw about twenty, mostly women."[28]

Mrs. Wong Kiang Sze, a 66-year-old widow, witnessed the Japanese shooting of her son-in-law, age 46, and the capture of her son, age 42, who never returned. "My son-in-law was an accountant," she said, "and my son was a clerk in the courts. My son-in-law was in the refugee zone when shot by the Japanese and neither he nor my son were soldiers, or in the military service. I begged on my knees that my son-in-law be spared, but it was no use." She added: "I saw piles of dead bodies in Nanjing at this time although I did not see anyone else killed."[29]

This same day Morrow, Crowley, and Chiu interviewed another widow, Mrs. Loh Sung Sze, age 45, who had witnessed her husband's murder by Japanese soldiers. "He was bayonetted in the neck, kidney, forehead, and altogether in seven places," she told them. She gave the name of her father, also living in Nanjing, who saw the murder and could testify to it.[30]

The interviews, a barrage of horrific stories, went on until after midnight.

The next morning, April 7, Sutton met Bates for Sunday services at the Christian Church of Nanjing University. Around two hundred Chinese students filled the chapel, with women in the pews on the right side and men on the left. A choir was singing as Sutton took his place. A young Chinese man gave an "excellent" thirty-minute sermon, in English. Bates presided at communion and then read the passage from the Gospel according to St. John in which Jesus feeds the multitudes with only five loaves of bread and two fishes. "I am the bread of life," Bates intoned. "Whosoever comes to me will never be hungry, and whosoever believes in me will never be thirsty." Sutton was impressed by the congregation. "They are clean looking devout people," he wrote in his notebook.

After lunch with Bates, Sutton went back to room 312 at the hostel, where dozens of Chinese waited their turn and Chiu, Morrow, and Crowley were still at work. One man described a place outside the city wall where, he said, a thousand victims—maybe Chinese soldiers—were machine-gunned by Japanese soldiers. He offered to lead Morrow and Sutton to it. He was followed by another witness, Wu Chien Tin, who recounted a similar story of mass slaughter in the western section of Nanjing. Another man had a story about being drafted from the refugee zone into a "labor gang" where weaker men were shot for not working fast enough or for misunderstanding directions.[31] He escaped but later witnessed the Japanese in a designated refugee area engage in a ploy to coerce more victims. They persuaded some sixty Chinese men with offers of good jobs, after which they marched the men to a vacant lot, lined them up, and shot them.

A 24-year-old man named Wing Pan Sze told of witnessing Japanese soldiers round up women from a communal house in the refugee zone where he was then living. "This one girl," he said, "who managed to get back to the house told me that she had seen one other girl raped and after being raped the Japs stuck weeds into her vagina and the girl had died from this treatment." Subsequently, on a visit to his grandmother who lived nearby, he witnessed a husband protesting as the Japanese dragged his wife away.

> The husband followed them trying to stop them [when] the Japs grabbed him, stuck wire through his nose and then tied the other end of the wire to a tree, just like one would tie up a bull. The Japs then bayoneted this man [in] many places over the body. This man's mother also came out and rolled on the ground crying, the Japs did not like this so they continued to bayonet the son. They told the mother to go into the house or they would kill her. The son died from his wounds on the spot. I saw it all as I was standing in the door watching the whole affair.[32]

A 25-year-old man recalled being coerced by Japanese soldiers to carry loot as they pillaged houses. The Japanese examined the hands of the Chinese men once they had finished this work and, if they had callouses, bayoneted them. "I say this because I was there and my hands were also examined," he told Henry Chiu. As the Japanese marched him and the others along, he saw "many dead Chinese lying along the road and elsewhere. I would say that I saw about a hundred dead Chinese among them many children. Most of them had been bayoneted to death, including the children."[33]

Colonel Morrow and a Chinese army colonel acting as translator interviewed Chen Fu Pao, age 27, who, on December 14, 1937, was among thirty-nine Chinese men taken from the refugee area by the Japanese. Without callouses on their hands, he and another man were spared from the execution that followed. He witnessed buildings being set on fire and two rapes, one of a 16 year-old-girl and the other of a pregnant woman he knew well since he had been sharing a house with her and her husband. Recruited to clean up after the Japanese slaughter of a group of Chinese, he told his interviewers, "I helped throw the bodies in the pond." Four months later the Red Swastika Society began pulling the remains from the pond for proper burial.[34]

Also on this Sunday, Mrs. Woo Chang Sze, age 31, testified to Henry Chiu about her experiences in the two weeks after the Japanese entered Nanjing. She had moved with her family to a house across from the American Embassy that had been occupied by a German doctor, which they and others seeking refuge there thought would be safe. Japanese soldiers came to the house and herded all the residents to the third floor, except a girl of 18, the daughter of the gatekeeper. Three soldiers raped her and left. The girl died soon after from bleeding and was buried by her father.[35]

US Embassy Records

That afternoon Sutton left his colleagues in room 312 and went to the US Embassy to research documents there. After January 8, 1938, when US Embassy staff returned to Nanjing, they kept records of their cable traffic with Washington and the Japanese Foreign Ministry and became a repository for copies of the frequent protests to Japanese officials by the leaders of the Safety Zone Committee and others. At the embassy, which was in transition from Chongqing, one of the staff, David C. Berger, allowed Sutton to peruse multiple volumes of this unique record. In three of them Sutton discovered cables and reports that corroborated what Bates and others had been telling him. The Safety Zone Committee had been systematic in ensuring that its observations, in all their gruesome detail, would be officially on the record. Sutton even found copies of the series of letters that Dr. Bates had sent the Japanese Embassy during the last two weeks of December 1937. On December 17 Bates protested the "reign of terror" being inflicted on the city, giving specific examples of physical violence and looting. The next day he reported rapes in six different university buildings and the terror of the thousands of women seeking refuge in dormitories there. On December 21 he wrote the Japanese that many hundreds of Chinese men had been taken away for forced labor and that his own house had been looted, for the fourth time. The American flag at the American School, he said, had been torn down and trampled and death threats issued to anyone who dared display the flag again.

In the embassy records Sutton discovered important confirmation of atrocity incidents as reported by the Safety Zone Committee and private individuals like Dr. Bates and Minnie Vautrin. Soldiers' attacks on the few Westerners left in the city were also recorded. In a notorious instance, Secretary Allison from the US Embassy was slapped twice in the face by a soldier attempting to obstruct Allison's entry into a military building that was the scene of an alleged rape.[36] Witnesses affirmed that Allison had done nothing to provoke such aggression. After complaints about the "Allison Incident" reached the desk of Secretary of State Cordell Hull, the controversy ended with a formal apology delivered to Allison in person by a special envoy, Japan's consul general in Shanghai (in morning coat, striped trousers, and a top hat), with the assurance that the commanding officer and twenty men of the unit involved had been court-martialed. During this time massacres, rapes, and lootings continued and Japanese soldiers began roughing up Westerners, including members of the Safety Zone Committee, if they ventured into the city center.[37]

The embassy material also documented damage to American property and interests. In the first three weeks of the Japanese invasion of the city, any unguarded building was likely to be looted, with no restraint regarding the grounds of the American Embassy (which had two compounds) or those of the German and Italian Embassies. The fourteen Americans in the city during this time had their residences repeatedly looted by soldiers; automobiles were stolen, even from the embassies. At the University of Nanjing approximately a hundred compounds and buildings were looted, at times more than once a day. The soldiers took breeding animals from the agricultural economics department and tools from its shop and vocational training classes and wantonly broke gates, windows, and doors. The British had more assets in Nanjing than Americans, Germans, or Italians, a factor that contributed to the Japanese ban on any British seeking to return to the city and attempting to protect their holdings.

In his review of the embassy records, Sutton realized that, like Morrow, he had struck gold, for they contained proof that the protests of the Safety Zone Committee and others had reached the highest levels in Tokyo. Telegrams in 1938 to the embassy in Nanjing from Joseph Clark Grew, the US ambassador in Tokyo, referred to the reports in detail and to conversations in which Grew had discussed them with officials of the Gaimusho (Ministry of Foreign Affairs), including Foreign Minister Hirota Koki. In a February 12 note to Grew, Hirota admitted the problem: "In Nanking various cases have been found which are considered as having occurred on account of inadequate control in that city."[38] Although the embassy was reluctant to part with any original records, Sutton wanted volumes 2, 8, and 9 brought to Tokyo and submitted in evidence, which, with Keenan's help, became possible.[39]

The embassy staff agreed to witness Bates's signing of his opium reports and the delivery of the documents to Sutton the next day at the hostel. Arrangements were also made for Lewis Smythe to make a brief signed statement when he returned to Nanjing in early June; this document would also be witnessed by one of the embassy staff and forwarded to Sutton at IPS.[40]

Instead of watching a Hollywood movie at the hostel, Sutton, Morrow, Chiu, and Crowley spent the evening conducting interviews and then discussing who among the witnesses might take the stand in Tokyo. So far, the testimonies reiterated the same atrocities, to which just a few victims might effectively testify, leaving a selection of affidavits to be submitted to the court as documentary evidence.

On April 8 the Chinese Division team was back again in room 312, where Sutton interviewed Mrs. Shui Fang Tsen (Chen), age 75.[41] In 1937 she had been director of the dormitory at Ginling College, inside the safety zone, where more than ten thousand women had sheltered. The Japanese soldiers, she said, did not respect the safety zone. One girl, age 21 or 22, was captured and held overnight by five of them, and when she was returned she had been raped so many times she could not walk. The worst night, said Mrs. Tsen, was December 17 when soldiers carried away eleven girls. The next morning eight were returned, but no one saw the others again. Minnie Vautrin kept watch at the school gates, facing off against Japanese soldiers when they arrived in December. But, as Mrs. Tsen testified, they ignored all protests and warnings and invaded the campus to loot and plunder and take away girls and women. A member of Nanjing's International Red Cross Committee, Vautrin wrote letters of complaint to the American Embassy, which had no effect.

Sutton's day was interrupted by a government invitation to tour shrines. His Chinese guide brought him first to the tomb of Hongwu, the first Ming emperor, who ruled from 1368 to 1398. Sutton carefully recorded this information in his notebook for his wife and family and picked up a stone chip from the shrine as a souvenir. The shrine was inside a huge pagoda, set on the southern slope of the Purple Mountain, which was covered with budding cherry trees. The paths in the surrounding park were dotted with large, fanciful statues of elephants and dragons.

Next he was led to the tomb of Dr. Sun Yat-sen, founder of the Republic of China, who died in Beijing in 1925. Following his guide, Sutton showed his fitness by climbing what seemed like hundreds of stairs to the huge mausoleum, situated under a massive pagoda roof. At the top he found an inspiring view of the surrounding landscape of wooded mountains and valleys, with the center city to the south and boats visible on the Yangtze. Unknown to Sutton, at the base of the mountain, extending to the river, was a large, gated tract with several rundown buildings and a small air field—the remnants of Unit Ei 1644.

Continuing his tour, Sutton went inside the Sun Yat-sen mausoleum to admire the marble statue of the great ruler and to view his sarcophagus, placed in a small rotunda, with the leader's reclining effigy in marble on top. The Japanese had been careful not to damage the shrine, to preserve respect for the puppet government. China had regained its heritage, and Sutton sensed that the city, perhaps the whole country, was awakening to its future.

Sutton spent his evening at the hostel talking with Reverend Mills. As Mills described, after their entry into Nanjing on December 13, 1937, the Japanese took over public buildings and public utilities, monopolized control of essential foodstuffs and raw materials, and imposed a puppet currency so that the Chinese immediately lost half the value of the holdings they had in national currency. Sutton, pleased at how this information could fit into the argument for Japan's "economic aggression," asked Mills if he could write a summary of it. Mills thought he could do this by the following week and send it to Sutton in Tokyo.[42]

In a final meeting with Bates, Sutton asked him as well to consolidate his information on Japanese economic exploitation, on drug commerce, and about plunder in Nanjing and send it to him.

Return to Shanghai

On April 8 Sutton and Morrow ended their week of investigation in Nanjing. Leaving Henry Chiu and Jack Crowley to finish more victim interviews, on April 9 the two prosecutors took the overnight train to Shanghai, where they checked in at the American Club on Foochow Road. SCAP's public relations office had already informed the news media about their trip. The headlines on the front page of the *China Press* that morning read: "Morrow Concludes China Tour, Gathers Evidence for Trial."[43] The story focused exclusively on the Rape of Nanking and described Morrow and Sutton as interviewing as many as 120 witnesses a day. In the *Shanghai Evening Post*, the same story ran on the front page, with reference to the "hundreds" of documents Morrow and Sutton were bringing back to Tokyo.[44] Next to it was an article on plague outbreaks on the Hunan-Jiangxi border and in Fujian to the south, just as Dr. King had described. The situation of refugees in China added to the chaos. Shanghai officials were in the process of repatriating 200,000 people to Ningbo, the first plague target in 1940, and not a site where Sutton could practically pursue his present inquiry.[45]

A handwritten note from Pollitzer, dated April 4, was waiting for Sutton at the office of the Theatre Judge Advocate. Pollitzer and Winston Yung had been in Shanghai that day and had to leave the next morning. Once Pollitzer reached Beijing, he would have Yung's report about the first three plague attacks authenticated and then send it to Sutton as trial evidence. The two physicians expected to return to Shanghai in several weeks, and Pollitzer hoped Sutton could meet with them then.

Sutton had not forgotten the plague charges. On his final day in Shanghai, his top priority was to track down Nurse Bannan, the eyewitness of the Japanese attack on Changde. At the office of the China Council of the Presbyterian Church in Shanghai, in the Missions Building, Sutton met with Dr. E. E. Walline, the council's secretary. Walline recalled that a missionary couple by the name of Bannan had long served in Changde but had departed for the United States, leaving a forwarding address in Wooster, Ohio. Walline advised Sutton to contact the Presbyterian Board of Foreign Missions, which kept records of its hospital and mission personnel. Sutton carefully wrote down the address: 136 Fifth Avenue, New York City.

In his note to Sutton, Pollitzer had mentioned Dr. Heinrich Jettmar, who had been involved in the public health response in Quzhou. He thought that Jettmar might be reached in Shanghai through UNRRA. Sutton instead located him at his hotel. Jettmar was another Austrian physician who, like Pollitzer, had been captured by Russians in World War I and sent to work in a Siberian military hospital. Jettmar, too, had become an itinerant public health worker during the interwar years, with a long career of fighting plague in Siberia and then in China. In 1931, he told Sutton, he was involved in trying to quell an epidemic that claimed thirty thousand victims. After that his path diverged from Pollitzer's. In 1932 Jettmar returned to Vienna for two years of further medical study. In 1937 he came back to China as an epidemiologist for the League of Nations and later worked at the German Medical Academy in Shanghai. He spoke with Sutton just before he decided to return to Vienna to become a university professor.

Unlike Pollitzer, Jettmar doubted it could be "positively shown" that the Japanese had attacked any city with plague. Arriving in Quzhou some weeks after its outbreak began, he was asked to examine globules the size of spider eggs collected from the tops of rickshaws and roofs. When he injected this material into guinea pigs, none became sick or died. That was all he knew. In his notebook, Sutton jotted that Jettmar's "evidence would be of no value to the trial." Still, he would include the interview in his trip report.

At the last minute, Sutton dashed off to the office of the National Christian Council to track down a thesis on "opium suffocation in China." Then, at the suggestion of the Australian Embassy, he went to the China Inland Missions to quickly review their war crimes files but found little of use from either source.

Despite some effort, Sutton was unable to reach Dr. Bobby Lim for his insights on the plague attacks, especially the one on Changde. With American backing, Lim had embarked on a major project to establish new hospitals throughout China, and so passed out of Sutton's reach, although he later became a source of information on Chinese military casualties during the war.

Once Sutton was sure of the roster of witnesses he needed from China, he would come back, assemble them, and escort them to Tokyo. It had been an exhilarating month of investigation, with good indicators for how he could build the case for the Rape of Nanking, while also developing the opium trafficking charges. The Chinese burial records, the reports of the Safety Zone Committee, and Timperley's book had made all the difference in affirming the details of the Nanjing Massacre. In addition, the American missionaries and Chinese survivors could tell their stories in court. The one disappointment of the trip had been the lack of clear evidence for the plague attacks. He would gladly argue the charge, but it lacked all best evidence: official reporting, professional eyewitnesses, and victim testimony. In a poor country that seemed continually beset by epidemics, perhaps Dr. King was simply wrong in blaming the Japanese.

With his suitcase packed full with documents, Sutton had no room for his souvenirs—the curios, vases, little paintings, and embroidered jackets he had bought for family and friends. Confident of a return trip, he left them for safekeeping at the desk of the Cathay Mansions Hotel and, with Morrow, flew back to Tokyo.

6

TOKYO

THE RUSH TO TRIAL

DESPITE THE DISCONCERTING FEBRUARY LEAK TO THE *STARS AND STRIPES*, Lieutenant Colonel Arvo Thompson continued to interview General Ishii, with some results on technical information.[1] He learned, for example, that Unit 731 had requisitioned the same factory in Harbin that made Ishii's porcelain water filter devices to manufacture their porcelain bombs, while army ordnance manufactured metal bomb prototypes. But Ishii still refused to admit that his center had been involved in anything but defensive activities, and Thompson's questioning of him was less than aggressive. Relying on US intelligence but without raising the King report from 1942 or the plague-infected fleas already described by Dr. Naito, Thompson tentatively queried Ishii about the possible plague attacks:

> *Thompson:* We have heard from Chinese sources that plague was started in Changteh, China, in 1941, by airplanes flying over and dropping plague material and a plague resulted. Do you know anything about that?
>
> *Ishii:* No. It is impossible from a scientific point of view to drop plague bacteria from airplanes.

Thompson: But rats, rags, and bits of cotton infected with plague were dropped and later picked up by the Chinese and that was how it was to have started.

Ishii: If you drop them from airplanes they will die. There is no chance of a human being catching plague as a result of dropping organisms from an airplane.[2]

Ishii denied that there had been any outdoor field tests of plague and insisted that only minor laboratory research on caged rats was conducted, with inconclusive results.

As Thompson reported to G-2, the only time that the general looked "genuinely fearful" was when he spoke of his horror of falling into Soviet hands. Late in the war he and his staff were given cyanide pills by the army, to avoid torture and execution should they be captured by the invading Soviet forces. Since fleeing Harbin, Ishii had been on the run and, as his faked death suggested, he was wary of discovery and revelations about his past. In his career, Ishii had been in charge of thousands of workers and soldiers at all levels. In addition, he had maintained ties at the Tokyo Army Medical School, spending three months there each year and recruiting hundreds of physicians and medical students to do rotations of research at Unit 731. After the article in the *Stars and Stripes,* old antagonists and potential blackmailers knew that he was alive, and so did Soviet prosecutors.

Instead of bluntly encouraging Ishii to seek US protection, Thompson posed a question. "As the Soviet Army crossed into Manchuria last August," he asked, "were your achievements all lost?"

Ishii bristled with indignation. "Let me assure you," he replied, "that we left nothing behind for the Russians. Our unit existed to counter their threat of germ weapons. Why would we want them to have any advantage? Besides, I myself gave the order that everything had to be destroyed."

When asked who of his subordinates had escaped to Japan, Ishii insisted proudly, "The best scientists are here." In fact, the Soviets had captured two of his top scientific experts: Dr. Kawashina Kiyoshi, Ishii's contemporary and an expert in the mass production of bacteria, and Dr. Karasawa Tomio, the young Unit 731 biologist who had helped organize the germ attacks on Central China.[3]

Although he offered no names, Ishii agreed to ask his "best scientists" if they would be willing to answer a brief questionnaire on strictly technical subjects that Thompson had prepared. In the next few weeks, eight former Unit 731 scientists responded with answers of varying substance and length. Although all claimed to be writing from memory, some of them provided a precise level of detail (for example, about pathogen research and bomb design) that convinced Thompson they had come away from Pingfan and other centers with valuable records. With steady attention and without judgment (his own wartime mission had had the same offensive goals as theirs), he persuaded Ishii and several of his former subordinates to speak more freely about their work. Their relationship so improved that Thompson and the G-2 and CWS officers assisting him were on friendly terms with Ishii, taking tea and eating meals at his home, where the interrogations of Ishii were always conducted.[4] More interviews, notes, and sketches added to Thompson's final report. None of the Unit 731 scientists and certainly not General Ishii admitted to germ attacks on civilians or to human experimentation, but their data pointed to large outdoor field tests or perhaps limited, experimental warfare.

The Chemical Warfare Interviews

While Sutton and Morrow were in China and Thompson was conducting his inquiry, Lieutenant Colonel John E. Beebe, Jr., an intelligence officer from the CWS Tokyo office, was deep into an investigation of what the Japanese high command knew about chemical warfare in China. For months, directed by G-2, Beebe had been working on a comprehensive evaluation of Imperial Japan's chemical weapons capability—the G-2 follow-through from the 1945 Scientific Intelligence Survey.

On April 2 at Sugamo Prison, Beebe was permitted to interview former premier and war minister Tojo Hideki. In response to Beebe's questioning, Tojo insisted that although chemical stocks had been produced, none had been used, and such materials could not have been used without his permission. In 1942 he had heard President Roosevelt's warning to Japan that if it used chemical weapons, US forces would retaliate in kind: "I thought, as I had from the beginning, that the use of gas would be disadvantageous for Japan because of tremendous America's industrial capacity and this statement of the President strengthened my own ideas."[5]

Tojo admitted that the Japanese did use "harassing agents," such as sneezing agents, tear gas, and smoke (as opposed to what he called "casualty agents"). When asked what harassing agents were banned by international treaties, he replied that police forces all over the world, including in the United States, used them with impunity to quell riots. Then he raised the *tu quoque* ("you also") argument, accusing the United States of hypocrisy in charging Japan with war crimes when its own actions had violated treaties against aggression. "How about the atom bomb?" he asked Beebe. In using tear gas or smoke, had the Japanese done anything nearly as horrendous as the attacks on Hiroshima and Nagasaki?

Changing the subject, Beebe showed Tojo Japanese field reports that Chinese soldiers had died of asphyxiation from gas attacks, with blood running out of their noses and mouths. Tojo attributed these deaths to the Chinese overreactions to harassing agents and to their fatal inexperience with using gas masks. Then he stubbornly returned to America's use of the "atom bomb."[6]

Putting it as a "theoretical question," Beebe then asked whether Emperor Hirohito would have had to consent to gas warfare in China. Tojo replied, "In such a decision, the cabinet would have had to have approved and the Emperor also. Of course, no such decision was made."[7] If evidence indicated otherwise—which Colonel Morrow's case research for China was showing—the Japanese high command and Hirohito might be held responsible.

Beebe then asked about biological weapons and specifically about Ishii. Tojo misidentified him as a lieutenant general (his old rank) in the army's Medical Department who was investigating water purification and doing work on bacterial warfare. In Tojo's words, Ishii's "understanding of bacteriology is excellent, so, from first to last, he was always doing researches in the field of bacteriology."[8]

Using what he knew from Thompson, Beebe pressed on:

Q. Were you advised of the progress of his experiments in making bombs capable of disseminating bacteria?

A. All over the world, we understood, nations were experimenting with bacteriological warfare and we had him experimenting in this field also. However, it was absolutely not used. It was never used. This is a greater problem than chemical casualty agents and its use was absolutely forbidden.

Q. By whom?

A. I, as War Minister, forbade it.

Q. Was its use against the Chinese ever permitted?

A. No, it was not permitted.

Q. Was experimental work with bacteria, using humans—that is, Chinese soldiers, or American soldiers, or Russian soldiers, ever permitted?

A. No, it was not.

Q. Were you kept informed on the progress of the work of General Ishii?

A. I heard about it once, I think, but I didn't hear often, since I made a strong fight against allowing the use of such things.

Tojo's concluding assertion was that his policy was to forbid the use of both chemical and biological warfare.[9]

On April 11 Lieutenant Colonel Beebe returned to Sugamo to interrogate another defendant, Field Marshal Hata Shunroku, the former war minister who in 1941–1944 commanded the China Expeditionary Force. Hata, too, insisted that Japanese forces in China had used only harassing agents, which required no special permission, but never phosgene, mustard gas, or lewisite, the agent invented by the Americans in 1918.[10] Four other army officers Beebe interviewed professed to have "no memory" of lethal chemicals being used and disparaged the Chinese claims and any involvement of the General Staff. One, the former commander of Japan's Chemical Warfare School in Narashino, which had trained over three thousand officers, told Beebe, "If gas were used in China it was just on the spur of the moment and not on the orders of high authorities." [11] By these accounts, the deaths from mustard and lewisite of hundreds of Chinese soldiers at Iching in 1941 and many other Japanese chemical attacks never happened. Colonel Beebe's next assignment was to find out how seriously the Chinese Division intended to pursue its chemical and biological warfare charges. For this, he needed to meet with Colonel Thomas Morrow and David Nelson Sutton after they arrived back from China.

IPS and the Preparation for Trial

While Nelson Sutton was still in Shanghai, British prosecutor Arthur Comyns Carr, the head of the Executive Committee, wired him to send the China affidavits by courier, although he could have delivered them in person two days later. When Sutton arrived back at IPS on April 14, he found his colleagues as anxious as Comyns Carr about being prepared for the trial opening on May 3. SCAP's decision to add judges from India and the Philippines to the tribunal had added to the pressure. The new judges would likely miss the opening of the tribunal and their prosecutors were late in discussing the defendant list and the indictment.

In March, the prosecutors from the Netherlands and France had arrived with new input relevant to their cases against Japan. Japanese leaders had to be held accountable for the thousands of civilians abused and killed in the Netherlands East Indies. The French were bringing charges for Japanese atrocities against prisoners of war and civilians during their brief war against the Japanese in Indochina in 1945. The colonial situation for both these allies had grown chaotic. British forces, many of them Indian, had been assigned the demobilization of the Japanese in the East Indies and the rescue of Allied prisoners of war, but political disagreement between the Dutch government and the new Republic of Indonesia leaders had erupted into armed conflict, which put British troops in danger.[12] In Indochina, the responsibilities for Japanese disarmament and repatriation, initially shared by General Chiang Kai-shek and Britain's Lord Mountbatten, the Allies' area commander, had been passed to the French.[13] But in 1945 Ho Chi Minh's independent Vietnam and resistance groups north and south were already battling French forces.

By mid-April the number of defendants who would stand trial had increased to twenty-six, up from the initial eighteen proposed by Alan Mansfield of the Evidence Committee. These candidates included four premiers (Tojo, Hirota, Koiso, and Hiranuma), two foreign ministers (Togo and Matsuoka), four war ministers (Araki, Hata, Itagaki, and Minami), two navy ministers (Nagano and Shimada), five generals (Matsui, Doihara, Kimura, Muto, and Sato), one admiral (Oka), one colonel (Hashimoto), two ambassadors (Oshima and Shiratori), three economic leaders (Hoshino, Kaya, and

Suzuki), plus the former imperial advisor Marquis Kido and the radical propagandist Okawa.

The draft of the indictment, which named each defendant and the crimes of which he was accused, was still undergoing revisions. While adhering to the charter (and therefore in synchrony with Nuremberg), Comyns Carr and the others began emphasizing the crime of murder as a consequence of Japanese belligerence, to introduce a universally accepted category that would offset the novelty of Class A crimes of aggressive war.[14] To keep the indictment from becoming lost in case details, Chief of Counsel Keenan appointed Solis Horwitz, his deputy counselor, to compose an overview analysis of key criminal events and of suspect personalities "to show the relationship between the two in such manner as will display most graphically the development of our case."[15] Despite this effort, simplification proved elusive; the number of counts reached fifty-five, as compared with Nuremberg's four charges, that is, for crimes against peace, conspiracy to wage aggressive war, violation of the laws of war, and crimes against humanity.

In their deliberations the IPS committees made little reference to the defense, which barely had a presence at the IMTFE until, on April 5, the International Defense Section (IDS) was formally established to provide counsel for the major war criminals. Most of the Class A suspects at Sugamo had legal counsel, but, for security reasons, no Japanese lawyers were allowed to interview any client before the indictment was filed, whereas IPS prosecutors—and select military personnel like Lieutenant Colonel Beebe and GHQ staff—had been permitted many hours to interrogate suspects.

The defense team was led by three high-caliber Japanese attorneys: Kiyose Ichiro, who had served in the prewar Diet for eight terms; Takayanagi Kenzo, a university professor who had studied with Roscoe Pound at Harvard; and Uzawa Somei, president of Meiji University. But they were wary of the Anglo-American legal bias of the judges and prosecutors and of being short on legal representation as the number of defendants grew.[16] In response to their concern, the Japanese government asked for British and American counsel. Since by law British barristers were not allowed to practice in foreign jurisdictions, the responsibility passed to the Americans. On March 11 Washington notified Keenan at IPS that fifteen US defense attorneys, principally civilians, would soon be flying to Tokyo, but delays prevented them from arriving. Six American defense lawyers already in Tokyo struggled with pretrial preparations as they awaited the final word on indictments. Three weeks before the trial was set to begin, the defense had yet to assemble, and even its housing provisions were uncertain.

On April 22 a US Navy officer, Captain Beverly Coleman, was appointed chief of the defense team and defense counsel for Tojo.[17] The choice led to a fractious rivalry between navy and army attorneys that reflected poorly on both. Most of the Japanese defendants, men who had until recently exercised great authority, had strong views about how they wanted to be represented in court, views about style and dignity that did not always match what American trial lawyers thought were in their best interests. Only two of the American counsel spoke Japanese, which imposed a "terrific burden" on communication with their Japanese counterparts.[18] Some defendants, disdaining the rest of the accused, were adamantly against their cases being part of any joint defense. Others refused to testify in court. Still others, like former foreign minister Matsuoka and Admiral Nagano, who helped plan the Pearl Harbor attack, were seriously ill and almost too frail to stand trial.

Soviet Participation

The absence of the Soviet Union was a significant problem for the Anglo-dominated Executive Committee, which could not easily ignore a major power. By early April Soviet representatives to the IMTFE had still not appeared in Tokyo. Soviet jurists had been tardy in arriving at Nuremberg, but, in comparison, Moscow's reluctance to participate in the Tokyo trial seemed to reflect Stalin's resentment about being excluded from the Occupation. Another complication was the Soviet Union's relationship with Japan, dating back to the sixteenth-century expansion of the Russian Empire into Asia, which was characterized by alternating phases of amiable economic cooperation and surprise hostilities, like Japan's 1904 attack on Port Arthur (Lüshunkuo) and its subsequent victory over Russia in northeastern China.[19] The late nineteenth-century development of the Trans-Siberian Railway and regular ferry traffic across the Sea of Japan, and later the additional rail systems the Japanese built for Manchukuo, all helped trade relations. In the 1920s and into the 1930s the progressive values of Soviet communism attracted many Japanese followers, until Japan cracked down on communism and allied itself with fascist Germany and Italy.

In 1937 and 1938 the two countries clashed violently in Siberian-Manchurian border disputes and then devised an uneasy peace. In April 1941 their diplomats brokered the Soviet-Japanese Neutrality Pact, binding for five years, until 1946. After Germany attacked the Soviet Union in June 1941, violating their 1939 Treaty of Non-Aggression, the Neutrality Pact kept Stalin out of war with Japan and allowed him to concentrate on the defeat of Nazi Germany. In early 1944 discussions in Washington about the Allied control of postwar Japan began with new expectations of the Soviet Union, namely, that its participation depended on whether it would take up arms against Japan.[20] At the Teheran conference in 1943, Stalin intimated he was willing to break the pact with Japan. At the Yalta conference in February 1945, Stalin assured President Roosevelt and Prime Minister Churchill that in six months he would be ready to violate the Neutrality Pact and declare war on Japan, and he repeated the promise at the Potsdam Conference in July 1945.

True to his word, as Germany collapsed in the spring of 1945, Stalin ordered his generals to reposition their armed forces from Europe to Siberia and the border with Manchuria.[21] During May, June, and July, four entire armies, accompanied by large specialized air and ground units, were transferred to the Far East in preparation for an invasion. In addition to the long Siberian-Manchurian border, the Soviets had access to Manchuria via Mongolia on the west; on the east, they had the benefit of their major port, Vladivostok. By early August Stalin's generals had amassed 1.5 million Soviet troops in Siberia, all of them inoculated against plague, endemic in Manchuria and Mongolia. The Soviet forces came equipped with 25,000 field guns and mortars, 5,500 tanks and self-propelled artillery, about 3,800 airplanes, a naval force of 600 combat vessels and submarines, and 1,500 naval aircraft.[22] Given the already heavy Soviet casualties of the war (estimated at twenty million or more military and civilian dead) and the country's already enormous arms expenditures, the effort signaled a major intent: to fight through to Japan's Home Islands and Tokyo.

But the defeat of Japan was suddenly accomplished without Soviet participation or advance warning when on August 6 the United States dropped an atomic bomb on Hiroshima. After learning of the Hiroshima bombing, on August 7 Stalin nonetheless signed the order for his troops to attack Manchukuo in two days. On August 9, before dawn, the Soviet military launched a surprise attack that surrounded the Kwantung Army from three sides, east from the Mongolian steppes, and south and west from Soviet Siberia. Calculating that their ground troops and tanks might take weeks to conquer central Manchuria and reach the Yellow Sea, the Soviets used their air force to drop advance troops in Harbin, Kirin, Chang-chun, Mukden, Darien, and Port Arthur. But the Kwantung Army, weakened by its involvement in the war against China, offered little resistance. The Soviet "lightning invasion" of Manchuria was finished in just over a week.[23] After accepting the surrender of Japan's Kwantung Army on August 16, the Soviets proclaimed that eighty thousand Japanese had been killed in the campaign, as opposed to eight thousand Soviet soldiers. Japanese sources calculated Soviet losses at thirty-two thousand, with many more of Japanese soldiers captured than the Soviets wanted to admit.[24]

The Manchurian invasion raised concerns about Soviet expansionist goals, already being felt in Eastern Europe. Not forgotten among the Allies was the Soviet invasion of Finland in 1939 and how, under the 1939 Treaty of Non-Aggression with Hitler, Stalin had entered into a secret pact to divide Poland.[25] The Soviet invasion of Manchuria continued with a brutal easterly drive to Sakhalin and the Kuril Islands, where tens of thousands of Japanese and Koreans became trapped as forced laborers, and on into northern Korea. While the IMTFE was being organized, Red Army troops lingered in Manchuria past the agreed-on February 15 deadline for evacuation, provoking Chinese and US anxiety about the Soviet role in China's civil war. The Kwantung Army had left behind weapons that the Soviets, without consulting the Nationalist Chinese, were seizing as reparations, perhaps to hand over to Communist Chinese forces. It was reported, to the consternation of General Chiang Kai-shek, that entire Japanese-built factories had been dismantled and shipped by train across the Soviet border. A Soviet mandate on August 30, 1945, ordered the acquisition of Manchurian industrial trophies: equipment for automobile manufacture, metallurgy and coal mining, electric power stations, chemical and rubber plants, and construction.[26]

A pressing problem not only for Japan but for prosecutors at the IMTFE was the Soviet treatment of POWs captured in Manchukuo. In August 1945 some 2.7 million Japanese lived there, among them 1.5 civilian settlers, with the rest in the Kwantung Army. According to Japanese government records, 1.3 million of them, the great majority men, were missing following the invasion. On August 23, just days after the Japanese surrender, Stalin secretly ordered the apprehension of 500,000 Japanese men "physically fit to work in the conditions of the Far East and Siberia."[27] To compensate for their war dead in Europe, the Soviets had done much the same to millions of German prisoners. The Soviet failure to repatriate the captured Japanese began a long dispute with Japan, which claimed that many captives had been put in labor camps, in violation of international laws regarding the treatment of POWs and against the spirit of the Potsdam Agreement to which the other Allies had agreed.[28] Many of those captured likely died from hunger and cold during the bitter Siberian winter of 1945–1946.

Although the defeated Kwantung Army left behind conventional armaments, the possibility that it had been developing advanced biological weapons emerged only when, on the outskirts of Harbin, the Red Army discovered the wreckage of Pingfan, with its bombed-out buildings, remnants of prison cells (their walls scrawled with desperate pleas), a crematorium and laboratories, and a mass grave of Chinese victims in a cattle pasture. As the Soviets moved eastward and captured fleeing Japanese, they apprehended dozens who had worked at Unit 731 and Unit 100, and, through interrogations of captives, they gradually began to understand the scope of Ishii's program.

On April 13, just as the IPS finalized its list of twenty-six defendants, the Soviet judge and a large team of prosecutors arrived in Tokyo, with a contingent of over fifty functionaries—clerks, interpreters, chauffeurs, cooks, gardeners, and others "of no particular description." With an acute housing shortage in Tokyo, SCAP struggled to find them accommodations. As one US official put it, "The Russians inundated us."[29] Their large IPS division, in military uniform, was given offices at the Meiji Building, where, since few spoke English, they were relatively isolated.

Before the arrival of its IMTFE contingent, the Soviet Union had promoted propaganda about the unjust domination of Japan by its capitalist victors and launched appeals to the Japanese communists who were soon to become a third of the new Japanese parliament. White Russians living in Japan were encouraged to reclaim their nationality and join the Soviet fold. From Moscow, Ambassador Averell Harriman of the United States suggested that the Soviets had three reasons for "dissatisfaction" with the Occupation, the foremost being that "Japan like Germany might some day be utilized by Western Powers [as] a springboard for attack on USSR." Another cause for their disgruntlement could be their feeling that the Soviet Union had not been accorded enough consideration in the disposition of Japan: "Being new rich with a lingering inferiority complex and feeling of gauche uncertainty in international society, USSR is inordinately sensitive re appearance as well as substance of prestige." Finally, Harriman thought, the US presence left the Soviets little leeway for expanding their influence, except for exploiting Japanese communists' postwar unrest. "We appear, however," the ambassador wrote, "to be housecleaning and encouraging liberal tendencies in Japan. This has the effect of stealing Communist thunder because fundamentally USSR prefers crusading against reaction to competing with liberalis[m]."[30]

As part of his "housecleaning," General MacArthur was determined to dismantle the imperial government's paramilitary structures that, since the 1920s, had promoted "thought police" and led to the imprisonment of tens of thousands of communists, socialists, anarchists, Korean nationalists, Christians, pacifists, and liberals.[31] Yet provisions in the Instrument of Surrender that protected Japan's central government posed obstacles to MacArthur's goal of preventing its reversion to a police state. Within SCAP, an in-house quarrel pitted liberals in the Government Section (GS) against anticommunist militarists, first among them General Charles Willoughby at G-2. MacArthur tolerated his old friend's opinions, while, with his civil reformers, he concentrated on strategies to balance guarantees of free speech against the risks of civil disorder.

At the IPS, ideological differences seemed to play little part. The Soviet Union had signed the Instrument of Surrender and, as a signatory, was entitled to its place at the trial. The Soviets' first message to the Executive Committee, delivered by Associate Prosecutor Sergei Alexandrovich Golunsky, was accepted without question, even though it went against previous deliberations. As was its right, the Soviet Union insisted on adding two more defendants to the already finalized list of twenty-six. One was General Umezu, the army chief of staff who had signed the Surrender Instrument aboard the USS *Missouri* on September 2, 1942. The second was the former foreign minister Shigemitsu, who had also signed the surrender agreement and had been on an earlier list from the Drafting Committee.

In formulating their charges, the Soviet prosecutors decided to emphasize aggressive war and conspiracy to wage aggressive war—the Class A crimes. Four defendants already chosen—Doihara, Hiranuma, Itagaki, and, at the top, Tojo—were identified as the major planners against the Soviet state. The examples cited were two conflicts instigated by Japan in the unsettled period just before the Neutrality Pact of 1941. The first was the Battle of Lake Khasan (Changkufeng) in July 1938 at the convergence of the Soviet, Korean, and Manchukuo borders, which Doihara and Itagaki had helped plan; along with Hiranuma, they had also supported the 1938–1939 battle at Nomonhan (Khalkin-gol), the second conflict on which the Soviets would base their charges.

At the time of the two battles, Shigemitsu was ambassador to the Soviet Union and Umezu was head of the Kwantung Army in Manchuria, roles not forgotten by the Soviets despite the rise to greater power by both men. Specific charges for these two new defendants had to be written into the indictment, which was hastily being readied for printing. Keenan rushed a memo to his entire IPS staff that he needed "all information of evidentiary value" about Shigemitsu and Umezu to complete the text. The Soviet prosecution also presented the charge that the Japanese, dating from the 1930s, conspired to attack the Soviet Union and seize its eastern territories. Golunsky and his division came prepared with documents, maps, and a long list of witnesses, yet their assumption seemed to be that the accused were already guilty as charged and that any evidence, even from shaky sources, would do. Their carelessness in witness selection, for example, and with historical details would later undermine their case.[32]

Class C Crimes: Sutton Prepares for the Tribunal

Immersed in his IPS duties, Nelson Sutton concentrated on drafting a report on all he had learned about the Class C crimes against humanity committed by Japan against China. With Prosecutor Hsiang of the China Division and Pedro Lopez, the newly arrived associate prosecutor for the Philippines, he would be framing the overall case argument for Class C crimes, which would draw on the material for both the Rape of Nanking and the Rape of Manila. The Nazis' systemic planning and perpetration of mass civilian deaths was being argued at Nuremberg, with examples from the Holocaust, but neither the Nanjing nor Manila atrocities was the result of a state genocidal policy. Instead, both would be represented as examples of Japan's overall aggressive warfare—its consistent pattern of excessive brutality and destruction. In addition, Sutton was helping Henry Hauxhurst write the brief on Japan's economic aggression in China. Evidence on Japan's exploitation of Manchukuo would be complemented by testimony about the post-1937 puppet government in Nanjing, with Miner Searle Bates and Reverend Mills listed as witnesses.[33]

Before drafting China's Class C crimes summary, Sutton met in Frank Tavenner's office with Colonel Morrow, Judge Hsiang, and Henry Chiu to review the results of the month-long China investigation. Together the team had accumulated over fifty documents containing evidence for the Nanjing Massacre and opium enslavement. Some were twenty or thirty pages long and nearly half were in Chinese; more might be coming from the war crimes commissions in China and other sources. All this material needed to be certified, translated, and readied for copying—if the trial opened May 3 as scheduled, the beginning arguments for the China case would follow three or four weeks later. Although China's case argument was a substantial part of the prosecution's presentation and would likely go on for a month or more, a basic problem loomed: Chinese-Japanese and Chinese-English translators were scarce, forcing reliance on English-speaking witnesses and already translated documents.[34]

As for witnesses, Morrow had a list to back up the chemical warfare charges he was developing. In addition, he and Sutton agreed that the two policemen, Harold Frank Gill and Peter Lawless, were good choices to testify about the opium enslavement charges, with perhaps Bates as an addition. Compelling as atrocities, the opium commerce charges also fit the Class B category, as an example of Japanese economic exploitation.

For the Nanjing massacre charges, Sutton was narrowing the list of victims interviewed in Nanjing, trying to decide who might be most effective in court. He was optimistic that he would have the key safety zone advocates. In addition to those he had found in Nanjing, he had tracked down the surgeon Robert O. Wilson in California and Reverend John Magee, who was in China, and persuaded them to testify.

As for the plague attacks, Sutton was less confident that he had "best evidence" of atrocities. On the positive side, the King report, official and relevant, showed that people in three cities had died from the disease, but the deaths might have been caused by natural outbreaks. He could call on at least three experts with public health credentials—Drs. Peter King, W. I. Chen, and Robert Pollitzer. But the witness he wanted most was the missing Nurse E. J. Bannan.

After the Chinese Division meeting, Sutton turned his attention to composing the Class C crimes overview—the brief on atrocities committed by the Japanese in China that ultimately ran to sixty-seven pages of text and affidavits.[35] He began by consulting the indictment draft and noted that the criminal acts he was describing were in group 2, counts 44–50 and 53–55, inclusive. Categorically these were murder and massacre, torture, rape, robbery, looting, and the wanton destruction of property. These atrocities, he would argue, had occurred in every province occupied by the Japanese and had continued from 1937 until 1945. Far from being unknown, the incidents had been "brought home not only to the commanding generals in China, but to the government in Tokyo, and no effective action was taken to correct the situation." To broaden his argument to fit the overall prosecution strategy, he described these crimes as part of "the Japanese pattern of warfare." The phrase was important, for it emphasized that the leadership of the Japanese government, represented by the defendants, was ultimately responsible for the atrocities.

Sutton presented the "Rape of Nanking" as the "first and outstanding instance" of this pattern and went on to underscore the guilt of the defendant General Matsui, the commanding officer on December 13, 1937, when the city fell and the "orgy of crime and violence" by soldiers began.[36]

To emphasize the torture of defenseless Chinese civilians, Sutton included details from the joint statement of the chair and vice chair of the Red Swastika Society in Nanjing:

> Indignities of every nature were committed by Japanese soldiers against Chinese civilians although Chinese civilians were abject and pitiful in their submissive attitude. They were kicked and beaten, made to stand undressed in the cold, had water poured down their noses, their bodies stabbed and burned, and subjected to all forms of human torture. Upon

> discovery of family relationships among the Chinese, a son would be required to have intercourse with his mother, a father with his daughter, a brother with his sister, in the presence of and to the delight of the Japanese soldiers.[37]

Sutton added that, from December 13, 1937, to February 6, 1938, "thousands of Chinese women in Nanking ranging in age from eleven to seventy-seven years of age were horribly, and in many cases repeatedly raped by Japanese soldiers." As Dr. Bates recounted, the International Committee estimated that by January 10, 1938, the number raped was twenty thousand. In his summary he stated that "Japanese soldiers frequently desecrated the bodies of the victims who had been raped and killed by inserting a stick or bottle or other foreign substance in the female organ and leaving the body exposed to public view."[38] Sutton made specific mention of Japanese soldiers invading the grounds of Ginling College and raping women who had sought refuge there and carrying off other women to officers' quarters "to be raped and horribly debauched."

Sutton reported that, to date, he had selected four witnesses to give the "overall picture": Professor Miner Searle Bates, Reverend John Magee, Dr. Robert Wilson (who would come from California), and Mr. Hsu Chieh-chen, the textile merchant. Four affidavits from the eyewitnesses, plus a report from the Nanjing safety zone, would be submitted as evidence for the court. These same four witnesses would speak to the issue of Japanese robbery, looting, and wanton destruction of property.

Sutton again emphasized that Japanese authorities had been well informed about these atrocities. Daily submission of reports and complaints to Japanese consulates had been made by the International Committee for the Nanking Safety Zone; summaries of those reports were cabled daily by the Japanese consular offices in China to the Japanese Foreign Office in Tokyo; and copies of the reports were forwarded to the office by air mail. The paper trail included dispatches from American consular officials to Tokyo, which Sutton had. None of these complaints, it seemed, ever evoked denials from Japanese officials. Sutton attached a list of Chinese provinces where similar, documented atrocities had occurred and added ten personal statements, the longest from Bates. While working on his summary of Class C crimes in China, Sutton drafted the report that Keenan had in March (through Frank Tavenner) requested on Imperial Japan's "Economic Aggression in China." In it, Sutton combined evidence about the commercialized opium "enslavement" of the Chinese with other information about Japanese exploitation of China's raw materials, agriculture, labor, public utilities, trade routes, and other resources. Sutton, who proved a quick study, summarized the findings as follows.

> We have set out here all of the information secured from the persons whom we were requested to interview with regard to KOA-IN (China Affairs Bureau) and such additional facts relative to this company as we were able to secure for our time and efforts were devoted primarily to other fields. It clearly appears that upon the release of strictly military control of occupied territory KOA-IN was the means by which Japan exercised complete control over the industrial life of the occupied areas of China and that there was a carefully worked out and well executed plan by the Japanese Government to despoil China and her natural resources and to completely control for the benefit of the Japanese Government and Japanese citizens all economic affairs in China.[39]

CWS and Military Intelligence

On April 19 Sutton took a break from his report writing and went with Colonel Morrow to the Chemical Warfare Service office on the fifth floor of the Mitsubishi Building, built in 1894 between the Imperial Palace and Tokyo Station. There they met with Lieutenant Colonel Beebe, who had just finished his interviews with Tojo, Hata, and the four more junior Japanese Army officers about Japan's chemical warfare.

From his investigation, Morrow felt confident that there was plenty of evidence that Japan had used chemicals in violation of international treaties, and he was in the process of writing a summary of his findings for Chief of Counsel Keenan.[40] A possible imperial connection to chemical warfare hovered, in that the emperor's uncle, Prince Naruhito Higashikuni, had been with the Second Army in China at the time of the chemical attacks at Wuhan, after the conquest of Shanghai.[41] The Japanese use of chemicals in China seemed to have varied by battlefield terrain and objective, for example, whether to use mustard gas as a lingering contaminant around villages. Nonetheless, the facts supporting Chinese allegations dating from 1937 through at least 1944 seemed solid.[42]

Sutton discussed the ambiguity of the proof for the plague attacks on China and explained that he had not located the key missing witness from Changde, Nurse Bannan, who might be tracked through the Presbyterian Board of Foreign Missions. Sutton's expectation was that, if this eyewitness were found and confirmed, China's charges of Japanese germ warfare stood a better chance of being brought to court. Beebe offered to help, and Sutton promised that the next day he would give him the address of the Presbyterian Board in New York, to help move ahead with the search for Nurse Bannan. He also promised to deliver to Beebe a copy of the report on "Bacterial Warfare" he was preparing for Keenan and MacArthur.

While Sutton and Morrow were meeting with Colonel Beebe, a metamorphosis was taking place in the organization of SCAP's military intelligence. The change would affect how an officer like Beebe or his superior at CWS, Colonel Geoffrey Marshall, might configure their intelligence roles versus the IMTFE and its mandate to prosecute war crimes. In the first months of the Occupation, the conflict between SCAP's military and civil divisions had at times slowed or hindered MacArthur's reform agenda. The crux of the problem was the antagonism between conservative voices, like General Willoughby's at G-2, and those of liberals like Charles Hades in the Government Section. The contest boiled down to which division best protected American interests: the one that gave priority to national security or the one that promoted open democratic institutions.

In mid-April 1946, through internal deliberations, SCAP found an organizational solution to the conflict. A new chain of command was created that allowed the civil divisions to bypass the constraints of the Military General Staff (which housed G1–4) and report directly to MacArthur via a new deputy chief of staff. In this way, the Military Division kept its own separate line of communication to the chief of staff, Major General Paul J. Mueller, and MacArthur. Thus, Willoughby's authority or that of any SCAP military official to obstruct the civil section was blocked.

Yet, owing to changes emanating from Washington, this organizational split eventually helped Willoughby expand his authority at SCAP and better promote his conservative beliefs. After the war Willoughby had resented that his rival, Brigadier General Elliot Thorpe, had been given the double advantage of heading intelligence at the Counter-Intelligence Corps in AFPAC (U.S. Army Forces in the Pacific) and also leading SCAP's Civil Intelligence Section. Willoughby felt hampered by not being able to restrain the ongoing purges of police, military officers, and ultranationalists that he believed were robbing the new Japanese state of its necessary central authority. The release of communists from Japanese jails scandalized him.

In early 1946 a policy change at the War Department worked in his favor when the US Congress and the public began to agitate for more cuts in the military budget. One complaint was that the army payroll supported too many generals who, with the war over, were seen as nonessential expenses. In response, the Pentagon issued reductions in rank for hundreds of officers who had received wartime promotions, which meant demotions for both Willoughby and Thorpe. Thorpe, believing that his loss of status from brigadier general to colonel would destroy his ability to deal with his Japanese contacts, opted for retirement.[43] Willoughby, whose demotion would be from major general to brigadier, took the prospective downgrade in stride and stayed put, waiting for his time to come. With Thorpe gone, he was among the few with the intelligence background to handle Thorpe's responsibilities, and he had the support of General MacArthur. Meanwhile, he continued to run G-2, which included his in-house spy network to track communist agents in Japan and Korea and a new team that united his ATIS translation service with War Department intelligence. Picking up from where those conducting the Scientific Intelligence Survey had left off the previous October, Willoughby was responsible for coordinating the exploitation of Imperial Japan's chemical and biological weapons capabilities. Lieutenant Colonel Beebe and his technical staff were chronicling every detail of Imperial Japan's chemical weapons research and development, for a planned set of six volumes. After Arvo Thompson finished his report, Willoughby saw value in continued G-2 relations with General Ishii and his Unit 731 scientists. Both these lines of inquiry identified Japanese chemical and biological warfare information as vital to US national security and therefore necessary to keep in the strictest secrecy.

Unaware of Willoughby's agenda, Nelson Sutton continued to collect documents about the Japanese plague attacks. From Robert Pollitzer, he had received a copy of Dr. Yung's report on the first three plague attacks, signed in Beijing by Yung and witnessed by Pollitzer. (The judge advocate in Shanghai had received and signed for the report and then forwarded it by air to Sutton in Tokyo.) Yung's credentials were more impressive than Pollitzer's: he was the director of the Department of Epidemic Prevention in China's National Health Administration, as well as a senior technical expert at the Army Medical Administration, Ministry of War. Sutton added Yung to the list of potential witnesses, but without Bannan or an equivalent eyewitness he doubted he could make a case.

On April 25 Sutton submitted his final report on allegations of Japanese bacteriological warfare to General MacArthur.[44] He had just been told to coordinate his reports to Keenan with SCAP, and this was the first item he shared with both. The report and letter were copied to Colonel Morrow, who was engrossed in a summary of Japan's military aggression in China in 1937–1945, integrating into it his chemical warfare charges.

The starting point of Sutton's thirty-seven-page report was Dr. Peter King's summary of the plague attacks as it appeared officially in March 1942, complete with the reference to the Japanese using the Chinese as human guinea pigs. Sutton described his meetings with both King and Chen, who had done the autopsy on the young man in Changde, and their descriptions of the first three attacks—on Ningbo, Chu-hsien (Quzhou), and Kinhwa (Jinhua). Although these two experts "could not positively determine that the bubonic plague which occurred in these instances was caused from germs which had been dropped from the planes," they were both "thoroughly satisfied" as to the Japanese source of the November 4, 1941, attack on Changde. Sutton's narrative then shifted to that city, to Nurse Bannan and to Dr. Pollitzer, whose career description from the previous April he submitted in full, including the letter from the League of Nations undersecretary.

The rest of Sutton's report was a collection of affidavits, document certifications, and extracts from the plague attack article in 1942 that ranged from individual clinical cases to autopsy reports and inconclusive tests on laboratory animals. Also included were figures from the Chinese Health Administration showing the spread of plague from Quzhou to two local villages and its reoccurrence in 1941–1944, with total cases of infection numbering 717 and deaths 651.[45] Along with it was Pollitzer's account of the subsequent spread of plague among rats and people in Changde and two adjoining villages. In addition, a merchant passing through Changde had contracted pneumonic plague, which led to a virulent outbreak some thirty miles north of the city, in which sixteen villagers died.[46] Buried in the report was Pollitzer's assertion that "the cause of the [Changde] epidemic was due to the scattering of infective material, probably infective fleas, by an enemy plane."[47]

As witnesses Sutton proposed King, Pollitzer, Chen, and Yung, who had written up events in the first three targeted cities. Sutton was clear, though, that he would have preferred firsthand accounts of the alleged attacks. With some confusion about the attack dates, he advised "That Mrs. E. J. Bannan be secured as a witness or an affidavit be secured from her in the States giving full and complete details relative to the grain and other substances dropped from the plane in Changteh November 4, 1941, and 7 December [*sic*] before the outbreak of plague in that city." He then suggested that "other witnesses be secured or affidavits from the other witnesses to testify to the fact that grain and other substances were actually dropped from Japanese planes in the cities in which the plague later appeared, the quantity of grain and other substances dropped from the planes, and other circumstances."[48]

In a cover letter to Keenan, Sutton commented: "On the present state of the record, it is respectfully recommended that that no attempt be made to establish the use of bacteria warfare by the Japanese against China." Yet he again alluded to the possibility of new evidence: "Should additional witnesses be located who can testify that grain or other substances were actually dropped from a Japanese plane on Changteh on November 4, 1941, then it would be proper to re-consider the matter in the light of additional evidence, for obviously the Japanese were not interested in providing 'manna' for the Chinese people." And he added: "Efforts are being made to secure additional evidence." This was likely a reference to Colonel Beebe's helpful offer and to whatever additional information might be sent to Prosecutor Hsiang from the Nanjing Procurator. His last sentence, though, was definitive: "As the case now stands, in my opinion the evidence is not sufficient to justify the charge of bacterial warfare."[49]

On May 1 Sutton sent a copy of his final report on bacterial weapons, with the cover letter to Keenan, to Colonel Beebe at the CWS office, with an inquiry about locating Bannan. "We will be very interested to learn the result of your further investigation of this matter," he wrote, "and particularly the report or statement which you may be able to secure from her."[50]

Without Sutton's knowing, G-2 had already located Bannan and sent Lieutenant Colonel Arvo Thompson to San Francisco to conduct an interview on April 22. Owing to a confusion at the time of the Changde epidemic, the eyewitness statement written by the Reverend Edward J. Bannan, the business director of the Changde Presbyterian Hospital, had been attributed to his wife, who was the hospital's nurse superintendent. On May 1 Thompson sent a wire to G-2's Technical Intelligence Section assuring his colleagues there that, based on his interview with Mr. Bannan, the evidence for Japanese biological warfare was "not conclusive."[51]

Case Evidence

Having put much energy into defendant selection and the indictment, the Executive and Evidence Committees had prepared the IPS for the court's opening on May 3. But they had lagged in articulating the uniform standards for case presentations. When the Evidence Committee met on April 25, its first action was to reaffirm the "best evidence" rule, drawn explicitly from British Common Law.[52] This standard would require that primary documents and firsthand testimony be selected over secondary or more suspect evidence. Stating the rule was less on behalf of the Anglo-American prosecutors who knew it well than for the new arrivals with other legal traditions—the Dutch, the French, and especially the Soviets.

With encouragement from the Evidence Committee, Roy Morgan, head of the Investigation Division, formulated basic IPS guidelines for selecting the Japanese government documents, the extracts from exhibits, and excerpts from interrogations necessary for the indictment as well as the chronological events ("incidents" as they were called) that would organize its overall narrative.

The question of balancing witness testimony against written documents remained. Even with text translation difficulties, it was less cumbersome to submit documents than to arrange to put a witness on the stand, especially one who did not speak English. In these early days the IMTFE had yet to create a system for transporting those selected to testify and arranging where they would stay. Given the acute housing shortage, the only accommodations were a house big enough for twenty-five in Ito, a coastal resort east of Tokyo, or a wing at Sugamo Prison, an awkward arrangement. A witness officer was in charge and the General Secretariat could likely find solutions. But the fact remained that witnesses made demands on time and resources that paper documents did not.

Another question was raised, this one about using sworn affidavits in place of the witnesses, a substitution that could provoke objections because it eliminated the possibility of cross-examination. Struggling with the issue, one member asked whether witnesses should be "discarded" when there was sufficient documentary evidence. In the end, in the name of efficiency, members decided that "the policy of this committee is that Documentary Evidence, including affidavit Evidence, shall be used in preference to Oral Evidence, and that Witnesses be reduced to an absolute minimum."[53] The committee, however, could not dictate numbers—which was good for Sutton. Given the centrality of the Chinese case, which Keenan and MacArthur supported, he saw every reason to put at least a dozen witnesses on the stand.

The larger problem for the IPS was the coordination of evidence for the disparate charges to be made by each of the participating nations. A single coherent framework was needed, and for that, information had to be shared. Roy Morgan told the Evidence Committee that he wanted the draft forms of briefs from every division completed and sent to him as soon as possible, in order to get them printed and circulated.

Management of the overall case, though, was lacking. Chief of Counsel Keenan seemed not to have thought ahead about the question. Newly returned from two weeks in China, he tried to delegate this responsibility to Carlisle Higgins, his deputy assistant, but Higgins was overwhelmed with IPS administration. Keenan then considered another member of his staff, John Fihally, the trial lawyer from Justice, but Fihally was perfecting his case against Tojo, based on many interrogations, and still had responsibilities that called him back to Washington. Keenan himself was focused on his opening statement for the prosecution, which he wanted to resound the way Justice Jackson's had at Nuremberg.

To solve the case management problem, Keenan recruited Eugene D. Williams, a rotund, bespectacled criminal trial lawyer in his late fifties who, like Keenan, was no stranger to headlines. In the 1930s, as assistant attorney general for Los Angeles County when Earl Warren was the attorney general, he had been a prosecutor in a celebrated corruption case that took down a "Special Intelligence Unit" at the Los Angeles Police Department—a covert organization that protected incumbent city politicians by intimidating and even murdering their opponents.[54] The police chief was tried and convicted for attempting to kill a private investigator by wiring his car with explosives. The case sparked the recall of the city's mayor, Frank Shaw, the first in US history.

What also reassured Keenan about Williams was his wartime connection with the Justice Department. After Pearl Harbor, Earl Warren, then the newly elected governor of California, became one of the driving forces behind the Japanese internment program, which was administered by the Department of Justice and the War Department. Warren's initiative (although he later regretted the internments) was considered patriotic by many, and Williams benefited by becoming chief of the Department of Justice Lands Division. During and after the war, the Justice Department supervised as many as eleven Japanese detention centers and camps, from California, New Mexico, and Idaho to Texas and Wisconsin. With no background in international law, Williams was contemplating retirement when he left Justice to join the IMTFE.[55]

In a preliminary memo to the IPS staff, Keenan explained that he wanted to designate Williams his special assistant, with the task of "over-all supervision of the presentation of the entire case."[56] To help him, Keenan would provide "one or two excellent secretaries to be available to him at all times." Williams would have an office close to Keenan's in the Meiji Building, so that, owing to "the vital nature of his work," he could keep in daily contact with the chief of counsel. Keenan urged all members of the IPS to give Williams their "entire and unqualified cooperation." He further advised Williams to consult with Roy Morgan, another lawyer from Justice, who in Keenan's opinion probably had "the best over-all general knowledge of any individual" at IPS.

In a memo on April 30, Keenan announced that Williams was now officially special assistant to the chief of prosecution, in charge of "the overall supervision of the presentation of the entire case." To this he added an imperative: "All members of the staff whose assignments involve matters of the preparation or presentation of evidence will consult and cooperate with Mr. Williams as to such matters."[57] The assignment also meant that Keenan was more able to distance himself from the IPS and its day-to-day agenda.

Just as Williams took up his new post, General Willoughby's waiting game at G-2 paid off, giving him a great increase in his authority at General Headquarters. With General Thorpe gone, after much deliberation SCAP decided on an organizational overhaul of its intelligence service. It created the Civil Intelligence Division (CID) that combined Thorpe's two intelligence units (the CIC and the CIS) and, that done, put MacArthur's acolyte Willoughby in charge. The creation of this new division and General Willoughby's appointment signaled a critical juncture in the Occupation, when military intelligence began turning to US postwar national security goals and away from a focus on Japan as the defeated enemy. Willoughby's rule of CID and G-2 would allow him in the long run to have influence on a broad range of ongoing reforms—Japanese educational policy, the purges, and police decentralization—about which he had fixed, conservative, even oppositional views. More immediately, Willoughby stood ready to promote his ongoing scientific intelligence projects on Japanese chemical and biological weapons and, using his authority and influence, keep them secret from Soviet competitors and public scrutiny.

7

THE TRIAL BEGINS

ON MAY 3, 1946, THE IMTFE OFFICIALLY OPENED, WITH FILM CAMERAS whirring and flashbulbs popping. The spectacle was planned to attract the world's attention, which it did, although not as a well-orchestrated triumph for justice. The courthouse was located inside the large former War Ministry building, in the Ichigaya District of Tokyo. The War Ministry was positioned high on a hill and protected by a fence and armed Allied guards. Starting at 7 a.m., two lines formed, one at the side entrance for the Japanese, the other at the main door for the Allies and their guests. The defendants, on public view for the first time since Japan's defeat, were driven over in a bus from Sugamo Prison. Two hours later, the nine judges (minus the two for India and the Philippines) arrived in limousines.

At a cost of a million dollars, the ministry's gymnasium and assembly area for cadets had been transformed into a replica of the Nuremberg court, high-ceilinged, with oversized windows, in grand European style. The judges' bench, banked by a lower row of desks for secretaries and assistants, loomed over the sunken main floor, where the alternating drama and boredom of the proceedings would unfold. On the main floor were podiums and tables for attorneys and a slightly elevated witness box. Facing the judges on a raised platform was the defense docket, with twenty-eight simple wooden chairs. To the right of the platform was the spectator gallery for the Japanese, with room for 500; to the left was the gallery for Allied VIPs, which held 160.[1] Every seat in the courtroom, from the bench to the galleries and the pit and press box, was provided with earphones. A glass-enclosed booth on a balcony near the VIP section had been wired for translation, with a choice of English, Japanese, and Russian. Higher up in the same area was the camera booth. Leaflets instructed visitors to not smoke, to rise and remain silent as the judges entered, to use only the earphones provided for translation, and, at the end of a session, to remain in their places until the defendants had filed out.

By 10 a.m. all the gallery seats were filled and the press box on the ground floor was jammed with a mix of Western and Japanese reporters. Nearly all the IPS prosecutors were there. For Sutton, who had started his career presenting cases in makeshift courts in feed stores, the event was magical. In his enthusiasm, he collected his colleagues' autographs in one of his little brown notebooks: Frank Tavenner, Colonel Thomas Morrow, Solis Horwitz, Osmond Hyde, Grace Kanode Llewlyn (the first of just two women to address the court), Britain's Arthur Comyns Carr, Australia's Alan Mansfield, New Zealand's Ronald Quilliam, and one of the two newly arrived Soviet prosecutors, Major General A. N. Vasiliev.[2]

At 10:30 the klieg lights hanging from the ceiling were switched on and the filming began. Spectators and news reporters leaned forward expectantly as twenty-six well-guarded defendants (two were still in transit) filed into the courtroom.[3] Their drab, wrinkled clothes spoke volumes about how far they had fallen. Suffering from tuberculosis, the bald, slight General Matsui, notorious for his role at Nanjing, moved as if in a trance. Shigemitsu Mamoru, the diplomat, walked slowly, leaning on his cane. General Umezu, the "Ivory Mask," lived up to his sobriquet. Ill with tuberculosis, Matsuoka Yosuke, the former foreign minister who had promoted ties with Nazi Germany, looked near death. General Muto, chief of staff under General Yamashita in Manila, looked stunned, as did Baron Hirota, the career diplomat who had been foreign minister during the time of the Nanjing Massacre. The propagandist Okawa Shumei, who in the late 1920s had advocated the Japanese takeover of Asia, seemed tearful and disoriented. Only Tojo, recovered from his self-inflicted gunshot wound, carried himself with confidence. By consulting the seating chart distributed throughout the courtroom, the spectators could identify the suspects as they seated themselves in the dock.

With the defendants in place, the IMTFE judges were expected to make their entrance. Instead, the nine of them waited for forty minutes in chambers for the two missing defendants, General Itagaki, former commander in Singapore, and General Kimura, accused of POW abuses in Burma. Just released from custody by British command, they were on a plane from Bangkok that was late in arriving.[4]

Finally, impatient with the delay, Court President Sir William Webb led the judges into the hushed, packed courtroom and up the stairs to the bench. Webb had determined the order of the judges' seating, in consultation with MacArthur. Webb was at the center, with the only microphone on the bench reserved for him. On his immediate left was China's Judge Mei Ju-ao, who had argued successfully to be seated in a place of privilege. Next to Mei was Judge I. M. Zarayanov from the USSR, followed by France's Henri Bernard and New Zealand's Harvey Northcroft. On Webb's right was the US judge, John Higgins, and next to him Britain's Lord Patrick (whom Mei had displaced), followed by Judge Edward Stuart McDougall of Canada and the Netherlands' Bernard Röling. The two end seats were reserved for the most junior members, the Philippines' Judge Delfin Jaranilla and India's Judge Radhabinod Pal, still to arrive.

President Webb made a brief opening statement, which was then translated into Japanese. He spoke of the bench's commitment to administer justice fairly. "To our great task," he said, "we bring open minds on both the facts and the law. The onus will be on the prosecution to establish guilt beyond a reasonable doubt." To finish, he waxed even more grandiloquent: "There has been no more important criminal trial in all history."[5]

At 11:30, after Webb's statement, a recess was called until 2:30 p.m.; the two missing defendants had landed at Atsugi Airport and were being sped to the court. By 2:30 they were seated with the other defendants in the dock, and at 2:35 Chief of Counsel Keenan began the presentation of the indictment on behalf of the Allied nations represented at the trial, as well as Portugal and Thailand.[6] All forty-eight pages of it would be read to the court by a relay of readers, a process expected to take nearly two days. The defense would then respond, and each defendant would plead guilty or not guilty as charged. Depending on the judges' evaluation of the indictment and other matters of court business, the prosecution could expect to start its case argument in several weeks, perhaps a month.

On April 29 the defense had received its copy of the indictment. Captain Beverly Coleman, its chief counsel, asked for two weeks to review the charges. Only six defense attorneys were in Tokyo, he pointed out, and few defendants had received adequate legal counsel. Webb refused the request, agreeing with Chief Prosecutor Keenan that three days was plenty of time to determine the pleas of the accused.

Following a brief preamble by Keenan, the prosecution began by reading count 1, from which the other fifty-four counts, more or less coherently expressed, had been derived. From January 1, 1928, until September 2, 1945, the charge went, the defendants together and with others participated in a common plan, whose object was

> that Japan should secure the military, naval, political and economic domination of East Asia and of the Pacific and Indian Oceans, and of all countries and islands therein and bordering thereon and for that purpose should alone or in combination with other countries having similar objects, or who could be induced or coerced to join therein, wage declared or undeclared war or wars of aggression, and war or wars in violation of international law, treaties, agreements and assurances, against any country or countries which might oppose that purpose.

And so, the charge continued, to the detriment of the Japanese people, the defendants engaged in a conspiracy with Nazi Germany and Fascist Italy to "secure the domination and exploitation by the aggressive States of the rest of the world, and to this end to commit, or encourage the commission of crimes against peace, war crimes, and crimes against humanity as defined in the Charter of this Tribunal, thus threatening and injuring the basic principles of liberty and respect for the human personality." All this was to the detriment of the Japanese people. Further it was charged, "The mind of the Japanese people was systematically poisoned with harmful ideas of the alleged racial superiority of Japan over other peoples of Asia and even of the world."

At 3:40 p.m. Webb called for a short recess to allow the press to photograph the defendants. When the court reconvened at 4 p.m., the reading of the charges continued. Just as a clerk was describing Japan's December 7, 1941, attack on Pearl Harbor initiating an illegal "war of aggression," the propagandist Okawa Shumei, who was seated directly behind Tojo in the dock, reached forward and slapped the former premier on the head. Caught on camera, the premier winced and grimaced. As Okawa reached to strike Tojo again, two military policemen took hold of him and dragged him from the courtroom. Given the uproar that followed, President Webb called for a recess until the next morning. US journalists assessed the IMTFE commencement harshly—one called it a "third string road show" much inferior to Nuremberg—and some among the judges, particularly New Zealand's Northcroft, were dismayed by the bright lights and pandering to the media.[7]

The Japanese press, though, was respectful and published the indictment in full. British Embassy officials in private doubted the indictment would "ever be understood by more simple Japanese who start with different conceptions of life, death, and personal conduct."[8] Yet this was a cynical interpretation. For many Japanese, the charges opened their eyes to the complicity of their major leaders in violations of law that ran to "mass murder, rape, pillage, brigandage, torture, and other barbaric cruelties upon the helpless citizens of the overrun countries." Counts 37 to 52 were grouped as "Murder," and, within each, names were named.[9] In count 45, twelve defendants were charged with permitting their armed forces in Nanjing "to slaughter the inhabitants contrary to international law [and thus] killed and murdered many thousands of civilians and disarmed soldiers of the Republic of China." The same defendants were accused of murder in similar attacks on four other Chinese cities.[10] The final two counts addressed the culpability of top officials, whether for directly ordering these hideous war crimes (count 54) or for so neglecting their duties that atrocities were committed (count 55). The indictment charges turned high state individuals into run-of-the-mill criminals, the intent of Chief of Counsel Keenan, who on the first day of court described the Japanese defendants as "gangsters" who should be "exposed for what they are: plain ordinary murderers."[11]

The IPS Prepares

Back at the Meiji Building, the Chinese Division team held daily meetings to organize its presentation. Judge Hsiang would make the opening statement.

He and Henry Chiu would handle the opium charges, while four to five American attorneys, including Thomas Morrow and Nelson Sutton, would fill in to argue the rest of the case. Sutton's special responsibility was to make sure that, in the appropriate sequence, the many pertinent documents were translated and ready for submission.

The Chinese Division, like the others at IPS, was under pressure to adapt its evidence to a standard format that would allow Keenan's special assistant Eugene Williams to coordinate the overall case argument. As chair of the Evidence Committee, Alan Mansfield worked closely with Williams and with Roy Morgan of the Investigation Division to develop a coherent strategy. To begin, all IPS attorneys were instructed to prepare a summary brief of each interrogation they had conducted.[12] Some thirty IPS staff had been assigned to question over 150 witnesses, defendants, and others; the results of their labors had to be incorporated into the case framework.

Morgan had beforehand promoted this kind of standardization, and his files were full of interrogation material, but irregularities threatened. The problem was not with the Anglo-American prosecutors, or the Chinese Division, which was being helped by Sutton and Morrow, or the newly arrived Indian and Filipino jurists, who were familiar with common law and the English language. It was the French, Dutch, and, in particular, Soviet lawyers who needed to conform to IPS legal culture, dominated as it was by the Americans, the British, and the Commonwealth nations.

On Saturday, May 4 (in the absence of Mansfield, who was at court), Eugene Williams chaired an ad hoc Evidence Committee meeting to reinforce the message about IPS teamwork. He had just circulated a "top priority" memo containing a "Form of Brief" template that he wanted each prosecutor to fill out so that their input would conform to a common pattern and design. It was highly specific in its requirements: each attorney had to append his name and the subject number of his case to a general summary of evidence and to "indicate precisely the group of counts of the indictment to which the evidence relates . . . in order that those examining the briefs may readily ascertain what counts of the indictment have or have not been proved." For supplementary information, they should attach appendices and refer to them in the case summary.[13]

To help them focus, Williams asked the division attorneys to write a general statement of the "ultimate facts" they believed their case evidence was establishing:

> Following "best evidence" standards, prosecutors should make a specific statement of each fact they sought to prove, followed by a detailed statement of the exact evidence by which it is to be proved. As for instance, a Certain Document (with a statement of the foundation evidence to enable the document to be introduced); a Certain Witness (with a brief statement of the exact things to which he will testify); a statement of any matter of which the Court is expected to take judicial notice; a Map or Chart, together with the evidence by which you expect to establish its authenticity; explanations you are prepared to give which will excuse the production of better evidence.[14]

Williams cited a model for the "Form of Brief" he wanted: the one being drafted by Colonel Morrow entitled "All China Military Aggression 1937–1945."

Williams chose the metaphor of American football to explain his role as special assistant: "I think that my relationship to the subject is very much similar to a combined job of quarter-back and you men are going to be the backs who are carrying the ball. All I am going to do is to make a suggestion here and there and try to co-ordinate it so that there will be a team instead of individuals at work."[15] He urged all speed in arranging for document translation and preparing charts and maps, and that witnesses be chosen in a way that would hasten the trial. The prosecution, he announced, would open June 3. He also warned against leaking any of this game plan to the defense.

That same Saturday, in response to a stern memo from Mansfield, Chief of Counsel Keenan circulated detailed instructions for the interrogation summaries. He required that each be broken down according to subject matter—he gave thirteen categories of charges—and that its relevant facts and events should be made clear. Each summary had to indicate the name of the person briefing the interrogation as well as the person who had conducted it.[16] Keenan also required that the staff indicate the evidentiary value in the text of each interrogation, with page, serial, and file number noted. Later that day he sent out another memo, this one to clarify his thirteen subject categories, which consolidated the fifty-five indictment counts.[17] Since the Soviets had belatedly introduced Shigemitsu and Umezu as defendants, Keenan also asked that the other IPS prosecutors check each interrogation "for all information of evidentiary value" against them. Keenan wanted these summaries handed in to Roy Morgan at the Investigation Division.

Sutton meanwhile was concentrating on his magnum opus: "Brief of Atrocities, Class C Offenses." He listed the "Crimes Against Humanity" as "1. Murder and massacre, 2. Torture, 3. Rape, and 4. Robbery, looting and wanton destruction of property."[18] Included in the brief were affidavits about Nanjing from Miner Searle Bates, Lewis Smythe, George Fitch, Hsu Chuan-Ying, and others, plus evidence from the UN War Crimes Commission and the Chinese Ministry of Justice relating to crimes committed in nine Chinese provinces. Sutton included the devastation caused by Japan's commerce in opium. Excluded was any mention of the plague attacks, which he had set aside.

Sutton's central theme was Japan's brutal "pattern of warfare":

> The commission of these atrocities by Japanese soldiers in city after city and province after province in China, and the continuation of this type of conduct month after month and year after year from 1937 to 1945, establishes clearly that this method of warfare was approved and assented to not only by the generals in command of the Japanese troops in China but by the Japanese High Command and the Japanese Government in Tokyo. Their responsibility for these crimes which shock the conscience of humanity is inescapable. This was the Japanese pattern of warfare.[19]

Repressed Evidence

Unknown to Sutton, the Military Intelligence Division of the War Department in Washington was circulating a top secret report that emphasized the centrality of germ weapons to US national security. Called *Biological Warfare: Activities and Capabilities of Foreign Nations*, the report asserted that the Soviet Union, France, and Great Britain could wage large-scale biological warfare within five years. "Biological warfare," the authors, who included General Alden Waitt of CWS, stated, "is a demoralizing, silent, and insidious weapon which can be used in a 'sneak attack' far more destructive than the strike at Pearl Harbor."[20] In a concluding statement, intelligence analysts stated that significant quantities of biological agents were immediately available to the "probable enemy" of the United States, referring to the Soviets. The US should be prepared, the report urged, "to strike the enemy's populated areas."[21]

The report also contained an update on the Japanese germ warfare program based on the Murray Sanders and Arvo Thompson inquiries. Three maps of the Pingfan Institute indicated its dimensions, and the Boeki Kyusuibu (Anti-epidemic Water Purification Bureau) front organization was described. Eight experimental Japanese bacterial bombs were discussed, with the porcelain *Ha* bomb of special interest, given the American investment in anthrax. At the back of the report was an international "BW Who's Who" list that, for Japan, named General Ishii, General Kitano Masaji, commander of Unit 731 after Ishii, and Colonel Masuda, once head of Unit Ei 1644 in Nanjing. About the plague attack on Changde, the report observed that, although qualified American investigators thought it highly probable the Japanese had conducted germ warfare, "authoritative opinion does not accept this conclusion unanimously."[22]

In its *Daily Intelligence Summary*, G-2 in Tokyo began circulating the essence of Thompson's findings to its officers and staff. The first article briefly outlined the organization of Boeki Kyusuibu, with its mission to prevent and control epidemics, after which it cited General Ishii on how the defensive measures became necessary owing to Soviet sabotage with anthrax, typhus, and cholera.[23] Three more brief summaries followed—adding details about Pingfan, research on causative agents, including at the Army Medical College in Tokyo, bombs and artillery shells, and the close working relationship of Unit 731 with the local Kempeitai, as an intelligence network and to apprehend saboteurs.[24] Taking the claims of Ishii and his cohort at face value, the final summary concluded: "Despite intensive investigations at Pingfan in the possibilities of offensive BW, the Japanese were never prepared to employ BW as a practical weapon."

Instead of these reports, which remained within intelligence channels, Sutton received a curious fragment of information from the Chinese

Division. On May 9 he found a note on his desk from Judge Hsiang and with it several translated pages of testimony.[25] On April 17–19, in a small town west of Tokyo, Mr. C. C. H. Hataba had been interrogated by an unidentified agent, likely American. Hataba identified himself as a former member of the Epidemic Prevention Section of the Ei 1644 Forces in Central China. He had served from May 1942 to March 1943, when he deserted out of revulsion for the section's true, inhumane mission. To reinforce his testimony, Hataba sketched a map of the EI 1644 base in downtown Nanjing and described its purpose: to culture microbes of cholera, typhus, plague, and dysentery for bacteriological warfare. The enclave, he said, had a "culture room of microbes in 4 storied building. Plus canteen, cooking room, hospital, warehouse, soldiers' quarters, air unit, flying field." Further, he testified that "the object of such an operation is to . . . spread the epidemics artificially in order to kill and demoralize the enemy. It is an inhumane act which also badly affects the inhabitants."

Starting in May 1942, Hataba recounted, the Japanese Army caused "a great scourge" throughout the Zhejiang and Jiangxi Provinces. As they drew back their forces, they wanted to leave only devastation for the KMT troops. "They were angry, too," he said, "at the Chinese who had sheltered your Doolittle pilots, so they executed them. It is said that they brought in General Ishii to infect the region with terrible diseases. He had made his reputation with the plague attacks [of 1940–1941] and promised the army he could do even worse killing and get away with it again. I believe it is correct that spreading cholera proved a disaster for their own troops, the general was demoted and another man was made chief in Harbin." As Hataba reported, "Other diseases killed many Chinese peasants in this area, very strangely and suddenly. Too many to remember."

Hataba, who had not witnessed any germ attacks, offered the name of Tatsuzawa Tadao, a member of his unit who "flew to the front lines to scatter microbes." Sutton immediately jotted a note to ask Legal Services to locate this pilot, whose testimony could verify Hataba's account.

Prosecutor Hsiang left another document for Sutton, on Japan's use of chemical weapons—incidents, types of munitions and agents, and casualties, including seventy-seven attacks on Changde in 1943, with projectiles, combining sneezing agents and vesicants. The report described the mustard gas and tear, sneezing, and suffocating gases manufactured and used, sometimes in combination, by Japanese troops in battles identified by locales and units. The total gas casualties for the Chinese were listed as 36,968, with 2,086 deaths. In October 1941 a chemical attack at Ichang (Yichang) in Hebei Province caused 1,600 casualties and 600 deaths. "Large quantities of Japanese poisonous shells," the summary concluded, "were captured from the Japanese Army between March and July, 1945, in various theaters of war in China."[26]

Then, in a single paragraph, the summary referred to the 1940–1941 plague attacks and identified a Dr. Kawahara as the leader of more than thirty bacterial specialists who, in 1939, arrived in Nanjing to direct aerial germ attacks and sabotage in Central China. It described a Japanese hospital in Shanghai as the producer of "bacteria of plague, cholera, typhoid, dysentery, etc." In retreat, the Japanese organized saboteurs to poison wells.[27]

The two documents from Hsiang, which pointed to a large military program, still offered no hard evidence that would make Sutton revise his conclusion, on file with Roy Morgan at the Investigation Division, that the evidence for the plague attacks was insufficient.

On May 5 Colonel Morrow's report on Japanese chemical warfare in China for Chief of Counsel Keenan went to General Headquarters and General Charles Willoughby at G-2.[28] It was then forwarded to Major General Alden Waitt, the chief chemical officer at the CWS in Washington. It corroborated the army's own verification of the lethal Japanese chemical attacks on Ichang in 1941, which not even Waitt doubted, and went beyond them while, following Sutton, biological warfare was downplayed.

Apparently unaware that his research on Japanese chemical warfare might trouble army officials, Morrow focused on organizing the overall case for Japan's crimes against peace in China. On May 13 he and Kenneth N. Parkinson, another IPS attorney, submitted to Keenan their "Form of Brief" on "All China Military Aggression, 1937–1945."[29] The draft meticulously described the relevant counts of the indictment as they related to China's charges against Japanese defendants. The summary covered the Sino-Japanese War from July 7, 1937, until Japan's official surrender in 1945. It listed the major cities conquered in the Japanese offensive (Beijing, Tianjin, Shanghai, Nanjing, Hankou, Canton, Changsha, Kengyang, Guilin, and Liuchow) and included Japan's blockade of the China coast as well as the land invasions. The draft drew heavily on Nelson Sutton's position

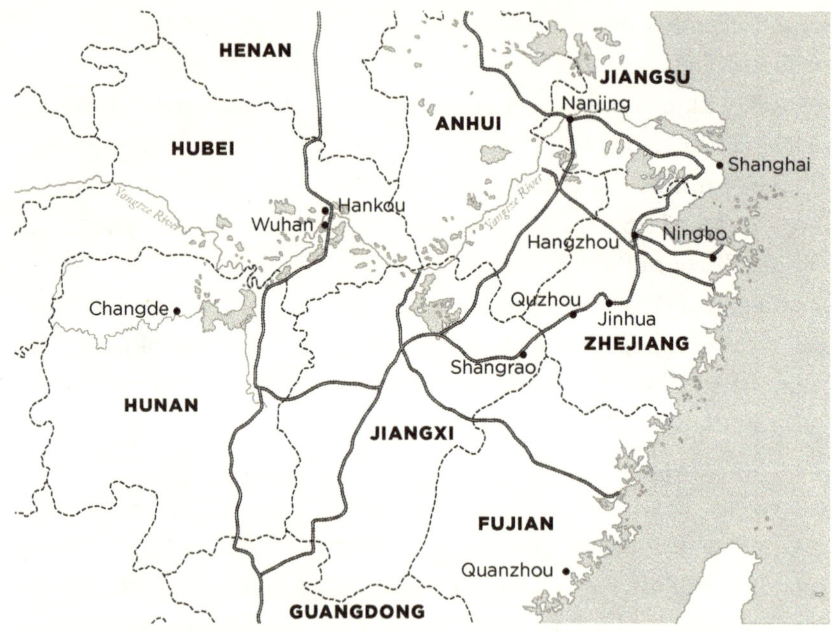

MAP 2 CHINESE WAR ZONE, 1937–1945
Key cities, provinces, and railway lines are indicated.

papers and his suggested witnesses—Dr. Bates, the Reverend Mills, Colonel David Barrett, the editor John B. Powell, and even Dr. Robert Lim, the surgeon general of the Chinese Army, who, although no longer needed as a source on the plague attacks, could offer statistics on Chinese troop casualties.[30]

Into the argument, Colonel Morrow inserted Japanese chemical warfare, a violation of The Hague Conventions: "This waging of war by Japan in China was characterized by gross violations of international law and treaties, by massacre of civilians and Chinese soldiers, prisoners of war, and by the outlawed use of poison gas."[31]

Starting with his own list of Chinese witnesses, Morrow quoted testimony from Major General Chang, deputy director of China's Army Medical Corps, who stated that the Japanese used poison gas at Ichang (outside Shanghai), where he "personally saw men who were burned about the eyes, arm pits, and the crotch whose cases were diagnosed by himself. He saw 30 or 40 soldiers affected this way."[32] A photographer at the scene, Major Yang Chu Nien, a gas defense officer of the 34th Army group, could testify to having observed soldiers badly blistered by vesicants. Brigadier General Wang Chang Ling, director of the army's gas defensive administration, could testify that in 1943 he found on a battlefield 15-centimeter howitzer shells containing highly lethal hydrocyanic (prussic) acid, banned after World War I, and that he saw a dozen soldiers suffering from gas poisoning by the Japanese, three of whom died. The general still had his notebook containing his notations of analyses of the contents of the shells. Finally, the director of a museum of chemical munitions near Chongqing was willing to describe the spent Japanese vesicant bombs and shells that he and others had brought back from battles.

As for official data, Major Woo Chia Shing of the Chinese Army, a custodian of records obtained from the Japanese Ministry of War, stated that 26,968 persons were injured by poison gas in the Sino-Japanese War, of whom 2,086 died. These records, the major said, showed that the Japanese used the gas 1,312 times in ten battles. In its complaint to the League of Nations in 1938, China had identified Field Marshal Hata and General Matsui, both indicted by the IPS, as the principal "defendants" responsible for chemical warfare in China.

Morrow then referred to a secret Japanese chemical plant that shipped many chemical weapons, including mustard and lewisite, to China.[33] In addition, he could offer documents from Japanese officials showing that, with the permission of the high command, gas weapons were used in battlefield "emergencies."

Also on May 13, Sutton received a message emanating from the Central Liaison Office of G-2, to which Legal Section had forwarded his inquiry about the pilot from Unit 1644. It read: "Tatsuzawa Tadao, a lance corporal of the 'Ei' 1644 Force, cannot report as directed, because the said Force has not yet been repatriated from China."[34] A potential witness to back up Mr. Hataba's statement had come up missing.

The next day Sutton found out that he had lost another witness. On his desk was the summary of the interrogation of Mr. E. J. Bannan by Lieutenant Colonel Arvo Thompson regarding the alleged plague attack on Changde in 1941, an interrogation conducted on April 22, three days after Sutton had forwarded the Presbyterian Church contact to Beebe at CWS intelligence in Tokyo.[35] General Willoughby in Tokyo and General Waitt at CWS in Washington had received their copies a week before Sutton.

Mr. Bannan remained certain that the outbreak of plague in Changde was caused by a deliberate Japanese experiment in bacteriological warfare. Pressed by Thompson, though, he did say that the evidence regarding the incident "was not conclusive but was strongly circumstantial." Bannan insisted, as in his original statement, that in thirty years he had never seen any comparable plague in Hunan Province. Nor did he believe that the Changde outbreak could have inadvertently spread from Ningbo over the long routes that separated the two cities, given the weeks required for such a journey. Bannan's wife Phyllis, who accompanied him to the interrogation, supported his version of the outbreak.

In his conclusion, rather than deepening his suspicions of General Ishii, Thompson dismissed Bannan's testimony for its reliance on "assumptions, suspicions, and unexplained facts." One of those assumptions was that the Japanese had used infected fleas to start the epidemic. As Thompson summarized:

> Interrogation of Mr. and Mrs. E. J. Bannan did not elicit additional information regarding the Changteh incident to that previously on file in intelligence records. The evidence connecting the Changteh plague outbreak with the plane incident, supposedly a Japanese attempt at biological warfare, is strongly circumstantial but not conclusive. The possibility of origin of the Changteh plague outbreak by natural spread from other endemic areas, as a result of the disorganization of normal trade and travel routes by war, has not been conclusively eliminated.[36]

The value of this lost witness was more than Sutton knew, for Bannan had credentials like Bates and others on the Nanjing Safety Zone Committee. After studying at the Princeton Theological Seminary, the Reverend Bannan had served in Changde since 1909 and been the hospital's business director since 1922, earning outstanding testimonials. In 1937 one church supervisor listed his strengths: "Fine legal mind, very efficient in dealing with questions of justice; consecrated, eager, effective missionary."[37] With equal praise, Phyllis Bannan had served even longer at the hospital and, with her husband, had endured the worst of the war, barely escaping bombings but never abandoning their mission.[38] Shortly after their interview in San Francisco, the Bannans returned to Changde, committed to rebuilding the war-damaged hospital.

Meanwhile, at the court, the defense counsel introduced the taboo subject of the atomic bombing of Hiroshima. If Japanese leaders could be individually accused of bombing Pearl Harbor, they contended, then the same culpability should apply to the decision to bomb Hiroshima. As prosecutor Major Ben Bruce Blakeney argued, "Show us the charge, produce the proof of the killing contrary to the laws and customs of war, name the man whose hand dealt the blow, produce the responsible superior who planned, ordered, permitted or acquiesced in this act, and you have brought a criminal to the bar of justice." Webb huffily dismissed the argument, with its obvious accusation of President Truman.

In his first statement to the bench, on May 14, Associate Prosecutor Hsiang spoke passionately in response to the defense about the wrongs done to China. After killing thousands and thousands of Chinese people in 1937, "Japan sent her soldiers all over China killing millions and millions of soldiers as well as children, women, and helpless civilians—noncombatants. If that were not war, what is a war—what is a war, I wonder?"[39]

Defense counsel objected that Hsiang was indulging in rhetoric, but Webb protected him, saying, "I have not noticed that Judge Hsiang has exceeded that direction." Yet when Hsiang began to extol China's battle against communists as a "war of resistance," Webb cut short his digression, which veered too close to the current civil war.[40]

On May 31 Lieutenant Colonel Thompson submitted his final report on his interviews with Ishii and his scientists to G-2 and General Waitt. Thompson suspected that Ishii's scientists were still hiding technical documents and clinical samples derived from the autopsies of human "patients" and that, with further persuasion, they might yield them.[41] General Willoughby agreed the investigation should continue.

So, too, did General Waitt at CWS in Washington. Hiroshima had seriously challenged the future of chemical warfare operations by outclassing them, and Waitt sought innovations that might be competitive. Advanced chemical weapons, he believed, could match the strategic capability of an atom bomb. The UK Chemical Defence Advisory Board had already pondered the future of chemical weapons and settled on nerve gases (lethal, easily disseminated, and odorless) as its advantage in the new nuclear age.[42] With claims that chemicals (along with biologicals) were "weapons of mass destruction," Waitt foresaw similar possibilities for the CWS program, provided it had unrestrained latitude for first use. According to the US Army's *Rules of Land Warfare*, the United States, not having ratified the Geneva Protocol of 1925, was not prohibited from the use of "toxic or nontoxic gases, or the use of smoke or incendiary materials," but President Truman had continued the Roosevelt policy of "retaliation only."[43] What Waitt sought was complete permission to attack the enemy first, based on his belief that massive enemy aggression was nearly inevitable.

If Japan were to be prosecuted for chemical warfare, as Waitt knew through G-2 that Colonel Morrow was proposing, the publicity could cause a reprise of World War I revulsion against noxious gases. It could emerge that the Japanese military had used chemical weapons against Chinese civilians, for example, to flush them out of hiding places or lay siege to resistant villages, which would link the US chemical program to another barbarity. The revelation that Japanese munitions contained hydrocyanic acid, the killing agent in Zyklon-B used to exterminate Jews in Nazi concentration camps, could only arouse more antipathy.

If China's chemical warfare charges went forward, the entire, dark history of Japan's CW munitions industry could also emerge, to the detriment of Waitt's plans to increase US production and include nerve agents. During 1940–1942, the peak years of Japanese chemical weapons production, six thousand workers at the factory at Okunoshima—known as "The Island of Great Hardships"—were required to produce some 1,200 tons of toxic gases annually as fill for 7.5 million weapons. Workers chronically suffered from leaks of gases that caused debilitating skin and bronchial diseases and death. Starting in the late 1930s, Japan's high command authorized the creation of massive arsenals of grenades, mortar shells, and heavy artillery shells for shipment to Manchukuo, a mobilization that had to have had the approval of the high command, perhaps even the emperor.[44] Under the Kwantung Army in Manchukuo, Unit 516 was based in Qiqihar expressly for testing these chemical weapons on Chinese and Manchu captives. A corollary to Unit 731, Unit 516 at times cooperated with it in joint experiments, such as measuring the effects of phosgene gas on humans and conducting on-site autopsies at testing grounds to learn about reactions in the nervous system.[45]

In mid-May, volume 1 of the CWS report on Japanese chemical warfare was issued, with Lieutenant Colonel Beebe as coauthor.[46] Volumes 2–6 had already been completed, making this one a culminating statement. Apparently intended for broad distribution, the report was a whitewash. It took at face value the denial of Japanese officers that lethal chemicals had ever been used and presented a redacted summary of forty-seven battle attacks in China from Japanese sources that referred only to the use of "special smoke"—as if Japanese mustard gas, lewisite, phosgene, and prussic acid had never been shipped for use in China.

In line with this report and G-2's agenda to mask Japanese chemical warfare, the Chinese Division's chemical warfare charges against Japan were soon deleted from the IPS case argument. With intervention from CWS and G-2, the May 13 "All China Military Aggression" draft that laid out those charges—and had been praised by Eugene Williams—was transformed into a May 24 version that removed them. All the "best evidence" that Morrow had assembled—the promised eyewitness testimony, hydrocyanic acid analyses, diaries, photographs, and victim counts—was eliminated, leaving only a vague reference to Japan's use of "poison gas."

The revised May 24 brief cautioned that some facts about Japanese chemical warfare could be "referred to and briefly used in evidence but not over-emphasized." Inserting phrases taken from Colonel Beebe's interviews with Tojo and Hata, it backed off from any reference to the Geneva Protocol:

> It does appear that 1) gas was used only in emergencies and for the most part tear, sneezing, and vomiting gas was used and not the vesicants, 2) the amount of casualties inflicted on the Chinese as evidenced from their statistics was a very small proportion of the total casualties suffered by the Chinese during the war, which is well over 3,800,000 according to their own records, and 3) in their interrogations Generals Hata and Tojo refer to the fact that in the United States we have used poisonous gases such as sneezing, vomiting and tear gasses in labor disputes and General Tojo in his interrogation about gas, raises the

question, "How about the atomic bomb?" which he claims is a much more outrageous weapon of warfare than poisonous gas.[47]

As Tojo warned, prosecuting Japan's use of chemical weapons could reignite defense accusations about Hiroshima and Nagasaki—just when SCAP was keeping those catastrophes secret from the Japanese public. Also in his interview, Tojo had stated that the emperor would have had to give consent to chemical warfare, a line of inquiry that SCAP would be most reluctant to encourage.

The May 24 case outline also distanced the prosecution from China's initial complaint to the League of Nations about Japanese chemical warfare in 1937: "The reference to the use of poison gas in this warfare appears to have been made in the form of a complaint by the Chinese to the effect that the Japanese army used gas in Shanghai three and four October 1937, but which the Japanese emphatically deny. We do not intend to offer this in evidence but merely invite the committee's attention."[48]

The CWS in Tokyo promised to provide IPS with its new report on Japanese chemical weapons (the whitewashed volume) and excerpts from documents provided by a Chinese military office on gas warfare defense—information that would validate the argument that the Japanese Army had used only tear gas and other nonlethal agents.[49]

On June 1 a top secret cable arrived from the office of the War Department Chief of Staff (General Dwight Eisenhower), or WARCOS, in Washington, addressed to Keenan, with copies to General MacArthur, his chief of staff, and G-2. It asked whether IPS had considered US Army rules of land warfare that protected its right to use chemical weapons, with deference to the Geneva Protocol but without strict adherence to it. "Your views are requested," the message stated, "whether prosecution of that sect[ion] will reverse US position."[50] No reply was asked for, since the question answered itself. IPS prosecution of the Japanese for the first use of chemical weapons, with the court's defining it a war crime, could limit the army's latitude for the same option.

Under US influence, China's charges of chemical warfare against Japan disappeared from IPS case arguments, although in appendix D of the indictment, in reference to the Hague Conventions and the Treaty of Versailles, it was tersely noted that "In the wars against China, poison gas was used. This allegation is confined to that country." With its accusations of Japanese chemical warfare reduced to a "complaint" and its germ weapons charges without proof, the Chinese Division pursued prosecution for the more flagrant Japanese crimes resulting from "aggressive war" and "crimes against peace." The enormity of their 3.8 million "total casualties" would carry their arguments, not Japan's disregard of arms control treaties.

During this intrusion of the CWS in Tokyo (which answered to G-2) into the domain of the prosecution and the arrival of the message from WARCOS, Chief of Counsel Keenan was at the Fujiya ("Fuji View") Hotel, two hours by car west of Tokyo, on Lake Kawaguchi. On May 20 he had left with Captain James Robinson and two other IPS lawyers to concentrate on composing his opening speech at the trial, scheduled for June 5.[51] He returned to Tokyo just in time to receive an order from General Willoughby that represented a much more serious G-2 invasion of the IPS than the May 24 case revision did.

That spring, General Willoughby, having consolidated his power as head of G-2, had created a Central Interrogation Center under his direct control and meant specifically "to regulate interrogations of Japanese and foreign nationals in Japan, in accordance with existing War Department Policies."[52] On June 4, 1946, Keenan sent a memo to his staff informing them of a stringent new requirement: "Hereafter no interrogations of Japanese or other enemy aliens will be performed in Japan by agencies of any country, except by prior authority of and under the direct supervision of the Assistant Chief of Staff [Willoughby], G-2, General Headquarters."[53]

From then on, the IPS had to make its requests for interrogations in writing and await permission from a G-2 officer. The requests would go first for clearance to Roy Morgan at the Investigation Division and be passed to G-2 to await approval and any necessary arrangement for an appointment. As Keenan informed his staff, "American intelligence officers and interpreters will be present to assist in all authorized interrogations."[54] Most prosecution interviews with the Japanese and "enemy aliens" had been conducted in the previous six months; Willoughby's new rule ensured that military intelligence could control or block new inquiries by any division, for example, the Soviet Union's (the focus of G-2's interest), but also any American or Chinese initiative that appeared to threaten US national security. For General Ishii and his network of scientists in Japan, the G-2 regulation enhanced their protection against any open inquiry.

Sutton Returns to China

During the revision of China's military aggression brief by Morrow, Nelson Sutton was highly distracted. On May 23 Keenan had instructed him to return to China and collect witnesses for the trial. A week later, after checking their availability and clearing paperwork, he flew in an army C-47 plane to Shanghai, where he just missed seeing Henry Chiu and Jack Crowley, who were flying back to Tokyo after more information gathering in China.[55]

Sutton had ten days to round up the witnesses he had identified on his previous trip and possibly find new ones. Dr. Robert Pollitzer, Dr. Peter King, and the others related to the plague charges were no longer on his list, nor were any of the Chinese military Colonel Morrow had interviewed about Japanese chemical warfare. Sutton's guides for this trip were Captain Luke Lea, Jr., Keenan's military aide, and Lieutenant Douglas Waldorf, both original Keenan IPS attorneys, with assistance from Lieutenant Joe Alexander from the Investigation Division. At IPS, Captain Lea had made a name for himself as a problem solver, while Waldorf from early days was an insider to SCAP intelligence on Japanese war crimes.

Now that the IMTFE had begun, Sutton found that doors opened easily for him. In Shanghai he began by seeking cooperation from the office of the Judge Advocate General of the US Forces in China, where it was suggested he contact Captain George Plotkin, now in charge of the Opium and Narcotics Investigation. Plotkin, whom he knew from his last trip, promised a new report on the Koa-in and the Japanese opium market.

Sutton went next to the director of China's Foreign Office, with a request that authorities in Nanjing expect his imminent arrival to secure witnesses. At the British Consulate he obtained permission for Harold Frank Gill, his Shanghai police expert on Japanese opium trafficking, to go to Tokyo. Sutton then conferred with J. Franklin Ray, Jr., the director of UNRRA in China, which employed George Fitch. Fitch, acting director of UNRRA's Henan Regional Office, was in remote Kaifeng beyond radio or telegraph contact; communication with him would take an estimated week to ten days. Sutton requested the US Army dispatch a plane to fetch him.

Albert A. "Pete" Dorrance, an old China hand and newly recommended witness, was working for UNRRA in Nanjing to set up a large shipment and warehouse operation. A former executive of the Standard Oil Company at Hankow (Hankou), in 1938 he had witnessed the Japanese slaughter of hundreds of Chinese after the city was defeated. Ray warned Sutton that neither Fitch nor Dorrance could be spared for more than two weeks. Sutton also telephoned Colonel David Barrett, General George Marshall's military attaché in Nanjing, to ask if he would be a witness at the trial. Barrett was willing, but the decision was up to the general. All these connections were made in three days, during which Sutton also managed to deliver letters to the wives of Judge Hsiang and Henry Chiu and take the two women to lunch at the Cathay Mansions Hotel, where he had stored his souvenirs from the previous trip.

On June 4 Sutton flew to Nanjing, where, although the temperature was in the 80s, he kept up the same vigorous pace. First he met with Dr. Wong Wen Hao, former minister of economics and now vice president of the Executive Yuan, the national governing council of which T. V. Soong, brother of Madame Chiang Kai-shek, was president. Sutton wanted to convince Wong to be a witness on Japanese economic aggression. Wong declined, citing pressure from his official duties, whereupon Sutton urged him to help find a suitable substitute. After a visit to the Chinese Foreign Office, Sutton went to the American Embassy to meet again with Colonel Barrett. Afterward, for the first time, he met Dr. Lewis Smythe, the sociologist from Nanjing University whose survey report had so impressed him.

The next day a US Army officer was dispatched by plane to Kaifeng to bring George Fitch to Nanjing. Sutton was simultaneously trying to enlist the help of the Chinese chief of staff, General Chen Cheng, in locating two witnesses on his list. Sutton then tried to convince the vice minister of national defense, General Ching Teh Tsun, to testify as a witness to the Marco Polo incident, but the general was unsure he could help.

On June 6, meeting Sutton at his hotel, George Fitch agreed to testify, with the understanding that Director Ray at UNRRA approved. James McCallum, although back in China, was away from Nanjing for another ten days; when he returned, Smythe would help him execute an official affidavit for use at the trial. After a meeting at the Chinese Foreign Affairs office "to secure a top man from China to testify on the subject of economic aggression," Sutton had a long meeting with the minister of justice and two officials from the Criminal Justice division. Arrangements were made with the ministry and the mayor of Nanjing for Sutton and Luke Lea to vet fifteen potential witnesses over the next three days.[56] One who made the cut was Wu Chang Teh, a 38-year-old former policeman who had been marched with hundreds of other men outside the city gates and narrowly avoided being executed along with them.[57]

Next, Sutton reunited with Miner Searle Bates and Smythe. When they explained that the university could not spare both to testify in Tokyo, Sutton chose the more authoritative Bates. Smythe instead submitted an affidavit outlining his experience as secretary of the Nanjing Safety Zone Committee and affirming the committee's regular submission of reports to the Japanese Embassy, with duplicates to the American Embassy—and the fact that the Japanese officials "at no time denied the accuracy of these reports."[58]

The highlight of Sutton's trip was an appointment in Nanjing with General George Marshall. As Sutton wrote in his trip notes, "I was privileged to have a delightful conference with him lasting more than an hour in the late afternoon of June 7." He described the general, dressed in civilian clothes and with a hole in his sock, as "approachable" and "friendly" but also "high minded." Marshall, much interested in the trial and how the Japanese public would react, would allow Colonel Barrett to travel immediately to Tokyo to testify but could not spare him for long. Sutton had caught Marshall, still attempting to mediate an end to China's civil war, in a rare moment of ease: a fifteen-day truce between Nationalist and Communist forces in northern China had just gone into effect.

On June 8 Sutton, Lea, and Waldorf flew from Nanjing to Shanghai with Bates, Fitch, Dorrance, Dr. Hsu Chuan-Ying, vice chair of the Red Swastika Society in Nanjing, and Wu Chang Teh, the policeman nearly killed in the massacre. In Shanghai, finding US Army billeting and meals for the American witnesses proved difficult. No such accommodations were available for the Chinese witnesses, who were lodged for three nights at the Shanghai Hotel, where Sutton paid out of pocket for their meals and rooms. To circumvent the red tape of Chinese travel restrictions, Lea appealed to an aide to General Marshall, who arranged special invitational orders for all in the group to proceed to Tokyo. Just in time, Captain Plotkin delivered to Sutton the promised report on the Japanese opium cabal. Mrs.

Hsiang and Mrs. Chiu gave him letters for their husbands and a package for Henry Chiu. On his final night, an elated Sutton celebrated with Lea, Waldorf, and Joe Alexander at a dinner at a popular Viennese restaurant.[59]

As the time for departure approached, the number of passengers on the flight to Tokyo grew. At the last minute General Ching, the vice minister of defense, was allowed to come, with an aide, which required sending the C-47 to Nanjing to pick them up. Peter Lawless, the Beijing policeman, had arrived in Shanghai to join the group. Along with Dr. Hsu Chuan-Ying, Hsu Chieh-Chen, the textile merchant interviewed by Sutton the previous March, was onboard. Another witness, Wang Len Chai, brought from Chongqing to testify about the 1937 Lukouchiao (Marco Polo Bridge) incident, was included, along with Shang Teh-Yi, who had survived as the Japanese machine-gunned captive Chinese on the banks of the Yangtze and later "climbed over corpses" to escape. So, too, was Captain Liang Ting-Fang, who had witnessed the slaughter of captured Chinese civilians. In addition, Captain Lea was asked to escort a prisoner, Admiral Sakonji Seizo, a former minister of state, to Tokyo. Known as a peace advocate who had urged Japan's early acceptance of the Potsdam Declaration, Sakonji was wanted by the British but would not be prosecuted. With the plane overbooked, Waldorf and Alexander were left behind to take a later flight.

Crowded into the plane, Sutton, Lea, the fifteen witnesses and Admiral Sakonji left Shanghai's Kiangwan Airport at 10:15 a.m. on June 12. To add to the excitement, as they flew, the plane passed within twenty miles of a volcano erupting over Japan, which did not stop Sutton from double-checking that each witness candidate had signed the required "acceptance of service."[60] The flight arrived at Atsugi Airfield at 4:20 p.m., after which the witnesses were driven to their housing in the city and Sutton went back to the Hotel Koronada, still exhilerated. At every step, the US Army had come through for him and for the IPS.

Sutton, had he been less modest, might have expected some public fanfare for all his labor. Chief of Counsel Keenan, though, had already claimed credit, announcing to the press that his research in China had produced key witnesses to the Nanjing Massacre and Japan's aggression in Manchuria, who were being flown in to testify at the tribunal.[61]

Sutton's trip to China caused him to miss Keenan's June 5 opening statement at the IMTFE. The chief prosecutor's rambling, five-hour speech was derided by critics in the press, in contrast to the praise that had been heaped on Justice Jackson's proclamation at Nuremberg.

Following Keenan's speech, the defense posed its objections, which went directly to the legitimacy of the court, starting with the appointment of Webb, who had led Australia's prosecutions of Japanese war criminals. Webb stepped aside to let the other judges decide the question in chambers; they concluded that the court had to respect MacArthur's authority in approving judges. (Later Filipino judge Delfin Jaranilla, a survivor of the Bataan Death March, would face a similar objection with the same outcome.) The defense then protested the inaccuracies of the Japanese-English translations, citing them as full of ambiguities and mistakes. No one doubted the language problem; over a hundred translators would eventually be working for the Language Section. Nonetheless, the trial moved on to the prosecution phase.

The Prosecution Struggles

Meanwhile Sutton awaited the arrival of two key witnesses, Dr. Robert Wilson and the Reverend Magee, whose testimony on Nanjing would be integrated into the general statement of the prosecution's case, after which Prosecutor Hsiang would follow with his opening presentation of the China brief. After Hsiang, more of Sutton's witnesses would take the stand, and documents from the China Division investigation, including affidavits, would be submitted as evidence and read into the court record.

On June 9, forbidding any public announcement, Chief of Counsel Keenan departed for Washington to his office at the War Crimes Branch (Civil Division) of the War Department. The Associated Press, though, learned he had suddenly left. Unaware, SCAP's Public Relations Office was about to repudiate the story when Frank Tavenner, alerted to the problem, advised the office to simply tell the truth and then, with his usual courtesy, he wrote an apology to Keenan for intervening.[62] Most of the IPS attorneys, including committee heads, learned only from the newspapers that Keenan would be absent for a month on a mission to obtain evidence—or, as one article insinuated, to "rest" at Saratoga Springs, the famous New York gambling resort.[63]

In Keenan's absence, on June 13 Brigadier Henry Nolan of Canada began the outline of the prosecution case, a ponderous four-and-a-half-hour discourse, with maps, that reached far back in Japanese history, starting with 660 B.C. The weather had turned hot, and in the stifling courtroom, defendants, spectators, and even President Webb dozed off.[64] Without simultaneous translation, the tempo of oral communication was slow, determined by a red light that flashed whenever the translators (including for the Soviet judge) needed a speaker to pause. Just after three o'clock, when Nolan briefly described the Japanese chemical warfare program, no one seemed to notice.

Despite Eugene Williams's urgings that prosecutors organize their evidence early, Nelson Sutton and Henry Hauxhurst were still shaping the case for Japan's economic exploitation of China. And, despite the Executive Committee rule to limit witnesses, on June 25 Sutton asked that four additional Chinese (three bankers and a power company executive) be summoned from Shanghai to testify. Permission was granted. Sutton then was permitted to add a prominent Chinese metallurgist who had been the director of the North China Iron and Steel Administration. Sutton's expectation was that his witnesses for Nanjing would be on the stand before July 5 and those testifying to Japan's economic exploitation of China soon after.

Distracted by administrative duties, Carlisle Higgins, the acting chief of counsel in Keenan's absence, turned to Frank Tavenner to help mobilize the IPS divisions, whose submissions of briefs were running late, no matter how many memos Williams issued on the importance of deadlines. Tavenner immediately put the IPS attorneys on notice that daily office hours would be lengthened, that they would have to work Sundays, and that all leaves were canceled. His next demand was to have the prosecutors and their assistants write the dossiers for the top Class A "aggressive war" defendants, which remained incomplete. Then, setting a July 26 deadline, he urged all the IPS divisions to file their affidavits and their opening statements with the Language Division as soon as possible so that translations into Japanese could begin.

After four months under Keenan's erratic authority and now with his prolonged departure, the discontent of the Anglo prosecutors reached a boiling point. The New Zealand associate prosecutor, Brigadier Ronald

Quilliam, in messages to his secretary of internal affairs, listed his frustrations with IPS: ambitious and lazy American attorneys were assigned to help him, the essential Allied military witnesses had been demobilized and gone home, valuable evidence had been shipped to the United States, and from the start the IPS failed to institute standards for interrogation. All these were due, Quilliam believed, to "the fundamental error" of appointing Keenan.[65] Most infuriating, as others agreed, was the series of press conferences Keenan had given in Hawaii on his way back to Washington. In them he represented himself as the court's authority—disparaging Webb and the IPS prosecutors.

On June 20, prompted by the Anglo contingent, Carlisle Higgins held a meeting of the associate prosecutors, at which it was decided, with the Philippines prosecutor Lopez dissenting, that Keenan should be given notice of their complaints and required to "refrain from making any statements to the Press in the future." Such a demand was futile, given Keenan's position and his well-known appetite for publicity. For Quilliam and Canada's prosecutor, Brigadier Nolan, the problem ran deeper; they questioned Keenan's competence and whether he should return from Washington at all. Quilliam cited his lax direction of IPS and his "condition of health," a veiled reference to his rumored drinking problem. Britain's Arthur Comyns Carr apparently shared this assessment, but he was reluctant to provoke Keenan. Quilliam and Nolan's further discussions with Higgins confirmed their suspicions about Keenan's alcoholism: "We learnt that Mr Keenan has for some years been addicted to drink, but that for twelve months prior to his appointment as Chief of Counsel he had totally abstained. However, from the middle of December last [1945], a few days after his arrival in Tokyo, he had been drinking to excess habitually."[66] As Quilliam reported, perhaps with exaggeration, Higgins, Eugene Williams, and Frank Tavenner agreed that Keenan should resign.

Other calamities were disrupting the IMTFE. Eighteen American lawyers had recently joined the original six defense lawyers at the International Defense Section. Failing to reach agreement on a common approach, eight of them, including lead counsel Captain Beverley Coleman, resigned. On June 27 defendant Matsuoka, once Japan's representative to the League of Nations and its close contact with Hitler and Mussolini, died at age 66 of tuberculosis at Tokyo Imperial University Hospital. The brief on his interrogation that had been readied as part of count 5 (the Axis conspiracy charge) was now useless.[67] The current Japanese premier sent a wreath to Matsuoka's funeral and other prominent government officials paid their respects, to the consternation of IPS attorneys.

The Chinese Division, scheduled to present its case first, remained under intense pressure. On June 29 Williams circulated an agenda of deadlines for each phase of the China case, stipulating that it would start in three days, on July 2, with military aggression, then proceed to atrocities and economic oppression and be finished by August 31. Yet the more than fifty documents Sutton and Morrow brought back from China, plus other material, had not yet been listed for Williams; some were still awaiting translation. In addition, the Chinese Division and the Language Section were struggling with a serious translation problem regarding the testimony of Chinese witnesses not fluent in either English or Japanese.[68]

As the summer became increasingly hot and humid, the klieg lights necessary for filming the trial were turning the Ichigaya courtroom into an oven and bringing some defendants and even judges to what looked like near collapse. On July 15 President Webb adjourned the court early to allow for air conditioning repairs, and it remained in recess for more than a week.[69]

With the delays, Sutton's witnesses grew restive. To begin, Colonel Barrett was soon needed by General Marshall in Nanjing; a few days after Sutton's visit, Marshall had received two nearly simultaneous messages, one from General Zhou Enlai, negotiator for the Communists, the other from General Hsu Yungchang, negotiator for the KMT. Each accused the other side of having broken the truce in China with unprovoked attacks.[70] A new US ambassador, John Leighton Stuart, a Presbyterian missionary who had been president of Yenching University in Beijing, had just arrived to help with mediation.[71] Barrett was allowed to submit his written testimony about the 1937 Marco Polo Bridge incident and return to Nanjing.[72]

Some of Sutton's witnesses, like Dr. Wilson, wanted the same option to sign affidavits rather than wait to testify. Sutton urged patience but failed to caution them about making public statements, even to officials. While waiting to testify, his prize American witnesses were interviewed by an officer of SCAP's Public Relations Section, who then forwarded their statements to the press. Banner-headline stories quoting the eyewitnesses to the

Nanjing atrocities quickly appeared. GHQ was infuriated and Carlisle Higgins, who saw the breach as nothing less than contempt of court, warned against any future communication with the press not directly authorized by GHQ.[73] On July 19 Tavenner assured Sutton that the Nanjing presentation could start in three days; instead, as the witnesses fretted and Tokyo broiled, it became six days. Prosecutor Alan Mansfield's goal of a "swift and simple trial" was fast becoming an illusion.

8
THE ATROCITIES

ON THE EVENING OF JULY 14, 1946, IN HIS SIXTH-FLOOR DAI-ICHI OFFICE, General MacArthur met with Special Assistant Eugene Williams of IPS and two prosecutors, Britain's Arthur Comyns Carr and Australia's Alan Mansfield.[1] They were there to talk about two crises involving Chief of Counsel Joseph Keenan, absent in Washington. The tribunal's US justice, John P. Higgins from the Superior Court of Massachusetts, had discovered cables full of scathing criticisms that Keenan had sent to colleagues in Washington. Already discontented with the workings of the court, Judge Higgins was determined to resign. After just two months in Tokyo and only five days in the courtroom, he decided that the judges were mediocre—except for President Webb—and the defense attorneys too disadvantaged to protect their clients. (Surreptitiously, Higgins had paid them a parting visit to wish them good luck.) Not even personal entreaties from MacArthur or the judge's mentor, Speaker John McCormack of the US House of Representatives, could convince Higgins to stay at the IMTFE. Writing to his wife, he reserved his sharpest criticism for Keenan: the "inability to organize and lack of tact on his part are the chief reasons for the failure of the presentation of the case."[2]

Higgins officially quit the bench on July 13, with a cover story given the press about his being needed back in Massachusetts: his replacement at the state court had suddenly died, and the acting chief justice was too elderly and frail to maintain the post for the two years that Higgins predicted the IMTFE would take. To replace him, President Truman quickly nominated Major General Myron C. Cramer, the US Army judge advocate general who had assisted Secretary of War Henry Stimson in formulating the standards for Nuremberg. The defense strongly objected to the substitution of Cramer. At the IPS, the Australian, Canadian, New Zealand, and Dutch prosecutors also protested the appointment of a new judge who had missed nearly two months of proceedings. Mansfield was set to resign over the controversy. Comyns Carr, along with the Chinese, French, and Soviet attorneys, could not conceive of a bench without an American judge. Williams remained neutral.

MacArthur's meeting on July 14 with the three lawyers lasted an hour and fifteen minutes and, unbothered by the lack of air conditioning at the Dai-Ichi Building, the general spoke for nearly the entire time. He told the three attorneys that he was obliged to approve the US nomination of Cramer, just as he had those of other governments. This appointment, he said, had the strong backing of President Webb, which surprised Mansfield, who then changed his mind about resigning from IPS.

The other problem was Keenan's behavior, about which MacArthur spoke plainly. He knew Keenan was "a drunkard" but praised the work he believed the chief of counsel had done in securing coordination among the representatives of eleven different countries. The assertion must have shocked his listeners, who had done most of the work to mobilize the IPS. The bottom line, as MacArthur saw it, was that since Keenan was the nominee of the US government, he could not interfere. The IPS staff would have to live with him.

In Washington, far from the upheaval caused by the departure of Judge Higgins, on July 18, 1946, the State-War-Navy Coordinating Committee issued Directive 216/3, regarding the "coordinated exploitation of Japanese intelligence targets of interdepartmental and international concern."[3] With the approval of the Joint Chiefs, a military commander could protect intelligence information that might jeopardize US foreign relations, which was tantamount to allowing "information of value" to justify political cover. In the same time frame, the JCS wired a message to SCAP ordering restricted Allied access to intelligence or other sources affecting "U.S. advantages in the field of scientific research and development."[4] Limited sharing would be allowed the United Kingdom (excluding Eire) and the Commonwealth nations, but Washington wanted the Soviet Union, France, the Netherlands, and China excluded. In Tokyo, General Willoughby was already committed to keeping a close watch on Japanese scientific information, especially concerning germ weapons.

The Prosecution Proceeds: The Chinese Case

On July 22, its recess over, the IMTFE was scheduled to continue the prosecution's aggressive war charges, centered on Japan's initiation of war with China in 1937.

That same day marked Judge Cramer's first appearance on the bench and, as predicted, the defense disputed General MacArthur's authority to approve a replacement. Its argument was that since the charter allowed him to appoint only eleven tribunal judges, he had already met his quota. As President Webb pointed out, a precedent had been set when Judge Henri Bernard was appointed to replace the original French candidate, which the defense had not protested. Still the defense complained that Bernard had not missed weeks of court presentations and arguments, and the point was made that Cramer had a bias: his son-in-law had been a civilian prisoner in one of the Japanese POW camps. To complicate matters, two defense lawyers informed the court their clients had no objections to Cramer. While Cramer absented himself, the other judges retired to vote in chambers and, by a majority decision, declared him "eligible to sit as a member of the Tribunal." Perhaps in unintended symbolism of their nations' postwar antagonisms, Cramer and the Soviet Union's I. M. Zaryanov were the only two judges who wore military uniforms on the bench.

Finally allowed to sound the opening salvo for the Chinese Division, Colonel Thomas Morrow called the first witness, General Ching Teh Tsun, China's vice minister for national defense, who had been deputy commander of its 29th Army in 1937. General Ching, in June escorted to Tokyo by Nelson Sutton, had submitted a sworn statement that directly implicated two defendants, General Dohihara Kenji and General Matsui Iwane, in the

Marco Polo Bridge incident of 1937. President Webb soon halted Ching's testimony when it became obvious that the witness's every sentence was being translated from Chinese into Japanese and then into English and that Morrow's questions of him were also being done in relay, from English to Japanese to Chinese. This cumbersome method, the best that the Language Section could arrange, infuriated Webb. Judge Mei Ju-ao's secretary temporarily filled in while the Language Section rushed to find Chinese-English translators.

On the morning of July 25, Chief of Counsel Keenan was back from Washington, where he had visited with President Truman. Made aware of the discontent at IPS that had percolated up to MacArthur, he blamed his assistant Carlisle Higgins for playing a part, although Higgins protested he had been merely a "witness" to the controversy.[5] The next day in court, without consulting any IPS staff, Keenan took to the podium to request a change in the rule for submitting affidavits, a matter on which Alan Mansfield, as head of the Evidence Committee, was preparing a formal motion.[6] Keenan's jumping the gun, which proved unsuccessful, smacked of spite toward Mansfield and so infuriated Eugene Williams that, as he reportedly confided to Higgins and Frank Tavenner, he was prepared to resign. Yet the British, Chinese, and Philippine prosecutors were firmly on Keenan's side, and the Soviet, Dutch, French, and Indian attorneys diplomatically distanced themselves from the Australian and New Zealand dissenters, while Canada's Brigadier Henry Nolan retreated to neutral ground. In court, defense counsel was actively objecting to the prosecution's language and tactics, fraying Webb's already short temper. With little stomach for atrocities, Webb went so far as to reprimand the much respected Colonel Morrow for "inflammatory" descriptions of the Japanese treatment of POWs.

In the midst of these disruptions, after Williams told Webb in chambers that the Nanjing witnesses were liable to quit Tokyo, Sutton was finally able to shepherd his Nanjing witnesses to the courtroom. Starting on July 25, he had a goal of presenting eight witnesses in five days, and in this he succeeded. His April report of China's Class C charges had laid out the case evidence; his job was to make sure it was heard in its entirety, despite defense objections and a cantankerous court president. The Nanjing surgeon Robert O. Wilson, who had traveled from California, was called to the stand first. He told the court how, after the city fell, his hospital was for the next six weeks "full to overflowing" with wounded Chinese soldiers and civilians and with women who were victims of rape. Next, Dr. Hsu Chuan-Ying from the Red Swastika spoke in halting but adequate English about the impossibility of burying the hundreds of decaying bodies individually—or of untying the bound hands of the dead so that they might be "unloosed" in their graves, following Chinese custom, a detail that unnerved Webb. Testimony from the Chinese victims followed, with their stories of nearly being killed by machine guns or bayonets, of mass slaughter and women raped—matching the many affidavits submitted to the court that exemplified the "Japanese pattern of war."

Next came the testimony of Miner Searle Bates, which surpassed even Sutton's high expectations. Guided by Sutton, the slim, bespectacled Bates gave a lucid overview of the Japanese invasion, from the killing and rapes that took place at his next-door neighbors' home to the wholesale slaughter of Chinese men lured into believing they were being hired as laborers and on to the rape of dozens of women in dormitories at his own university. When Bates remarked that his campus was right next to the Japanese Embassy, journalist Arnold Brackman, covering the trial, noted that "a suppressed gasp went up among spectators and others. . . . Not only had the Japanese high command in Nanking been aware of the deplorable situation, but so had Japanese officials in the embassy."[7]

Although intensely cross-examined by defense lawyer William Logan, Bates kept his composure. Logan (who represented Marquis Kido, advisor to the emperor) pressed him on whether his reports to the Japanese Embassy had been forwarded to Tokyo.[8] When Bates said that he himself had not seen those messages, Logan seemed to have scored an important point, namely, that Japan's high government leaders had been ignorant of the atrocities. But Bates added that, thanks to records from the US Embassy in Nanjing (those obtained by Sutton), he had recently been enlightened by important communications from 1938. In them, Joseph Grew, then US ambassador in Tokyo, wrote that he had learned about the atrocity reports from the Japanese Foreign Ministry and that he had discussed them with Baron Hirota, the foreign minister, who now sat at rigid attention in the dock. In addition to Grew's cables, the embassy records included dozens of reports filed by the International Safety Zone Committee and private individuals like Bates and Minnie Vautrin—all entered into evidence by Sutton.

According to the press, General Matsui's eyes were riveted on Bates as he testified about Nanjing and identified Matsui as the Japanese commander during the massacre.[9] Thanks to Sutton, the text of Matsui's interrogation at Sugamo the previous March, in which he denied knowledge of his soldiers' crimes, had been entered in evidence. Bates's testimony demolished his claim. Worse for Matsui was the June 20, 1946, affidavit of a Japanese consular official, Okazaki Katsuo, which Sutton had also included in his Class C war crimes brief. In Nanjing at the time of its conquest in December 1937, Okazaki had met frequently with General Matsui about the ongoing chaos caused by the troops and had shown him the reports sent by the Safety Zone Committee to the Japanese Embassy, which were forwarded to the Foreign Ministry in Tokyo. According to Okazaki, Matsui took responsibility for the massacre, saying that there were "no excuses to be made."[10]

Finally on July 29 Sutton called to the stand Mr. Hsu, the 33-year-old textile merchant from Shanghai he had interviewed at the start of his China investigation in March. Sutton began by asking Hsu to assure the court that he understood the content of his affidavit and had signed it. In his haste Sutton forgot to show the document to Hsu and had to be reminded to do so by Webb. Hsu repeated what was in his affidavit, that he had been taken captive with others near the Burma-Yunnan highway, and that, by feigning death, he had narrowly escaped Japanese slaughter by machine gun fire, although he had been bayonetted in the back. When Sutton asked the witness to remove his shirt to show the scar, defense counsel William Logan objected and President Webb, visibly put off, agreed that showing wounds was unnecessary. The defense declined to cross-exam the witness.

At this high point for IPS, Chief of Counsel Keenan wrote a letter to President Truman that "Our trials are proceeding now at a very satisfactory pace and we expect that the prosecution will conclude its case sometime in the month of September."[11]

The Chinese case presentation, though, faced a serious disruption, from the Soviet Division. On August 2 Associate Prosecutor Sergei Golunsky told Roy Morgan that his government would soon allow Henry Pu Yi, the last of the Manchu emperors of China, to testify at the IMTFE about his puppet governance of Manchukuo.[12] Months before, Golunsky seemed not to know Pu Yi's whereabouts, but a long affidavit provided by the Soviet Division showed that the previous June, on Golunsky's order, the former "emperor of Manchukuo" (as he had been declared by the Japanese) had been interrogated in the Siberian city of Khabarovsk.[13] The prosecution expected that Pu Yi would add to the case for Japanese military expansionism, although there was a question as to whether, as a Soviet captive, he could speak freely.

With the date of Pu Yi's arrival uncertain, the Chinese Division pursued its case with witness testimony on Class C war crimes, which was reported internationally. Captain Liang Ting-Fang testified about the wholesale killing of Chinese men, tied five in a group, shot, and thrown into the Yangtze River. A. A. "Pete" Dorrance, the Standard Oil executive living in Hankou in 1938, told of how, from the bridge of an American gunboat, he saw the Japanese execution of hundreds of Chinese. "It was an extremely impersonal action," he recalled. The Japanese soldiers "would indifferently kick the Chinese into the river and shoot them when their heads came up."[14] Dorrance, head of Hankou's American Chamber of Commerce and active on relief and policing committees, added credible details about the numerous bodies of Chinese, their hands bound, piled in the streets after the Japanese stormed the city.

On August 15 Associate Prosecutor Hsiang gave his opening statement. In it, he emphasized China's case for crimes against humanity. Since Henry Pu Yi was scheduled to appear in court the next day, Hsiang delayed fully arguing the charge for opium enslavement. As a preliminary, he spoke of the three international treaties signed by Japan to suppress opium that had been entered into evidence. The Chinese case for Japan's systemic drug assault on its society pointed most directly at Prince Konoe, who had committed suicide the previous December, but it also incriminated key cabinet members. In 1938, Konoe had created the Koa-in (Asian Affairs Board); its four vice presidents (the ministers of war, the navy, finance, and foreign affairs) organized the production and distribution of opium and reaped enormous profits from its sales. A half dozen of those one-time officials were seated in the dock.

That afternoon, Prosecutor Hsiang also deferred to the testimony of Reverend John G. Magee, the missionary who had waited weeks to testify about the Nanjing Massacre. While on the stand, Magee looked down to check his notes and inadvertently caused a furor. All written material had to be made accessible to the court, the defense objected, or how would it know the witness's sources? President Webb concurred. Continuing without his notes, Magee offered a unique perspective on Nanjing during the massacre. Soon after the invasion, he had been asked by a vice consul from the Japanese Embassy to help identify foreign properties in the city, in order to post notices to protect them from the Japanese Army. Traveling around the city by car, at one point they were blocked from taking a shortcut by bodies piled in an alley. Along another street they came across stacks of 300 to 500 bodies that had been set on fire. The main boulevard leading to the railway station, he added, was littered with bodies. That December, Magee testified, he took motion picture films of sixty men being marched away by the Japanese while women, on their knees, pleaded for their lives. This testimony alone caused a hush in the courtroom, and more like it would come later.

In the meanwhile, the appearance of Henry Pu Yi before the IMTFE gave the world the spectacle of yet another Asian emperor fallen from power. In 1935 Emperor Hirohito had entertained Pu Yi at the Imperial Palace, a well-publicized visit that many Japanese remembered. Pu Yi's arrival in Tokyo revived unfounded rumors that Hirohito would be called to testify in court about their relationship. Serendipitously, Pu Yi's projected appearance coincided with a US Army production of Gilbert and Sullivan's satire *The Mikado* at the Ernie Pyle Theater.[15] Until this time, the musical had been banned in Japan. Now Japanese officials cooperated by supplying authentic Meiji-era costumes and Japanese women sang in the chorus. Members of the imperial family even took in one performance, seated discreetly in the balcony. To audiences of mostly US soldiers unfamiliar with ideas of monarchy, the six-foot-tall American playing the emperor of Japan sang, "My object all sublime, I shall achieve in time, to make the punishment fit the crime, the punishment fit the crime."

For a week (from August 16 to 23) Pu Yi gave an elaborate account of his fourteen years as head of Manchukuo, one that denied any collaboration with Japanese authorities. The prosecution, which had called him as a witness, began to wonder about his credibility as a prisoner of the Soviet Union who might be relinquished to the Chinese government and put on trial. The IPS had in hand a translation of the April 1, 1938, "Regent's Ordinance," signed by Pu Yi, that outlined the full dimensions of his authority, which included running the government, overseeing the budget, and declaring war.[16] Years later, in his autobiography, Pu Yi regretted his testimony. "My difficulty was," he wrote, "that I was in constant fear of eventual punishment in China for what I might say."[17]

The Soviets returned Pu Yi to Siberia, with their ability to produce a trial-worthy witness in doubt. The Chinese case continued, but it was hampered by the slow processing of documents. It was already mid-August when Sutton finally gave Eugene Williams a list of evidence documents regarding Japanese atrocities in China—seventy-three items, nearly all witness affidavits, plus a dozen documents from the Procurator's Office, the Red Swastika Society, and American Embassy records.[18] The consecutive translation of witness testimony so slowed down court proceedings that the IPS decided to increase the reading of already translated and distributed documents into evidence. To that end, Sutton started editing the texts as he waited for lulls in the proceedings to take to the podium.

On August 29 his chance came, and Sutton began by reading selections from the affidavit of Lewis Smythe, the University of Nanjing sociologist. Immediately Logan from the defense objected, on the grounds that he wanted Smythe to appear in court as a witness who could be cross-examined. President Webb overruled the objection; Smythe, he said, was one of many testifying to the same alleged events and, unless the defense wanted the trial to "go on for years," written statements in this instance had to be acceptable.

Following Smythe's affidavit, Sutton moved on to the eyewitness account of George Fitch, who had signed a personal statement and returned to the United States. After the gruesome details provided by Fitch, Sutton read the affidavit of Mrs. Shui Fang Tsen about the widespread rapes at Ginling College. He continued by reading the portion of the diary of John McCallum that proclaimed, "Never have I heard or read of such brutality. Rape! Rape! Rape!—we estimate at least 1,000 cases a night and more by day."[19]

Sutton then entered into evidence a barrage of other incriminating documents: thirteen statements from Chinese eyewitnesses and victims, excerpts from the Safety Zone Committee reports, charts of the burial places of victims, and the Nanjing procurator's estimate that at least 260,000 people had been killed in about seven weeks.[20] His goal, which he achieved, was to overwhelm the defense with evidence of the atrocities.

After a break for lunch, Sutton presented translated material from IPS Document 1706, Exhibit 327, the "Summary Report on the Investigation of Japanese War crimes Committed in Nanjing, Prepared by the Procurator of the District Court." With the court's permission, Sutton began reading excerpts. The catalogue of destruction and degradation was dreadful. Still, Sutton read on: "A woman was killed for refusing intercourse. For amusement a father was forced to assault his daughter. In another case, a boy was forced to assault his sister. An old man was forced to assault his son's wife. Breasts were torn off, and women were stabbed in the bosoms. Chins were smashed, and teeth knocked out. Such hideous scenes are unbearable to watch."

To this, Sutton added graphic phrases from the report about widespread plunder and the burning of homes "too numerous to mention." At this point, President Webb, having had his fill of horrors, called for a fifteen-minute recess.

When the court resumed at 3 p.m., Sutton continued reading from the procurator's report, starting with a category called "Particulars Regarding Other Atrocities." A fragment of information had come in from the Nanjing procurator—just a sentence about the testing of poison serums at Unit 1644. Sutton decided to put it into the record: "The enemy's TAMA division carried off their civilian captives to the medical laboratory, where the reactions to poisonous serums were tested. This detachment was one of the most secret organizations. The number of persons slaughtered by this detachment cannot be ascertained." (He chose to omit the next three lines in Document 1706, which began with "The sacrifice of cats and dogs for experiments is unbearable for a human person, much less the use of fellow victims.")

Sutton then changed the subject to the procurator's updated estimates of the carnage in Nanjing: "The materials investigated up to this time discloses more than 300,000 persons killed, more than 4,000 houses burnt or destroyed, 20–30 persons raped or killed for refusing intercourse, and 184 persons missing. The rest of the material is still in the process of investigation." He was about to continue when President Webb asked him, "Are you going to give us any further evidence of these alleged laboratory tests for reactions to poisonous serums? That is something entirely new, we haven't heard before. Are you going to leave it at that?"

Knowing that he had nothing more at hand, Sutton answered, "We do not at this time anticipate introducing evidence on that subject." The statement by the unit deserter C. C. H. Hataba would stand alone until and unless the Nanjing procurator or another source came up with supporting evidence; should that happen, the Chinese Division could in theory add it under its Class C charges.

Two defense attorneys, Alfred Brooks and Michael Levin, had already protested the high numbers of murdered Nanjing victims the prosecution claimed. They now faulted Sutton with presuming that "a mere assertion unsupported by any evidence" should be taken seriously by the court. What if the "poisonous serums" were actually vaccinations? Webb agreed, saying that "the statement to which the defense objects, namely that there were tests with poisonous materials on Chinese, is rejected as evidence." Even so, Sutton had placed the charge on record, which the Nanjing officials must have intended by forwarding information consonant with Prosecutor Hsiang's original charge about the plague attacks of 1940 and 1941.

That day and the next, Sutton continued reading into evidence the details of the Nanjing Massacre. One was an account by a German Embassy official of twenty thousand women and children slaughtered, with the corpses dumped into ponds after the Japanese refused to allow their burial. Another was testimony from the US Embassy records, taken from a 1938 report by the US ambassador, Nelson T. Johnson, who described Japanese massacres of Chinese men whether they were ex-soldiers or not. When Sutton moved on to descriptions of looting, defense attorney William Logan rose to object that the court should be told that the Chinese did much of this looting themselves. Webb urged him to be patient and wait until it was time for the defense case. Sutton continued, laying the groundwork for China's Class B charges of economic destruction.

By late afternoon, when Sutton's presentation ended, the atmosphere in the courtroom was somber. The next day, his picture was featured in the Tokyo papers and the *Pacific Stars and Stripes* ran an AP story describing how, "for the second successive day, the prosecution attorney David Nelson Sutton read into the record stories of rape, murder, burning and looting which occurred as the Japanese swept into Nanking."

With Sutton's presentation, the court could not ignore the criminality of rape, but the recitation of those and other atrocities had been an ordeal for an upstanding Christian man who would prefer such crimes did not exist. His work was not finished. The Chinese Division case preparations were running two months behind the agenda Eugene Williams had circulated in early July. The chronic backlog of documents needing translation had created a "critical situation." Instead of respecting the listed order for processing, prosecutors were going directly to the IPS Language Division to skip the line. Frustrated, Williams circulated a warning that "the translation and document divisions have been directed not to process any documents other than such as appears on the definitive list provided for each subject unless such processing receives my personal approval in writing."[21]

An effective witness during this phase was John B. Powell, the respected American editor of the *China Weekly Review*, recommended to Sutton by Colonel Barrett and examined in court by Colonel Morrow. Crippled by his POW experience in Shanghai's Bridge House Jail, he had returned to live in America while his son, John W. Powell, took over as the journal's new, contrarian editor. In 1937, before his capture, he had traveled behind the lines to report on the Japanese advance from Shanghai to Nanjing and spoke as an eyewitness to war, despite President Webb's skepticism about a journalist's qualifications to do so.[22]

In addition to technical delays, in mid-September another terrible heat wave hit Tokyo and the air conditioning at Ichigaya again failed. On September 19 President Webb recessed the court for a week, time enough, he thought, to repair the air conditioning system. The court resumed a week later, but in less than two hours the system broke down, and Webb declared another week's recess. The judges were chauffeured back to the Imperial Palace Hotel where the air conditioning was functioning; the defendants were bused back to Sugamo where the screens installed on their windows to keep out mosquitoes kept out breezes as well. Although accustomed to southern summers, Sutton was photographed smiling in the Tokyo sun, without his suit jacket, which was most unusual for him.

While the IMTFE was in recess, Colonel Morrow left the IPS to return home to civilian life. He had done yeoman's work in establishing the IPS, worked hard on the China investigation, and helped present key witnesses for China's case. Following the rules, he had spoken to the court of the millions of Chinese soldiers killed in the war by Japan and said nothing of its chemical warfare that violated international treaties. Although unreconciled to the suppression of information on Japanese chemical and biological warfare, he was a good soldier and left on friendly terms with his colleagues and with Keenan, with no sign he held him accountable.[23]

During this same time, G-2 was circulating the gist of Arvo Thompson's research on Japanese germ weapons via its *Daily Intelligence Summary.* Despite Ishii's denials, the final posting concluded that "from the scope of the research and the progress made, it is evident that BW research and development in the Kwantung Army BKE was conducted on a large scale, was officially sanctioned, and was supported by the highest military authority."[24]

In the defendants' box, those authorities, among others, were Generals Tojo Hideki and Umezu Yoshijiro, who knew General Ishii from their time in Manchukuo, and Field Marshal Hata Shunroku, in charge of the China Expeditionary Force in 1940–1942.

The Soviets and Unit 731

In September 1946, far from Tokyo's suffocating heat, Soviet Army officers in Khabarovsk were interrogating two physicians, Major General Kawashima Kioshi and Major Karasawa Tomio, both former researchers at Unit 731, in an attempt to augment the Soviet case against the IMTFE defendants.

The first to be questioned was Kawashima, age 53, a former chief medical officer of the Kwantung Army and then head of production at Unit 731 during the war years.[25] An interpreter and a stenographer assisted the Soviet interrogator, Captain Nitikin. "You will be held responsible," the captain began, "under USSR Criminal Code if you make any false statements. Do you understand?"

"Yes, I understand," Kawashima replied. He had already told the Soviets about his work at Unit 731 but had been careful not to incriminate himself or others. Without success, Nitikin tried to get him to implicate another Soviet captive, Lieutenant General Kajitsuka Ryuiji, former chief medical officer of the Kwantung Army, and to admit that General Umezu and members of the General Army Staff had visited the unit to instruct General Ishii Shiro about "special maneuvers." Kawashima claimed he knew about no maneuvers except expeditions to provide water purification for the troops. His work was focused on vaccine production, nothing else. Within the hour he was led back to prison.

Four days later General Kawashima's interview was resumed, this time with a tape recorder and a new interrogator, a Colonel Kudriavtsev, who had interrogated Pu Yi in the same room the previous June and signed his affidavit.[26]

"We are questioning you as an important witness," Kudriavtsev began, "in regard to major Japanese war criminals by request of the Soviet representative of the IMTFE." After repeating what he had said previously about the unit's water purification expeditions, Kawashima then admitted he knew more: "Besides the above-mentioned duties, the Ishii unit was also in charge of secret work on a special mission concerned with the study and use of bacilli as a war weapon." He remembered, he said, being told when he arrived in 1941 that the unit's tests for dropping infected fleas from airplanes had proved "technically easy" and gave "extremely effective results." The only field test he saw was on twenty Manchu prisoners who were exposed to the fleas. The scientist in charge later told him that the rate of infection was low.

Kawashima also recalled a staff meeting early in 1941 at which General Ishii described the General Staff Office's encouragement of the study of fleas for bacterial warfare. In June of that year there were 130 officers and 2,000 noncommissioned officers at Pingfan. In August 1942 Dr. Kitano Masaji from Unit 100 took over as the new director, while Ishii remained in Beijing, and the research and experiments continued as before.

The Soviet interview with Major Karasawa, conducted by a Captain Peters, took place soon after and was more productive.[27] Karasawa, age 35, was a career army physician who had worked at Unit 731 from 1939 to 1944, after which he was transferred to the Kwantung Army's 44th division. Before being assigned to Unit 731, he specialized in anti-epidemic protection for Japanese soldiers in China and knew nothing about Ishii's program until he was posted to Manchukuo. He described how, after the Soviet invasion in 1945, General Ishii took a train headed for Korea and escaped to safety in Japan, but he himself was captured on September 1, 1945.

Karasawa spoke at length about the unit's warfare preparations and activities and identified General Umezu, commander of the Kwantung Army and Lieutenant General Kasahara, then chief of staff, as having visited Pingfan in 1943. He described Umezu as providing "leadership" for Ishii's work and, without hesitation, was able to give a detailed description of Unit 731's eight departments, four subdepartments, and a separate enclave (Unit 100) built in 1936 outside Changchun, the capital of Manchukuo, on the same scale as Pingfan. The First Department, concentrated on bacteriological research, found that plague and anthrax were the most powerful infective microbes for warfare. The Second Department engaged mainly in outdoor experiments, supplied with germ agents by the Fourth Department, whose goal was mass production.

The young Dr. Karasawa portrayed himself as more of a follower than a leader. As he told Captain Peters, between August and December 1940, Ishii took around a hundred subordinates to Central China for a "test." To assist them, Karasawa said he manufactured 70 kilograms of typhoid bacilli culture and 50 kilograms of cholera bacilli, and that 5 kilograms of fleas infested with plague bacilli were produced and shipped for spraying in a zone occupied by the Chinese Army. One result of the "experiment" was the plague outbreak in Ningbo.[28]

On the subject of human experimentation, Karasawa was repentant. "I participated in this work," he began, "so I hate to say anything about it, but I will explain it because it will be a burden on my mind if I don't." Then he recounted that for several years scientists at Pingfan were interested in how germs could spread via open wounds. As he explained:

> A bomb filled with bacteria was placed on the ground and about twenty Manchurians were tied to poles or made to sit down on the ground at a proper distance (that is, enough distance to prevent men's death) from the bomb, which was electrically exploded. By the bomb blast, which was caused by the explosion of the bomb, and its fragments, the plague bacilli and anthrax bacilli penetrated through the wound into human bodies. The wounded were kept in the laboratory until the symptoms of the disease appeared and when they were taken ill, they were given medical treatment and their cases were studied, but most of them died in agony. The experiment obtained results just as expected. The directors of this experiment were Lieutenant General Ishii and Colonel Ikari.[29]

These two interviews by the Soviets, giving details about biological attacks and grotesque tests on captives, expanded the range of Japanese war crimes that might be prosecuted at the IMTFE. In late September in Tokyo, after receiving the transcripts of the Kawashima and Karasawa interrogations, Golunsky had his assistant prosecutor Vasiliev take them to the office of the chief of counsel, where they seemed to vanish without a reaction—at least from the Soviet perspective.[30]

In the fall of 1946 Alva Carpenter at Legal Section was hearing much the same stories as the Soviets in Khabarovsk. Inflammatory letters kept arriving from Japanese individuals who wanted to tell General MacArthur about medical experiments on American POWs by Ishii and about others who had worked for the Imperial Army on germ weapons.

Reports of Japanese medical atrocities to Legal Section were not that rare. The previous May an anonymous letter had accused Japanese Army officers of intentional POW deaths at the Sagamigahara (Tokyo) Army Hospital. Carpenter quickly opened a case file in preparation for prosecution.[31] At Yokohama, a Japanese physician was put on trial for performing medical surgery without anesthesia on Allied prisoners at the Omori prison camp.[32] Along the same lines, messages were coming to SCAP about the murders of eight POWs in medical experiments at the Kyushu Imperial University hospital to the south. Doctors there, it was claimed, had substituted seawater for their victims' blood and conducted vivisection. Carpenter created a new case file and in July enlisted the Japanese Central Liaison Office in Tokyo in the apprehension of eight suspects, including three surgeons, a nurse, and the university president.[33] On further investigation, he issued arrest warrants and planned a trial at Yokohama.

In August Legal Section received a letter that accused Ishii's scientists of the dissection of "many prisoners of Allied Forces" at the Mukden prisoner-of-war camp and of infecting POWs with glanders, a rare disease of horses especially lethal to humans (known as stableboy's disease). Carpenter added it to other messages in which Japanese physicians mutually accused one another of war crimes.[34] Allegations surfaced that American POWs at Mukden had been victimized by physicians at a certain Unit 100, referred to as the "Kwantung Army Quarantine Stables," connected to Unit 731.[35] As he often did to find suspects, Carpenter asked the Japanese Government Liaison Office to obtain the full military and biographical histories and the addresses of those named.[36] On August 8 Legal Services began an investigation of one suspected scientist, Yamaguchi Motaji, associated with both Unit 100 and Unit 731. In the various testimonials, General Ishii was repeatedly accused as the chief criminal.

The Court Continues

On September 4 David Nelson Sutton's name was again in the news. He and Arthur Sandusky, another American lawyer at IPS, had added to Prosecutor Hsiang's case for the Japanese opium enslavement. "Court Told Japan Turned Manchuria into a Drug Market" ran the headline in the *Nippon Times*.[37] The Chinese prosecution ended in late September. With little public acknowledgment, Sutton had proved to be an important architect of the Chinese brief, assembling evidence and witnesses for its Class C charges, extending them to the Class B category, and then integrating them into the Class A war crimes with the "pattern of war" argument. The end of the Chinese case was a relief for some outside IPS. Rather than reiterating Japanese atrocities, President Webb wanted the IMTFE to take the higher ground and focus on the responsibility of government leaders for provoking ruinous wars—with Nuremberg as his model. On October 1 the verdicts handed down at Nuremberg dominated the world news and resonated strongly in Tokyo. The results were execution for twelve defendants, prison sentences for seven, and three acquittals. The main conclusion of the fifty-thousand-word judgment was that aggressive war is "the supreme international crime."[38]

After China's case was argued, the other nations offered their evidence for war crimes related to Japan's aggression in the East. The Netherlands prosecutor, W. G. Frederick Borgerhoff-Mulder, formerly a judge at the Special War Criminals Court established in 1945 at The Hague, made a straightforward argument about the Japanese invasion of the Dutch East Indies to secure its oil. The French prosecutor Robert Oneto went next to the podium. His insistence on making his presentation in French—an official language at Nuremberg—caused a furor. President Webb led a walkout of the bench, while the French judge Henri Bernard, who supported Oneto (and whose spoken English was also poor), threatened to resign. Supported by Keenan, Oneto was finally allowed to continue in French and presented evidence of Japan's aggression against Indochina in 1944–1945, after the fall of Germany and the Vichy government, when Vietnamese and liberated French soldiers fought side-by-side against the Imperial Army.

The Soviet prosecutors, next at the podium, had a difficult time, especially compared to the performance of their attorneys at Nuremberg. The previous February one of their star jurists, 35-year-old Lev Nikolaevich Smirnov, had with films, photographs, and eyewitness testimony presented dramatic evidence of Nazi crimes against the peaceful populations of the Soviet Union, Yugoslavia, Poland, and Czechoslovakia. Smirnov elicited stunning testimony from carefully chosen witnesses, among them a Red Army physician captured and forced with other POWs to march four days with almost no food and no water, a Russian peasant whose family had been killed by Nazi soldiers, a Polish survivor of Birkenau who described the Nazi murders of children, and a Russian Orthodox priest who gave a dramatic account of the siege of Leningrad.[39] Although the Soviet Union was reluctant to recognize Jews as the primary and unique victims of Nazism, Smirnov called Jewish death camp survivors to the stand, including a survivor of Treblinka who described the three trainloads of victims that arrived each day, with an estimate of ten to twelve thousand murdered by the end of the war.[40]

In Tokyo, as at Nuremberg, the Soviets were focused on Class A war crimes, but at the IMTFE they had little choice but to limit their charges to just two Japanese acts of aggression, the Battle at Lake Khasan in 1938 (the Changkufeng Incident for the Japanese) and the other more extensive 1939 conflict at the Khalkin-gol River (the Nomonhan Incident). Associate Prosecutor Golunsky opened the Soviet case with a statement nearly two hours long that began with the Russo-Japanese War of 1905 and the claim that Japanese militarists had started it by illegally attacking Russia. Although irrelevant to the IMTFE, the historical reference resonated with the American argument that Japan's strike on Pearl Harbor was a "crime of surprise attack" as defined and codified by the Third Hague Convention of 1907.[41] Golunsky skipped past the Soviet invasions of Finland and Poland in 1939, arguably also contrary to the convention. His statement then ended in 1940, before the Soviet-Japanese Neutrality Pact of 1941, which, with Allied urging, the Soviets had violated by invading Manchuria in 1945. Nor did he mention that, in 1941, the Soviets had protested Nazi Germany's surprise invasion of its borders as a violation of the same treaty—which would have introduced too much political complexity about reversals in Soviet alliances.

The defense, as it would later show, had made careful note of past Soviet infractions. The Soviet prosecution's handling of witness testimony also left it open to criticism. Originally planning to call as many as seventy witnesses to reinforce the charge of aggressive warfare, prosecutors chose written testimony instead, to their disadvantage. Golunsky, for example, introduced an affidavit from a Russian collaborator who attested to Japan's intention to invade Siberia and capture Vladivostok. But the defense revealed that this individual had been tried and executed by the Soviets three weeks before, under the USSR decree of April 19, 1943, against war crimes, including collaboration.[42]

As President Webb pointed out, the court normally reserved the right to examine a deponent, but affidavits alone had been allowed, for instance, in the Chinese Division's presentation of the Nanjing atrocities. Webb decided to allow this affidavit to stay in evidence. When Golunsky then introduced another affidavit, it emerged that it was signed by a Russian who was sentenced to death. Challenged by the defense, Golunsky confessed to not knowing the actual fate of the witness. To make matters worse, two Japanese deponents Golunsky meant to call were apparently too ill to appear in court. Webb became openly exasperated with the Soviet prosecutors, and the spectators at Ichigaya seemed relieved when the day's presentation ended.[43]

The Soviet problem with witnesses continued. One Japanese witness called to testify afterward committed suicide; another was described as "somewhere in Germany." Five Japanese witnesses whose affidavits had been submitted to the court could not be brought to Tokyo "for considerations of state security."[44]

The Reward

On October 1 Nelson Sutton was rewarded for his work for the Chinese Division with a six-day leave for rest and recuperation at the Fujiya Hotel, where Chief of Counsel Keenan had retreated the previous May to write his opening speech. Located west of Tokyo, the hotel, built to elaborate standards in the late nineteenth century, was run by the US Eighth Army.

Its Hakone Sengoku golf course, once a favorite of Hirohito's, had become a favorite of Joseph Keenan, Roy Morgan, Pedro Lopez, and many US Army brass.

On the slow train from Tokyo, Sutton was struck by Japanese life outside the city and filled his diary with details to share with his family. He noted the fields of long-headed millet, sorghum, and sweet potatoes, the rice paddies, the horse-drawn carts, a woman drawing water from a well, and the many destroyed areas of the landscape. The people, he observed, looked "tired, thin, hungry." Yet he also observed signs of progress: "high steel towers carrying electric transmission lines criss-cross the landscape," he wrote, and electric freight trains, their box cars about three-quarters the size of those in America, were running. Passing through Yokohama, he found the landscape divided between signs of wartime destruction and the American takeover. He saw hundreds of concrete smokestacks "with no smoke emerging" and "twisted iron on acres of cement floors of former factories," plus "acres of army vehicles—trucks of all kinds in all states of repair" and oil tanks, over which the American flag flew. On the train, young Japanese men wearing armbands that read "Boy," passed through the cars lighting cigarettes for passengers.

The hotel had over a hundred well-appointed rooms, modern toilets, a restaurant, and a bar and lounge with magnificent views of Mount Fuji. There were daily newspapers, mail and telegram service, massages, tennis courts, an outdoor pool and hot springs, and nightly entertainment, including American movies. Graceful young women in kimonos poured tea in the lobby. These comforts came with the serenity and coolness of the mountains (the hotel was 1,400 feet above sea level).

Sutton's room was the "Pear Room" with a picture of a pear tree in blossom on the door. It had two twin beds and a lovely view of waterfalls in the rock garden. He counted twenty-three guest families, some with children. Sutton mixed easily with the officers and other civilian visitors. In his diary he wrote the names of people with whom he dined and their home states (Michigan, New York, Colorado, and Pennsylvania), and he met a lieutenant colonel whose family was from the Richmond area. Virginia Bowman, a secretary for the Executive Committee, was there with another woman from IPS. Sutton lunched with them and showed them the souvenirs he had purchased for his family from the hotel arcade: a brooch for 2,800 yen and other, less costly souvenirs, a bowl, two plates, a fanciful ivory image, a blue cloisonné vase, and a Chinese tray with mother-of-pearl inlay.

The point of Sutton's six days of vacation was to avoid thinking about war crimes. The time was crammed full of entertaining distractions: pool parties, hiking trips, a ping pong tournament, nightly dinner dancing to music by a string orchestra, and a tour of a princely villa. Sutton took advantage of the hotel's golf course, playing eighteen holes on Tuesday and Thursday. Thursday was capped off by a Japanese show featuring a foot juggler, which was followed by a swimming party and then sandwiches and coffee. On Saturday he played thirty-six holes (scores 96 and 98), after which he had a three-quarter-hour soak in a hot tub and a massage. Late in the evening on Sunday, October 6, Sutton returned to Tokyo; the army driver dropped off Miss Bowman at her hostel before bringing Sutton to the Hotel Koronada.

The next day he became immersed in a new phase of struggle at the IPS, one in which a staff shortage put maximum stress on his colleague Frank Tavenner. American attorneys had begun leaving during the summer and their numbers continued to drop. Roy Morgan at the Investigation Division was set to return to North Carolina to his wife and young son. Chief of Counsel Keenan was again away in Washington, invited to speak at the American Bar Association annual meeting.[45] The Nuremberg trial had just ended, a great success that in less than a year had demonstrated the threat of aggressive war to individuals, nations, and civilized life. Keenan could not promise that the Tokyo trial would set precedents beyond Nuremberg's. In the end, he missed the ABA meeting and a friend presented his speech for him.

Sutton Assists at IPS

Committed to the IPS, Sutton took on a new assignment, to assist Prosecutor Pedro "Pete" Lopez of the Philippines, a former resistance fighter and, in 1945, the leader of his country's delegation to the United Nations. The Philippines was a favored country at SCAP. When it became an independent nation on July 4, General MacArthur returned to Manila for the celebration, and he chose Filipino guards for his office at Dai-Ichi. At the IPS, the Philippines was respected but a junior player.

Sutton's assignment was to help Lopez formulate his country's Class C war crimes charges against Japan. The atrocities in the Philippines had been as grotesque as those in China—the fanatic soldiers with bayonets, swords, and machine guns seemed part of the same Japanese pattern of warfare, which Lopez had seen firsthand. The evidence included documentation of individual murders—of a blind woman stripped naked and hung, of a woman raped and stabbed to death—and of mass killings: 800 defenseless men, women, and children machine-gunned at St. Paul's College in Manila, another 2,500 shot or bayoneted at Calambra, 100 people in a church in Ponson killed in the same way, another 169 villagers slaughtered in Matina Pang. In his presentation, Lopez planned to cover the Bataan Death March, even though several American attorneys already expected to present it for the US case. He had the advantage of fourteen thousand pages of documents from the earlier trials of Generals Yamashita and Homma.[46] The Philippine justice Delfin Jaranilla, a Bataan survivor, had agreed to absent himself from the court during this phase of the trial.

After Lopez, Alan Mansfield, the prosecutor for Australia, would follow with more Japanese government documents showing that individual defendants in the dock—Tojo, Kimura, Muto, Sato, Togo, and Shigemitsu—were responsible for these and other atrocities in the Pacific.

As an IPS expert on Class C war crimes, Sutton helped Lopez calculate the civilian death statistics. By official count, the total came to 130,000, likely an underestimate given the lack of records in rural areas and the chaos during the 1945 "Rape of Manila."

Meanwhile, the Chinese were moving forward with their own trial for the Nanjing Massacre.[47] The precepts of the London Charter that defined the crimes of aggressive war, of violations of customary rules of war, and those against humanity had become Chinese law. Since General Matsui had already been indicted for war crimes at the IMTFE, the Chinese settled for Lieutenant General Tani Hisao, former commander of the Japanese Sixth Division, which had entered Nanjing with Matsui's troops. After a long delay, Legal Section helped arrange for him and twelve other Japanese suspects to be transported to Shanghai. On September 9, 1946, Tani was arrested there, and within weeks he was indicted in Nanjing. The Chinese government used the prospect of the tribunal not only to show, like other victors, that it represented justice and social order but also for communitarian ends, to encourage ordinary citizens to speak up about what they had suffered at the hands of the Japanese military. Its efforts to gather evidence about the Nanjing Massacre were energetic. Teams of investigators directed by the KMT government or by the city "carried out the investigations into the charges—they interviewed thousands who had experienced the massacre, dug up graves, took measurements, and combed the international press from that time. The prosecution pulled out piles of testimonials, tables, pictures, and evidence along with other documents to prove Tani's responsibility for the events."[48] Despite all this fact finding in Nanjing, Sutton heard no more about Unit 1644 and its poison experiments or the germ weapons onslaught of 1942 to punish the Chinese for saving the Doolittle pilots that was described by C. C. H. Hataba, the deserter from the unit.

After Sutton was assigned to work with Lopez, the United States took more than a month, from October 23 to November 27, to argue its charge against Japan for the sudden attack on Pearl Harbor, which for Americans was the foremost example of "aggressive war." A wealth of evidence—Japanese government documents, decoded cables, war maps of reconnaissance flights, and the diaries of Japanese sailors describing their secret mobilization weeks in advance of the attack—supported the charge, which involved not just Pearl Harbor but the synchronized attacks at the same time on Shanghai's international settlement, Kota Bharu in Malaya, Singora in Thailand, Singapore, Guam, and Hong Kong. The US presentation left little doubt about the efficient organization of the Japanese high command or its blatant disregard of international treaties, especially the ban on surprise attack in the Third Hague Convention.

Japan's Germ Warfare: Emerging Crimes

At Legal Section, accusations about General Ishii's biological weapons program continued to arrive. In a letter to General MacArthur dated October 4, a former military physician named Ueki Hiroshi from Kyoto intimated that many people like himself knew about Pingfan's criminal activities.[49] "Former Lt-Gen Ishii Shiro, an army medical doctor," he wrote, "established a large scale human experimental station in the suburb of Harbin . . . and executed brutal experiments on many Allied [POWS]." The letter contained a list of fifteen of Ishii's subordinates, with their titles. Colonel Masuda was noted as chief of administration. Other top officials were named—among them Dr. Ota Kiyoshi, Dr. Ikari Tsuneshige, and Dr. Kikuchi Hitoshi—who like Ishii were in Japan and within the reach of the law. "The placing of [Ishii's] name on the war crime suspect list was inevitable," the doctor wrote, "but lately, he is using bribes to escape the consequences."

During this time, Legal Section located the former commander of Unit 100, Dr. Wakamatsu Yujiro, in Osaka and brought him in for questioning.[50] Accused in a letter to SCAP of conducting glanders experiments on POWs, the self-effacing Wakamatsu denied any wrongdoing. Nonetheless, Alva Carpenter, the head of Legal Section, opened case File No. 330 for all information about Ishii, Wakamatsu, and others implicated in Japanese biological weapons. In it, Carpenter included allegations about medical experiments on POWs both in Manchuria and in Japanese hospitals.

On October 28 Tavenner asked Sutton to come to his office, room 304 at the War Ministry, which was next door to Sutton's. There he gave him copies of the two affidavits from Khabarovsk that the Soviets had delivered to the chief of counsel's office the previous month.[51] They appeared to be mostly paraphrased excerpts, not fully translated, and relating primarily to plague and fleas. One statement was signed by Major Karasawa, likely the same Unit 731 leader mentioned in the document given by Prosecutor Hsiang to Sutton with the Hataba statement about Unit 1644.

Even though truncated, Dr. Karasawa's testimony was incriminating. After identifying his superiors, he stated "how the Japanese Army had spread the Pest [plague] bacilli-infected fleas over Free China in 1940." (Next to this phrase, Sutton jotted on his copy, "Have this completely translated.") Further, according to the synopsis of the interview, Karasawa stated "how experiments were carried out on the living bodies of those Manchurians who had been sentenced to death at ADACHI laboratory [100 kilometers from Harbin] in 1943 and 1944 in order to find out how they could make them infected with the various germs through the wounds of their bodies." Then the text quoted Karasawa directly:

> Lt. General Ishii had been in Hanchow [Hangzhou] from August until December 1940 with about 100 subordinates for the purpose of experiments. I produced 70 kilograms of the abdominal typhoid's virus and

> 50 kilograms of cholera virus and the 2nd Division [of Unit 731's Fourth Division] produced 5 kilograms of Pest bacilli-infected fleas. The experiment was carried out by diffusing those virus[es] from airplanes over the Chinese occupied area. After the experiment, Pest broke out in Ningpo [Ningbo]. Neither cholera nor typhoid was effective, but it proved that Pest virus was effective.[52]

In a separate statement, Major General Kawashima, the former chief of the Production Division for Unit 731, confessed that the unit's secret duty was to research germs for use in war. He then focused on three methods for spreading plague—to drop fleas from airplanes, to drop bombs that contained live fleas, and to spread fleas directly on the ground by guerrillas or as Japanese troops were withdrawing from an area. He confirmed Karasawa's account of experiments on humans, describing one in which plague-infected fleas were dropped on twenty Manchu prisoners. Major General Ishii, he recalled, told his scientists that the General Staff in Tokyo had directly instructed improvements in germ warfare research.

In addition to these two witnesses, the Soviets had interviewed another captured Japanese officer, Lieutenant General Hata Hikosaburo, former chief of staff of the Kwantung Army under General Umezu and, after him, under General Yamada.[53] When pressed to reveal what he knew about the "top secret" bacterial weapons, Hata denied that General Headquarters had anything to do with using such weapons on his watch. He did, though, admit to "the possibility of applying the materials for bacterial warfare only in the following cases: To use them behind the enemy in a strategic view, or mix them in water before retreat for the purpose of spreading them to communicate disease or cause infectious diseases among men and domestic animals by communicating the diseases to animals or insects." Hata identified General Ishii as the leader of Epidemic Prevention and Water Supply Department and stipulated that he had been directly subordinate to the commander of the Kwantung Army, whether Umezu or Yamada. Hata traced Ishii's chain of command up to the War Ministry and its Military Affairs Bureau and described the Army Medical School in Tokyo as in charge of bacterial warfare training and experiments. "Concerning the problem of the preparation for bacterial warfare," he said, "Lieutenant General Ishii kept direct connection with the authorities in Tokyo."

In his testimony Hata implicated other IMTFE defendants besides Umezu who had led the Kwantung Army during Ishii's development of his biological warfare program. General Minami Jiro had been commander from 1934 to 1936. General Koiso Kuniaki had been chief of staff from 1932 to 1934. Former premier Tojo had also served as chief of staff in 1937–1938.[54]

Tavenner told Sutton that the Soviets were offering to put the two Unit 731 scientists, Kawashima and Karasawa, on the stand. But the other IPS staff he consulted were against it.[55] The defense counsel would be sure to question the credibility of any witnesses held captive by the Soviets. In addition, finding Kwantung Army or General Staff records to link the defendants to the alleged secret activities of General Ishii would be difficult. With two or possibly three unreliable witnesses and no documents, the prosecution was where it was in April, when Sutton, writing about the plague allegations, concluded that the "weakness of the case is that we do not now have sufficient evidence." The three Soviet affidavits went into the Investigation Division files, with no plans for IPS action.

On November 4, without Colonel Morrow to help, Sutton submitted his version of the brief, "All Military Aggression in China Including Atrocities Against Civilians and Others," to Chief of Counsel Keenan. Thorough as it was, its fifty-seven pages contained no reference to Japanese chemical or biological warfare and deleted any mention of appendix D, paragraph 9, in the indictment, affirming the Japanese use of poison gas in China. Sutton started the summary with a flourish: "The China Incident [of 1937] was a war. It was a war begun in violation of solemn treaty obligations and repeated official assurances. It was a war waged in violation of every rule of organized warfare and in a manner which shocked the conscience of humanity. The acts of the defendants violated the inexorable rules of human conduct. Their acts were sins against humanity. 'The wages of sin is death.'"[56]

In nine months at IPS, Sutton had learned a great deal about Japanese war crimes but little about Japanese germ warfare. All the information was fragmentary, and much was obviously hidden: King and Pollitzer on the plague attacks, poison inoculations at the Tama Division, Morrow's failed inquiry about General Ishii, Hataba's testimony about Ei 1644, Reverend Bannan's eyewitness account of the Changde attack, the three affidavits from the Soviet Division. It seemed that terrible atrocities had taken place, but he was a trial lawyer without trial-worthy evidence.

9

THE SOVIET DIVISION VERSUS US MILITARY INTELLIGENCE

On November 12, 1946, the Nuremberg tribunal concluded and the celebratory report of US Judge Francis Biddle was released to the press. Biddle described a judicial process that moved quickly, with increasing cooperation among judges who took no breaks. Justice was served, yet Biddle was not naïve about the future of armed conflicts: "War is not outlawed by such pronouncements, but men learn a little better to detest it when as here, its horrors are told day after day, and its aggressive savagery is thus branded as criminal."[1]

In his congratulations to the court, President Truman approved Biddle's recommendation that the trial should become the basis for "a general codification of offenses against the peace and security of mankind"—a fitting task for the governments of the United Nations.[2] To his praise for Chief of Counsel Robert Jackson, Truman added: "I am convinced that the verdict for which you worked will receive the accolade of civilized people everywhere and will stand in history as a beacon to warn international brigands of the fate that awaits them."[3]

Nearly a year had passed since Chief of Counsel Joseph Keenan's arrival in Tokyo, when IPS had only twenty-two lawyers (compared to over two hundred six months later), Japanese suspects were daily committing suicide, and the text of the Tokyo Charter had yet to be finalized. Yet progress had been slow. The prosecution phase, begun the previous June, continued; with the delays caused by translation, document processing, and contention between opposing counsel, it was expected to go on for another month or more. Except for tribunal president William Webb and a few others, the judges intermittently left the bench with empty seats, whether for reasons of illness (the UK's Lord William Patrick and New Zealand's Erima Northcroft had chronic health problems) or personal matters (Radhabinod Pal's wife in India was ill), although the quorum of seven was always met.

As the year 1947 approached, Keenan wrote home to his wife about how good life was in Japan, part of an effort to encourage her to visit.[4] He was, he said, enjoying the beauty of his office in the Meiji Building, which had a view of Mount Fuji, his comfortable accommodations at Hattori House, and the many social events sponsored by the embassies, the US Army, and the Japanese government. He had much to entertain him: golf at the Fujiya Hotel, a British reception in honor of Princess Elizabeth's marriage (he saved the engraved invitation as a souvenir for his daughter), and weekend trips to the country residence of General Robert Eichelberger, head of the Eighth Army and MacArthur's second-in-command. General Zinovi Pechkoff, the charismatic French ambassador who was much liked by MacArthur, had invited Keenan for an intimate dinner at his residence.[5] Keenan told the general that, in his view, no death sentences would be handed out at the trial's end, not out of lenience but to avoid making "heroes of these people."[6] If anything annoyed Keenan about the IMTFE, it was the dominance of the Anglo judges on the bench, creating "a situation where we have one vote and the British Commonwealth five."[7]

Immersed in day-to-day difficulties at the IPS, Frank Tavenner remained anxious about the growing shortage of attorneys—only seventy-five staff lawyers were left. Tavenner wrote about the problem to Captain Luke Lea, Keenan's former military aide now at the War Department's War Crimes Branch in Washington, who remained in close contact with Keenan.[8] The IPS was apparently being dismantled. Osmond Hyde, who had worked with Tavenner on the Axis Powers argument, had returned to the Justice Department. Six more attorneys were leaving within the week, with no replacements. At age 48, an American prosecutor had died suddenly of a heart attack in a corridor at the War Ministry Building where the Ichigaya court was located; Tavenner had discovered his body, and the shocking loss much troubled all the staff.[9] The Australian lead prosecutor, Alan Mansfield, who had urged a "swift and simple trial," announced he was resigning. New Zealand's Brigadier Ronald Quilliam also wanted to return home. Associate Prosecutor Sergei Golunsky was recalled to Moscow, putting General A. N. Vasiliev in charge of the Soviet Division.[10] Leaving the British to prosecute its war crimes charges, the Indian Division was packing up, with no plan to return.

The last weeks of the prosecution were, Tavenner felt, in danger of "going off the rails," while ahead loomed the defense phase, for which little preparation had been made, and, following that, the rebuttal and the closing arguments. In the previous weeks he had been relying on a core group: "All the Americans that were left—the only ones who could be depended on for work in the court room—were Carlisle [Higgins], Horwitz, Sutton, Woolworth and myself."[11]

Higgins, Keenan's assistant chief of counsel and Tavenner's good friend, was in poor health "due to the grind he has been under and the difficulties of his position."[12] Keenan's distrust of him after the attempted palace coup in July had endured; still, Tavenner was optimistic that Keenan would with time soften his attitude. Tavenner also explained away the chief of counsel's unimpressive handling of witnesses in court as the result of fatigue. Keenan, Tavenner diplomatically reflected, "has done a tremendous amount of work, and for this and other reasons he needs a rest. He will devote his time to prepare his argument on the law of the case for conclusion of prosecution's evidence—not [be] involved in testimony part to come."

Other American attorneys made no excuses for Keenan. Robert Donihi, a junior member of the original IPS team and among those about to decamp, had found Keenan's temperament difficult and, in retrospect, thought others felt the same: "Many of the lawyers hated him. At least one threatened violence. His verbal assaults on his own counsel had estranged even his best friends. In general, there was a depressed feeling at all times among those working for Keenan."[13]

Tavenner himself treaded carefully. For example, believing that Keenan's closing argument needed documentary material from Nuremberg, he asked Captain Lea to obtain the relevant briefs. "Will you discretely inquire and handle these matters," he requested, "in such a manner that it will not be seen as coming from me?"[14]

The loss of attorneys forced Eugene Williams, Keenan's special assistant, to reshuffle the list of IPS assignments to prepare for cases against individual defendants.[15] He relied on the small remaining Anglo-American contingent, and when he assigned cases to the Soviet and Filipino prosecutors, he gave them extra American support. Assisted by Captain James J. Robinson, Pedro Lopez, the associate prosecutor for the Philippines, would examine the cases against Generals Muto, Kimura, and Itagaki. Colonel Gilbert Woolworth, already delegated to the Soviet Division, would help General Vasiliev with the cases against the defendants former foreign minister Shigemitsu and General Umezu.

While Tavenner and Williams struggled at IPS, Keenan reflected loftily that "a few good workers are infinitely more desirable than the larger crowd of men who have no great desire to work at all."[16] And, as December approached, he scheduled yet another trip back to Washington—his wife was too ill to join him for the Christmas holidays as he had hoped, and he told friends he had his law firm's business to manage. Before leaving, he wrote a brief memo directing the IPS attorneys what to do in his absence. The memo started with a chiding reference to General MacArthur's impatience with the slowness and lack of "efficiency" of the tribunal."[17] Keenan then issued directions for his depleted staff. He favored Brigadier Henry Nolan, the reserved Canadian prosecutor, and assigned him and Tavenner to review the records of individual defendants. Eugene Williams, with Solis Horwitz and Alfred Comyns Carr, would continue to prepare responses to the defense motions that would begin at the end of the prosecution's case.

As for IPS organization, Keenan increasingly relied on Willis Mahoney, his executive assistant in charge of administration, a responsibility originally delegated to Carlisle Higgins. Keenan told the staff that, in his absence, the assistant chief of counsel would be authorized to act on his behalf, but he avoided mentioning Higgins by name.

Keenan also stipulated that Australia's prosecutor Alan Mansfield, assisted by Captain Robinson, would oversee arguing the Class B and C war crimes—a phase Keenan expected to miss since he would be in Washington "on authorized assignment." Mansfield's role had become difficult, which Keenan knew. Pedro Lopez was showing signs that his fury at the Japanese was causing him to expand his case argument for Class C crimes, which risked the ire of President Webb, who was easily repulsed by reiterations of Japanese atrocities and wanted the court to emphasize Class A crimes. Lopez also risked curtailing Mansfield's case presentation on the overall B and C crimes. "Considerable friction has arisen regarding the proposed length of Lopez' section and Mansfield's section," Tavenner confided to Lea. "I do not know where the argument will end. It is a very critical situation, threatening an open break which could lead to serious difficulties."

As an advisor to Lopez, Nelson Sutton would have been in the middle of the emerging conflict, but on November 6 he was granted a sixty-day leave of absence to return to Virginia, where his mother, in her late seventies, had fallen ill and his law practice needed his attention. Before leaving, he had made a note to himself to request the appearance of C. C. H. Hataba, whose affidavit had described Unit 1644 and the Chekiang germ campaign of 1942, but with no apparent follow-through.[18] Sutton was away for two months, missing the fracas Lopez was causing and, more important, changes in IPS organization as the Soviet Division began agitating about presenting Unit 731 evidence.

Just about to depart for Washington, Keenan called a meeting of all the associate prosecutors.[19] Citing pressure from MacArthur and Washington to speed up the trial, he demanded that Lopez and Mansfield drop their Class B and C charges, on the grounds that most of the crimes, especially about POW abuse, had been adjudicated in minor tribunals in Manila and elsewhere. After angry resistance from his prosecutors, especially Lopez and Mansfield, Keenan backed off his request.

On December 4, after Keenan left, Tavenner wrote Sutton an update on how the Lopez-Mansfield problem was resolved:

> You probably know about the difficulty between Lopez and Mr. Keenan over Lopez' opening statement. It finally fell to me to try to tone it down, and, much to the surprise of everyone, Lopez agreed to the recommendations made and [Solis] Horowitz [*sic*] is helping him with the revision. It is lurid enough even with the modifications, and I am still a little uneasy as to what attitude Sir William [Webb] will take.[20]

Left out of Tavenner's letter was the news that, after eight months as Keenan's special assistant, Eugene Williams had decided to return to California. If Keenan was surprised or dismayed, he gave no sign of it. In preparation for his departure, Williams circulated a memo to announce that he was relinquishing "all authority in connection with the preparation or presentation of the prosecution's case." In his place, Keenan had assigned Tavenner:

> Under the direction of Mr. Keenan, Mr. Frank S. Tavenner, Jr. will have over-all charge of the preparation of the cases against individual defendants, both as it relates to the presentation of additional evidence at the close of the prosecution case and in preparation for cross-examination of defendants. Therefore, any and all problems in connection with that matter should be taken up with him promptly and directly.[21]

Tavenner predicted that the great challenge to come was the defense phase, during which the prosecution's legal and investigative personnel would be taxed "to the utmost" by the cross-examination of an estimated one hundred witnesses.[22] To strengthen their overall presentation, Williams urged IPS attorneys to "cooperate in exchanging information." He had a special concern for the Soviet Division, noting that General Vasiliev, responsible for the charges against former prime minister Shigemitsu and General Umezu, was still asking the other divisions that "all material regarding them be brought to his attention."[23]

Generally unknown at IPS, where the Soviet Division kept relatively isolated, Vasiliev was eager to promote germ warfare charges against the Japanese. In a parting memo, Williams handed off the potential controversy to Tavenner:

> General Vasiliev is somewhat disturbed because in the Chinese phase certain evidence provided by the Russians was not used to prove that the Japanese resorted to bacteriological warfare. He says the Russians have two witnesses now in Vladivostok who are available to supplement what evidence we have here. I informed him that I had reviewed the evidence available during the Chinese case and had reached the conclusion that it was not sufficient to warrant opening that issue. He is disturbed,

> however, and would like to have a definite decision reached. I think you should take this matter up with him.[24]

The insufficient evidence Williams referred to was Sutton's April 1946 report on his China investigation, all that had been available as the Chinese Division argued its case, but not the totality of what had accumulated in the Investigation Division file. On December 13 Tavenner wrote a diplomatic but discouraging memo to Vasiliev, explaining that he and the IPS staff had given "careful consideration" to the Kawashima Kioshi and Karasawa Tomio affidavits "regarding the activities of the Ishii Detachment in experimenting with bacteria as a means of attack." As backup, he cited Alan Mansfield, the former head of the Evidence Committee now in charge of the Class B and C crimes. Since, however, G-2 was in control of any new interrogations (as per the June 3, 1946, order to IPS), Tavenner's decision necessarily relied on General Willoughby's consent, which the Soviet Division ought to have understood. Informed, probably by G-2, of Lieutenant Colonel Arvo Thompson's inquiry the previous spring, Tavenner used it to argue to Vasiliev that no links had been found to any defendants in the dock:

> Upon directing investigation of Japanese records and reports on the subject of bacteriological warfare, I learned that an experienced investigator was sent directly from the United States to Japan where he conducted a seven-week investigation of this detachment, and no evidence was brought to light which would indicate that these experiments were being made at the direction of the General Staff in Tokyo or that any reports have been received relating to these experiments. We do not consider the evidence now available is sufficient to justify an awareness that any of the accused can be associated with this activity by any of the criteria adopted by the Court with reference to atrocities and prisoner of war offenses.[25]

Tavenner also downplayed the prospects of future IPS inquiries: "Although our investigation will continue for the purpose of obtaining additional evidence, the chance of success in light of the investigation already made is so slight that it is not considered wise or reasonable to request the U.S.S.R. to produce the witnesses under these circumstances."[26]

For the moment, Tavenner had deflected General Vasiliev's request, but he underestimated the Soviet Division, which would persist in its efforts to present its two Japanese biological warfare witnesses and to hope for US cooperation.

At Legal Section, Alva Carpenter was finding that the chances of new revelations about Japanese biological weapons were improving, with his case file No. 330 on Ishii and his cohort fast expanding. In September Carpenter had been alerted to the Kawashimi and Karasawa affidavits handed in by the Soviets and the alleged criminal dimensions of Ishii's Unit 731.[27] In early December Unit 100's former leader, Major Wakamatsu Yujiro, while denying any wrongdoing of his own, provided more names for LS to track.[28] With leads from the CWS, Dr. Ota Kiyoshi, a top Unit 731 scientist who had mobilized the 1941 plague attack on Changde, was found and interviewed in Tokyo, where he gave little away about his past.[29]

While the Legal Section investigation proceeded, newspaper headlines around the world announced the beginning of twelve new U.S. military tribunals in Nuremberg, allowed under the Allied Control Council Law No. 10. The first of them, the Doctors' Trial, was to prosecute Nazi physicians for mass murders and medical experimentation on prisoners of war and concentration camp victims.[30] On December 9 Brigadier General Telford Taylor, the chief of counsel, gave an opening statement in which he articulated the unique historical role of this war crimes tribunal. Speaking of the "the nameless dead" who "were treated worse than animals," Taylor emphasized the importance of evidence as a means of rescuing victims otherwise consigned to oblivion: "For them, it is far more important that these incredible events be established by clear and public proof, so that no one can ever doubt that they were fact and not fable; and that this Court, as the agent of the United States and as the voice of humanity, stamp these acts and the ideas which engendered them, as barbarous and criminal."[31]

After accusing the defendants of "wholesale murder and unspeakable cruel torture," Taylor enumerated Nazi medical experiments, for example, on human reactions to freezing, infectious diseases, poisons, mustard gas, and experimental antibacterial drugs.[32] For those who knew about Unit 731's human experimentation—Ishii's scientists and the widening circle of American officials learning about his program—the similarity to crimes being prosecuted at the Doctors' Trial, where the more monstrous defendants were nearly sure to hang, was striking.

Smirnov Arrives in Tokyo

The international world in which the Allied representatives lived and worked in Tokyo allowed surprising social connections. The Soviet delegation enjoyed a reputation for high-spirited parties, where SCAP, IPS, and defense staff were welcome; vodka flowed freely and mounting Cold War tensions were set aside.[33] In a letter to his wife, Chief of Counsel Keenan wrote, "I see quite a bit of the Russians" and referred to the Soviet envoy to the Allied Council for Japan, Lieutenant General Kusma Derevyanko, as "my old friend."[34] Derevyanko, who had signed the Japanese Surrender Instrument for the Soviet Union, had been the representative of the Soviet Armies Supreme Command at GHQ, with quarters at the Imperial Hotel, where he socialized with other elite Allied officers. At the council, whose offices were at the Meiji Building, he was continually at odds with the US representative and ACJ chairman George Atcheson, Jr., a fervent anticommunist.[35] Keenan seemed oblivious to any contention. About the IPS Soviet Division, he commented, "The Russians still keep a complete staff here in this work and evidence real interest in it for some reason or other."

One reason the Soviet Division maintained a full staff was its determination to reinforce its patently weak case against the Japanese. A new addition to the division was 35-year-old attorney Lev Nikolaevich Smirnov, who had performed outstandingly at Nuremberg with vivid presentations of evidence of Nazi atrocities. In addition to showing a bar of soap made from the body of a death camp victim and a sample of processed human skin, he offered voluminous proof from Soviet files, for example, some 54,784 depositions about mass slaughter, and then introduced the equally weighty US records. His otherwise stern look softened as he elicited moving testimony from survivors. His expression became again severe as he brought out photographs that graphically documented the slaughters in Poland and the Soviet Union—pictures of baskets of decapitated heads, streets lined with the hanging bodies of victims, and mass graves. Smirnov also showed a German film of the massacres at Lidice in Czechoslovakia in 1942.

"For four days," as US prosecutor Telford Taylor recounted, "the courtroom was an echo chamber of unthinkable torture and uncountable killings throughout the German-occupied areas in the Soviet Union and in Poland, Yugoslavia, and Czechoslovakia."[36] (The effect was like that produced by Sutton with his evidence for Japanese atrocities in China.) In his presentation, Smirnov spoke of the indoctrination of Nazi followers in words that touched Taylor: "It was necessary to train persons deprived of both heart and conscience, perverted creatures who had deliberately cut themselves off from the basic concepts of morality and law."[37] The same might be said of General Ishii and his cohort and would be if Smirnov had his way in Tokyo.

Regarding Japan's criminal germ weapons program, the Soviet prosecutors could pursue any argument and submit new proof at almost any time in the court proceedings. Along with other liberal rules, the IMTFE allowed the introduction of "mitigation evidence" (which in Anglo-American law usually follows a verdict) in the final stages of the trial. Until the end of the rebuttal phase, the Soviet Division could spontaneously enter the affidavits of Kawashima and Karasawa in evidence and even summon the two scientists to testify about the Japanese threat of germ warfare against the Soviet Union. From the Soviet vantage, the charge had important potential, for if the Kwantung Army, laying waste to southeastern China with germ weapons, planned to do the same to Soviet Siberia, the Soviet invasion of Manchuria in August 1945 could be interpreted as having prevented a "bacteriological holocaust."[38] Smirnov arrived in Tokyo with what he claimed was new documentation from Manchuria that confirmed the Kawashima and Karasawa affidavits and the interrogation of Lieutenant General Hata, the former Kwantung Army chief of staff. The Soviets had discovered Kwantung Army records describing its cooperation with Unit 731 and how the local Japanese military police rounded up "special consignments" of victims for Ishii's experiments—as many as seven hundred per year from 1938 to mid-1945. The Soviets were also holding captive more of Ishii's former staff than just Kawashima and Karasawa, along with Kwantung Army commander Yamada Otozo.

With Smirnov's arrival, the Soviet Division began to petition even more vigorously for access to General Ishii and other former Unit 731 scientists in Japan. In early January, with the conclusion of the prosecution's case delayed, Vasiliev repeated his interview request to Lieutenant Douglas L. Waldorf, who had ultimately succeeded Roy Morgan as head of the IPS Investigation Division. Waldorf passed the message to Frank Tavenner, who was in charge of the overall prosecution case and, in Keenan's continued absence, emerging as the main IPS decision maker. On January 7 Tavenner forwarded the request to G-2, which responded immediately with a demand for a written application. Two days later Vasiliev complied, writing Tavenner to emphasize that the Soviets had information relating to Japanese preparations for germ warfare and about the "mass murder of people as a result of these experiments."[39] He made specific reference to General Ishii and to Dr. Ota, identified as the leader of the plague attack on Changde—about which the Soviets had no doubts—and also to Major General Kikuchi, Unit 731's research director.

In his petition, Vasiliev made clear the Soviet intention to prosecute: "To present these materials as evidence to the Military Tribunal it is necessary to conduct a number of supplementary interrogations of persons who worked previously in the Anti-Epidemic Group (Manshu) N731 of Kwantung Army." His hope was that the United States would cooperate in these charges or at least aid the Soviet initiative. Vasiliev earnestly urged discretion, writing that he believed "it would be expedient to take preliminary measures preventing the spreading of information concerning this investigation before the investigation is completed and the materials are presented to the Tribunal." He advised that the witnesses be sworn to secrecy and that interrogations be conducted somewhere sequestered, not at the busy War Ministry building, where the trial was being conducted and whose upper floors had become a honeycomb of IPS division and SCAP offices.

On January 13 Tavenner consulted with Colonel Gilbert Woolworth, the US prosecutor assigned to assist the Soviet Division, who had his own G-2 contacts. As Tavenner informally wrote Vasiliev:

> I sent your memorandum to Colonel Woolworth on Saturday [January 12]. Went in a few minutes ago and talked to him. I find that Colonel Woolworth has already talked over the substance of your communication with a colonel in G-2 who has gone to General Willoughby, G-2 Assistant Chief of Staff, who is at present confined to his quarters by sickness.

> Colonel Woolworth expects to receive a report tonight or tomorrow morning, so I think we may as well postpone further consideration of the matter until the report is received.[40]

Smirnov was quickly invited to a 9 a.m. meeting on January 15 at a US government office at the War Ministry.[41] The meeting was called by Lieutenant Colonel Robert McQuail of G-2; Lieutenant Waldorf from the Investigation Division at IPS and Major Owen Keller from Tokyo's CWS office were also there. After describing the thoroughness of the Kawashima and Karasawa interrogations, Smirnov explained his goal of interviewing General Ishii as well as Dr. Ota and Dr. Kikuchi. He spoke of their "horrible crime of killing 2,000 Manchurians and Chinese" and their preparations for mass attacks on China, with plans to attack Siberia. Smirnov, who said nothing about the Kwantung Army records, confirmed what G-2 had suspected, that the Japanese had left Unit 731's Pingfan and other facilities in ruins, with all documents destroyed.

McQuail expressed no interest in a US-Soviet collaboration. After the meeting, he reported to Willoughby that, in his opinion, the Soviets had acquired little technical information from their captive Japanese officers; G-2 and CWS had the advantage of access to General Ishii and more and better scientific experts than the Soviet Union.

The Chinese Division seemed to have no role in these communications between the Soviet Division, IPS, and G-2. In its case against Japan, the Chinese prosecutors became focused on Japan's aggressive war crimes rather than the problematic subjects of biological or chemical warfare. In Washington, the vision of China as America's democratic ally in Asia was disintegrating, which had repercussions for the Chinese at the IMTFE. General George Marshall was recalled to Washington, signaling the end to US mediation to resolve the civil war and a growing ambivalence about military support for Generalissimo Chiang Kai-shek. Yet it was Prosecutor Hsiang Che-chun's position and that of his government that, if Japan were to become the US bastion of democracy in Asia, China could only benefit from friendly relations with its neighbor, a position that argued for a quick end to the IMTFE and an early peace treaty for Japan.[42]

On January 24, after presenting its case against Tojo, the prosecution took up its charges against General Umezu, who was the last on the alphabetical list of defendants. If the Soviet prosecutors had wanted to hold him responsible for Unit 731 war crimes, the opportunity was theirs. Instead they let Umezu be represented solely as a Class A warmonger who had also condoned the abuse of enemy captives. Without taking the stand, the "Ivory Mask" as usual impassively heard out the charges. At 4:12 p.m., with the case against Umezu completed, Carlisle Higgins announced to Sir William Webb, "Mr. President, the prosecution will now rest."

As the defense readied itself, civic unrest was growing outside the Ichigaya courthouse. General MacArthur, although he expressed his reluctance, banned the planned February 1 strike of 2.4 million government workers—those in transportation, light, gas, water, and postal services—who wanted a triple increase in pay and the resignation of the current conservative cabinet.[43] The left-of-center Japan Congress of Industrial Unions (Sanbetsu Kaigi) was at the root of this and previous strikes—confirming for General Willoughby his prediction of the communist threat to the Occupation. Although government worker salaries were about half those of others, MacArthur argued that Japan was too "impoverished" to allow the shutdown. With the Eighth Army ready to intervene with bayonets, the strike was canceled. But the backlash was solid public support for the Japan Socialist Party, which, to Willoughby's chagrin, became "the strongest force in the National Diet."[44]

On January 29 the defense counsel began its presentation of motions and arguments—and then collapsed in disagreement as to how individual cases should be represented in the general, joint argument. Another problem was the split between the American defense attorneys and their Japanese colleagues about what constituted persuasive documentary evidence and witness testimony. The Japanese approach, quantity of documents over quality and bravado declarations over reserved demeanor, unfortunately prevailed.[45]

That same day, Higgins and Tavenner sent an urgent telegram to Keenan in Washington about the continuing decline in IPS staff. The week before, Sutton had returned from Virginia, but many US lawyers had left for good. "Our American legal staff," they wrote, "is depleted to the extent we cannot operate at all effectively without immediate help. We have been expecting additions to the staff since the middle of December and had hoped they would be here to become acquainted with the background of the case in order to be of assistance in the cross examination of accused and defense witnesses. The few working members of the staff left here have labored day and night. All are extremely tired. We need help."[46]

With little help on the way, Higgins and Tavenner made do with the IPS staff they had, reviewing and reassessing individual case assignments. Vasiliev and Woolworth remained focused on Umezu, while Vasiliev by himself was assigned to Shigemitsu.[47] The heaviest responsibility went to British prosecutor Comyns Carr, who was given the cases for three major defendants, Baron Hirota, Marquis Kido, and General Araki. Sutton received a coveted assignment: the cross-examination of Field Marshal Hata Shunroku, former commander of the Japanese forces in China and implicated in the 1942 execution of the Doolittle pilots in Shanghai.

The defense counsel's disorganization created more delays, and, at its request, on February 3 President Webb called for a three-week adjournment of the court. In this lull, Sutton and others from IPS went on a tour of the Imperial Palace grounds, where he saw the emperor's biological laboratory and noted, "He studies jelly fish." The group had the chance to beat eight-hundred-year-old metal drums over six feet in diameter and to visit the imperial stable where Sutton, a practiced equestrian, saw Snow, the emperor's signature white stallion, and another prize, a horse that was "the grandson of Man O'War."[48]

On February 11, Prosecutor Hsiang came to Sutton's office at the War Ministry building to introduce three additions to the Chinese Division; Henry Chiu, much missed by Sutton, had left, leaving a gap. Foremost among the new recruits was Judson T. Nyi (Ni Zhengyu), counsel to the Ministry of Justice, who had studied law at Stanford University and at Johns Hopkins; Nyi had been a student of Judge S. Francis Liu, the eminent scholar with whom Sutton had lunched in Shanghai in April 1946. Liu, just a few weeks before, had spent a weekend at Sutton's home in Virginia, along with Luke Lea.[49] Grateful for the new Chinese prosecutors, Tavenner immediately gave them specific case tasks.[50] But the shortage of attorneys at IPS still, he felt, threatened the prosecution's case.

On February 12, Frank Tavenner was advised by Willis Mahoney that Keenan wanted him to be in exclusive charge of courtroom proceedings during the defense phase, with Carlisle Higgins relegated to case preparation with Comyns Carr. On February 25, in a terse radiogram to Tavenner from Washington, Keenan officially appointed him acting chief of counsel, completely bypassing Higgins, his assistant counsel and Tavenner's good friend.[51] Tavenner immediately wired Keenan for clarification as to his title, his exact duties, and whether "full authority" was in his hands. In the past he had been given considerable authority, but Keenan seemed to be making a change that was intended to last for some time. With some hesitation, Tavenner announced Keenan's decision the next day at an IPS staff meeting. As Sutton noted, Tavenner told the surprised group, "We must work as one team."

At exactly this same juncture, the defense counsel at the IMTFE opened its joint case for all defendants by laying out the five divisions of its upcoming argument. It would start with Division 1, the "general problems" in Japan's political and economic history, then move on to Division 2, on matters concerning Manchuria and Manchukuo; then to Division 3, on China; to Division 4, on the Soviet Union; and finally to Division 5, on the Pacific War. The defense intended to argue that the Japanese government had acted only in self-defense "against provocative acts of other nations threatening and interfering with Japan's recognized and legitimate rights in Asia and her right of national existence."[52] Its overarching claim was that the Allies had created the war of aggression charges post facto, and that there could be no crime without a pertinent law (*nullem crimen sine lege*) and, by extension, no punishment either (*nulla poena sine lege*)—age-old arguments raised by Germany after World War I and again by the defense at Nuremberg.[53] The Japanese defense would also contest the court's right to indict individual state officials and to ignore the immunity accorded diplomats "from time immemorial." To wage war to protect one's country, the defense asserted, was no crime. It also claimed that "killing in warfare does not and never has constituted murder, whatever the circumstances of its inception."[54]

In between the introduction of many documents and witnesses, the defense again enlivened the court proceedings with the claim that the United States had committed a war crime by using nuclear bombs on Hiroshima and Nagasaki. President Webb supported the prosecution's objection that waging aggressive war had nothing to do with the choice of weapons but with its unprovoked nature, a distinction inherent in the Nuremberg and Tokyo Charters.[55] When the defense moved on to argue that, in 1937–1945,

Imperial Japan fought the spread of communism in China as a threat to its national security, Webb criticized the argument as irrelevant, although it remained part of the defense strategy.

At the IPS, Frank Tavenner continued to be in charge. On March 28, in an unexpected letter from Washington, Keenan at last fully explained why he had made him acting chief counsel. "I returned from the hospital yesterday," Keenan began, "after undergoing a serious operation for which I had to prepare for many weeks preceding." His illness, about which he was vague, dated back nearly a year, but he felt he was well on his way to a complete cure. In the interim, he wanted Tavenner to have full command of the prosecution case and rely on Brigadier Nolan and Willis Mahoney for assistance. He acknowledged the "differences of views and perhaps exhibitions of temperament" at IPS and continued, "I know, however, Frank, that you have excellent judgment and a fine sense of fairness." He then closed with a warm compliment: "It has been a source of a great deal of comfort to me in my illness to know you were there, able and willing to carry on."[56]

Tavenner, who had written Keenan about his unease with the informality of the February promotion, wrote back that he had been completely unaware that Keenan was "required to go through such a siege of illness." "I shall always be grateful," he added, "for your expression of friendship and confidence."[57] Tavenner, Nolan, and his chief administrator Mahoney worked well together; as Mahoney reassured Keenan, Tavenner was competently directing the prosecution, and morale at the IPS was high.[58] Carlisle Higgins, though, had decided to return to law practice in North Carolina.

Morale may have been high that spring among the Americans at IPS but not at the Soviet Division. The Japanese defense was basing its self-defense argument not only on Western trade and immigration restrictions that forced its territorial expansion but on Soviet military aggression that demanded Japan's military presence in China. The defense opened its "general problems" argument with a broadside at the historic Soviet disregard of treaties, citing "Soviet aggression against Finland, its expulsion from the League of Nations, its aggression against the Baltic states, its aggression against Manchuria, and its wartime occupation of Iran (with the British) to guarantee an oil supply to the Soviet military and industry."[59] The defense was also set to argue that Soviet communism had been a destabilizing geopolitical threat, a claim that resonated with the rising Cold War tensions in Europe. Following its five-part agenda, further attacks on the Soviet case would be made sometime in May, when the Soviet Division, if it wished, could reinforce its case with new evidence of Japanese aggression.

On the stand, defense witnesses often made sweeping contentions that were then undermined by incriminating facts from the prosecutors. After a month the court insisted that defense witness testimony had to be submitted in writing three days in advance; if approved, the statement would be read in court with a simultaneous translation, after which cross-examination and reexamination would proceed as usual. When the court rejected what it considered an overload of irrelevant documents, the defense again collapsed. In the tumult of this period, the British, Canadian, and New Zealand judges, frustrated by President Webb's autocratic style, threatened to quit the court. Webb had long shunned their advice as well as their company. A New Zealand official persuaded Judge Erima Northcroft, a major critic of Webb's, that it would be a scandal for Britain and its dominions to sabotage the court by resigning.[60] That reasoning prevailed as Webb became more conciliatory, and the crisis passed, although the judges were far from unified in their assessments of the trial.

As the defense resumed arguing its case, the IPS concentrated on organizing its response to each issue raised by defense counsel, from Japan's self-defense argument and its claims to have honored the Hague Conventions of 1899 and 1907 to the specific charges against each defendant. As Frank Tavenner described to his former colleague, Osmond Hyde, "the grind has been terrific" and he remained short of staff.[61] Tavenner intervened with US Army officials to keep Captain Robinson, a mainstay from the original IPS team, from being recalled to Washington.[62] He had to beg New Zealand prosecutor Quilliam, still irked with Keenan and missing home life, not to leave. Nelson Sutton, too, although committed to the trial, was yearning for home. A timely letter from Luke Lea in Washington buoyed his spirits. "I want you to know that all your friends are gratified," Lea wrote, "with the position you are taking before the Tribunal and the work you are doing. We get excellent reports and I, as one of your devoted friends, am very proud of you."[63]

The "grind" at IPS continued, with Tavenner and the IPS staff working every night and most weekends to respond to the defense. With Williams,

Higgins, and Mansfield gone, Tavenner put Sutton in charge of case preparation, but the job proved beyond him. On May 26 Tavenner wrote an urgent plea to Keenan to use his influence at the Justice Department to send back a former IPS prosecutor, G. Osmond Hyde.[64] Willis Mahoney also wrote Keenan a letter in support of the reappointment of "Ozzie." In it he faulted Sutton for his lack of "orderly administrative ability" and inability to direct the overall case argument: "While he works late into the night and gets along beautifully with his associates and knows how to turn out his work, by reason of a nervous temperament he scatters his ability and for that reason Frank must constantly be alert to assist him."[65] No help came from Keenan; Hyde stayed at the Justice Department and the grind continued, with Tavenner himself eventually participating in over fifty cross examinations of defense witnesses, twice that of any other IPS lawyer.

While the defense case kept the IPS busy, Tavenner kept a watchful eye on the Soviet Division, repeatedly reminding prosecutor Vasiliev to be clear about his division's arguments, to keep up with deadlines, and handle the necessary Russian translations.

MacArthur's Petition to the JCS

Throughout the winter the Soviet Division had persisted in asking IPS for access to the Unit 731 scientists, a sign that their intentions to prosecute held firm. On February 7 Willoughby at G-2 reacted by sending a collection of briefing papers on their requests to the chief of staff at SCAP, requesting a decision from MacArthur as to whether Soviet counsel should be allowed to interrogate Ishii and other BW scientists.[66] Willoughby was against granting any contact, on the grounds that advanced scientific weapons information was at risk. He was convinced that the US acquisition of Japanese human experimentation data warranted giving Ishii and the others the official immunity from war crimes allowed Nazi scientists.

MacArthur passed Willoughby's memo to the State-War-Navy Coordination Committee and its Subcommittee for the Far East (SFE) to deliberate the question and formulate a policy. The subcommittee organized a working group to respond, the first of two it would commission. The Soviet Union was an ally whose request had to be taken seriously, yet the previous July, the Joint Chiefs of Staff had put restrictions on sharing scientific information with the Allies, except the British and Commonwealth members. Recognizing this, in a few weeks the working group formulated basic rules for Soviet access that maximized intelligence benefits for G-2 and the Chemical Warfare Service and minimized disclosing valuable information. First, the interrogations could be done only after the Japanese scientists had yielded as much information as possible to CWS—a measure that required another Detrick inquiry and would delay Soviet access. Second, the Japanese scientists had to be warned against revealing any significant information to the Soviets. Third, the interrogations had to take place under G-2 monitoring with the understanding that they could not be used for any war crimes prosecution. The interrogations allowed by SFE 188, as the policy was initially called, would be granted "as an amiable gesture toward a friendly government."[67] The United States would thus proceed slowly toward cooperation on this sensitive matter.

Frustrated by a continued lack of access to Ishii, the Soviet Division sought another route of appeal. On March 7 the Chief of Staff's Office at SCAP received a formal request from Lieutenant General Derevyanko at the Allied Council (Keenan's "friend") for the Soviet prosecutors to interview Unit 731 officers Ishii and Ota—in order to investigate Japanese war crimes against the USSR.[68] The right to extradite them was also requested, with the implication that the Soviet Union, as it had the right to do, might proceed with its own war crimes trial, on its own territory. In his request, Derevyanko underscored Soviet knowledge of G-2's and SCAP's ongoing protection of doctors whose crimes were as repulsive as any being exposed in Nuremberg. As a member of the Allied Council, Derevyanko had recently been personally rebuffed by General MacArthur for questioning one of the general's policy decisions.[69] Now he could prod SCAP and Washington, too, with the threat of scandal.

Meanwhile, more deliberations about the terms of Soviet access to Ishii's scientists continued to be held at the SWNCC subcommittee and full committee levels before being passed to the Joint Chiefs of Staff. On March 20 the JCS granted approval of the working group terms and the policy decision was immediately wired to SCAP.[70] With input from General Willoughby, a message went from SCAP to General Derevyanko informing him that Soviet interrogations would be allowed, subject to G-2's schedule and provided no war crimes investigation was involved.[71]

G-2 remained unsure what the Soviets had retrieved from the wreckage of Pingfan and other sites. Intelligence flagged the issue in March, reporting news from Manchuria in its *Daily Intelligence Summary* for officers and staff. On request, the Chinese Nationalist government had reported from Changchun (which had been Manchukuo's capital) that "surrendering Japanese troops had wrecked the top secret chamber of the Bacteriological Research Institute in former Kwantung Army headquarters . . . and the disease bacteria cultivation room of the Lu Yuan (Green Garden) Hospital."[72] Despite the destruction of buildings and records, it was known that the Japanese had been conducting research on a variety of diseases, especially plague, cholera, and "horse-nose cancer," understood to be glanders.[73] The planned methods for spreading the germs seemed mostly sabotage: "dropping bacteria packages by parachute over enemy territory; throwing into water sources; injecting into fruit; placing inside desks of superior officials; throwing among crowds." Still, it remained that research documents were missing and likely destroyed.

At the same time, Legal Section was making progress in locating Japanese biological warfare scientists capable of filling in more details. They seemed relatively eager to talk about the human experimentation they had witnessed, although they blamed it on their superiors, especially Unit 100's Dr. Wakamatsu. In a January 28 interview, Dr. Naito Ryiochi, Colonel Murray Sanders's guide in 1945, accused General Ishii of ordering the Unit 731 medical atrocities and using POWs in experiments; he then offered the names of others who could be interrogated.[74] On February 10 Naito returned to give a full summary of Ishii's malevolent career, a copy of which was sent to General MacArthur.[75] Shortly after, others lined up behind Naito to talk about experiments on human captives, always putting the blame on higher-ups. In one account, Dr. Wakamatsu and a Major Yamaguchi were described as "responsible for the deaths of 13 persons as the result of secret experiments."[76] In another, a worker from Unit 100 described an experiment with glanders performed by physicians on a victim who appeared to be a Russian soldier.[77] Not long after, Dr. Masuda Tomosada (Ishii's protégé and former head of Unit 1644) made a statement denouncing his former mentor as well as two former colleagues, Dr. Ota Kiyoshi and Dr. Ikari Tsuneshige.[78] Messages went out from Legal Services to the Japanese government that names and addresses of anyone involved in the germ weapons program should be provided. The ensuing weeks were taken up with interrogations focused on Unit 100 and possible links between animal research and experiments on humans, possibly including US POWS, Carpenter's main interest. In a coup for the Legal Section, Dr. Ota and Dr. Ikari were soon found and interrogated.[79]

Dr. Fell's Promise

In line with the JCS directive, arrangements were made for Dr. Norbert Fell, chief of Camp Detrick's Field Division, to come to Tokyo in April to make further inquiries. Only when he was satisfied and had reported his findings back to SWNCC would Colonel Lev Smirnov, the designated Soviet interrogator, be allowed to conduct his interviews.

On April 13 Dr. Fell was in Tokyo, meeting with Ishii and his cohort to determine just what weapons "booty" they had to offer. He gave the Japanese scientists an outline of the desired medical and technical details, the kind of information that would enhance US strategic antipersonnel weapons research and also data on anticrop agents, in which Detrick had invested heavily during the war. The Americans' intermediary was Dr. Kamei Kanichiro, a business entrepreneur who was close to Dr. Naito and knew about Sanders's earlier investigation.[80]

On April 22, in the presence of Kamei and G-2's Lieutenant Colonel McQuail, Dr. Fell questioned Dr. Masuda, once Ishii's right-hand man, with little result. Afterward, Kamei revealed to Fell that Masuda had admitted to Unit 731 human experimentation on "Manchurian criminals," but those involved in these experiments had vowed never to speak of them. Kamei told Fell, "I feel sure that if you handle your investigation from a scientific point of view, you can obtain detailed information."[81] Kamei was confident that the Japanese BW scientists had much to offer, even from memory.

A week later Fell was interviewing Naito, Masuda, and a third Ishii scientist, Kaneko Junichi, all previously interviewed by Colonel Murray Sanders in 1945. When Fell confronted them with the Kawashima and Karasawa affidavits (somehow acquired from IPS by G-2) and their descriptions of medical atrocities, Masuda admitted to having heard about human experimentation, but the other two hesitated. After the three conferred in private, Naito explained the problem to Fell. "We are afraid some of us will be prosecuted as war criminals," he said. "We do not know how much (the other scientists) will be willing to give us. If you can give us documentary immunity, possible we can get everything."[82]

On the spot, Fell assured them that "war crimes were not involved." This phrase from the SWNCC/JCS directive was accepted as enough of a guarantee of immunity to reassure his nervous informants. Thereafter the Japanese scientists started offering new disclosures, for example, about the plague-infected flea attacks on China, typhoid fever spray experiments, and human research on hemorrhagic fevers. Masuda and Naito volunteered to contact other Unit 731 scientists in Japan to involve them in passing on important information. In expectation of SCAP protection, the network of those willing to talk to Fell expanded to nearly two dozen. Major General Kikuchi, former chief of Unit 731's First Division, for example, cooperated fully when he found out that the Soviet prosecutors had asked to interview him. General Ishii, though, remained intransigent. When Fell interviewed him at his home, where he was confined to bed, he found the general as wily as he had been with Thompson. Implying he controlled a great store of hidden information, Ishii insisted on a written guarantee of immunity.

In mid-April, persuaded by Willoughby that Ishii's program required the utmost secrecy, General MacArthur gave G-2 complete control over Legal Section's File 330, the repository of dozens of documents about Unit 731.[83] In a memo that declared the file secret, Willoughby announced that, regarding further inquiries: "Every step, interrogation or contact must be coordinated with this section as per the order of the Commander-in-Chief and Chief of Staff."[84] Legal Section head Alva Carpenter was advised that "no action [could] be taken on prosecution or any form of publicity of this case without G-2 concurrence." Yet Willoughby wanted more: heeding Ishii's ultimatum, he felt that an official immunity bargain with the US government was necessary to obtain a maximum of information and that the supreme commander should intervene.

At this point in his career, General MacArthur was in an especially strong position. After a year and a half as SCAP, he had achieved nearly all the goals of US postsurrender policy. Japan's military power was destroyed and a representative government was in place, with a modern constitution. Emperor Hirohito was protected from indictment; unable to reach a decision, the previous October the State-War-Navy Coordinating Committee tried and failed to relegate the decision to the IPS, which MacArthur had previously decided lacked the necessary authority.[85] Free elections had been held, with women voting. He had liberated political prisoners and implemented land reform. Overall, political power had been decentralized and police oppression eliminated, and he had seen to the separation of church from state. Revered throughout Japan, MacArthur was known as the "Second Emperor."

In January the wartime Armed Forces of the Pacific (AFPAC) had been reorganized as Far East Command (FECOM), which greatly enlarged MacArthur's sphere of responsibility. It consolidated his control of the US Armed Forces in the region and the British Commonwealth Occupation Force and, territorially, gave him the Ryukyus Command, the Philippine Command, and, in the Pacific Islands, the Marianas-Bonin Command.[86] His prospects for becoming the next president of the United States, backed by the Republican Party, looked bright. The one policy goal that still eluded him was the punishment of the war criminals, as understood in the Potsdam Declaration. The IMTFE lumbered on without closure. The crimes of the Ishii program and its connection to the high command and possibly the emperor was an unanticipated complication that needed resolution.

Pressured by Willoughby, General MacArthur decided to use his authority to alert the highest military officials in Washington. On May 6, 1947, he sent a two-page top secret radiogram to the War Department's General Intelligence Division, requesting action by the Joint Chiefs of Staff on an immunity agreement for the Unit 731 scientists.[87] Fleet Admiral William Leahy, head of the JCS, had known him for years; Fleet Admiral Chester Nimitz, representing the navy, had won the war with him in the Pacific; in the 1930s Army Chief of Staff Dwight Eisenhower had been MacArthur's aide in the Philippines. The request for a decision revealed that SCAP had secretly been protecting scientists whose hideous crimes matched those being prosecuted in Nuremberg and, further, involved mass killings of Chinese civilians by germ warfare. In his brief message, MacArthur made his military peers and presumably President Truman complicit in this knowledge.

MacArthur's radiogram laid out the situation frankly. First, the Japanese scientists interviewed by Dr. Fell had confirmed the scope of information in the Kawashima and Karasawa interviews:

> Experiments on humans were known to and described by three Japanese and confirmed tacitly by Ishii; field trials against Chinese Army took place on at least three occasions; scope of program indicated by report of reliable informant Masuda that 400 kilograms of dried anthrax organisms destroyed at Pingfan in August 1945; and research on use of BW against plant life was carried out. Reluctant statements by Ishii indicate he had superiors (possibly General Staff) who knew and authorized the program.[88]

Among the IMTFE defendants, these superiors included General Umezu, Tojo and others who had led the Kwantung Army in the 1930s, and General Hata, who had commanded the Zhejiang-Jiangxi campaign in 1942.

Willoughby's belief that Ishii's cooperation was crucial to national security was evident in MacArthur's request:

> Ishii states that if guaranteed immunity from "war crimes" in documentary form for himself, his superiors and subordinates, he can describe the program in detail. Ishii claims to have extensive theoretical high-level knowledge including strategic and tactical use of BW on defense and offense, backed by some research on best BW agents to employ by geographical areas of Far East and the use of BW in cold climates.[89]

The radiogram further stated that "persuasion, exploitation of Japanese fear of the USSR, and desire to co-operate with the US" had been effective in gaining information and that the same methods could continue to be used.

MacArthur then suggested two contrasting responses. One was to offer official documented immunity to Ishii and his associates, which would likely guarantee the "complete story" of BW plans and theories. A JCS/SWNCC ruling to allow them immunity from criminal prosecution in exchange for valuable information would follow the SWNCC directive 216/1 for Japan.

The alternative was to take a softer approach that relied on trust and avoided a signed agreement: "Additional data, possibly including some statements from Ishii probably can be obtained by informing Japanese involved that information will be retained in intelligence channels and will not be employed as 'war crimes' evidence." The phrase "in intelligence channels" offered the US government's institutional guarantee of secrecy with a diminished risk of scandal. This way, the arrangement of G-2's control of witness interrogation and of File 330 information might simply continue.

While SWNCC deliberated MacArthur's message, it still remained for G-2 to discover what further evidence the Soviets had by observing their interrogations of a few of Ishii's men and Ishii himself. On May 13 Soviet prosecutor Lev Smirnov was allowed an on-the-record interrogation of Dr. Murakami Takashi, a former 731 division leader, at the FECOM Central Interrogation Center in Tokyo.[90] General Ishii was unavailable, reportedly ill, and Murakami, prepared by the Americans the previous May, was chosen for the first interview. The SWNCC restraints had been made clear. The interview transcript could not be used as an IMTFE affidavit, and Smirnov had no right to call anyone he interrogated to testify as a war crimes witness. Dr. Fell from Camp Detrick and Lieutenant Colonel McQuail from G-2 attended the interrogation, with two interpreters and a stenographer. G-2 would prepare the typed transcript and deliver it to the Soviet Division.

In 1941 Murakami had taken over as chief of Unit 731's 2nd Section, in charge of research. Like the others in his cohort, he had been warned to reveal no secrets to the Soviets. His most repeated phrase turned out to be "My memory is poor." He could not remember any mass production of fleas, the meetings to plan the expedition to China in 1942, the expedition itself, whether Ishii had directed it, if the Kwantung Army ever gave orders to the unit, or if experiments on captives had ever been conducted there. Murakami did remember being in Nanking in 1942, but only as part of an anti-epidemic effort to protect retreating troops. He was able to describe and even sketch porcelain anthrax bombs but denied that they were ever filled with real bacteria, only with simulants to gauge what harm the enemy might do. He portrayed himself as an "average doctor" and an administrator who took his orders from Ishii and no one else.

"What we cannot comprehend," the exasperated Smirnov commented, "is why you don't say the truth."

"I can't tell you what I don't know," Murakami answered, and the interview ended.

On May 16 Colonel Smirnov returned to the Central Interrogation Office to question Dr. Ota, head of the 2nd Section at Unit 731 prior to Murakami and at the Ei 1644 Unit in Nanjing in the 1940s.[91] His research had included a series of anthrax aerosol tests on Chinese male captives. In 1941 he had led the plague attack on Changde, and in 1942, along with Murakami, he had participated in the Zhejiang-Jiangxi campaign.

Warned by the Americans, Ota evaded Smirnov's questions. He described Unit 731 as devoted only to defensive BW research and the Ei 1644 branch as committed solely to anti-epidemic prevention among troops. He denied knowing anything about bacteriological warfare or extensive sabotage in China. Again, like Murakami, Ota played the humble administrator. "We just performed our assigned duties," he told Smirnov, "and were ignorant of the nature and source of the orders." When Smirnov read him Karasawa's description of bomb experiments with Manchu captives, Ota responded, "I don't know anything about it. I have never heard about it, and I have never seen any."

After Ota denied that any Chinese captives were imprisoned at Unit 731, Smirnov showed him a map of the enclave and asked him to identify certain unmarked buildings. Ota replied that they were warehouses for chemicals; in fact, they were the unit's prison and crematorium.

"You are not answering truthfully," Smirnov scolded Ota. "It is strange that you should conceal the facts."

"I am not trying to conceal," Ota insisted, and he was allowed to leave.

Smirnov had learned nothing from the two scientists and, as far as the Americans could tell, he knew little more than what was in the two Soviet affidavits. It was agreed that he would be allowed to interview General Ishii later, as soon as the general felt well enough.

Without a signed immunity bargain, Ishii was speaking freely with CWS and G-2 officers, even entertaining them at his home, while G-2 reinforced its relationship with twenty other Unit 731 scientists, paying for restaurants, hotel accommodations, and personal gifts, enough to win their trust.

10
NATIONAL SECURITY VERSUS MEDICAL ETHICS

WHILE G-2 ARRANGED THE IPS SOVIET DIVISION'S ACCESS TO UNIT 731 scientists, the State-War-Navy Coordinating Committee in Washington began a long debate about MacArthur's May 6 request for an Ishii immunity agreement. As with the decision to allow Soviet access for interrogations, the pros and cons were discussed throughout multiple bureaucratic levels, beginning with the Subcommittee for the Far East and its working group, with policy recommendations to be returned to the SWNCC. After SWNCC review, the recommendations would go to the Joint Chiefs of Staff for consideration. Consultations with staff at the War Department and different US War, Army, Navy, and State Department offices were part of the process. The working policy draft (called SWNCC 188) would reach a final version, approved by the Joint Chiefs, and be sent to SCAP as a directive. The subject was sensitive and the decision would not be rushed.

The committee's goal was to craft a policy position that would avoid two risks. One was the risk to US national security as General Charles Willoughby and most military advisors saw it, which involved strategic arms competition with the Soviets. The other risk was scandal, about which Robert A. Fearey of the Department of State, a former political advisor at

SCAP, warned. For weeks the press in Nuremberg had been reporting on the Doctors' Trial and the medical horrors of Nazi death camps.[1] Should word leak that the US government and General MacArthur had granted official immunity to Japanese scientists as monstrous as any Nazi sadists, public denunciation of President Truman, the administration, and General MacArthur was the guaranteed outcome.

The defense counsel at Nuremberg had fought back with proof that, during the war, the US Office of Scientific Research and Development had conscripted hundreds of prison inmates for a study of malaria.[2] The US government's justification at the time was that the research was merited for the protection of the health of soldiers, who were willing to sacrifice their lives for the nation. In the dock at Nuremberg, Dr. Karl Brandt, the Reich's general commissioner for health and sanitation, defended himself with the same argument, stating: "The general need for experiments on human beings, and only those are relevant here, has been recognized by all nations as a military necessity."[3] Even as the Doctors' Trial continued, US Public Health researchers were exploiting vulnerable populations—southern blacks, the mentally ill, children, prostitutes, and the poor—in infectious disease studies.[4] But the United States recoiled from associating its medical research with the Nazi state-run crimes that ranged from mass euthanasia of disabled people and so-called undesirables (such as alcoholics, homosexuals, and vagrants) to subjecting concentration camp prisoners to fatal experiments of high-altitude oxygen deprivation and freezing exposure, injections of malaria, typhus, and jaundice, limb amputation, bone removal, poison injections, and full-body exposure to aerosols of mustard gas. Predictably, SWNCC discussions about Unit 731 focused on potential "embarrassment" should an official US cover-up of similar Japanese medical atrocities become public.

In late 1946, months before MacArthur's immunity request, the news media had exposed Operation Paperclip, causing a furor over the US government's employment of hundreds of ex-Nazis in defense industry sectors throughout the nation.[5] Albert Einstein, the celebrated physicist, led a group of forty concerned citizens that appealed to President Truman, Secretary of War Robert Patterson, and Secretary of State James Byrnes to question why "potentially dangerous carriers of racial and religious hatred" should be rewarded with US citizenship and given "key positions in American industrial, scientific, and educational institutions."[6] Distinguished nuclear physicist Hans Bethe, a German Jewish refugee who had worked on the Manhattan Project, criticized the moral standards of these bargains with "die-hard Nazis." "Do we want science at any price?" he asked.[7]

Balanced against the possibility of a Unit 731 scandal was the perceived growing threat of the Soviet Union, which preoccupied the Joint Chiefs and the White House. Early in 1947, in reaction to the possible fall of Greece to communism, the Truman Doctrine was introduced to affirm America's central role in an enduring conflict between free peoples and totalitarian regimes. Soviet communism was perceived as a domestic threat as well. On March 21, 1947, Truman signed Executive Order 9835, a sweeping requirement for federal agencies to use the FBI to investigate the loyalty of federal employees (nearly 2.4 million in total).[8] The Loyalty Review Board was created to investigate individual biographies, including school and college records. With its mission to investigate communist subversion and propaganda, the House Un-American Activities Committee (HUAC), a permanent congressional committee since 1945, helped by contributing its files on likely suspects.

Atomic scientists were closely monitored, owing to fears, which proved realistic, of secrets being leaked to the Soviet Union; the stakes of nuclear supremacy were nothing less than existential.[9] In anticipation of Soviet nuclear advances, the United States moved toward increasing its arsenal from twenty-nine to fifty-five atomic bombs.[10] Just as the SWNCC began evaluating MacArthur's request regarding immunity, the Senate Committee on Armed Services was reviewing the Truman administration's "Unification Bill," the basis for the upcoming National Security Act that would unite the armed services under a secretary of defense and create the National Security Council and the Central Intelligence Agency. Every legislative debate over national security, including this one, was deeply influenced by anxiety over nuclear arms competition and its dreaded implications.[11] The preparation for total war seemed urgently necessary for America's survival as the dominant, democratic world power.

As chief chemical officer, Major General Alden Waitt argued that chemical and biological weapons were part of this preparation. His organization had, in fact, exploited Operation Paperclip.[12] As early as September 1945 Gerhard Schrader, who in 1936 had synthesized tabun nerve gas, was writing scientific reports for US-UK combined intelligence, although he later refused Allied recruitment. Chemist Friedrich Hoffman, unsurpassed in his knowledge of organophosphates, was recruited first by the British in their Operation Matchbook (their version of Operation Paperclip); then, in 1947, he relocated to Edgewood Arsenal for top secret work on the new nerve agents. Over thirty other German chemists and technicians (including former Nazis) had been relocated to Edgewood to assist with munitions production. Building on German research, scientific teams there and at Britain's Porton Down discovered more about why the nerve agents were so lethal: they inhibited a key enzyme in the nervous system called acetyl cholinesterase, causing convulsions, constricted breathing, and rapid death. Assisting the Allied Chemical Weapons Tripartite coalition of the United States, Great Britain, and Canada, the Australians hired several dozen German chemists for their program. Together the US-led coalition made progress with offensive research and also developed masks, suits, and antidotes to protect their troops from nerve gas attacks.

In addition to US national security, the Joint Chiefs of Staff's vision of the coming role of Japan affected the SWNCC response to the immunity request. With the crumbling of European empires in Asia, the United States was positioned to become the heir to regional power, using direct economic support as well as military and covert action to secure its position.[13] But the deterioration of Chiang Kai-shek's Kuomintang forces in their battle against Mao Zedong's Communist Party army undermined that ambition. Following significant incursions into northern China in 1946, by early 1947 the disorganized Chinese Nationalist forces had been pushed south and seemed close to collapse. After critics at home pointed out that Generalissimo Chiang had absorbed considerable American support "without any noticeable effect," the Joint Chiefs advised giving China only "carefully planned, selective and well-supervised assistance," limited to ammunition and replacement parts for US equipment already supplied to the Nationalists.[14] As it communicated to SWNCC, the JCS saw that the potential fall of Chiang would give the USSR hegemony throughout Asia. This grim possibility reinforced the importance of Japan as a democratic ally that offered the Ryukyu Islands, including Okinawa, as a US military outpost, a complement to US bases in the Philippines.

In Tokyo the SCAP anticommunist intelligence apparatus that Willoughby had established in 1945—his regional espionage and surveillance networks—fit the new Truman Doctrine. In June he expanded his mission by creating a "Loyalty Desk" inside G-2's Public Safety Division, under its Civil Intelligence Division. A miniature, military version of Truman's Loyalty Review Board, its purpose was to conduct security checks on Occupation personnel. Willoughby also created a "Domestic Subversion Desk" to identify "disaffected" Americans at SCAP.[15] The timing was right. Japan's newly revised democratic constitution (which came into effect on May 3, 1947) positioned it as an American ally against the growing threat of communism in the East. A "soft" Cold War was in the making, a precursor to radical changes in MacArthur's initial Occupation vision for a neutral, pacifist Japan.[16] Within SCAP, generals who thought like Willoughby had come to control most of the sections and had fixed ideas about Japan's future. As an Australian diplomat in Tokyo observed: "They see the Japanese nation, not as a sick society, but as a demobilized army. They are preoccupied with the Russian danger and the associated danger of Communism within Japan. The only change they deeply desire is to change Japan from a former enemy into a future ally, and they believe this is comparatively simple to contrive."[17]

Abrupt, secret interventions by General Willoughby, like the classification of Legal Section's File 330 on General Ishii the previous April, had larger consequences. Owing to the file's subject matter, Alva Carpenter, the head of Legal Section, was drawn into the SWNCC interagency deliberations on immunity. On June 6, in response to an inquiry from the War Crimes desk at the War Department, he conferred with Frank Tavenner at the International Prosecution Section and then sent Washington a bland communication that summarized Tavenner's rationale for not prosecuting.[18] Carpenter explained that "anonymous letters, hearsay, rumors" were the only evidence against Ishii and his cohort and thus no charges would be levied at the IMTFE; the matter had been decided the previous December, he stated, alluding to Tavenner's dismissive response to General A. N. Vasiliev. "The alleged victims," he added in defense of the decision, "are of unknown identity. Unconfirmed allegations are to the effect that criminals, farmers, women and children were used for BW experimental purposes."

To his reply, Carpenter attached Tavenner's brief summaries of the General Kawashima and Major Karasawa affidavits, which included no details of atrocities. Tavenner left out mention of the third Soviet interrogation, of Lieutenant General Hata, the former Kwantung Army chief of staff, who had named defendants General Minami, General Koiso, and Premier Tojo. Following Tavenner's lead, Carpenter declared that none of the accused in the dock could be "associated with acts charged." Carpenter also warned that Soviet prosecutors might, given their independent investigation of Japanese germ warfare, confront some Tokyo defendants with criminal evidence from Manchuria, which could risk Ishii's exposure.

After a brief period of open publications and defensive research, in 1947 the US biological weapons program reverted to wartime secrecy and offensive planning. As army chief of staff at the time, General Dwight Eisenhower held a press conference to emphasize its national security mission, and James Forrestal, once he became the new secretary of defense in September, reinforced the policy reversal, which shielded the reactivated US program from public scrutiny.[19] As former Camp Detrick scientist Theodor Rosebury, a wartime architect of the program, protested, "The Army, having lifted ever so slightly the lid of the germ-warfare Pandora's box, slammed it shut again under strict secrecy regulations."[20] The British and the Canadians, America's wartime biological weapons partners, remained Cold War collaborators in the pursuit of an offensive capability that might match that of atomic weapons, a touted but unrealistic goal.[21]

The Defense Counsel Attacks

In Tokyo that spring and summer, as defense lawyers presented their arguments, the prosecutors took turns fighting back. The aggressiveness of the defense surprised the Chinese, who had not expected any great challenge to their case.[22] More surprised and dismayed were the Soviet prosecutors. The defense persisted in emphasizing the Soviet history of geopolitical aggression and communist revolution and, going further, extrapolating that history into the Cold War present. One defense attorney raised the Truman Doctrine as confirming Japanese fears of Soviet communism in the 1930s.[23] Portraying Imperial Japan as the protector of Asia, another defense counsel brought up Winston Churchill's Iron Curtain speech to illustrate how Soviet regional interference continued to cause upheaval and suffering.[24] A heated courtroom exchange erupted about the Soviet Union's refusal to allow the defense to obtain testimony from USSR prisoners of war, including nine Japanese generals.[25]

Whatever the personal beliefs of Frank Tavenner regarding Soviet communism, he was responsible for leading all the prosecution divisions, out of respect for the court's international objectives. Cold War politics, though, intruded at Ichigaya when Willoughby's G-2 cooperated with the defense, certainly with SCAP's approval. Soviet counsel had argued that the Japanese continually conspired to aggress into eastern Siberia, demonstrated by the increase in Kwantung Army forces in Manchuria and Korea in 1941. From G-2, the defense learned of Japanese General Staff records about the wartime superiority of Soviet military strength in the border area. On June 2–3, relying on classified documents, Lieutenant Homer Blake from G-2 testified for the defense that from 1943 to 1945 Japanese forces in the North were seriously undermanned and underequipped, relative to the Soviet Far Eastern Army.[26] While on the stand, Blake confirmed the authenticity of more documents acquired through G-2 that made the same point for the 1930s.

The defense was again helped by the US military regarding the Soviet violation of its 1941 Neutrality Pact with Japan. An affidavit by US Major General John Deane testified to Joseph Stalin's repeated promises to break the pact—at the Teheran Conference in 1943, at the Moscow Conference in 1944 (where Deane, as military attaché, had been an observer), at Yalta in February 1945, and at Potsdam in July 1945, where Stalin stipulated late August as the time for his invasion of Manchuria. Tavenner, as surprised as the Soviet Division by Deane's statement, offered to help Vasiliev handle the objection.[27] The court accepted the affidavit but only after three hours of debate between the defense and prosecution.[28]

Another surprise came when the defense submitted an affidavit from General George C. Marshall, who in January had become Truman's secretary of state.[29] Marshall stated that Japan had kept faithfully to the Neutrality Pact, even allowing Soviet ships carrying US Lend Lease materials to proceed unimpeded to Vladivostok.[30] The hypocrisy of the Soviet Union was the point in the defense's *tu quoque* argument. Incensed, Prosecutor Vasiliev protested that "our country has deserved the right not to be insulted in this Tribunal."[31]

New Zealand prosecutor, Ronald Quilliam, who had prolonged his stay at IPS, commented on the Soviet Division's performance during this phase:

> The Russian counsel do not willingly accept advice, and are rather secretive about their plans and the information possessed by them. They press their own point of view with great persistence. Of course the language difficulty must produce some misunderstanding, but that does not account for all the difficulties that arise. Further, if they were not so sensitive it would help. Unfortunately, however, they claim to be the only true democrats and the only peace-loving people, and at any rate since the revolution, to have an unblemished record. They therefore strongly resent any suggestion which appears, however remotely, to reflect on their conduct as peace-loving democrats. For all these reasons the Russian Phase is taking an inordinate time and a great deal of irrelevant material is being introduced on both sides.[32]

Tavenner felt the Soviets lacked rigor and were a detriment to the overall prosecution case.[33] For the three weeks of the Soviet phase, he attended each session, often accompanied by Judge Hsiang, whom he described as a "consoling presence," and actively assisted with cross-examinations to compensate for confusions due to language differences and legal misunderstandings. The Soviet phase ended without its division introducing evidence about Unit 731 as part of the Japanese threat of aggressive war. Its prosecutors had barely been able to represent their original case.

CWS and Military Intelligence in Tokyo

In Washington, General Waitt, while advising the War Department on MacArthur's immunity request, remained a G-2 ally. In an early June telephone call, he and Willoughby agreed on "the extreme value of the intelligence information obtained and the danger of publicity on this subject."[34] Camp Detrick's Dr. Norbert Fell, a division chief who specialized in infectious diseases, would continue to investigate the Ishii program, in the utmost secrecy.[35]

General Waitt had reason to worry about adverse publicity. In line with Secretary of War Patterson's policies, his postwar vision emphasized close military and corporate business cooperation. But, with the Truman reorganization of US defense, by mid-July 1947 Patterson was gone while the congressional focus on wartime military excesses and corruption continued. Waitt soon became entangled in a Senate investigation of the Garsson brothers, two contractors who during the war had bilked the US government out of millions of dollars, a good deal of it through CWS contracts. Photographs had surfaced from the marriage in 1944 of one of the Garsson daughters to a CWS major; in them CWS chief General William Porter, Alden Waitt, and other CWS officers were caught celebrating the event at the Hotel Pierre in New York.[36] Testifying before Congress, Waitt defended the record of the service, which under his leadership had become the Army Chemical Corps—the upgrade that President Franklin Roosevelt had adamantly opposed in 1937.

Despite the bad press, Waitt held on to his post and the CWS budget, which the year before had sunk to $933,000, regained its wartime high of $2.4 million, thanks to a turn toward Cold War thinking.[37] Immediately after the war, chemical and biological weapons were virtually missing from US national security planning. The very first resolution of the United Nations in 1946 concerning "weapons capable of mass destruction" referred only to "atomic arms."[38] As Cold War tensions in Europe mounted and the Truman Doctrine took hold in Washington, Waitt's ideas about a coming total war and the strategic promise of biological and chemical weapons struck a chord. President Truman withdrew the Geneva Protocol of 1925 from Senate consideration. At Detrick, the program to adapt lethal pathogens to bombs and spray generators was revived, with hopes the air force would become a major client. The discovery of German nerve gases gave the Chemical Corps a new research direction. As US partners, the British were also developing nerve gas munitions and, in 1946, embarked on a project called "Red Admiral" to make a thousand-pound cluster bomb that could inflict a 50 percent death rate on an industrial area of one hundred square miles.[39] Whether biological or chemical weapons could actually compete with nuclear arms or even with conventional bombs was a matter of theory, but theory was enough to loosen congressional purse strings to institutionally invest in these innovations.

Still in Tokyo, more successful in his inquiry than either Sanders or Thompson, Dr. Fell was discovering ample evidence of forced human experimentation. At Camp Detrick the scientific understanding of the impact of especially lethal infectious diseases on humans was crucial yet difficult to measure without research that exposed test subjects to mortal danger. In its inhalatory form, anthrax was known to kill over 90 percent of those infected, with no hope of cure, which made it the premier US biological weapon. But how its spores did their damage was poorly understood, and how the pathogens of other disease candidates like plague, tularemia, and typhoid fever might be better used as bomb and spray weapons lacked human research. The Unit 731 experiments on "prisoners" could hold the key. As Fell reported to General Waitt and General Willoughby, with just verbal assurance of protection, he had found it "finally possible to get the key Japanese medical men who had been connected with B.W. to agree to reveal the entire story."[40]

As part of that story, Fell's Japanese informants promised theoretical and mathematical models about particle-size and droplet distribution of disease microbes by bomb and aircraft sprays, which they called "bacterial rain." As Fell knew, these models had been developed through tests on human subjects. In addition, the scientists promised full accounts of twelve field "trials" against Chinese civilians, including the plague attacks on China and the Zhejiang-Jiangxi campaign of 1942, with maps of targets and a summary of results. Supplied with questions telegraphed from Detrick, Fell was able to find out about Japanese crop destruction agents and plans to destroy agriculture over the border in Siberia and throughout Manchuria; in the event they had to flee, Unit 731 scientists had intended to leave behind a new kind of "scorched earth." In addition, ten Unit 100 scientists agreed to write about experiments on animal diseases, including anthrax and glanders. General Ishii, described by Fell as "the dominant figure in the B.W. program," would write "a treatise on the whole subject."

Fell reckoned that the top prize for the United States, to be shared with the collaborating UK and Canadian BW programs, would be the collection of eight thousand slides of pathological sections from more than two hundred human cases of disease intentionally caused by BW agents: "Data on human experiments, when we have correlated it with data we and our Allies have on animals, may prove invaluable, and the pathological studies and other information about human diseases may help materially in our attempts at developing really effective vaccines for anthrax, plague and glanders."[41]

The former Unit 731 pathologist who secretly held this collection was Ishikawa Tachiomaru, the professor at Kanazawa University once reported to have sheltered Ishii. He promised to write a report by the end of August. In addition, six hundred pages of Japanese documents on human plague cases were available for translation.

As Ishii's scientists overcame their hesitations, Fell reported that they confirmed details of the Kawashima and Karasawa testimonies concerning experiments on "Manchurian coolies who had been condemned to death for various crimes." As Fell wrote: "The human subjects were used in exactly the same manner as other experimental animals, i.e., the minimum infectious and lethal dosage of various organisms was determined on them, they were immunized with various vaccines and then challenged with living organisms, and they were used as subjects during field trials of bacteria disseminated by bombs and sprays."[42]

Fell accepted the scientists' assertions that, except for when they tested the blood of some American POWs in Mukden for antibodies, they had conducted no medical experiments on American prisoners of war. Carpenter would eventually concur; some forty-six affidavits he had collected for File 330 apparently contained no supporting evidence for such experiments.[43]

In discussions with Fell, the Japanese informants explained how, late in the war, the Japanese launched balloon bombs toward the west coast of the United States and Canada, in one instance killing people having a picnic. At the time, US and Canadian germ warfare experts (including Detrick's Murray Sanders) investigated the balloons on-site and became concerned that "a biological weapon would introduce a particularly virulent strain of bacteria capable of being distributed by any number of vectors, human, animals, vegetation, and even the wind."[44] The Japanese scientists promised a brief report describing how their balloon project, planned for Siberia, proved impractical, like the conventional balloon bombs.

Smirnov Confronts Ishii

On June 13 Colonel Lev Smirnov went to the FECOM Central Interrogation Office to interview General Ishii, now well enough (or finally willing) to leave his home.[45] As usual, Lieutenant Colonel Robert McQuail from G-2 was there for the interrogation, this time with two interpreters and a stenographer.

Colonel Smirnov started by allowing General Ishii to discourse about the different kinds of glassware used in the Unit 731 laboratories and the size in centimeters of the "steam kettles" used for disinfection, after which he bragged about a cultivating apparatus he had invented—a square box with ten compartments into which a melted agar-agar solution was poured. In his element, Ishii described his institute's mass vaccine production—for 600,000 people, he claimed, in response to a plague outbreak in Manchukuo's capital, Changchun.

Switching the subject, Smirnov asked if his unit's Fourth Section had been equipped to mass produce bacteria for warfare. "Nonsense!" Ishii replied. The aim of Unit 731, he insisted, was solely to protect Japanese soldiers and in response to fears of the different kinds of epidemics endemic in China—cholera, plague, and anthrax—and to the threat of germ attacks from the Soviet Union.

Smirnov pressed his point, telling Ishii that other scientists who had once worked for him had described the frequent testing of BW bombs. Ishii shrugged off the insinuation by arguing that to prepare adequate defenses, one had to know the enemy's capability, in this case, bacteriological bombs. "Defensive and offensive acts are synonymous in the primary stage," he said, "but I am ignorant of any large scale operations."

When Smirnov tried to determine if experiments on bacterial virulence and stability had been conducted, Ishii pleaded ignorance. Pushed about the plague attacks on China, he claimed he knew nothing. Smirnov countered by saying that he had the names of three men who had testified to having participated in the attack on Ningbo in October 1940. Ishii said he knew nothing about it since he spent every autumn in Tokyo on administrative business. Besides, he added, plague had been rampant in China that year. As for the scenario of a plane dropping plague-infected fleas, he replied, "I feel it is based upon imagination."[46]

"How can you deny these things?" Smirnov asked impatiently, and then he exaggerated what Murakami Takashi and Ota Kiyoshi had revealed in his recent interviews of them. "Your subordinates who were interrogated in Tokyo have confirmation as to the expeditionary unit. Even Col Murakami and Col Ota have made a similar statement."

"They are telling lies," Ishii retorted.

Smirnov then confronted him about atrocities: had prisoners been used for medical experiments? Ishii said he knew nothing about this. In response, Smirnov read Major General Kawashima's description from his September 1946 interview in Khabarovsk:

> From 150 to 200 criminals were confined in two guard houses, and the number of criminals which was delivered annually to the unit amounted to 500 to 800, and therefore, while I was with the unit, approximately 1,000 to 1,200 criminals were received by the unit. The experiments on them were performed before they were executed. Should an experimental subject survive, then he was used for some other experiment. The virulence of cholera, typhoid, typhus, plague was experimented on these criminals. I, personally, have seen the guardhouses and the condition within, and I have personally witnessed some of the human experiments which were conducted at the [Anda] Experimental Field. Since I have seen these facts, I testify to these being the truth.[47]

"That is not true," Ishii protested.

Exasperated, Smirnov ended the interrogation. Ishii had given nothing away, as his US handlers had requested. The prospects for Soviet and US cooperation on Japanese germ warfare charges, never more than dim, had vanished.

At the same time, in Nuremberg, Telford Taylor, chief of counsel at the Doctors' Trial, was listening to the closing argument of one of his prosecutors that described Nazi experiments with old blood serum on Buchenwald inmates and experiments with typhus on other captives. The details of the case involved the Nazi plan (never completed) to investigate biological warfare through the experiments conducted on human beings to discover "under what conditions inhaled aerosoles [*sic*] or dispersed droplets of certain pathogenic germs caused diseases in men."[48] This question had frustrated US and British BW researchers during the war and still did. The hope at Detrick was that Ishii's experiments would advance this knowledge, without creating moral qualms.

Legal Points

On June 20 1947, Dr. Fell sent his final report to G-2 and CWS.[49] Willoughby received it with thanks and told him he had brought it to the attention of General MacArthur and the chief of staff; he also commended Fell for his "discreet use of Military Intelligence Division Confidential Funds."[50]

The same day that Fell submitted his report, the War Crimes Branch in Washington, in response to Alva Carpenter's message of June 6, asked him to be precise about whether evidence at Legal Section warranted the opinion that the "Japanese BW group headed by Ishii did violate rules of land warfare." Under the US *Rules of Land Warfare* current in 1947, the United States respected The Hague Conventions of 1899 and 1907, which forbade the use of poison in war, and the rules extended this ban "to the use of means calculated to spread contagious diseases."[51] Further, it was held that civilian populations should "not be injured in their lives or liberty."[52] Regulated violence was the essence of war; military necessity, however, did not "admit of cruelty-that is, the infliction of suffering merely for spite or revenge; nor of maiming or wounding except in combat."

The War Crimes Branch of the War Department wanted "soonest clarification and further detail" about the nature of the Unit 731 war crimes, not, though, to prosecute but to advise the services and therefore the SWNCC and the Joint Chiefs of Staff about an immunity bargain: "We are satisfied evidence in possession [of] Legal Section does not repeat not warrant such charge against and trial of Ishii and his group. Must have information re all possible proof Ishii BW group participation in activities that could be considered war crimes under rules of land warfare before reaching decision."[53]

As soon as he received the query, Carpenter again conferred with Tavenner. Then, on June 27, he responded in detail in a top secret memo that, rather than emphasizing the weakness of the case, underscored the known criminal nature of the Japanese biological warfare activities.[54] To begin, Carpenter summarized the plague attacks of 1940–1941, noting that "strong circumstantial evidence" indicated that the Japanese had used plague-infected fleas on the targeted cities, thus backing the King report of 1942. He noted further that the Karasawa interview from the Soviets corroborated these attacks, as well as the germ warfare in the 1942 Zhejiang-Jiangxi campaign.

Carpenter then described how, directed by Ishii and his colleague Dr. Ikari Tsuneshige, "laboratory experiments were made 7 or 8 times during 1943 and 1944 with plague and anthrax bacilli on human beings." The local gendarmerie "furnished Manchurians for these experiments who had been sentenced to death." Relying on the Karasawa affidavit, he cited that "it clearly appears that Ishii detachment had [a] secret mission of studying use of bacilli as a war weapon" and had been experimenting with dispersing plague-infected fleas from airplanes and bombs—testing them on animals and humans alike. Moreover, "IPS [is] of the opinion that the foregoing information warrants a conclusion that the Japanese BW group headed by ISHII did violate the rules of land warfare, but this expression of opinion is not a recommendation that the group be charged and tried for such. KARAZAWA affidavit would necessarily need corroboration and testing for trustworthiness by a thorough investigation before prosecutive action is decided upon."[55]

Carpenter concurred that war crimes likely had been committed. But he defended Tavenner's decision in 1946 that no case could be made against any defendant: "IPS did not include any evidence re BW in its case in chief because at the time of closing case it could not assure the Tribunal under its rulings that the accused or some of them would be shown to have been associated with acts of the BW group."[56]

Less than a year later, those high-level associations with Unit 731 could be made. Assigning command responsibility for Ishii's war crimes, Carpenter named four defendants who had served as leaders of the Kwantung Army—a prestigious position as the army grew in the 1930s—and therefore would have had direct knowledge of Ishii and his many activities. As army commanders there were Umezu Yoshijiro (1939–1944) and Minami Jiro (1934–1936). In the earliest days of Ishii's enterprise (1932–1934), Koiso Kuniaki had been chief of staff. In 1937–1938, when the program was rapidly developing, the chief of staff had been Tojo Hideki, who, like Umezu had served in the Kwantung Army in the early 1930s. Either count 54 charging direct orders or count 55 charging General Yamashita's crime of failure to control subordinates would suffice, if charges were brought.[57]

Carpenter finished his dispatch with the IPS rationale that Ishii should be securely protected because Soviet options for courtroom revelations remained open: "Since seeing translation of Karasawa affidavit IPS [it is] more certain than before that Soviet prosecutor will endeavor in cross examination of one or more of the accused to lay foundation for the use in rebuttal of some of the evidence above recited and other evidence on this subject which may have resulted from their independent investigation in Manchuria and Japan."[58]

Later, in a message on June 30 titled "BW Group," Frank Tavenner reemphasized his concern about Soviet intentions: "The Soviet Prosecutor probably will endeavor in cross-examination of one or more accused to lay foundation for the use in rebuttal of the above-mentioned evidence and other evidence which may have resulted from their independent investigation."[59] General Umezu was the likely target. Tavenner sent Carpenter the full Kawashima and Karasawa affidavits and advised he forward them to Washington, which Carpenter did that day.[60] After a visit from McQuail to his office, Tavenner shared his memo and the affidavits with him.

On July 3 Willoughby wrote Tavenner a thank-you note for his "past cooperation and assistance and information on the difficult and sensitive subject which you recently gave to Lieutenant Colonel McQuail." He expressed his concern over "publicity which may result in endangering intelligence information of extreme importance to the United States." He ended his note emphasizing the alliance he and Tavenner had struck: "Your kind offer to keep me informed of new developments and to provide copies of your documents for intelligence purposes is appreciated." In a second note, Willoughby assured Tavenner: "Your cooperation will assist greatly in the successful carrying out of a very profitable project."[61] These words were no small assurance from the general who ran the Loyalty Desk.

A crackdown on military spending in Washington soon pushed General Willoughby to justify whether the Unit 731 project was indeed worthwhile. Willoughby first fired off a protest letter to MacArthur, which he copied to Major General Stephen J. Chamberlin, the War Department's director of intelligence, formerly in charge of plans and operations (G-3) for MacArthur during the war in the Pacific.[62] "My dear Steve," was how Willoughby addressed his letter to Chamberlin. In it, Willoughby extolled the achievements of the Fell inquiry, arguing that the three or four thousand dollars expended on the Unit 731 scientists for hotels, entertainment, and gifts was a "mere pittance," given the national security worth of "the fruit of twenty years' [Japanese] laboratory tests and research." "If we cannot maintain these people, as at present," he wrote, "loss of face combined with our inability to satisfy what they want, will destroy a relationship so far successfully developed." He knew of "no more destructive way to kill intelligence procurement on an international level than these [budget] restrictions." His appeal a success, Willoughby was able to keep his budget for continuing investigations of Japanese germ weapons—science at a bargain price—and keep the information in intelligence channels, away from the IMTFE.

Summer Stasis

Tavenner's rapprochement with Willoughby took place in Chief of Counsel Keenan's absence, during a relatively quiet period for the IPS. After much debate among the judges, on June 23, 1947, President Webb had declared a six-week recess to allow the defense more time to organize. The upcoming Pacific War phase would take another six weeks, and as long as three months was predicted for the individual defense presentations. Throughout this time the Soviets could conceivably spring their Unit 731 evidence, but they kept their intent secret.

In Washington, SWNCC's Subcommittee for the Far East continued into the summer to debate its response to MacArthur's May request regarding an immunity bargain.[63] At first those in the discussion saw the Ishii group as unlikely to be prosecuted since the evidence was "insufficient."[64] China, for example, had not sought to bring charges.[65] Yet, as represented by MacArthur, war crimes had been committed that, should they come to light, ought to come to justice. A single sentence in the August minutes summarized the position of the representatives from the military services: "The value to the U.S. of Japanese BW data is of such importance to national security as to far outweigh the value accruing from 'war crimes' prosecution."[66]

SFE members accepted Carpenter's conclusion that the Japanese BW group, headed by Ishii, did violate the rules of land warfare. They recognized that "this Government is at present prosecuting leading German scientists and medical doctors at Nuremberg for offenses which included experiments on human beings which resulted in the suffering and death of those experimented on."[67] On August 20, in the middle of the subcommittee debates, seven defendants in the Doctors' Trial at Nuremberg, notably Karl Brandt, were sentenced to death by hanging.

Yet the chance of biological weapons competition from the Soviet Union troubled the debates in Washington. In the 1930s the Soviet Union had supported defensive and offensive bacterial weapons projects at research institutes in Moscow and, to the east, in the Urals—efforts that were halted by Stalinist purges of military medical and public health officials in 1937.[68] As World War II ended, Allied forces captured two German officers with intelligence information about Soviet wartime efforts to test pathogenic aerosols—efforts perhaps to be revived.[69]

In the summer of 1947 the US Office of Naval Intelligence put together a report about Japan's wartime germ weapons program, including its medical experimentation, and sent it to the chairman of the Joint Chiefs of Staff, Admiral William Leahy, and the then secretary of the navy, James V. Forrestal, in line to become the secretary of defense.[70] The report's argument was that a communist Japan dominated by the Soviet Union could revive the Unit 731 program in five years and that, independently, also in five years, the Soviet Union could emerge as a serious biological warfare threat.

The SWNCC subcommittee solemnly acknowledged the "forbidden fruit" aspect of the horrific Unit 731 data: "This Japanese information is the only known source of data from scientifically controlled experiments showing the direct effect of BW agents on man." Since "any war crimes trial would completely reveal such data to all nations, it is felt that such publicity must be avoided in the interests of defense and national security."[71] Yet the committee stopped short of approving an official immunity bargain, leaving the status quo of G-2's protection of Ishii and his scientists. With the reorganization of the armed forces under the National Security Act of 1947, the SWNCC became the State-Army-Navy-Air Force Coordinating Committee (SANACC) and continued without resolution to argue the two sides of the immunity bargain debate.

Taking a break from Washington, General Waitt traveled to London, where he told the UK Inter-Service Sub-committee on Biological Warfare how "in the course of the War Crimes Prosecution in Tokio [*sic*], considerable evidence about Japanese activities in B.W. had been unearthed."[72] The Chemical Corps plan was to share that information with Porton Down.

In Tokyo, with the court adjourned, Frank Tavenner took a break from worrying about the Soviet prosecutors. With Keenan still in Washington, he decided to bring his wife Sarah and also Nelson Sutton's wife Frances and daughter Fran for an extended visit to Japan. Initially, the War Department's policy had been to prohibit any relatives of employees from staying less than a year, but favors were allowed. Earlier in the year, Tavenner had pulled strings for prosecutor Quilliam's wife to come to Tokyo while her husband, who had wanted to quit, put in extra weeks at IPS during the defense phase. Now Sutton, Tavenner's mainstay, was waxing homesick. As he wrote to a business associate, he had underestimated how long the trial would keep him in Tokyo: "As you know, I came here for a period of four to six months, but once into the case the responsibility has grown so that there has been no opportunity to leave. Mr. Keenan's return could alter that situation, but this is doubtful. This is my seventeenth month, and there is nothing in the world that I would prefer more than to be home."[73]

Tavenner arranged accommodations for the visitors at the Fujiya Hotel outside Tokyo, where Sutton had vacationed the year before. Sutton wrote his wife to bring two new summer suits from his tailor in Richmond, and on July 15 he went to Yokohama to meet the Liberty ship, the refurbished wartime cargo boat that was bringing both the two Sutton women and Mrs. Tavenner from Seattle. In his notes he described the festive scene: "Army band on dock playing gay music and everybody on the ship was crowded on the side next to the dock waving and calling to their folks who lined the upper portion of the pier. It seems to me that every other person was taking pictures."[74]

Sutton made sure his wife and daughter were fingerprinted and photographed for their American residency cards, after which he escorted them to the hotel, where they had rooms in the Flower Palace, the resort's most elite quarter. The US Army car pool was at their disposal, by lottery; eventually Sutton bought a secondhand Ford from an army officer to make touring easier. For six months the two women filled their days with visits to parks and shrines in the countryside and to the school for Japanese girls created by the United Christian Missionary Society of the Disciples of Christ, their church back in Virginia. Sarah Tavenner often joined the Sutton women on their tours. She and Sutton's daughter, then 18, became so close that people sometimes mistook them for mother and daughter.[75] The wife and son of Pedro Lopez, the Philippine prosecutor, were also living at the hotel. On weekends the three families socialized and ate dinner together and Sutton and Lopez played golf. The Sutton women occasionally came to Tokyo for special events—art shows, receptions, and dances—but the hotel protected them from exposure to Tokyo's destroyed landscape, honky-tonk street life, the emerging signs of political unrest—and the war crimes tribunal.

After Colonel Smirnov's frustrating interview with Ishii, the Soviet Division stopped requesting access to the Japanese BW scientists, but it gave no indication it would back away from biological weapons charges against Japan. As acting chief of counsel, Tavenner maintained frequent communication with Soviet prosecutor Vasiliev—partly out of anxiety about possible germ weapons charges and partly because he worried that the Soviet Division, if unprepared for the rebuttal phase, would undermine the prosecution's overall case. Solis Horwitz stepped in to give the Soviets technical help while Colonel Gilbert Woolworth remained on assignment to the division. At Tavenner's request, Nelson Sutton began assisting Vasiliev in framing the Soviet rebuttal and summation. Whether Tavenner or Vasiliev confided in Sutton about the Soviet's possible surprise introduction of Unit 731 evidence is unclear, although Sutton had seen copies of the Kawashima and Karasawa affidavits and knew about the division's earlier intent to bring the two as witnesses. That Tavenner, who was exceptionally discreet, would tell his junior colleague about his interaction with G-2 and MacArthur's May immunity request would be unlikely.

Whether Tavenner confided in China's prosecutor Judge Hsiang is equally doubtful. The Chinese Division appeared "pliant," as the British had predicted, and yet increasingly competent in arguing charges for Japanese crimes against peace. At stake for China in this immediate postwar period were not only its relationship with the United States but its future role in the region, as a neighbor to Japan and to the new border nations (India, Vietnam, Burma, Thailand, and Laos) and to the Soviet Union and the divided Korea.[76] The years of war had changed China fundamentally and permanently, in ways not yet completely understood, except that its past of Western legations and leases was over.[77]

On August 10 Chief of Counsel Keenan, recovered from his operation, returned to Tokyo, with Captain Luke Lea. In Keenan's absence of more than six months, the question had arisen of what to do with the Class A Japanese prisoners still languishing in Sugamo Prison. Much earlier, Tavenner had warned Keenan that legal representatives for numerous unindicted prisoners were demanding their release.[78] G-2 and Legal Section were also in favor of ending the long imprisonment. That SCAP would sponsor another Tokyo trial was doubtful. When pressured for a decision, MacArthur told the JCS that he was reluctant to replicate the IMTFE's "cumbersome, slow, costly, and generally unsatisfactory organization prescribed [that] renders such procedures open to criticism."[79] An alternative would be to prosecute the remaining inmates in minor B and C trials under his jurisdiction, through the Legal Section.

While in Washington, Keenan had reviewed a selection of fifty individual case files, sent to him from IPS, to evaluate each suspect's culpability. He was no sooner back in Tokyo than he called a press conference in which he promised an "appropriate, lawful tribunal" to prosecute the large number of imprisoned Class A suspects still in Sugamo.[80] At IPS Pedro Lopez alone was enthusiastic about another major trial; the other prosecutors, impatient for closure, were displeased that Keenan had spoken without consulting them. As if to disturb his staff even more, Keenan immediately staged a second news conference to claim that he had consistently tried to hasten the IMTFE proceedings, specifically by blocking redundant prosecution presentations on atrocities in the Pacific, only to have a "behind the scenes revolt" by certain IPS attorneys thwart his efforts.[81] Lopez and others were incensed. In time, as might have been predicted, MacArthur's reluctance to stage a major trial won out. Nineteen of the fifty suspects on Keenan's list were identified for possible indictment in minor trials run by Legal Section, and the remaining thirty-one were released for a lack of convincing evidence.[82] Of the nineteen, none was ever brought to trial. Alva Carpenter at Legal Section had trouble organizing judges to participate, and support from Washington faltered. This lapse was good news for Ishii and his group, however far-fetched the possibility that Carpenter would circumvent G-2's protection of them.

As autumn began, a parade of defendants was about to take the stand at Ichigaya and there was no time for infighting at IPS. Seventeen would speak in their own defense. The other eight, including Shigemitsu and Umezu, elected not to testify; still, defense counsel planned to introduce voluminous evidence in support of them and all the defendants.[83] International media attention and public interest, which had drifted away from Tokyo, was expected to return, especially when the celebrity defendant, former premier Tojo, took the stand.

Prompted by Tavenner, Keenan called for the formation of a committee to prepare for what came after the defense phase, the prosecution's rebuttal.[84] Brigadier Quilliam was appointed its chairman, with Alfred Comyns Carr and Nelson Sutton as associates. Sutton was to collect and organize the information. Each attorney was to give him "at the earliest practicable date" a report of relevant defense evidence for the accused, which would then be evaluated and redistributed. The committee in effect had the power to reject new division evidence that did not strengthen the general case, a possible restraint on Soviet ambitions. To prepare for the rebuttal, Tavenner, who was interested in totalitarian ideologies, asked Sutton to write a refutation of the defense's argument that Imperial Japan was "anticommunist" and only on that basis in league with Nazi Germany. Sutton produced a detailed commentary that pointed out, among other inconsistencies, the Japanese attempt early in the war to involve the Soviet Union as an ally against "capitalist imperialism."[85]

The defense witnesses were no sooner ready to testify than Ben Chifley, Australia's prime minister, ordered President Webb to leave Tokyo to resume attendance at the High Court in Canberra before it completed its 1947 session on December 15, or else step down. The order meant that Webb would miss ten or more of the individual defense presentations, an absence that could cast doubts on the court's legitimacy. After his personal entreaties to Chifley were rebuffed, MacArthur asked New Zealand judge Erima Harvey Northcroft to take Webb's place, but Northcroft (who had once threatened to quit the court) refused. Instead, US justice General Myron Cramer, less volatile than Webb but more distrusted by the defense, became acting president of the tribunal, and the proceedings moved ahead.

Given the assignment of preparing for the cross-examination of Field Marshal Hata Shunroku, Sutton had little time to spend with his wife and daughter. As he wrote to his law partner in West Point, he spent long days in court and all his nights gathering documents and preparing the questions to be asked the defendant. Unfortunately, he finished his work an hour before Hata's counsel announced that the general would not take the stand but would instead rely on witnesses.[86]

During this time Sutton also continued work with the Chinese Division to develop its charges against General Itagaki Seishiro for his role in the Mukden conflict in 1931 and for later brutalities against Chinese soldiers and civilians. As he wrote in a letter on October 10: "I have been in court each day this week with the Chinese Division, who are handling the Itagaki Phase, trying to guide them in a general way and sometimes with not too much success in my efforts to reduce the number of questions on cross-examination."[87] According to one observer, Judge Judson Nyi, an assistant Chinese prosecutor, managed the Itagaki interrogation well.[88] Unknown to the defense, Nyi was relying on the newly discovered diaries of the late Prince Saionji, a confidant of Emperor Hirohito who had recorded the emperor's criticisms of Itagaki's excesses in China. IMTFE evidence was supposed to be shared, and Chief of Counsel Keenan and Solis Horwitz were both in favor of giving the defense open access to prosecution files. Tavenner, though, was wary of "fishing expeditions" and, in this instance of hiding a source, exercised no control over the Chinese Division.

During this same time, in tribute to his IPS performance, Sutton was made a member of the Committee on Judicial Ethics of the Virginia State Bar. The honor perhaps compensated for jolting news from home that his son Nelson, who was now in his final year of college, had eloped with a young woman Sutton had never met. From West Point, his assistant Louise Medlin wrote urging him not to judge his son harshly: "He apparently did not know when you and his mother would return and he *wanted to get married*."[89]

"Valuable Information"

In Washington, the SWNCC agreed that more information should be procured from Ishii and his scientists—implying that better results might justify official immunity.[90] General Willoughby and General Waitt again cooperated to arrange for more intense, data-focused interrogations. On October 28, 1947, two pathologists, Dr. Edwin V. Hill, chief of Basic Sciences at Camp Detrick, and Dr. Joseph Victor, arrived in Tokyo to start interviews of twenty-two cooperative Japanese BW scientists.[91] Most were conducted and recorded at G-2 headquarters; they focused on "medical science," not the organization of the Unit 731 program, its relation to the Japanese General Staff or the emperor, or germ attacks on Chinese civilians.

To begin, Hill and Victor interviewed Dr. Masuda, former head of Ei 1644 in Nanjing, on his scientific knowledge of dysentery.[92] On November 3–4 they interviewed Dr. Ueda, a bacteriologist, about ways to increase infectivity through mucin (mucosal substances).[93] As in most of these interviews, the scientists showed no hesitancy in describing their research on humans—Chinese, Manchus, Koreans, and Russians. For example, Dr. Masuda noted that, after being injected with dysentery, one captive subject developed symptoms on the third day and hanged himself on the fourth.[94]

On November 7 Hill and Victor traveled to Kanazawa, the fortress town on the Sea of Japan, to meet Professor Ishikawa, who had promised to give them the Unit 731 pathology collection that in 1943 he had brought to Japan. As Hill and Victor reported:

> The pathological material . . . consisted of specimens from approximately 500 human cases, [only] 400 of which have adequate material for study. The total number of human cases which had autopsies at Harbin was less than 1,000 in 1945, according to Dr. Kozo Okamoto [interviewed separately]. This number was about 200 more than were present in Harbin at the time Dr. Ishikawa returned to Japan. As a result of inventory of specimens which were first submitted, it was evident that much material was being withheld. However, it required only slight encouragement to obtain an additional collection of specimens which was considerably greater than that first submitted.[95]

The collection was unique, but, after spending a week examining it, Hill and Victor found that it "was in a completely disorganized condition. It was necessary to arrange this material by case number, tabulate the number of specimens and inventory the number of specimens." Of the 850 recorded cases, there was adequate material for only 401 and none for 317. Samples were included from another 64 autopsies, victims of an "external plague epidemic" of unspecified origin. Finally, 11 recorded suicide cases out of a total of 30 had been autopsied and tissue samples preserved, for no particular purpose. The most valuable data were from the 31 complete human test cases of anthrax, the 42 of plague, and the 20 of glanders.[96]

Returning to Tokyo for the last two weeks of November, Hill and Victor completed the remaining interviews. When they asked for explicit descriptions of the testing methods, the Japanese responses led them into a world of forced human experiments and hundreds of autopsies and vivisections, embellished with random references to "sacrificed" subjects. Dr. Kitano Masiji, who took over Unit 731 command from Ishii in 1942 until early 1945, and Dr. Kasahara Shiro, his assistant, offered a report on *songo* fever that described the deliberate infection of captives who were then quickly killed to study the effects of the disease on their livers, spleens, and kidneys, or subject to vivisection, given the details of the report. Kitano and Kasahara also discussed experiments in which blood from a *songo*-infected captive was injected into horses to test for transmissibility, which proved effective. This was followed by the injection of blood from a sick horse into humans, which proved positive in just two of eight experimental subjects—all of them like the others "sacrificed." Dr. Hayakawa Kiochi, a veteran of the suicide team at Nomonhan, presented data on brucellosis studies at Pingfan; after six months at the University of Michigan in 1939, Hayakawa had conducted experiments in Singapore on mite-borne scrub typhus in humans.

Of special interest to the Americans was a glass aerosol chamber large enough to accommodate several adults at a time to test the virulence of anthrax spores. As Hill reported from one scientist:

> The octagonal shaped chamber used for human experimentation had a capacity of 26 cubic meters. For the generation of the aerosol, an insect type sprayer similar to the flit gun was used. In some cases, the atomizer is located within the chamber, but operated manually from the outside, whereas in other cases it is located outside of the chamber and the aerosol produced is conducted to the chamber through a rubber hose. . . . Individuals were placed inside the chamber and then the bacterial aerosol was introduced in the manner stated above.[97]

Crude experiments of various kinds were conducted in the chamber not just with anthrax but with plague, typhus, smallpox, glanders, dysentery, brucellosis, gas gangrene, and cholera.

General Ishii was Hill and Victor's main informant.[98] In his interview on November 22 he held forth on a variety of "scientific" experiments, including subjecting ten to twenty human subjects to gas gangrene, testing meningococcus on thirty-five "patients," and using the porcelain bomb to test anthrax dispersal on five or six other subjects. He described influenza experiments with twelve human subjects, using material derived from ferret lungs, obtained, he claimed, from an American source. He listed the methods as "injected, inhaled, nasal instillation, injected intrapulmonary, painted pharynx." As a variation, smallpox virus taken from a natural case in Manchuria was dried, and ten subjects inhaled this material from paper bags. All became ill and, as he recalled, "about four died." Ishii also offered less detailed comments on tests involving glanders, plague, tetanus, and tularemia.[99]

On December 12, 1947, Hill sent his summary report to General Waitt in Washington, with a copy to G-2.[100] In concluding his report, Hill wrote: "Evidence gathered in this investigation has greatly supplemented and amplified previous aspects of this field." He justified the information gained as an economic bargain, echoing Willoughby's earlier argument:

> It represents data which have been obtained by Japanese scientists at the expenditure of many millions of dollars and years of work. Information has accrued with respect to human susceptibility to those diseases as indicted by specific doses of bacteria. Such information could not be obtained in our own laboratories because of scruples attached to human experimentation. These data were secured with a total outlay of yen sign 250,000 (around $3000) to date, a mere pittance by comparison with the actual cost of the studies.[101]

The report summary noted that the Japanese had "carried out a series of laboratory and field trials on human beings, several hundred subjects being employed during a period of three or four years." The autopsy data were envisioned as a complement to animal studies: "Although the results obtained were somewhat fragmentary since the number of subjects was not sufficiently large to permit the framing of statistically valid conclusions, nevertheless, this information should provide invaluable supporting evidence to our assessments of the probable effects of B.W. on humans which must necessarily be extrapolated from experiments on animals."[102]

The findings of the Hill and Victor Report, with all their war crimes implications, were forwarded to British BW experts and then summarized for individual UK chiefs of staff, who kept the information secret.[103]

As Hill assured Willoughby and Waitt: "No question of immunity guarantee from war crimes prosecution was ever raised during the interview."[104] The cooperation of the Japanese scientists had earned his respect. "It is hoped," he continued, "that individuals who voluntarily contributed this information will be spared embarrassment because of it and that every effort will be taken to prevent this information from falling into other hands."

11
OPEN AND CLOSED TRIALS

STARTING IN EARLY SEPTEMBER 1947, EACH OF THE JAPANESE defendants, in alphabetical order, had the right to make his case to the court. Somewhat strangely, General Umezu Yoshijiro convinced his defense counsel to argue that US POWs at Mukden had indeed received humanitarian care and, on September 8, to offer in evidence an order he had issued in February 1943, when he commanded the Kwantung Army in Manchukuo. It instructed the army's Boeki Kyusuibu, the Anti-infection Water Purification Bureau, to improve medical services at the Mukden camp where Allied prisoners were being held.[1] A defense witness then took the stand to praise the bureau for its success in providing medical services in Burma.[2] The claims passed without comment from the Soviet prosecutors and others who knew the secret maleficent purpose of Ishii Shiro's Boeki Kyusuibu.

On September 10 Lawrence McManus, the attorney for General Araki Sadao (Ishii's early supporter), went further by announcing that his client "had condemned the use of poison gas or bacteria as a crime and contended that the destructive power of weapons should be limited and that war damage upon women, children and other non-combatants should be avoided at all costs."[3] Spoken on behalf of a defendant who had strongly advocated war on China, the assertion passed as if unnoticed by the prosecution.

This phase of the defense, which lasted until mid-January, proceeded with more predictable arguments for each of the accused. For the short-staffed IPS it was a difficult period of preparing for objections and cross-examinations. Still on the job, David Nelson Sutton handled background paperwork and had several opportunities to question witnesses. His best moment came in his interrogation of General Miyano Masatoshi, a witness testifying in lieu of Field Marshal Hata Shunroku. At issue was the treatment of the captive Doolittle pilots and their sham trial. Sutton knew the material well; in March 1946, in Shanghai, he had visited the US trial of the Japanese soldiers indicted for the crime and had worked hard to prepare the case against Hata. At the podium, he confronted the witness with the surviving victims' testimony about repeated abuses, among them water torture, being stretched on racks, and brutal beatings, and the circumstances of their trial. After first claiming ignorance, Miyano admitted that Hata had ordered the sham trial of the pilots, which allowed no defense counsel or translation into English and lasted less than two hours. Having sent an affidavit to exonerate the Japanese officers tried in Shanghai, Hata had already taken some responsibility for the pilots' fates. His leadership of the Zhekiang-Jiangxi Campaign seemed by comparison inconsequential.

A vindication for the Chinese Division and Judge Mei Ju-ao, and for Sutton, too, was the appearance on the stand of the defendant General Matsui Iwane, a patient at the US Army's 361st Station Hospital. Ten years before, as field commander in China, Matsui had triumphantly proclaimed: "Now the flag of the Rising Sun is floating over Nanking and the Imperial Way is shining forth in the area south of the Yangtze. The dawn of the renaissance of Eastern Asia is about to take place. On this occasion, it is my earnest hope that the 400 million people of China will reconsider."[4] Now a broken man dying of tuberculosis, Matsui apologized for the Nanjing Massacre and then was rushed back to the hospital.

The much anticipated high point of the defense case came with the testimony of former premier Tojo, which began on December 26 in a packed courtroom. Spectators had lined up for tickets at six that morning, and scalpers were selling them for 500 yen apiece, about the cost of an afternoon at a kabuki theater.[5] Mrs. MacArthur sat in the front row with her nine-year-old son Arthur. President William Webb had returned from Australia just in time to hear Tojo expound on his innocence and patriotism.

Chief of Counsel Joseph Keenan took charge of Tojo's cross-examination, only to find the defendant better prepared than he was and with a sharp tongue.[6] As a rising star in the military in the early 1930s, he had been nicknamed *kamisori* (straight razor) Tojo for his scathing retorts, and he spared Keenan none of them.[7]General Pechkoff, head of the French mission, was at the trial and described the disaster the cross-examination became for the chief of counsel: Tojo sat in the defendant's chair as if he were a president officiating at a meeting of his council of ministers, while Keenan appeared nervous and unable to phrase questions that were clear, pertinent, and succinct.[8] Tojo had used his prison time to prepare not only his defense but his attack. As the last defendant to testify (Umezu having declined), he finished on a note of triumph, to the open satisfaction of some of the other Japanese leaders on trial.

The press was brutally critical of Keenan's performance, and he fled to a resort outside Tokyo to recover. Frank Tavenner, left in charge of the IPS staff, remained anxious about the Soviet prosecution. The Rebuttal Committee, busy reviewing each division's case materials, had rejected most of the over forty items submitted by the Soviets (none concerning Unit 731) as repetitious or irrelevant—as Tavenner paid close attention to every detail. With General Umezu's defense still to be heard, the Soviets unnerved Tavenner by suggesting that the general's Japanese counsel be barred from the court because of his possible war crimes, a proposal Tavenner promptly rejected.[9] As before, Umezu let witnesses speak on his behalf, while the Soviet prosecutors let pass another opportunity to accuse him of collusion with Ishii in the Unit 731 war crimes. The rebuttal phase to come, though, still offered them their final chance to introduce new evidence.

The defense rested its case on January 12, 1948. By this time, heightened Cold War tensions in Europe and the violent emergence of new states from old colonies were creating global turmoil. Burma and Malaya, now autonomous, were wracked by internal divisions. The independent Philippines, where the United States held a ninety-nine-year lease on designated military bases, was once again ruled by oligarchs, who were fighting the Hukbalahap communist insurgents who had fought the Japanese. Indonesia still battled colonial Dutch troops. In India, millions were dying in the

Hindu-Moslem slaughter accompanying the partitioning of Pakistan. In China, KMT forces, on retreat from the North, were losing the civil war to the Chinese Communists. The Soviet Union and the United States still shared the trusteeship of Korea, but not for long. In 1948 South Korea would become the Republic of Korea, under US-backed Syngman Rhee, North Korea would become the Democratic People's Republic of Korea, under communist leader Kim Il-Sung, and the stage would be set for conflict.

In February the State-Army-Navy-Air Force Coordinating Committee further delayed its response to MacArthur's request for an immunity decision, explaining that it was awaiting the Chemical Corps assessment of the Hill and Victor Report.[10] Through the committee, Fleet Admiral William Leahy, head of the Joint Chiefs of Staff and close to President Truman, had been informed about Unit 731 human experimentation, and so, too, had the other chiefs and a network of SANACC consultants throughout government who kept these particularly gruesome war crimes and the mass disease attacks on the Chinese top secret.

In Tokyo, as the IMTFE rebuttal phase began, the prosecution staffs rushed to reinforce their arguments with extra evidence. Relying on US aerial surveillance, the IPS acquired photographs of the route of the Bataan Death March, images showing that sources of natural water along the route had been available but were cruelly denied to the captives. Since the defense phase months before, the Chinese Division had been accumulating evidence on the collusion of individual defendants (General Umezu among them) in plots to conquer and exploit China after taking control of Manchuria.[11] Although the spreading conflict between the KMT and the CCP made it difficult to find new facts in China, the discovery in Japan of the Prince Saionji diaries, transcribed by his secretary, Baron Harada, had strengthened the Chinese cross-examination of General Itagaki Sheishiro and would be used again to prove he had suppressed firsthand accounts by Japanese military of the extensive rapes, murders, and lootings committed by their troops in China.[12] The Saionji diaries also bolstered the Chinese shift to a focus on Japanese leadership and policy affecting China, from the cabinet cabal that organized the opium trade to Marquis Kido Koichi's awareness of the Nanjing Massacre, and the Foreign Ministry's foreknowledge of the Mukden incident in 1931.

If their performance at the Nuremberg International Military Tribunal was any indication, the Soviet Division might opt to spring a surprise witness to raise the accusation of germ weapons. On August 26, 1946, just before Nuremberg's final hearings, Major General Walter Schreiber, a high-ranking physician captured by the Soviets, was called to the stand to testify about German biological weapons, for which no evidence had been presented.[13] Schreiber accused Dr. Kurt Blome, a former Nazi deputy surgeon general, of preparing for bacteriological warfare at a secret research facility in Poland, outside the city of Poznan, specifically by doing research on plague bacteria and testing pathogenic sprays. The Soviet Union's interest in this subject was that its troops had discovered the Poznan laboratory; its prosecution was eager to pin a germ weapons charge on Reichsmarschall Hermann Göring, and perhaps embarrass the Americans for their wartime BW program, now reported in the US press.

Under cross-examination, though, Schreiber could not substantiate any connection between the high command and the Poznan laboratory or the grotesque medical experiments on captives he vividly described as having taken place elsewhere. Within the year Dr. Blome was tried but acquitted at the Nuremberg Doctors' Trial, and, simultaneous with SWNCC deliberations about General Ishii, Blome was hired under Operation Paperclip to work at a secret US research facility in West Germany, not the last time a risk of scandal would be taken for the Army Chemical Corps.[14]

In Tokyo, the Soviet Division did call a surprise witness, but not Major General Kawashima Kioshi or Major Karasawa Tomio or anyone else from Unit 731. Instead it presented a Soviet prisoner of war, Lieutenant Colonel Horst von Petersdorff, a former Nazi spy, to testify about Japanese plans to wage war against the USSR in Siberia, plans allegedly shared with Berlin.[15] In a repeat of a familiar pattern, the defense counsel criticized the credibility of the Soviet witness and an irritated President Webb, who saw little value in evidence accrued from espionage, sided with them.

While the rebuttal phase continued, Tavenner planned ahead to orchestrate the case summations. Months before, to give the defense extra time to prepare, the court decided that the prosecution would deliver its summation first, not second, as Keenan had expected. With Keenan once again in Washington, Tavenner created a Summation Committee and appointed five members: Canada's Brigadier Henry Nolan, Britain's Alfred Comyns Carr, China prosecutor Hsiang Che-chun, Solis Horwitz, and Nelson Sutton, and he added himself as an ex-officio member.[16] In this final phase, the IPS staffers shared the review of defense material relevant to each division's summation text; they conducted line-by-line checks of defense statements, combed transcripts, and checked the accuracy of every reference. After this, they passed their evaluations to the committee members. Like others, Sutton found a good number of defense allegations "unsupported," especially those involving the Chinese Division charges, his specialty.

To carry out a rigorous assessment of the division summations, Tavenner assigned staff to edit each draft submission beforehand and enlisted the five committee members to make the final evaluations. In addition, he continued to monitor the Soviet input. In one instance, he corrected A. N. Vasiliev's description of a defendant's wanting the Tri-Partite Pact with Germany to be exclusively against the Soviet Union when evidence had shown the opposite.[17] Lev Smirnov took charge, to fortify the argument that the agreement was purposefully hostile to his country.[18]

From its inception, the IMTFE had frustrated Soviet expectations. Prosecutors Sergei Golunsky and Vasiliev had arrived in Tokyo wanting to make a case for Japanese aggression against the Soviet border prior to the Neutrality Pact of 1941; General Doihara Kenji, General Itagaki, and Baron Hiranuma Kiichiro stood broadly implicated, but the Soviet charges lacked weight. Proving that Tojo had planned to violate the Neutrality Pact had not been as successful as the Soviets wanted, and General Umezu and Foreign Minister Shigemitsu Mamoru, their late additions to the defendant list, had both escaped charges of atrocities. For these reasons, the Soviet Division might be motivated, as Vasiliev and Smirnov had indicated earlier, to introduce charges against the Japanese for crimes involving germ weapons, especially if the buildup of Unit 731 activities in Manchuria were presented as anti-Soviet aggression. Or, to give their case drama, they could introduce the mass killing and inhumane medical experimentation as Class C crimes against humanity, stemming from the Class A aggressive war crimes. But no one knew the Soviet plan.

The Chinese Division stayed allied with American prosecutors, even as the military strength of the Kuomintang government seemed to deteriorate. A rousing statement on December 25 by Mao Zedong candidly laid out the successful military tactics and planning of the CCP forces in the civil war.[19] In a January message to the secretary of state, Ambassador John Leighton Stuart observed that China's politics were not improving; the recent National Assembly elections showed "little of the substance of democracy"—given the inevitable landslide produced by "Kuomintang control over all branches of government, complete lack of effective opposition, and the ignorance and political inexperience of the people."[20] All this was in addition to widespread demonstrations against worsening economic conditions.

At the IMTFE, the rebuttal phase was completed by the final week of February. The Soviet Division argued its part without raising the Unit 731 charges that so concerned Frank Tavenner, General Willoughby, and officials in Washington. With little delay, the trial moved directly to the prosecution's summation, for which the IPS divisions had been preparing.

On February 24 with collaborative work still ahead, Vasiliev nonetheless wrote Tavenner a note of appreciation: "In the period of strenuous and responsible work connected with rebuttal as well as with writing and processing of the prosecution's summation 'Japanese aggression against the U.S.S.R.' and with personal briefs of the accused Shigemitsu and Umezu your assistants and other members of your staff rendered us great help being always very considerate and attentive."[21]

In addition to thanking each of the clerical staff by name, Vasiliev thanked three IPS attorneys: Solis Horwitz, David Nelson Sutton, and Gilbert Woolworth, the army colonel with G-2 connections.

A day later Tavenner responded to Vasiliev's message:

> I want to take this opportunity to express both personally and officially my congratulations on the very excellent summations you and your associates of the USSR have presented [to the committee]. They reflect painstaking care and great legal skill in their preparation.
>
> It has been a matter of great gratification that the presentation of this case has demonstrated as well that it has been the work of the team, a team which at all times has striven to pursue one goal—the establishment of a precedent which should be a milestone on the road to world peace.[22]

Tavenner's reference to "painstaking care and great legal skill" was diplomatically phrased, given the time US lawyers had devoted to the Soviet court presentations and Tavenner's personal vigilance. His mentioning of world peace was ironic; the Soviet Union was on the brink of withdrawing from the Allied Control Council that had unified the Four Powers in Europe, and, after months of contention, it would soon declare a blockade of Berlin. It also had become the ally of Mao's CCP forces in China.

As soon as the rebuttal phase at the IMTFE was over, the debate between representatives of the Department of State and the War Department at SANACC drew to an end. At the Chemical Corps, General Waitt registered satisfaction with the Hill and Victor Report, and, thanks to Soviet lack of action at the IMTFE, the JCS was liberated from any responsibility for an official immunity agreement. On March 4 the Subcommittee for the Far East noted: "While it is true that an additional six weeks will be devoted to argument in this case, it may be assumed that for the purpose of the matter at issue, the trial is at an end."[23] On trust alone—as MacArthur had proposed—and without scandal, the Chemical Corps had acquired "information of value" from the Unit 731 scientists for its biological weapons program, which was just beginning to revive. The Subcommittee for the Far East drafted a message to General MacArthur, to the effect that his request for official immunity was now irrelevant, and sent it for approval to the Joint Chiefs of Staff.[24] On March 13 the message was sent directly from the JCS to General MacArthur with a recommendation that he could, if he considered it necessary, resubmit his "within intelligence channels" request.[25] With SCAP in control of any future trials and G-2 in control of the Japanese BW witnesses and files, the message was an empty bureaucratic gesture, like the SWNCC recommendation in October 1946 that MacArthur could relegate the decision to indict Emperor Hirohito to the IPS.

With no new evidence allowed at the IMTFE, the agreement for US government protection in exchange for valued weapons information was described as a "fait accompli." Ishii and his scientists—Naito Ryiochi, Masuda Tomsada, Wakamatsu Yujiro, Ota Kiyoshi, Kitano Masiji, and their like were beyond international criminal prosecution. De facto immunity extended to the thousands who over the years had participated in Ishii's program, not only in Manchuria but at the Tokyo Army Hospital and the branch plants in China, Burma, and Singapore, and had remained sworn to silence, at least in public.[26] On March 12, 1948, the prosecution summary ended. With widely varying input and energy, the eleven Allied nations had made their cases. It fell to an assistant Soviet attorney, Colonel Alexander T. Ivanov, to pronounce the final words: "Your Honor, this concludes the prosecution's case."

For the next month, the defense presented its summation. Despite altruistic efforts by prosecutor Horwitz to help its lawyers locate documents, the final statement went badly. George Yamaoka, the lead counsel, tried to maintain order, but two of his American colleagues were barred from court after altercations with President Webb, and disagreements persisted between American and Japanese defense counsel. Finally, on April 14, the defense summary concluded.

Two days later Frank Tavenner, as acting chief of counsel, delivered the trial's closing words, in response to the defense summation. The Ichigaya courtroom was overflowing with spectators, staff, and the press. On this final day David Nelson Sutton sat at the conference table where he had spent many months elbow-to-elbow with his IPS colleagues, ceaselessly jotting notes, his briefcase and papers at hand, becoming a major contributor to the court process, imperfect though he knew it was.

At the podium, Tavenner, in a dark three-piece suit, began reading his prepared text, which emphasized the universal theme of moral choice. The defendants in the dock, he said, had chosen to turn their nation into a "symbol of evil." Dismissing the characterization of them as gangsters (the absent Keenan's favorite epithet), Tavenner portrayed them as an elite, "the brains of an empire," and contrasted them to the "hoodlums" tried at Nuremberg.[27] Rather than leading Japan to "an honored life in the family of nations, willing to settle differences that might arise in an amicable and lawful manner," they had chosen "a program of aggrandizement and war" and brought "death and injury to millions of people." Tavenner declared that the defendants bore the guilt of this choice of evil over good, "a guilt perhaps greater than that of any group of men who have stood before the bar of law in the entire history of this world."[28]

Tavenner's words marked the end of two years of legal proceedings. President Webb banged his gavel and the crowd stood as the judges exited. The public theater of the trial was over and the courtroom emptied.

At the War Ministry and their Meiji Building offices, IPS attorneys began packing their files and, after farewell drinks and dinners, headed home. Each of the countries they represented—the United States, China, Great

Britain, the Soviet Union, France, Australia, New Zealand, Canada, the Netherlands, India, and the Philippines—and the country they had come to know, Japan, had become part of a much changed and still changing world. The lines of the Cold War conflict had been drawn, with the United States and the Soviet Union as the opposing world superpowers. The European colonial empire in Asia, destroyed in the war, was being replaced by new nations, no matter how fiercely the colonial powers, like the Netherlands and France, fought to hold on. The old global order of European domination, against which Judge Radhabinod Pal had railed, was being replaced by East and West ideological polarities, with the most of the less privileged nations of the world becoming client states, if not pawns, for one side or the other.

The IPS job on behalf of justice was done. As the long-serving Nelson Sutton wrote a friend on April 19, "the case has gone to the 'jury'"—the court's eleven judges.[29]

The court judges still had months of work ahead of them. The IMTFE had been in session for two years and ninety-eight days and had heard 419 witnesses (109 for the prosecution and 310 for the defense) and 16 defendants. The court had accepted 775 depositions and affidavits from those not required to testify. The court record consisted of 49,058 pages, 3,915 exhibits, and an additional 30,000 pages of material not copied into the record. To further process this material, a team of translators took over Hattori House, which for security was surrounded by barbed wire. Not only the extensive case documents but disagreements among the justices delayed the court's judgment until November 4, 1948. Its final statement was 1,228 pages long and took seven days to read aloud for the record. The commentary raised the absence of Emperor Hirohito as a defendant in the trial as a possible negative influence on court deliberations—the personal opinion of President Webb, Judge Mei, Judge I. M. Zarayanov, Judge Bernard Röling, and Judge Pal that, made public, criticized MacArthur's protection of the emperor. Webb and the others believed that the involvement of Hirohito in decisions to wage aggressive war was too obvious to ignore; without his directives, they felt, his military leaders could not have proceeded to commit their crimes against peace.[30]

Sentencing was announced on November 12. The mixed criteria for selecting defendants—a combination of cabinet members, figures chosen to represent different charges, and others demanded by individual nations—made for erratic punishments, although, unlike Nuremberg, not one of the accused was acquitted. The court condemned seven defendants to death by hanging. Five of them (Tojo and Generals Itagaki, Doihara, Kimura, and Muto) were convicted of count 54, for ordering, authorizing, and permitting war crimes. Tojo's penalty had been predicted. Itagaki's command in China had been characterized by the "pattern of warfare" Sutton had argued. Doihara was condemned for abuses of POWs and opium trafficking. Kimura was linked to Pearl Harbor and the deaths on the Siam-Burmese Railway. Muto, cleared of any criminal role at Nanjing, received the death sentence for his command at Manila. The two others (Baron Hirota Koki and General Matsui) were found guilty under count 55, the failure to command that had doomed General Yamashita in Manila in 1946.[31] Evidence of Koiso's brutal wartime rule of Korea convinced the judges of his guilt, while Hirota and Matsui were both tainted by their involvement in the Rape of Nanking. The decision to execute Hirota, which turned on a 6–5 vote, was appealed without success to the US Supreme Court.[32] Three defendants were convicted for aggressive war against the USSR: General Doihara, General Itagaki, and Baron Hiranuma, who was sentenced to life imprisonment.

Sixteen other defendants were also sentenced to life imprisonment. Among them were Generals Umezu, Koiso, and Minami, all former leaders of the Kwantung Army in Manchukuo who had overseen Japan's germ weapons program, and General Hata, the field commander in China who, in charge of the Zhejiang-Jiangxi campaign, must have approved General Ishii's strategic germ attacks. Umezu, ill with colon cancer and absent from Ichigaya when his sentence was pronounced, was convicted of crimes against peace but not of any specific crimes against the Soviet Union. Marquis Kido, the emperor's advisor, also received a life sentence.

The other late Soviet addition to the defendants list, former foreign minister Shigemitsu, received a seven-year sentence, as close to acquittal as the court came; like Matsui, who had been just a field commander in China, he was not convicted of count 1 of the indictment, the crime against peace, with its connotation of high authority. Togo Shigenori, the well-known foreign minister, was sentenced to twenty years.[33] The propagandist Okawa Shumei, who had slapped Tojo's head on the court's opening day, had spent the trial years confined to a psychiatric hospital, where he completed a translation of the Koran; he was discharged and became a free man shortly after the verdicts were announced. Two defendants, General Matsuoka Yosuke and Admiral Nagano Osami, had died during the trial.

President Webb made public the dissent among the judges that had troubled these sentencing decisions. Judge Pal of India, in an opinion that ran over a thousand pages, argued the injustice of the major colonial powers defining war crimes for a defeated Asian nation. Alone among the judges, Pal also commented that item 9 of the indictment's appendix D, concerning the use of poison gas in China, "had been abandoned by the prosecution" with "no evidence to support this charge . . . addressed at the hearing."[34] Judge Henri Bernard from France and Judge Röling from the Netherlands felt the sentencing was too harsh. Webb was in principle against execution, and the Soviet Union's Zarayanov was restrained by his country's 1947 prohibition of the death penalty. China's Judge Mei and Judge Delfin Jaranilla from the Philippines, of the same mind as the US judge General Myron Cramer, weighted the sentences toward execution or life in prison.

On November 12, 1948, President Webb put down his gavel for the last time and the IMTFE concluded. Returning to Washington, Chief of Counsel Keenan was thanked in person by President Truman. Afterward, on December 2, 1948, Truman sent him a letter to express his "deep appreciation" for his service in Tokyo. (The letter was written for Truman by Attorney General Tom Clark, Keenan's former boss at the Justice Department who was soon to become a Supreme Court justice.) "You have," it said, "carried out a most difficult and responsible assignment with credit to both your country and yourself, and at the same time have contributed immeasurably to the cause of humanity and the further development of international law."[35]

General MacArthur was empowered by article 17 of the Tokyo Charter to reduce any of the court's sentences; despite pleas from Great Britain, Australia, Canada, India, and the Netherlands, he refused to choose clemency for any defendant.[36] Envisioning a dramatic accomplishment of the "punish the war criminals" directive, MacArthur wanted the seven condemned defendants executed on December 7, the anniversary of Pearl Harbor. As a last resort, defense lawyers appealed to the US Supreme Court, arguing that MacArthur had overreached his SCAP authority by establishing the

IMTFE. On December 20, with Justice Robert Jackson recusing himself, the Supreme Court rejected the appeal, deciding that since the Allies at the Moscow Conference of 1945 had legitimately empowered MacArthur, his actions and the IMTFE were beyond its jurisdiction.

Shortly after midnight on December 22, the seven defendants sentenced to be executed were hung at Sugamo Prison. No media reports or photographs were allowed. Their bodies were put in plain wooden caskets, which were then taken to a crematorium for incineration, after which their ashes were scattered. As at Nuremberg, the Allies wanted no burial sites that could become future shrines for war criminals.

Work at Legal Section continued during this time, but the drive for minor war crimes tribunals was near its end. As soon as the Tokyo trial concluded, the countervailing trend to release prisoners from Sugamo began, and in a few years it would lead to the wholesale parole of all surviving IMTFE defendants. On November 29 an internal SCAP memo declared that Legal Section's Case File 330 was to be boxed and shipped to Washington. "No further investigation," the memo instructed, "[is] to be conducted by this Division. Case closed."[37]

The Cold War and the Asia Pacific Region

Back in February 1946, when David Nelson Sutton arrived in Tokyo, the United States was holding on to Franklin Roosevelt's great hope that China would be America's unified ally in the Far East. By 1948 the American hopes for China had greatly dimmed. Generalissimo Chiang Kai-shek seemed to keep delegating his authority to incompetent and corrupt officials and to be unable to implement social and economic reforms. As Ambassador Stuart reported from Nanjing in the summer of 1948, Chiang's determination and courage, which suited his wartime leadership, were proving "a hindrance for him in problems calling for very different mental processes."[38] It could be, as Stuart's secretary suspected, that the aging Chiang was becoming senile. Yet no alternative leader had emerged, and the Chinese legislature seemed incapable of governing. Inflation was out of control; people lacked jobs and food; masses of university students and workers were protesting. Meanwhile, Mao Zedong's Communist forces had taken much of Manchuria and North China. "The situation in general," Stuart observed, "continues to deteriorate alike in its military, economic and psychological aspects."[39]

Even as the United States passed the China Aid Act, a last-ditch effort by congressional sympathizers to back the Nationalists, the best idea the Joint Chiefs of Staff had was to send US experts to help with operational planning. Neither approach could prevent the inevitable. That November, while the IMTFE verdict was being read aloud in Tokyo, a coterie of Allied ambassadors met secretly in Nanjing to discuss what they might do "with respect to the issuance of evacuation warnings."[40] The question was whether the Generalissimo could effectively move the government to another venue or would just take his personal entourage.

On April 25, 1949, Communist forces took Nanjing. The US Embassy compound in Nanking was invaded at 6:45 a.m. by twelve armed soldiers who woke Ambassador Stuart in his bedroom.[41] Meanwhile, Generalissimo Chiang and the Republic of China government fled, ultimately to establish their base in Taiwan.

By this point, the Joint Chiefs of Staff envisioned Japan's strategic importance. It lay in "her manpower and industrial potential, which could be exploited by any controlling power; also to her geographic position dominating the exits and entrances of the Sea of Japan, the East China and Yellow Seas, and, to a lesser degree, the ports of Asia north of the Shanghai-Woosung area. . . . In addition, Japan would provide staging areas from which to protect US military power against Soviet territory in Asia."[42]

By the year's end, the People's Republic of China (PRC) was China's new government, with Beijing as its capital. As its leader, Mao Zedong was committed to his alliance with the Soviet Union and the mission "to strengthen the people's state apparatus, which refers mainly to people's army, people's police and people's courts."[43] Such prosecutions of Japanese war crimes as were conducted emphasized "reeducation" over punishment and communist doctrine over law.

On September 23, 1949, President Truman announced that the Soviet Union had successfully tested its first atomic bomb, "Joe-1," which ended the American nuclear monopoly. This news followed soon after the USSR takeovers in Czechoslovakia and Hungary, its blockade of Berlin, and the creation of NATO (the North Atlantic Treaty Organization) to assure the military defense of Western Europe.[44] The Truman administration's position paper on "Soviet Intentions and Capabilities" reflected the view then held by many in influence: "The avowed intention of the USSR is to engage in 'competition' with the US until the US is destroyed, or forced to capitulate. The Soviet concept of 'competition' with the US is—demonstrably—to wage a relentless, unceasing struggle in which any weapon or tactic which promises success is admissible."[45] The US relationship with the Soviet Union was defined as a new total war: "It consequently cannot be described as a 'political struggle,' or a 'cold war,' or a 'limited war.' In the eyes of the Kremlin, it is war in the broadest sense of the term, a war to the death."

Anticipating a Third World War, strategists at the Joint Chiefs of Staff configured multiple nuclear offensive operations, with names such as Pincer, Reaper, and Dropshot, to destroy the Soviet petroleum industry, its electric power system, and its iron and steel industry. General Curtis LeMay, who had led the incendiary raids on Japan, envisioned attacking seventy Soviet targets with over a hundred atomic bombs in thirty days of attack, supplemented by enormous conventional forces.[46] Operation Dropshot, although never approved by the Joint Chiefs, nonetheless illustrated the strategic vision: "The atomic offensive would require nineteen American and seven British heavy and medium bomb groups with a total of 780 bombers, 144 reconnaissance planes and seventy-two weather reconnaissance aircraft. Seventy-five to 100 atomic bombs would be used against atomic assembly facilities, storage points, and heavy bomb air fields."[47]

If any nation in the Far East was to be a stable democratic US ally, it was Japan—with a population that was educated, disciplined, and skilled in science and technology. In 1947 Soviet specialist George F. Kennan, head of the Policy Planning Staff at the US State Department, had with foresight fashioned a US "containment policy" that included rebuilding Japan as a stable, capitalist bulwark against communism and the Soviet Union—a model that would prevail.[48]

At the start of the Occupation, MacArthur's purge of Japanese ultranationalists had radically changed the military, police, and government bureaucracies and affected the formation of cabinets and election outcomes. In the world of corporate finance, the purge had caused a "veritable revolution."[49] Even before it was completed, 49 corporate monopolies (*zaibatsu*) comprising 1,200 companies were dissolved. In November 1946 MacArthur launched a second attack, this time on 137 companies that were secret or "masked" offshoots of the dissolved monopolies.

As 1949 approached, MacArthur could no longer ignore Washington directives to move Japan toward Kennan's model by initiating a conservative "reverse course" that countermanded his original reform agenda. In late 1948 a purposeful reinforcement of the *zaibatsu* and crackdown on labor unions, along with a new national centralization of the police and of education, signaled the advent of a capitalist-leaning Japan reliant on old notions of authority and influence.[50] In February 1949 US envoy Joseph Dodge, a Detroit banker, arrived in Japan to implement nine strict principles of economic stabilization; for the power he wielded, he soon became known as another "supreme commander." Although his reign was short-lived, Dodge ushered in austerity policies that curbed inflation; they also caused increased unemployment—one million people lost their jobs—and generated widespread public protests.[51] In June 1950 MacArthur, advised by G-2 and with the cooperation of the Japanese government, launched a "Red Purge" against communists who were leading among the electorate and emboldening the radical labor unions and antigovernment movements.[52]

The United States, even as it manipulated Japan's economy, promised protection and future stability in exchange for important geopolitical concessions.[53] In the likely event that Mao Zedong defeated Generalissimo Chiang, the Americans offered Japan a nuclear power counterbalance to the coming alliance between Communist China and the Soviet Union.

The Khabarovsk Trial: Truth or Propaganda?

On February 24, 1949, the Far Eastern Commission in Washington announced a new policy: no further international trials should be initiated against Japanese Class A suspects held in custody. Dozens of prisoners remained in Sugamo, and the feeling was mounting at SCAP that it was time to put aside war crimes and focus on Japan's future. A follow-up March 31 recommendation from the FEC encouraged Allied nations to conclude "if possible" all trials by September 30. Australia, determined to finish its slate of minor war crimes tribunals, disregarded the policy. Still the path was laid for the eventual release of all Japanese prisoners as a move toward normal relations with the West and a peace treaty that would allow Japan to regain its autonomy.

For the Soviet Union, Japanese war crimes still meant unfinished business. At the IMTFE its division had been unable to mount the case it wanted, on its own terms, free of a belligerent defense, an intrusive chief judge, and US military intelligence. Its criticisms of the IMTFE as an "American imperialist farce," which had appeared in the Soviet press during the trial, had intensified at the end of the rebuttal phase and continued into 1948 while the court deliberated its verdicts.[54] Nothing prevented the Soviet judiciary from holding its own Japanese war crimes trial within its own national boundaries. With Stalin's encouragement, the Soviet choice was to focus on Japanese germ warfare as a way of reviving the charges of Japan's aggression and conspiracy against the Soviet Union that had been weakly represented at the IMTFE.

From December 25 to 30, 1949, a little over a year after the IMTFE ended, the Soviet Union put twelve of its captive Japanese BW scientists and military officers on trial in the Siberian city of Khabarovsk.[55] Colonel Lev N. Smirnov, formerly of the IPS Soviet Division and now state counselor of jurisprudence of the third class, was appointed state counsel for the prosecution at the trial; the opportunity to present Japan's atrocities, denied him at Tokyo, would be allowed at Khabarovsk. Solomon Rosenblit, another Soviet lawyer who had been at both Nuremberg and Tokyo, wrote the indictment.

In Khabarovsk the Soviets presented the case they might have made at the IMTFE, complete with credible eyewitnesses and official documents, and even simultaneous translation. The trial drew on the Presidium Decree of April 1943 that authorized the early USSR trials in the Ukraine and Russia and became part of the Allied Control Council agreement in Europe. The trial, though, was closed to foreign media. Tickets were distributed to local factory workers and soldiers, and the proceedings were broadcast on the radio. When the crowds overwhelmed the courtroom on the second day, outdoor loudspeakers were set up for those willing to bear the cold.

The twelve accused at Khabarovsk were Japanese officers and laboratory employees who had been involved in germ warfare research or operations. Foremost among them were Major General Kawashima and Major Karasawa, whose 1946 affidavits had been shared with IPS; they were accused of both germ warfare and performing inhumane medical experiments. In addition, the Soviets charged other captives: the former Kwantung Army chief of medical administration, a former chief of the army's Veterinary Service, a lieutenant colonel who had been a section chief at Unit 731, a former chief of a branch of that unit, a chief of the Fifth Army's medical service, two scientific researchers from Unit 100, and two laboratory assistants in their mid-20s. In reserve, the prosecution had twelve more Japanese captives, most of them low-level employees, who were called as witnesses.

As at Nuremberg and Tokyo, the accused had defense counsel, but the defendants all pled guilty and their lawyers were limited to explaining the mitigating circumstances that had pushed them toward crime.[56] Four defense lawyers were from Moscow and eight from the Khabarovsk area; in the proceeding, they played mainly "secondary, decorative roles."[57] To review the scientific evidence of biological weapons, the trial relied on a committee of experts drawn from the Academy of Medical Sciences of the USSR, from the army's Medical Services, and from the department of microbiology of the Khabarovsk Medical Institute.[58] As with the trials against Nazis, the dreadful evidence of criminal behavior had no need for embellishment with propaganda—which gave this trial a chance to establish the historical truth of the Unit 731 war crimes.

The Khabarovsk court acknowledged that the IMTFE had effectively prosecuted the three classes of war crimes—aggressive war, crimes in violation of the customs of war, and crimes against humanity. This trial, though, was intended to establish Japan's biological warfare activity as a crime of planned, unprovoked aggression against the Soviet state, on a mass scale akin to Nazi atrocities. The conclusion to the indictment read: "The preliminary investigation in the present case has established that, in planning and preparing aggressive war against the U.S.S.R. and other states, the Japanese imperialists intended to employ on a wide scale for the accomplishments of their aims, and in part did employ, a criminal means of mass extermination of human beings—the weapon of bacteriological warfare."[59]

Further, the indictment highlighted the medical atrocities suppressed at the IMTFE: "It has likewise been established that, to accomplish their criminal plans, the Japanese militarists did not stop at any atrocity, even performing inhuman experiments on living people and exterminating several thousand prisoners by forcibly infecting them with lethal bacteria."[60]

Also with moral implications, accusations of the United States for secretly continuing its biological warfare program were an important part of the Soviet agenda. News of the US wartime program had appeared in the postwar press, and after 1945 dozens of technical articles from Camp Detrick were available in scientific journals. The 1942 Rosebury-Kabat framework for the US wartime program, complete with a list of the best microbial agents to develop as weapons, had been openly published.[61] For the Soviet Union, the resistance of G-2 and CWS in Tokyo to Soviet access to General Ishii and the other Japanese scientists indicated the American intent to develop the secret, still tentative "criminal means of mass extermination," possibly on a par with atomic weapons. In the 1930s the Soviet Union had started its own BW research in conjunction with its chemical program, only to have it collapse in 1937 when its leaders, along with a generation of biologists and physicians, were arrested in Stalinist purges.[62] That was the buried past. Now, with the Soviet Union's weapons research successfully concentrated on nuclear weapons, the prosecutors could claim moral superiority: in this court they would criminalize the development of germ weapons and any state plans and "conspiracy" to use them in war.

To align their charges with the crime of aggressive war, the Khabarovsk prosecutors made a special point of eliciting from the defendants the admission that, with the USSR as its target, Japan had purposefully positioned Units 731 and 100 and at least four smaller detachments near the Soviet border. Those who testified described sabotage against the Soviet troops in Siberia that was carried out from the late 1930s through 1942 and involved a range of tactics: from dumping anthrax spores into a tributary of the Argun River to spreading pathogens in the Soviet frontier districts.[63]

Heavily implicated at the trial was the absent General Ishii, identified as the creator of Unit 731, overseer of inhumane medical experimentation, and the engineer of mass attacks in China—all facts suppressed at the IMTFE by US military intelligence, as Smirnov well knew. Ishii's ignominious flight from Manchuria became part of the trial record when a young technician described what he witnessed at Unit 100 on August 20, 1945: Ishii and five of his cohort stopped at the unit's stable where they hastily fed glanders-infected grain to sixty horses. After releasing the horses to the countryside, they fled by train to Korea and, from there, to safety in Japan.

Emperor Hirohito entered into the prosecution's case when two defendants, Major General Kawashima, the top researcher at Unit 731, and Lieutenant General Takahashi, a former chief of the Kwantung Army's Veterinary Service, testified that, by a secret order, the emperor himself in 1936 had established Units 731 and 100 and approved their offensive BW missions.[64] On direct examination, Takahashi described the military chain of command from General Umezu at the Kwantung Army to himself at the Veterinary Administration and then to Wakamatsu at Unit 100.[65]

The Soviet prosecutors remained intent on proving charges against General Umezu, even though he had died a prisoner in Tokyo earlier that year. Among the incriminating new documents they introduced was a secret order by Umezu to establish in Manchuria four new branches of Unit 731, whose BW development goals—from bomb attacks to sabotage with germ-filled fountain pens—were testified to by the defendants. In another order, issued in 1940, General Umezu authorized the secret transport of Unit 731 personnel and equipment to Central China.[66] Testimony supported Ishii's plague attack on Ningbo that same year—a witness described the film of Ishii descending from the specially equipped plane returning from its mission.

The Soviets also presented documents of Japanese military orders to attack Changde with plague in 1941 and for Ishii's expert teams to participate in the Japanese retreat from Zhejiang and Jiangxi in 1942 by spreading disease throughout the area—by bombs, sprays, and the poisoning of wells and other sabotage. The apparently beneficent distribution of food to Chinese peasants, for example, was filmed for the edification of the Japanese public, without revealing that it was laced with lethal pathogens. One defendant, formerly the chief of information and intelligence for the Thirteenth Japanese Army, testified that Japanese scientists from Ei 1644 had taken part in germ warfare during the campaign.[67]

The Soviets' prize defendant was General Yamada Otozoo, the former commander-in-chief of the Kwantung Army. Two years before he took General Umezu's place, he had seen the 1940 film about the organization of the Ningbo attack, the one starring General Ishii. In his testimony, the contrite Yamada took responsibility for overseeing Unit 731's inhumane medical experiments and preparations for war against the Soviet Union. He admitted permitting the experiments that resulted in the violent killing of the Chinese, Russians, and Manchurians captured by the Kempeitai and by officers under his authority.

The descriptions of Japanese experiments were as horrific as those recounted in Nuremberg. A laboratory researcher at Unit 100 described experiments on humans with inoculations of anthrax and glanders. Another witness testified about experiments in which human subjects were forced to keep their arms and feet in special boxes filled with ice until their limbs froze solid. One researcher described how ten prisoners were tied to stakes and then subjected to a bomb attack. The shrapnel, contaminated with pathogens of gas gangrene (a bacterial infection usually caused by *Clostridium perfringens*), killed them all within a week. As for the systematic nature of the slaughter, the testimony at the trial revealed that from 1939 to 1945, at least six hundred victims were murdered per year, most of them Chinese and Manchu but with Russians and Koreans included.[68] The Soviet spectators at the trial reacted with shouts of anger and tears.[69]

On the evening of December 29, Lev Smirnov presented the case summary, simultaneously translated into Japanese, that had been frustrated at the Tokyo trial. To begin, Smirnov represented the Anti-Comintern Pact signed by Japan with Germany in 1936 as a treaty "directed primarily against the U.S.S.R."—part of a criminal conspiracy to seize the Soviet Far East—and quoted words to that effect that from the IMTFE's final verdict in 1948.[70]

Then, drawing on his arguments at Nuremberg, he stressed the similarity between Nazi medical atrocities and those of Ishii's detachment—the obvious comparison that the JCS and SWNCC had feared would become public. He recalled how the Soviet Army, marching westward "in single combat with Hitlerite Germany," discovered "the smoking ruins of Treblinka, the gas chambers at Majdanek, and the incinerators at Oswiecim [Auschwitz]—the vile death industry that was called into being by criminal German fascism." And, he reminded his audience, "fascist physician-experimenters tested on their helpless victims lethal, infectious and poisonous substances, they subjected living people to slow freezing in ice baths, and put people to a painful death in pressure chambers."

He accorded the greatest significance, though, to the Poznan institute in Poland, Germany's belated effort at offensive germ warfare, aimed at a future of "murdering millions of the civilian population and causing them the direst suffering." Not once, but twice, he argued, the Soviet Union had saved the world from the horrors of bacteriological warfare. The first was "the crushing blow of the Soviet Armed Forces that then saved mankind from the horrors of bacteriological warfare into which Hitlerite miscreants were preparing to plunge the world." The second was after the invasion of Manchuria in 1945, when "the Soviet Army, faithfully performing its duty as an ally, with a swift blow shattered the major striking force of criminal Japanese—the Kwantung Army—it again saved mankind from the horrors of bacteriological warfare."[71]

Smirnov pointedly compared the Soviet record on arms control to that of the United States and the fact that the Americans chose to protect General Ishii and other Unit 731 criminals. The Soviet Union had signed and ratified the Geneva Protocol of 1925, along with the majority of "other civilized states." Then Smirnov raised the threat of nuclear bombs:

> Being a genuine bulwark of peace and herald of the ideas of socialist humanism, the Soviet Union, marching at the head of democratic forces of the world, emphatically repudiates the employment of inhuman means of mass extermination. This is exactly why, despite all the efforts of the instigators of a new war in the Anglo-American bloc, the Soviet Union has been for a number of years striving in the United Nations organization to secure the absolute prohibition of atomic weapons.[72]

In addition to the punishment of the criminals in the dock, Smirnov urged that the court's verdict should sound a warning:

> Let all those who are contemplating new crimes against mankind, and preparing new means for the wholesale extermination of human beings, remember that the world had not forgotten the lessons of World War II. Peace and security is being guarded by millions of common people, by the mighty front of democratic forces headed by the great Soviet Union. It is a mighty and all-conquering force, which will be able to check and sternly punish all instigators of a new war.[73]

Smirnov was finally able to declare that "the atrocities committed by these miscreants from the secret bacteriological units of the Japanese Army verily have no equal." Given their crimes, the senior Khabarovsk defendants were fortunate in that the Soviet Union in May 1947 had abolished the death penalty, at least temporarily.[74] The maximum punishment in 1949 was twenty-five years in a labor camp, which five defendants received, among them General Yamada and Dr. Kawashima, the senior Unit 731 researcher, while his junior colleague Dr. Karasawa and four others were given fifteen to twenty years, and the rest, lower in the hierarchy, were allowed lighter sentences.

Representatives of the People's Republic of China attended the proceedings but as onlookers. Mao had just visited Moscow to discuss with Stalin the terms of the new Sino-Soviet Friendship, Alliance, and Mutual Assistance agreement, a replacement for a similar treaty concluded with the KMT in 1945. For Mao, an important goal was to regain the rights to ports and railways in Northeast China that Generalissimo Chiang had signed away.[75] China was also in need of loans to recover from the long years of war. In return, the Soviets wanted China as a junior partner in the region, for example, as a surrogate it could advise in achieving a communist takeover of Korea. Mao, though, was reluctant to be led. Rather than adopting the Khabarovsk tribunal as a model, the PRC would forge its own approach to prosecuting Japanese war criminals, based on a combination of "benevolence" and ideological reeducation aimed at turning the marauding Japanese "devils" into responsible socialists.[76] The People's Republic would emphasize "communist educational persuasion" over harsh penalties or long sentences.[77] At this time, former IMTFE judge Mei, who had opted to remain in the PRC, advised the release of prisoners even if they were thought guilty, as a show of good will toward Japan, whose favor Mao sought to cultivate.[78]

The Soviets issued multilingual press releases, including for Tokyo, while the Khabarovsk trial was ongoing. The news must have shaken Ishii and his cohort, as well as G-2. SCAP's response was an immediate and complete denial. On December 27 the *New York Times* ran a story under the headline "No Knowledge, MacArthur Says." Confusing the issue, his headquarters told the press that no cases were known in which the Japanese used American soldiers in germ warfare experiments, nor had any Americans held prisoner at Mukden "ever accused their captors of having used them as 'guinea pigs' in biological warfare tests." That much was generally accurate, but SCAP's public relations office denied any truth to the Khabarovsk testimony on medical atrocities: "The headquarters added that the Japanese had done some experiments with animals but that there was no evidence they had ever used human beings." In the West, every effort was made to discredit the Khabarovsk trial.[79] Joseph Keenan, the often absent IPS chief of counsel, denounced it as a Soviet "show" trial. The Netherlands judge, Bernard Röling, who had played tennis with General Willoughby but knew nothing of G-2's protection of Ishii, criticized the trial's "lack of proof."[80]

In Tokyo, as the news from Khabarovsk was breaking, street demonstrations erupted in protest of the Soviet Union's continued failure to repatriate hundreds of thousands of Japanese POWs captured in Manchuria in 1945 and diverted media attention from the trial's revelations. By the end of 1949 the Soviet government had, in fact, returned most of the Japanese men captured in Manchuria, but, in order to undermine the power of Japanese communists, the Occupation's "Red Purge" was just beginning.[81] Taking advantage of the situation, the right-wing press reported many stories of abuse told by those repatriated which reinforced animosity toward the Soviet Union, whose bid to prosecute Emperor Hirohito, along with Ishii, Kitano, Wakamatsu, and Kasahara, found no support in Japan or the West.

In Japan, the main source of the Khabarovsk revelations in Japan was the communist newspaper *Akahata*, which for over two months reported on the trial and its implications. Since the Japanese public relied mostly on GHQ for its information, the news of the trial was largely unavailable. When a communist member of the Diet raised the issue of war crimes linked to biological weapons and the several thousands who may have served as guinea pigs for the Kwantung Army program, its secretary dismissed him with the comment that such matters had been taken care of by the Allied nations, in conformity with the Potsdam declaration, that is, at the IMTFE.[82] A few months later, the deputy who raised the question was banned from government by the Occupation's anticommunist purge.

Undeterred, in July 1950 the Soviets distributed a book-length summary of the Khabarovsk trial proceedings and key documents, translated into English and other languages. It included case summaries and edited transcripts of witness testimony and pleas, as well as photographs of incriminating Japanese documents, such as General Umezu's orders to ship Unit 731 staff and microbes to China. Also mentioned was David Nelson Sutton's August 1946 reading into the record of the poisoning of Chinese captives by the Tama Division in Nanjing, followed by the accusation that the American-dominated prosecution staff had suppressed the charges because "certain influential persons . . . were evidently interested in preventing the exposure of the monstrous crimes of the Japanese militarists."[83]

Unfortunately, by using the trial for anti-American propaganda, the Soviets diminished its credibility. A week after it ended, Colonel Mark Raginsky, who like Rosenblit had accompanied Lev Smirnov from Nuremberg to Tokyo, launched a frontal attack on General MacArthur, accusing him in the Soviet press of protecting Japanese BW war criminals "with a view to using them in another world war."[84] A string of similar caustic comments followed: Joseph Keenan was called an "advocate of plague" for protecting Emperor Hirohito, the United States was accused of putting war criminals back in power and turning Japan into a "chief operational base" for aggressive war against the Soviet Union and China, aided by an American expansion of the bacteriological warfare program.[85] If the Soviets had intended to separate fact from myth and use criminal law to rescue the nameless victims from historical oblivion—as Telford Taylor had urged at Nuremberg—their effort failed.

With the Tokyo trial's failure to prosecute the Unit 731 atrocities and the Khabarovsk trial cast in disrepute in the West, Imperial Japan's germ warfare program and its nameless victims disappeared from history, with little chance of being fixed in public memory by the judgment of an open court perceived by the world as unbiased.

EPILOGUE

THE FALLOUT

AFTER 1948 THE IMTFE JURISTS LEFT TOKYO FOR THEIR HOME countries. Joseph Keenan resumed his legal work in Washington and, his health problems intensifying, died in 1954 from heart disease.[1] Also returning to Washington, Frank Tavenner became chief counsel for the US House Un-American Activities Committee (HUAC), gaining a reputation for steady service during its heated and controversial investigation into the alleged communist infiltration of the entertainment industry.[2] After running Legal Section, Alva Carpenter became an attorney for the Senate Internal Security Subcommittee, whose Cold War investigations paralleled those of HUAC.[3] Solis Horwitz also gravitated to Capitol Hill, as counsel for the House Armed Services Committee; he later became assistant secretary of defense for administration and finally a professor at the University of Pittsburgh. Roy Morgan, the former head of the IPS Investigation Division, embarked on a successful career as a corporate intermediary for American and Japanese businesses. Carlisle Higgins was appointed an associate justice of the North Carolina Supreme Court and stayed on the court for twenty years.

IPS stalwart David Nelson Sutton returned to his family and private practice in West Point, Virginia. Although little acknowledged, his work on the Nanjing Massacre proved a major contribution to the trial and to the legal memory of China's many wartime victims. The recognition of rape as a war crime was reinforced with his recitation of evidence from the Nanjing Massacre, the kind of gruesome detail that made President Webb and spectators recoil. After his service at the Tokyo trial, he was elected head of the Virginia Bar Association. Without political ambition, he rejected a bid to run for governor.[4] Colonel Thomas Morrow, the war hero not permitted to argue against chemical warfare at the IMTFE, returned to his judgeship in Ohio, where he died in 1950.

Sir William Webb, the IMTFE president, returned to the High Court of Australia and in 1954 was made a knight commander of the Order of the British Empire. Also returning to Australia, Alan Mansfield was knighted and became the Supreme Court justice for Queensland and then Queensland's governor. In Great Britain, Arthur Comyns Carr, too, was knighted and, no longer shy of controversy, became president of the Liberal Party. Judge Erima Harvey Northcroft, who envisioned a more independent tribunal, resumed his place on the New Zealand Supreme Court.

Judge Mei Ru-ao and Prosecutor Hsiang Che-chun and others at the Chinese Division disappeared into Mao's People's Republic of China, which, having abolished the Ministry of Justice, had little use for their talents. After the end of the Cultural Revolution in 1976, both reemerged as respected jurists and offered commentaries on the IMTFE.[5]

After leaving Tokyo, Soviet associate prosecutor Sergei Golunsky became Foreign Minister Andrei Gromyko's legal advisor, accompanying him to San Francisco in 1951 for the signing of the peace treaty with Japan, to which neither of the two Chinas was invited. Protesting the failure of the international community to recognize Mao's People's Republic, Gromyko refused to add his signature. In Moscow, Lev Smirnov—veteran of the Smolensk, Nuremberg, Tokyo, and Khabarovsk trials—rose to become the chief justice for Russia, the pinnacle of the Soviet judiciary. On leaving China in 1949, Dr. Robert Pollitzer joined the World Health Organization in Geneva, where he became recognized as a world expert on plague. Pollitzer stood by the King report and its assertions of Japanese plague attacks.[6] Retreating from China's politics, Dr. Robert Lim became the director of medical research at Miles Laboratories in Elkart, Indiana, while Colonel David Barrett retired back home in Colorado and taught courses on Shakespeare at the state university at Boulder. The Reverend Edward J. Bannan and his wife Phyllis served as medical missionaries in Changde until 1951, then retired to Southern California. Also leaving China, in 1950 Miner Searle Bates became a professor at the Union Theological Seminary in New York.

General Douglas MacArthur's sojourn in Japan ended abruptly with a sudden political fall from grace. Starting in June 1950, he led the US Eighth Army in the conflict with North Korea and China. On April 12, 1951, President Truman fired him for acting without consultation with Washington, as had long been the general's habit as SCAP. MacArthur had just called on the Chinese commander to surrender "or else," with the implication that he personally would escalate the conflict over the border to China and risk war with its ally the Soviet Union, the other nuclear power.[7] Truman was not averse to escalation. He had deployed a squadron of planes carrying atomic bombs to the western Pacific, and his field commanders and Pentagon chiefs supported their use.[8] But he would not tolerate MacArthur's tendency to insubordination.

Major General Willoughby (he had been promoted in 1948) left Tokyo when MacArthur did and found a new calling as a consultant to Spain's fascist president, Francisco Franco. He continued to write books, notably his panegyric to MacArthur in 1954.[9] Amid accusations of corruption, General Alden Waitt of CWS retired from the army to San Antonio, Texas, where he became an active advocate for the arts. In 1951 Lieutenant Colonel Arvo Thompson committed suicide in Tokyo.

The overall impact of the IMTFE faded quickly.[10] Japanese ambivalence about the trial became colored by resentment that foreign victors had passed judgment on Japan's conduct of the war.[11] Of the eighteen defendants sentenced to prison, fourteen were paroled by 1955, with great public approval.[12] The four others, like General Umezu Yoshijiro, had died while incarcerated or they, too, would have been freed. Released in 1950, Shigemitsu Mamoru reentered politics and in 1954 was again appointed Japan's foreign minister. The idea that Japan itself might institute war crimes trials, as was done in Germany, had no place in this newly reconstituted nation.

Free from legal threats, Japanese biological weapons scientists fared well.[13] On his army pension and family inheritance, General Ishii Shiro continued to live a comfortable life, visited by some former Unit 731 researchers, shunned by others, occasionally consulted by the Chemical Corps, intermittently frightened by blackmailers, and closely watched by US intelligence. He died of throat cancer in 1959, after converting to Catholicism. Ishii's protégé Dr. Masuda took up general medical practice in the Tokyo suburbs, not far from his old boss, and died in a motorcycle accident in 1952.

Benefiting from the Occupation's business-friendly "reverse course," Dr. Naito Ryiochi became the principal founder of a large, successful blood supply company, initially called the Blood Bank of Japan (Nihon Burrado Banku) and later the Green Cross Corporation (Midori Jūji). He hired Dr. Kitano Masiji, Unit 731's second commander after Ishii, as chief of the company's Tokyo branch. The Korean War, during which the Americans needed blood products, greatly improved the company's fortunes. Over the years it engaged in a joint venture with Cutter Laboratories, the California pharmaceutical company, and set up branches in Switzerland, Germany, China, and the United Kingdom.[14] Naito was made a member of the New York Academy of Sciences; in 1963 he received an award from the Japanese Science Society for his work on artificial blood products; and in 1977 he was awarded the Order of the Rising Sun. Another entrepreneur, Dr. Hayakawa Kiyoshi, who had supervised human experimentation at Pingfan and Singapore, started his own vaccine venture, Hayakawa Medical Company.

Dr. Ishikawa Tachiomaru, who had shared his Unit 731 pathology data with Drs. Hill and Victor, became president of the Kanazawa Medical School. Dr. Ota Kiyoshi, a leader of the plague attack on Changde in 1941 and in charge of aerosol anthrax experiments on humans, established a general medical practice. Dr. Kashahara Shiro, the Unit 731 researcher once sought by the Soviets, became vice president of the Kitasato Hospital and Research Unit in Tokyo. Dr. Yoshimura Hisato, who had conducted freezing experiments on Chinese captives, became head of the Kyoto Prefectural University of Medicine and advised the Japanese government on an expedition to the South Pole. Many other Unit 731 and Unit 100 scientists taught at medical schools or worked in business or government.[15]

Dr. Wakamatsu Yujiro, former commander of Unit 100, conducted research on streptococcal infections in children for the Japanese National Institute of Health. The institute started hiring Ishii scientists in 1946, even as the United States deliberated on the immunity bargain.[16] From 1947 to 1983 seven of its eight directors had served in one or another of the biological warfare units. Questionable human research ethics seemed characteristic of projects that involved members of the former Unit 731 cadre. In the 1980s the sale of HIV-contaminated blood products by Green Cross (which guaranteed only "pure Japanese blood") led to the infection of more than a thousand hemophiliac patients and the deaths of 493, causing an international scandal.[17]

In 1956, in a conciliatory gesture toward Japan, the Soviets paroled the twelve Japanese defendants from the Khabarovsk trial. Major Karasawa Tomio died before he could return home; it was rumored he hanged himself. His older colleague Major General Kawashima Kioshi and the others, including General Yamada, arrived back safely and slipped into anonymity.

In 1978 fourteen of those found guilty at the IMTFE were honored at the Imperial Shrine of Yasukuni, the Shinto memorial. These included the seven executed defendants, plus the two who died of illness during the trial (Matsuoka and Nagano), and the four who died while imprisoned (Shiratori, Koiso, Togo, and Umezu). The rationale was that they had all died "of a foreign hand" while in service to their country—not unlike the thousands of Japanese soldiers and civilian war dead the shrine also honors. After the war, India's judge Radhabinod Pal gave lectures in Japan denouncing the "Western imperialism" that had dominated the IMTFE. To celebrate his being a "hero of Japanese nationalism," a statue of him was erected at the Yasukuni Shrine.

The Cold War and the Superpower Arms Race

During a brief euphoric period after World War II, the United Nations acted idealistically to promote universal criminal law and arms control. Reaching back to the League of Nation efforts in 1924 to codify international law, in 1947 the UN International Law Commission began determining how the precedents of Nuremberg could inform the General Assembly. The commission agreed on the three Nuremberg Charter categories—crimes against peace, war crimes, and crime against humanity—and there was consensus that they had become part of international law, without, however, the reinforcement that the criminal prosecution of Unit 731 atrocities would have added.[18] The Nuremberg Code of 1947 grew out of the US trial of Nazi doctors and began a new, more humane era in Western medical research and law. In 1948 the UN Genocide Convention articulated the prohibition on the annihilating attacks on racial, ethnic, religious, and national minorities suffered by victims of the Holocaust.[19] Along with another committee on international criminal jurisdiction, the International Law Commission worked on draft proposals for an international criminal court—more permanent than Nuremberg or Tokyo—but Cold War tensions made the idea untenable.[20]

In August 1948 the UN Commission on Conventional Armaments defined "weapons of mass destruction" (WMD) as "atomic explosive weapons, radioactive material weapons, lethal chemical and biological weapons, and any weapons developed in the future which have characteristics comparable in destructive effect to those of nuclear or other weapons mentioned above."[21] This definition, based on a draft submitted by the United States, was meant to promote the United Nations as a forum for arms control. But the new, competitive era of WMD proliferation had begun and would continue unabated for another four-plus decades, during which nuclear weapons of increasing potency became the currency of power.[22] By 1992 the Soviet stockpile of nuclear warheads had reached 40,723; the United States was at 23,254.[23]

In this same epoch biological and chemical weapons were integrated into the Cold War value placed on potential strategic weapons for the total war of the future. The disdain many US military officers felt for both types of weapons ought to have put an end to them in 1945, when the US CBW programs were being dismantled, but will and foresight were lacking. In his 1950 autobiography, Fleet Admiral William Leahy expressed his moral repugnance for the use of bacteriological weapons as a violation of "every Christian ethic" and "all of the known laws of war."[24] Yet in 1947, as head of the Joint Chiefs of Staff, Leahy acquiesced in allowing General Ishii and his cohort to be protected by G-2, in the name of national security and the future of the Chemical Corps. Using similar reasoning, Leahy believed that the "United States must have more and better atom bombs than any potential enemy."[25]

In the midst of the Korean War (1950–1953), China and North Korea began accusing the United States of using germ weapons (including infected fleas and anthrax aerosols) on civilian targets, allegedly with help from General Ishii.[26] The matter was taken to the United Nations, where

China refused an International Committee of the Red Cross investigation and instead guided a team led by British sinologist Joseph Needham to the war zone to review evidence; although the Needham team was persuaded, the charge was later revealed to be largely Chinese propaganda. Not admitted publicly at the time, Camp Detrick's germ weapons were too rudimentary to be integrated into US Army or Air Force war plans.[27] While this lack of development did not entirely preclude the possibility of covert US battlefield experiments, the charges remained speculative.[28] Instead of plague-infected fleas or anthrax bombs, the American military relied on its tried-and-true incendiaries, including napalm, and conventional and cluster bombs, and equipped ground soldiers with flame-throwers. By the time of the 1953 armistice, the Korean peninsula had become "a smouldering ruin" with some three million inhabitants killed.[29]

After the Korean War armistice, the US Army's secret biological warfare program grew steadily until it comprised a dozen research stations and testing sites and hundreds of research and development contracts with universities and industry.[30] Doubled in size to a thousand acres, in 1956 Camp Detrick became Fort Detrick. In parallel, the resources for US research, development, and testing of chemical weapons increased and the latitude for the use of both types of weapons in war expanded. In 1956 the National Security Council issued directive 5062/1, which affirmed that the United States would be "prepared to use chemical and biological weapons in general war," with the president (at that time Dwight D. Eisenhower) empowered to make the decision for first use. The phrase "retaliation only" was deleted from the army's *Law of Land Warfare* manual. After the 1964 Gulf of Tonkin Resolution, which gave President Lyndon Johnson the right to wage all-out war against North Vietnam, the scale of the US BW program expanded to include large-scale aerial tests to disperse lethal pathogens over thousands of miles.

President Richard Nixon, sworn into office on January 20, 1969, was faced with a public energized by the environmental movement and protesting the US use of herbicides in the Vietnam War. The year before, an air force jet on a test run near Dugway Proving Ground accidently released gallons of VX nerve gas over grazing land in Skull Valley, Utah. The emission reportedly killed hundreds of sheep, an accident quickly reported in the press.[31] Members of Congress and the public were shocked to find out about secret strategic chemical warfare tests and were alarmed by news of leaking CW munitions to be transported across the country by rail and dumped in the Atlantic, off the populous East Coast. These threats to the public made the Chemical Corps more vulnerable to restraints than it had been in years. To begin, the use of Agent Orange in Vietnam was stopped—but not before 73 million liters had been sprayed over some thousands of acres and thousands of Vietnam civilians and US ground troops were exposed, with controversial health consequences.[32]

After an extensive review of the BW program by his national security advisor Henry Kissinger and with the support of the secretaries of defense and state and senior scientists outside government, President Nixon decided to end the biological warfare program.[33] After more than twenty years, it had failed to convince the military establishment that it served any important need, while the proliferation of biological weapons could pose a serious threat to US and international security.[34]

On November 25, 1969, President Nixon renounced biological weapons on behalf of the US government and restricted the US program to "research and development for defensive purposes." To meet this directive, a new institution was created at Fort Detrick, the US Army Medical Research Institute of Infectious Diseases (USAMRIID). Nixon's decision came just as microbiology and genetic engineering were on the brink of revolutionary advances, which Detrick's warfare program, involving thousands of scientists in hundreds of laboratories, would have necessarily exploited. In that day's National Security Decision Memorandum 35, Nixon reaffirmed the US renunciation of the first use of lethal chemical weapons, as well as incapacitating ones.[35] Excluded were riot-control agents (like tear gas) and herbicides, which the Pentagon insisted on using in Vietnam. The Geneva Protocol of 1925 would also be resubmitted to the Senate for its advice and consent.[36]

To the press, Nixon declared: "Biological weapons have massive unpredictable and potentially uncontrollable consequences. They may produce global epidemics and impair the health of future generations. I have therefore decided that the U.S. shall renounce the use of lethal biological agents and weapons, and all other methods of biological warfare."[37] US nuclear weapons were enough of a deterrent. And, as Nixon put it, "Mankind already carries in its own hands too many seeds of its own destruction."

The international sequel to Nixon's decision was the 1972 Biological and Toxin Weapons Convention (BWC) that banned their development, production, possession, and transfer. Most of the world's nations signed the BWC and reinforced an important norm against state biological warfare programs. In 1975 the United States and Japan both finally ratified the Geneva Protocol prohibiting the use of chemical or biological weapons in war.

Unknown to the outside world, a small, influential cadre in the Soviet Union believed that biological weapons remained essential to its national security goals—and that the United States, despite Nixon's renunciation, was covertly expanding its offensive program.[38] In 1972 the Soviets embarked on an enormous arms initiative called Biopreperat, established by its Central Committee, to twin an accelerated development of its retrograde microbial sciences with a secret buildup of germ weapons. Vast in its proportions, the Soviet program was deeply secret, even within its own government, and a threat to the world and its own people.[39] In 1973 its high-risk testing caused a smallpox outbreak in an Aral Sea port. In 1979 an accidental release of virulent anthrax spores from a military facility caused the documented deaths of nearly one hundred people in the eastern city of Sverdlovsk.[40]

Post-Cold War Ideals and Threats

At the end of the Cold War (as happened at the end of World War II), the realization dawned that strategic weapons had brought the world to the brink of catastrophic destruction, with the added understanding that safeguards were far from foolproof.[41] Nuclear weapons had proliferated to the United Kingdom, France, China, Israel, South Africa, and India, with Pakistan to come and other nations, such as North Korea, suspected of having nuclear capability. In secret the Soviets had created an enormous germ weapons capability, and a half dozen small nations were suspected of having developed biological weapons. Tons of chemical munitions produced by nations large and small had been stockpiled around the world, with destabilizing consequences. Aided by the West, Saddam Hussein had resorted to mustard gas in the Iran-Iraq War and then launched nerve gas attacks on Kurdish villages, without being held accountable.[42]

In the late 1980s Soviet president Mikhail Gorbachev and US president Ronald Reagan agreed to a bilateral agreement to reduce the risks of nuclear war beyond earlier restrictions on atmospheric testing. In 1991 their two nations signed START I, which barred a deployment of more than six thousand nuclear warheads and implemented limits on intercontinental ballistic missiles and bombers.[43]

Another major arms control accomplishment of the era was the almost universally supported Chemical Weapons Convention of 1993. Aimed at ending all state CW programs by banning chemical weapons and production facilities, it was promoted by then president George H. W. Bush. This treaty, complementing the Biological Weapons Convention, came with its own standing organization in The Hague, the Organization for the Prohibition of Chemical Weapons (OPCW). One responsibility of the OPCW was to oversee the verified destruction of declared CW stockpiles by member states. In addition to its expanded munitions and production facilities, Russia had accumulated 40,000 metric tons of nerve agent. The Americans, having retreated from chemical weapons in the Nixon era, were only slightly less burdened, with 31,000 metric tons of nerve and mustard agents. Both nations agreed to a timetable to meet the treaty's terms and led the way for other nations to do the same. By article 1 of the convention, Japan was obliged to destroy or remove at least 700,000 chemical weapons left behind in China by its Imperial Army.[44] Included were the mustard gas munitions left behind at Qiqihar, the scene of Ishii's early experiments on captive Chinese.[45]

In the internationalist atmosphere of the early 1990s, European nations, led by the British, aimed to reinforce the Biological Weapons Convention with mandatory compliance measures.[46] But, as after World War I and World War II, the euphoria of idealism dissipated rapidly and US support for a stronger convention was undercut by fears that on-site inspections would jeopardize national security and commercial secrets. Nonetheless, the number of states committed to the Biological Weapons Convention stood as a firm declaration of an international norm. Those party to it exceeded 150, with only Israel, Egypt, Syria, North Korea, and a few small states holding back. International cooperation among BWC member nations became active and many of them introduced national "enabling legislation" to enforce the treaty's provisions within their borders. On a parallel track, the Chemical Weapons Convention, ratified by 180 of the world's nations, came into force in 1997, with the Americans on board. By the beginning of the new century, though, the predictable outliers—North Korea, Israel, Egypt, Libya, and Syria—still refused to join, although Libya and Syria eventually did so.

Following the Cold War, the fallout from decades of WMD proliferation continued to have repercussions. For the United States, small enemy states and terrorists who might gain access to these weapons technologies became the new threat, with Iraq, Iran, Libya, Syria, and North Korea high on the suspect list. Following Saddam's defeat in the Gulf War of 1991, cease-fire conditions required disarmament under supervision by inspectors from the United Nations Special Commission (UNSCOM).[47] By 1995 Iraq's fledgling nuclear capability was destroyed, along with its chemical weapons and production capability, but suspicions of Saddam's hidden germ weapons, especially anthrax, persisted, and, although unfounded, they ultimately became part of the US rationale for its Iraq invasion of 2003.

In a macabre twist, in 1995 a Japanese cult called Aum Shinrikyo (Supreme Truth), with a global membership in the tens of thousands, staged a small sarin nerve gas attack in a Tokyo subway station that killed twelve people and terrified at least a thousand others.[48] Japanese officials rushed to create strict national laws against WMD possession and use and to prosecute the cult leaders. In another strange turn, during the administration of President Bill Clinton, the threat of bioterrorism assumed new importance, with growing fears of Iraqi terrorists attacking the United States with germ weapons, especially anthrax and smallpox, although no evidence existed that Saddam had renewed production of the former or developed the latter.[49] Dozens of federal offices dedicated to preventing bioterrorism in particular and terrorism in general were created in the 1990s and funding for biodefense projects grew, boosting defensive research at Fort Detrick's USAMRIID, in medical research centers, and in small commercial start-ups.

Following the Clinton years, the George W. Bush administration faced the worst terrorist event perhaps ever experienced by Americans—the September 11, 2001, al-Qaeda airplane attacks on Manhattan's World Trade Center and the Pentagon. That national trauma was followed within a month by reports of seemingly random deaths and illness from exposure to anthrax, a highly uncommon disease. With the FBI and police investigating, it was discovered that five anthrax letters had been sent from within the United States to media centers in Florida and New York City and to US Senate offices in Washington, DC, where, amid rising panic, thousands were treated with antibiotics.[50] The three mailed envelopes that were retrieved contained fine powders of lethal spores and crudely printed letters intimating that al-Qaeda terrorists had sent them, which raised alarms about foreign bioterrorism.

The immediate US reaction to the 9/11 attacks was to join with the United Kingdom to invade Afghanistan, seen as al-Qaeda's main base; later a NATO-led coalition and other nations also joined the war. Then, in 2003, the United States made the unilateral decision to invade Iraq. In the rush to war, the Bush administration believed that, without intervention, Saddam's suspected stores of anthrax weapons posed a dire threat to US security. In anticipation of American soldiers being deployed to Iraq, two million troops were required to have anthrax vaccinations, which, for a small minority, caused harmful side effects; the requirement prompted a number of officers and enlisted men and women to quit the service.[51] In that same rush to war, influential medical advisors to the White House promoted the dubious idea that smallpox-infected terrorists sent by Saddam Hussein might invade the United States; as a safeguard, a plan was put into action to vaccinate thousands of American "first responders" against the disease, a first step to a mass vaccination of the entire US public. When the vaccine, known to pose health risks, was linked to three deaths, state medical authorities halted the plan.[52] By then the Iraq War, later widely regarded as a waste of lives and money, was under way, with no sign of Iraqi germ warfare.

Yet fears of bioterrorism continued in the United States, and federal funding for medical research on defenses against anthrax, plague, tularemia, the Ebola virus, and other select agents increased sharply, from hundreds of millions in 2000 to around $7 billion a year in 2003, a level maintained for more than a decade although no significant incidents of bioterrorism occurred.[53] With federal support, the number of maximum containment laboratories (Biosafety-level 4 or BSL-4) increased from four to seventeen, and hundreds of BSL-3 laboratories sprung up around the nation. Fort Detrick became the site of perhaps the largest such military laboratory in the world (835,000 square feet) and of another large new laboratory, exclusively for the Department of Homeland Security and FBI high-security research.

Meanwhile, FBI inquiries into the source of the anthrax letters continued, ranging from tracing leads in Afghanistan to commissioning the genetic fingerprinting of the powdered spores. In 2008 the FBI was ready to indict a mentally unstable USAMRIID anthrax expert who likely had sent the letters as a hoax. But the suspect, a civilian microbiologist named Bruce Ivins, committed suicide and the case was closed.

For years no similar anthrax letter attacks occurred. Instead, the hazards of infections from pathogens once developed for germ weapons increased inadvertently. Chronic safety failures—the mailing of virulent *Bacillus anthracis* to an unprotected lab, mechanical breakdowns, the death of a University of Chicago researcher from a laboratory plague strain—generated citizen protest in Frederick, Maryland, about risks posed by Fort Detrick, and in Boston, where a BSL-4 lab was planned to open in a minority neighborhood, and in California and the state of Washington where other groups had similar concerns about accidental emissions.[54] Late in the administration of President Barack Obama, the US Centers for Disease Control, reacting to incidents of anthrax spills and the unguarded storage of smallpox samples there, promised more vigilant biosafety measures—and a possible reduction in high-containment research.[55] Meanwhile, for a decade of accidental mailings of live anthrax spores to around two hundred private, academic, and federal laboratories, the US Army ordered suspensions and demotions for ten of its employees.[56]

Unexpectedly, chemical warfare emerged as a more lethal threat than bioterrorism. In August 2013, during the civil war in the Syrian Arab Republic, a sarin attack killed nearly a thousand people in Ghouta, outside Damascus. Despite international investigations, whether Assad's military or insurgents were responsible for the atrocity remained unclear. Nonetheless, pressured by Russia and the United States, Syrian president Bashar al-Assad quickly arranged his nation's ratification of the Chemical Weapons Convention and, with OPCW and international assistance, the destruction of its chemical stockpiles.[57] As the OPCW reported, though, Syria subsequently resisted compliance with the treaty. In April 2017, a second sarin attack on rebel-held Sheikoun in northern Syria killed more than 600 civilians. As with Ghouta, ambiguity surrounded the attack, leaving identification of the murderers to future investigations and, hopefully, legal retribution.[58]

The Revelations in Japan: Justice Denied

The late 1960s and early 1970s marked a new phase in international revelations about the horrors of Unit 731. One influence was President Nixon's decision in 1969 to end the US BW program. Even before his announcement, neglected documents, like China's King report of 1942 on the plague attacks, were rediscovered and circulated to bolster the argument for an international ban, promoted by the British, which culminated in the Biological Weapons Convention of 1972.[59]

Another decision by President Nixon opened the door to a mutual reassessment of Japan and China's wartime history. Nixon's February 1972 visit to the People's Republic of China and his agreement with Chairman Mao Zedong to an "ideological truce" radically reconfigured Asia-Pacific geopolitics.[60] By the Shanghai Communiqué, the United States and China stood united against any expansion of the Soviet sphere; and, by recognizing that "there is but one China and that Taiwan is part of China," the United States left it to the PRC to "peacefully resolve" the troublesome question of unity.[61] Japan, which had been thriving as a US Cold War ally, soon followed with its recognition of the People' Republic; Deng Xiaoping, the leader of then impoverished China, greeted this gesture with joy and admiration for Japan's "hardworking people."[62]

In 1973 journalist Yoshinaga Haruko tracked down ageing veterans of Ishii's program for a Tokyo Broadcasting System exposé called "A Bruise—Terror of the 731 Corps," which aired in 1976 and was reported in the *Washington Post*.[63] In addition, in the midst of controversy about wartime cover-ups in Japanese textbooks, Morimura Seiichi wrote a novel based on Unit 731, *The Devil's Gluttony*; serialized in *Akahata*, the Communist Party newspaper, and then published in book form, it became a best seller, with the arrogant monster General Ishii at its center.[64] Around this same time, Professor Tsuneishi Kei-ichi of Kanagawa University and other Japanese academics began dedicating themselves to documenting Ishii's program and revealing the postwar activities of its scientists in Japan, as well as the secrets of Japan's wartime chemical weapons.[65]

For Americans, the first revelations that the United States government had covered up Ishii's war crimes came from American journalist John W. "Bill" Powell, the son of the disabled Shanghai journalist who had testified at the beginning of the IMTFE. As the new editor of the *China Weekly Review*, which his father had started, the younger Powell reported on the Chinese germ warfare accusations against the United States during the Korean War, to the dismay of American authorities. Returning to the United States in 1953, Powell and his wife were subjected to intimidating public interrogations by the Senate Internal Security Subcommittee; for one of these sessions Alva Carpenter organized an audience of angry former Korean War POWs to intimidate the couple.[66] In 1956, at the height of the Cold War congressional "witch hunts," Powell was charged with sedition and for having threatened US troop morale during the Korean War by circulating his journal. After a mistrial was declared in 1959, all charges against him were dropped for lack of evidence, but he remained blacklisted from journalism. Nonetheless, Powell persisted in combing declassified documents about US germ weapons until, in 1980, he wrote an article for a small scholarly journal discussing the US cover-up of Japan's wartime program.[67] In an expanded version, his research was published in the *Bulletin of the Atomic Scientists*, along with a supportive commentary by former Netherlands IMTFE judge Bernard Röling, then age 75.[68]

Powell's second version was richer in documentation than his first. Reproduced in it was General Ishii's sketch of Pingfan and a photocopy of General Willoughby's letter of March 27, 1947, arguing against Soviet requests to interview Ishii.[69] Powell described the human experiment details in the 1947 Hill and Victor Report submitted to SCAP, Willoughby, and General Alden Waitt. He also cited Alva Carpenter's letter of June 27, 1947, acknowledging the Ishii group's criminal violation of the rules of land warfare. Reproduced was the first page of that letter, in which Carpenter cites Frank Tavenner's affirmation that the Karasawa affidavit corroborated the plague attacks in China but that, even with human experimentation admitted, these actions did not justify war crimes prosecution.[70]

Continuing on, Powell presented the excerpts from the SWNCC deliberations that (1) argued for the "vital importance" of human experimentation data, (2) fretted that similarities to the Nazi doctors' crimes might be revealed at the Tokyo war crimes trial, and (3) agreed that "this Government would retain in intelligence channels all information given by the group on the subject of BW."[71] After this factual account, Powell raised the suspicion of an American cover-up of Japanese germ experiments on US POWs, which generated congressional hearings but no hard conclusions.

After Powell's article was published, British and American investigators followed up with more detailed expositions of the Ishii war crimes and the US cover-up and congressional hearings on possible abuses of POWS.[72] Although the hearings were inconclusive, the investigative works set the stage for more revelations coming from Japan and China in the next decade.

Memory and Justice

In the early post–Cold War years, international criminal justice and human rights, sidelined for decades, gained new prominence.[73] With this change, the intellectually neglected subject of genocide became a focus for philosophical discussion and political action.[74] In Japan, the time arrived for the recognition of war crimes.[75] The surge in popular interest followed decades of government suppression of imperial wartime atrocities, in contrast to the German proclivity to keep the memory of Nazi war crimes alive through trials, memorials, and public education. Each year, as a nation, Japan commemorated just two wartime events, the August 6 bombing of Hiroshima and the emperor's August 15 announcement of surrender—remembrances of Japanese victimization and defeat.

The newly public Japanese remembrances of war with China were marked by competing versions of history and at times by violent reactions to any insinuation that Imperial Japanese soldiers or the emperor could be responsible for war crimes.[76] The Rape of Nanking, for which David Nelson Sutton had assembled thorough evidence at the Tokyo trial, was the most contentious issue, dismissed by conservative nationalists as Chinese propaganda. Unlike the fringe group of Holocaust deniers in Germany, those Japanese who claimed that Nanking was a hoax had a large audience supported by powerful right-wing politicians.[77] Many facts, though, were a matter of legal record, which was not so for the Unit 731 war crimes. The persistent, selective secrecy surrounding Japanese government archives, combined with the scattering of documents after the war, contributed significantly to ignorance about Unit 731. Although most of the Japanese Foreign Ministry documents returned by the United States after

1952 were opened to the public, those concerning the use of chemical weapons and biological warfare and experimentation were closed or redacted, along with other documents kept "private."[78]

Nothing, though, could stop the testimony of aging Japanese veterans who, in the early 1990s, began to publicly express regret for their participation in the germ weapons atrocities.[79] At the beginning, small numbers of Japanese men who had worked in different capacities at Pingfan and the other research facilities came forward to confess what they had done and the systemic atrocities they had witnessed. At meetings and conferences and in a traveling exhibit organized by peace activist organizations in Japan, these and other witnesses admitted performing vivisections, "sacrificing" the survivors of medical experiments, and conducting bomb tests on captives.[80] An estimated 450,000 Japanese, mostly students, saw a total of 159 such expositions. In person and on video, the witnesses described transporting Chinese captives to Unit 731 for experiments—often in black vans called "ravens"—and disposing of prisoners' bodies in incinerators; the tasks were made so routine that their moral sensibilities were numbed. An anonymous telephone line was created for other veterans to add their stories. General Ishii's driver (Koshi Dadao) spoke up, appearing at the expositions and on television to describe how, with Ishii at his side, he used a truck to deliver victims to their deaths at Unit 731.[81]

In China, new documents about Unit 731 and its branches surfaced, allowing a new look at the criminality of Ishii's activities.[82] In 1946 the Nanjing Prosecutor's Office had prepared three indictments of Japanese officers for atrocities committed at Unit 1644's Nanjing facility and had located two witnesses.[83] One was C. C. H. Hataba (Chimba Osam), the deserter whose statement Prosecutor Hsiang had given to David Nelson Sutton. None of this witness testimony found its way to a Chinese court—not during the time of the KMT government, when war disrupted the courts, or after the creation of the PRC, which instead of highlighting atrocities, chose to be magnanimous in judging the thousands of Japanese left behind after the war, rather than alienating its close neighbor.[84]

The belated revelations of Unit 731 horrors generated active interest in China, which in the 1980s began a phase of "Reform and Opening Up" to fight economic stagnation. In 1986, at Harbin, a museum in honor of victims was built on the Pingfan ruins; it grew and became a partner with the memorial museums at Nagasaki and Nanking.[85] In 1987 a concerned group of Chinese citizens wrote an open letter to Beijing on the question of reparations due the Chinese victims of Japanese germ warfare who, with their families, were beginning to tell their stories. It took time, but in 1995 a group of Chinese and Japanese activists united with the goal of bringing a law suit against the Japanese government on behalf of just over a hundred plaintiffs to force an admission of guilt and financial compensation. Based in Shanghai, Chinese activist Wang Xuan was a leader of the legal venture; her family was from a village near Quzhou, the target of the first plague attack in 1940, and had suffered from the plague outbreaks. Preparation for the lawsuit uncovered public health records indicating Chinese BW victims in the tens of thousands or more. Encouraged by Wang, in 2001 Captain Li Xiaofang of the Chinese Army embarked on a four-year investigation of dozens of what were called "Rotten Leg" villages, where elderly survivors of the Zhejiang-Jiangxi Campaign still suffered from ulcers caused by glanders.[86] Over a hundred testimonies and photographs from dispersed villages corroborated the germ weapons attacks of 1942 described by Japanese veterans, by witnesses at the Khabarovsk trial, and by Ishii and his scientists to US military scientists in 1947.

In 2002 the Tokyo District Court acknowledged that the Chinese plaintiffs' argument was valid: Unit 731 scientists had "used bacteriological weapons under the order of the Imperial Japanese Army's headquarters."[87] Yet the court decided that no compensation was due because the peace treaty of 1952 had absolved Japan of its responsibilities with regard to wartime damages. Furthermore, in the Sino-Japan Joint Communiqué of 1972, in which Japan apologized for its wartime aggression and recognized Beijing, China in return gave up its right to seek war reparations. The plaintiffs went forward with appeals. In May 2007 the second, final one failed—ten years after the case was initiated, by which time twenty-four of the plaintiffs had died.[88]

In 1950, after returning to his law practice in Virginia, David Nelson Sutton reflected on the IMTFE, asking with some skepticism whether it was really "the most important trial in history," as President Webb had declared on its opening day. Few more than Sutton knew its drawbacks. With great diligence and despite obstacles, he had brought together every piece of trial-worthy evidence he could find to argue the prosecution case, but only within the boundaries allowed by the Occupation. Relying on a quote from Justice Robert Jackson, Sutton took a positive stance: "If it be true as has been so well said that 'The fundamental problem confronting the world is to establish world order under the rule of law,' then the fact that eleven nations including the greatest nations in this world have in our day worked together in this one trial for over thirty months to administer justice under law should give us hope."[89] He also advised patience: "International criminal law is still in its infancy. . . . It may take a long time to develop an ordered and workable system for the trial and punishment of offenders against international law."[90]

Even while it was ongoing, American and British dominance at the IMTFE opened it to the criticism that it had yielded only "victors' justice" that ignored the culpability of Allied forces and left many victims unheard.[91] Yet military secrecy was a great hindrance to justice, one that was protected and escaped attention. Sutton lived until 1974 (ten years longer than Frank Tavenner), long enough to hear about the Nixon decision and the admission that the US biological warfare program posed a threat to the nation and the world. As Sutton likely guessed and as Tavenner certainly knew, to protect that program US military intelligence had actively invaded the Tokyo trial proceedings and suppressed an entire category of war crimes perpetrated against Chinese civilians. The rule of law could hardly have been more abused in the name of national security.

The post–Cold War 1990s revived not only remembrances of war crimes but the progressive movement to create an "ordered and workable system" for the international prosecution of new atrocities. To find justice through ad hoc tribunals for those slaughtered in the former Yugoslavia and Rwanda was a struggle for all involved: the United Nations, nongovernmental organizations, the international community at large, legal scholars, and the surviving victims and witnesses.[92] A variety of tribunals were created to settle the scores of other human rights abuses and atrocities: truth and reconciliation hearings began in South Africa and a war crimes tribunal for massacres was held in Cambodia. Belatedly, a Truth and Reconciliation Commission in South Korea addressed the massacres of thousands of civilians, many occurring in 1950 when then president Syngman Rhee launched a violent antileftist campaign.[93]

Another "constitutional moment" of idealism joined by public enthusiasm seemed to have arrived. The United Nations went back to its International

Law Commission's proposals from the early 1950s proposing a permanent international criminal court.[94] More work by the commission culminated in the drafting in 1998 of the Rome Statute, involving a coalition of 120 states, to codify the jurisdictional and procedural rules of an International Criminal Court (ICC) and define the crimes it should address. (Among them, article 8 of the statute refers to criminal sanctions against "employing poison weapons.") In 2003 the ICC opened as "the first permanent international criminal court with a distinct legal foundation, jurisdictional reach, structure, and set of rules."[95] As a legal experiment, it was built from scratch, independent of the United Nations but often caught between the UN Security Council and states disrupted by war and genocide, and lacking the support of three major powers, the United States, Russia, and China.[96] Once in operation, with a limited budget, the ICC proceeded slowly, finally choosing its first case, on behalf of child soldiers in the Congo wars, while continuing to investigate dozens of other criminal allegations—although not without criticism for its apparent bias toward African criminal transgressions.[97]

In his address to the review conference on the ICC in 2010, UN Secretary General Ban Ki-moon, a South Korean born in 1944, heralded a new age:

> The old era of impunity is over. In its place, slowly but surely, we are witnessing the birth of a new Age of Accountability. It began, many decades ago with Nuremberg and the Tokyo Tribunals. It gained strength with the international criminal tribunals for Rwanda and the former Yugoslavia, as well as the so-called "hybrid" tribunals in Sierra Leone, Cambodia and Lebanon. Now we have the ICC, permanent, increasingly powerful, casting a long shadow.[98]

The court's "long shadow" is its potential for deterring future war crimes. The idealists—Robert Jackson, Hersch Lauterpacht, and Telford Taylor, and we must add David Nelson Sutton—would have approved. Yet every nation that refuses to join the court also resists the commitment to accountability and transparency necessary to guarantee justice for victims.

With the passage of time, an international court resolution of the Unit 731 war crimes seems impossible; the delay in justice at Tokyo led to a denial of justice that seems almost intractable. Still, unresolved crimes always call for resolution, to restore the sense of social order on which individual and institutional relationships depend. A grass-roots movement in the new age of social media could revive a court process.[99] At the least, a diplomatic initiative is needed. For two cultures in which apologies carry great significance, Japan should stand ready to offer an official statement of healing and China would do well to accept it.[100] Given its central role in the IMTFE cover-up of Japan's germ weapons atrocities, the United States ought to seize the opportunity to take a leadership role in acknowledging the injustice and also apologize.[101] The alternative is to allow a persistent, corrosive insult to China. Such an affront, committed when Japan and China were wrecked by war and lacked autonomy, makes no sense in the twenty-first century of Asian politics, when both nations exert regional and global influence beyond any Allied imaginings and have a shared future to build.[102]

The larger problem remains the protection of fair judicial process from political powers that use secrecy to obstruct the vindication owed to victims, however compelling or existential state interests might seem. More than seventy-five years ago, a young man named Kung Tsao-shang died of plague because he visited his sick mother in Changde. His was the only victim's name featured in Tokyo trial records, because the report of his autopsy was part of the public health record passed to Sutton. The thousands of other victims killed in Japan's mass disease attacks and in its years of medical experimentation became "too many to remember." Where in this negligence does one find justice or, as Telford Taylor phrased it, the voice of humanity?

ACKNOWLEDGMENTS

ALL BOOKS ARE COLLABORATIVE VENTURES, WITH COLLEAGUES one meets face-to-face and with authors and witnesses to history whose ideas live in their writings.

The organizers of several key conferences helped shape the ideas for this book. In 2005 Raymond Jeanloz, chair of the Committee on International Security and Arms Control at the US National Academy of Sciences, led a group of us to Harbin to place a wreath at the Unit 731 memorial to victims, the event that sparked the beginning of this project. In the following decade the annual Geneva workshops on chemical and biological weapons disarmament, sponsored by the Pugwash Conferences on Science and World Affairs, broadened my education, as did my participation in the World Economic Forum's Global Agenda Council on Nuclear, Biological, and Chemical Weapons, and my long-term association with the Harvard-Sussex Program on Chemical and Biological Weapons. A number of scholars have held conferences and edited books based on the proceedings. For including my contributions, I thank Bratislav Friedrich and Florian Schmaltz for the meeting on the hundredth anniversary of Ypres cohosted in 2015 by the Fritz Haber Institute of the Max Planck Society and the Max Planck Institute for the History of Science; Brian Balmer, Jason Dittmer, and Alex Mankoo for high-energy meetings on politics and science at University College, London; Brian Balmer and Caitriona MacLeish for a parallel series on the history of CBW at Sussex University; and Filippa Lentzos, King's College, for organizing contemporary oral histories and articles on the politics of CBW policy into book form. Earlier invitations to apply a social science perspective to problems of international justice and national security came to me from Kamari Clark, Mark Goodale, Sally Merry, Reto Wollenmann, Peter Lavoy, Anne Clunan, Susan Martin, and Margaret Harrell.

I also thank other scholars and fellow investigators in the fields of arms control, military history, law, and medical ethics. First among them are Matthew Meselson and Julian Perry Robinson, whose dedication to the elimination of biological and chemical weapons has brought great good to the world. Starting in the 1960s, usually behind the scenes, Meselson in particular successfully dedicated himself to the radical changes in US policy necessary for the eventual global ban on both weapons. Tomoko Steen, Walter Grunden, Ulf Schmidt, Mary Kaldor, Sally Falk Moore, Richard Samuels, Barry Posen, Philip Heymann, Gregory Koblentz, Martin Furmanski, Michael Franzblau, John van Courtland Moon, Benjamin Garrett, Amy Smithson, Jo Husbands, Rogelio Pfirter, and William King have been colleagues and teachers of the highest caliber. I thank Carter Wilkie for directing me to the diaries of Ambassador John Leighton Stuart, his grandfather. Wang Xuan, whom I was fortunate to meet, has been admirable in pursuing legal redress for the Chinese victims of Japanese biological warfare. My appreciation goes as well to the MIT Center for International Studies and the Security Studies Program, which together have provided a welcoming base for writing about CBW threats and realities. I thank also Ketian Zhang, Ji Lie, Jacob Russell, and Yong-Bee Lim for their expert, valuable research assistance. For years, Janet Montgomery at Harvard University, an internet wizard, has helped greatly with her efficient responses to my many inquiries.

Among the many archivists who helped me, my special thanks go to James Zobel at the MacArthur Memorial Archive and Library; William Cunliffe at the National Archives, College Park; Edwin Moloy, Anna Martin, and Atanos Sabov at the Harvard University Law School, and Jennifer Barr at the Presbyterian Historical Society in Philadelphia. My sincerest thanks go to archivist Sandy Ropper at Harvard University, who long has been intrepid, resourceful, and imaginative in finding source documents that otherwise seem impossible to locate. The University of Virginia Law Library Tokyo War Crimes Trial Project (noted throughout as UVALL), initiated by Elizabeth Ladner, is an essential resource that allows the papers of Frank S. Tavenner, David Nelson Sutton, Roy Morgan, and other principal actors at the IMTFE to be accessed online with ease. John McClure, director of research services at the Virginia Historical Society (VHS), which houses many of Sutton's papers, was most helpful. Suzanne Corriell, who organized the Sutton Collection of the Far East Military Tribunal at the University of Richmond Muse Law Library, greatly assisted, as did Joyce Manna Janto and Katherine Kepfer.

For years of legal advice, I thank Zick Rubin. I also thank Anita O'Brien and Vicky Cullen for extra editorial assistance and Martin Hinze for his capable, on-time mapmaking. I thank Anne Routon for her long-term enthusiasm for this book project and, at Columbia University Press, Miriam Grossman and Leslie Kriesel for their constant help and series editor Tom Christensen and book editor Stephen Wesley for their encouragement. My most heartfelt appreciation goes to my spouse and best friend, the aforementioned Matthew Meselson, for his expertise and fine guidance.

SOURCE NOTES

THE PROLIFERATION OF INFORMATION ABOUT WORLD WAR II, WAR CRIMES, AND the Nuremberg and Tokyo tribunals that began in the 1990s has been accelerated by its new availability on the internet, from hundreds of sources. A great step forward was the introduction in 1999 of the Japanese Imperial Army Disclosure Act by Senator Dianne Feinstein of California. The subsequent release of new documents on biological and chemical weapons from throughout the US government has made the National Archives and Records Administration at College Park, Maryland, essential for researchers. With the work of Edward Drea, Greg Bradsher, William Cunliffe and an entire staff, the Japanese war crimes materials became not only coherently organized but easily accessible.

A difference exists between access to original material from the IMTFE in Tokyo and that for the Nuremberg IMT, the better-known tribunal. Records for Nuremberg have been available for years, for example, at the Avalon Project at Yale Law School and similar repositories at other universities mentioned in the notes to this book. Much more could be done for the IMTFE archives. A good beginning is the digitized University of Virginia Law Library project, without which this book could not have been written; more should be done to expand this kind of repository. The fundamental work of R. John Pritchard, Neil Boister,

Robert Cryer, and others in organizing and providing commentary on the enormous material generated by the Tokyo trial remains the best substitute for having been there, except, perhaps, for Arnold Brackman's vivid account in *The Other Nuremberg*, a treasure of modern journalism. For background, the authors of the meticulously documented SIPRI volumes on the problem of chemical and biological weapons have made a lasting contribution to history. Finally, there is hardly a better way to research the Pacific War and the Occupation of Japan than to consult the MacArthur Memorial Library and Archive in Norfolk, Virginia.

The online resources on peace, international law, war, and arms control are another important resource. The invaluable book series *Foreign Relations of the United States* (*FRUS*) published by the Office of the Historian of the US Department of State, is available through the National Archives (https://www.archives.gov). The United Nations, the International Red Cross, the Truman Presidential Library, the International Criminal Court, the Federation of American Scientists, the Carnegie Endowment, and many academic centers offer reliable information on these important subjects. So, too, do independent journalists like Shoji Kondo, who wrote on Japan's secret germ weapons and created a CD-ROM collection of key documents, most from US archives, in *Japanese Biological Warfare, Unit 731: Official Declassified Records* (Tokyo: Kashiwa Shobō, 2003).

Another great boon to knowledge is the literature being written from the Asian perspective, only some of which informs this book. More bridges are needed to understand the full history of the war years and their aftermath. The many changes in the Asia Pacific region since the end of World War II can be missed by Western audiences more familiar with the old hegemonies than the rise of new Asian ones. Many IMTFE documents anglicize or misspell the names of Japanese and Chinese places and people (including Chinese Division lawyers) or reverse the traditional order of surname first maintained in Japan and China. When possible, I have corrected errors and indicated modern alternatives for old spellings in the archives (Hankou for Hankow, for example). I have kept the traditional word order in Japanese and Chinese personal names, except for authors who have chosen to publish differently, but have not added accents for Japanese words except as they appear in documents. The place name Manchuria is used in the text when relevant to the Chinese Division case at the Tokyo trial, which involved Japan's colonization and renaming of Northeast China (also known as the Three Eastern Provinces), or when in historical documents foreign observers assume that Manchuria is a real rather than a concocted name.

ACRONYMS

ACJ	Allied Council for Japan
ATIS	Allied Translation and Interpreters Service
BW	biological warfare
CCP	Chinese Communist Party
CIC	Counter-Intelligence Corps
CINCPAC	commander-in-chief of the Pacific
CIS	Civil Intelligence Section (SCAP)
CW	chemical warfare
CWS	U.S. Army Chemical Warfare Service (1918–1946)
FEC	Far Eastern Commission
FO	Foreign Office (British)
FRUS	*Foreign Relations of the United States* (State Department)
G-2	US Military Intelligence
GHQ	General Headquarters (Japan)
GS	Government Section (SCAP)
ICC	International Criminal Court
ID	Investigation Division (IPS)
IMT	International Military Tribunal

IMTFE	International Military Tribunal for the Far East
IPS	International Prosecution Section
JCS	Joint Chiefs of Staff
KMT	Kuomintang (Chinese Nationalist Government)
LS	Legal Section (SCAP)
NARA	US National Archives and Records Administration
OSRD	Office of Scientific Research and Development (US)
POW	prisoner of war
PRC	People's Republic of China
PRO	UK Public Records Office (Kew)
ROC	Republic of China
SACSEA	supreme allied commander, South East Asia
SANACC	State-Army-Navy-Air Force Coordinating Committee (SWNCC replacement)
SCAP	Supreme Commander for the Allied Powers (MacArthur and his organization)
SWNCC	State-War-Navy Coordinating Committee (1944–1947)
UK	United Kingdom
UN	United Nations
UNRRA	United Nations Relief and Rehabilitation Administration
UNWCC	United Nations War Crimes Commission
US	United States
USSR	Union of the Soviet Socialists Republics
UVALL	University of Virginia Law Library, Tokyo War Crimes Trial Collection
VHS	Virginia Historical Society

PRINCIPAL CHARACTERS

US Government

Harry S. Truman, US president succeeding Franklin D. Roosevelt in 1945

Henry L. Stimson, secretary of state under President Herbert Hoover and secretary of war under Presidents Roosevelt and Truman

General George C. Marshall, Truman's army chief of staff and later secretary of defense

General Douglas MacArthur, supreme commander for the allied powers (SCAP)

Major General Charles A. Willoughby, chief of military intelligence (G-2) in Tokyo

Alva Carpenter, head of Legal Section under SCAP

Chemical Warfare Service (CWS)

General Amos A. Fries, founder of the Chemical Weapons Service in 1918

Major General Alden C. Waitt, chief chemical officer, Chemical Weapons Service/ Army Chemical Corps

Theodor Rosebury, senior scientist in US wartime biological warfare program

Colonel Murray Sanders, CWS microbiologist who interviewed Unit 731 scientists for the 1945 Scientific Intelligence Survey

Lieutenant Colonel Arvo Thompson, CWS veterinarian who interviewed Ishii scientists in late 1945 and early 1946

Dr. Norbert Fell, chief of Camp Detrick Field Division who interviewed Ishii scientists April–June 1946

Dr. Edwin V. Hill, chief of Detrick Basic Science who interviewed Ishii scientists October–November 1947

Dr. Joseph Victor, Detrick pathologist who assisted Dr. Hill

Lieutenant Colonel John E. Beebe, CWS staff in Tokyo

International Prosecution Section (IMTFE)

Joseph B. Keenan, chief of counsel

Carlisle Higgins, deputy chief of counsel

Frank S. Tavenner, US associate prosecutor and later acting chief of counsel

Roy Morgan, head of Investigation Division

David Nelson Sutton, US associate prosecutor and assistant to the Chinese Division

Colonel Thomas H. Morrow, US associate prosecutor

Hsiang Che-chun, associate prosecutor, China

Alan J. Mansfield, associate prosecutor, Australia, Evidence Committee chair

Alfred S. Comyns Carr, associate prosecutor, Great Britain, Executive Committee chair

Brigadier Ronald H. Quilliam, associate prosecutor, New Zealand

Brigadier Henry Nolan, associate prosecutor, Canada

Sergei Alexandrovich Golunsky, associate prosecutor, Soviet Union

A. N. Vasiliev, assistant and successor to Golunsky in October 1946

Pedro Lopez, associate prosecutor, Philippines

Henry Hauxhurst, associate prosecutor, United States

Solis Horwitz, US deputy counsel

Eugene Williams, special assistant to Keenan

Captain James Robinson, US associate counsel

IMTFE Judges

Sir William Webb, Australia, court president

Mei Ju-ao (Ru-ao), China

John P. Higgins, United States (until July 1946)

Major General Myron Cramer, United States (from July 1946)

Ivan Michyevich Zaryanov, Soviet Union

Lord William Patrick, United Kingdom

Erima Harvey Northcroft, New Zealand
Delfin Jaranilla, Philippines
Bernard V. Röling, Netherlands
Judge Radhabinod Pal, India
Edward S. McDougall, Canada
Henri Bernard, France

Japanese BW Scientists

Major General Ishii Shiro
Naito Ryiochi, interlocutor for Sanders and Fell and Green Cross founder
Miyagawa Yonetsugi, well-connected bacteriologist and friend of Naito
Masuda Tomosada, Ishii protégé in charge of Nanjing's Unit 1644
Kawashima Kioshi, Unit 731 production head captured by the Soviets
Karasawa Tomio, assistant in 1942 Zhejiang-Jiangxi Campaign captured by the Soviets
Ota Kiyoshi, leader of 1941 plague attack on Changde and of anthrax experiments
Ishikawa Tachiomaru, Kanazawa Medical School professor with Unit 731 autopsy data
Wakamatsu Yujiro, head of Unit 100 for animal research
Kitano Masiji, researcher at Unit 100 and commander of Pingfan August 1942–March 1945
Kashahara Shiro, Unit 731 collaborator with Kitano on *songo* fever experiments
Kajitsuka Ryuji, medical chief of Kwantung Army sentenced to twenty-five years at Khabarovsk
Hayakawa Kiyoshi, conducted brucellosis experiments on humans
Yoshimuro Hisato, conducted freezing experiment on humans at Pingfan and Anda site

Chinese Leaders

Generalissimo Chiang Kai-shek, head of the Kuomintang and Republic of China
Mao Zedong, leader of the Chinese Communist Party and head of the People's Republic of China

IMTFE Defendants

General Araki Sadao (1877–1966), former minister of war, member of the Supreme War Council, minister of education, and close advisor to Premier Tojo; advocated war on China and was claimed by General Ishii as a supporter. Life imprisonment; paroled in 1955.

General Doihara Kenji (1883–1948), commander of the Kwantung Army overseeing Pingfan, 1938–1940, and of Singapore, 1944–1945; involved in opium commerce in Manchuria and running brutal POW camps. Sentenced to death.

Colonel Hashimoto Kingoro (1890–1957), involved in the 1931 aggression in northeastern China and the Nanjing Massacre. Life imprisonment; paroled in 1954.

Field Marshal Hata Shunroku (1879–1962), leader, from 1937, of Japanese forces in China, including the Zhejiang-Jiangxi campaign. Life imprisonment; paroled in 1954.

Baron Hiranuma Kiichiro (1867–1952), militarist who became president of the Privy Council in 1945. Life imprisonment; paroled in 1952.

Baron Hirota Koki (1878–1948), planned the invasions of Southeast Asia and the Pacific Islands during the 1930s and was foreign minister during the Nanjing Massacre. Sentenced to death.

Hoshino Naoki (1892–1978), chief of financial affairs in Manchukuo, 1932–1934; involved in opium commerce. Life imprisonment; paroled in 1955.

General Itagaki Sheishiro (1885–1948), held responsible for POW camps, commanded Japanese troops in China, and led the War Council in 1943. Sentenced to death.

Kaya Okinori (1889–1977), early advocate of drug trafficking in China and plunder of Chinese natural resources and industry; arranged financing of the Siam-Burma Death Railway. Life imprisonment; paroled in 1955.

Marquis Kido Koichi (1889–1977), lord keeper of the Privy Seal; held ministerial positions during the war and was a close advisor to the emperor; secret diary revealed government decision making to the IPS. Life imprisonment; paroled in 1955.

General Kimura Heitaro (1888–1948), chief of the Kwantung Army, 1940–1941, when General Ishii's empire was expanding. As field commander in Burma, held responsible for brutalization of Allied POWs there. Sentenced to death.

General Koiso Kuniaki (1880–1950), chief of staff of the Kwantung Army, 1932–1934, when Ishii's research was beginning, and Japan's rule of Korea during the war, where he was known for brutal suppression. Sentenced to life imprisonment; died while in prison.

General Matsui Iwane (1878–1948), field commander of the China Expeditionary Force, 1937–1938; held responsible for the Nanjing Massacre, although not for count 1, crimes against peace. Sentenced to death.

Matsuoka Yosuke (1880–1946), led the Japanese exit from the League of Nations in 1933; president of the South Manchuria Railway, 1935–1939; as foreign minister in 1939–1941, helped orchestrate the Axis alliance. Died during trial.

General Minami Jiro (1874–1955), commander of the Kwantung Army in 1934–1936 and held responsible as high-level official for Japanese instigation of war with China in 1937. Life imprisonment; paroled 1954.

General Muto Akira (1892–1948), director of the Military Affairs Bureau, 1939–1942, and army chief of staff in the Philippines, 1944–1945; held responsible for commanding troops at the 1945 Rape of Manila. Sentenced to death.

Admiral Nagano Osami (1880–1947), held responsible as the key planner of the December 1941 surprise attacks on Pearl Harbor, Hong Kong, Manila, and other targets. Died during trial.

Admiral Oka Takasumi (1890–1973), chief of the Naval Affairs Bureau; held responsible for planning the Pearl Harbor and other December 1941 attacks and for the infamous "hell ships" on which thousands of POWs and civilian slave laborers died, as well as the shooting of survivors of torpedoed Allied ships. Life imprisonment; paroled in 1954.

Okawa Shumei (1886–1957), propagandist who promoted war on China and the Allies; broke down in court on the first day and was considered unfit to stand trial. Released in late 1948 from a psychiatric hospital.

General Oshima Hiroshi (1886–1975), diplomat who spent most of his career in Nazi Germany, promoting Axis ties. Life imprisonment; paroled in 1955.

General Sato Kenryo (1895–1975), a leader of the Military Affairs Bureau (1942–1944) and an army commander in China and Indochina; held responsible for the abuse of POWs and civilian slave laborers transported to work on the Siam-Burma Railway. Life imprisonment; paroled in 1956.

Shigemitsu Mamoru (1887–1957), Japan's foreign minister (1943–1945) and signer of the September 2, 1945, Surrender Instrument; ambassador to the Soviet Union (1936–1938) at the time of border battles between the two countries and selected as a defendant by the USSR prosecutors at the IMTFE. Sentenced to seven years; paroled in 1950.

Admiral Shimada Shigetaro (1883–1976), navy minister (1941–1944); like Admiral Oka, held responsible for Pearl Harbor and other December 1941 surprise attacks, for POW transports and the killing of survivors of torpedoed Allied ships. Life imprisonment; paroled in 1955.

Shiratori Toshio (1887–1949), a career diplomat who favored the Axis alliance and Japanese military expansion. Life imprisonment; died while in prison.

General Suzuki Teiichi (1888–1989), chief of the China Affairs Bureau (Koa-in); held responsible for economic exploitation of China, for opium commerce, and for slave labor of POWs and civilians. Life imprisonment; paroled in 1955.

Togo Shigenori (1884–1948), foreign minister in 1941–1942; involved in Japan's failure to communicate an advance warning of the Pearl Harbor attack to the United States. Sentenced to twenty years in prison; died while in prison.

General Tojo Hideki (1884–1948), chief of the Manchukuo secret police (1935) and chief of staff of the Kwantung Army (1937–1938); knew General Ishii and about his program. As premier (1941–1944), was also head of the Ministries of Foreign Affairs, Home Affairs, and Education and took responsibility for the war. Sentenced to death.

General Umezu Yoshijiro (1882–1949), commander of the Kwantung Army (1939–1944); oversaw General Ishii's program and in 1944 became army chief of staff; on September 2, 1945, signed the Surrender Instrument. Life imprisonment; died while in prison.

NOTES

Prologue: General Ishii and Germ Warfare

1. Noriko Kawamura, *Emperor Hirohito and the Pacific War* (Seattle: University of Washington Press, 2015), 70–85; Akira Iriye, *Pearl Harbor and the Coming of the Pacific War: A Brief History with Documents and Essays* (Boston: St. Martin's Press, 1999), 6; John Dower, *War Without Mercy: Race and Power in the Pacific War* (New York: Random House, 1986), 262–66; Christopher Howe, *The Origins of Japanese Trade Supremacy: Development and Technology in Asia from 1540 to the Pacific War* (London: Hurst, 1996), 421–25.
2. Edwin P. Hoyt, *Japan's War: The Great Pacific Conflict, 1853–1952* (New York: McGraw-Hill, 1986), 192–95.
3. Peter Williams and David Wallace, *Unit 731: The Japanese Army's Secret of Secrets* (New York: Free Press, 1989), 63–80.
4. N. Charles Rothschild, "New Species of Siphonapera from Egypt and the Sudan," *Entomologist's Monthly Magazine* 39 (1903): 83. This type of flea was discovered in Egyptian cotton bales in 1903 and named *Pulex cheopsis*, in reference to the tomb of the pharaoh Cheops. In 1911 Rothschild changed the name to *Xenopsylla cheopsis*.
5. Sheldon H. Harris, *Factories of Death: Japanese Biological Warfare, 1932–1941, and the American Cover-up* (New York: Routledge, 2002), 13–25.

6. Kei-ichi Tsuneishi, "C. Koizumi: As a Promoter of the Ministry of Health and Welfare and an Originator of the BCW Research Program," *Historia Scientiarum* 26 (1984): 95–113.
7. Harris, *Factories of Death*, 41.
8. Ibid., 335.
9. Tsuneishi, "C. Koizumi," 96–98.
10. Tsuneishi Kei-ichi, "Reasons for the Failure to Prosecute Unit 731 and Its Significance," in *Beyond Victor's Justice?: The Tokyo War Crimes Revisited*, ed. Yuki Tanaka, Tim McCormick, and Gerry Simpson, 177–205 (Leiden: Martinus Nijhoff, 2011), 179–84.
11. *Materials on the Trial of Former Servicemen of the Japanese Army Charged with Manufacturing and Employing Bacteriological Weapons* (Moscow: Foreign Language Publishing House, 1950), 203–18.
12. Archie Crouch, "Biological Warfare in China: One Family's Encounter," n.d., Sheldon H. Harris Papers, Hoover Institution on War, Revolution, and Peace, box 7, folder 1.
13. Crouch's recollections of wartime Ningbo are corroborated by another missionary, Maybelle Smith. See Diaries of Mrs. Maybelle (Elleroy) Smith, Yale University Library China Records Project, Miscellaneous Personal Papers Collection, 1938–1942, box 195, folders 6–8.
14. SIPRI (Stockholm International Peace Research Institute), *The Problem of Chemical and Biological Warfare*. Vol. 1: *The Rise of CB Weapons* (New York: Humanities Press, 1971), 112–16, 342–47.
15. Theodor Rosebury, *Peace or Pestilence* (New York: McGraw-Hill, 1949), 109–10.
16. Ibid., 101. British plague experts in India scribbled derisive comments on the report's cover, such as "please return when you have finished smiling at the attached" and "glance at this muck."
17. John W. Dower, *Embracing Defeat: Japan in the Wake of WWII* (New York: Norton, 1999), 21.
18. Williamson Murray and Peter R. Mansoor, eds., *Hybrid Warfare: Fighting Complex Opponents from the Ancient World to the Present* (New York: Cambridge University Press, 2012), 351.
19. Tohmatsu Haruo, "The Strategic Correlation Between the Sino-Japanese and Pacific War," in *The Battle for China: Essays on the Military History of the Sino-Japanese War*, ed. Mark Peattie, Edward Drea, and Hans van de Ven, 423–45 (Stanford, Calif.: Stanford University Press, 2011), 427; Carroll V. Glines, *The Doolittle Raid: America's Daring First Strike Against Japan* (Atglen, Penn.: Schiffer Military/Aviation History, 1991).

20. Glines, *Doolittle Raid*, 150–53.
21. "Former Japanese Army Targeted Pacific for Germ Bombs," Kyodo News Service, November 28, 1993. Newly discovered General Staff logs from 1944 and 1945 showed ongoing interest in Ishii's microbial bombs and infected fleas for use in the Pacific Theater, the only obstacles being "a lack of capacity for producing fleas and rats as media for cultivating bacteria, and a shortage of airplanes for transporting germ bombs."
22. Kei-ichi Tsuneishi, "Unit 731 and the Human Skulls Discovered in 1989: Physicians Carrying Out Organized Crimes," in *Dark Medicine: Rationalizing Unethical Medical Research*, ed. William R. LaFleur, Gernot Böhme, and Susumu Shimazono, 72–82 (Bloomington: Indiana University Press, 2007), 77.

Introduction: Lasting Peace and the Protection of Civilians

1. SIPRI, *The Problem of Chemical and Biological Warfare*. Vol. 3: *CBW and the Law of War* (New York: Humanities Press, 1973), 151–54.
2. US General Orders No. 100, issued in 1863, also known as the Lieber Code, was written by Columbia University law professor Francis Lieber. It was replaced in 1914 by *The Law of Land Warfare*, the army field manual.
3. James B. Scott, ed., *The Hague Conventions and Declarations of 1899 and 1907* (New York: Oxford University Press, 1915), 101–2; Stephan Hall, "'The Persistent Spectre': Natural Law, International Order, and the Limits of Legal Positivism," *European Journal of International Law* 12 (2001): 269–307; Antonio Cassese, "The Martens Clause: Half a Loaf or Simply Pie in the Sky?" *European Journal of International Law* 11, no. 1 (2000): 187–216.
4. Mario Sartori, *The War Gases* (New York: Van Nostrand, 1943).
5. Avalon Project, Documents on Law, History, and Diplomacy, Yale Law School, http://avalon.law.yale.edu/19th_century/dec99-02.asp.
6. James J. Robinson, "Surprise Attack: Crime at Pearl Harbor and Now," *American Bar Association Journal* 46 (September 1960): 976.
7. Rudolf Hanslian, *Der deutsche Gasangriff bei Ypern am 22 April 1915* (Berlin: Verlag Gassschutz und Luftschutz, 1934); SIPRI, *The Problem of Chemical and Biological Warfare*. Vol. 1: *The Rise of CB Weapons* (New York: Humanities Press, 1971), 127–30. The reckoning of accurate battlefield casualties including deaths from chemical attacks proved difficult at Ypres and throughout the war.
8. Olivier Lepick, *La Grande Guerre Chimique* (Paris: Presses Universitaires de France, 1998).
9. SIPRI, *The Problem of Chemical and Biological Warfare*, 1:26–58.

10. Ibid., 49.
11. In his poem "Dulce et decorum est," British poet Wilfred Owen, killed in battle in 1918, made famous the image of a dying soldier drowning "as in a green sea" of gas. The poem, published posthumously in 1920, and John Singer Sargent's oil painting *Gassed* became popular emblems of battlefield suffering.
12. Margaret MacMillan, *The War That Ended Peace: The Road to 1914* (New York: Random House, 2013).
13. Margaret Macmillan, *Paris 1919: Six Months That Changed the World* (New York: Random House, 2001); Norman A. Graebner and Edward M. Bennett, *The Washington Treaty and Its Legacy: The Failure of the Wilsonian Vision* (Cambridge: Cambridge University Press, 2011).
14. James F. Willis, *Prologue to Nuremberg: The Politics and Diplomacy of Punishing War Criminals of the First World War* (Westport, Conn.: Greenwood Press, 1982).
15. Mark Peattie, *Nan'yō: The Rise and Fall of the Japanese in Micronesia, 1885–1945* (Honolulu: University of Hawaii Press, 1984). The Japanese had established trade routes in this area and by 1939 had equipped the islands for staging military attacks.
16. Bruce A. Elleman, *Wilson and China: A Revised History of the Shandong Question* (New York: Routledge, 2015), 27. In fact, the previous year China had secretly agreed to allow Japan to temporarily keep Shandong (romanized at the time as Shantung) in exchange for sharing improved railway access and mining technology.
17. Frederic J. Brown, *Chemical Warfare: A Study in Restraints* (New Brunswick, N.J.: Transaction Books, 2006), 52–56.
18. David Kennedy, "The Move to Institutions," *Cardozo Law Review* 8, no. 5 (April 1987): 841–988.
19. Bruce Ackerman, *The Future of Liberal Revolution* (New Haven, Conn.: Yale University Press, 1992), 46–54.
20. The court heard fifty cases between 1922 and 1932. The website of the International Criminal Court documents the history of the PCIJ, including a commemorative volume in 2012, http://www.icj-cij.org/pcij/?p1=9.
21. William A. Schabas, *An Introduction to the International Criminal Court* (Cambridge: Cambridge University Press, 2004), 2–5.
22. The Avalon Project at Yale University Law School also documents the league's history, http://avalon.law.yale.edu/20th_century/leagcov.asp.
23. Andrew Gordon, *A Modern History of Japan: From Tokugawa Times to the Present* (New York: Oxford University Press, 2002), 177–78.
24. Christopher Howe, *The Origins of Japanese Trade Supremacy: Development and Technology in Asia from 1540 to the Pacific War* (London: Hurst, 1996), 268–97.

25. Elleman, *Wilson and China*, 46–48.
26. SIPRI, *The Problem of Chemical and Biological Warfare*. Vol. 4: *CB Disarmament Negotiations, 1920–1970* (New York: Humanities Press, 1971), 46–47; Richard M. Price, *The Chemical Weapons Taboo* (Ithaca, N.Y.: Cornell University Press, 1997), 78–98.
27. Brown, *Chemical Warfare*, 45. Supporting Fries were Representative Julius Kahn, chair of the House Military Affairs Committee, and Senator George Chamberlain, chair of the Senate Military Affairs Committee.
28. Ibid., 56–61.
29. Ibid., 61–69. At the Washington Conference, public outcry led the United States to shift its position from restraints on chemical weapons to a full ban of their use in war.
30. SIPRI, *The Problem of Chemical and Biological Warfare*, 3:21–27.
31. League of Nations, *Report of the Temporary Mixed Commission for the Reduction of Armaments*. Part 4: *Chemical Warfare*, July 30, 1924, 29–30. Available at Northwestern University Library/Digital Collection, http://digital.library.northwestern.edu/league/le000313.pdf.
32. Ibid., 30; Mark Wheelis, "Biological Sabotage in World War I," in *Biological and Toxin Weapons: Research, Development and Use from the Middle Ages to 1945*, ed. Erhard Geissler and John van Courtland Moon), 35–62 (New York: Oxford University Press, 1999), 46.
33. Étienne Aucouterier, *La guerre biologique: aventures francaises* (Paris: Etudes Metériologiques, 2017).
34. John R. Walker, "The 1925 Geneva Protocol: Export Controls, Britain, Poland, and Why the Protocol Came to Include 'Bacteriological Warfare,'" Harvard-Sussex Program Occasional Paper No. 5, June 2016, http://www.sussex.ac.uk/Units/spru/hsp/occasional%20papers/HSPOP_5.pdf.
35. John Norton Moore, "Ratification of the Geneva Protocol on Gas and Bacteriological Warfare: A Legal and Political Analysis," *Virginia Law Review* 58, no. 3 (March 1972): 419–509.
36. Brown, *Chemical Warfare*, 45.
37. Ibid., 85.
38. Ibid., 118.
39. Walter E. Grunden, *Secret Weapons and World War II: Japan in the Shadow of Big Science* (Lawrence: University Press of Kansas, 2005), 178–82.
40. Ibid., 56–82.
41. The goal of the Japanese military to exploit modern science extended to nuclear physics, where its achievements were forestalled by a lack of coordination between its army and navy and with industry. Ibid., 59–79.

42. Howe, *Origins of Japanese Trade Supremacy*, 398–403.
43. John Buckley, *Air Power in the Age of Total War* (Bloomington: Indiana University Press, 1999).
44. Giulio Douhet, *Command of the Air*, trans. Dino Ferrari (London: Faber & Faber, 1942), 6–7. For his American counterpart, see Alfred Hurley, *Billy Mitchell: Crusader for Air Power* (Bloomington: Indiana University Press, 1975).
45. The International Treaty for the Renunciation of War as an Instrument of National Policy, http://avalon.law.yale.edu/20th_century/kbpact.asp.
46. Kirsten Sellars, *Crimes Against Peace and International Law* (Cambridge: Cambridge University Press, 2013), 32.
47. The Convention relative to the Treatment of Prisoners of War, dated July 27, 1929, and known as the Geneva Convention of 1929, had its roots in an 1864 treaty promoted by the International Committee of the Red Cross and subsequent accords, https://ihl-databases.icrc.org. Until early 1938, the Red Cross also actively worked against the proliferation of chemical weapons. See Daniel Palmieri, "How Warfare Has Evolved—a Humanitarian Organization's Perception: The Case of the ICRC, 1863-1960," *International Review of the Red Cross* 97 (2015): 994–95.
48. Brown, *Chemical Warfare*, 110–21. The final resolution among delegates allowed limited preparedness in the way of materials and training to protect individual or collective preparation.
49. Ibid., 120. The MacDonald Plan for disarmament, submitted by the British, included these provisions and was accepted in May 1932 by newly elected president Franklin Roosevelt. Echoing former president Herbert Hoover, Roosevelt called for the complete elimination of all "offensive weapons: war planes, heavy mobile artillery, tanks, poison gas." See US Department of State, *Peace and War: United States Foreign Policy, 1931–1941* (Washington, D.C.: Government Printing Office, 1942), 180–84.
50. Edwin P. Hoyt, *Japan's War: The Great Pacific Conflict* (New York: McGraw-Hill, 1986), 81–102.
51. Noriko Kawamura, *Emperor Hirohito and the Pacific War* (Seattle: University of Washington Press, 2015), 37–48. The emperor appeared ambivalent about the military takeover of Manchuria, describing it in public as an act of "self-defense," while in an internal communication he criticized the "current military's insubordination and violence." He likely missed a crucial opportunity to assert his authority over the military by endorsing the initial conflict. See Herbert P. Bix, *Hirohito and the Making of Modern Japan* (New York: HarperCollins, 2000), 239–40.

52. Marius B. Jansen, *The Making of Modern Japan* (Cambridge, Mass.: Harvard University Press, 2002), 576–85.
53. Richard J. Samuels, *Machiavelli's Children: Leaders and Their Legacies in Italy and Japan* (Ithaca, N.Y.: Cornell University Press, 2003), 141–51. Kishi Nobusuke, the genius planner of industrial growth in Manchuria, was imprisoned for three years after the war and then, in 1957–1960, served as prime minister.
54. Mark Driscoll, *Absolute Erotic Absolute Grotesque: The Living, Dead, and Undead in Japanese Imperialism, 1895–1945* (Durham, N.C.: Duke University Press, 2010), 266. The Japanese total war economy depended on colonized Chinese and Koreans and disadvantaged Japanese, especially lower-class women.
55. Arthur K. Kuhn, "The Lytton Report on the Manchurian Crisis," *American Journal of International Law* 27, no. 1 (January 1933): 96–100. Kuhn pointed out that the league council drew on article 11 of the covenant, which framed the incident as "a matter of concern," rather than the more forceful article 10, which refers to "external aggression" and "territorial integrity," or article 11, which would have allowed greater latitude in interpretation and intervention.
56. The five-person commission was led by V.A.G.R. Bulwer-Lytton, the British representative to the league, with members from the United States, Germany, Italy, and France. In the spring of 1932 its members spent six weeks in Manchukuo conducting interviews.
57. *FRUS* (*Foreign Relations of the United States*), Secretary of War Stimson, September 22, 1939, Occupation of Manchuria by Japan and Statement of Policy by the United States (Washington), 1931–1941, 5–8.
58. Henry L. Stimson and McGeorge Bundy, *On Active Service in Peace and War* (New York: Harper & Brothers, 1947), 220–63. Constrained by the policies of President Herbert Hoover, Stimson made his ideas public via a letter to a US senator.
59. Harriet L. Moore, *Soviet Far Eastern Policy 1931–1945* (Princeton, N.J.: Princeton University Press, 1945), 13–15,
60. Hoyt, *Japan's War*, 98–101; Jansen, *Making Modern Japan*, 584.
61. "Lytton Report, 1932," United Nations Office at Geneva (UNOG) Registry, Records and Archives Unit, Printed Documents (League of Nations), 1932; Sir John Simon (secretary of state for foreign affairs), "The Lytton Report. Japan and the League of Nations," November 1932, PRO CAB 24/235.
62. Stewart Brown (UPI), "Japan Stuns World, Withdraws from League," February 24, 1933, UPI Archives, http://100years.upi.com/sta_1933-02-24.html.
63. Gordon, *Modern History*, 189–200.
64. These two resignations (Japan and Germany) were officially effective in 1935.
65. SIPRI, *The Problem of Chemical and Biological Warfare*, 4:175–89.

66. Bix, *Hirohito*, 318–27. Baron Hirota Koki, later indicted at the IMFTE, was Japan's foreign minister at this time.
67. SIPRI, *The Problem of Chemical and Biological Warfare*, 4:189–92.
68. "Communication from the Chinese Delegation, Geneva August 8, 1938," League of Nations File C.251. M.149. 1938.VII, Geneva, August 8, 1938.
69. League of Nations, Official Journal, November 1938, 102nd Session of the Council, Fourth Meeting (19 September), 54. The original plea concerning Japanese chemical attacks on the Shandong front made by China the previous May was followed by a tepid league resolution asking members for more information. After more requests from China, the league responded with a second resolution on September 19.
70. Ibid., "Resolution and Report on the Sino-Japanese Dispute Adopted in September, 1938," 2, University of Virginia Law Library, Tokyo War Crimes Trial Collection (UVALL), sec. 13, folder 59, MSS1 Su 863a, http://imtfe.law.virginia.edu.
71. Robert E. Park, "The Social Function of War," *American Journal of Sociology* 46, no. 4, (1941): 558.
72. Ian Buruma, *Year Zero: A History of 1945* (New York: Penguin Press, 2013).
73. John W. Dower, *War Without Mercy: Race and Power in the Pacific War* (New York: Random House, 1986), 295–97; Werner Gruhl, *Imperial Japan's World War Two* (New Brunswick, N.J.: Transaction Books, 2007), 85, 143.
74. E. Bartlett Kerr, *Flames Over Tokyo: The U.S. Army Air Forces' Incendiary Campaign Against Japan 1944–1945* (New York: Donald I. Fine, 1991).
75. Telford Taylor, *The Anatomy of the Nuremberg Trials* (New York: Alfred A. Knopf, 1992), 28–33.
76. Ibid., 29–32. Roosevelt's treasury secretary, Hans Morgenthau, Jr., and his staff preferred summary execution. With the approaching end of the war, news of the abuse and killing of Allied prisoners of war and the liberation of the Nazi concentration and death camps heightened the spirit of revenge and increased assaults on defeated Nazis and their collaborators (Buruma, *Year Zero*, 75–127).
77. Gary Jonathan Bass, *Stay the Hand of Vengeance: The Politics of War Crimes Trials* (Princeton, N.J.: Princeton University Press, 2000), 58–105. Kaiser Wilhelm died June 4, 1941, in the Nazi-occupied Netherlands, at age 82.
78. Kirsten Sellars, "Treasonable Conspiracies at Paris, Moscow, and Delhi," in *Trials for International Crimes in Asia*, ed. Sellars, 25–54 (Cambridge: Cambridge University Press, 2016), 43–45.
79. Article 1 of the Decree of the Presidium of the Supreme Soviet of the USSR, April 19, 1943, read: "On measures of punishment for the German-fascists villains guilty in murders and tortures of Soviet civilians and imprisoned Red

Army military, for spies, traitors to the Fatherland from among the Soviet citizens and their accomplices of April 19, 1943."

80. Arieh J. Kochavi, *Prelude to Nuremberg: Allied War Crimes Policy and the Question of Punishment* (Chapel Hill: University of North Carolina Press, 1998), 64–68.
81. Ibid., 66–71. Chosen as representatives of the Nazi invaders, three Germans and a collaborator were accused of using mobile "gas cars" to execute thousands of Soviet citizens, shooting wounded Soviet POWs, and destroying cities and towns. The trial and the hangings that followed were open to the Western press, and the proceedings were published in English. A full-length film, *The Trial Goes On*, full of graphic images of citizens murdered by the Nazis, was distributed to Soviet cinemas.
82. George Ginsburgs, "Moscow and International Legal Cooperation in the Pursuit of War Criminals," *Review of Central and East European Law* 21, no. 1 (1995): 10–14.
83. Stimson and Bundy, *On Active Service*, 587. On January 19, 1945, Secretary Stimson briefed Roosevelt on the War Department's recommendations for military tribunals, to which Roosevelt agreed.
84. Raphael Lemkin, *Axis Rule in Occupied Europe. Laws of Occupation. Analysis of Government. Proposals for Redress* (Clark, N.J.: Lawbook Exchange, 1944; repr. 2005); "Genocide," *American Scholar* 15, no. 2 (April 1946): 227–30. In his book, Lemkin, a Jewish lawyer who had emigrated from eastern Europe to the United States, introduced the term genocide to define as criminal the Nazis' systemic mass obliteration of millions in targeted national, racial, and religious groups. Although not integrated into the Nuremberg trials, it became the basis for the UN Convention on the Prevention and Punishment of Crimes of Genocide of 1948. See Irving Louis Horowitz, *Taking Lives: Genocide and State Power*, 3rd. ed. (New Brunswick, N.J.: Transaction Books, 1980), 184.
85. Frits Kalshoven, "Arms, Armaments, and International Law," *Collected Courses of the Hague Academy of International Law* 191 (1985): 309–11.
86. United Nations, "1945: The San Francisco Conference/United Nations, History," http://www.un.org/en/sections/history-united-nations-charter/1945-san-francisco-conference/index.html.
87. United Nations, "1941: The Declaration of St. James' Palace," http://www.un.org/en/sections/history-united-nations-charter/1941-declaration-st-james-palace/index.html. The signatories were Great Britain, Canada, Australia, New Zealand, and the Union of South Africa, along with the exiled governments of Belgium, Czechoslovakia, Greece, Luxembourg, the Netherlands, Norway, Poland, and Yugoslavia, and General Charles de Gaulle of France.

88. Luc Reydams and Jan Wouters, "The Politics of Establishing International Criminal Tribunals," in *International Prosecution,* ed. Luc Reydams, Jan Wouters, and Cedric Ryngaert, 6–80 (New York: Oxford University Press, 2012), 15; Mark J. Osiel, "In Defense of Liberal Show Trials—Nuremberg and Beyond," in *Perspectives on the Nuremberg Trial,* ed. Guénaë Mettraux, 704–26 (New York: Oxford University Press, 2008).
89. Hersch Lauterpacht, "The Law of Nations and the Punishment of War Crimes," *British Yearbook of International Law* 21 (1944): 58–95. Lauterpacht also argued that military courts were legitimate in occupied enemy territory or the theater of war (66, n. 1).
90. Taylor, *Anatomy of the Nuremberg Trials,* 34–42.
91. Ibid., 629. Justice Robert Jackson advocated the conspiracy definitions and with his British colleagues quelled objections from the French and Soviet representatives. The Soviet Union had already considered the concept. See Sellars, "Treasonable Conspiracies."
92. Taylor, *Anatomy of the Nuremberg Trials,* 8–11.
93. Nuremberg Charter, sec. 6.
94. Taylor, *Anatomy of the Nuremberg Trials,* 126.
95. Isaiah Berlin, "Political Ideas in the Twentieth Century," *Foreign Affairs* 28, no. 3 (1950): 378.
96. Nancy Rosenblum, "Justice and Experience of Injustice," in *Break the Cycle of Hatred: Memory, Law and Repair,* ed. Martha Minow, 77–106 (Princeton, N.J.: Princeton University Press, 2002), 88.
97. Peter Burian, "Introduction: The Natural History of Law," in *The Complete Aeschylus,* vol. 1: *The Oresteia,* ed. Peter Burian and Alan Shapiro, 3–37 (New York: Oxford University Press, 2011), 6.
98. Jackson's opening speech was given on November 21, 1945, and is available on film at the Robert H. Jackson Center, https://www.roberthjackson.org/collection/speeches/.
99. Jackson's reference was to Shakespeare's *Macbeth,* act 1, scene 7:

    . . . in these cases,
    We still have judgment here, that we but teach
    Bloody instructions, which being taught, return
    To plague th'inventor. This even handed justice
    Commends th'ingredients of our poison'd chalice
    To our own lips.

100. Reydams and Wouters, "The Politics of Establishing International Criminal Tribunals," 201; Osiel, "In Defense of Liberal Show Trials," 704–26.

101. Taylor, *Anatomy of the Nuremberg Trials*, 56.
102. Francesca Gaiba, *The Origins of Simultaneous Interpretation: The Nuremberg Trial* (Ottawa: University of Ottawa Press, 1998).
103. Winston Churchill, "Sinews of Peace," March 5, 1946, Westminster College, Fulton, Mo. The text of the speech and Stalin's response, plus the British Foreign Office assessment, are available at http://nebraskastudies.org/0900/media/0901_0102iron.pdf. Churchill mentioned Soviet aggression in Manchuria and Pakistan, as well as the "iron curtain" descending from "Stettin in the Baltic to Trieste in the Adriatic."
104. IMTFE transcripts, Dissenting Opinion of the Member from India on the Judgment, 21:1085–1102. This view was central to the Japanese defense at the Tokyo trial as well as to broader criticisms. See Richard H. Minear, *Victor's Justice: The Tokyo War Crimes Trial* (Princeton, N.J.: Princeton University Press, 1971).
105. Charles S. Maier, "The End of Empire and the Transformations of the International Systems," in *History of Humanity. Scientific and Cultural Development*. Vol. 7: *The Twentieth Century*, ed. Sarvepalli Gopal and Sergei L. Tikhvinsky, 21–55 (Paris: UNESCO, and New York: Routledge, 2008).
106. John W. Dower, *Embracing Defeat: Japan in the Wake of World War II* (New York: Norton, 1999), 414–15.
107. Kirsten Sellars, "Introduction," in *Trials for International Crimes in Asia*, ed. Sellars (Cambridge: Cambridge University Press, 2016), 1–24.
108. William Manchester, *American Caesar: Douglas MacArthur 1880–1964* (Boston: Little, Brown, 1978), 184.
109. Ambassador Francis Huré, interview, April 23, 2015; Francis Huré, *Portraits de Pechkoff* (Paris: Edition de Fallois, 2006), 124–47. Huré was an assistant to the French ambassador to occupied Japan, Zinovi Pechkoff.
110. William Kirby, "Traditions of Centrality, Authority, and Management in Modern China's Foreign Relations," in *Chinese Foreign Policy: Theory and Practice*, ed. Thomas W. Robinson and David Shambaugh, 13–29 (New York: Clarendon Press, 1996), 17.
111. "Situation in China," War Cabinet Joint Intelligence Sub-committee, 8 June 1942, UK Public Records Office (PRO) PREM 143/1. Churchill calculated that a "small diversion of assault shipping and air forces to this theatre might pay a handsome dividend by keeping China in the war and by engaging Japanese forces in the process of attrition."
112. Albert Feuerwerker, "The Foreign Presence in China," in *Cambridge History of China: Republican China, 1912–1949*. Vol. 12, ed. John K. Fairbank, 128–207 (Cambridge: Cambridge University Press, 1983).
113. Stephen G. Craft, *V. K. Wellington Koo and the Emergence of Modern China* (Lexington: University Press of Kentucky, 2004), 163–64, 190–91. Koo signed for China

at the creation of the League of Nations and was later ambassador to the United Kingdom.

114. Tim Maga, *Judgment at Tokyo: The Japanese War Crimes Trials* (Lexington: University Press of Kentucky, 2001), 28–29.

115. Kenneth W. Condit, *History of the Joint Chiefs of Staff. The Joint Chiefs of Staff and National Policy*. Vol. 2: *1947–1949* (Washington, D.C.: Office of Joint History, Office of the Chairman of the Joint Chiefs of Staff, 1996), 235.

116. Barak Kushner, *Men to Devils, Devils to Men: Japanese War Crimes and Chinese Justice* (Cambridge, Mass.: Harvard University Press, 2016), 66–67, 88–102. Kushner points out that the Japanese colonial hold on various parts of China made the relations between the two nations and the Japanese process of surrender more complicated than for the Western Allies.

117. The declaration text can be found at http://www.unmultimedia.org/searchers/yearbook/page.jsp?volume=1946-47&bookpage=1. The term "United Nations" was suggested by President Roosevelt and was used here for the first time.

118. Neil Boister and Robert Cryer, *The Tokyo International Military Tribunal: A Reappraisal* (New York: Oxford University Press, 2008), 17–18.

119. Kushner, *Men to Devils*, 77–84.

120. Maga, *Judgment Tokyo*, 29. China's request for several tribunals was perceived as "a huge and expensive operation" that UN Commission chairman Sir Cecil Hurst rejected, while Pell responded by helping create the commission's special Far East panel.

121. Timothy Brook, *Documents on the Rape of Nanking* (Ann Arbor: University of Michigan Press, 1999); Iris Chang, *The Rape of Nanking: The Forgotten Holocaust of World War II* (New York: Basic Books, 1997); Joshua A. Fogel, ed., *The Nanjing Massacre in History and Historiography* (Berkeley: University of California Press, 2000).

122. Julia Lovell, *The Opium War: Drugs, Dreams, and the Making of China* (Basingstoke/Oxford: Picador, 2011). The long colonial history involved the Chinese Qing dynasty and its mercantile interests in the opium trade, not just British and Japanese profiteering. Under Chiang Kai-shek, the Chinese rendition depicted only the exploitation of China by foreign powers.

123. Motohiro Kobayashi "An Opium Tug-of-War: Japan Versus the Wang Jingwei Regime," in *The Opium Regimes: China, Britain, and Japan, 1839–1952*, ed. Timothy Brook and Bob Tadashi Wakabayashi, 344–59 (Berkeley: University of California Press, 2000).

124. Brown, *Chemical Warfare*, 200–201; US Military Intelligence Division, *Enemy Tactics in Chemical Warfare*, Special Series no. 24 (Washington, D.C., War Depart-

ment, 1 September 1944). Of 1,600 chemical casualties, some 600 were estimated killed.

1. MacArthur in Japan: "Punish the War Criminals"

1. Marshall to MacArthur, "WAR 48342," August 12, 1945, MacArthur Memorial Archives, RG-9, box 160, folder War Department, August–September 1945; To MacArthur from Marshall, August 13, 1945, MacArthur Archives, RG-9, box 160, folder War Department, August–September 1945. The latter message included four documents, among them the text of the Instrument of Surrender, the message Hirohito should announce to his constituents, and the terms of "General Order No. 1" for the decommissioning of Japanese forces throughout Asia and the Pacific. The appointment of MacArthur as SCAP was noted as approved by "Prime Minister (Churchill), Generalissimo Chiang Kai-Shek and Generalissimo [*sic*] Stalin." SCAP became used interchangeably for MacArthur himself and his organization.
2. Mark Selden, "A Forgotten Holocaust: U.S. Bombing Strategy, the Destruction of Japanese Cities, and the American Way of War from the Pacific War to Iraq," in *Bombing Civilians: A Twentieth-Century History*, ed. Yuki Tanaka and Marilyn Young, 76–96 (New York: New Press, 2009).
3. Charles A. Willoughby and John Chamberlain, *MacArthur 1941–1951* (New York: McGraw-Hill, 1954), 293.
4. The text of the Surrender Instrument is available at the US National Archives, https://www.archivesfoundation.org/documents/japanese-instrument-surrender-1945/.
5. After the US entry into the war, Franklin Roosevelt and Winston Churchill created the Combined Chiefs of Staff to coordinate service strategies. Admiral William Leahy and General George C. Marshall suggested a unified command to complement the existing British Chiefs of Staff Committee. The JCS was given statutory authority after the war by the National Security Act of 1947.
6. Henry L. Stimson and McGeorge Bundy, *On Active Service in Peace and War* (New York: Harper & Brothers, 1947), 414–15.
7. Walter R. Borneman, *MacArthur at War: World War II in the Pacific* (New York: Little, Brown, 2016), 451–52.
8. Douglas MacArthur, *Reminiscences* (New York: McGraw-Hill, 1964), 282–83. On August 30 MacArthur received by cable two Joint Chiefs of Staff directives (1328/3 and 1328/4) stipulating the general Occupation goals. See Takemae Eiji, *Inside GHQ: The Allied Occupation of Japan and Its Legacy*, trans. Robert Ricketts

and Sabastian Swann (New York: Continuum, 2002), 52–60. Throughout September 1945 the SWNCC and JCS sent MacArthur explicit policy directives, including seventeen pages of instructions cabled on September 25 (MacArthur Archives, RG-9, box 160, folder War Department, August–September 1945).

9. Commander in Chief, U.S. Pacific Fleet and Pacific Ocean Area (CINPAC), "Report of Surrender and Occupation of Japan," 11 February 1946, NARA, World War II Command Files, RG 38, entry UO-09D 19, box 255, 8–9. This document summarizes monthly US Navy reports concerning policy for the first months of the Occupation, from September to December 1945.

10. Borneman, *MacArthur at War*, 499; Robert L. Eichelberger, with Emma Gudger Eichelberger, and Jay Luvaacs, *Dear Miss Em: General Eichelberger's War in the Pacific, 1942–1945* (Westport, Conn.: Greenwood, 1972), 305. Major General Eichelberger, then in command of the Eighth Army, worried that MacArthur's "refusal to guard himself might prove an embarrassment."

11. From Marshall to MacArthur, "W 48342," 12 August 1945, MacArthur Archives, RG-9, box 160, folder War Department, August–September 1945. Although not to MacArthur's liking, newly freed POWs General Jonathan Wainwright, who had surrendered the Philippines, and Lieutenant General Arthur Percival, who had surrendered Singapore, were also on deck. The State Department had notified the Japanese government that "the Emperor will be required to authorize and insure the signature by the government of Japan and the Japanese Imperial Headquarters" and otherwise carry out the surrender terms.

12. Admiral Stuart S. Murray, "Reminiscences of the Surrender of Japan and the End of World War II," Battleship Missouri Memorial, Pearl Harbor, Hawaii, 1974, https://ussmissouri.org/learn-the-history/surrender/admiral-murrays-account.

13. Arnold C. Brackman, *The Other Nuremberg: The Untold Story of the Tokyo War Crimes Trails* (New York: William Morrow, 1987), 413.

14. "Statement by General MacArthur to Surrender Delegates Aboard Battleship *Missouri*," in *The Political Reorientation of Japan, September 1945 to September 1948*. Vol. 2, ed. Government Section SCAP (Washington, D.C.: US Government Printing Office, 1949), 736.

15. Reflecting the US assessment of national status, after China came the United Kingdom, the Soviet Union, Australia, Canada, France, the Netherlands and New Zealand.

16. William Manchester, *American Caesar: Douglas MacArthur, 1880–1964* (Boston: Little, Brown, 1978), 452. The observation was made by Toshikazu Kase, secretary of the Japanese Foreign Ministry, who assisted Shigemitsu at the signing.

17. "Report of Surrender," 31.
18. *FRUS (Foreign Relations of the United States), Diplomatic Papers, 1945, The British Commonwealth, the Far East.* Vol. 6, "Tokyo, September 17, 1945—Text of Statement Issued Today by General Douglas MacArthur"; ibid., "Memorandum of Telephone Conversation, by the Acting Secretary of State [Washington,] September 17, 1945.
19. Willoughby and Chamberlain, *MacArthur 1941–1951*, 302. MacArthur's order to Eichelberger to raise the flag was: "Have our country's flag unfurled and in the Tokyo sun let it wave in full glory, a symbol of hope for the oppressed and as a harbinger of victory for the right."
20. James J. Robinson, "Surprise Attack: Crime at Pearl Harbor and Now," *American Bar Association Journal* 46 (September 1960): 979.
21. Peter Williams and David Wallace, *Unit 731: Japan's Secret Biological Warfare in World War II* (New York: Free Press, 1989), 91–112.
22. R. W. Home and Morris F. Low, "Postwar Scientific Intelligence Missions to Japan," *Isis* 84 (1993): 527–37.
23. "Mission to Tokyo by Karl T. Compton," 8 October 1945, Office of the President 1930–1959 (Karl Compton), MIT Archives, box 59, folder 15, 2–3.
24. Boris Pash, *The Alsos Mission* (New York: Charter Books, 1969).
25. Samuel A. Goudsmit, *Alsos* (New York: Henry Schuman, 1947), 109.
26. Erhard Geissler, "Biological Warfare Activities in Germany, 1923–1945," in *Biological and Toxin Weapons: Research, Development and Use from the Middle Ages to 1945*, ed. Erhard Geissler and John van Courtland Moon, 91–126 (New York: Oxford University Press, 1999).
27. Jonathan Tucker, *War of Nerves: Chemical Warfare from World War I to Al-Qaeda* (New York: Random House, 2005), 24–41.
28. Annie Jacobsen, *Operation Paperclip: The Secret Intelligence Program That Brought Nazi Scientists to America* (New York: Little, Brown, 2014), 106.
29. Ibid., 175–76.
30. Frank N. Buscher, *The U.S. War Crimes Trial Program in Germany, 1946–1955* (New York: Greenwood Press, 1989), 19.
31. Walter Grunden, *Secret Weapons and World War II: Japan in the Shadow of Big Science* (Lawrence: University Press of Kansas, 2005).
32. Edward Drea, *MacArthur's Ultra: Codebreaking and the War Against Japan, 1942–1945* (Lawrence: University Press of Kansas, 1992).
33. The General Staff divisions (G-1 to G-4) applied throughout the army and within General Headquarters in Tokyo. G-1 concerned administration, G-2 intelligence, G-3 operations, and G-4 logistics.

34. See Charles A. Willoughby, *Maneuver in Warfare* (Harrisburg, Pa.: Military Service Publishing, 1939).
35. Frank Kluckhohn, "Heidelberg to Madrid—the Story of General Willoughby," *The Reporter* (New York Journal), August 19, 1952, http://www.maebrussell.com/Articles%20and%20Notes/Charles%20Willoughby.html. Kluckhohn, a journalist who knew Willoughby from the war and the Occupation, interviewed him for this article. Among other facts, he found out that Willoughby's elite roots, by his own admission, had been fabricated. Instead of being the son of a baron, he was likely born to working-class German parents and "orphaned" before his migration to America. See also Kenneth J. Campbell, "Major General Charles A. Willoughby: A Mixed Performance," December 14, 2004, Arlington National Cemetery website, http://www.arlingtoncemetery.net/cawilloughby.htm.
36. Borneman, *MacArthur at War*, 490.
37. Takemae, *Inside GHQ*, 18–21; Willoughby and Chamberlain, *MacArthur 1941–1951*, 58, 98–99. The core group for ATIS comprised FBI-trained agents who before the war were sent to the Philippines to spy on the Japanese.
38. Grant K. Goodman, *America's Japan: The First Year 1945–1946*, trans. Barry D. Steben (New York: Fordham University Press, 2005), 28–29.
39. Williams and Wallace, *Unit 731*, 91–112.
40. "B.W. Bomb (Japanese)," 20 May 1944, PRO WO 188/690.
41. *The Japanese and Bacterial Warfare*, ATIS Research Report No. 84, 24 July 1944, MacArthur Archives, RG-3, box 119, folder 7.
42. "Japanese Bacteriological Warfare in China" PoW interrogation, China G-2, 12 December 1944, NARA, RG 319, MFB.
43. *Japanese Violations of the Laws of War*, ATIS Research Report No. 72, 15 June 1945, MacArthur Archives, RG-3, box 119, folder 4.
44. Ibid., 9. Fragments of notes found in the Philippines referred to an "MK bacterial bomb weighing one kilogram." A 396-page manual concerning field service, dated August 1941, with many pages missing, had a section "Subject Matter—Bombing, Gas and Bacteria," but these pages had been torn out.
45. "Japanese Biological Warfare," Military Intelligence Project 2263, 26 July 1945, NARA, RG 202, entry 201, box 202, 30.
46. Ibid., 2.
47. "Mission to Tokyo by Karl T. Compton," 9–10. Compton and Edward L. Moreland, dean of electrical engineering at MIT and head of the army's Scientific and Technical Advisory Section under MacArthur, were together asked to form the group, under the aegis of the section. Moreland headed the mission and worked closely with Thorpe at CIC.

48. Ibid., 8.
49. R. W. Home and Morris F. Low, "Postwar Scientific Intelligence Missions to Japan," *Isis* 84 (1993): 527–37.
50. Takemae, *Inside GHQ*, 91–198.
51. G-2 [Washington] to the Office of the Surgeon General, "Japanese Attempts to Secure Virulent Strains of Yellow Fever Virus," 3 February 1941, NARA, RG 112, Federal Security Agency.
52. Sheldon H. Harris, *Factories of Death: Japanese Biological Warfare, 1932–1945, and the American Cover-up* (New York: Routledge, 2002), 203. Dr. Miyagawa reportedly was close to Prince Konoe, then Japan's premier, and to the minister of health and welfare, Koizumi Chikahiko, General Ishii's early mentor.
53. *Report on Scientific Intelligence Survey in Japan*. Vol. 5: *Biological Warfare*, September and October 1945, US Army Military History Institute (US Army Heritage & Education Center), Carlisle, Pa., D810 B3 R46 1945a. Authored by Colonel Sanders, it is known as the Sanders Report.
54. Supplementary Biological Warfare Information, Interrogation of Gen. Umezu Yoshijiro by Lt. Col. Murray Sanders and Lt. H. Youngs, 9 November 1945, 3, NARA, RG 331, file 385, TSC, AG Section. In this memorandum, Sanders submitted three other equally inconclusive interrogations of Japanese general staff.
55. To CINCAFPAC/SCAP from Washington, 4 September, 1945, MacArthur Archives, RG-9, box 160, WD1205.
56. B. V. A. Röling and Antonio Cassese, *The Tokyo Trial and Beyond* (Cambridge, Mass.: Polity Press, 1993), 80, 85.
57. Ibid., 33–34.
58. Another suicide was Hashida Kumihiko, a former minister of education. Togo Shigenori, a former foreign minister, suffered a heart attack but survived to stand trial.
59. Brackman, *The Other Nuremberg*, 50–51.
60. The Nuremberg Charter stipulated the "killing of hostages" only.
61. Philip R. Piccigallo, *The Japanese on Trial: Allied War Crimes Operations in the East, 1945–1951* (Austin: University of Texas Press, 1979); Sandra Wilson, Robert Cribb, Beatrice Trefalt, and Dean Aszkielowicz, *Japanese War Criminals: Politics of Justice After the Second World War* (New York: Columbia University Press, 2017); Kersten von Lingen, ed., *Trials in the Wake of Decolonization and Cold War in Asia* (London: Palgrave Macmillan, 2016).
62. Ibid., 124.
63. Ibid., 263–65. More than 2,200 war crimes trials were held against more than 5,500 accused, with over 4,400 convicted and around 1,000 executed.

64. Willoughby and Chamberlain, *MacArthur 1941–1951*, 311–14.
65. Carroll V. Gline, *The Doolittle Raid: America's Daring First Strike Against Japan* (Atglen, Pa.: Schiffer Publishing, 1991).
66. Ibid., 81. The account is cited as Richard E. Cole, response to questionnaire, Air Force Office of Information, March 28, 1957. Cole remembered that "Japan looked very pretty and picturesque from what I could see. We flew at treetop level until our target area then pulled up to twelve hundred feet, dropped our bombs, and lowered to treetop level again, People on the ground waved to us. It was about 12:15 Tokyo time, the weather was clear but a little hazy, which limited forward vision. We could see the moat, the Imperial Palace, and downtown Tokyo."
67. United Nations War Crimes Commission, "Trial of Lieutenant-General Shigeru Sawada and Three Others. United States Military Commission, Shanghai (27th February, 1946–15th April, 1946)," in *Law Reports of Trials of War Criminals*. Vol. 5 (London: His Majesty's Stationery Office, 1948), 1–24.
68. John W. Dower, *War Without Mercy: Race and Power in the Pacific War* (New York: Random House, 1986), 49.
69. "Indictment Against Lieutenant General Masaharu Homma," *Historical Bulletin* (Philippine Historical Association), 11, no. 3 (September 1967): 304–15.
70. Dower, *War Without Mercy*, 53–57.
71. Takemae, *Inside GHQ*, 172.
72. "Trial of Jap War Criminals Nears," *News-Palladium* (Benton, Mich.), October 20, 1945, 1.
73. Manchester, *American Caesar*, 414–15. The author notes, "Ironically, the chief survivors of the prewar oligarchy were the members of Laurel's [Japanese] puppet government, who were safe in Baguio with Yamashita." After the war, the same landed oligarchy took control of the Philippines.
74. Aubrey Kenworthy, *The Tiger of Malaysia: The Story of General Tomoyuki Yamashita and "Death March" General Masuhara Homma* (New York: Exposition Press, 1953); Tim Maga, *Judgment at Tokyo: The Japanese War Crimes Trials* (Lexington: University Press of Kentucky, 2001), 18–27; Allan A. Ryan, *Yamashita's Ghost: War Crimes, MacArthur's Justice, and Command Accountability* (Lawrence: University Press of Kansas, 2012).
75. Manchester, *American Caesar*, 484–88.
76. John J. McCloy to General Douglas MacArthur, 19 November 1946, MacArthur Archives, RG-5, box 2, folder 2. McCloy, about to leave government, went on to become the first high commissioner of Germany.
77. *The Report of the Meeting of the Ministers of Foreign Affairs of the Union of the Soviet Socialist Republics, the United States of America, the United Kingdom* (Moscow,

December 16–December 26, 1945). The report is available at the Yale Law School Avalon Project, http://avalon.law.yale.edu/20th_century/decade19.asp. The meeting established a UN commission for the control of atomic energy—to keep it for peaceful ends—and "the elimination from national armaments of atomic weapons and of all other major weapons adaptable to mass destruction." It also acknowledged the special interest of the Soviet Union in the new, neighboring governments of Bulgaria and Rumania—governments that the Americans and British felt should be "more representative."

78. *FRUS, 1946, The Far East*. Vol. 8: The Joint Chiefs of Staff to General of the Army Douglas MacArthur, at Tokyo, January 5, 1946. This directive to MacArthur promised that the SWNCC would send him "early political guidance for meetings of the joint commission [on Korea]."
79. From Sir George Sansom to the Foreign Office, 31 January 1946, PRO FO 371/54082.
80. Dower, *War Without Mercy*, 124–31.
81. John W. Dower, *Embracing Defeat: Japan in the Wake of WWII* (New York: Norton, 1999), 280–86. Dower underscored the influence of Brigadier General Bonner Feller, chief of SCAP's Psychological Warfare Branch.
82. Sodei Ringirō, *Dear General MacArthur: Letters from the Japanese During the American Occupation*, ed. John Junkerman, trans. Shizue Masuda (New York: Rowman & Littlefield, 2006), 67.
83. Sansom (Tokyo) to MacDermot, 31 January 1946, PRO FO 371/54082. MacArthur compared the emperor to Charlie McCarthy, the famous ventriloquist dummy, a puppet "who had neither begun the war nor stopped it."
84. Joint Chiefs of Staff to CINCAFPAC, 30 November 1945, MacArthur Archives, RG-9, box 159, folder War Crimes, September 1945–June 1946.
85. Devin O. Pendas, "Transitional Justice and Just Transitions: The German Case 1945–1950," *European Studies Forum* (Spring 2008): 57–64. Many Soviet-organized trials were held in Germany in the name of socialism and the new communist order.
86. Neil Boister and Robert Cryer, *The Tokyo International Military Tribunal: A Reappraisal* (New York: Oxford University Press, 2008), 221. The authors note that international courts by their nature "are complex entities with various different organs, participants, agendas, and philosophies."
87. Executive Order 9660, "Conferring Certain Authority on the Chief of Counsel in the Preparation and Prosecution of War Crimes Against the Major Leaders of Japan and Their Principal Agents and Accessories," 10 Federal Registry, 29 November 1945.

88. Robert Donihi, "War Crimes," *St. John's Law Review* 66, no. 3 (1991): 740–48. Donihi was a liaison to the State Department representatives at SCAP. His recollections about Keenan were not always consistent.
89. Memo on History Outline of the Investigative [*sic*] Division, 26 July 1946. UVALL, box 2, folder [IMTFE] (IPS) 1946 Japan.
90. Donihi, "War Crimes." By Keenan's order, Carlisle Higgins replaced the original deputy, John Darsey, a US assistant attorney general who had competed for the chief of counsel position.
91. Takemae, *Inside GHQ*, 169.
92. Robinson, "Surprise Attack," 979; Telford Taylor, *The Anatomy of the Nuremberg Trials* (New York: Alfred A. Knopf, 1992), 116.
93. Solis Horwitz, "The Tokyo Trial," *International Conciliation* (November 1950): 494.
94. Joseph B. Keenan, Chief of Counsel, International Prosecution Section, Assignment Chart, 28 December 1945, UVALL, box 1, folder General Reports and Memoranda for 1945. Keenan's chart stipulated that all other requests for information should go the Investigation Division and that the Documents Division would be the repository for case files on all individuals named by the IPS. Grace Llewlyn, one of the few IPS women prosecutors, was on this early team.
95. James J. Robinson, "Surprise Attack: Crime at Pearl Harbor and Now (Part II)," *American Bar Association Journal* 46 (October 1960): 1085–91.
96. Takemae, *Inside GHQ*, 150. The State Department's Robert A. Fearey was involved in this work.
97. The emphasis on Japanese wartime cabinet members contrasted with the tendency in Nuremberg to view Hitler's cabinet as relatively divorced from decision making and to focus instead on his political cronies and military and Gestapo heads. See Taylor, *Anatomy*, 78–115.
98. Edward Drea, "Introduction," in *Researching Japanese War Crimes: Introductory Essays*, ed. Edward Drea et al., 3–20 (Washington, D.C.: National Archives and Records Administration for the Nazi War Crimes and Japanese Imperial Government Interagency Working Group, 2006), 9–11.
99. IPS Doc. No. 2594.A, "Instructions for the disposition of documents" (IMTFE *Prosecution documents which were either not offered or were rejected*, Microfilm reel 1, Bierce Microforms, University of Akron), 1–2. Code books, registers of personnel, and those concerning general affairs might be temporarily preserved until no longer of use. On the other hand, documents "especially desirable to preserve for future use (for example, black-list of leftists, etc.) should, as a suggested plan, be ingeniously moved to another place." Page 3 of this IPS document includes a

Japanese government memo, dated August 20, 1945, indicating that the order had been successfully executed, although it alludes to "blunders," such as leaving papers in the back of drawers or inserted under the legs of desks to stabilize them, that require "careful examination."

100. Yukiko Koshiro, *Imperial Eclipse: Japan's Strategic Thinking About Continental Asia Before August 1945* (Ithaca, N.Y.: Cornell University Press, 2013), 4.

101. Kluckhohn, "Heidelberg to Madrid," 4. As Kluckhohn reported, the arrival of Thorpe's counterintelligence was, according to Willoughby and perhaps because of him, delayed six weeks so that "the writer and others who were in Tokyo when the occupation began watched the Japanese Foreign Office, Radio Tokyo, and the military openly burning in the streets documents and records they did not want our authorities to see, with no counterintelligence men there to stop them."

102. Boister and Cryer, *The Tokyo International Tribunal*, 103–14.

103. In power at the height of Japanese wartime aggression and the inventor of Japan's opium cabal in China, Konoe saw himself as part of Japan's rebirth and had been working on the new constitution.

104. Horwitz, "Tokyo Trial," 480; Brackman, *The Other Nuremberg*, 63. The diary was not always to Kido's benefit. On December 8, 1941, he wrote that the attack on Pearl Harbor was a "grand success" after which he "deeply felt the blessings of Divine Grace." IMTFE Document No. 1623 (90), Exhibit 1239, page 1 (IMTFE *Prosecution documents which were either not offered or were rejected*).

105. Dower, *Embracing Defeat*, 310–17. Known officially as the "Imperial Rescript on the Construction of a New Japan," Hirohito's statement was ambiguous enough in Japanese to allow a continuing claim to divinity. It also bemoaned the despondency into which his people had fallen and urged acceptance of the Occupation reforms as a means to prosperity.

106. CINCAFPAC ADV (MACARTHUR) to WARCOS (JOINT CHIEFS OF STAFF), 24 January 1946, MacArthur Archives, RG 9, WC75.

107. Yuma Totani, *The Tokyo War Crimes Trial: The Pursuit of Justice in the Wake of World War II* (Cambridge Mass.: Harvard University Asia Center, 2008), 52–58. It was October 1946 before the SWNCC advised MacArthur to hand the Australian list back to IPS, which he had already rejected as an authoritative body.

108. J. B. Keenan and B. F. Brown, *Crimes Against International Law* (Washington, DC: Public Affairs Press, 1950), 1.

109. Alternate judges were allowed at Nuremberg, so that eight judges normally sat on the bench. With nine to eleven judges predicted for the IMTFE, doubling that number was considered impractical.

110. The entire record of the IMTFE is available at the US National Archives Collection of World War II War Crimes Records, RG 238.7, http://www.archives.gov/research/guide-fed-records/groups/238.html#238.7.

111. Totani, *Tokyo Trial*, 30–31; "The New Zealand Member [Northcroft], International Military Tribunal for the Far East to the Prime Minister, 11 March 1946," *Documents on New Zealand External Relations*. Vol. 2: *The Surrender and Occupation of Japan*, ed. Robin Kay (Wellington, N.Z.: P. D. Hasselberg, 1982), 1532.

2. Spoils of War: Secret Japanese Biological Science

1. Denis Piszkiewicz, *The Nazi Rocketeers: Dreams of Space and Crimes of War* (Westport, Conn.: Praeger, 1995).
2. Michael J. Neufeld, "Wernher von Braun, the SS, and Concentration Camp Labor: Questions of Moral, Political, and Criminal Responsibility," *German Studies Review* 25, no. 1 (February 2002): 57–78.
3. Roy Sloan, *The Tale of Tabun: Nazi Chemical Weapons in North Wales* (Llanrwst: Gwasg Carreg Gwalch, 1998), 34.
4. Ulf Schmidt, *Secret Science: A Century of Poison Warfare and Human Experiments* (New York: Oxford University Press, 2015), 92–94.
5. Robert K. Merton, "Science and the Social Order," in *The Sociology of Science: Theoretical and Empirical Investigations* (Chicago: University of Chicago Press, 1973), 254–66.
6. Schmidt, *Secret Science*, 81–94; Robert Harris and Jeremy Paxman, *A Higher Form of Killing: The Secret History of Chemical and Biological Weapons* (New York: Hill and Wang, 1982), 57–62.
7. Clarence G. Lasby, *Operation Paperclip: German Scientists and the Cold War* (New York: Athenaeum, 1971); Linda Hunt, *Secret Agenda: The United States Government, Nazi Scientists, and Project Paperclip, 1944–1990* (New York: St. Martin's Press, 1991); Annie Jacobsen, *Operation Paperclip: The Secret Intelligence Program that Brought Nazi Scientists to America* (New York: Little, Brown, 2014).
8. John Gimbal, *Science, Technology, and Reparations: Exploitation and Plunder in Postwar Germany* (Stanford, Calif.: Stanford University Press, 1992).
9. The postwar immunity of some criminal scientists in Germany needed only institutional protection. See Benno Müller-Hill, *Murderous Science: Elimination by Scientific Selection of Jews, Gypsies, and Others in Germany, 1933–1945*, trans. George R. Fraser (New York: Oxford University Press, 1988.)
10. Karl Taylor Compton, "Mission to Tokyo," draft for *Report on Scientific Intelligence Survey in Japan 1945*, MIT, Office of the President, Personal Papers of

Karl T. Compton and James R. Killian, box 56, folder 15, 23. As Compton recounted, "My 200 pounds was too much for the floor of one of their laboratories; I broke through and nearly went out of sight, to the great consternation of the admirals. I won't get the purple heart, but for several days I was decorated with the Red Elbow and the Black and Blue Shin."

11. *US Navy Technical Mission to Japan Report* (San Francisco: US Navy Technical Mission, 1946).
12. Jeanne Guillemin, *Biological Weapons: From State-Sponsored Programs to Contemporary Bioterrorism* (New York: Columbia University Press, 2005), 27–39.
13. Theodor Rosebury and Elvin A. Kabat, with the assistance of Martin H. Boldt, "Bacterial Warfare," *Journal of Immunology* 56, no. 1 (1947): 7–96.
14. Truman, on becoming vice president, was succeeded on the committee by New York senator James Mead, http://www.senate.gov/artandhistory/history/common/investigations/Truman.htm.
15. Guillemin, *Biological Weapons*, 65–66.
16. General Brehon Somervell, Commander of the Army Services Forces, to the Chief of Staff, "Research and Development in Biological Warfare," 11 August 1945, NARA, Correspondence File of Dr. G. W. Merck, RG 165, Records of the War Department, General and Special Staffs.
17. Keith E. Eiler, *Mobilizing America: Robert P. Patterson and the War Effort, 1940–1945* (Ithaca, N.Y.: Cornell University Press, 1998), 463.
18. Leo P. Brophy, Wyndham D. Miles, and Rexmond C. Cochrane, *The US Army in World War II. The Technical Services: The Chemical Warfare Service: From Laboratory to Field* (Washington, D.C.: Office of the Chief of Military History, US Army, 1959), 431–34.
19. Military Intelligence Division, War Department, "Biological Warfare: Activities and Capabilities of Foreign Nations," 30 March 1946, NARA, RG 319, Records of the Army Staff.
20. Alden Waitt to the Surgeon General, US Army, "Peacetime Progress of Research and Development in Biological Warfare," 8 October 1945, NARA, RG 165, box 186, Records of the War Department, General and Special Staffs.
21. Frederic J. Brown, *Chemical Warfare: A Study in Restraints* (New Brunswick, N.J.: Transaction Books, 2007), 166. Major William Porter, later chief of CWS, taught from 1933 to 1937. Waitt taught from 1937 to 1940.
22. Brown, *Chemical Warfare*, 122.
23. Ibid., 124–25. The occasion was Roosevelt's veto of a bill, initiated by the War Department, to change the name of CWS to the Chemical Corps, to give it more permanent status.

24. Alden H. Waitt, "Poison Gas in This War," *New Republic* 106, no. 17 (April 27, 1942): 563–65.
25. See Alden H. Waitt, *Gas Warfare* (New York: Duell, Sloan and Pierce, 1944), 24.
26. Jonathan Tucker, *War of Nerves: Chemical Warfare from World War I to Al-Qaeda* (New York: Random House, 2006), 84–102.
27. John Bryden, *Deadly Allies: Canada's Secret War 1937–1947* (Toronto: McClelland & Stewart, 1989), 179–83. As early as 1943 the Allies were alerted to German nerve gases and had produced some close in formula to the German ones and even established atropine sulphate as an antidote. But CWS chief General Porter "had his sights firmly fixed on mustard gas" as a way to defeat Germany and Japan.
28. Ibid., 186–87.
29. Ibid., 192–93.
30. "660 Japan," 16 March 1945, NARA, RG 175, box 182, Station Series, 1942–1945.
31. The report, called *A Study of the Possible Use of Toxic Gas in Operation Olympic*, was submitted to the chief of the Chemical Warfare Service on 9 June 1945. Labeled top secret, it was later corrected by handwritten insertions of the words "retaliatory" and "as a retaliatory measure" to eliminate language indicating the proposed first use. In 1996 a declassified copy was made available by the Pentagon to military historians Thomas B. Allen and Norman Polmar, who had filed a Freedom of Information Act request for it (Thomas Allen, personal communication, 6 October 2016). See Allen and Polmar, "The Most Deadly Plan," *Proceedings Magazine* 124, no. 1 (January 1998), published online by the US Naval Institute, http://www.usni.org.
32. John Ellis van Courtland Moon, "Project Sphinx: The Question of the Use of Gas in the Planned Invasion of Japan," *Journal of Strategic Studies* 3, no 3 (1989): 303–23.
33. Brown, *Chemical Warfare*, 279–85.
34. "Appreciation of Biological Warfare," 11 November 1946, ACW, NARA, RG 319, entry 154, box 10, sec. 111-B, part 1. Anticrop agents were described as having logistical problems. For example, the 31 million acres of wheat in the Ukraine would take 31,000 to 62,000 tons of agents to destroy them (5). Nonetheless, Detrick would continue to develop them.
35. W. Seth Carus, *Defining "Weapons of Mass Destruction,"* Occasional Paper No. 8, Center for the Study of Weapons of Mass Destruction, National Defense University (Washington, D.C.: National Defense University Press, 2012), 9–11.
36. "Appreciation of Biological Warfare," 4.
37. Guillemin, *Biological Weapons*, 40–74.

38. Brian Balmer, "Killing 'Without the Distressing Preliminaries,'" *Minerva* 40 (2002): 72.
39. "A Review of German Activities in the Field of Biological Warfare," 12 September 1945, ALSOS Mission, Report No. B-C-H-H/305, Washington, D.C., NARA, RG 112 C-4, 49. Kurt Blome, the director of BW activities in Germany, was introduced to his position with a warning to work only on defensive measures: "[Chief of Defense Field Marshal] Keitel told Blome that Hitler had strictly forbidden any work on offensive preparations for BW and added his own opinion that it was a foolish method of waging war in any event."
40. Ibid., 67.
41. Ibid., 47. They noted that one of their principal informants, Professor H. Kliewe, "left files full of detailed laboratory protocols and notes which have been of the greatest help in preparing this report."
42. *Report on Scientific Intelligence Survey in Japan.* Vol. 5: *Biological Warfare, September and October 1945*, appendix 29, supplement 1-b, US Army Military History Institute (US Army Heritage & Education Center), Carlisle, Pa., D810 B3 R46 1945a, 4. Referred to as the Sanders Report. See also Peter Williams and David Wallace, *Unit 731: Japan's Secret Biological Warfare in World War II* (New York: Free Press, 1989), The Naito Document, appendix A, 257–61.
43. Jacobsen, *Operation Paperclip.*
44. Williams and Wallace, *Unit 731*, 133. The authors devoted an entire chapter to Sanders, including his wartime adventures in sabotage on behalf of the US Army and the Legion of Merit he received in 1946 (121–140).
45. Sanders Report, 6.
46. *Reports: US Naval Mission to Japan 1945–1946*, "Bacteriology and Chemistry in the Japanese Navy." Intelligence Targets JAPAN (DNI) of 4 September 1945, FASCICLE M-1, TARGET M-10, November 1945, Chief of Mission Clifford G. Grimes USN, Summary, 1.
47. Sanders Report, 7.
48. Williams and Wallace, *Unit 731*, 134.
49. Ibid. Sanders recounted this story when interviewed by the Japanese press in 1983 ("MacArthur Guaranteed War Crimes Immunity," *Asahi*, August 14, 1983).
50. Sanders Report, 2.
51. Ibid., 3. On Naito's deception see "Green Cross Founder Hid Info about Unit 731: letter," *Asian Political News*, August 17, 1998.
52. Note by Chairman, B.W.I.C., "Japanese Biological Warfare Intelligence," 18 January 1946, PRO CAB 81/58, 2.

53. Takemae Eiji, *Inside GHQ: The Allied Occupation of Japan and Its Legacy* (New York: Continuum, 2002), 161–64. During the war in the Pacific, Willoughby employed hundreds of Nisei from Hawaii and California as translators who were sent out with military detachments. See Charles A. Willoughby and John Chamberlain, *MacArthur, 1941-1951* (New York: McGraw-Hill, 1954), 98–99.
54. Takemae, *Inside GHQ*, 165–66.
55. Elliott R. Thorpe, *East Wind, Rain* (Boston: Gambit, 1969), 91–95.
56. Takemae, *Inside GHQ*, 161–63.
57. Ibid., 146.
58. Ibid., 238–39. MacArthur followed the declaration with instructions to the new Japanese government to compose a new constitution with five basic reforms: voting rights for women, encouragement of labor unions and abolishment of child labor, reform of education, the elimination of secret inquisition and abuse, and the promotion of fair income distribution and ownership of the means of production and trade.
59. Charles L. Kades, "The American Role in Revising Japan's Imperial Constitution," *Political Science Quarterly* (Summer 1948): 215–47; Richard B. Finn, *Winners in Peace: MacArthur, Yoshida, and Postwar Japan* (Berkeley: University of California Press, 1992), 89–122. Finn noted that "if Japan's constitution could be said to have a father, Kades would have a strong claim."
60. Finn, *Winners in Peace*, 116. Kades approved the language of the article after its review by the Japanese. The last phrase, concerning the "belligerency of the state," is attributed to MacArthur.
61. Takemae, *Inside GHQ*, 147–52.
62. Major General Alden H. Waitt, "Recent Technological Developments of the Chemical Warfare Service," 21 May 1946 (Washington, DC: US Industrial College of the Armed Forces), 8.
63. William W. Ralph, "Improvised Destruction: Arnold, LeMay, and the Firebombing of Japan," *War in History* 13 (2006): 495–522. Higher authorities at the Pentagon and Secretary Stimson himself (except for an order not to bomb Kyoto) put no restrictions on LeMay's plans for bombing more cities. The rationale that Japanese home industry was central to factory production—a justification for destroying residential urban centers—was questionable. By 1944 shortages of oil, bauxite, steel, and aluminum had sharply decreased munitions production.
64. George C. McGhee, *On the Frontline in the Cold War* (Westport, Conn.: Praeger, 1997), 88. McGhee, a consultant to General LeMay, saw the first clear aerial photographs of the attack.

65. E. Bartlett Kerr, *Flames Over Tokyo: The U.S. Army Air Forces' Incendiary Campaign Against Japan 1944–1945* (New York: Donald I. Fine, 1991), 189–204.
66. Ralph, "Improvised Destruction," 514. See also Ronald W. Clark *The Role of the Bomber* (New York: Thomas Y. Crowell, 1977).
67. Henry Stimson, secretary of war, "Statement on the Bombing of Japan" August 6, 1945. Available at the Project of the Nuclear Age Foundation, http://www.nuclearfiles.org/menu/library/correspondence/stimson-henry/corr_stimson_1945-08-06.htm.
68. Henry DeWolfe Smyth, *Atomic Energy for Military Purposes. The Official Report on the Development of the Atomic Bomb Under the Auspices of the United States* (Princeton, N.J.: Princeton University Press, 1945). The report was in bookstores in September, made the best-seller list, and went through eight printings.
69. Richard Rhodes *The Making of the Atomic Bomb* (New York: Simon & Schuster, 1986), 750.
70. Brown, *Chemical Warfare*, 149–66.
71. "Claim CWS Head 'Whitewashes' His Own Office," *Chicago Tribune*, July 21, 1946.
72. Barclay Moon Newman, *Japan's Secret Weapon* (New York: Current, 1944). See also Sheldon H. Harris, *Factories of Death: Japanese Biological Warfare, 1932–1945, and the American Cover-up* (New York: Routledge, 2002), 232; Roger B. Jeans, Jr., "Alarm in Washington: A Wartime 'Expose' of Japan's Biological Warfare Program," *Journal of Military History* 71 (April 2007): 411–39.
73. Brian Balmer, *Britain and Biological Warfare: Expert Advice and Science Policy, 1930–1945* (London: Palgrave, 2001), 70–73.
74. Compton, "Mission to Tokyo, 1945."
75. Ibid.
76. Clark M. Clifford, *American Relations with the Soviet Union: A Report to the President by the Special Counsel to the President*, 24 September 1945, Truman Library, https://www.trumanlibrary.org/4-1.pdf.
77. Rexmond C. Cochrane, *Biological Warfare Research in the United States*. Vol. 2, part D, xxiii: *Chemical Plant Growth: History of the Chemical Warfare Service in World War II (1 July 1940–16 August 1945)* (Washington, D.C.: Office of Chief, Chemical Corps, 1947), 48.
78. George W. Merck, "Biological Warfare: Report to the Secretary of War by George W. Merck, Special Consultant for Biological Warfare, January 3, 1946," *Military Surgeon* 98 (1946): 237–42; reprinted in the *Bulletin of the Atomic Scientists* 2, no. 7/8 (October 1, 1946): 16–18.
79. *Washington Post*, January 6, 1946.
80. Gerard Piel, "BW," *Life Magazine*, November 18, 1946.

81. Jacob Darwin Hamblin, *Arming Mother Nature: The Birth of Catastrophic Environmentalism* (New York: Oxford University Press, 2013), 26–27.
82. Neil O'Brian, *American Editor in Early Revolutionary China: John William Powell and the China Weekly/Monthly Review* (New York: Routledge, 2003), 216–17.
83. Theodor Rosebury, *Peace or Pestilence: Biological Warfare and How to Avoid It* (New York: McGraw-Hill, 1949), 4. Having left the Detrick program, Rosebury complained that, in contrast to the 1945 Smyth Report on nuclear weapons, "all we have on [US] germ warfare is a few niggardly official handouts, some obscure technical reports, and a scattering of newspaper and magazine stories in which solid substance is hard to find under the froth of conflicting opinion and speculation."
84. "Biological Warfare. Report to the Secretary of War by Mr. George W. Merck, Special Consultant for Biological Warfare," 3 January 1946, US National Academy of Sciences Archives, http://www.nasonline.org/about-nas/history/archives/collections/cbw_files_list.html. See also From J. S. M. Washington to Cabinet, "Secret Cyber Telegram," 17 December 1946. PRO CAB 105.51. This message from the CWS describes Japanese field tests and tests for sabotage but no capacity for "operational use."
85. Williams and Wallace, *Unit 731*, 134, 160.
86. Ibid., 145.
87. Arvo T. Thompson, "Report on Japanese Biological Warfare Activities," 31 May 1946, Adjutant General's Office, Washington, D.C., NARA 765017. Known as the Thompson Report. In a supplemental section, Thompson included diagrams of experimental bombs sketched by Ishii, for example, the I Bomb and the RO Bomb for bacterial liquid, the HA Bomb for anthrax, the U Bomb for sprays, the Old Type Uji Porcelain Bomb for liquid, and the GA Glass Bomb for bacterial liquid, plus the TYPE 50 UJI "Improved Porcelain" bomb also for bacterial liquid.

3. International Prosecution Section: Toward the "Swift and Simple Trial"

1. Travel Orders, IJ-Tokyo*ABM, 28 January 1946, UVALL, sec. 1, folder 2, MSS1 Su 863 a.
2. Ronald L. Heinemann, *Harry Byrd of Virginia* (Charlottesville: University of Virginia Press, 1996), 175–76. Byrd's political control of Virginia relied heavily on the exclusion of the black vote; despite his resistance to the Supreme Court decision outlawing segregation (*Brown* v. *Board of Education, Topeka, Kansas*, 1954), the case marked "the death knell of the machine" (325).

3. "Supplement to the Assignment or Selection of the 30 to 40 Most Likely Suspects," 18 December 1945, UVALL, Tavenner Papers, box 1, folder General Reports and Memoranda from 1945.
4. Takemae Eiji, *Inside GHQ: The Allied Occupation of Japan and Its Legacy*, trans. Robert Ricketts and Sabastian Swann (New York: Continuum, 2002), 259.
5. "Japanese War Crimes," 15 January 1946, PRO FO 371/57422.
6. Suzannah Linton, "Rediscovering the War Crimes Trials in Hong Kong, 1946–48," *Melbourne Journal of International Law* 13, no. 2 (2012): 296–97.
7. Peter Dennis, *Troubled Days of Peace: Mountbatten and South East Asia Command, 1945–1946* (Manchester, UK: University of Manchester Press, 1987), 11–12.
8. UK Embassy Washington (M. E. Reed) to Foreign Office, 25 January 1946, PRO FO 371/57423.
9. From Moscow to Foreign Office, 8 February 1946, PRO FO 371/57423. The US chargé d'affaires in Moscow had been urging the Soviets to send their representatives to Tokyo on the mistaken assumption that the IMTFE organization, laid out in the Tokyo Charter, was still open to discussion.
10. Robert Donihi, "War Crimes," *St. John's Law Review* 66, no. 3 (1991): 733–71.
11. Walter R. Borneman, *MacArthur at War: World War II in the Pacific* (New York: Little, Brown, 2016), 404.
12. Document 656, "The New Zealand Member, International Military Tribunal for the Far East, to the Acting Prime Minister," Tokyo, February 7, 1946, from E. H. Northcroft in *The Surrender and Occupation of Japan. Documents on New Zealand External Relations*, ed. Robin Kay (Wellington, N.Z.: P. D. Hasselberg), 2:1520–21.
13. From UK Liaison Mission to Foreign Office, 16 February 1946, PRO FO 371/57423.
14. Solis Horwitz, "The Tokyo Trial," *International Conciliation*, no. 465 (1950): 477–98.
15. From UK Liaison Mission to Foreign Office, 16 February 1946.
16. Arnold C. Brackman, *The Other Nuremberg: The Untold Story of the Tokyo War Crime Trial* (New York: William Morrow, 1987), 69–79. Brackman, then a young journalist, describes each of the IMTFE judges. In-depth analyses of the roles of Northcroft, Henri Bernard, Lord Patrick, Bernard Röling, and India's Judge Radhabinod Pal can be found in Yuki Tanaka, Tim McCormack, and Gerry Simpson, eds., *Beyond Victors' Justice: The Tokyo War Crimes Trial Revisited* (Leiden: Martinus Nijhoff, 2011), 79–144.
17. Brackman, *The Other Nuremberg*, 73.
18. From UK Liaison Mission to Foreign Office, 16 February 1946.
19. Brackman, *The Other Nuremberg*, 66–67.
20. Yuki Tokatori, "The Forgotten Judge at the Tokyo War Crime Tribunal," *Massachusetts Historical Review* 10 (2008): 139.

21. From Keenan to Honorable Tom C. Clark, Atty. General, 21 January 1946, MacArthur Archives, RG-9, box 159, folder War Crimes, September 1945-June 1946. Clark had been Keenan's superior at the Department of Justice Criminal Division. As attorney general he dined weekly with Truman and often played poker with him. See Oral History Interview with Tom C. Clark, Washington, D.C., by Jerry N. Hess, Harry S. Truman Library, 8 February 1973, https://www.trumanlibrary.org/oralhist/clarktc.htm.
22. James Burnham Sedgwick, "The Trial Within: Negotiating Justice at the International Military Tribunal for the Far East, 1946–1948," Ph.D. diss., University of British Columbia, 2012.
23. B.V.A. Röling and Antonio Cassese, *The Tokyo Trial and Beyond: Reflections of a Peacemonger* (Cambridge, Mass.: Polity Press, 1993), 85.
24. Susan J. Pharr, "A Radical US Experiment: Women's Rights and the Occupation of Japan," in *Democratizing Japan: The Allied Occupation*, ed. Robert E. Ward and Sukamoto Yoshikazu, 221–52 (Honolulu: University of Hawaii Press, 1987). On brothels, see Takemae, *Inside GHQ*, 67-71.
25. Shana Tabak, "Grace Kanode Llewellyn: Local Portia at the Tokyo War Crimes Tribunal," *George Washington University Law School International and Comparative Law Perspectives* (2013): 7–9, http://ssrn.com/abstract=2475116. Helen Grigware Lambert summarized the defense against the defendant Hoshino. Eleanor Bontecou helped prepare IMTFE cases at the War Department. Another woman lawyer, Eleanor Jackson, later married *Scientific American* publisher Gerard Piel and became a celebrated civil rights advocate.
26. Telford Taylor, *The Anatomy of the Nuremberg Trials* (New York: Alfred A. Knopf, 1992), 215.
27. Keenan to Leslie Biffle, US Senate, 10 March 1946, Joseph Berry Keenan Papers, Harvard Law School Library, Series II, box 2, folder 1.
28. "US Indictment Draft," UK Liaison Japan to Foreign Office, 15 February 1946, PRO FO 371/57423. The "Japanese Imperial Government" is listed last as charging Tojo et al. with crimes against peace, war crimes, and crimes against humanity. The idea had apparently been floated at a meeting of the Far Eastern Commission.
29. Foreign Office to Scott Fox, UK Liaison Mission in Tokyo, 15 February 1946, PRO FO 371/57423.
30. Far Eastern Dept. (Mr. Beckett), 8 February 1946, PRO FO 371/57423. The disdain for Japanese law and justice was common. See Judith Shklar, *Legalism: Law, Morals, and Political Trials* (Cambridge, Mass.: Harvard University Press, 1987), 176–86.

31. Alvin D. Coox, "The Lake Khasan Affair of 1938," *Soviet Studies* 25, no. 1 (July 1973): 51–65.

32. Alvin D. Coox, *Nomonhan: Japan Against Russia* (Stanford, Calif.: Stanford University Press, 1988); Stuart Goldman, *Nomonhan, 1939: The Red Army's Victory That Shaped World War II* (Annapolis, Md.: Naval Institute Press, 2012).

33. Harriet L. Moore, *Soviet Far Eastern Policy 1931–1945* (Princeton, N.J.: Princeton University Press, 1945), 122–25, 200–201.

34. From Foreign Office to Washington, 31 December 1945, PRO FO 371/57423.

35. Kayoko Takeda, *Interpreting the Tokyo War Crimes Tribunal: A Sociopolitical Analysis* (Ottawa: University of Ottawa Press, 2010), 85.

36. Cecil Uyehara, personal communication, June 5, 2012. As a 19-year-old university student with a British mother and Japanese father, Uyehara worked as the supervisory translator at IPS, under Commander Carr, a US Navy language officer. In line with other critics, Uyehara observed, "almost every translation had to be reworded, rearranged, if not completely rewritten."

37. Morgan to Kenneth Brim, 19 March 1946, UVALL, box 11, folder 2, MSS 93-4.

38. Borneman, *MacArthur at War*, 388–89.

39. Brackman, *The Other Nuremberg*, 85–86.

40. "Report of Valentine C. Hammack and Henry A. Hauxhurst," 6 March 1946, UVALL, box 8, folder 4, MSS 78-3. The report concluded that Hoshino was "a major war criminal and as such should be included in the indictment."

41. David Nelson Sutton to Mr. Joseph B. Keenan, Chief of Counsel, 4 March 1946, "Summary of Interrogation of Mr. Shozo Murata and Recommendation as to Him," UVALL, sec. 3, folder 12, MSS1 Su 863 a.

42. Ibid.

43. Sutton to Keenan, Chief of Counsel, "Summary of Interrogation of Hatta, Yoshiaki, and Recommendation as to Him," 7 March 1946, UVALL, sec. 3, folder 12, MSS1 Su 863 a.

44. "Serum Plane's Cargo Is Va. Attorney," *Washington Post*, March 17 1946.

45. Interview with Judge Xiang Zhejun (Associate Prosecutor Hsiang), *Baidu*, March 6, 2014, http://baike.baidu.com/view/476490.htm [in Chinese]; Xiang Longwan and Marquise Lee Houle, "In Search of Justice for China: The Contributions of Judge Hsiang Che-chun to the Prosecution of Japanese War Criminals at the Tokyo Trial," in *Historical Origins of International Criminal Law*, ed. Mortan Bergsmo, Cheah Wui Ling, and Yi Ping (Brussels: Torkel Opshal Academic EPublisher, 2014), 2:143–75, http://www.fichl.org.

46. Barak Kushner, *Men to Devils, Devils to Men* (Cambridge, Mass.: Harvard University Press, 2015), 72–87.

47. Ibid., 137–42. Although legislation modeled on the Tokyo Charter was passed in late 1946, according to Japanese records, only around 883 Japanese were tried in Nationalist courts, with an emphasis on personal injuries to specific Chinese citizens rather than prosecution for Class A aggressive war charges or violations of treaties or crimes against humanity.
48. "[United Nations] List of War Crimes," IPS Doc. 1700, n.d., UVALL, sec. 7, folder 23, MSS1 Su 863 a.
49. Kushner, *Men to Devils*, 155. Kushner covers the extradition of Tani Hisao, head of the Sixth Army at Nanjing, and his trial and execution (155–64).
50. P. Z. King, "Bacterial Warfare," *Chinese Medical Record* 61, no. 3 (July–September 1943): 259–63.
51. Vernon Bennett Link and Theodore J. Bauer, *A History of Plague in the United States of America*, Public Health Monograph No. 26 (Washington, D.C.: U.S. Government Printing Office, 1955). From 1900 to 1946 the total number of US cases was under 500, with most of those occurring before 1925.
52. Rexmond C. Cochrane, *The Use of Gas in the Meuse-Argonne Campaign*, Study No. 10 (Army Chemical Center, Md.: US Army Chemical Corps Historical Office, Office of the Chief Chemical Office, 1958), 77–79, 90.
53. "Minutes of Meeting of Executive Committee with Interrogators," March 5, 1946, UVALL, box 1, folder 3, MSS 93-4.
54. Ibid., 2.
55. "Minutes of the Evidence and Defendants Committee Meeting," 6 March 1946, UVALL, box 1, folder 3, MSS 93-4.
56. Keenan to Members of the Legal Staff, "Documentary Evidence," 9 March 1946, UVALL, box 1, folder 5, MSS 78-3.
57. Chief of Counsel to All the Staff, "Assignments," 23 February 1946, UVALL, box 1, folder 4, MSS 78-3.
58. Mansfield to Keenan, "List of Defendants," 2 March 1946, UVALL, box 1, folder 5, MSS 78-3.
59. Hattori Satoshi and Edward J. Drea, "Japanese Operations from July to December 1937," in *The Battle for China: Essays on the Military History of the Sino-Japanese War of 1937–1945*, ed. Mark Peattie, Edward J. Drea, and Hans Van de Ven, 156–80 (Stanford, Calif.: Stanford University Press, 2011), 177.
60. Mansfield to Keenan, 1.

4. The Investigation for Evidence in China

1. Keenan would later fund the French associate prosecutor Robert Oneto to search for evidence in Indochina and Paris and a similar trip to Burma by the

adjunct Burmese attorney, U. E. Maung. Maung's inquiry, unlike Oneto's, was especially productive in that he brought back evidence of the beheading of Allied pilots, the shooting of POWs, the rape and forced concubinage of two English women, and conditions at the Rangoon jail that were worse than "the Black Hole of Calcutta." ("Burma 11 October 1946," PRO FO 371/57429).

2. "SCAP Locates and Question General Ishii. Medic Whom Communists Claim Experimented on PWs Lives in Tokyo," *Pacific Stars and Stripes*, 27 February 1946, UVALL, box 1, folder 1, MSS2012-1. Kalischer, who later covered the Vietnam War and worked for CBS, was following up on a January 6 article in the same paper, in which communist sources, dismissing reports of Ishii's death, claimed that he had conducted bubonic plague experiments on American and Chinese POWs.
3. Morrow to Keenan, 2 March 1946, Subject Sino-Japanese War, Sheldon H. Harris Collection, Hoover Institute, Stanford, Calif., box 2, folder 5.
4. Chinese Ministry of Education, *China Handbook 1937–1943*, ed. Hollington K. Tong (New York: Macmillan, 1942), 679–84.
5. Morrow to Keenan, 2 March 1946.
6. Morrow to Keenan, "Assignment 'B,'" 8 March 1946, Harris Collection, box 2, folder 5. Morrow reviewed the interrogation assignments before mentioning his meeting with Thompson and G-2's Lieutenant Colonel D. S. Tait, who referred him to Colonel Geoffrey Marshall, chief chemical officer at GHQ.
7. *Basic Agreement Between the Government of China and the UNRRA* (Shanghai: International Publishers, 1946).
8. IPS Document 2081, Exhibit 4349, 10 November 1944.
9. McEwen to Sutton, "Possible Leads for China Trip," 8 March 1946, UVALL, sec. 1, folder 3, MSS1 Su 863 a. Lieutenant McEwen was a fellow investigator at ID, on leave from Aetna Casualty and Surety Company, Hartford.
10. All the opium accords were cited by the prosecution and noted in the court's final verdict. See *International Military Tribunal for the Far East. Judgment of 4 November 1948*, 55–57.
11. Timothy Brook, "Opium and Collaboration in Central China, 1938–1940," in *The Opium Regimes: China, Britain, and Japan, 1839–1952*, ed. Timothy Brook and Bob Tadashi Wakabayashi (Berkeley: University of California Press, 2000), 323–43; Motohiro Kobayashi, "An Opium Tug-of-War: Japan Versus the Wang Jingwei Regime" in ibid., 344–59.
12. Travel orders, March 6 and 8, 1946, Virginia Historical Society, Sutton Collection, box 1, folder 3.
13. James Burnham Sedgwick, "The Trial Within: Negotiating Justice at the International Military Tribunal for the Far East, 1946–1948," Ph.D. diss., University of British Columbia, 2012, 141–42.

14. Immunization certificate (Sutton), VHS, Sutton Collection, box 16, folder 75.
15. Albert C. Wedemeyer, *Wedemeyer Reports!* (New York: Henry Holt, 1958). Assigned to command US forces in China, Wedemeyer advised putting severe pressure on Chiang and Mao to end the civil war, advice that was disregarded.
16. Marcia R. Ristaino, *The Jacquinot Safe Zone: Wartime Refugees in Shanghai* (Stanford, Calif.: Stanford University Press, 2008).
17. Copies of Sutton's many notebooks, the source in this book for background detail on his time in Japan and his China trips, are at the University of Richmond Law Library, Sutton Collection, addition 2, old folder 1.
18. Exhibit 319.
19. See F.S.C. Northrup, "Obstacles to a World Legal Order and Their Removal," *Brooklyn Law Review* 19, no. 1 (December 1952): 2.
20. H. J. Timperley, *What War Means: The Japanese Terror in China, A Documentary Record* (London: Victor Gollancz, 1938), published in the United States as *Japanese Terror* (New York: Modern Age Books, 1938).
21. John Rabe, *The Good Man of Nanjing: The Diaries of John Rabe*, ed. Erwin Wickert, trans. John E. Woods (New York: Vintage, 1998).
22. Farrell to Sutton, "German Ambassador Stahmer," 14 April 1946, UVALL, sec. 1, folder 3, MSS1 Su 863 a.
23. David Nelson Sutton, Report from China: German-Japanese Collaboration in China—Stahmer, 23 April 1946, UVALL, sec. 1, folder 3, MSS1 Su 863 a. Marked by hand to give to Tavenner, Keenan, and Hsiang. IPS interviewed Stahmer later that month.
24. David D. Barrett, *Dixie Mission: The United States Army Observer Group in Yenan, 1944* (Berkeley: University of California Press, 1970).
25. In early August 1946 John B. Powell testified at the IMTFE about his captivity at the Bridge House Jail. In the 1980s his son John W. "Bill" Powell wrote on Unit 731 (see chapter 12 on his work).
26. Affidavit of Harold Frank Gill and Affidavit of Su Yeh Yueh, 6 April 1946 (IPS Document 1419), UVALL, sec. 7, folder 22, MSS1 Su 863 a.
27. The etiquette of seating meant more to Mei than Sutton perhaps knew; later that spring the judge successfully argued to sit next to President Webb on the IMTFE bench, leaving the American judge on Webb's right but displacing the judge from the United Kingdom on the left. A popular Japanese film version of the trial dramatized Mei's victory for Chinese status. See Barak Kushner, *Men to Devils, Devils to Men: Japanese War Crimes and Chinese Justice* (Cambridge, Mass.: Harvard University Press, 2015), 79–80. Sutton notes that "Lambert" sat at Mei's right but is unclear whether this is James G. Lambert or Helen Lambert, both from IPS.

28. Mei Ju-ao, "China and the Rule of Law," *Pacific Affairs* 5, no. 10 (October 1932): 863–72.
29. United Nations War Crimes Commission, "Trial of Lieutenant-General Shigeru Sawada and Three Others," in *Law Reports on Trials of War Criminals* (London: His Majesty's Stationery Office, 1948), 5:1–24.
30. IPS Doc. No. 626-A, "Military Ordinance /'Gunrei'/ No. 4 of the Japanese Expeditionary Forces in China," IMTFE *Prosecution documents which were either not offered or were rejected*, Microfilm reel 1, Bierce Microforms, University of Akron, 1. "Death shall be the military punishment," the ordinance read, unless extenuating circumstances justified life imprisonment or more than ten years' confinement.
31. Philip R. Piccigallo, *The Japanese on Trial; Allied War Crimes Operations in the East, 1945–1951* (Austin: University of Texas Press, 1979), 71–73.
32. Charles A. Willoughby and John Chamberlain, *MacArthur 1941–1951* (New York: McGraw-Hill, 1954), 76. Robertson, involved first in the wartime lend-lease program in the Pacific, was assistant secretary of state from 1952 to 1959 in the Eisenhower administration, during which he advised continued military intervention to overthrow Mao's CCP in China. He was also the father of Pat Robertson, the right-wing televangelist.
33. "Opium," 23 March 1946, UVALL, sec. 12, folder 51, MSS1 Su 863 a.
34. Report from China, n.d., UVALL, box 2, folder 2 (item 40), MSS1 Su 863 a.
35. Lim's father, after studying in Edinburgh, served as personal physician to Sun Yat-sen, the founder of the modern Chinese state. Born in Singapore, Robert Lim was a British citizen with three degrees from Edinburgh University, one in general medicine from 1919, a Ph.D. in medicine in 1920, and a doctorate in science in 1924. His work in emergency military medicine during the war provided China with thousands of trained medical and nursing personnel. See John R. Watt, *Saving Lives in Wartime China: How Medical Reformers Built Modern Healthcare Systems Amid War and Epidemics* (Boston: E. J. Brill, 2013), 123–58.
36. Ibid., 46–47.
37. R. Keith Schoppa, *In a Sea of Bitterness: Refugees During the Sino-Japanese War* (Cambridge, Mass.: Harvard University Press, 2011). In chapter 12 the author described the great differences in public health responses in Ningbo and Quzhou, which may have led to late reporting of plague cases in the latter.
38. Dr. P. Z. King Statement and Accompanying Documents, 4 April 1946, UVALL, box 2, folder 1, MSS 78-3, 1. The text of King's March 31, 1942, report was validated by an official at the Health Administration at Sutton's request.
39. P. Z. King, "Bacterial Warfare," *Chinese Medical Record* 61, no. 3 (July–September 1943): 259–63.

40. Peter Williams and David Wallace, *Unit 731: Japan's Secret Biological Warfare in World War II* (New York: Free Press, 1989), 99–100.
41. Dr. Paul K. Fildes, "Paragraph for BW Intelligence Summary No 1," PRO WO 188/690, 58986.
42. W. K. Chen, "Plague Epidemic in Changteh," 29 March 1946, UVALL, box 1, folder 5, MSS 78-3.
43. King to Sutton, 28 March 1946, University of Richmond Law School, Sutton Collection, Working and Personal Series, old folders 1–60, folder 17.
44. United Nations War Crimes Commission, *History of the United Nations War Crimes Commission and the Development of the Laws of War* (London: His Majesty's Stationery Office, 1948), 130.
45. Annick Perrot and Maxime Schwartz, *Pasteur et ses lieutenants* (Paris: Odile Jacob, 2013), 180–91. Yersin trained with Louis Pasteur in Paris. The bacillus he discovered in 1894 in Hong Kong was first called *Bacterium pestis,* then in 1900 *Bacillus pestis,* and then in 1923 *Pasteurella pestis,* in honor of the Pasteur Institute. Finally, in 1970 the World Health Organization announced it would be called *Yersinia pestis* in honor of Yersin. In 1894, also in Hong Kong, the Japanese microbiologist Kitasato Shibasaburo, a student of Robert Koch, claimed to have discovered the bacillus first, but Yersin's claim and the accuracy of his work proved superior. See also Myron Eichenberg, *Plague Ports: The Global Urban Impact of Bubonic Plague, 1894–1901* (New York: New York University Press, 2010), 68–70.
46. John Frith, "The Discoveries of the Plague Bacillus and Its Vectors," *Journal of Military and Veterans Health* 2, no. 3 (August 2012): 4–8. In 1898 in India, Paul-Louis Simond from the Pasteur Institute discovered that the fleas on diseased brown rats also infected humans with plague, although the idea of the flea as vector was for years after dismissed by the British and others.
47. Carsten Flohr, "The Plague Fighter: Wu Lien-teh and the Beginning of the Chinese Public Health System," *Annals of Science* 53 (1996): 360–81.
48. Wu Lien Teh, Chun Wing Han, and Robert Pollitzer, "Plague in Manchuria," *Journal of Hygiene* 21, no. 3 (May 1923): 307–58. The material for this article was from the Plague Prevention Service Laboratory, Harbin. The upsurge in plague was traced to the increased European demand for the pelts of tarabagan marmots that carried the disease. New German dyes allowed the pelts to be dyed to resemble sable and ermine, which increased their market value and drew many new, inexperienced hunters to Mongolia.
49. R. Pollitzer, "Plague and Plague Control in China," *Chinese Medical Journal* 66, no. 6 (June 1948): 328–33.

50. Wu Lien Teh and Wang Jimin, *The History of Chinese Medicine: Being a Chronicle of Medical Happenings in China from Ancient Times to the Present Period* (Shanghai: National Quarantine Service, 1936).
51. Movietone News distributed footage of the events, http://www.usspanay.org/newsreels.shtml.
52. From Major Roger Depo to Sutton, "The Panay and Ladybird Incident," 30 April 1946, UVALL, box 4, folder 4, MSS 78-3.
53. Dr. P. Z. King Statement and Accompanying Documents. In appendix 2, Pollitzer wrote King on December 30, 1941: "As unanimously stated by the inhabitants of Changteh, an enemy airplane, appearing in the morning of November 4th, 1941 and flying unusually low, scattered over certain parts of the city fairly large amounts of grain admixed to which were other materials as discussed below."
54. Ibid., appendix 1.
55. W. W. Yung "Summary Report on the Origin of Plague in Northern Chekiang in 1940" (Document 1895), n.d., UVALL, box 10, folder 5, MSS 78-3.
56. Sketched Map of Chang-Peh [*sic*] City, n.d., UVALL, box 6, folder 4, MSS 78-3.
57. Pollitzer to Sutton, 3 April 1946, University of Richmond Law Library, Sutton Collection, Working and Personal Series, old folders 1–60, folder 17.
58. Ibid., 4.
59. Carolyn Crouch Finster, personal communication, September 12, 2012. Born in Ningbo in 1940, Finster grew up with stories of her father's adventures in China, to which he never returned after 1946.

5. The Best Witnesses

1. Barak Kushner, *Men to Devils, Devils to Men: Japanese War Crimes and Chinese Justice* (Cambridge, Mass.: Harvard University Press, 2015), 147–52. Sakai would be found guilty and executed for all three types of crime defined by the Tokyo Charter, notably for the 1941–1943 murders of 100,000 civilians in Guangdong and Hainan Provinces.
2. IPS Exhibit 324.
3. Suping Lu, *They Were in Nanjing: The Nanjing Massacre Witnessed by American and British Nationals* (Hong Kong: Hong Kong University Press, 2004), 19–41.
4. Ibid., 226–27.
5. Minor Searle Bates, "Open Letter on the Narcotics Problem in Nanking," 22 November 1938, Yale University Divinity School Library, RG 10, box 4, file 52; M. S. Bates, "The Narcotics Situation in Nanking and Other Occupied Areas," *Amerasia* 3 (January 1940): 525–27.

6. *FRUS, Diplomatic Papers, 1939, The Far East; the Near East and Africa.* Vol. 4, January 14, 1939, 430.
7. Timothy Brook, ed., *Documents of the Rape of Nanjing* (Ann Arbor: University of Michigan Press, 1999), doc. 21, 49–50.
8. H. J. Timperley, letter to M. S. Bates, 29 January 1938. Yale Divinity School Library, Nanking Massacre Project Special Collection, RG 10, box 4, folder 65. Their book correspondence is filed under NMPO092-NMPO102.
9. Lu, *They Were in Nanjing*, 58–63.
10. E. W. Jeffery, "Report on the Conditions at Nanjing Dated November 4th, 1938," PRO File 13815, FO371/22156, 4.
11. J. Kinloch, "Notes on Visit to Nanking by J. Kinloch," 3-16 September 1938, PRO File 11032, FO371/22155, 2.
12. Keiichi Tsuneishi and Tomizo Asano, *Germ Warfare Troops and Two Medical Researchers Who Committed Suicide* (Tokyo: Shinchosha, 1982); Sheldon Harris, *Factories of Death* (New York: Routledge, 2002), 135–50.
13. Lewis S. C. Smythe, "War Damage in the Nanking Area, December 1937 to March 1938," Nanking International Relief Committee, June 1938. See also Lu, *They Were in Nanjing*, 178–82.
14. Lewis S. C. Smythe, letter to his wife, Margaret (Mardie), "Chicks and Folks," 21 December 1937, Yale Divinity School Library, Nanking Massacre Special Collection, RG 8, box 103.
15. Lu, *They Were in Nanjing*, 362.
16. Lewis S. C. Smythe, "War Damage in the Nanking Area," 7, n. 3; "Statement of Lewis S. C. Smythe," 7 June 1946, UVALL, sec. 7, folder 29, Su 863 a.
17. Field Diary Kept by Member of Japanese Medical Corps, NARA, RG 153, entry 180, box 5, War Crimes Branch, China War Crimes File, 1945–48.
18. Lu, *They Were in Nanjing*, 281.
19. Ibid., 98.
20. Statement of Chu Yong Ung and Chang Chi Hsiang, Court Document 1719, Exhibit 314. All Nanjing Massacre interviews and others not noted here can be found at UVALL, sec. 7, boxes 25, 27, 30, and 31.
21. Testimony of Hu Tu Sin, IPS Document 1724, Exhibit 316.
22. Testimony of Shang Teh Yi, IPS Document 1735 (no exhibit number indicated).
23. For a detailed description of Pudong and other camps where missionaries were interned, see Sonia Grypma, *China Interrupted: Japanese Internment and the Reshaping of a Canadian Missionary Community* (Waterloo, Ont.: Wilfrid Laurier University Press, 2012).

24. Suping Lu, ed., *A Mission Under Duress: The Nanjing Massacre and Post-Massacre Social Conditions Documented by American Diplomats* (Lanham, Md.: University Press of America, 2012), 150–51.
25. Lu, *They Were in Nanjing*, 278–79.
26. Kushner, *Men to Devils*, 82–84.
27. Wu Tsung-Yen and Hsu Chuan-Ying, "A Factual Account of the Massacre of Chinese Civilians and Disarmed Soldiers at Nanking by Japanese Soldiers and the Burial of Dead Corpses in Nanking," 6 April 1946, UVALL, sec. 7, folder 26, MSS Su 863 a. Sutton later attached to this statement another document, prepared in March 1946: "Chart Showing Burying of Victims by Red Swastika Society, Nanking," Court Document 1704, Exhibit 376.
28. Testimony of Clang [*sic*] Kia Sze, IPS Document 1740, Exhibit 322.
29. Testimony of Wong Kiang Sze, IPS Document 1741, Exhibit 315.
30. Testimony of Loh Sung Sze, IPS Document 1739, Exhibit 312.
31. Testimony of Li Fu Pao, IPS Document 1729, Exhibit 311.
32. Testimony of Wing Pan Sze, IPS Document 1731, Exhibit 320.
33. Testimony of Woo King Zai, IPS Document 1732, Exhibit 313.
34. Testimony of Chen Fu Pao, IPS Document 1742, Exhibit 1.
35. Testimony of Woo Chang Sze, IPS Document 1730, Exhibit 321.
36. Lu, *They Were in Nanjing*, 209–16.
37. Ibid., 203–20.
38. *FRUS, Press Releases*. Vol. 18, 19 February 1938, Koki Hirota to American Ambassador Joseph C. Grew, 12 February 1938, 11.
39. IPS Document 1906, Exhibit 328. Keenan's assistant Luke Lea later picked up the original three volumes in Shanghai for Sutton to use in the trial. Later the embassy grew concerned about the delayed return of volume 9, the only one actually submitted as evidence. See David C. Berger (US Embassy, Nanjing) to Sutton, "Return of Volume IX," 8 October 1946, VHS, Sutton Collection, box 1, folder 9 (Memoranda, Orders, Correspondence, 1946).
40. IPS Document 1921, Exhibit 306.
41. Testimony of Shui Fang Tsen, IPS Document 1736, Exhibit 308.
42. Mills to Sutton, 12 April 1946, UVALL, sec. 1, folder 4, MSSI Su 863 a.
43. "Morrow Concludes China Tour, Gathered Evidence for Trial," *China Press*, April 10, 1946, Virginia Historical Society, Papers, 1919–1965, of David Nelson Sutton, Box 14, folder 60.
44. "Tokyo Trial to Hear Full Story on N'king Rape," *Shanghai Evening Post and Mercury*, April 10, 1946, Virginia Historical Society, Sutton Papers, Box 14, folder 61.

45. R. Keith Schoppa, *In a Sea of Bitterness: Refugees During the Sino-Japanese War* (Cambridge, Mass.: Harvard University Press, 2011), 51–52.

6. Tokyo: The Rush to Trial

1. LTC Arvo T. Thompson, "Report on Japanese Biological Warfare (BW) Activities," 31 May 1946, NARA, RG 319, Box 2097, IWG Ref. Collection, Dugway "A," item 2, JWC 2236.
2. Ibid. Stenographic Transcript of Interrogation of Lt. General SHIRO ISHII in Tokyo by Lt. Colonel A. T. Thompson on 6 February 1946. Lieutenant General Kitano, who took over from Ishii at Pingfan (Heibo in Japanese) in 1942, was interviewed briefly the same day and claimed no knowledge of the authority or funding for biological weapons research there.
3. Kajitsuka Ryuiji, the medical chief of the Kwantung Army, who had worked closely with Ishii's program, was also missing, along with the Kwantung Army's commander, General Yamada Otozoo.
4. Peter Williams and David Wallace, *Unit 731: Japan's Secret Biological Warfare in World War II* (New York: Free Press, 1989), 145–61.
5. Interrogation of General Hideki Tojo, 2 April 1946, NARA, RG 496, entry 53, box 342, 4.
6. Ibid., 7–10. Included in the Japanese field report were captured instructions from Generalissimo Chiang Kai-shek that advised troops not to confuse smoke with toxic gases "and make an unnecessary fuss about it, but hold calmly to your position and receive the attack." The Japanese military used Chiang's unrealistic instructions, plus examples of the "very primitive" Chinese knowledge of gas warfare, the poor quality of their gas masks and training to use them, and the panic that gas attacks caused, to explain to their troops the advantages of chemical warfare. See *Intelligence Report on Japanese Chemical Warfare* (Tokyo: Office of the Chief Chemical Officer, GHQ, 15 May 1946), 1: appendix 1. Available at the Combined Arms Research Digital Library, https://server16040.contentdm.oclc.org/cdm4/item_viewer.php?CISOROOT=/p4013coll8&CISOPTR=2071&CISOBOX=1&REC=2.
7. Interrogation of General Hideki Tojo, 4.
8. Ibid., 11.
9. Ibid., 12.
10. Interrogation of General Shunroku Hata, 11 April 1946, NARA, RG 496, entry UD UP53, box 342, folder C-306. Beebe concluded his interview with Hata without questioning him concerning the use of germ weapons during the

Zhejiang-Jiangxi campaign of 1942, which would have been under Hata's command. Beebe himself might not have known about it.

11. Interrogation of Takeshige Yokoyama, 17 April, 1946, NARA, JWC, RG 496, entry UD UP53, box 342, folder C 305.

12. *FRUS, 1946, The Far East.* Vol. 8, The British Ambassador (Halifax) to the Secretary of State, January 26, 1946. The ambassador noted the continued failure to reach a settlement on constitutional issues and in particular "the lawless conditions arising therefrom which are causing a mounting toll of lives both among the British forces and among the peaceful inhabitants of the Netherlands East Indies."

13. Ibid., The Secretary of State to the French Ambassador (Bonnet), April 10, 1946. The Combined Chiefs of Staff left it to the French and Chinese to arrange the handover of authority.

14. A. S. Comyns Carr, "The Tokyo War Crimes Trial," *Far Eastern Survey* 18, no. 10, (1949): 109–14; Kirsten Sellars, *"Crimes Against Peace" and International Law* (Cambridge: Cambridge University Press, 2013), 197–201. Perhaps the inclusion of the word "murder" and its connotations, less pronounced at Nuremberg, was due to American influences. General MacArthur frequently referred to the deaths at Pearl Harbor as murders, and Chief of Counsel Keenan and some of his staff often used the term in their court presentations.

15. Keenan to Horwitz, 23 February 1946. UVALL, sec. 1, folder 2, MSSI Su 863 a.

16. Arnold C. Brackman *The Other Nuremberg: The Untold Story of the Tokyo War Crimes Trial* (London: Collins, 1987), 82–83.

17. "Announcement of Captain Beverly M. Coleman as Defense Counsel," 22 April 1946, UVALL, box 1, folder Defense Counsel Memoranda, Letters, 1946–1947. Defense counsel G. Carrington Williams contributed this material to the university archive.

18. Solis Horwitz, "The Tokyo Trial," *International Conciliation* (November 1950): 473–584.

19. Yukiko Koshiro, *Imperial Eclipse: Japanese Strategic Thinking About Continental Asia Before August 1945* (Ithaca, N.Y.: Cornell University Press, 2013), 1–2. The author's argument is that, prior to the war's end, Japan saw its neighbor the Soviet Union as its possible arbiter with the West.

20. Ibid., 180.

21. John Despres, Lilita Dzirkals, and Barton Whaley, *Timely Lessons of History: The Manchurian Model for Soviet Strategy* (Santa Monica, Calif.: Rand, 1976), 15–16.

22. Raymond L. Gartoff, "Marshal Maliovsky's Manchurian Campaign," *Military Review* 46 (October 1966): 50–61; see also Lilita I. Dzirkals, *"Lightning War" in*

Manchuria: Soviet Military Analysis of the 1945 Far East Campaign (Washington, D.C.: US Department of Defense, 1976).

23. By September 2 the last Japanese troops in the area surrendered—or so Stalin, who had negotiated surrender terms with Generalissimo Chiang, claimed in a public address that day. Japanese surrender in Manchuria and China was, however, by no means a simple process, in that Soviet troops were invading the Kuril Islands, and KMT and CCP forces were competing for the rights to control surrendered areas. See Koshiro, *Imperial Eclipse*, 244–48; Takemae Eiji, *Inside GHQ: The Allied Occupation and Its Legacy*, trans. Robert Ricketts and Sebastian Swann (New York: Continuum, 2002), 86–89.
24. Despres, Dzirkals, and Whaley, *Timely Lessons of History*, 37; David Glantz, *The Soviet Strategic Offensive in Manchuria: "August Storm"* (London: Frank Cass, 2003), xix. The Japanese count of Soviet casualties was 32,000, although there was no doubt the Kwantung Army had been routed.
25. Robert Service, *Stalin. A Biography* (Cambridge, Mass.: Harvard University Press, 2004), 400–403; Brackman, *The Other Nuremberg*, 238.
26. Sherzod Muminov, "Eleven Winters of Discontent: The Siberian Internment and the Making of the New Japan, 1945–1956," Ph.D. diss., Cambridge University, 2015, 14.
27. Ibid. Over 600,000 Japanese prisoners of war, among them a few army nurses, were sent to distant Siberian work camps and to camps in Ukraine and Uzbekistan, while most older people, other women, and children fled to Japan or China. See Andrew E. Barshay, *The Gods Left First: The Captivity and Repatriation of Japanese POWS in Northeast Asia* (Berkeley: University of California Press, 2013); Lori Watt, *When Empire Comes Home: Repatriation and Reintegration in Postwar Japan* (Cambridge, Mass.: Harvard University Press, 2009).
28. Tsuyoshi Hasegawa, *The Northern Territories Dispute and Russo-Japanese Relations* (Berkeley: University of California Press, 1998), 2:517–18.
29. Brackman, *The Other Nuremberg*, 90.
30. *FRUS: Diplomatic Papers, 1945, The British Commonwealth, the Far East.* Vol. 6, The Ambassador in the Soviet Union to the Secretary of State, October 30, 1945, 809.
31. Takemae, *Inside GHQ*, 295–96.
32. Koshiro, *Imperial Eclipse*, 270–73. The author suspected that at least one former Japanese officer testified to Japan's anti-Soviet conspiracy in return for favored treatment as a Soviet prisoner of war.
33. Hauxhurst to Keenan, "Report on Economic Aggression in China (Greater East Asia) 1932–1945," 18 May1946, UVALL, box 3, folder 2, MSS 93-4.

34. Brackman, *The Other Nuremberg*, 151–52.
35. David Nelson Sutton, "Brief of Atrocities–Class C Offenses–Crimes Against Humanity Committed by Japanese Troops in China, 1937–1945," n.d., UVALL, sec. 5, folder 19, MSS1 Su 863 a.
36. The role of Prince Asaka and other subordinates to Matsui in Nanjing on December 13, 1937, when the city fell and chaos broke out was ignored in Sutton's brief, just as it was by Bates and other American witnesses.
37. Sutton, "Brief of Atrocities," 5.
38. Ibid., 6
39. David Nelson Sutton, "Economic Aggression Report," 1 May 1946, UVALL, sec. 1, folder 5, MSS1 Su 863 a, 12.
40. Morrow to Keenan, "Evidence of Japanese Use of CW agents in China," 4 May 1946, NARA, RG 496, entry 53, box 343.
41. "Library of Congress, Report of CW in the Wuhan Operation," *The Times*, June 11, 1985. This AP story reported in London and carried globally recounted a Japanese scholar's discovery at the Library of Congress of a 142-page imperial Japanese report about the use of lethal chemicals at Wuhan.
42. Victor A. Utgoff, *Challenge of Chemical Weapons: An American View* (New York: St. Martin's Press, 1991), 29–32.
43. Takemae, *Inside GHQ*, 163–64.
44. Sutton to General Douglas MacArthur and Joseph B. Keenan, "Bacteria Warfare," 25 April 1946, University of Richmond Law Library, Sutton Collection, Personal and Working Series, old folders 1–60, folder 13.
45. Ibid., 18.
46. Ibid., 20. See R. Pollitzer and C. C. Li, "Some Observations on the Decline of Pneumonic Plague Epidemics," *Journal of Infectious Diseases* 72, no. 2 (1943): 160–62. Families in six villages were fatally affected.
47. Sutton to MacArthur and Keenan, "Bacteria Warfare," 29.
48. Ibid., 37. In King's statement, as in Sutton's report, Bannan was referred to as "Mrs." His name was often misspelled as Bannon.
49. Sutton to Keenan (cover letter), "Bacteria Warfare," 25 April 1946, University of Richmond Law Library, Sutton Collection, Personal and Working Series, old folders 1–60, folder 13.
50. Sutton to Lt. Col. John Beebe, "Bacteria Warfare," 1 May 1946, University of Richmond Law Library, Sutton Collection, Personal and Working Series, old folders 1–60, folder 13.
51. Washington, D.C. (SERVCHNM) to CINCAFPAC (PASS TO G-2 TECHNICAL INTELLIGENCE SERVICE), 2 May 1946, University of Richmond Law

Library, Sutton Collection, Personal and Working Series, old folders 1–60, folder 13/39.

52. "Minutes of the Third Meeting of the Evidence and Defendants Committee," 25 April 1946, UVALL, box 1, folder 1, MSS 93-4.
53. Ibid., 2.
54. *People v. Kynette,* 15 Cal. 2d 731, Tuesday 07/30/1940, http://scocal.stanford .edu /opinion/people-v-kynette-23692. Like Keenan, Williams was known for front-page criminal cases, for example, the successful prosecution of a barber who had drowned his wife to collect her insurance money, after he first failed to kill her by exposing her feet to rattlesnakes. Williams's recruitment was reported by AP on April 13, 1946, with emphasis on the notorious barber case and was picked up by local newspapers. One, the *Harrisburg Telegraph,* led with the headline "Williams Will Direct Case Against Tojo."
55. Justice Department facilities were in addition to US Army Centers and special War Relocation Authority Centers. See Tetsuden Kashima, *Judgment Without Trial: Japanese American Imprisonment During World War II* (Seattle: University of Washington Press, 2003), 10–13.
56. Chief of Counsel, "Conference with Mr. Eugene Williams," 22 April 1948, UVALL, box 2, folder 1, MSS1 78-3.
57. Keenan to Staff, "Assignment," 30 April 1946, UVALL, sec. 1, folder 4, MSS1 Su 863 a.

7. The Trial Begins

1. The court entrances and the restrooms were segregated and the War Ministry cafeteria was off-limits except for Allied officials and their guests.
2. D. N. Sutton, Memo at Tokyo #3, Opening Session, VHS Sutton Collection, box 11, folder 49.
3. Arnold Brackman, *The Other Nuremberg: The Untold Story of the Tokyo War Crimes Trial* (New York: Collins, 1987), 98–111.
4. Itagaki had surrendered Singapore to British General Lord Louis Mountbatten, supreme allied commander of SEAC (Southeast Asia Command) from 1943 to May 1946. Kimura nearly missed being indicted because of the six-week delay in the British releasing him to the IMTFE. "Item 1—Kimura Heitaro," 29 March 1946, UVALL, box 8, folder 6, MSS 78-3.
5. IMTFE transcripts, 1:1–21. See the twenty-two volumes of R. John Pritchard and Sonia M. Zaide, eds., *The Tokyo War Crimes Trial: The Complete Transcripts of the Proceedings of the International Military Tribunal for the Far East* (New York: Gar-

land, 1981). Transcribed copies of the trial's proceedings are available at the US National Archives, http://www.archives.gov/research/captured-german-records/war-crimes-trials.html#asia. For a reference guide, see Paul S. Dull and Michael Takaaki Umemura, *The Tokyo Trials: A Functional Index to the Proceedings of the International Military Tribunal for the Far East*, Center for Japanese Studies, Occasional Papers No. 6 (Ann Arbor: University of Michigan Press, 1957). A valuable selection of documents also appears in Neil Boister and Robert Cryer, eds., *Documents on the Tokyo International Military Tribunal* (Oxford: Oxford University Press, 2008).

6. A copy of the May 3, 1946, indictment text was kept by Sutton and is available at UVALL, sec. 6, folder 20, MSS1 Su 863 a.
7. Arthur S. Comyns Carr, "The Judgment of the International Military Tribunal for the Far East," *Transactions of the Grotius Society* 34 (November 1948): 142.
8. British Embassy Tokyo to Foreign Office, "Indictment of Japanese Major War Criminals," 17 May 1946, PRO FO 371/57427.
9. Neil Boister and Robert Cryer, *The Tokyo International Military Tribunal: A Reappraisal* (Oxford: Oxford University Press, 2008), 157–59.
10. Count 46 referred to Canton, count 47 to Hankow, count 48 to Changsha, count 49 to Hengyang, and count 50 to Kweilin and Liuchow. The defendants for all these counts were listed as ARAKI, HASHIMOTO, HATA, HIRANUMA, HIROTA, ITAGAKI, KAYA, KIDO, MATSUI, MUTO, SUZUKI and UMEZU.
11. Brackman, *The Other Nuremberg*, 84–85. Brackman quotes Keenan's press release at the time of the indictment.
12. "Fourth meeting of the Evidence and Defendants Committee Chaired by Mr. Justice Mansfield who requests summary of interrogations," 2 May 1946, UVALL, box 1, folder 1, MSS 93-4.
13. "Proceedings of the Meeting Held in Room 364 at 9:30 A.M. on 4th May 1946," 4 May 1946, UVALL, box 1, folder 1, MSS 93-4, 2.
14. Ibid., 3.
15. Ibid., 2.
16. Keenan, "Evidence Memo," 4 May 1946, UVALL, box 1, folder 1, MSS 93-4.
17. Keenan, "Briefing of Interrogations," 4 May 1946, UVALL, box 1, folder 1, MSS 93-4. The thirteen categories were military aggression in Manchuria; military aggression in all China from 1937; economic aggression in China and Greater East Asia; methods of corruption and coercion in China and other occupied territories; Japan's general preparation for war; organization of Japanese politics and public opinion for war; collaboration between Japan, Germany, and Italy and aggression against French Indo-China and Thailand; aggression against

the Soviet Union; relations between Japan, Netherlands, and Portugal; murder; offences against prisoners of war and civilians; Japanese constitution; and the function of various offices held by defendants.

18. Sutton, "Brief of Atrocities, Class C Offenses CRIMES AGAINST HUMANITY COMMITTED BY JAPANESE TROOPS IN CHINA 1937–1945," n.d., University of Richmond Law School, Sutton Collection, Working and Personal Series, old folders 1–60, folder 4.
19. Ibid., 18–19.
20. Military Intelligence Division, War Department, Washington, D.C., *Biological Warfare: Activities and Capabilities of Foreign Nations,* 30 March 1946, NARA, RG 319, entry 154, box 10, sec. 111–13, part 111, 1.
21. Ibid., Addendum, "Appreciation of Biological Warfare," 1.
22. Ibid., 16.
23. "Development of Japanese Biological Warfare," USAFPAC, *Daily Intelligence Summary* #1561, 30 July 1946, MacArthur Archives, RG-4, box 33, folder 5.
24. "Development of Japanese Biological Warfare," USAFPAC, *Daily Intelligence Summary,* #1562, 31 July 1946, MacArthur Archives, RG-4, box 33, folder 5; "Development of Japanese Biological Warfare," USAFPAC, *Daily Intelligence Summary* III #1563, 1 August 1946, MacArthur Archives, RG-4, box 33, folder 5; "Development of Japanese Biological Warfare III," USAFPAC, *Daily Intelligence Summary* IV #1564, 2 August 1946, MacArthur Archives, RG-4, box 34, folder 1.
25. "Testimony regarding crimes committed by a Japanese Force," 11 May 1946, University of Richmond Law Library, Sutton Collection, Working and Personal Series, old folders 1–60, folder 17. No US Army officer witnessed the affidavit, which was translated by a T. Yamamoto. Hataba's address in Japan was noted as Shizuoka-ken, Ogasagun, Kawashiro-mura, Kurasawa, 358.
26. "A General Account of Japanese Poison Warfare in China, 1937–1945," n.d., University of Richmond Law School, Sutton Collection, Working and Personal Series, old folders 1–60, folder 17. In the upper right corner of the cover page Sutton jotted, "From Judge Hsiang 5/8/46."
27. Ibid., 2.
28. "Japanese Use of Chemical and Biological Weapons Against China," 5 May 1946, NARA, RG 496, entry 53, 343. Noted as from Keenan to GHQ, AFPAC (G-2), and Chief Chemical Officer.
29. Mr. Kenneth N. Parkinson and Colonel Thomas H. Morrow to Mr. Joseph B. Keenan, Chief of Counsel "Trial Brief," 13 May 1946, UVALL, box 2, folder 12, MSS 93-4.
30. Ibid., 9.

31. Ibid., 1.
32. Ibid., 7.
33. Ibid., 8. The Ichang mustard attacks were investigated and verified by an American officer. See Frederic J. Brown, *Chemical Warfare: A Study in Restraints* (New Brunswick, N.J.: Transaction Books, 2006), 247. See Walter E. Grunden, *Secret Weapons and World War II: Japan in the Shadow of Big Science* (Lawrence: University of Kansas Press, 2005), 178–83, for further historical support of Morrow's evidence.
34. Central Liaison Office G-2 to Legal Section, "Tatsuzawa Tadao," 5 May 1946, University of Richmond Law School, Sutton Collection, Working and Personal Series, old folders 1–60, folder 17.
35. Arvo T. Thompson to Chief, Special Projects Division, CWS, "Interrogation of Mr. E. J. Bannon [*sic*] regarding Plague Incident in Changteh, China," 22 April 1946, University of Richmond Law School, Sutton Collection, Working and Personal Series, old folders 1–60, folder 17.
36. Ibid., 3.
37. Rev. Edward Joseph Bannan (Summary Record), 1 August 1952, Presbyterian Historical Society, Philadelphia, Pa., RG 360, box 11, folder 39.
38. Phyllis Kurtz Bannan, "Excerpts from letter to her children," 27 December 1943, Presbyterian Historical Society, Philadelphia, Pa., RG 360, box 11, folder 40.
39. IMTFE transcripts, 1:272–73.
40. Ibid., 274, 277.
41. Peter Williams and David Wallace, *Unit 731: Japan's Secret Biological Warfare in World War II* (New York: Free Press, 1989). See photograph facing p. 149.
42. Ulf Schmidt, *Secret Science: A Century of Poison Warfare and Human Experiments* (New York: Oxford University Press, 2015), 174–90.
43. *Rules of Land Warfare. 1 October 1940. War Department Field Manual FM27-10.* (Washington, D.C.: US Government Printing Office, 1947), para. 29, 8–9.
44. Herbert P. Bix, *Hirohito and the Making of Modern Japan* (New York: HarperCollins, 2000), 361–62.
45. Sheldon H. Harris, *Factories of Death: Japanese Biological Warfare, 1932–1945, and the American Cover-up* (New York: Routledge, 2002), 331–35.
46. *Intelligence Report on Japanese Chemical Warfare*." Vol. 1 (Tokyo: Office of the Chief Chemical Officer, GHQ, 15 May 1946). Available at the Combined Arms Research Digital Library, https://server16040.contentdm.oclc.org/cdm4/item_viewer.php?CISOROOT=/p4013coll8&CISOPTR=2071&CISOBOX=1&REC=2. Its first appendix is a heavily edited translation of "Lessons from the Chinese Incident,"

with maps, which had been used at the Narashino CW school to describe battle plans, including for the lethal Ichang attack in 1941.

47. Parkinson and Morrow, All China Military Aggression, 1937–1945, 24 May 1946, UVALL, box 3, folder 4, MSS 93-4, 32.
48. Ibid.
49. Ibid., appendix D, no. 9.
50. WARCOS to CINCAFPAC (FOR KEENAN IPS), ACTION: INTL PROSEC SECT, 1 June 1946, MacArthur Archives, RG-9, box 101, folder WD, 1–10 June 1946.
51. James Burnham Sedgwick, "The Trial Within: Negotiating Justice at the International Military Tribunal for the Far East, 1946–1948" (Ph.D. Thesis, University of British Columbia, 2012), 172–73.
52. "General Order 26 (G-2)," 2 June 1946, UVALL, box 1, folder 4, MSS 78-4.
53. Chief of Counsel (Keenan) to Staff, "Interrogations," 4 June 1946, UVALL, box 3, folder 1, MSS 78-3. As Keenan warned: "This order applies to all interrogations wherever conducted."
54. Ibid.
55. Sutton to Keenan, "Trip to China to secure witnesses," 13 June 1946, VHS, Sutton Collection, box 1, folder 6, (Administration Memoranda). For Sutton's trip notes, see D. N. Sutton, China, 31 May–12 June 1946, University of Richmond Law Library, Sutton Collection, old addition 2, folder 3.
56. The minister then asked that two criminal case files sent to IPS be returned, as the two accused were soon to go on trial. He said he would like the remainder of 150 other case files to also be returned—an indication of the volume of material China was reviewing.
57. Testimony of Wu Chang Teh, IPS Document 2119, Exhibit 207.
58. Testimony of Lewis S. C. Smythe, 7 June 1946, IPS Document 1921, Exhibit 306.
59. Sutton wrote in his diary that "the proprietor [is] an artist at preparing and cooking food."
60. Invitational Travel Orders, by Command of Lieutenant General Gillem, 20 June 1946, Shanghai China, UVALL, sec. 1, folder 6, MSS 1 Su 863 a. The travel orders were listed for Fitch, Bates, Gill, Lawless, Dorrance, Captain Liang Ting-Fang, Dr. Hsu Chuan-Ying, Dr. Sun K. Chen, Wang Len Cai, Shang Teh-Yi, Chen Fu Pao, Wu Chang Teh, Hsu G. J. [Chieh-Chun], and [General] Ching Teh-Tsun.
61. "Rape of Nanking," n.d., UVALL, box 1, folder 1, MSS 2012-1, item 227. Given its content, the United Press article likely appeared June 9, 1946.
62. Tavenner to Keenan, 10 June 1946, UVALL, box 3, folder 1, MSS 78-3.
63. Brackman, *The Other Nuremberg*, 115.

64. "Even the Judge Dozes as Tojo's Trial Proceeds," *Chicago Tribune*, June 14, 1946. In the afternoon Webb awoke and testily urged Nolan to "cut it shorter" and soon after adjourned the court for the day.
65. R. H. Quilliam to Mr McIntosh, 17 June 1946, *Documents on New Zealand External Relations*. Vol. 2: *The Surrender and Occupation of Japan*, ed. Robin Kay (Wellington, N.Z.: P. D. Hasselberg, 1982), 1597–1600.
66. Ibid., 25 June 1945, 1601–04.
67. Commander John Shea, "Summary Brief of Interrogation of Matsuoka, Yosuke," 24 May 1946, UVALL, box 2, folder 3, MSS 78-3.
68. Kayoko Takeda, *Interpreting the Tokyo War Crimes Tribunal: A Sociopolitical Analysis* (Ottawa: University of Ottawa Press, 2010), 19–21.
69. Roy L. Morgan to John Gold, Chief of Police, Winston-Salem, 16 July 1946, UVALL, box 11, folder 2, MSS 93-4.
70. *FRUS, 1946 The Far East: China*. Vol. 9. The Mission of General of the Army George C. Marshall to China to Arrange the Cessation of Civil Strife and to Bring About Political Unification. "Memorandum by General Chou En-lai to General Marshall," Nanjing, 12 June 1946, 1034–35; ibid., "Memorandum by General Hsu Yung-chang to General Marshall," 1035.
71. Ibid., "Joint Statement of General Marshall and Dr. Stuart," 10 August 1946.
72. G. Yamaoka to All Defense Counsel, 8 May 1947, UVALL, box 2, folder 1, MSS 78-4. Barrett's affidavit was entered as evidence on August 7, 1946, with the understanding that he could be called later as a witness. It was not until May 12, 1947, that he was cross-examined by the defense, which was unable to shake his testimony.
73. Higgins to Staff, Memo re No Publicity, 1 July 1946, UVALL, box 1, folder 7, MSS 1 Su 863 a; R. H. Quilliam to Mr McIntosh, 2 July 1946, *Documents on New Zealand*, 1608.

8. The Atrocities

1. R. H. Quilliam to Mr McIntosh, 15–16 June 1945, *Documents on New Zealand External Relations*. Vol. 2: *The Surrender and Occupation of Japan*, ed. Robin Kay (Wellington, N.Z.: P. D. Hasselberg, 1982), 1621–26.
2. Yuki Takatori, "The Forgotten Judge at the Tokyo War Crimes Trial," *Massachusetts Historical Journal* 10 (2008): 129.
3. Thomas Haycroft, "Plague, Politics, and Policy: The Decision to Grant Immunity to Suspected Japanese Biological Warfare War Criminals," master's thesis, US Joint Military Intelligence College, 1999, 62–68.

4. Washington (Joint Chiefs of Staff) to CINCAFPAC (MacArthur), 24 July 1946, NARA, RG 153, entry 145, box 73, 000.5, 2.
5. Robert Donihi, "War Crimes," *St. John's Law Review* 66, no. 9 (1991): 746.
6. R. H. Quilliam to Mr McIntosh, 26 July 1946, *Documents on New Zealand External Relations,* 1631–34.
7. Arnold Brackman, *The Other Nuremberg: The Untold Story of the Tokyo War Crime Trials* (New York: Collins, 1987), 193.
8. Ibid., 194.
9. "History Professor Gives Account of Nanking Rape," *Pacific Stars and Stripes,* July 30, 1946.
10. Affidavit of Katsuo Okazaki, attached to [Sutton] "Brief of Atrocities Class C Offenses. Crimes Against Humanity Committed by Japanese Troops in China 1937–1945," n.d., UVALL, sec. 5, folder 19, MSS 1 Su 863 a.
11. Letter from Joseph B. Keenan to Harry S. Truman, 1 August 1946, accompanied by a reply from Matthew Connelly, 8 August 1946, Official File, Truman Papers, Harry S. Truman Presidential Library and Museum, https://www.trumanlibrary.org/whistlestop/study_collections/nuremberg/documents/index.php?documentid=2-6&pagenumber=2.
12. Morgan to District Court Judge Johnston J. Hays, Williamsboro, N.C., 2 August 1946, UVALL, box 11, folder 2, MSS 93-4. Morgan wrote: "General Golunsky, who is Minister of Justice in Russia, and associated with our prosecution, has just left my office. He brought me news of the fact that Russia was willing to turn over to us the former Emperor of Manchuria, one Henry Pu Yi, who will make a very outstanding witness as to Japan's military aggression of Manchuria and how they set him up as Emperor there."
13. Affidavit of Ai-Sin-Cho-Lo PU YI, IPS Document No. 2456, UVALL, box 1, folder 1, MSS 2012-1.
14. "Tells of Japs 'Assembly Line' Killing of 5000," AP Tokyo, Japan, 7 August 1946 (AP), UVALL, box 1, folder 1, MSS 2012-1.
15. Samuel L. Leiter, "Performing the Emperor's New Clothes: *The Mikado, The Tale of Genji,* and Lesé Majesté," in *Rising from the Flames: The Rebirth of Theater in Occupied Japan,* ed. Samuel L. Leiter, 125–63 (London: Rowman & Littlefield, 2009).
16. Exhibit No. 436. "Regent's Ordinance" *Manchukuo Government Gazette,* vol. 1, 1 April 1932, 7–10.
17. Henry Pu Yi, *The Last Manchu. The Autobiography of Henry Pu Yi Last Emperor of China,* ed. Paul Kramer, trans. Kuo Ying Paul Tsai (New York: G. P. Putnam's Sons, 1967), 228.

18. Sutton to Mr. Eugene Williams, "Atrocities Against Civilians and Others in China-Order of Presentation of Evidence," 12 August 1946, UVALL, box 6, folder 5, MSS 78-4.
19. IMTFE Document 2466, Exhibit 309. Diary Notes Written by Mr. J. H. McCullen, Japanese Occupation of Nanjing—December 1938-January 1939.
20. Document 1702, Exhibit 324. The mortality figures presented were the Tsung-shan-tang, 112, 266; Red Swastika Society, 43,071; Shia Kwan District, 26,000; stated by Mr. Lu Su, 57,400; stated by Mssrs. Jui, Chang, and Young, 7,000 or more; stated by Mr. Wu, Epitaph on the Tomb of Unknown Victims, 3,000 or more. Total 260,000.
21. Eugene D. Williams, "Processing of Documents," 12 September 1946. UVALL, box 3, folder 4, MSS 78-3.
22. Peter Williams and David Wallace, *Unit 73: Japan's Secret Biological Warfare in World War II* (New York: Free Press, 1989), 150–52.
23. Morrow to Keenan, 17 October 1946, Harvard Law School Library, Joseph Berry Keenan Papers, box 1, folder 11. As his family remembered, Morrow remained discontented about the evidence suppression. William C. Morrow (grandson, personal communication), June 8, 2007.
24. "Development of Japanese Biological Warfare," *Daily Intelligence Summary* No. 1562, 31 July 1946, MacArthur Archives, USAFPAC *Daily Intelligence Summary*.
25. IPS Document 9305, "Questionnaire" (Kawashima), 12 September 1946, UVALL, box 6, folder 1, MSS 78-3.
26. IPS Document 9309, "Interrogation Report-P.O.W.-Kwantung Army, Major General Kawashima, Kiyoshi, at Khabarovsk on September 12–16, 1946," NARA, RG 153, entry 145, box 73.
27. IPS Document 9306, "Statement of Major Karasawa, Tomio," n.d., presumably in mid-September 1946, NARA RG 153, entry 145, box 73.
28. Ibid., 8–9.
29. Ibid., 11.
30. Peter Williams and David Wallace, *Unit 731: The Japanese Army's Secret of Secrets* (New York, Free Press, 1989), 184. In 1939 Ikari Tsuneshige was the leader of Ishii's suicide team at Nomonhan. For their book, the authors interviewed Soviet prosecutor Mark Raginsky, who claimed nothing was heard for three months after the affidavits were brought to Keenan's office in September 1946.
31. As early as May 1946 Carpenter was alerted to medical atrocities involving US POWs at Sagamigahara (Tokyo) Army Hospital, which became part of case file #290. See "SAGAMIGAHARA Army Hospital," 8 May 1946, NARA, RG 331, entry 1331, box 1771.

32. Philip R. Piccigallo, *The Japanese on Trial: Allied War Crimes Operations in the East, 1945–1951* (Austin: University of Austin Press, 1979), 93. The physician was Fujii Hiroshi. Piccigallo described other such trials throughout his book.
33. "Apprehension of Suspected War Criminals," 11 July 1946 (SCAPIN 1062), NARA, RG 331, entry UD 1098, box 4; "Apprehension of Suspected War Criminals," 22 July 1946 (SCAPIN 1075), ibid.
34. "Report on War Criminals," 23 August 1946, NARA, RG 331, entry 1771, box Nishimura, Takeshi.
35. "Affidavit of Takeshi KINO," 26 June 1946, NARA, RG 331, entry 1331, box LS/ID.
36. Carpenter's requests began in July 1946 and continued for months: "Motiji YAMAGUCHI et al.," 6 July 1946, NARA, JWC, folder 331, entry 1295, box 1434; "Motoji Yamaguchi et al.," Legal Section Case 330, 11 November 1946, NARA, JWC, RG 331, entry 1331, box 1762.
37. "Court Told Japan," 4 September 1946, UVALL, sec. 14, box 64, MSS 1 SU 863 a.
38. Brackman, *The Other Nuremburg*, 244.
39. The Robert Jackson Center film archive contains footage of Lev Smirnov at Nuremberg IMT, http://www.youtube.com/watch?v=oLAPq5Ydg5U&list=PL87B9A36B3B515FB6.
40. Telford Taylor, *The Anatomy of the Nuremberg Trial* (New York: Knopf, 1992), 313–18.
41. James J. Robinson, "Surprise Attack: Crime and Pearl Harbor and Now," *American Bar Association Journal* 46 (September 1960): 974.
42. Brackman, *The Other Nuremburg*, 240.
43. Ibid., 242.
44. Communication from Major General Vasiliev, 21 October 1947, UVALL, box 6, folder 1, MSS 78-3.
45. Joseph B. Keenan, "Our Relations in the Far East as They Appear in the International Military Tribunal for the Far East," paper delivered at American Bar Association Meeting, October 30, 1946, read by Ottowell Sykes Lowe. Earl Gregg Swem Library, William and Mary College, Japanese War Trials Papers, 1945–1948, folder F, item 10.
46. Barak Kushner, *Men to Devils, Devils to Men: Japanese War Crimes and Chinese Justice* (Cambridge, Mass.: Harvard University Press, 2015), 71.
47. Ibid., 153–64. Kushner also described the highly-publicized trial involving the "100 Man Killing Contest," which found three low-level Japanese officers guilty of mass beheadings, and the trial and release of a top Japanese general, Okamura Yasuji, before the pursuit of war criminals in China ran down (164–82).

48. Ibid., 158.
49. To General MacArthur from Ueki Hiroshi, 4 October 1946, received by ATIS 11 October 1946, in LS file 330, NARA WC 242/28.
50. Legal Section, Investigative Division, NARA, RG 331, box 1434, 20, case 330.
51. IPS Documents 9305 and 9306.
52. IPS Document 9306.
53. "Statement of Hata Hikosaburo," 10 October 1945 (Harbin), UVALL, box 2, folder 1, MSS 78-3.
54. Williams and Wallace, *Unit 731*, 32. The authors reported that Tojo watched Ishii's movies of Unit 731 experiments until he developed an aversion to them. Their source was Tsuneichi Keiichi, *The Germ Warfare Unit That Disappeared* (Tokyo: Kai-Mei-sha, 1981), 162.
55. Memorandum for Major-General A. N. Vasiliev, Subject: Bacteriological Warfare, 13 December 1946, UVALL, box 3, folder 7, MSS 78-3. Whether Tavenner consulted with Associate Prosecutor Hsiang is undocumented. At his meeting with Tavenner, Sutton jotted a note to consult with Hsiang, but no record seems to exist that he did so.
56. Sutton, "All Military Aggression in China Including Atrocities Against Civilians and the Summary of Evidence and Note of Argument" (IPS Document 9580), 4 November 1946, UVALL, box 3, folder 6, MSS 78-3, x. The phrase, from Paul to the Romans 6:23, ends, "but the gift of God is eternal life in Christ Jesus Our Lord."

9. The Soviet Division Versus US Military Intelligence

1. "Correspondence Between Harry S. Truman and Francis Biddle 12 November 1946," Harry S. Truman Presidential Library and Museum, Truman Papers Official File 325b, International Military Tribunal-Nuremberg, 6, http://www.trumanlibrary.org/whistlestop/study_collections/nuremberg/documents/index.php?documentid=3-7&pagenumber=6.
2. Ibid. Truman was also impressed by Biddle's description of the change in attitude of defendants and their counsel from indifference to "a determination to fight for their lives" that helped assure the fairness of the trial and lead to a better overview of evidence.
3. "Correspondence Between Harry S. Truman and Robert Jackson Accompanied by Related Correspondence October 17, 1946," Harry S. Truman Presidential Library and Museum , Truman Papers Official File 325b, International Military Tribunal-Nuremberg, Correspondence, http://www.trumanlibrary.org

/whistlestop/study_collections/nuremberg/documents/index.php?documentdate=1946-10-17&documentid=2-7&pagenumber=1).

4. Keenan to Mrs. Joseph B. Keenan, 4 November 1946, Harvard Law Library Special Collections, Joseph B. Keenan Papers, box 2, folder 6. Keenan began his letter by inviting his wife to come with their daughter to spend the Christmas holidays in Tokyo, where he was sure, because of insider connections, he could find them comfortable accommodations and even take them on a tour of China and possibly India.
5. Pechkoff, a close friend of General de Gaulle and the French liaison to SCAP, paved the way for MacArthur to receive the Légion d'Honneur. Thanks to MacArthur's admiration for Pechkoff, General Willoughby, "on a strictly personal basis, without authority from Washington," was updating the French military on GHQ defense plans. See "Le Capitaine de Frégate GILLY à M. le Général Pechkoff, Tokyo, le 10 octobre 1947," Ministre des Affaires Étrangères Archives Séries E, Asie-Océanie Japon, vol. 190/4, 128–29.
6. Pechkoff, le 8 octobre 1947, Ministre des Affaires Étrangères Archives, Séries E, Asie-Océanie Japon, vol. 190/4, 124.
7. Keenan to Mrs. Keenan. He respected the Indian prosecutors and the French and Canadian judges and thought Pedro Lopez "an experienced and able man, and I think quite a kindly and understanding one." He also appreciated the "large and beautiful" personally autographed portrait of Chiang Kai-shek given him by Judge Hsiang of the Chinese Division.
8. Tavenner to Lea, 21 November 1946, UVALL, box 3, folder 6, MSS 78-3.
9. James Burnham Sedgwick, "The Trial Within: Negotiating Justice at the International Military Tribunal for the Far East, 1946–1948," Ph.D. diss., University of British Columbia, 2012, 53.
10. Keenan to Golunsky, 18 October 1946, Harvard Law Library Special Collections, Joseph B. Keenan Collection, box 2, folder 4.
11. Tavenner to Lea, 21 November 1946.
12. Ibid.
13. Robert Donihi, "War Crimes," *St. John's Law Review* 66, no. 3, article 9 (1991): 762. Donihi, close to John Darsey from Justice, criticized Keenan for marginalizing Darsey. For other critical opinions from staff, see Sedgwick, *The Trial Within*, 63–64.
14. Lea quickly followed up, communicating through other IPS staff. See "Telecon," 18 December 1946, UVALL, box 3, folder 7, MSS 78-3.
15. Eugene Williams, "Preparation of Cases Against Individual Defendants," 21 November 1946, UVALL, box 3, folder 6, MSS 78-3.

16. Keenan to Mrs. Keenan.
17. Keenan, "Memo to Associate Prosecutors and Assistant Counsel of the American Staff," 27 November 1946, UVALL, box 3, folder 6, MSS 78-3.
18. "Testimony Regarding Crimes Committed by a Japanese Force," 11 May 1946, University of Richmond Law Library, Sutton Collection, Personal and Working Series, old folders 1-60, folder 17. On his copy Sutton jotted: "11/4/46 requested Hataba appearance" without any more information recorded.
19. R. H. Quilliam to A. H. McIntosh, 2 December 1946, *Documents on New Zealand External Relations*. Vol. 2: *The Surrender and Occupation of Japan*, ed. Robin Kay (Wellington, N.Z.: P. D. Hasselberg, 1982), 1649–51.
20. Tavenner to Sutton, 4 December 1946, UVALL, box 3, folder 6, MSS 78-3. Tavenner apparently also helped Mansfield edit his presentation.
21. Eugene D. Williams to Mr Tavenner et al., "Circulation of Information," 4 December 1946, UVALL, box 3, folder 7, MSS 78-3.
22. Tavenner to Keenan, "Update of Trial Situation," 6 December 1946, UVALL, box 3, folder 7, MSS 78-3.
23. Williams to Tavenner.
24. Williams, "Trial Strategies," 4 December 1946, UVALL, box 3, folder 7, MSS 78-3.
25. "Memorandum for Major-General A. N. Vasiliev, Subject: Bacteriological Warfare," 13 December 1946, UVALL, box 3, folder 7, MSS 78-3. Tavenner made a generalized use of the word experiments that obscured whether he was referring to human experimentation or preparations for biological warfare or both.
26. Ibid.
27. "Statement of Major Tomio Karsaw [*sic*]," 12 September 1946, NARA, folder 331, entry 1901, box 1.
28. "Yamaguchi et al" Legal Section Case 330, 3 December 1946, NARA, RG 331, entry 1331, box 1762.
29. "Interrogation of Dr. Kiyushui Ota," 2 December 1946, NARA, RG 112, entry 295A, box 6, folder 27: Subject: Bacteriological Warfare.
30. *Trials of War Criminals Before the Nuernberg [Nuremberg] Military Tribunal Under Council Control Law No. 10*. Vol. 1: *The Medical Case* (Washington, D.C.: US Government Printing Office, 1952). Transcript available at the US National Archives, Records of the U.S. Nuernberg War Crimes Trials, United States of America v. Karl Brandt et al (Case 1), Nov. 21, 1946-Aug. 20, 1947, microfilm publication M887 (Medical Case). See Robert Jay Lifton, *The Nazi Doctors: Medical Killing and the Psychology of Genocide* (New York: Basic Books, 2000). Following the London Charter, the counts against the defendants were organized as A.

crimes of aggression, B. war crimes (largely involving POWs), and C. crimes against humanity involving civilians. The court decided that crimes of aggression were beyond the scope of the charges.

31. Documentation and commentary on the twelve Nuremberg Military Trials, including Taylor's opening address, is widely available. See, for example, the University of Georgia online archive, http://digitalcommons.law.uga.edu/cgi/viewcontent.cgi?article=1000&context=nmtl.
32. A photocopy of the Doctors' Trial indictment ("The United States against Karl Brandt et al.") is available through Harvard Law School, http://nuremberg.law.harvard.edu/php/search.php?DI=1&FieldFlag=1&PAuthors=336).
33. Sedgwick, *The Trial Within*, 239–41.
34. Keenan to Mrs. Keenan. Derevyanko was especially high-spirited. At a party at the Imperial Hotel for an Occupation general, Beata Sirota, the SCAP translator who helped introduce women's rights into the Japanese constitution, recalled how Derevyanko picked her and his secretary up, one under each arm, and carried them. See Beata Sirota Gorden, *The Only Woman in the Room: A Memoir* (New York: Kodasha International, 1997), 27.
35. "Report by the British Commonwealth Member, Allied Council for Japan, September 1946," *Documents on New Zealand External Relations*, 2:1200–1202; "Report by the British Commonwealth Member, Allied Council for Japan, May 1947," ibid., 1229. The council's member for the British Commonwealth, Macmahon Bell, described chronic "clashes" and "bickering" between Atcheson, from the State Department, and Derevyanko. Atcheson's career was cut short by his death in a plane accident on August 16, 1947, while he was on route to a meeting in Washington. Derevyanko was soon thereafter recalled to Moscow.
36. Telford Taylor, *The Anatomy of the Nuremberg Trials* (New York: Knopf, 1992), 314. Smirnov was also given the onerous task of arguing that the Germans had killed Polish officers in the Katyn Forest massacre in 1940, a crime committed by the Soviet Army (470–71).
37. Ibid., 313–14.
38. Valentyna Polunina, "The Khabarovsk Trial," in *Trials for International Crimes in Asia*, ed. Kirsten Sellars (Cambridge: Cambridge University Press, 2016), 121–44.
39. Maj-General Vasiliev to Maj-Gen Willoughby through IPS, "Memorandum," 9 January 1947, NARA, RG 153, entry 145, box 73.
40. Tavenner to Vasiliev, "Memorandum," 13 January 1947, UVALL, box 4, folder 1, MSS 78-3.
41. LTC McQuail to G-2, "Bacteriological Experiments," 17 January 1947, NARA, RG 331, entry 1901, box 1.

42. Xiang Longwan and Marquise Lee Houle, "In Search of Justice for China: The Contributions of Judge Hsiang Che-Chun to the Prosecution of Japanese War Criminals at the Tokyo Trial," in *Historical Origins of International Criminal Law*. Vol. 2, ed. Morten Bergsmo, Cheah Wui, and Yi Ping (TOAEP Torkel Opsahl Academic EPublishers, 2014), 155–56.
43. Eiji Takemae, *Inside GHQ: The Allied Occupation of Japan and Its Legacy*, trans. Robert Ricketts and Sebastian Swann (New York: Continuum, 2002), 318–21; David Flath, *The Japanese Economy* (New York: Oxford University Press, 2005), 75.
44. Takemae, *Inside GHQ*, 321.
45. Solis Horwitz, "The Tokyo Trial," *International Conciliation*, no. 465 (November 1950): 526.
46. "Telecon," 29 January 1947, UVALL, box 4, folder 1, MSS 78-3.
47. Okawa, confined to a mental institution, was assigned to Tavenner and Tojo to Dunnigan; Lopez, Robinson, and Edwards were assigned Muto, and Robinson and Edwards were to handle Itagaki.
48. Sutton Diary, Memo 1947–8, 18 February 1947, University of Richmond Law School, Sutton Collection, addition 2.
49. The second was Daniel A. Ao, dean of the Souchow University Law School, with a degree from Lincoln University Law School in California, and the third was Wu Hsueh-yi, who was fluent in Japanese. In a memo to Tavenner, Hsiang described all their credentials (Hsiang to Tavenner, "New Technical Assistants of Chinese Division," 12 February 1947, UVALL, box 4, folder 2, MSS 78-3).
50. Frank S. Tavenner to Mr. Chen-Chun Hsiang, Judge Judson T. Y. Nye, Dr. Daniel A. Ao, and Mr Hsuah-Yi Wu, "Assignments for New Technical Assistants of Chinese Division," 13 February 1947, UVALL, box 4, folder 2, MSS 78-3. Tavenner directed Judge Nye to cover the Lytton Report and the other three "gentlemen" to address aspects of the Manchurian and China phases that had not been read into the record.
51. Keenan to Tavenner, Radiogram, 25 February 1947. UVALL, box 4, General Reports and Memoranda from February 1947, MSS 78-4. "You are to take complete charge of all matters in the courtroom in my absence," Keenan wrote. Tavenner immediately asked for clarification as to his duties to be communicated to the Chief of Staff. See: Tavenner to Keenan, 26 February 1947, UVALL, box 4, folder 4, MSS 78-4.
52. Horwitz, "Tokyo Trial," 526.
53. See Beth Van Schaak, "*Crimen Sine Lege*: Judicial Lawmaking at the Intersection of Law and Morals," *Georgetown Law Journal* 97 (2008): 119–92.

54. Opening Statement of Division 1 (Defense), n.d., UVALL, box 4, folder 3, MSS 78-4, 5; see also IMTFE transcripts, 7:17004–28.
55. For a view from a defense lawyer, see George F. Blewett, "Victor's Injustice: The Tokyo War Crimes Trial," *American Perspective* 4, no. 3 (Summer 1950): 282–92.
56. Keenan to Tavenner, 28 March 1947, UVALL, box 4, General Reports and Memoranda for March 1947, MSS 78-4. Keenan acknowledged Tavenner's friendship with Higgins and the difficulty the decision might cause.
57. Tavenner to Keenan, 16 May 1947, UVALL, box 4, folder 4, MSS 78-3.
58. Willis Mahoney to Keenan, 22 April 1947, UVALL, box 4, folder 5, MSS 78-3.
59. Opening Statement of Division 1 (Defense), 4.
60. "The Former Chief Justice (Myers) to the New Zealand Member, International Military Tribunal for the Far East," 24 April 1947, *Documents on New Zealand External Relations*, 1667–68.
61. Tavenner to G. Osmond Hyde, 9 May 1947, UVALL, box 4, folder 5, MSS 78-3.
62. Tavenner to War Department, "Captain Robinson Leave," 13 February 1947, UVALL, box 4, folder 8, MSS 78-3.
63. Luke Lea to Sutton, 18 April 1947, David Nelson Sutton Collection, University of Richmond Law Library, General and Personal Correspondence, folder 107.
64. "Trial Update on the Soviet Phase," UVALL, box 4, folder 5, MSS 78-3.
65. Willis Mahoney to Joseph B. Keenan, "Tavenner's Work," 22 April 1947, UVALL, box 4, folder General Reports and Memoranda from May 1947; Keenan to Tavenner, "Ozzie Hyde," 3 June 1947, UVALL, box 5, folder 1, MSS 78-3. As Keenan explained, Hyde wanted to remain on the Justice Department payroll while working at IPS, an arrangement Justice refused. Hyde remained at Justice rather than accept the $10,000 yearly salary offered by IPS.
66. "Memo for Record on Russian Request to Interrogate Japanese on Bacteriological Warfare," 7 February 1947, NARA, RG 331, entry 1901, box 1.
67. "State-War-Navy Coordinating Subcommittee for the Far East, Request of Russian Prosecutor for Permission to Interrogate Certain Japanese" (SFE 188), 26 February 1947, NARA, RG 166, box 628, SWNCC 351.
68. Lt. General Derevyanko, USSR/Allied Council for Japan to SCAP, 7 March 1947, NARA, RG 331, entry 1901, box 1.
69. "Report by the British Commonwealth Member, Allied Council for Japan, February 1947," *Documents on New Zealand External Relations*, 1218. On February 6, 1947, MacArthur consulted with ACJ representatives about a letter he intended to send to the prime minister to urge a general election, following the destabilization caused by MacArthur's cancellation of the February 1 strike, and before the new May constitution. Derevyanko thought the letter should be delayed

pending the council's deliberations. "General MacArthur replied with some feeling that he could not hold up his action to enable it to be debated." The meeting finished at 11:30 a.m. and, as planned, MacArthur's letter was issued to the press at 1:30.

70. Army OPD, Policy and Plans, to CINCFE, "Request of Russian Prosecutor for Permission to Interrogate," 26 March 1947, NARA, RG 163, entry 421, box 25. The number of the directive under SWNCC had been 351/1, which became JCS 1753 and then, with the final directive for SCAP, WAR 94446.
71. SCAP to LTG Derevyanko, USSR/Allied Council Japan, "Memorandum 1087," 10 April 1947, NARA, RG 331, box 1.
72. *Daily Intelligence Summary* #1759, 25 March 1947, MacArthur Archives, RG-6 FECOM, Intelligence 12.
73. The letter also mentioned that "intestinal suffocation" and tubercular bacteria were being studied.
74. "Motoji Yamaguchi et al.," 28 January 1947, NARA, RG 331, entry 1294, box 1434, and entry 1331, box 1772.
75. "Shiro Ishii, His Rise to Power," 10 February 1947, NARA, RG 331, entry 1294, box 1434. Ishii faced allegations that he and his two brothers had stolen money, uniforms, and equipment from the Japanese Army. See Sheldon Harris, *Factories of Death: Japanese Biological Warfare, 1932–1945, and the American Cover-up* (New York: Routledge, 2002), 246.
76. Motoji Yamaguchi et al., "Statement by Takeshi Kino," 6 March 1947, NARA, JWC, RG 331, entry 1331, box 1772.
77. Motoji Yamaguchi et al., "Affidavit of Mamoru Ouchi," 14 March 1947, NARA, RG 331, entry 1294, box 1434, folder 19.
78. "Statement by Tomosada Masuda," 13 March 1947, NARA, RG 331, entry 1331, box 1772.
79. "Interrogation of Ikari, Tsunoshigo," 10 May 1947, NARA, IWG Collection, Dugway "A," item 6, JWC 228/10; "Interrogation of Ota, Kiyoshi (aka Ota Akira)," 10 May 1947, NARA IWG Collection Dugway "A," item 6, JWC 228/09. A third Ishii scientist was also interviewed that day: "Interrogation of Murakami, Takashi," 10 May 1947, NARA IWG Collection Dugway "A," item 6, JWC 228/08.
80. Harris, *Factories of Death*, 266–69.
81. "Interrogation of Tomosada Masuda," 22 April 1947, NARA, IWG Reference Collection, Dugway "A," item 6, JWC 228/02.
82. Norbert E. Fell, Chief, Field Division, to Assistant Chief of Staff G-2 [Willoughby], GHQ, Far East Command, Through Technical Director, Camp Detrick, 24 June

1947, memo on meetings 26, 29, and 30 April and 1 May 1947, NARA, IWG Collection, Dugway "A," item 6, JWC 228/02.

83. G-2 to LS, "Legal Section Invest Div Report 330," 17 April 1947, NARA, RG 259, folder 8.
84. "Motoji YAMAGUCHI et al.," 17 April 1947, NARA, RG 331, entry 1294, box 1434.
85. SCAP FILE List 000.5 (ts) War Crimes File #1, Sep. 1945–Dec. 1946, NARA, RG 331, 1891, 1; Yuma Totani, *The Tokyo War Crimes Trial: The Pursuit of Justice in the Wake of World War II* (Cambridge, Mass.: Harvard University Asia Center, 2008), 52–58.
86. Takemae, *Inside GHQ*, 126–27.
87. CINCFE to WDGID, "OPERATIONAL PRIORITY," 6 May 1947, NARA, RG 165, entry 421, box 25.
88. Ibid., 1.
89. Ibid.
90. "Interrogation of Murakami, Takashi, 13 May 1947," UVALL Tavenner Papers, General Reports and Memoranda, 10 June 1947, box 5.
91. "Interrogation of Ota, Kiyoshi, 16 May 1947," UVALL Tavenner Papers, General Reports and Memoranda, 14 July 1947, box 5. Tavenner was obviously kept advised of Smirnov's efforts.

10. National Security Versus Medical Ethics

1. Ulf Schmidt, *Karl Brandt: The Nazi Doctor. Medicine and Power in the Third Reich* (London: Continuum, 2007), 362–63; Arthur L. Kaplan, ed., *When Medicine Went Mad: Bioethics and the Holocaust* (Totowa, N.J.: Humana Press, 1992).
2. Schmidt, *Karl Brandt*, 376–77. The project was revealed in a *Life Magazine* article in June 1945. During the war the US Army had been a major sponsor of human research, seeking to protect troops by learning more about how to cure or prevent malaria, Dengue fever, sand fly sickness, and sleeping sickness, with medical studies conducted on prison populations in Massachusetts, New Jersey, New York, Texas, Georgia, and Pennsylvania. Compensation for the prisoners was either $100 in cash or consideration for parole or sentence reduction, at the risk of debilitation and perhaps death.
3. Records of the U.S. Nuernberg War Crimes Trials, United States of America v. Karl Brandt et al (Case 1), Nov. 21, 1946–Aug. 20, 1947, NARA, microfilm publication M887 (Medical Case), 2383.
4. US Centers for Disease Control, "Findings from a CDC Report on the 1946–1948 U.S. Public Health Service Sexually Transmitted Disease (STD) Inocu-

lation Study," 30 September 2010, http:/www.hhs.gov/1946inoculationstudy/findings.html. The study was discovered by Susan Reverby through research on her book *Examining Tuskegee: The Infamous Syphilis Study and its Legacy* (Chapel Hill: University of North Carolina Press, 2009), which recounts the thirty-year US research exploitation of black men in the South.

5. Clarence G. Lasby, *Project Paperclip: German Scientists and the Cold War* (New York: Scribner's, 1975), 191–204. Lasby describes the divided ranks among the Federation of American Scientists that caused the outcry to disappear in a matter of months. See also Linda Hunt, *Secret Agenda: The United States Government, Nazi Scientists and Project Paperclip, 1944–1990* (New York: St. Martin's Press, 1991), 36.
6. Lasby, *Project Paperclip*, 191–93. Einstein was joined by Dr. Norman Vincent Peale, Rabbi Stephen Wise, and other respected figures.
7. H. A. Bethe and H. S. Sack, "German Scientists in Army Employment," *Bulletin of the Atomic Scientists* 3, no. 2 (February 1947): 65, 67. Because Bethe's mother was Jewish, he could find no employment in Nazi Germany in the 1930s and immigrated to America. In 1967 he was awarded a Nobel Prize. Published in conjunction with this letter was a commentary by Samuel Goudsmit, head of Alsos, whose parents had been killed by the Nazis. He argued that such bargains were in the national interest. See Samuel A. Goudsmit, "German Scientists in Army Employment," *Bulletin of the Atomic Scientists* 3, no. 2 (February 1947): 64, 67.
8. Ira Katznelson, *Fear Itself: The New Deal and the Origins of Our Time* (New York: Norton, 2013), 458–66.
9. Allen Weinstein and Alexander Vassiliev, *The Haunted Wood: Soviet Espionage in America—the Stalin Era* (New York: Random House, 1999).
10. Katznelson, *Fear Itself*, 428.
11. Ibid., 246–47.
12. Jonathan B. Tucker, *War of Nerves: Chemical Warfare from World War I to Al-Qaeda* (New York: Random House, 2005), 114–17.
13. Charles S. Maier, "The World Economy and the Cold War in the Middle of the Twentieth Century," in *The Cambridge History of the Cold War*. Vol. 1, ed. Melvyn P. Leffler and Odd Arne Westad, 44–66 (Cambridge: Cambridge University Press, 2009), 61.
14. Kenneth W. Condit, *History of the Joint Chiefs of Staff. The Joint Chiefs of Staff and National Policy*. Vol, 2: *1947–1949* (Washington, D.C.: Office of Joint History, Office of the Chairman of the Joint Chiefs of Staff, 1996), 237.
15. Takemae Eiji, *Inside GHQ: The Allied Occupation of Japan and Its Legacy*, trans. Robert Ricketts and Sebastian Swann (New York: Continuum, 2002), 164.

16. John W. Dower, "Occupied Japan and the Cold War in Asia," in *The Truman Presidency*, ed. Michael J. Lacey, 366–409 (Cambridge: Cambridge University Press, 1989).
17. "Report by the British Commonwealth Member, Allied Council for Japan, April 1947," May 6, 1947, in *Documents on New Zealand External Relations.* Volume 2: *The Surrender and Occupation of Japan*, ed. Robin Kay, 1226–28 (Wellington, N.Z.: P. D. Hasselberg, 1982), 1228.
18. Alva Carpenter, Legal Section, SCAP to War (WDSCA WC), 6 June 1947, NARA, RG 153, entry 145, box 73.
19. Seymour Hersh, *Chemical and Biological Warfare: America's Hidden Arsenal* (Indianapolis: Bobbs-Merrill, 1968), 202; Jeanne Guillemin, *Biological Weapons: From the Invention of State-Sponsored Programs to Contemporary Bioterrorism* (New York: Columbia University Press, 2005), 92–93.
20. Theodor Rosebury, *Peace or Pestilence: Biological Warfare and How to Avoid It* (New York: McGraw-Hill, 1949), 9.
21. Donald Avery, "The Canadian Biological Weapons Program and the Tripartite Alliance," in *Deadly Cultures: Biological Weapons Since 1945*, ed. Mark Wheelis, Lajos Rózsa, and Malcolm Dando, 84–131 (Cambridge, Mass.: Harvard University Press, 2006).
22. Barak Kushner, *Men to Devils, Devils to Men* (Cambridge, Mass.: Harvard University Press, 2016), 81–82. See also Ni Zhengyu, "Ni Zhengyu huiyilu, danpo congrong li haiya," in *Nanjing datusha shiliaoji*. Vol.7: *Dongjing shenpan*, ed. Yang Xiawu (Jiangsu renmin chubanshe, 2005).
23. IMTFE transcripts, 9:20478–79.
24. Ibid., 23778.
25. Arnold Brackman, *The Other Nuremberg: The Untold Story of the Tokyo War Crimes Trial* (New York: Collins, 1987), 338–39.
26. IMTFE transcripts, 10:23436.
27. Tavenner to Vasiliev, "Deane Affidavit," 4 June 1947, UVALL, box 5, folder 1, MSS 78-3.
28. Document 1627, Affidavit of General George C. Marshall; Tavenner to Vasiliev, "Memorandum," 4 June 1947, UVALL, box 5, folder 1, MSS 78-3. Advised in advance, Tavenner offered to help the Soviet Division present objections to the affidavit.
29. Valentyna Polunina, "The Khabarovsk Trial: The Soviet Riposte to the Tokyo Tribunal," in *Trials for International Crimes in Asia*, ed. Kirsten Sellars, 121–44 (Cambridge: Cambridge University Press, 2016), 124.
30. IMTFE transcripts, 19:46778.

31. Ibid., 10:23792.
32. R. H. Quilliam to A. D. McIntosh, *Documents on New Zealand External Relations*, 3 June 1947, 1672.
33. Tavenner to C. Higgins, 2 July 1947, UVALL, box 5, folder 2, MSS 78-3. Tavenner wrote that Russians indulged in too much cross-examination and lacked rigor: "I have the distinct feeling that our case has been strengthened all along the line except in the Russian phase." He noted that so far approximately 125 witnesses had testified for the defense and 55–60 of them were cross-examined.
34. "Intelligence Information on Bacteriological Weapons G-2," 9 June 1947, NARA, RG 153, entry 145, box 73.
35. "Brief Summary of New Information," 29 June 1947, NARA, IWG Reference Collection, Dugway "A," item 5, JWC 227.
36. "Claim CWS Head 'Whitewashes' His Own Office," *Chicago Tribune*, 21 July 1946.
37. Rexmond C. Cochrane, *Biological Warfare Research in the United States*. Vol. 2, part D, XXIII: *Chemical Plant Growth: History of the Chemical Warfare Service in World War II (1 July 1940–15 August)* (Washington, D.C.: Office of Chief, Chemical Corps, 1947), 508–12.
38. United Nations (UN) General Assembly Resolution 1(I), "Establishment of a Commission to Deal with the Problem Raised by the Discovery of Atomic Energy," January 24, 1946. See also W. Seth Carus, *Defining "Weapons of Mass Destruction,"* Occasional Paper No. 8, National Defense University Center for the Study of WMD (Washington, D.C.: National Defense University Press, 2012).
39. Brian Balmer, *Britain and Biological Warfare: Expert Advice and Science Policy, 1930–65* (London: Palgrave, 2001), 79–85.
40. Norbert E. Fell to Chief, Chemical Corps, "Brief Summary of New Information About Japanese B.W. Activities," 20 June 1947, NARA, RG 175, entry 67A4900, box 196.
41. Ibid.
42. Ibid.
43. "Case File #330; Ishii Shiro, 1946–1948," Legal/Investigative Division, NARA, RG 331, entry 1331, box 1772.
44. Ross Coen, *Fu-go: The Curious History of Japan's Balloon Bomb Attacks on America* (Lincoln: University of Nebraska Press, 2013), 92.
45. "Affidavit Interrogation of Ishii Shiro," 13 June 1947, UVALL, box 5. folder 2, MSS 78-315.
46. Ibid., 13.
47. Ibid., 15.

48. Closing Brief for the United States of America Against Siegfried Handloser, Nurnberg [Nuremberg], June 16, 1947, James M. McHaney et al., Military Tribunal No. 1, Case 1, 34. Available at Harvard Law School Library Nuremberg Trial Project, http://nuremberg.law.harvard.edu/documents.
49. Fell, "Brief Summary."
50. G-2 (Tokyo) to G-2 (Washington), "Report of Bacteriological Warfare," 22 June 1947, NARA, RG 319, entry 164, folder 6.
51. *Rules of Land Warfare (1 October 1940)*, War Department Field Manual, FM 27–10 (Washington, D.C.: US Government Printing Office, 1947), rule 28, 8.
52. Ibid., rule 19, 6.
53. War Branch to Legal Section, "Draft Reply to C63169 & C62432," 20 June 1947, NARA, RG 331, entry 1901, folder 1.
54. CINCFE-Legal Section to WAR, "Incoming Classified Message," 27 June 1947, NARA, RG 163, entry 146, folder 73.
55. Ibid.
56. Ibid.
57. Left unmentioned was Field Marshall Hata, commander during the Zhejiang-Jiangxi campaign of 1942, when Ishii, Masuda, Ota, Karasawa and others orchestrated mass germ attacks on Chinese civilians.
58. CINCFE-Legal Section to WAR.
59. Tavenner to Carpenter, "BW Group," 30 June 1947, NARA, RG 331, entry 1294, box 1434. Tavenner's initial terse summaries deleted mention of human experimentation, but full translations of the two Soviet interviews were soon substituted, while the watered-down summaries of the Hata and Dr. King affidavits first presented were deleted.
60. Ibid.
61. Willoughby to Tavenner, "Report," 29 July 1947, UVALL, box 5, folder 2, MSS 78-3; Willoughby to Tavenner, "Matter Assigned to Lt. Col. McQuail," 3 July 1947, UVALL, box 5, folder 2, MSS 78-3.
62. "Report on Bacteriological Weapons," 17 July 1947, NARA, RG 319, entry NM347A, box 4; Willoughby to Chamberlin, 22 July 1947, ibid.
63. Sheldon Harris, *Factories of Death: Japanese Biological Warfare, 1932–1945, and the American Cover-up* (New York: Routledge, 2002), 297–305. Using archives then available, Harris outlined in detail the tensions between State and military representatives at SWNCC committees in the summer and fall of 1947.
64. "SFE 188/2, Interrogation of Certain Japanese by Russian Prosecutor," 8 August 1947, NARA, RG 165, entry 468, box 587. This estimate was shared with the JCS and SCAP.

65. "Interrogation of Certain Japanese by Russian Prosecutor (Comments on SWNCC 351/2/D)," 8 August 1947, NARA, RG 353, entry 514, box 89. By this argument, which was from State and Fearey, an unwritten agreement could suffice.
66. "Note by the Acting Secretary," SFE 188/2, State-War-Navy Coordinating Committee for the Far East, 1 August 1947, NARA, RG 153, entry 145, box 73; "SFE 188/2 Interrogation of Certain Japanese by Russian Prosecutor," 1 August 1947, NARA, RG 165, entry 468, box 587.
67. Memorandum to Commander J. B. Cresap, 15 July 1947, NARA, RG 153, entry 145, box 73.
68. Valentin Bojtzov and Erhard Geissler, "Military Biology in the USSR, 1920–45," in *Biological and Toxin Weapons: Research, Development and Use from the Middle Ages to 1945*, ed. Erhard Geissler and John Ellis van Courtland Moon, 153–67 (New York: Oxford University Press, 1999); Guillemin, *Biological Weapons*, 134–36; John Hart, "The Soviet Biological Weapons Program," in *Deadly Cultures: Biological Weapons Since 1945*, ed. Mark Wheelis, Lajos Rozsa, and Malcolm Dando, 132–56 (Cambridge, Mass.: Harvard University Press, 2006); Milton Leitenberg and Raymond Zelinskas, with Jens H. Kuhn, *The Soviet Biological Weapons Program: A History* (Cambridge, Mass.: Harvard University Press, 2012). In *The Dead Hand: The Untold Story of the Cold War Arms Race and Its Dangerous Legacy* (New York: Doubleday, 2009), David E. Hoffman places the Soviet proliferation of germ weapons in the Cold War context.
69. Col. Walter Hirsch, M.D., "Soviet BW and CW Preparations and Capabilities," US Army Chemical Intelligence Branch, 15 May 1951, Washington, D.C.; Heinrich Kliewe, "Bacterial War" (Der Bakterienkrieg), 19 January 1943, Alsos Mission, report no. CC-H/303 (Washington, D.C.: War Department), 1945.
70. Office of Naval Intelligence to Chairman, JCS and Secretary of Navy, "Naval Aspects of Biological Warfare," 8 August 1947, NARA, RG 330, entry 199, folder 103.
71. "Interrogation of Certain Japanese by Russian Prosecutors," 1 August 1947, NARA, RG 331, entry 1901, folder 1, appendix B, 7.
72. "B.W. Research in the United States. Draft Report to the Chiefs of Staff," 4 December 1947, PRO WO 188/705.
73. Sutton to Herbert Trotter Woodstock, 2 July 1947, Virginia Historical Society, Sutton Papers, MSS1 Su 868a, 20–21.
74. Sutton to L. Medlin, 29 July 1947, University of Richmond Law Library, Sutton Collection, General and Personal Correspondence, folder 106.
75. Author interview with Mrs. Frances Sutton Oliver (Sutton's daughter), October 28, 2011, Chesapeake, Va.

76. See M. Taylor Fravel, *Strong Border, Secure Nation: Cooperation and Conflict in China's Territorial Disputes* (Princeton, N.J.: Princeton University Press, 2008).
77. Diane Lary, *The Chinese People at War* (Cambridge: Cambridge University Press, 2010), 195.
78. "Update on Trial Situation," 3 December 1946, UVALL, box 3, folder 7, MSS 78-3.
79. MacArthur to JCS, Priority, 12 May 1947, NARA, RG 331, entry 1289, box 1416.
80. The announcement was reported back to Washington that day, with suggestions that personnel were being diverted to review the suspects' records. "Telecon Conference," 13 August 1947, UVALL, box 5, folder 4, MSS 78-3.
81. R. H. Quilliam to A. H. McIntosh, *Documents on New Zealand External Relations*, 13 September 1947, 1693. Quilliam, citing the *Nippon Times* article, noted the outrage felt at IPS.
82. Yuma Totani, *The Tokyo War Crimes Trial: The Pursuit of Justice in the Wake of World War II* (Cambridge, Mass.: Harvard University Asia Center, 2008), 72–77. Totani argued that the detainee problem might have been solved with successful trials had MacArthur and Keenan paid attention to it earlier.
83. Those who would testify were Tojo, Matsui, Koiso, Minami, Araki, Hashimoto, Itagaki, Kaya, Muto, Oka, Oshima, Shimada, Suzuki, and Togo. The others declining to testify were Dohihara, Hiranuma, Hirota, Hoshino, Kimura, and Sato.
84. "Memorandum to the Members of the Staff," 24 September 1947, UVALL, box 5, folder 5, MSS 78-3.
85. Sutton, "Rulings of the Court on Defense Evidence of Communism in China," 9 September 1947, UVALL, box 5, folder 5, MSS 78-3.
86. Sutton to John Paul Causey, 24 September 1947, University of Richmond Law Library, Sutton Collection, General and Personal Correspondence, folder 106.
87. Sutton to L. Medlin, 10 October 1947, University of Richmond Law Library, Sutton Collection, General and Personal Correspondence, folder 106.
88. Brackman, *The Other Nuremberg*, 366.
89. L. Medlin to Sutton, 11 October 1947, University of Richmond Law Library, Sutton Collection, General and Personal Correspondence, folder 107. Emphasis in the original.
90. "Note by Acting Secretary," SFE 188/3, State-War-Navy Coordinating Committee for the Far East, 8 September 1947, NARA, RG 153, entry 145, box 73.
91. To General Alden C. Waitt from Edwin V. Hill and Joseph Victor, "Summary Report on BW Investigation," 12 December 1947, NARA, Reference Collection-Japanese Biological Weapons in WWII, RG 395, entry 6909-C, box 1, BW. Referred to as the Hill and Victor Report.
92. Ibid., tab I.

93. Ibid., tab P.
94. Ibid., tab J.
95. Ibid., 3.
96. The records of these data were organized in three separate books, labeled *Report of 'A'* (anthrax, 406 pages), *Report of 'Q'* (plague, 745 pages), and *Report of 'G'* (glanders, 372 pages), with laboratory notes and clinical drawings from the experiments and autopsies, with an English translation. Declassified copies of the three books eventually went to the Library of Congress, Science and Technical Report Section, Washington, D.C. (S49 275, 1947).
97. Hill and Victor Report, tab B.
98. Ibid., tabs AA, AB, A, D, J, L, M, N, O, V, W, and X.
99. The Hill and Victor Report credited Ishii with offering information about tuberculosis, on which human experimentation was done, but his transcribed interviews mention nothing about the disease.
100. Contrary to what Sanders believed in 1945, the Japanese had explored a wide range of disease agents—botulism, brucellosis, Fugu toxin, smallpox, tick encephalitis, tularemia, tsutsugamushi, and others. The known Japanese studies before these interviews were on anthrax, cholera, glanders, plague, and certain plant diseases, as well as salmonella, songo, tetanus, typhoid, and typhus.
101. Hill and Victor Report, 3
102. Ibid.
103. "B.W. Research in the United States."
104. Hill and Victor Report, 4.

11. Open and Closed Trials

1. IMTFE transcripts, 12:4545–47.
2. Defense Document 2470, Exhibit 3100, "Sworn Testimony of Tsuneo Yasuda," 2 September 1947.
3. IMTFE transcripts, 12:28110 and 28239–44.
4. Robert J. C. Butow, *Tojo and the Coming of the War* (Princeton, N.J.: Princeton University Press, 1961), 102.
5. Arnold C. Brackman *The Other Nuremberg: The Untold Story of the Tokyo War Crimes Trial* (London: Collins, 1987), 389.
6. Ibid., 391. John W. Fihelly, who had devoted months to interrogating Tojo, was scheduled to conduct his cross-examination. Keenan asked the court if he could share the cross; when the court refused, Keenan took over the questioning. Keenan had similarly upstaged Comyns Carr in the cross-examination of

Marquis Kido, but unlike Comyns Carr, who stayed to assist the chief counselor, Fihelly stalked out of the courtroom and left Keenan on his own.

7. Ibid., 42.
8. "Cher Jean" personal letter from Pechkoff, n.d., noted as his first letter of 1948. Ministre des Affaires Étrangères Archives, Séries E, Asie-Océanie Japon, vol. 190/4, no. 41, 183–84.
9. Rebuttal Committee, Report on the Materials Submitted by the U.S.S.R. Division, 9 December 1947, UVALL, Tavenner Papers, box 6, General Memoranda and Reports for December 1947; Tavenner to Vasiliev, "Counsel for Umezu," 23 December 1947, UVALL, Tavenner Papers, box 6, General Memoranda and Reports for December 1947. The Soviets also argued that Umezu's assistant counsel was a relative of his and therefore too biased to represent him.
10. "Undated memo by Army seeking SFE working group meeting," February 1948, NARA, RG 165, entry 468, box 628.
11. "Report on Unintroduced Evidence—China Phase" from James T. C. Liu to Frank S. Tavenner, Judge C. C. Hsiang, Mr. David Nelson Sutton, and Judge Judson T. T. Nyi, 22 April 1947, UVALL, box 4, folder 4, MSS 78-3. This memo, marked "Urgent," refers to over a hundred pages of documents implicating nearly half the defendants.
12. Brackman, *The Other Nuremberg*, 366. As it prepared for the rebuttal phase, the Chinese Division complained that not enough emphasis was being put on Japanese policy regarding aggressive war in China and on Japanese sources for such charges. See Chinese Division to Rebuttal Committee, "China Phase and Itagaki," 5 December 1947, UVALL, Tavenner Collection, box 6, General Reports and Memoranda for December 1947.
13. *Nuremberg Trial Proceedings*, vol. 21, Two Hundred and Eleventh Day, 26 August 1946. Available at the Avalon Project, http://avalon.law.yale.edu/imt/08-26-46.asp.
14. Annie Jacobsen, *Operation Paperclip: The Secret Intelligence Program That Brought Nazi Scientists to America* (New York: Little, Brown, 2014), 323–49. Major General Schreiber, after three years as a Soviet prisoner, was released to the West, where the Chemical Corps hired him to work first in Germany and then at the School of Aviation Medicine at Randolph Field in Texas. In 1952 his involvement in medical atrocities was exposed and, with US protection, he was sent to another position in Buenos Aires.
15. Lieutenant Colonel von Petersdorff had been the assistant German military attaché to Japan and a spy involved with Richard Sorge, the German journalist and embassy official known as a Soviet mole. President Webb refused to consider this testimony because spy rings were not germane to the trial.

16. "Summation Committee," 12 March 1948, UVALL, box 6, folder 7, MSS 78-3.
17. Tavenner to Vasiliev, "Memorandum," 5 February 1948, UVALL, box 6, folder 6, MSS 78-3. "I would like to see the change made," Tavenner wrote, "because otherwise it will conflict with a lot of the evidence which will be recited."
18. Smirnov to Tavenner, "Transferring Materials Concerning the Tripartite Pact and the Anti-Comintern Pact," 19 September 1947, UVALL, box 5, folder 5, MSS 78-3.
19. *FRUS, 1948, The Far East: China*. Vol. 7. The Ambassador in China (Stuart) to the Secretary of State, Nanking, January 9, 1948.
20. Ibid., January 15, 1948.
21. Vasiliev to Tavenner, 24 February 1948, UVALL, box 6, folder 6, MSS 78-3.
22. Tavenner to Vasiliev, 25 February 1948, UVALL, box 6, folder 6, MSS 78-3.
23. "Interrogation of Certain Japanese by Russian Prosecutor (SANACC 351/3)," 4 March 1948, NARA, RG 153, entry 145, box 73.
24. "Interrogation of Certain Japanese by Russian Prosecutor," 12 March 1948, NARA, RG 165, entry 468, box 587. The subcommittee's decision paper 188/5 was transmitted to JCS as SANACC 351/3.
25. "Outgoing Classified Message [CM OUT 976050] to MacArthur from JCS," 13 March 1948, NARA, RG 153, entry 145, box 73.
26. Zachary D. Kaufman, "Transitional Justice for Tojo's Japan: The United States Role in the Establishment of the International Military Tribunal for the Far East and Other Transitional Justice Mechanisms for Japan After World War II," *Emory International Law Review* 27 (2014): 780.
27. Years later scholar Inoue Kiyoshi would use Tavenner's characterization to argue that the emperor, far from being a cog in the machine, was an intelligent actor who failed his people. See Yuma Totani, *The Tokyo War Crimes Trial: The Pursuit of Justice in the Wake of World War II* (Cambridge, Mass.: Harvard University Asia Center, 2008), 203.
28. A film of Tavenner's statement is available at the University of Virginia Law School, Tokyo War Crimes Trial site, http://lib.law.virginia.edu/imtfe/content/tavenner-lectern-giving-final-summation-during-tokyo-war-crimes-trials.
29. From Sutton to Lewis Jones, 19 April 1948, University of Richmond Law School, Sutton Collection, General and Personal Correspondence, old file 108.
30. Herbert P. Bix, *Hirohito and the Making of Modern Japan* (New York: HarperCollins, 2000), 236–86.
31. In all, these were Dohihara, Hirota, Itagaki, Kimura, Matsui, Muto, and Tojo.
32. Ian Buruma, *Wages of Guilt: Memories of War in Germany and in Japan* (New York: Farrar Straus Giroux, 1994), 164.

33. Koiso, Hata, Hoshino, and Shigemitsu were unusual in that they were found guilty under count 55 but not condemned to death.
34. IMTFE transcripts, Separate Opinions, 22:1058–59.
35. Letter from Harry S. Truman to Joseph B. Keenan accompanied by related correspondence, December 2, 1948, Harry S. Truman Presidential Library and Museum, Truman Papers, Official File. OF 325a, Office of U.S. Chief of Counsel for Prosecution of Axis Criminality.
36. Relay from US Embassy, London to SCAP, 19 November 1948, MacArthur Archives, RG-9, box 160, folder War-Crimes, 19 November 1948–29 May 1950. Nine British government officials and advisors signed the message.
37. "Memo: Case 330," 26 November 1948, NARA, RG 261, box 4.
38. Stuart to the Secretary of State, Nanking, 17 July 1948, in Kenneth W. Rea and John C. Brewer, eds., *The Forgotten Ambassador: The Reports of John Leighton Stuart, 1946–1949* (Boulder, Colo.: Westview Press, 1981), 258.
39. Ibid., 19 June 1947, 117.
40. *FRUS, 1948, The Far East: China*. Vol. 7. The Ambassador in China (Stuart) to the Secretary of State, Nanking, 7 November 1948.
41. Ibid., 25 April 1949, 320. Stuart, who understood Mao's allegiance to Stalinist principles of state government, nonetheless believed a productive dialogue with him was possible, which the State Department did not. Stuart left Nanjing in late July and departed China on August 2.
42. Kenneth W. Condit, *History of the Joint Chiefs of Staff. The Joint Chiefs of Staff and National Policy*. Vol. 2: *1947–1949* (Washington, D.C.: Office of Joint History, Office of the Chairman of the Joint Chiefs of Staff, 1996), 267.
43. *FRUS, The Far East: China*. Vol. 7. The Ambassador in China (Stuart) to the Secretary of State, Nanking, 6 July 1949, 335. Stuart quoted from Mao's article "On People's Democratic Dictatorship."
44. Richard Rhodes, *The Making of the Atomic Bomb* (New York: Simon and Schuster, 1986), 766–67.
45. "Soviet Intentions and Capabilities," 20 February 1950, Public Papers of the Presidents, Harry S. Truman, 1945–1953, Harry S. Truman Library and Museum, http://iats-coe2.missouri.edu/~whistlet/newDoctrine/documents/outputfulldoc.php?documentid=78.
46. Steven T. Ross, *American War Plan 1945–1956* (London: Routledge, 2013), 119.
47. Ibid., 127; Ira Katznelson, *Fear Itself: The New Deal and the Origins of Our Time* (New York: Norton, 2013), 447.
48. Takemae Eiji, *Inside GHQ: The Allied Occupation of Japan and Its Legacy*, trans. Robert Ricketts and Sebastian Swann (New York: Continuum, 2002), 457–58.

49. Ambassador Pechkoff to the Minister of Foreign Affairs, 19 September 1947, Ministre des Affaires Étrangères Archives, Asie-Océanie Japon Séries E, vol. 188-1. Pechkoff also reported that the crackdown on the media affected 117 newspapers, 225 publishers, 15 theaters and cinemas, and 6 radio stations—with about 2000 people eliminated from their positions, in addition to the 193,000 others purged at that time.
50. Takemae, *Inside GHQ*, 457–515.
51. John W. Dower, *Embracing Defeat: Japan in the Wake of World War II* (New York: Norton, 1999), 540–46.
52. Takemae, *Inside GHQ*, 478. The Red Purge in Japan coincided with the start of Wisconsin senator Joseph McCarthy's anticommunist "witch hunts" in Washington.
53. Ian Buruma, *Inventing Japan, 1853–1964* (New York: Modern Library, 2003), 152.
54. V. Berezhkov, "The Tokyo Trial," *New Times*, January 28, 1948, 6; A. Trainin, "From Nuremberg to Tokyo," *New Times*, March 17, 1948, 11–13; M. Markov, "Falsification of History at the Tokyo Trial," *New Times*, April 21, 1948, 10; M. Raginsky and S. Rozenblit, "What People Expect of the International Military Tribunal in Tokyo," *Pravda* (Soviet Press Translations), July 15, 1948, 421; Philipp R. Piccigallo, *The Japanese on Trial: Allied War Crimes Operations in the East, 1945–1951* (Austin; University of Texas Press, 1979), 146–49.
55. *Materials on the Trial of Former Servicemen of the Japanese Army Charged with Manufacturing and Employing Bacteriological Weapons* (Moscow: Foreign Language Publishing House, 1950).
56. Valentyna Polunina, "The Khabarovsk Trial: The Soviet Riposte to the Tokyo Tribunal," in *Trials for International Crimes in Asia*, ed. Kirsten Sellars, 121–44 (Cambridge: Cambridge University Press, 2016), 134.
57. Boris G. Yudin, "Research on Humans at the Khabarovsk War Crimes Trial," in *Japan's Wartime Medical Atrocities: Comparative Inquiries in Science, History and Ethics*, ed. Jing-Bao Nie, Nanyan Guo, Mark Selden, and Arthur Kleinman, 59–78 (New York: Routledge, 2010), 64.
58. From a Western perspective, the experts might have lacked credibility. Leading them was Nikolai N. Zhukov-Verezhnikov, a microbiologist under the influence of Trofim Lysenko, Stalin's favored biologist who, in rejecting modern genetics, set Soviet biology back decades. Yet the experts' assessment of the harm posed to communities by the plague attacks and the campaign of 1942 focused sensibly on public health threats, such as community contagion, given the poor sanitary conditions in China (*Materials on the Trial of Former Servicemen*, 395–404).

59. Ibid., 9.
60. Ibid., 28.
61. Theodor Rosebury and Elvin A. Kabat, with the assistance of Martin H. Boldt, "Bacterial Warfare," *Journal of Immunology* 56, no. 1 (1947): 7–96.
62. Valentin Bojtzov and Erhard Geissler, "Military Biology in the USSR, 1920–45," in *Biological and Toxin Weapons: Research, Development and Use from the Middle Ages to 1945*, ed. Erhard Geissler and John Ellis van Courtland Moon, 153–67 (New York: Oxford University Press, 1999), 159.
63. *Materials on the Trial of Former Servicemen*, 462.
64. Ibid., 10.
65. Ibid., 326–27.
66. Ibid.
67. Ibid., 25.
68. Ibid., 57.
69. "The 20th Century's Forgotten Villains," *Moscow Times*, April 27, 2001.
70. *Materials on the Trial of Former Servicemen*, 407–8.
71. Ibid., 411.
72. Ibid., 409–10.
73. Ibid., 410–11.
74. Yudin, "Research," 62. Since the death penalty was to be restored January 12, 1950, the prosecutors may have rushed the trial to a conclusion to avoid appearing vengeful against Japan or risking retribution. See Georgy Permyakov, "Death Zone," *Tikhookkeanskaya zvezda* [Pacific Ocean's Star], February 29, 2000. A translator at the IMTFE, Permyakov has been widely cited.
75. Nakajima Mineo, "Sino-Soviet Confrontation in Historical Perspective," in *The Origins of the Cold War in Asia*, ed. Akira Iriye and Yonosuke Nagai, 203–23 (New York: Columbia University Press, 1977), 208–9. Disagreements notwithstanding, in 1950 the two leaders signed a treaty of amity that endured until the 1960s. See Austin Jerslid, *The Sino-Soviet Alliance: An International History* (Chapel Hill: University of North Carolina Press, 2014).
76. Barak Kushner, *Men to Devils, Devils to Men: Japanese War Crimes and Chinese Justice* (Cambridge, Mass.: Harvard University Press, 2015), 19–23.
77. Ibid., 248–99.
78. Ōsawa Takeshi, "The People's Republic of China's 'Lenient Treatment' Policy Towards Japanese War Criminals," in *Trials for International Crime in Asia*, ed. Kirsten Sellars, 145–66 (Cambridge: Cambridge University Press, 2016), 156.
79. Jing-Bao Nie, "The West's Dismissal of the Khabarovsk Trial as 'Communist Propaganda': Ideology, Evidence and International Bioethics," *Journal of Bioethical Inquiry* 1, no. 1 (April 2004): 32–42.

80. "Joseph Keenan Meets the Press," *American Mercury* 70 (1950): 457–58; Piccigallo, *Japanese on Trial*, 156; Bernard V. A. Röling, *Recueil des Cours*, vol. 100 (Leiden: Académie de Droit International, 1961), 431, n. 6.
81. Sherzod Muminov, "Eleven Winters of Our Discontent: The Siberian Internment and the Making of the New Japan, 1945–1956," Ph.D. diss., Cambridge University, 2015, 210–11.
82. Arnaud Doglia, *L'Arme Biologique Japonaise, 1880–2010* (Berne: Peter Lang, 2016), 196–200.
83. *Materials on the Trial of Former Servicemen*, 409–10, 466.
84. M. Raginsky, "Monstrous Atrocities of the Japanese Imperialist," *New Times*, January 8, 1950, 3–7.
85. Piccigallo, *Japanese on Trial*, 154–56, 252. Piccigallo cites nine such articles appearing in the Soviet press in 1950 and 1951, and five news articles from 1950 indicating that the PRC concurred with demands to punish Japanese BW criminals and stop US "remilitarization" of Japan.

Epilogue: The Fallout

1. "Joseph B. Keenan, Prosecutor, Dies," *New York Times*, December 9, 1954.
2. "F. S. Tavenner, Jr. House Panel Aide: Un-American Activities Unit General Counsel Dies," *New York Times*, October 22, 1964. The trials and blacklisting of folk musician Pete Seeger and playwright Arthur Miller were among the more notorious consequences of the committee investigations.
3. The Senate Special Subcommittee to Investigate the Administration of the Internal Security Act and Other Internal Security Laws (1951–1977) was also known as the McCarran Committee, after its first chair, Nevada senator Patrick McCarran. It had a formal agreement with the FBI to investigate possible suspects, which the HUAC did not.
4. Author interview with Mrs. Frances Sutton Oliver (daughter of David Nelson Sutton), October 28, 2011, Chesapeake, Va. In subsequent years her son William S. Oliver also answered queries from the author about Sutton at the IMTFE.
5. Interview with Judge Xiang Zhejun (Hsiang Che-chun), March 6, 2014, *Baidu*, http://baike.baidu.com/view/476490.htm; *Barak Kushner, Men to Devils, Devils to Men: Japanese War Crimes and Chinese Justice* (Cambridge, Mass.: Harvard University Press, 2015), 343, nn. 39, 49. The first reference is to fragments of Mei's diaries that appeared in 2005, the second to a publication from 1962.
6. Robert Pollitzer, "Plague Studies. 1. A Summary of the History and a Survey of the Present Distribution of the Disease," *Bulletin of the World Health Organization*

4, no. 4 (1951): 485; see also Robert Pollitzer, *Plague,* World Health Organization Monograph Series No. 22 (Geneva: WHO, 1954).

7. Major General Charles A. Willoughby and John Chamberlain, *MacArthur, 1941–1951* (New York: McGraw-Hill, 1954), 422–24.
8. John Tirman, *The Deaths of Others: The Fate of Civilians in America's Wars* (New York: Oxford University Press, 2011), 89–90.
9. Willoughby and Chamberlain, *MacArthur,* 424.
10. Yuma Totani, *The Tokyo War Crimes Tribunal: The Pursuit of Justice in the Wake of World War II* (Cambridge, Mass.: Harvard East Asian Monograph, 2008), 77; Kushner, *Men to Devils,* 230–31, 314–15. For competing versions of history in Asia, see Thomas U. Berger, *War Guilt and World Politics After World War II* (New York: Cambridge University Press, 2012), 175–229.
11. Ian Buruma, *Wages of Guilt: Memories of War in Germany and in Japan* (New York: Farrar Straus Giroux, 1994), 164.
12. Awaya Kentaro, "The Tokyo Tribunal, War Responsibility and the Japanese People," trans. Timothy Amos, *Asia Pacific Journal* 4, no. 2 (2006), http://apjjf.org/-Awaya-Kentaro/2061/article.html.
13. Peter Williams and David Wallace, *Unit 731: The Japanese Army's Secret of Secrets* (New York: Free Press, 1989), 236–47; Sheldon H. Harris, *Factories of Death: Japanese Biological Warfare 1932–45 and the American Cover-up* (New York: Routledge, 2002), 337–44.
14. Arnaud Doglia, *L'Arme Biologique Japonaise, 1880–2010* (Berne: Peter Lang, 2016), 178. The Blood Bank of Japan was established in 1950 at Osaka, with encouragement from the Japanese Red Cross, GHQ, and the minister of health. In 1955 Cutter Laboratories was at the center of a scandal involving the sale of live-virus polio vaccine that infected some 40,000 inoculated and killed ten. See Paul A. Offit, *The Cutter Incident: How America's First Polio Vaccine Led to the Growing Vaccine Crisis* (New Haven, Conn.: Yale University Press, 2005).
15. The two former ministers interviewed by Sutton in 1946 also did well. Murata Shozo became president of the Japan Association for the Promotion of Overseas Trade and a special ambassador to the Philippines who worked for the restoration of relations between Japan, China, and the Philippines. In 1953 Hatta Yoshiaki became chair of the Japan Science Foundation and in 1957 was chair of the forerunner of the Japan Highway Public Corporation.
16. Takemae Eiji, *Inside GHQ; The Allied Occupation of Japan and Its Legacy,* trans. Robert Ricketts and Sebastian Swann (New York: Continuum, 2002), 427; Harris, *Factories of Death,* 338.
17. Eric A. Feldman, "HIV and Blood in Japan: Transforming Private Conflict Into Public Scandal," in *Blood Feuds: AIDS, Blood, and the Politics of Medical Disaster,*

ed. Eric A. Feldman and Ronald Bayer, 59–92 (Oxford: Oxford University Press, 1999); Harris, *Factories of Death*, 336–44. After paying compensation of $216 million, the company was absorbed by Yoshitomi Pharmaceutical Industries, Ltd. In addition to the Green Cross scandal, Harris noted thirty-seven cases of serious medical ethics violations in postwar Japan, including the policy in 1948 for the forced sterilization of mentally and physically disabled women without their consent.

18. George J. Annas and Michael A. Grodin, *The Nazi Doctors and the Nuremberg Code* (New York: Oxford University Press, 1992).
19. UN General Assembly, *Convention on the Prevention and Punishment of the Crime of Genocide*, December 9, 1948, United Nations, Treaty Series. Vol. 78, 277, http://www.refworld.org/docid/3ae6b3ac0.html; Ian Brownlie, *International Law and the Use of Force by States* (Oxford: Oxford University Press, 1963), 191–94. On POWS, see Francois Bugnion, "The Geneva Conventions of 12 August 1949: From the 1949 Diplomatic Conference to the Dawn of the New Millennium," *International Affairs* 76, no. 1 (2000): 41–50. For Northcroft's vision of a permanent international court as "the greatest possible means of insurance against unscrupulous use of power by victorious nations in the future," see "The Former New Zealand Member, International Military Tribunal for the Far East, to the Prime Minister," 17 March 1949, in Robin Kay, ed., *Documents on New Zealand External Relations*, Volume II, *The Surrender and Occupation of Japan* (Wellington, N.Z.: P. D. Hasselberg, 1982), 1736–37.
20. William A. Schabas, *An Introduction to the International Criminal Court* (Cambridge: Cambridge University Press, 2004), 8–9.
21. Commission on Conventional Armaments (CCA), UN document S/C.3/32/Rev.1, August 1948, quoted in *The United Nations and Disarmament, 1945–1965*, UN Publication 67.I.8, 28W, UN Office of Public Information; Seth Carus, "Defining 'Weapons of Mass Destruction,'" Occasional Paper No. 8, Center for the Study of Weapons of Mass Destruction, National Defense University (Washington, DC: National Defense University, 2012), 10.
22. Joseph Cirincione, *Bomb Scare: The History & Future of Nuclear Weapons* (New York: Columbia University Press, 2007), 19.
23. See Federation of American Scientists, *Status of World Nuclear Forces*, http://fas.org/issues/nuclear-weapons/status-world-nuclear-forces.
24. William D. Leahy, *I Was There. The Personal Story of the Chief of Staff to Presidents Roosevelt and Truman Based on His Notes and Diaries Made at the Time* (New York: McGraw-Hill, 1950), 339–442. Leahy felt the same repugnance for chemical weapons, even though his brother had directed the naval unit at Edgewood Arsenal's Chemical Warfare School.

25. Ibid., 441.
26. Kathryn Weathersby, "Deceiving the Deceivers: Moscow, Beijing, Pyongyang, and the Allegations of Bacteriological Use in Korea," *Cold War International History Project Bulletin* 11 (1998): 176–85; Milton Leitenberg, "New Russian Evidence as to Korean Biological Warfare Allegations: Background and Analysis," *Cold War International History Project Bulletin* 11 (1998): 185–99. See also *Report of the International Scientific Commission for the Investigation of the Facts Concerning Bacteriological Warfare in Korea and China: With Appendices* (Peking: World Peace Council, 1952). Known as the Needham Report.
27. Conrad C. Crane, "No Practical Capabilities: American Biological and Chemical Warfare Programs During the Korean War," *Perspectives in Biology and Medicine* 45, no. 2 (Spring 2002): 241–49.
28. Stephen Endicott and Edward Hagerman, *The United States and Biological Warfare: Secrets of the Early Cold War and Korea* (Bloomington: Indiana University Press, 1998), 172–78. See also Endicott and Hagerman's posting "Biological Warfare during the Korean War: Rhetoric and Reality" (2004), http://www.yorku.ca/sendicot/ReplytoColCrane.htm.
29. Bruce Cumings, *The Origins of the Korean War* (Princeton, N.J.: Princeton University Press, 1991), 1:xix. Among Americans, 34,000 died in the three years of the war, and among the Chinese forces perhaps 500,000, whereas the total Korean casualties were around three million. For an overview of civilian deaths, see Tirman, *The Deaths of Others*, 93–110.
30. Seymour Hersch, *Chemical and Biological Warfare: America's Hidden Arsenal* (Indianapolis: Bobbs-Merrill, 1968), 202.
31. Philip M. Boffey, "Nerve Gas: Dugway Accident Linked to Utah Sheep Kill," *Science*, 162, no. 3861 (1968): 1460–64.
32. Jeanne Mager Stellman, Steven D. Stellman, Richard Christian, Tracy Weber, and Carrie Tomosallo, "The Extent and Patterns of Usage of Agent Orange and Other Herbicides in Vietnam," *Nature* 422 (April 17, 2003): 681–87.
33. Joel Primack and Frank von Hippel, "Matthew Meselson and Federal Policy on Chemical and Biological Warfare," in *Advice and Dissent: Scientists in the Political Arena*, 143–164 (New York: Basic Books, 1974). Starting in the Kennedy administration as an ACDA (Arms Control and Disarmament Agency) consultant, Meselson, with colleague Milton Leitenberg, mobilized 5,000 scientists to urge a ban on the first use of biological and chemical weapons, an end to antipersonnel and anticrop agents in Vietnam, and a review of the CBW programs—goals accomplished in the Nixon administration.
34. On organizational problems, see Sonia Ben Ougrham-Gormley, *Barriers to Bioweapons: The Challenge of Expertise and Organization to Weapons Development*

(Ithaca, N.Y.: Cornell University Press, 2014). On the dangers of CBW research, see Jonathan D. Moreno, *Undue Risk: Secret State Experiments on Humans* (New York: W. H. Freeman, 1999).

35. National Security Decision Memorandum 35, November 25, 1969, https://2001-2009.state.gov/documents/organization/90919.pdf.
36. R. R. Baxter and Thomas Buergenthal, "Legal Aspects of the Geneva Protocol of 1925," *American Journal of International Law* 64, no. 5 (October 190): 853–79.
37. Editorial, *New York Times*, November 26, 1969.
38. Raymond L. Garthoff, "Polyakov's Run," *Bulletin of the Atomic Scientists* 56, no. 5 (September 2000): 37–40; Milton Leitenberg and Raymond A. Zilinskas, *The Soviet Biological Weapons Program. A History* (Cambridge, Mass.: Harvard University Press, 2012), 60–67. The Soviet Central Committee also established a secret program called "Foliant" to acquire a new class of chemical agents with greater toxicity, stability, persistence, and ease of production (508).
39. David Hoffman, *The Dead Hand: The Untold Story of the Cold War Arms Race and Its Dangerous Legacy* (New York: Doubleday, 2009).
40. Matthew Meselson, Jeanne Guillemin, Martin Hugh-Jones, Alexander Langmuir, Ilona Popova, Alexis Shelokov, and Olga Yampolskaya, "The Sverdlovsk Outbreak of 1979," *Science* 266, no. 5188 (1994): 1202–8; Jeanne Guillemin, *Anthrax: The Investigation of a Deadly Outbreak* (Berkeley: University of California Press, 1999).
41. Scott Sagan, *The Limits of Safety: Organization, Accidents, and Nuclear Weapons* (Princeton, N.J.: Princeton University Press, 1993); Hugh Gusterson, "Nuclear Weapons and the Other in Western Imagination," *Cultural Anthropology* 14, no. 1 (1999): 111–43.
42. Kenneth R. Timmerman, *The Death Lobby: How the West Armed Iraq* (Boston: Houghton-Mifflin, 1991), 111–12; Human Rights Watch, *Genocide in Iraq—the Anfal Campaign Against the Kurds*, http://www.hrw.org/reports/1993/iraqanfal/.
43. "Start I" text and other information is available at the *Nuclear Threat Initiative* website, http://www.nti.org/treaties-and-regimes/treaties-between-united-states-america-and-union-soviet-socialist-republics-strategic-offensive-reductions-start-i-start-ii.
44. Lisa Woollomes Tabassi, ed., *OPCW: The Legal Texts* (The Hague: T.M.C. Asser Press, 1999), 5. Japan was bound by article 1, no. 3, of the convention: "Each state party undertakes to destroy all chemical weapons it abandoned on the territory of another State Party, in accordance with the provisions of this Convention."
45. Harris, *Factories of Death*, 335.
46. Jez Littlewood, *The Biological Weapons Convention: A Failed Revolution* (Aldershot, UK: Ashgate, 2005).

47. Graham S. Pearson, *The UNSCOM Saga: Chemical and Biological Weapons Proliferation* (New York: St. Martin's Press, 1999); Amy E. Smithson, *Germ Gambits: The Bioweapons Dilemma, Iraq and Beyond* (Stanford, Calif.: Stanford University Press, 2011).
48. David E. Kaplan and Andrew Marshall, *The Cult at the End of the World* (New York: Crown, 1996); Robert Jay Lifton, *Destroying the World in Order to Save It* (New York: Metropolitan Books, 1999).
49. Judith Miller, Stephen Engelberg, and William Broad, *Germs: Biological Weapons and America's Secret War* (New York: Simon & Schuster, 2001). On threat perception, see Kathleen M. Vogel, *Phantom Menace or Looming Danger: A New Framework for Assessing Bioweapons Threats* (Baltimore: Johns Hopkins University Press, 2013).
50. Jeanne Guillemin, *American Anthrax: Fear, Crime, and the Investigation of the Nation's Deadliest Bioterrorism Attack* (New York: Times Books, 2011); David Willman, *Mirage Man: Bruce Ivins, the Anthrax Attacks, and America's Rush to War* (New York: Bantam, 2011).
51. Jeanne Guillemin, "Medical Risks and the Volunteer Army," in *Anthropology and the United States Military: Coming of Age in the Twenty-first Century*, ed. Pamela Friese and Margaret Harrell (New York: Palgrave, 2003), 29–48.
52. Guillemin, *American Anthrax*, 176–83.
53. Tara Kirksell and Matthew Watson, "Federal Agency Biodefense Funding, FY2013-FY2014," *Biosecurity and Biodefense* 11, no. 3 (September 2013): 196–216.
54. Guillemin, *American Anthrax*, 255–57.
55. "CDC Chief Admits Pattern of Safety Lapses after Mishandling Anthrax, Other Pathogens," *Washington Post*, July 16, 2014.
56. "Army Metes Out Punishment in Anthrax Scandal," *USA Today*, July 5, 2016.
57. The OPCW website offers descriptions of its chemical demilitarization projects in Libya, Syria, and elsewhere, at https://www.opcw.org.
58. "Britain, France Want U.N. Sanctions Over Syria Toxic Gas Attacks," *Reuters*, 25 October 2016. The OPCW website provides background on the 2017 strike.
59. SIPRI, *The Problem of Chemical and Biological Warfare*. Vol. 1: *The Rise of CB Weapons* (New York: Humanities Press, 1971), 217–19, 342–47.
60. Henry Kissinger, *On China* (New York: Penguin, 2012), 270–72.
61. *FRUS 1969–1976*. Vol. 17: *China, 1969–1972*, "Joint Statement Following Discussions with Leaders of the People's Republic of China: Shanghai, February 27, 1972."
62. "China and Japan Hug and Make Up," *Time*, November 6, 1979.
63. Doglia, *L'Arme Biologique*, 274–90. Doglia traces Japanese revelations from the 1980s onward, in academic conferences, the courts, and the press. In addition

to the testimonies of Ishii's former employees, a cousin who worked for him during the war wrote memoirs of him, pages of diary Ishii kept surfaced, and his daughter was interviewed.

64. Morimura Seiichi, *Akuma no hōshoku* [The Devil's Gluttony] (Tokyo: Kadokawa Shoten, 1983).

65. Tsuneichi Kei-ichi, *Kieta saikinsen butai: Kantōgun Dai 731 Butai* (Tokyo: Kai-meisha, 1981). Available in English as *The Germ Warfare Unit That Disappeared: The Kwantung Army's 731st Unit* (Arlington, Va.: US Army Intelligence and Threat Analysis Center, 1982); Kei-ichi Tsuneichi, "Unit 731 and the Human Skulls Discovered in 1989: Physicians Carrying Out Organized Crimes," in *Dark Medicine: Rationalizing Unethical Medical Research*, ed. William R. LaFleur, Gernot Böhme, and Usuumu Shimazono, 72–82 (Bloomington: Indiana University Press, 2007), 81. Peter McGill ("Japan Used Poison Gas," *Observer*, June 24, 1984) reported from Tokyo on new revelations of Japan's CW program and attacks against Chinese soldiers and civilians.

66. Williams and Wallace, *Unit 731*, 250–52.

67. John W. Powell, "Japan's Germ Warfare: The U.S. Cover-up of a War Crime," *Bulletin of Concerned Asian Scholars* 12, no. 4 (1980): 2–17.

68. Robert Gomer, John W. Powell, and Bert V. A. Röling, "Japan's Biological Weapons: 1930–1945," *Bulletin of the Atomic Scientists* (October 1981): 43–53. On November 19, 1980, after meeting Ruth Adams, editor of the *Bulletin*, and also being in touch with Gerard and Eleanor Jackson Piel, Powell sent his first article to Matthew Meselson asking for help in getting the piece "more attention." Meselson pointed to more data sources and, after editing the paper, sent it to Adams (Meselson, personal correspondence). Robert Gomer, a chemistry professor at the University of Chicago and a member of the *Bulletin*'s Board of Directors, wrote a preamble to the article attesting to the authenticity of Powell's documents.

69. Ibid., 46.

70. Ibid., 47.

71. Ibid., 48.

72. Hearing before the Subcommittee on Oversight and Investigation of the Committee on Veterans Affairs, House of Representatives, Ninety-Seventh Congress, Second Session, June 10, 1982; Robert Harris and Jeremy Paxman, *The Secret History of Chemical and Biological Warfare* (New York: Random House, 1982); John Bryden, *Deadly Allies: Canada's Secret War, 1937–1947* (Toronto: McClelland & Stewart, 1989); Williams and Wallace, *Unit 731*. See also Harris, *Factories of Death*. In 1995 US Army historian Benjamin Garrett guided Harris to the Dugway Proving Ground, source of the Japanese reports on anthrax, plague,

and glanders given to Hill and Victor, which had been thought lost. Benjamin Garrett, personal communication, September 15, 2016.

73. Luc Reydams and Jan Wouters, "The Politics of Establishing International Criminal Tribunals," in *International Prosecution*, ed. Luc Reydams, Jan Wouters, and Cedric Ryngaert, 6–80 (New York: Oxford University Press, 2012), 20.
74. Irving Louis Horowitz, "Stages in the Evolution of Holocaust Studies: From the Nuremberg Trials to the Present," *Human Rights Review* 10 (November 2009): 493-504.
75. Charles Maier, *The Unmasterable Past: History, Holocaust and National Identity* (Cambridge, Mass.: Harvard University Press, 1988); Buruma, *Wages of Guilt*; Mark Osiel, *Mass Atrocity, Collective Memory, and the Law* (New Brunswick, N.J.: Transaction Books, 1997).
76. Iris Chang, *The Rape of Nanking: The Forgotten Holocaust of World War II* (New York: Basic Books, 1997), 201–14. There was an assassination attempt in 1989 on the mayor of Nagasaki after he publicly expressed his view that Emperor Hirohito bore responsibility for the war.
77. Buruma, *Wages of Guilt*, 122.
78. Daqing Yang, "Documenting Evidence and Studies of Japanese War Crimes: An Interim Assessment," in *Researching Japanese War Crimes: Introductory Essays*, ed. Edward Drea, Greg Bradsher, Robert Hanyok, James Lide, Michael Petersen, and Daqing Yang, 21–56 (Washington, D.C.: National Archives and Records Administration for the Nazi War Crimes and Japanese Imperial Government Records Interagency Working Group, 2006), 27–29.
79. Buruma, *Wages of Guilt*, 134. Perhaps the death of Emperor Hirohito in 1989 liberated them from silence. Also, in 1991 Hirohito's discourse on the war from 1946, called *The Emperor's Monologue*, was finally published in full, revealing a monarch who was well informed, aggressive, and self-interested.
80. Hal Gold, *Unit 731 Testimony* (Rutland, Vt.: Tuttle, 1996), 150–250. The testimonies of the 1990s came to the author through faxes and photocopies from the Central Organizing Committee for the Unit 731 Exhibitions in Tokyo. In addition to twenty-one testimonials of varying length and detail, the book includes a lecture by Nishino Rumiko in December 1994 concerning venereal disease experiments on comfort women (159–66), confirmed at the Khabarovsk trial, and in witness research conducted by Morimura for his novel.
81. Ibid., 241.
82. Imperial Japan's criminal use of Chinese, Koreans, and others as "comfort women" for its troops was brought to new attention and generated action at the level of the Japanese government and the United Nations. See Maki Kimura,

Unfolding the "Comfort Women" Debates: Modernity, Violence, Women's Voices (London: Palgrave Macmillan, 2016), 10–20.

83. Fujii Shizue, *Unit 731: The Horror of Japan's Monstrous Biological Weapons* (Taipei: Weningtang, 1997), 43; Suzy Wang, "Medicine-Related War Crimes Trials and Post-war Politic and Ethics: The Unresolved Case of Unit 731, Japan's Bio-warfare Program," in *Japan's Wartime Medical Atrocities: Comparative Inquiries in Science, History, and Ethics*, ed. Jing-Bao Nie, Nanyan Guo, Mark Selden, and Arthur Kleinman, 32–58 (London: Routledge, 2010), 34–35.
84. Kushner, *Men to Devils*, 257–99.
85. See the museum's website, http://www.unit731.org/Harbin-museum.html.
86. Li Xiaofang, *Qixue kongsu: Qin-Hua Rijun xijunzhan tanju, biju shouhai xincunzhe shilu* (Blood Weeping Accusations, Records of Anthrax Victims) (Beijing: CCP Press, 2005). Eighty-one of those interviewed and photographed were men, nineteen women. The book includes commentaries by Wang Xuan, Sheldon Harris, and two American physicians, Michael Franzblau and Martin Furmanski, who diagnosed the glanders cases.
87. "Shouting the Pain for Japan's Germ Attacks," *New York Times*, November 23, 2002; "Japanese Court Rejects Germ Warfare Damages," *International Herald Tribune*, July 20, 2002.
88. Two major cases against Japan regarding Korean forced labor and "comfort women" (forced prostitution) were also dispensed with using this same argument of prior treaties (Wang, "War Crimes Trials," 49). Much earlier, in 1955, a case on behalf of atom bomb survivors presented in Japan eventually failed on the same grounds. See Yuki Taneko and Richard Falk, "The Atomic Bombing, The Tokyo War Crimes Trial and the Shimoda Case: Lessons for Anti-Nuclear Legal Movements," *The Asia Pacific Journal* 7, no. 3 (November 2, 2000), apjjf.org/_Yuki_Taneki/3245/article.html.
89. David Nelson Sutton, "The Trial of Tojo: The Most Important Trial in All History?," *American Bar Association Journal* 36, no. 2 (February 1950): 165.
90. Ibid.
91. Richard H. Minear, *Victors' Justice: Tokyo War Crimes Trial* (Princeton, N.J.: Princeton University Press, 1971). For a cultural analysis, see Yuki Takatori, "'Equal Punishment for All'—Japan's View of the Tokyo Trial," *Virginia Review of Asian Studies* 17 (2015): 1–20.
92. Gary Jonathan Bass, *Stay the Hand of Vengeance: The Politics of War Crimes Tribunals* (Princeton, N.J.: Princeton University Press, 2000).
93. Tirman, *The Deaths of Others*, 286–94. In four years the commission, inspired by Associated Press investigative journalism, found some two hundred cases of US

atrocities against civilians during the Korean War. Its results were suppressed in the conservative South Korean press and generally ignored in the United States.

94. M. Cherif Bassiouni "Searching for Justice in the World of Realpolitik," *Pace International Law Review* 12 (2008): 213–31.
95. Martha Minow, C. Cora True-Frost, and Alex Whiting, eds., *The First Global Prosecutor: Promise and Constraints* (Ann Arbor: University of Michigan Press, 2015), 360–61.
96. Iraq, Israel, Libya, Qatar, and Yemen also voted against the treaty.
97. Invited Experts on Africa Question, http://iccforum.com/africa.
98. Ban Ki-moon, "An Age of Accountability," address to the Review Conference on the International Criminal Court, Kampala, May 31, 2010, https://www.un.org/sg/en/content/sg/articles/2010-05-27/age-accountability.
99. Zachary D. Kaufman, "Transitional Justice Delayed Is Not Transitional Justice Denied: Contemporary Confrontation of Japanese Experimentation During World War II Through a People's Tribunal," *Yale Law & Policy Review* 26 (2008): 645–59.
100. J-B Nie, "The United States Cover-up of Japanese Wartime Medical Atrocities: Complicity Committed in the National Interest and Two Proposals for Contemporary Action," *American Journal of Bioethics* 6 (May–June 2006): 21–33. Nie proposed an American apology and compensation.
101. Katrien Devolder, "U.S. Complicity and Japan's Wartime Medical Atrocities: Time for a Response," *American Journal of Bioethics* 15, no. 6 (June 2015): 45. Following Nie, Devolder recommended the activation of a US presidential bioethics commission.
102. On China as a rising military and economic power, see Graham Allison, *Destined for War: Can America and China Escape Thucydides's Trap?* (New York: Houghton Mifflin Harcourt, 2017).

INDEX

GPSR Authorized Representative: Easy Access System Europe, Mustamäe tee 50, 10621 Tallinn, Estonia, gpsr.requests@easproject.com

www.ingramcontent.com/pod-product-compliance
Lightning Source LLC
Chambersburg PA
CBHW021847090426
42811CB00033B/2175/J

* 9 7 8 0 2 3 1 1 8 3 5 2 9 *